INTERNATIONAL RELATIONS THEORY

International Relations Theory

Realism, Pluralism, Globalism

Paul R. Viotti *U.S. Air Force Academy*

Mark V. Kauppi *University of Colorado at Colorado Springs*

MACMILLAN PUBLISHING COMPANY
New York
Collier Macmillan Publishers
London

To Linda and Kathleen

Copyright © 1987, Macmillan Publishing Company, a division of Macmillan, Inc.
Printed in the United States of America

MACMILLAN PUBLISHING COMPANY
866 Third Avenue, New York, New York 10022

Collier Macmillan Canada, Inc.

Library of Congress Cataloging-in-Publication Data

Viotti, Paul R.
  International relations theory.

  Includes bibliographies and index.
  1. International relations.   I. Kauppi, Mark V.
II. Title.
JX1391.V57   1987   327′.01   86-12580
ISBN 0-02-423020-0

Printing: 1 2 3 4 5 6 7 8   Year: 7 8 9 0 1 2 3 4 5

ISBN   0-02-423020-0

PREFACE

There are numerous works that are designed to introduce the student to international relations and world politics.* Some are thematic with chapters devoted to such topics as diplomacy, the making and implementation of foreign policy, the arms race, international organization, transnationalism, interdependence, and the management of global resources. Other works are encyclopedic in nature, a veritable "who's who" in the field, providing brief summaries of writers and approaches from ancient times to the present. Each approach has its place, and both serve important purposes.

This book takes a different approach. We make no claim to have covered every topic in the field, much less every writer or scholarly contributor. We do have four major purposes: (1) to discuss the underlying assumptions and images that influence scholarly work in the international relations field—images that we label *realism, pluralism,* and *globalism;* (2) to provide in the chapters and readings representative samples of theoretical works; (3) to introduce to the upper-division and graduate student key concepts used by scholars in their study of international relations; and (4) to encourage the student to scrutinize critically works dealing with international politics.

The fourth purpose is of particular importance. If a student leaves the classroom better equipped to analyze everyday events, to ask the right questions, to recognize underlying assumptions of written works by academics, government officials, and journalists, this would transcend any achievements made in memorizing which author is associated with what theory. Although we have attempted to avoid overwhelming the reader with names, particular authors are mentioned when it is necessary to highlight a critical concept, debate, trend, or theory. Important concepts in each chapter are highlighted in boldface type and are found in the glossary.

We fully recognize the problem of generalizing about a particular image of international relations when very often there are varying perspectives within any one image. Where such schisms exist, we attempt to point them out. Given the length of the work, it is impossible to cover every shade of opinion, every theoretical variation, every point of con-

---

*Although distinctions can be drawn between the terms *international relations* and *world politics* (or international *relations* and international *politics*), and different scholars do have different preferences in this regard, we use the terms interchangeably throughout this book.

tention, let alone every well-known scholar of international relations. Some readers will object because we have not discussed certain theorists, whereas others will perhaps disagree with our interpretation of a particular work. This is to be expected in an enterprise of this nature. We provide a broad overview of the field through presentation of the three basic images in the expectation that this will allow the professor to concentrate upon an area of the discipline he or she finds to be of particular interest and importance.

It is appropriate at the outset to comment on our own biases. We believe in the possibility and necessity of explaining the world around us, and that a rigorous social science should be the goal of scholars of international relations. Although different methods may be used, the goal of scholarly research should be to increase our understanding of how the world functions. To deny the possibility of explanation is to deny the relevancy of the works discussed in this book. We also contend, as do E. H. Carr and others, that values are relevant to the study of international relations. In our view there is a need for normative theory that can be a guide for policy choice. Empirical theory and normative theory operate in separate domains, but each has a role to play.

The idea for this book resulted from a conversation between the authors in 1982 as they strolled through the grounds of Schloss Solitud, located outside Stuttgart, West Germany. At the time Kauppi was teaching for the University of Southern California's masters program in international relations in Germany, and Viotti was an Air Force Academy professor on sabbatical serving as a political advisor at the U.S. European Command. The topic of the discussion was the perennial problem of how to present to our students a significant portion of the vast amount of literature that comprises the international relations discipline and to do so in a relatively coherent manner. After several years of classroom experimentation and numerous other conversations between the authors, the result is this textbook. We would therefore like to thank our former students who provided important feedback, insights, and criticisms. Kauppi is particularly appreciative of the opportunity Douglas T. Stuart gave him to teach the USC international relations theory core course.

We would also like to thank a number of individuals who commented on earlier drafts of various chapters: James Caporaso, James Dixon, Michael Dziedzic, Karen Feste, Schuyler Foerster, Kenneth Kemp, George Modelski, R. Craig Nation, Joseph Rallo, J. David Singer, William Tow, Malham Wakin, and Kenneth Wenker. Thanks also to those individuals who reviewed sections of the manuscript that deal with their work: Graham Allison, Ernst Haas, Robert Jervis, Henry Kissinger, James Rosenau, and Kenneth Waltz. We would also like to acknowledge James L. Busey and Douglas J. Murray for their suggestions and encouragement. As for any errors of fact, interpretation, or conceptualization, the authors of this textbook naturally accept full responsibility.

CONTENTS

CHAPTER ONE

Theory, Images, and International Relations:
An Introduction

Why do wars occur? Is nationalism the primary cause? Or ideology? Or the lack of world government? Or misperception? Or are people innately aggressive? How can stability (if not peace) be achieved? Why is there such tremendous social and economic inequality between different regions of the world? These are the sorts of questions that have preoccupied scholars and statesmen at various times over the millennia, whether the political entity in question was an ancient city-state or a modern nation-state, a centralized empire or a decentralized feudal system, a socialist or a liberal democratic society. Nor are these questions the private preserve of intellectuals, diplomatic practitioners, and assorted political pundits and commentators. At one time or another, most citizens reflect on one or more of these important queries.

The discipline of **international relations** addresses such questions. Despite the adjective *international*, the field is concerned with much more than relations between or among states. Other actors such as international organizations, multinational corporations, and terrorist groups are now all part of what could more correctly be termed **world politics.** Studies have also focused on factors internal to a state, such as bureaucratic governmental coalitions, interest groups, presidents, and politburos. The discipline ranges from balance of power politics and economic structures at the international level to the ideological and perceptual predispositions of individual leaders.

Given the tremendous diversity and complexity of *what* is studied, it is not too surprising that there is a multiplicity of views concerning *how* one studies international relations. The possible avenues go well beyond the realms of history and political science. They now include economics, psychology, social psychology, sociology, and anthropology. All this may seem rather intimidating to the student. If it is any consolation, it can also be intimidating to the professional in the field. As a result, many professionals tend to focus on one particular aspect of international relations, perhaps the foreign policy of the United States, the functioning of the United Nations and other international organizations, or decision making in crisis situations.

No matter how ambitious or modest an international relations research project may be, however, every scholar approaches it from a particular point of view. Although some would argue that values ought to be central, most academics strive (or at least claim to strive) to reduce the impact of personal values when it comes to **empirical** research. Nevertheless, personal background and the nature of academic training inevitably influence the manner in which scholars interpret and examine international relations. As the German scholar Max Weber once argued: "All knowledge of cultural reality is always knowledge from particular points of view." How research is conducted will be "determined by the evaluative ideas that dominate the investigator and his age."[1] In other words, each individual's work will be influenced by a particular doctrine, image of the world, ideology, paradigm, or perspective. One may strive to be value-free and objective, but at best these goals can be achieved only imperfectly.

Different perspectives on international relations naturally generate debates. In the 1930s **realists** and **idealists** argued over the nature of international politics and the possibility of peaceful change. In the 1960s the so-called second great debate between **traditionalists** and **behavioralists** dealt with the question of appropriate **methodology.** Traditionalists emphasized the relative utility of history, law, philosophy, and other traditional methods of inquiry. Behavioralists argued in favor of social science conceptualization, quantification of variables, formal hypothesis testing, and causal model building. More recently, **dialectical** approaches drawing on history and Marxist insights have been the subject of much discussion in certain journals in the field, although this debate is not yet widely reflected in the textbook literature.

In this book we deal with three alternative images or perspectives of international relations we label **realism, pluralism,** and **globalism.** Our depiction of the international relations field in terms of these three images compares in some respects to a categorization devised by James N. Rosenau: state-centric, multi-centric, and global-centric approaches to international politics.[2] We argue that these images have provided the basis for the development of theoretical works that attempt to explain various aspects of international relations. The image that one has of international relations is of critical importance. Each image contains certain assumptions about world politics—whether or not explicitly recognized by the researcher—concerning critical actors, issues, and processes in world politics. These images lead one to ask certain questions, seek certain types of answers, and use certain methodological tools in the construction and testing of hypotheses and theories. The advantage is that such images bring order to the analytical effort and make it more manageable. A potential disadvantage, however, is that alternative perspectives and insights may be ignored or overlooked. Although the realist, pluralist, and globalist images are not mutually exclusive in all respects, the differences in point of view and emphasis are much greater than any apparent similarities. The resultant attempts at theory building, therefore, also vary considerably.

In this chapter we first address the question of what is meant by the term *theory*. We then briefly discuss the three images as alternative perspectives that influence the construction of international relations **theory.**

WHAT IS THEORY?

The word *theory* means different things to different people. It may even mean different things to the same person. In common parlance, for example, something may be true "in theory" but not in fact or in a particular case or set of circumstances. In this rather loose usage, "in theory" equates to "in principle" or "in the abstract."

Another meaning, somewhat more consistent with usage in this volume, is theory as the task of making the world or some part of it more intelligible or better understood. Theories dealing with international relations usually aspire to achieve this goal. Making things more intelligible may, of course, amount to nothing more than better or more precise *description* of the things we observe. Although accurate description is essential, theory is something more.

For many people, theory is *explaining* or *predicting*. One goes beyond mere description of phenomena observed and engages in **causal** explanation or prediction based on certain prior occurrences or conditions. Thus, whenever A is present, then B can be expected to follow. "If A, then B" as hypothesis may be subject to empirical test—that is, tested against real-world or factual data. "If states engage in arms races, then the likelihood of war increases" is an example of such a hypothesis. Indeed, formal statement and testing of hypotheses through the use of a statistical methodology is seen by many as central to the theory-building process. Others prefer to rely on nonquantitative case and comparative case studies, historical methods, and reasoned argument—the so-called traditional methods of theory building.

War is an example of a topic of considerable theoretical concern among international relations theorists using a wide variety of methodological approaches to developing better causal theory. Quincy Wright's *A Study of War* was a pioneering effort. Kenneth Waltz's *Man, the State and War* examined causes in the context of three **levels of analysis.** Since the 1960s, J. David Singer and others sharing his preference for formal hypothesis testing through the use of statistical methods have been engaged extensively in studying the phenomenon of war. Bruce Bueno de Mesquita's *The War Trap* is an example of a relatively recent work in this continuing effort to gain a better understanding of war by building better theory.[3]

One view is that the underlying cause of war is the absence of any world government or central authority vested with the capability to enforce rules, settle disputes, and maintain peace among states. It is this anarchy or lack of common government that poses no obstacle and thus permits war to occur. As such, anarchy is the *permissive* cause of war.[4] Misperception may be the immediate or direct cause of a given war. Or, by contrast, war may break out not so much as the result of misperception or misunderstanding but because of hardheaded, rational calculation that the benefits of going to war appear to outweigh the costs.

Theory in a stronger or more formal sense will go beyond proposing the cause of war in such broad terms and will insist that the relations among variables be clearly specified and weighted with the precision one finds in an algebraic equation or set of related equations.[5] Such fully developed theory is not common to the social sciences that are often said to be at a lesser level of progress than are the natural sciences.

General theories that would provide a complete account of the causes of war are less common than *partial*, or *middle-range*, theories that are more modest in the scope of what is to be explained or predicted. Part of the war puzzle addressed by such middle-range theorists, for example, involves crises and decision making in crises. Are partial theories about such things as crisis decision making like building blocks that can at some future date be assembled into a fully developed, general theory of war? Some theorists would say yes and that the most productive enterprise for the present is the development of better middle-range theories. Not everyone would agree; some would argue that formulating general theory comes first, with partial theories being deduced or flowing from it.

The world of theory is an abstract one. Theories may exist apart from facts. Mathematical theorists, for example, deal entirely in the realm of abstraction, whether or not their work has direct relevance to problems of the world in which we live. Practical application for the work of mathematical theorists is sometimes found years later, if ever. **Empirical** theories in the social or natural sciences, by contrast, relate to facts and provide explanation or prediction for observed phenomena. Hypotheses associated with these theories are subject to test against real-world data or facts. The theorist need not have any purpose in developing such empirical theories other than satisfying his or her intellectual curiosity, although many will seek to make their work "policy relevant."[6]

Policy-relevant theories may have explicit purposes that stem from the value preferences of the theorist, such as reducing the likelihood of war or curbing the arms race. Acting on such theories, of course, is the domain of the policymaker, a task separate from that of the empirical theorist. Theorists who become policymakers may well make choices informed by what theories say will be the likely outcomes of implementing one or another alternative. Their choices may be informed by empirical theory or understanding of world events, but the decisions they make are still based on value preferences.

Normative theory deals precisely with values and value preferences. Unlike empirical theory, however, propositions in normative theory are not subject to empirical test as a means of establishing their truth or falsehood. Normative theory deals not with what *is*, the domain of empirical theory. Rather, normative theory deals explicitly with what *ought* to be—the way the world should be ordered and the value choices decisionmakers *should* make. Although the bulk of the effort in this volume is allocated to empirical theory within the context of separate images of world politics, we consider normative theory to be an important and policy-relevant, if often neglected, enterprise. Chapter Five deals explicitly with normative theories relevant to international relations and foreign policy choices. We also identify normative preferences often associated with the three images of international relations theory that are at the core of our effort.

ALTERNATIVE IMAGES

This section provides an overview of the two most striking or immediately apparent distinctions among the three images of international relations under consideration: (1) the key *actors*, or *units*, and (2) the *assumptions* made about them. In the succeeding chapters we go well beyond this brief examination of actors and underlying assumptions. The discussion of realism, for example, focuses on the concepts of power and the balance of power, the chapter on pluralism emphasizes decision making and transnationalism, and the treatment of globalism stresses the concept of dependency in a world capitalist context. We also discuss the intellectual precursors of these images, and philosophical and conceptual issues such as **determinism, voluntarism, system,** and system change. Although **normative** assumptions and implications of the three images are treated explicitly in Chapter Five, they are also woven throughout the discussion in earlier chapters.

We begin this introductory overview with a discussion of *realism*. As will become apparent, proponents of the other two perspectives have to a certain degree been forced to come to terms with this long-established tradition. Indeed, many of their arguments are addressed directly to the strengths and weaknesses of work by realists.

Realism—Major Actors and Assumptions

Realism is based on four key assumptions. First, *states are the principal or most important actors*. States represent the key **unit of analysis** whether one is dealing with ancient Greek city-states or modern nation-states. The study of international relations is the study of relations among these units. Realists who use the concept of **system** defined in terms of interrelated parts usually refer to an international system of states. What of non-state actors? International organizations such as the United Nations may aspire to the status of independent actor, but from the realist perspective this aspiration in fact has not been achieved to any significant degree. Multinational corporations, terrorist groups, and other transnational and international organizations are frequently acknowledged by realists, but the position of these non-state actors is always one of lesser importance. States are the dominant actors.

Second, the state is viewed as a *unitary actor*. For purposes of analysis, realists view the state as being encapsulated by a metaphorical hard shell. A country faces the outside world as an integrated unit. A common assumption associated with realist thought is that political differences within the state are ultimately resolved authoritatively such that the government of the state speaks with one voice for the state as a whole. The state is a unitary actor in that it is usually assumed by realists to have one policy at any given time on any particular issue. To be sure, exceptions occur from time to time, but to the realists these are exceptions that demonstrate the rule and that actually support the general notion of the state as an integrated, unitary actor.

Even in those exceptional cases in which, for example, a foreign ministry expresses policies different from policy statements of the same country's defense ministry, corrective action is taken in an attempt to bring these alternative views to a common and authoritative statement of policy. "End running" of state authorities by bureaucratic and nongovernmental, domestic and transnational actors is also possible, but it occurs unchecked by state authorities in only those issues in which the stakes are low. From the realist perspective, if the issues are important enough, higher authorities will intervene to preclude bureaucratic end running or action by nongovernmental actors that are contrary to centrally directed policy.

Third, given this emphasis on the unitary state-as-actor, realists usually make the further assumption that *the state is essentially a rational actor*. A rational foreign policy decision-making process would include a statement of objectives, consideration of all feasible alternatives in terms of existing capabilities available to the state, the relative likelihood of attaining these objectives by the various alternatives under consideration, and the benefits or costs associated with each alternative. Following this rational process, governmental decision makers evaluate each alternative, selecting the one that maximizes utility (maximizing benefit or minimizing cost associated with attaining the objectives sought).

As a practical matter, the realist is aware of the difficulties in viewing the state as a rational actor. Governmental decision makers may not have all the factual information or knowledge of cause and effect they need to make value-maximizing decisions. The process may well be clouded by considerable uncertainty as decision makers grope for the best solution. They also have to deal with the problem of human bias and misperception that may lead them astray. In any event, the choice made—if not always the *best* or value-maximizing choice in fact—is at least perceived to be a satisfactory one. It is a **satisficing** or suboptimal choice—less than a value-maximizing choice, but still good enough in terms of the objectives sought.

Fourth, realists assume that within the hierarchy of international issues, *national security* usually tops the list. Military and related political issues dominate world politics. A realist focuses on actual or potential conflict between state actors, examining how international stability is attained or maintained, how it breaks down, the utility of force as a means to resolve disputes, and the prevention of the violation of territorial integrity. **Power,** therefore, is a key concept. To the realist, military security or strategic issues are sometimes referred to as **high politics,** whereas economic and social issues are viewed by many of them as the more mundane, less important or **low politics.** Indeed, the former is often understood to dominate or set the environment within which the latter occurs.

Pluralism—Major Actors and Assumptions

The pluralist image consists of a different set of assumptions. First, *non-state actors* are important entities in international relations that cannot be ignored. International organizations, for example, can be independent actors in their own right. The organization's own decision makers, bureaucrats, and other associated groups have considerable influence in areas such as agenda setting—determining which issues are most important politically. International organizations are more than simply arenas within which sovereign states compete. Organizational power and autonomy are neither absolute nor nonexistent but something in between, varying from organization to organization. Similarly, other nongovernmental actors such as multinational corporations (MNCs) cannot be dismissed merely as being of only marginal importance, given an increasingly **interdependent** world economy.

Indeed, in some cases they are even capable of circumventing the authority of the state.

Second, for the pluralist, *the state is not a unitary actor.* Indeed, the realist view of the state as unitary actor is an abstraction that masks the essence of politics that is found principally within the state. The state is not some **reified** entity—an abstraction to be treated as if it were a physical being that acts with single-minded determination, always in a coherent manner. It is, rather, composed of individual bureaucracies, interest groups, and individuals that attempt to formulate or influence foreign policy. Competition, coalition building, conflict, and compromise among these actors are the stuff of politics. To speak of "U.S. foreign policy" is really to speak of a number of foreign policy decisions determined by competition among a number of actors. Pluralists disaggregate the state—break it into its component parts. They reject the notion of the state as an integrated entity, impermeable to outside forces. Both governmental and nongovernmental actors pass through this soft outer shell, sometimes taking actions with policy implications contrary to preferences of central state authorities. These are not just exceptional cases from the pluralist perspective. In fact, focusing on the state as if it were a unitary actor again misses the essence of politics. This is not only in terms of interactions *within* the state; equally important, it is the **transnational** dimension of state and nonstate actors that operate *across* national borders. The pluralist image thus offers greater complexity than the relatively simpler image of states as unitary actors interacting with one another.

Third, pluralists *challenge* the utility of the realist assumption of *the state as rational actor.* This follows logically from the pluralist image of the disaggregated state in which the foreign policy decision making process is the result of clashes, bargaining, and compromise between and among different actors. In some cases, a particular policy may be suggested in order to enhance the bureaucratic power, prestige, and standing of one organization at the expense of others. Although this may seem rational from the perspective of an individual bureaucracy, it can lead to poor, if not disastrous, foreign policies. The pursuit of individual, value-maximizing strategies at the organization level can lead to collective disaster at the nation–state level. Moreover, the decision-making process is typically one of coalition and countercoalition building, bargaining, and compromising that may not yield a best or optimal decision. Attempting to establish a consensus or at least a **minimum winning coalition** is a process far different in kind from the earlier simple description of what is usually meant by the term **rational.** Misperception on the part of decision makers as a result of incomplete information, bias, stress, and uncertainty about cause and effect is also a key focus of attention for some pluralist scholars. All such factors undercut the idea of a rational decision-making process.

Finally, for the pluralist, *the agenda of international politics is extensive.* The pluralist rejects the notion that the agenda of international politics is dominated primarily by military–security issues. Foreign affairs agendas have expanded and diversified over the past thirty years such that economic and social issues are often at the forefront of foreign policy debates. Former Secretary of State Henry Kissinger, himself a realist, noted in 1975 that

> progress in dealing with the traditional agenda is no longer enough. A new and unprecedented kind of issue has emerged. The problems of energy, resources, environment, pollution, the uses of space and the seas now rank with questions of military security, ideology, and territorial rivalry which have traditionally made up the diplomatic agenda.[7]

Not surprisingly, such a statement was made at a time of détente or relatively relaxed tensions between East and West. It may be that as international tensions decrease, economic and social, or **welfare,** issues tend to come to the forefront of international debate.

Globalism—Major Actors and Assumptions

Globalism, as we use the term, is a third perspective, fundamentally different from both the realist and pluralist images. In the 1970s, debate within the international relations discipline tended to focus on the realists and pluralists. Only recently has attention been paid to the globalist perspective. Globalists typically assume that the starting point of analysis for international relations is *the global context within which states and other entities interact.* Globalists emphasize the overall structure of the international system or, more colloquially, the "big picture." To explain behavior, one must first grasp the essence of the global environment within which such behavior takes place. This is a dominant theme within the globalist image, although some realists and pluralists also share this perspective. To understand the external behavior of states requires more than merely examining factors internal to a state. One must first grasp how the structure of the system conditions and predisposes certain actors to act in certain ways.

Second, globalists assume that it is not only useful but also imperative to *view international relations from a historical perspective.* It is only through an examination of history that one can understand the current environment within which world politics takes place. For many globalists, Marxists as well as non-Marxists, the defining characteristic of the international system is that it is **capitalist.** This requires the study of the rise of capitalism as it emerged in sixteenth-century Western Europe, its development, changes, and expansion to the point at which today we can speak of a **world capitalist system** that conditions and constrains the behavior of all states and societies. Some states and societies benefit from this capitalist system; others do not.

Third, although globalists recognize the importance of states-as-actors, international organizations, and transnational actors and coalitions, the particular focus of their analysis is on how these and other factors act as *mechanisms of domination* by which some states, classes, or elites manage to benefit from this capitalist system at the expense of others. More specifically, globalists are typically concerned with the development and maintenance of **dependency** relations among northern, industrialized states (North America, Western Europe, Japan, and, increasingly, the socialist states—the USSR and Eastern Europe) and the poor, underdeveloped, or industrially backward Third World or less developed countries (LDCs) of Latin America, Africa, and Asia. The basic argument is that these latter states and societies are underdeveloped not because they have failed to develop capitalist economic systems or because they are poorly integrated into the world capitalist system. On the contrary, it is not a matter of too little capitalism but too much. Far from being placed outside the mainstream of the world capitalist system, LDCs have become an integral part of it. The structure of the global political economy has developed in such a manner—intentionally and unintentionally—as to keep the Third World countries underdeveloped and dependent on the rich northern states. The LDCs play a crucial role in the economic well-being of such countries as the United States by providing cheap labor, raw materials necessary to fuel the American economy, and markets for American manufactured goods. As part of the world capitalist system, LDCs cannot choose their own path toward economic and political development. Autonomous development in these circumstances is not possible.

Finally, as should now be apparent, globalists emphasize to a greater extent than either realists or pluralists the critical *importance of economic factors* when it comes to explaining the dynamics of the international system. Realists, you will recall, subordinate economic factors to those of a political-military nature. Pluralists argue that this is an open question; they typically reject this high versus low politics dichotomy. Social and economic issues to pluralists are at least as important as the security concerns of the realists. Globalists, however, start with the assumption that economics is the key to understanding the creation, evolution, and functioning of the contemporary world system. Although the pluralist and globalist would seem to share common ground because both place importance on economic and social questions, they differ fundamentally in the ways in which they deal with them. The more fragmented pluralist image of multiple actors bargaining, compromising, and building coalitions within and across national borders contrasts sharply with the structural image of the globalist. The globalist would tell a pluralist that the outcome of bargaining among various actors is in most cases predetermined if it involves a **North–South** issue. Such interactions take place within the context of an exploitative and dependent relation that works, at the most general level, to the benefit of maintaining the world capitalist system and, more specifically, to the benefit of particular groups or classes.

TABLE 1.1 Alternative Images of International Relations: Underlying Assumptions

	Realism	Pluralism	Globalism
Analytic Unit(s)	1. State is the principal actor	1. State and non-state actors are important	1. Classes, states and societies, and non-state actors operate as part of world capitalist system
View of Actor(s)	2. State is unitary actor	2. State disaggregated into components, some of which may operate transnationally	2. International relations viewed from historical perspective, especially the continuous development of world capitalism
Behavioral Dynamic	3. State is rational actor seeking to maximize its own interest or national objectives in foreign policy	3. Foreign policy making and transnational processes involve conflict, bargaining, coalition, and compromise—not necessarily resulting in optimal outcomes	3. Focus is on patterns of dominance within and among societies
Issues	4. National security issues are most important	4. Multiple agenda with socioeconomic or welfare issues as, or more, important than national security questions	4. Economic factors are most important

Images of International Relations: Some Qualifications

We find the threefold division of realism, pluralism, and globalism to be a useful way to view the diverse images on which theoretical efforts are based in the field of international relations. We are the first to admit that this classification scheme also has its limitations. Accordingly, we offer several qualifications and clarifications.

First, each image should be viewed as an **ideal** or **pure type** in that each image emphasizes what a number of seemingly diverse theoretical approaches have in common.[8] For example, there are substantial differences in the works of Kenneth Waltz, Stanley Hoffmann, and the late Hans J. Morgenthau, but all three scholars share core assumptions of the realist perspective. What unites them as international relations theorists is more important for our purposes than what divides them.

Second, the overview of key assumptions of each of the three perspectives might give the impression that the three images are mutually exclusive in all respects. This is not the case. Realists such as Robert Gilpin, for example, do not deny the importance of economic factors in international relations; they simply differ with many pluralists and globalists as to the relative importance of political-military considerations compared to economic factors. Such globalists as Immanuel Wallerstein also recognize the significance of the state in international relations but prefer to emphasize economic trends and class relations. Similarly, many interdependence theorists of pluralist orientation do not deny the importance of the state as a key international actor, but they prefer to examine non-state actors as well as transnational, socioeconomic factors that they see as having reduced the autonomy of the state-as-actor. Even if the three images are not mutually exclusive in every respect, and even if every observer of international relations can agree that sensitivity to alternative perspectives on world politics is commendable, the reader may want to keep in mind how difficult it is to combine three images with so very different underlying assumptions from which all subsequent analyses, hypotheses, and theories derive.

Third, we readily confess that not all international relations specialists can be assigned conveniently to one particular image. Bruce Russett, for example, has written on dependency, international integration, and conflict between states-as-actors—each subject associated, respectively, with globalist, pluralist, and realist images. Robert Jervis has bridged two camps in his pluralist examination of psychological factors in foreign policy decision making and in his realist focus on national security questions associated with deterrence, arms races, and how the anarchical international system provides the environment within which wars occur. Recent works by Robert O. Keohane and Joseph S. Nye recognize the importance of insights from realism as well as insights derived from the pluralist perspective with which both were earlier identified.

Although we believe that the vast majority of writers within the international relations discipline tends to be associated with one of the three perspectives, notable exceptions do not, in our estimation, undermine the utility of the tripartite division of the field that we employ in this volume. We acknowledge a certain amount of conceptual eclecticism by scholars in the study of international relations, perhaps reflecting the absence of a single, dominant perspective and the continuing search for such an all-encompassing, singular image. Our focus here, however, is primarily on ideas, trends, and generalized images of international relations and only secondarily on the work of particular authors. Indeed, our references to work in the international relations field are meant to be representative of the images we discuss, not encyclopedic in scope. Just as it is hoped that the reader will come to appreciate the strengths and weaknesses of each of the three perspectives, so too do many specialists in the field weigh the relative utility of these alternative images in generating insights helpful in answering particular theoretical questions they may be asking.[9] Moreover, it is not surprising to find a certain amount of conceptual eclecticism in the work of a number of theorists whose interests have changed over the years.[10]

Fourth, the images tend to focus more on *what* is studied than on *how* to conduct such studies. A central argument we make is that quantitative and nonquantitative approaches to the study of international politics are methods that transcend the three images we have identified. Statistical methods, formal hypothesis testing, and **causal modeling** find their adherents within each of the perspectives as do the more traditional, nonquantitative, historical, philosophical, legal, case study, and comparative case study methods. Our point remains that these are *methods*, not images of international relations or world politics. Images may influence the choice of methods, but images and methods are not one and the same.

Although it is the subject of endless debates and much blood letting in academic circles, the behavioralist-traditionalist (or the "science"-traditionalist) dichotomy is not particularly useful for our purposes. One can argue over the relative merits of particular methods for answering political questions, but a more fundamental concern is the conceptual framework within which those methods are used. Are these methods informed by realist, pluralist, or globalist images of international politics, and how useful are these alternative images by which we order or make some sense of what we observe?[11]

Recent efforts to predict global futures through complex modeling, for example, reflect one or another of the three images we identify.[12] An image of international or world politics influences the selection of units or processes examined and **variables** identified and operationalized. Thus, for realists, states and state interactions are of key importance; for pluralists, transnational interactions to include communications flows across national borders may well be the central focus; and for globalists, patterns of class or North-South relations of dominance or dependence are perhaps most important.

Similarly, methods associated with the literature on **decision-making** and **public choice theory**—economic models applied to political decision making—transcend the three world images we identify.[13] Assumptions made about actors and processes are informed by realist, pluralist, and globalist images and color the use a particular method is given. Thus, **public** or **collective goods theory, game theory, econometrics,** and other approaches identified with the rapidly growing interdisciplinary field of **political economy** find their adherents among scholars holding diverse images and thus are not the exclusive preserve of realists, pluralists, or globalists.

Finally, we wish to state explicitly that the three images we identify are not *theories* of international relations.[14] Rather, they represent general perspectives on international relations out of which particular theories *may* develop. Assumptions of an image may become part of a theory (such as the realist assumptions of a unified, rational, state-as-actor in some realist works), but more often than not, they simply help to orient a scholar's research by highlighting certain units of analysis for investigation in the construction of a theory and help to determine what constitutes evidence in the testing of hypotheses.

SUMMATION

For the realist, states are the principal or most important actors on the international political stage and represent the key unit of analysis. States are viewed as unitary actors that behave in a generally rational manner. National security issues dominate the hierarchy of the international agenda. For the pluralist, by contrast, nonstate actors are also important entities. The state is disaggregated into its component parts and is continually subjected to outside elements, including state as well as nonstate actors. The hierarchy of world issues is also subject to change and is not always dominated by matters of military security. For the globalist, all actors must be viewed within the context of an overarching global structure. The defining characteristic of this structure is its capitalist nature; it must be viewed in a historical context with a particular emphasis on the role of dominant classes that transcend the particular confines of any one state. To understand the mechanisms of dependency whereby rich, industrialized states maintain poor LDCs in a subordinate position within this world capitalist system requires an appreciation of the paramount role played by economic factors.

We now turn to a more comprehensive discussion of the three images of international relations, giving in subsequent chapters summaries of major actors and assumptions, intellectual precursors and influences, key concepts and representative theoretical works, and criticisms.

NOTES

1. Max Weber, *Methodology of the Social Sciences*, trans. and ed. E. A. Shils and H. A. Finch (New York: Free Press, 1949), pp. 81, 84.
2. James N. Rosenau, "Order and Disorder in the Study of World Politics," in *Globalism Versus Realism: International Relations' Third Debate*, ed. Ray Maghroori and Bennett Ramberg (Boulder, CO: Westview Press, 1982), pp. 1–7.
3. Quincy Wright, *A Study of War* (Chicago: University of Chicago Press, 1942); Kenneth N. Waltz, *Man, the State and War* (New York: Columbia University Press, 1959); Bruce Bueno de Mesquita, *The War Trap* (New Haven, CT: Yale University Press, 1981).

4. Waltz, *Man, State, War*, pp. 232–38. Consistent with this view, anarchy is also a *necessary* condition for war to occur, but it is by no means *sufficient* as a sole cause of the phenomenon.

5. For a discussion on how to approach the study of international conflict, see the articles by Bruce Bueno de Mesquita, Stephen Krasner, and Robert Jervis in *International Studies Quarterly* 29, no. 2 (June 1985): 121–54. Bueno de Mesquita in particular calls for the development of rigorous, deductive, axiomatic theory.

6. For arguments challenging the supposed ability to determine in an objective manner what constitutes "facts," let alone "the real world," see Richard J. Bernstein, *The Restructuring of Social and Political Theory* (New York: Harcourt Brace Jovanovich, 1976).

7. Henry A. Kissinger, "A New National Partnership," *Department of State Bulletin*, 72 (17 February 1975): 199, Cited in Robert O. Keohane and Joseph S. Nye. *Power and Interdependence: World Politics in Transition* (Boston: Little, Brown, 1977), p. 3.

8. On ideal types, see Weber, *Methodology*, pp. 90–93. Cf. Max Weber, *Basic Concepts in Sociology*, trans. H. P. Secher (Westport, CT: Greenwood Press, 1962, 1969), pp. 52–55.

9. Whether different images of the world lead to the formulation of different questions or whether the questions themselves have resulted in these different mental constructs for dealing with them is arguable and may depend on the particular theorist.

10. See, for example, articles in W. Ladd Hollist and James N. Rosenau, eds., *World System Structure: Continuity and Change* (Beverly Hills, CA: Sage Publications, 1981). It is one thing to produce a work that is purposely eclectic, drawing on insights from a wide variety of sources, but this is different from attempting to reconcile underlying assumptions reflecting fundamentally divergent perspectives on world politics without relaxing one or more of these critical assumptions. For attempts at reconciliation, see Richard K. Ashley, *The Political Economy of War and Peace* (London: Frances Pinter, 1980); Nazli Choucri and Robert C. North, *Nations in Conflict: National Growth and International Violence* (San Francisco: W. H. Freeman, 1975); Richard W. Mansbach and John A. Vasquez, *In Search of Theory: A New Paradigm for Global Politics* (New York: Columbia University Press, 1981). See also John Gerard Ruggie, "Continuity and Transformation in the World Polity: Toward a Neorealist Synthesis," *World Politics* 35, no. 2 (January 1983): 261–285; and Robert O. Keohane, "Theory of World Politics: Structural Realism and Beyond," paper presented at the 1982 meeting of the APSA, Denver, September 1982; reprinted in *Political Science: The State of the Discipline*, ed. Ada W. Finifter (Washington, DC: American Political Science Association, 1983), pp. 503–540.

11. See the articles in Klaus Knorr and James N. Rosenau, eds., *Contending Approaches to International Politics* (Princeton, NJ: Princeton University Press, 1969). See also G. David Garson, "Marxism as Methodology," in his *Handbook of Political Science Methods*, 2d ed. (Boston, MA: Holbrook Press, 1976), pp. 9–20.

12. The dominant image among most world modelers, however, is a pluralist one informed by what Ashley calls "liberal positivist commitments." See Richard K. Ashley, "The Eye of Power: The Politics of World Modeling," *International Organization* 37, no. 3 (Summer 1983): 500.

13. See, for example, Bruno S. Frey, "The Public Choice View of International Political Economy," *International Organization* 38, no. 1 (Winter 1984): 199–223; Mancur Olson, *The Rise and Decline of Nations* (New Haven, CT: Yale University Press, 1982) and *The Logic of Collective Action* (Cambridge, MA: Harvard University Press, 1965). See also "Symposium: Mancur Olson on the Rise and Decline of Nations," *International Studies Quarterly* 27, no. 1 (March 1983): 3–37; and John A. C. Conybeare, "Public Goods, Prisoners' Dilemmas, and the International Political-Economy," *International Studies Quarterly* 28, no. 1 (March 1984): 5–22.

14. Nor are the images equivalent to the research program discussed by Imre Lakatos. Such a research program, if formulated for international relations, would be more specific than the images discussed in this book but more general than any particular theory we mention. See Imre Lakatos, "Falsification and the Methodology of Scientific Research Programmes," in *Criticism and the Growth of Knowledge*, ed. Imre Lakatos and Alan Musgrave (Cambridge: Cambridge University Press, 1970). Lakatos is attempting to refute what he sees as the relativism of Thomas Kuhn's influential *The Structure of Scientific Revolutions* (Chicago: University of Chicago Press, 1962).

SUGGESTED READINGS

Agnew, Neil M., and Sandra W. Pyke. *The Science Game: An Introduction to Research in the Behavioral Sciences.* Englewood Cliffs, NJ: Prentice-Hall, 1982.

Alker, Hayward R., Jr., and Thomas J. Biersteker. "The Dialectics of World Order: Notes for a Future Archeologist of International Savoir Faire." *International Studies Quarterly* 28, 2 (June 1984): 121–42.

Almond, Gabriel A., and Stephen J. Genco. "Clouds, Clocks, and the Study of Politics." *World Politics* 29, 4 (July 1977): 489–522.

Art, Robert J., and Robert Jervis, eds. *International Politics: Anarchy, Force, Political Economy, and Decision Making.* 2d ed. Boston, MA: Little Brown, 1984.

Ashley, Richard K. "The Eye of Power: The Politics of World Modeling." *International Organization* 37, 3 (Summer 1983): 495–535. A review essay.

Axelrod, Robert and Robert O. Keohane. "Achieving Cooperation Under Anarchy." *World Politics* 31, 1 (October 1985): 226–254.

Banks, Michael. "Two Meanings of Theory in the Study of International Relations." *The Yearbook of World Affairs.* 20 (1966): 220–40.

———. "Ways of Analyzing the World Society." In *International Relations: A Bibliography*, ed. A. J. R. Groom and Christopher R. Mitchell. London: Frances Pinter, 1978.

Bernstein, Richard. *The Restructuring of Social and Political Theory.* New York: Harcourt Brace Jovanovich, 1976.

Bronowski, Jacob. *The Origins of Knowledge and Imagination.* New Haven, CT: Yale University Press, 1978.

Bueno de Mesquita, Bruce, Stephen D. Krasner, and Robert Jervis. Articles in *International Studies Quarterly* 29, 2 (June 1985): 121–49.

Connolly, William E. "Theoretical Self-consciousness." *Polity* 2, 1 (1973): 5–35.

Conybeare, John A. C. "Public Goods, Prisoners' Dilemmas and the International Political Economy." *International Studies Quarterly* 28, 1 (March 1984): 5–22.

Dougherty, James E., and Robert L. Pfaltzgraff, Jr. *Contending Theories of International Relations.* 2d ed. New York: Harper & Row, 1981.

Eulau, Heinz. "Multilevel Methods in Comparative Politics." *American Behavioral Scientist* 21, 1 (September/October 1977): 39–62.

Frey, Bruno S. "The Public Choice View of International Political Economy." *International Organization* 38, 1, (Winter 1984): 199–223.

Garson, G. David. *Handbook of Political Science Methods.* 2d ed. Boston: Holbrook Press, 1976.

Guetzkow, Harold, and Joseph J. Valadez, eds. *Simulated International Processes: Theories and Research in Global Modeling.* Beverly Hills, CA: Sage Publications, 1981.

Habermas, Jürgen. "Technology and Science as Ideology." In *Towards a Rational Society.* Translated by Jeremy Shapiro. London: Heinemann, 1970.

Heath, Anthony. *Rational Choice and Social Exchange.* Cambridge: Cambridge University Press, 1976.

Hettne, Bjorn. "Conceptions of the Present World Order in the Social Sciences." *Cooperation and Conflict* 16 (1981): 109–18.

Hoffmann, Stanley. *Contemporary Theory in International Relations.* Englewood Cliffs, NJ: Prentice-Hall, 1960.

Holsti, K. J. *The Dividing Discipline.* Winchester, MA: Allen & Unwin, 1985.

Kaplan, Abraham. *The Conduct of Inquiry: Methodology for Behavioral Sciences.* New York: Harper & Row, 1964.

Keohane, Robert O., and Joseph S. Nye. *Power and Interdependence: World Politics in Transition.* Boston: Little, Brown, 1977.

Kindleberger, Charles P. "Dominance and Leadership in the International Economy: Exploitation, Public Goods, and Free Rides." *International Studies Quarterly* 25, 2 (June 1981): 242–54.

———. "On the Rise and Decline of Nations." *International Studies Quarterly* 27, 1 (March 1983): 5–10. A review essay on Mancur Olson, *The Rise and Decline of Nations.*

Knorr, Klaus, and James N. Rosenau, eds. *Contending Approaches to International Politics.* Princeton, NJ: Princeton University Press, 1969.

Knorr, Klaus, and Sidney Verba, eds. *The International System: Theoretical Essays.* Princeton, NJ: Princeton University Press, 1969.

Kubalkova, Vendulka, and A. A. Cruickshank. *Marxism–Leninism and Theory of International Relations.* London: Routledge & Kegan Paul, 1980.

Kuhn, Thomas S. *The Structure of Scientific Revolutions.* Chicago: University of Chicago Press, 1962.

Lakatos, Imre. "Falsification and the Methodology of Scientific Research Programmes." In *Criticism and the Growth of Knowledge,* ed. Imre Lakatos and Alan Musgrave. Cambridge: Cambridge University Press, 1970.

Lauren, Paul Gordon. *Diplomacy: New Approaches in History, Theory, and Policy.* New York: Free Press, 1979.

Lieber, Robert J. *Theory and World Politics.* Cambridge, MA: Winthrop, 1972.

Light, Margot, and A. J. R. Groom, eds. *International Relations: A Handbook of Current Theory.* Boulder, CO: Lynne Rienner Publishers, 1985.

McClelland, Charles A. "On the Fourth Wave: Past and Future in the Study of

International Systems." In *The Analysis of International Politics*, ed. James N. Rosenau. New York: Free Press, 1972.

————. *Theory and the International System*. New York: Macmillan, 1966.

Maghroori, Ray, and Bennett Ramberg, eds. *Globalism Versus Realism: International Relations' Third Debate*. Boulder, CO: Westview Press, 1982.

Moon, J. Donald. "The Logic of Inquiry: A Synthesis of Opposed Perspectives," In *Handbook of Political Science*, Vol. 1, ed. Fred I. Greenstein and Nelson W. Polsby. Reading, MA: Addison-Wesley, 1975.

Morgan, Patrick M. *Theories and Approaches to International Politics*. 3d ed. New Brunswick, NJ: Transaction Books, 1981.

Mueller, John E. *Approaches to Measurement in International Relations: A Non-Evangelical Survey*. New York: Appleton-Century-Crofts, 1969.

Olson, Mancur. *The Logic of Collective Action*. Cambridge: Harvard University Press, 1965.

————. *The Rise and Decline of Nations*. New Haven, CT: Yale University Press, 1982.

————. "Towards a Mature Social Science." *International Studies Quarterly* 27, 1 (March 1983): 29–37.

Nagel, Ernest. *The Structure of Scientific Explanation*. New York: Harcourt Brace Jovanovich, 1961.

Palmer, Norman D. "The Study of International Relations in the United States: Perspectives of Half a Century." *International Studies Quarterly* 24, 3 (September 1980): 343–64.

Parkinson, F. *The Philosophy of International Relations*. Beverly Hills, CA: Sage Publications, 1977.

Rapoport, Anatol. "Various Meanings of Theory." *American Political Science Review* 52, 4 (December 1958): 972–88.

Rogowski, Ronald. "Rationalist Theories of Politics: A Midterm Report." *World Politics* 30, 2 (January 1978): 296–323. A review article.

Rosenau, James N., ed. *International Politics and Foreign Policy: A Reader in Research and Theory*. 2d ed., rev. New York: Free Press, 1969.

Ruggie, John Gerard. "Collective Goods and Future International Collaboration." *American Political Science Review* 66 (1972): 874–93.

Simon, Herbert A. *Models of Thought*. New Haven, CT: Yale University Press, 1979.

Singer, J. David. *A General Systems Taxonomy for Political Science*. New York: General Learning Press, 1971.

————. *The Scientific Study of Politics: An Approach to Foreign Policy Analysis*. Morristown, NJ: General Learning Press, 1972.

Smith, Michael, Richard Little, and Michael Shackleton, eds. *Perspectives on World Politics*. London: Croom Helm, 1981.

Stinchcombe, Arthur L. *Constructing Social Theories*. New York: Harcourt Brace Jovanovich, 1968.

Sullivan, Michael P. *International Relations: Theories and Evidence*. Englewood Cliffs, NJ: Prentice-Hall, 1976.

Thompson, Kenneth W. *Masters of International Thought: Major Twentieth-Century Theorists and the World Crisis*. Baton Rouge: Louisiana State University Press, 1980.

————. "Toward a Theory of International Politics." *American Political Science Review* 49, 3 (September 1955): 733–46.

Toulmin, Stephen. *Foresight and Understanding: An Inquiry Into the Aims of Science*. New York: Harper & Row, 1963.

Waltz, Kenneth N. *Theory of International Politics*. Reading, MA: Addison-Wesley, 1979.

———. "Theory of International Relations." In *Handbook of Political Science*, Vol. 8, *International Politics*, ed. Nelson W. Polsby and Fred I. Greenstein. Reading, MA: Addison-Wesley, 1975.

Zinnes, Dina A. "A Consumer's Guide to Texts on Mathematical Modeling." *World Politics* 31, 3 (April 1979): 434–56. A review article.

———. "Three Puzzles in Search of a Researcher." *International Studies Quarterly* 24, 3 (September 1980): 315–42.

Thinking Theory Thoroughly

James N. Rosenau

James Rosenau addresses creative theorizing and develops nine principles to guide those who would engage in this enterprise.

It rarely happens, but now and again in academic life one is jolted into returning to fundamentals, into ascertaining whether one has unknowingly strayed from one's organizing premises. This happened to me recently when a graduate student inquired whether she should take an "independent reading" course under my direction. Noting that my competence was limited, I responded by asking what topics or problems she planned to investigate. Her answer startled me, perhaps partly because it was ungrammatical but mainly because I found it pedagogically challenging. Her answer was simple: "I would like you to teach me to think theory!" I agreed to take on the role of advisor.

At this writing, some eleven weeks, many conversations and much reflection later, I still find the assignment challenging, though now I am beginning to wonder whether the capacity to think theoretically, the inclination to perceive and assess the course of events as suggestive or expressive of larger forces, is a talent that can be taught. It may be, instead, a cast of mind, a personality trait, or a philosophical perspective that some acquire early in life and others do not.

If this is so, there is not much that a professor can do to teach students how to think theoretically. They can be introduced to the nature of theories, taught the various purposes theories can serve, exposed to the controversies over the relative worth of different theories, and instructed on the steps required for the construction of viable theories. And, to solidify the learning of these lessons, they can then be given assignments in which they have to formulate concrete hypotheses and tie them together into an actual theoretical framework. The learning of these skills underlying the design of theories is not, however, the equivalent of learning how to think theoretically. Or, more accurately, it is not the

From James N. Rosenau, *The Scientific Study of Foreign Policy*, rev. ed. London: Frances Pinter, 1980, pages 19–31. Reprinted by permission.

equivalent of what I understood my student as wanting me to teach her. In fact, she may only have been asking instruction on the dos and don'ts of theoretical design. But because of the way she worded her request I interpreted her as seeking more than an introduction to the procedures and techniques essential to creative theorizing. It seemed to me she was looking to acquire not a set of skills, but rather a set of predispositions, a cluster of habits, a way of thinking, a mental lifestyle—or whatever may be the appropriate label for that level of intellectual existence that governs the use of skills and the application of values—that she did not possess and that she thought she valued enough to want to make part of her orientation toward international phenomena. It is this more fundamental dimension of the life of the mind that I now suspect may not be teachable or learnable, a caveat that needs emphasis at the outset because the ensuing analysis amounts to nothing less than a pronouncement on how to think theoretically.

NINE PRE-CONDITIONS FOR CREATIVE THEORIZING

It follows that the task of disciplining ourselves and our students to think theoretically consists, first, of identifying the cognitive inclinations and perceptual impulses from which creative theory springs and, second, of then forming intellectual habits which assure the prevalence of these inclinations and impulses whenever we turn to theory-building endeavors. The central question examined in this paper follows: what are the mental qualities that best enable one to "think theory" and how can their acquisition be best assured? Nine such qualities strike me as especially conducive to the development of good theorists. Each of the nine seems equally important and there is some overlap among them. Accordingly, the sequence of their elaboration here should not be interpreted as implying a rank ordering.

> To think thoretically one has to avoid treating the task as that of formulating an appropriate definition of theory.

So as to clarify what is involved in thinking theoretically, let me start with the proposition that the task is not one of developing a clear-cut definition of theory. On balance, it is probably preferable to have a precise conception of the nature of theory rather than a vague one, but definitional exactness is not the only criterion of thinking theoretically and it may not even be a necessary requirement for such thought. I can readily imagine a young student thinking theoretically about international phenomena well before his or her first course on the subject turns to the question of what constitutes theory and the various uses to which it can be put. Indeed, I have had the good fortune of encountering a few students who were, so to speak, born theoreticians. From their very first comments in class as freshmen it was clear that they thought theoretically even though they have never had any methodological training or any exposure to the history of international relations.

Most of us are not so lucky. Most of us have to be trained to think theoretically and then we have to engage in the activity continuously in order to achieve and sustain a genuinely theoretical perspective. Hence, the fact that a few among us can maintain such a perspective without training and practice is a useful reminder that definitional clarity is not a prerequisite to creative theorizing.

The reminder is important because many of us tend to exaggerate the importance of exact definitions. To be clear about the nature of theory is not to guarantee the formulation of meaningful theory. Such clarity can be misleading. It can provide a false sense of security, a misguided confidence that one needs only to organize one's empirical materials in the proper way if one is equipped with a clear-cut definition of theory. It is my impression that much of the writing in our field derives from this premise that good definitions automatically yield good theories, as if the definitions somehow relieve the observer of the need to apply imagination and maintain philosophical discipline.

To be sure, much of the writing also suffers from loose and ambiguous conceptions of theory or from a confusion between theory and method. Such research would, obviously, be more valuable if it proceeded from a tighter and clearer notion of what the theoretical enterprise entails. So, to repeat, I am not arguing against definitional clarity. On the contrary, I believe it is highly appropriate to help students achieve such clarity by introducing them to the vast array of articles and books now available on the dynamics, boundaries, uses, and abuses of theory in the international field. But I am arguing for more than definitional clarity. I am arguing for caution and restraint in the use of definitions: in digesting the literature on theory and building a more elaborate conception of what it involves, one has to be careful not to lean too heavily on definitions and guidance. Also needed is a cast of mind, a mental set that focuses application of the definitions and facilitates creative theorizing.

> To think theoretically one has to be clear as to whether one aspires to empirical theory or value theory.

Progress in the study of international affairs depends on advances in both empirical and value theory. But the two are not the same. They may overlap; they can focus on the same problem; and values always underlie the selection of the problems to which empirical theories are addressed. Yet they differ in one overriding way: empirical theory deals essentially with the "is" of international phenomena, with things as they are if and when they are subjected to observation, while value theory deals essentially with the "ought" of international phenomena, with things as they should be if and when they could be subjected to manipulation. This distinction underlies, in turn, entirely different modes of reasoning, a different rhetoric, and different types of evidence.

The habit of making the necessary analytic, rhetorical, and evidential distinctions between empirical and value theory can be difficult for young students to develop. Indeed, it can be weak and elusive for any of us who have strong value commitments and a deep concern for certain moral questions. The more intensive are our values, the more are we tempted to allow our empirical inquiries to be guided by our beliefs rather than by our concern for observation. For this reason I have found that helping students become habituated to the is–ought distinction is among the most difficult pedagogical tasks. They can understand the distinction intellectually and they can even explain and defend it when pressed; but practicing it is another matter and often their empirical analyses slip into moral judgments without their being aware of it. It is as if they somehow fear that their values and the policy goals they want to promote will be undermined if they allow themselves to focus on observable phenomena. Such, of couse, is not the case. On the contrary, moral values and policy goals can be well served, even best served, by putting them aside and proceeding detachedly long enough to enlarge empirical understanding of the obstacles that hinder realization of the values and progress toward the goals.

This is the one line of reasoning on behalf of thinking theoretically that my most value-committed students find persuasive. If empirical theory is posited as a tool of moral theory, they can approach it instrumentally and see virtue in habituating themselves to distinguishing between the two. It takes a while, however, before the perceived virtues of habituation are translated into actual habits and, in fact, some never manage to make the transition, hard as they may try. Impatient with the need for change, convinced that time is too scarce to afford the slow pace of empirical inquiry, many simply give up and dismiss the is–ought distinction as one of those picayune obsessions to which some academics fall prey.

It is my impression that impatience with empirical theorizing is likely to be especially intense among Third World students of international relations. The newly developed consciousness of the long-standing injustices built into First World–Third World relationships, the lure of dependency theory, and perhaps a frustration over the central tendencies of social science in the First World have made Third World theorists particularly resistant to detached empirical theorizing. Their resistance gives a First World scholar pause: is his insistence on habituating oneself to the is–ought distinction yet another instance of false superiority, of projecting onto the developing world practices that have worked in industrial societies? It could be. Of late I have become keenly aware of the biases that may underlie my intellectual endeavors and thus I am not prepared merely to brush aside the idea that the is–ought distinction may be inappropriate to theorizing in much of the world. In this particular instance, however, I cannot even begin to break the habit. The relevance of the distinction strikes me as global, as independent of any national biases, as necessary to thinking theoretically wherever and whenever enlarged comprehension is sought. Empirical theory is not superior to moral theory; it is simply preferable for certain purposes, and one of these is the end of deepening our grasp of why international processes unfold as they do.

Aware that my own expertise, such as it may be, lies in the realm of empirical theory, the ensuing discussion makes no pretense of being relevant to thinking theoretically in the moral context. All the precepts that follow are concerned only with those mental qualities that may render us more thoroughgoing in our empirical theorizing.

> To think theoretically one must be able to assume that human affairs are founded on an underlying order.

A prime task of empirical theory is to explain why international phenomena are structured as they are and/or behave as they do. To perform this task one must assume that each and every international phenomenon is theoretically explicable, that deeper understanding of its dynamics could be achieved if appropriate instruments for measuring it were available. To assume that everything is potentially explicable is to presume that nothing happens by chance, capriciously, at random, that for every effect there must be a cause. That is, there must be an underlying order out of which international relations springs. If this were not the case, if events could occur for no reason, there would be little point in theorizing. If some events are inherently inexplicable, efforts to build creative theory are bound to fall short to the extent that they embrace phenomena that may occur at random. Indeed, in the absence of the assumption of an underlying order, attempts to fashion theory are futile, pointless exercises, a waste of time that could be better spent writing poetry, playing tennis, or tending the garden.

This is *not* to say that thought only acquires the status of theory when it purports to account for every event. As indicated below, theory is also founded on the laws of probability. Hence it only purports to account for central tendencies, but this claim is unwarranted if an assumption of underlying order is not made. That is, to think theoretically one must presume that there is a cause for every effect even though one does not seek to explain every effect.

I have found that most students have a difficult time becoming habituated to the assumption of an underlying order. They see it as a denial of their own freedom. To presume there is a cause for everything, they reason, is to deprive people of free will, perhaps even to relieve them of responsibility for their actions. The assumption of an underlying order does not, of course, have such implications. One's freedom of choice is not lessened by the fact that the choices made are not random and, instead, derive from some source. Yet, fearful about compromising their own integrity, many students cannot accept this subtlety and insist on the premise that people have the capacity to cut themselves off from all prior experience and to act as they please for no reason whatsoever. To support their resistance to the assumption of an underlying order, they will often cite instances of international history when the unexpected occurred or when a highly deviant, impetuous, and irrational action was undertaken, as if somehow irrationality and impetuosity are capricious and do not stem from any sources.

Besides patiently reassuring dubious students that there are no insidious threats in the assumption of an underlying order, resistance to the idea can be lessened, even broken in some instances, by pointing out how the assumption offers hope for greater understanding and deeper comprehension. To presume that there is a cause of every effect is to assume that everything is potentially knowable, that inquiry can pay off, that one is not necessarily destined to go down an intellectual path that dead ends, leads nowhere. The assumption of an underlying order, in other words, is pervaded with hope. We do not make it to allow ourselves to be hopeful, but it has that consequence. It enables us to view ourselves as totally in charge of our own investigations, limited only by our imaginations and the resources at our disposal. It allows us to approach the chaos we perceive in the world around us as a challenge, as an orderliness that has yet to be identified and traced. It permits us to dare to think theory thoroughly because the affairs of people are patterned and the patterns are susceptible to being uncovered.

> To think theoretically one must be predisposed to ask about every event, every situation, or every observed phenomenon, "Of what is it an instance?"

Of all the habits one must develop to think theoretically, perhaps none is more central than the inclination to ask this question at every opportunity. It must be a constant refrain, a melody that haunts every lurch forward in the process of moving from observations to conclusions. For to see every event as an instance of a more encompassing class of phenomena is to sustain the search for patterns and to avoid treating any phenomenon as inherently unique. To think theoretically is to be at home with abstractions, to generalize, to discern the underlying order that links otherwise discrete incidents, and such a mode of thinking cannot be achieved and maintained unless every observed phenomenon is approached as merely one instance of a recurring sequence.

Again students appear to have a hard time building up this habit. They are inclined to probe for the special meaning of an event, to explore it for what sets it apart from all other events, rather than to treat it as an instance of a larger pattern. They want to understand the Iranian revolution, not revolutions as a social process, and to the extent this is their preference, to that extent do they resist building up the impulse to always reach for more general theoretical insights. Indeed, I have had many students who simply do not know where to begin when asked to indicate of what pattern some event they regard as important is an instance. Their faces turn blank and their tongues turn silent. They are paralyzed. They do not know what it means to treat the event as merely an instance of something, as just part of a larger category. And so they stumble, mumble, or otherwise resist thinking in those elementary terms out of which theorizing springs.

My response here is twofold. First, I try to portray the pleasure, the sheer joy, to be had from taking steps up the ladder of abstraction. Fitting pieces into larger wholes offers, I believe, a special sense of satisfaction, a feeling of accomplishment not unlike that which accompanies solving a puzzle or resolving a mystery. Indeed, theory building can readily be viewed as puzzle solving, as uncovering the dynamics embedded deep in the interstices of human relationships, and there are few students who are not intrigued by the challenge of solving puzzles.

If appealing thus to the curiosity of students does not succeed in getting them to ask habitually "Of what is this an instance?" (and often it is not a sufficient incentive), I revert to a second line of reasoning which, in effect, amounts to an attempt to shame them into the habit. This involves pointing out the implications of stumbling and mumbling, of not being able to discern any larger class of phenomena of which the observed phenomenon is an instance. The implications are unmistakable: to be paralyzed by the question "Of what is this an instance?" is not to know what one is interested in, to be lacking questions that generate and guide one's inquiry, to be confused by the phenomena one claims to be worthy of investigation. Based on the presumption of an underlying order, I believe that no phenomenon exists in isolation, unique only unto itself, and thus I believe that we always have an answer to the of-what-is-this-an-instance question, whether we know it or not. Accordingly, the task is not one of figuring out an answer presently unknown to us; it is rather that of explicating an answer that we have already acquired but have yet to surface. I am arguing, in other words, that we do not get interested in an international phenomenon for no reason, that our interest in it stems from a concern about a more encompassing set of phenomena, and that there is therefore no need to be paralyzed by the question if we press ourselves to move up the ladder of abstraction on which our intellectuality is founded. Once shamed into acknowledging that their concerns are not confined to the lowest rung on the ladder, most students are willing to begin to venture forth and approach the phenomena they observe as mere instances of something else.

> To think theoretically one must be ready to appreciate and accept the need
> to sacrifice detailed descriptions for broad observations.

One cannot begin to mount the rungs of the ladder of abstraction if one is unable to forgo the detailed account, the elaborated event, the specific minutia. As indicated, the theoretical enterprise is committed to the teasing out of central tendencies, to encompassing ever greater numbers of phenomena, to moving up the ladder of abstraction as parsimoniously as possible. Thus theory involves generalizing rather than particularizing and, in so doing, it requires relinquishing, subordinating, and/or not demonstrating much of one's impulse to expound everything one knows. It means, in effect, that one must discipline one's self to accept simple explanations over complex ones.

These are not easy tasks. Most of us find comfort in detail. The more details we know, the more are we likely to feel we have mastered our subject. To forgo much of the detail, on the other hand, is to opt for uncertainties, to expose ourselves to the criticisms of those who would pick away at our generalizations with exceptions. The temptations to fall back on details are thus considerable and much concentration on the upper rungs of the ladder of abstraction is required if the temptations are to be resisted.

Happily this is less of a problem for beginning students than more mature ones who are introduced late to the theoretical enterprise. The former have yet to acquire extensive familiarity with details and they are therefore not likely to feel threatened by the loss of their knowledge base. They want to focus on the unique, to be sure, but at least it is possible to expose them to the case of theorizing before they find security in endless minutiae. Exactly how more mature scholars accustomed to the comforts of detail can be persuaded to be theoretically venturesome is, I confess, a problem for which I have yet to find anything resembling a solution.

> To think theoretically one must be tolerant of ambiguity, concerned about probabilities, and distrustful of absolutes.

To be concerned about central tendencies one needs to be accepting of exceptions, deviations, anomalies, and other phenomena that, taken by themselves, run counter to the anticipated or prevailing pattern. Anomalies ought not be ignored and often explorations of them can lead to valuable, path-breaking insights; but neither can anomalies be allowed to undermine one's focus on central tendencies. Empirical theories deal only with probabilities and not with absolutes, with how most phenomena are likely to respond to a stimulus and not with how each and every phenomenon responds. Theorists simply do not aspire to account for every phenomenon. They know there will be anomalies and exceptions; indeed, they are suspicious on those unlikely occasions when no exceptions are manifest. Rather their goal is to build theories in which the central tendencies encompass the highest possible degree of probability, with certainties and absolutes being left for ideologues and zealots to expound.

Although they engage in it continuously in their daily lives, students tend to be resistant to the necessity of thinking probabilistically when they turn to theorizing. More accurately, they tend to be reluctant to ignore the ambiguity, to be restless with anything less than perfect certainty, as if any exception to the anticipated central tendencies constitutes a negation of their reasoning. I have found this low tolerance of ambiguity difficult to contest. Many students, fearful of uncertainty, seem to get fixated on the exception, and it is very hard at that point to recapture their interest in central tendencies. The very rhetoric of their everyday language—that things are "completely" the case or that an observation is "absolutely" accurate—reinforces their inclinations to be intolerant of deviations. In this mood they recognize only the "whole truth" as valid and regard central tendencies as a partial rather than a legitimate form of knowledge.

I confess to perplexity over how to handle this obstacle to theorizing on the part of students. I have tried elaborating on the many ways in which probabilistic thinking underlies their daily lives. I have tried making analogies between the physicist and the political scientist, pointing out that the former does not aspire to account for the behavior of every atom any more than the latter aspires to accounting for every voter. I have tried sarcasm, stressing the noxious values that derive from a concern with absolutes. Neither alone nor in combination, however, do such techniques seem to have any effect on many students. Whatever its sources, their intolerance of ambiguity is apparently too deep-seated to yield to reasoning or persuasion. So, reluctantly, I have concluded that students with a low tolerance of ambiguity and a high need for certainty are unlikely to ever think theory thoroughly and that it is probably wasted energy to try to teach them to do so.

To think theoretically one must be playful about international phenomena.

At the core of the theorizing process is a creative imagination. The underlying order of world affairs is too obscure and too complex to yield to pedestrian, constricted, or conventional minds. Only deep penetration into a problem, discerning relationships that are not self-evident and might even be the opposite of what seems readily apparent, can produce incisive and creative theory. Thus to think theoretically one must allow one's mind to run freely, to be playful, to toy around with what might seem absurd, to posit seemingly unrealistic circumstances and speculate what would follow if they were ever to come to pass. Stated differently, one must develop the habit of playing and enjoying the game of "as if"—that is, specifying unlikely conditions and analyzing them *as if* they prevailed.

Put in still another way, it has always seemed to me that good theory ought never be embarrassed by surprises, by unanticipated events that have major consequences for the system on which the theory focuses. A Hitler–Stalin pact, a Nixon resignation, or a Sadat peace initiative should not catch the creative theorist unawares because part of his or her creativity involves imagining the unimaginable. One imagines the unimaginable by allowing one's variables to vary across the entire range of a continuum even if some of its extreme points seem so unlikely as to be absurd. To push one's thinking beyond previously imagined extremes of a continuum is to play the game of "as if," and it involves a playfulness of mind that mitigates against surprises as well as facilitates incisive theorizing.

How one teaches playfulness is, of course, another matter. In some important sense it is an intellectual quality that cannot be taught. One acquires—or perhaps inherits—creativity early in life and no amount of subsequent training can greatly enhance the imaginative powers of those with tunnel vision and inhibited mentalities. On the other hand, encouragement to playfulness can bring out previously untapped talents in some students. Many have become so used to being told what to think that their creative impulses have never been legitimated and, accordingly, they have never even heard of the existence of the "as if" game. So no harm can be done by pressing our students (not to mention ourselves) to be playful and flexible in their thinking, and just conceivably such an emphasis may produce some unexpected results.

> To think theoretically one must be genuinely puzzled by international phenomena.

Creative use of the imagination requires humility toward international phenomena. One must be as concerned about asking the right questions about the order underlying world affairs as finding the right answers. To focus only on answers is to be sure about the questions one wants to probe and this, in turn, is to impose unnecessary limits on one's capacity to discern and integrate the deeper structures of global politics. If, on the other hand, one is genuinely puzzled by why events unfold as they do, one is committed to always asking why they occur in one way rather than another and, in so doing, pressing one's theoretical impulses as far as possible.

I do not use the notion of "genuine puzzles" casually. They are not simply open-ended questions but refer, rather, to perplexity over specific and patterned outcomes. To be genuinely puzzled about the declining capacity of governments to govern effectively, for example, one does not ask, "Why do governments do what they do?" Rather, one asks, say, "Why are most governments unable to control inflation?" or "Why do they alter their alliance commitments under specified conditions?" Genuine puzzles, in other words, are not idle, ill-framed, or impetuous speculations. They encompass specified dependent variables for which adequate explanations are lacking. I do not see how one can begin to think theoretically if one does not discern recurrent outcomes that evoke one's curiosity and puzzlement. Some analysts believe they are starting down the road to theory when they start asking what the outcomes are, but such a line of inquiry leads only to deadends, or worse, to endless mazes, because one never knows when one has come upon a relevant outcome. Genuine puzzles can lead us down creative paths, however, because they discipline us to focus on particular patterns.

One cannot teach others to be puzzled. Again it is very much a matter of whether curiosity has been repressed or allowed to flourish at an early age. It is possible, however, to keep after students and colleagues with the simple question, "What genuinely puzzles you about international affairs?" Hopefully repetition of the question will prove to be sufficiently challenging to facilitate a maximum expression of whatever may be the curiosity potential students may possess.

To think theoretically one must be constantly ready to be proven wrong.

Perhaps nothing inhibits the ability to be intellectually puzzled and playful more than the fear of being embarrassed by the inaccuracies of one's theorizing. Many of us have fragile egos that are so sensitive to error as to lead us to prefer sticking close to conventional wisdom rather than risking speculation that may be erroneous. It is as if our stature as students depends upon the soundness of our observations.

Fragile egos are not readily bolstered and some students may never be capable of venturing forth. In my experience, however, there is one line of reasoning that some students find sufficiently persuasive to lessen their fears of appearing ridiculous. It involves the thought that our comprehension of international phenomena can be substantially advanced even if our theories about them prove to be woefully wrong. Such progress can occur in two ways. One is that falsified theory has the virtue of indicating avenues of inquiry which no longer need be traversed. Doubtless egos are best served by theoretical breakthroughs but if one presumes that knowledge is at least partly developed through a process of elimination, there is some satisfaction to be gained from having narrowed the range of inquiry through theory that subsequently proves fallacious.

Secondly, unsound theory can facilitate progress by provoking others into demonstrating its falsity and attempting to show how and why it went astray. Indeed, assuming that the erroneous theory focuses on significant matters, often the more outrageous the theory is, the more it is likely to provoke further investigation. Thus even if one cannot negotiate a theoretical breakthrough on one's own, one can serve one's ego by the possibility that one's errors may sustain the knowledge-building process. This is surely what one astute analyst had in mind when he observed, "It is important to err importantly."[1]

CONCLUSION: BRINGING IT ALL TOGETHER

Plainly, there is no easy way to evolve the habit of thinking theoretically. Indeed, if the foregoing nine precepts are well founded, it can be readily argued that theorizing is the hardest of intellectual tasks. Clearing away the confusion of day-to-day events and teasing out their underlying patterns is not merely a matter of applying one's mental skills. Sustained, disciplined, and uninhibited work is required, and even then theory can

be elusive, puzzles difficult to identify, details hard to ignore, and probabilities tough to estimate. And the lures and practices of non-theoretical
thinking are always present, tempting us to forgo the insecurities and
ambiguities of high levels of abstraction in favor of the comfortable precision available at low levels.

Yet the payoffs for not yielding to the temptations and persisting to
think theoretically are considerable. There is an exhilaration, an exqui-
siteness, to be enjoyed in the theoretical enterprise that virtually defies
description. Stimulated by the rarified atmosphere, energized by the
freedom to roam uninhibitedly across diverse realms of human experience, one gets giddy at high levels of abstraction. It is that special kind
of giddiness that comes from the feeling that one is employing all the
resources and talents at one's command, moving beyond anything one
has done before. And if one should be so fortunate as actually to achieve
a theoretical breakthrough, then the exhilaration, the excitement, and
the sense of accomplishment can approach the thrill of discovery that
Darwin, Einstein, Freud, and the other great explorers of underlying
order must have experienced at their moments of breakthrough.

For all the difficulties it entails, then, thinking theoretically is, on balance, worth the effort. And so, therefore, is the effort to teach others to
think thoroughly in this way. The habits of theoretical thinking may not
always be teachable, and they may not even be teachable at all; but if
our efforts successfully manage to reach only a few students, they are
worth undertaking. And it is even conceivable that in trying to teach others to think theoretically, we may refine and enlarge our own capacities
for comprehending the underlying order that sustains and alters the
human condition.

NOTE

1. Marion J. Levy, "'Does It Matter If He's Naked?' Bawled the Child," in Klaus
   Knorr and James N. Rosenau (eds.), *Contending Approaches to International
   Relations* (Princeton: Princeton University Press, 1969), p. 93.

CHAPTER TWO

Realism: The State, Power, and the Balance of Power

MAJOR ACTORS AND ASSUMPTIONS: A SUMMARY

In the previous chapter we stated that realism is an image of international relations that is based on four assumptions. Scholars or policy-makers who identify themselves as realists, however, do not all perfectly match the realism ideal type. We find, however, that the four assumptions identified with this perspective are useful as a general statement of the main lines of realist thought and the basis on which hypotheses and theories are developed.

To recapitulate, for the realist *states are the principal actors*, and the study of international relations focuses on these units. Nonstate actors such as multinational corporations and other **transnational** organizations are decidedly less important. International organizations, such as the United Nations or the NATO alliance (North Atlantic Treaty Organization), do not have independent standing because they are composed of sovereign, independent, or autonomous states that determine what these international organizations will do. In short, for the realist the focus is on states and interstate (or international) relations.

What, then, is the nature of this actor that is at the core of international relations? For purposes of analysis, the realist views the state as both *unitary* and *rational*. The state is said to be unitary because any differences of view among political leaders or bureaucracies within the state are ultimately resolved so that the state speaks with one voice. If there are exceptions in practice (as when one agency of government adopts a foreign policy line different from that of another agency of the same government), these cases either deal with trivial issues or are corrected in due course by the leadership. In any event, exceptions are precisely that—exceptions or marginal cases that in effect demonstrate the general rule that unitary states are the principal actors in world politics.

Realists also assume that states are rational actors. Given particular goals, states consider feasible alternatives to achieve these goals in the light of their existing capabilities. Realists recognize problems of lack of information, uncertainty, bias, and misperception, but it is assumed by realists that decision makers strive to achieve the best possible decision even with these constraints.

One may well ask if this characterization of the formulation of foreign policy is accurate. Could one not just as easily argue that history is better characterized as a "march of folly?"[1] Was it wise, for example, for Germany to invade Poland in 1939? Was it in Japan's interest to attack Pearl Harbor in 1941? Was the American conduct of the Vietnam war an example of rationality at work?

From the standpoint of **methodology,** the image of a unified, rational state is a realist *assumption,* not a description of the actual world. Assumptions, it is sometimes argued, should be viewed not in terms of descriptive accuracy but, rather, in terms of how fruitful they are in generating insights and valid generalizations about international politics. From this point of view, assumptions are neither true nor false; they are more or less useful in helping the theorist derive testable propositions or hypotheses about international relations. Once hypotheses are developed, they are tested against the real world. The image of the unified, rational state is, therefore, the starting point for realist analysis, not a concluding statement. Hans J. Morgenthau has explained the utility of the rational, unitary actor assumption as follows:

> We put ourselves in the position of a statesman who must meet a certain problem of foreign policy under certain circumstances, and we ask ourselves what the rational alternatives are from which a statesman may choose . . . and which of these rational alternatives this particular statesman, acting under these circumstances, is likely to choose. It is the testing of this rational hypothesis against the actual facts and their consequences that gives meaning to the facts of international politics and makes a theory of politics possible.[2]

Theorists use such simplifying assumptions as an aid to developing hypotheses and theories about the causes of various international political phenomena including war, arms races, the formation and maintenance of international organizations, and so on.

Finally, realists typically assume that among the array of world issues, *national security* tops the list for states. Military and political issues dominate the agenda and are referred to as high politics. States act to maximize what is often called the **national interest.** Put another way, states try to maximize the likelihood that they will achieve whatever objectives they have set. These objectives include high-political concerns of assuring state survival—security matters—as well as the more mundane or low-political objectives in such fields as trade, finance, monetary exchange, and health. States use the power they have to serve their interests or achieve their objectives. To most realists, the struggle for (or use of) power among states is at the core of international relations. In the words of Morgenthau, "International politics, like all politics, is a struggle for power. Whatever the ultimate aims of international politics, power is always the immediate aim."[3]

As an image of politics, therefore, realism is concerned with power and power politics among states, but as will become clear in subsequent discussion, many realists (including Morgenthau) have also been concerned with values and norms and the role they play in ordering international politics. In our view, realism is not the opposite of an idealism preoccupied with values to the exclusion of power considerations, although the degree of emphasis placed on power and values among realists varies widely. Indeed, some realists place a greater emphasis on values, norms, and formal rules agreed on by states than other realists who see relations of power and the balance of power as the dominant factors. This is true whether the theorist approaches the subject matter of international relations through historical case studies or through the use of quantifiable data in the pursuit of understanding such topics as the causes of war. The common denominator is a conceptual emphasis on a unitary, rational state and problems of national security.

Where did these assumptions of contemporary realist thought come from? They obviously did not appear out of thin air following World War II. Rather, they represent the culmination of thinking about international relations over the centuries. We now turn to some of the more notable intellectual precursors who have had a significant impact on the writings of contemporary realists.

INTELLECTUAL PRECURSORS AND INFLUENCES

Thucydides

Thucydides (471–400 B.C.) is usually credited with being the first writer in the realist tradition as well as the founding father of the international relations discipline.[4] Anyone who has taken a class in political philosophy would probably agree that the profound insights of many ancient Greek writers are not easily grasped on first reading. One might initially find this less a problem with Thucydides' *The Peloponnesian War* because this famous work chronicles twenty-one of the twenty-eight years of war between Athens and Sparta (and their respective allies) in the fifth century B.C. Taken simply as history, it is a masterful account of this era, filled with tales of heroism and brutality, victory and defeat, brilliance and stupidity, honor and deceit. These human traits are certainly exhibited not only in one particular war but in all wars throughout the ages. This is what makes *The Peloponnesian War* such a classic.

The task Thucydides set for himself, however, was much more ambitious than simply describing what was occurring. Particular events were dealt with in great and vivid detail, but his goal was to say something significant not only about the events of his own time but also about the nature of war and why it continually recurs. For Thucydides, the past was the guide for the future. He was less interested in the immediate causes of the Peloponnesian war than he was in the underlying forces at work. Leaders might point to a particular event to justify a policy, but for Thucydides this simply obscured more profound factors that operate throughout history. At heart, *The Peloponnesian War* is a study of the struggle for military and political power.

Thucydides was younger than Socrates and Sophocles and older than Aristophanes. In 424 B.C., during the eighth year of the Peloponnesian War, he was elected an Athenian general. While stationed in Thrace, he failed to prevent the Spartan capture of a city and was punished with twenty years of exile. Athens might have lost a general, but the world gained a historian.

As a member of one of the more notable Athenian families, Thucydides spent the rest of the war observing events, traveling, and interviewing participants. As an exile, he was detached yet obsessed with politics. Although concerned with accuracy, he gave precedence to understanding the motives and policies of the leaders on all sides of the conflict and used the technique of liberally reconstructing speeches and episodes. His purpose was to draw historical lessons for future statesmen who might read his work.[5] By analyzing the particular, he hoped to illuminate the general.

Why did war break out between Athens and Sparta? Thucydides states:

> I propose first to give an account of the causes of complaint which they had against each other and of the specific instances where their interests clashed [i.e., the immediate causes of the war]: this is in order that there should be no doubt in anyone's mind about what led to this great war falling upon the Hellenes. But the real reason for the war is, in my opinion, most likely to be disguised by such argument. What made war inevitable was the growth of Athenian power and the fear which this caused in Sparta [i.e., the underlying cause of the war].[6]

Thus, the real or underlying cause of the war was *fear* associated with a shift in the balance of power. Sparta was afraid of losing its preeminent role in the Hellenic world and therefore took countermeasures to build up its military strength and enlist the support of allies. Athens responded in kind. In the ensuing analysis, the situations, events, and policies Thucydides described lend themselves to comparison with such familiar notions as arms races, deterrence, balance of power, alliances, diplomacy, strategy, concern for honor, and perceptions of strengths and weaknesses.

Thucydides' emphasis on fear as a cause of the Peloponnesian War, fear that resulted from the increase in Athenian power relative to that of Sparta, is echoed throughout history. As statesmen perceive the balance of power to be shifting in their disfavor, they make efforts to rectify the situation that in turn cause fear, suspicion, and distrust on the part of their rivals. One could quite easily substitute for Athens and Sparta other historical examples such as France and Britain in the seventeenth and eighteenth centuries, Napoleonic France and the rest of Europe in the early nineteenth century, Germany and Britain after the Franco-Prussian War of 1870, and the Soviet Union and the United States since 1945. In all such historical examples, a good case can be made that fear is a dominant characteristic and a motivating factor for arms races and war itself.

One reason Thucydides is deemed a scholar of international relations, however, is that the cause of fear he identifies is not so much man's innate or basic nature as it is the nature of interstate politics. In a world in which no superordinate or central authority exists to impose order on all states—whether ancient city-states or modern states often encompassing large expanses of territory—"the strong do what they have the power to do and the weak accept what they have to accept."[7] Although fear may lead to war, power and capabilities relative to that of others determine the outcome.

Thucydides is sometimes unfairly criticized as an advocate of harsh and brutal wartime policies, one who rationalized such events as he described in the famous Melian dialogue. Thucydides, however, favored the democracy of the Golden Age of Pericles. In fact, the second half of *The Peloponnesian War* is a description of the degeneration of Athenian democracy and the resulting fanaticism that turned the war from a defensive effort to a war of conquest. The Melian dialogue reflects the latter phase of the war and should not be viewed as a personal preference on the part of Thucydides.

Machiavelli

By his own admission, the Italian political philosopher Niccolo Machiavelli (1469–1527) drew heavily from his study of ancient Greek and Roman writings. In some respects, the situation in sixteenth-century Italy, divided as the peninsula was into separate city-states, was similar to the Hellenic world of Thucydides. Machiavelli worked as a civil servant and diplomat until the Republic of Florence fell in 1512. During his enforced idleness, he put his time to good use by reflecting on the chaos and political instability of Italy.

Like Thucydides, Machiavelli wrote of power, balance of power, formation of alliances and counteralliances, and the causes of conflict between different city-states. His primary focus, however, was on what contemporary writers refer to as national security. For Machiavelli, survival of the state (identified with the ruling prince) was paramount. The prince could lose his state by not coping effectively with both internal and external threats to his rule. The German term **Realpolitik,** so central to realist thought, refers to power and power politics among states. Machiavelli's most famous work, *The Prince,* is a practical manual on how to gain, maintain, and expand power.[8] It is dedicated to the ruler of Florence at that time, Lorenzo di Medici.

One of the more controversial parts of Machiavelli's thesis is the notion that security of the state is so important that it may justify certain acts by the prince that would be forbidden to other individuals not burdened by the princely responsibility of assuring that security. The end—security of the state—is understood to justify any means necessary to achieve that end. **Machiavellianism** (or **Machiavellism**) has been condemned by many who consider such a view to be immoral. Others have argued, however, that the actions of statesmen do (and should) follow a code of conduct different from that of the average citizen. Thus, it has been observed that there are two separate and distinct ethics: first, conventional religious morality concerned with such matters as individual salvation (the ethics of ultimate ends) and, second, by contrast, the moral obligations of rulers who must take actions to provide for national security (the ethics of responsibility).[9] Following this interpretation, one can understand Machiavelli's view that rulers should be good if they can (good in the conventional sense) but be willing to practice evil *if necessary* (consistent with their obligations as rulers).

Another point of view is that Machiavelli wrote of the world as it *is,* not the world as it *should* or *ought* to be. Ethics and politics are divorced from each other. His advice to the prince, following this interpretation, was based on an analysis of history, of what actually occurs in the political realm, not on abstract ethical principles:

> Many have imagined republics and principalities which have never been seen or known to exist in reality; for how we live is so far removed from how we ought to live, that he who abandons what is done for what ought to be done, will rather learn to bring about his own ruin than his preservation. A man who wishes to make a profession of goodness in everything must necessarily come to grief among so many who are not good.[10]

For Machiavelli, in an amoral (if not immoral) world, what meaning does the preaching of conventional morality have? Indeed, an extreme statement of realist thinking is that considerations of power and power politics are the *only* relevant factors.

In the modern world, a convenient way to discredit an opponent is to accuse him or her of being Machiavellian. Nevertheless, it must be emphasized that Machiavelli did not encourage rulers to use violence for its own sake. In numerous passages he advises the prince not to be needlessly cruel because this may eventually undermine his rule.[11] The yardstick one should use is how a particular policy contributes to the security and stability of the state.

Hobbes

The political philosophy of the Englishman Thomas Hobbes (1588-1679) was developed during the first fifty turbulent years of the seventeenth century. After attending university in Oxford, he became a tutor to the son of a nobleman, and throughout his life he remained associated with the family. A Royalist, Hobbes left for France in 1641 at a time when Parliament was asserting its power against the monarchy. For three years he tutored the son of Charles I, the latter eventually being executed in 1649 during the English civil war. Hobbes returned to England in 1652, pledging loyalty to the republican regime.

Hobbes's famous work *Leviathan*, which was the first general theory of politics in English, was published that same year.[12]. Like Machiavelli, Hobbes had a pessimistic view of human nature. His primary focus was domestic politics, and his goal was to make the strongest case possible for the necessity for a powerful, centralized political authority. To illustrate his philosophical points, Hobbes posited that prior to the creation of society, men would live in a "state of nature" that would be a condition of war of "every one against every one." There would be "a continual fear and danger of violent death; and the life of man, solitary, poor, nasty, brutish, and short."[13]

Hobbes did not argue that such a state of nature had ever really existed. To him, the state of nature was the result of a thought experiment—imagining what the world would be like without governmental authority or any other social structure. Accordingly, he was interested in showing how people could escape from this hypothetical situation by agreeing to place all power in the hands of a Leviathan (a state authority, or supreme ruler) that would maintain order and end the anarchy of the state of nature. If governmental authority did not already exist, it would have to be created. In his words: "There must be some coercive power to compel men equally to the performance of their covenants, by the terror of some punishment, greater than the benefit they expect by the breach of their covenant."[14] Without order, he argued, civilization and all its benefits are impossible—no economic development, art, knowledge, or anything else of value.

Hobbes's impact on the realist view of international relations stems from this image of individuals in a mythical state of nature. His description is equally applicable to relations among states because in the state of nature as well as in international politics, there is no Leviathan or superordinate power to impose order. It is a condition of **anarchy**—the absence of central or superordinate authority over states that claim to be **sovereign** with a *right* to be independent or autonomous with respect to one another. In Hobbes's words:

> In all times, kings, and persons of sovereign authority, because of their independency, are in continual jealousies, and in the state and posture of gladiators; having their weapons pointing, and their eyes fixed on one

another; that is, their forts, garrisons, and guns upon the frontiers of their kingdoms; and continual spies upon their neighbours; which is a posture of war.[15]

As anarchy prevails in the state of nature, so too is anarchy a dominant characteristic of international politics. Without a Leviathan (or, in the language of contemporary international relations literature, a **hegemonic** power or world state), suspicion, distrust, conflict, and war are seemingly inevitable. In the absence of any **social contract** among (or authority over) them, there are no moral obligations to govern the relations of states.

Grotius

Hugo Grotius (1583–1645), a Dutch contemporary of Thomas Hobbes, offered a view of international relations alternative to those associated with Hobbes and Machiavelli. Grotius dealt with the essential anarchy of international relations by calling for the establishment (or acknowledging the existence) of laws or rules accepted by states as binding. That the relations of states *ought* to conform to such rules is a central tenet of the Grotian tradition in international relations.

To Grotians, values or norms, particularly when recognized as international law, are important in maintaining order among states. In this regard, some contemporary realists owe as much to Grotius and the Grotian tradition as they do to Thucydides, Machiavelli, and Hobbes.[16] Writings by the latter authors have contributed more to an understanding of power and the balance of power among states than to any Grotian sense that states are also constrained by international law, agreed-on rules, and other **normative** considerations.

Grotius dealt with the problems of international relations (including commercial transactions) from a very practical point of view. Given the importance of trade to his native Holland as a seafaring nation, he addressed this subject in his *Law of Prize and Booty* (1604–1605) and questions of freedom of navigation and territorial seas in his *Freedom of the Seas* (1609). Probably his most important work was his *Law of War and Peace* (1625), three volumes that dealt with war and questions of national security—central themes in much realist writing then and now.

What are the sources of international law? Grotius looked to the use of reason and to the "natural law" for general principles. He also looked to customary practice and to rules agreed on by governments that would be binding on states. Such treaties or formal convenants would be binding (in Latin, *pacta sunt servanda*) in the sense that states are obligated to follow them even in the absence of central authority to enforce their adherence. Changing circumstances might lead to the alteration of rules, but the important point is that to Grotians within the realist school, order in international relations and matters of war and peace involve both power *and* values. Power and the balance of power remain important, but they are by no means the only considerations.

Clausewitz

Carl von Clausewitz (1780–1831), a Prussian officer who rose to the rank of general and who served in the Napoleonic wars, thought the military element of a state's power to be extremely important but subordinate always to the political. Consistent with the writings of Machiavelli on war, Clausewitz argued in an oft-quoted phrase that war is "a continuation of political activity by other means."[17]

Much of Clausewitz's writing took place in the interwar period between the defeat of Napoleon in 1815 and Clausewitz's recall to duty in 1830 for service in East Prussia. Clausewitz died in 1831, never having completed his magnum opus *On War*. His legacy, nevertheless, remains a central contribution to the realist school. As significant as his view that the military is properly a political means was his exposition of societal (including social and economic) dimensions of national capabilities. At the same time, his focus on national security problems places him in the mainstream of realist thought.

Carr

Many students of international relations consider Edward Hallett Carr's *The Twenty Years' Crisis, 1919–1939* already a classic. Although Carr can be viewed as an intellectual precursor for realists, his work transcends narrow classification in that he has also been influential, as has Grotius, on the thinking of certain authors whom we would label pluralist.

The writings of Thucydides, Machiavelli, Hobbes, Grotius, and Clausewitz illustrate how great works are often written during the most difficult times. *The Twenty Years' Crisis* is no exception in that it was completed in the summer of 1939 with the shadow of war looming over Europe. As with other authors we have discussed, Carr was less interested in apportioning blame to particular leaders for the imminent onset of World War II than he was in attempting "to analyse the underlying and significant, rather than the immediate and personal, causes of the disaster."[18] Unless this were done, he argued, we would fail to understand how war could break out twenty short years after the signing of the Versailles Treaty in 1919. He dedicated his book "to the makers of the coming peace."

In attempting to understand "the more profound causes of the contemporary international crisis," echoes of Thucydides can be discerned. Carr, for example placed a great deal of emphasis on the role of fear in explaining World War I.[19] Similarly, he also argued (and quoted Machiavelli and Hobbes to this effect) that "the exercise of power always appears to beget the appetite for more power.... Wars, begun for motives of security, quickly become wars of aggression and self-seeking."[20] Just as Thucydides saw Athens at the outset of the Peloponnesian War claim "self-defense" and then turn into a more ambitious, aggressive power, so too Carr noted that during the course of World War I

> nearly every country participating ... regarded it initially as a war of self-defense; and this belief was particularly strong on the Allied side. Yet during the course of the war, every Allied government in Europe announced war aims which included the acquisition of territory from the enemy powers. In modern conditions, wars of limited objective have become almost as impossible as wars of limited liability.[21]

Carr differentiates between domestic and international politics, as realists do, noting that "in international politics, there is no organized power charged with the task of creating harmony."[22] The international Leviathan does not exist. Throughout *The Twenty Years' Crisis* Carr refers to the impact of Machiavelli and Hobbes on realist thinking. Although his work is best known as a critique of **utopian** or **idealist** thought, Carr also evaluates the more extreme versions of realism that posit the divorce of morality from politics in international relations. He argues that

> any sound political thought must be based on elements of both utopia [i.e., values] and reality [i.e., power]. Where utopianism has become a hollow and intolerable sham, which serves merely as a disguise for the interests of the privileged, the realist performs an indispensable service in unmasking it. But pure realism can offer nothing but a naked struggle for power which makes any kind of international society impossible.[23]

Hence, for Carr, politics is made up of two elements, inextricably intertwined: utopia and reality, values and power.

More than a third of the book is devoted to such Grotian topics as the role of morality in international relations, the foundations of law, the sanctity of treaties, the judicial settlement of international disputes, peaceful change, and the prospects for a new international order. Because Carr critically estimated the strengths and weaknesses of utopianism as well as realism, he can be viewed as an important influence on many contemporary international relations theorists, both realists and non-realists.

This brief overview of the intellectual precursors of realism illustrates a distinct realist preoccupation with war. A concern with the causes and consequences of conflict helps to explain why the realist perspective is held by statesmen throughout the world; over the centuries leaders have engaged in the very battles and struggles described by authors from Thucydides to Carr. Realism, from the statesman's point of view, is indeed realistic because it tends to correspond to personal experiences.

THE LEVELS OF ANALYSIS

Before examining some of the major concepts and ideas associated with realism, it is necessary to address briefly a question every scholar of international relations must first ask no matter what image or perspective one holds: Where should one focus his or her research efforts? Let us assume that we are rather ambitious and wish to explain the causes of war between states. Does one deal with individual decision makers or small groups of individuals engaged in the policy process? How important, for example, are such factors as the correctness of individual perceptions or bargaining skill in determining the decision to go to war? On the other hand, if one looks outside the individual or small decision-making group to the entire state apparatus, society as a whole, or the international political system of states, one is acknowledging the importance of external or environmental factors as well.

Work by Kenneth N. Waltz in the 1950s on the causes of war represented a path-breaking effort, given his identification of distinct **levels of analysis** and his attempt to specify the relations among these levels.[24] Was the cause of war to be found in the nature of individuals? (Are humans innately aggressive?) Or in the nature of states and societies? (Are some types of states more aggressive than others?) Or in the nature of the international system of states? Each answer reflects a different level of analysis—individual, state and society, or international (see Figure 2.1). Waltz's conclusion was that the *permissive* cause of war is the condition of anarchy in the international political system of states, whereas the *efficient* causes of any given war can be found as well at the other levels of analysis (individual or state and societal levels). Whether or not one agrees with his conclusion, the important point is that his analysis of the problem of war was at different levels. In 1961,

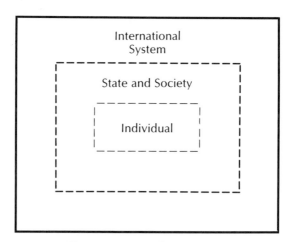

Figure 2.1. Levels of analysis.

the importance of the question of levels of analysis to the study of international relations was further discussed in detail in an often-cited article by J. David Singer. Singer argued that one's choice of a particular level of analysis determines what one will and will not see. Different levels tend to emphasize different actors and processes.[25]

But *which* level of analysis, one may ask, is most important? To take a specific example, let us assume that the foreign policies of most states exhibit relative constancy, or slowness to change. How is this constancy to be explained? Some scholars point to external factors such as the balance of power among states that is relatively slow to change in any major way. Others emphasize relatively constant factors within the state—the same decision makers or decision-making processes, with incremental or small changes being the rule.

Another example: How are arms races explained? Some scholars point to international factors such as the military expenditures and hostility of other states that lead to an increase in the production of weapons. Other researchers emphasize the importance of domestic factors such as bureaucratic competition between branches of the military services and budgetary processes that encourage a steady increase in expenditures.[26]

The easy answer to the question of which level of analysis should be emphasized is that all levels of analysis should be considered. Such a response is not particularly useful because it suggests that we have to study everything under the sun. Few scholars would even attempt such a task.[27] Instead, they tend to be selective as to what they examine. Among realists, however, there are two basic concepts that traditionally have been the foci of analysis at the state and international levels: **power** and **system.** In the following pages, we discuss how realists have attempted to define these terms. We then give examples of how theorists have used these concepts in generating insights and explanations of the causes of war. This is followed by a discussion of how realists deal with the concepts of **interdependence** and **change.** We conclude with a critique of the realist image of international relations.

POWER

Definitions

In discussing several of the more important intellectual precursors of realism, the concept of power was mentioned time and again. Any attempt to give the reader a more complete understanding of the realist image of international relations starts with a discussion of this crucial term. Power is the core concept for realists.

Having said this, it is rather ironic that even among realists there is no clear consensus on how to define the term *power*. Some realists understand power to be the sum of military, economic, technological, diplomatic and other *capabilities* at the disposal of the state. Others see power not as some absolute value determined for each state as if it were in a vacuum but, rather, as capabilities *relative* to the capabilities of other states. Thus, the power of the United States is evaluated in terms of its capabilities relative to the capabilities of the Soviet Union and other states.

Both of these definitions—whether treating capabilities of a state in isolation or relative to the capabilities of other states—assume a *static* view of power. Power is an attribute of the state that is the sum of its capabilities whether considered alone or relative to other states. An alternative, *dynamic* definition of power focuses on the interactions of states. A state's influence (or capacity to influence or coerce) is not only determined by its capabilities (or relative capabilities) but also by (1) its willingness (and perceptions by other states of its willingness) to use these capabilities and (2) its control or influence over other states. Power can thus be inferred by observing the behavior of states as they interact. The relative power of states is most clearly evidenced by the outcomes of their interactions.

Examples of diverse views of power are the following definitions drawn from the literature: power as the capacity of an individual, group, or nation "to influence the behavior of others in accordance with one's own ends," power as "man's control over the minds and actions of other men," and power as "the ability to prevail in conflict and overcome obstacles."[28]

Measurement

Given these definitional and conceptual disputes, it follows that attempts to measure power will also be divergent. If one understands power as being equivalent to capabilities, one looks for some way to measure military, economic, and other component elements. If one views power as actual control or influence, some measurement of capabilities may still be a useful "first cut" if one is engaged in predicting the outcome of interactions between or among states.

Even if one assumes that it is possible to measure these capabilities adequately through such indicators as defense expenditures or gross national product, the further problems of weighting and aggregating or adding up such diverse capabilities into a common measure of power remains. How should one weight different component capabilities? Which, for example, is the more important—military or economic capabilities—and how much more important? How does one measure geographic, technological, or diplomatic factors with any degree of precision? What about the unity and strength of a society, which one scholar claims is the "forgotten dimension of strategy"?[29] And, if capabilities are difficult to measure, are not *relative* capabilities between and among states even more difficult to specify?

Scholars who focus on power in the international system are well aware of these difficulties. Nevertheless, in order to use power as an analytical concept, certain measurements have been suggested. A. F. K. Organski, for example, has argued that gross national product, or national income, is perhaps the best yardstick of national capability. J. David Singer and his associates emphasize military, industrial, and demographic capacities as the critical variables required to indicate overall national capabilities.[30]

We must remember that the purpose in devising such formulas is not trivial. Measuring the power capabilities of states is a critical step in attempts to explain the behavior of states and the functioning of the international system with regard to matters of war and peace. Such concerns are evident in the ongoing Correlates of War project headed by Singer in which state power is a key variable. Similarly, Bruce Bueno de Mesquita utilizes Singer's national capabilities scores as key elements of his expected utility theory that seeks to explain the causes and outcomes of wars. The theory logically assumes that decision makers attempt to calculate the power capabilities of a rival before initiating armed conflict. The probability of success is a function of each state's relative power adjusted for such factors as alliance commitments. Bueno de Mesquita found, for example, that between 1816 and 1974, states with a positive expected utility score who intiated a war won 83% of the conflicts.[31]

Some would say that the view of power as a unitary concept calculated by aggregating component capabilities or relative capabilities misses the key point, which is that the power of a state is dependent on the *issue* involved. Consider, for example, the argument that some states such as Japan have substantial economic power but are militarily weak. Hence, in a particular area, the Japanese are powerful. Opponents of this disaggregation of power into its component capabilities note that persuasive as it may be on the surface, it is misleading because it overlooks the relations among the various power components. Thus, the *economic* capabilities of Japan as a global trader are said to be related to its *military* ties with the United States that assure Japan's freedom to engage in commerce.

Similarly, the fact that only Western European states are members of the European Economic Community (EEC) whereas Eastern European states are members of the Council for Mutual Economic Assistance (CMEA, or COMECON) is related to the military division between East and West that defines the underlying international political order in the region. Thus, from this perspective, whether addressing the power of Japan, Europe, or Third World countries, one cannot understand economic, military, political, or other component capabilities of power as if they were factors independent of one another. Much as military ties and divisions among states may define the framework within which economic relations take place, so military capabilities of states are bolstered (or weakened) by the strength or relative strength of their economies.

SYSTEM

In the preceding section we discussed the concept of power and attempts to measure state power. Using that discussion as a basis, we now move on to a discussion of the concept of system.

When applied to international relations, the term *system* has currency within each of the three images we have identified—realism, pluralism, and globalism. As one might expect, however, there is considerable diversity among theorists on both the *definition* of the term and the *uses* to which it should be put in the construction of international relations theory.

Thus, some theorists define a system in terms of various distributions of power or capabilities and other attributes. Others understand system to be the set of interactions among states and other non-state actors, a behavioral definition. Hence, we find a certain symmetry between definitions of power and definitions of system: static and dynamic.

However system may be defined, the uses to which the concept is put vary considerably. Some theorists are content to use systems as mere **taxonomies,** frameworks for organizing knowledge about international relations. Others are more ambitious. Beyond **heuristic** purposes—that is, contributing to common understanding of the subject—they may see utility in actually using the system concept to explain and predict outcomes of international relations.[32]

Some scholars view the concept of system as an abstraction. Systems are mental images that may help to describe, explain, or predict international phenomena. They are, in effect, superimposed on the real world by a scholar in order to make the real world more intelligible and easier to understand. Other theorists go beyond this and ascribe such properties to systems as **equilibrium,** or balance, of their component parts (such as among states). Critics, however, find little use in such notions as "equilibrating tendencies." Treating a system as if it were a concrete or tangible entity and ascribing properties to it is of questionable validity from this point of view. To do so, according to critics, is to be guilty of the methodological error of **reification**—treating abstractions as if they were real and had a life of their own.[33]

A response by some system theorists to this line of criticism is that dealing in abstractions is useful in the generation of propositions or **hypotheses** about international relations. These, in turn, can be tested **empirically** to determine whether or not they have factual support. To the extent, then, that use of the systems concept enables the theorist to describe, explain, or predict international phenomena, the use of the concept is justified.

The reader may or may not wish to visualize international relations or world politics as a system that is defined in terms of patterns of interactions, a particular structure, equilibrating tendencies, or some other characteristics. We do note, however, that the systems concept as an approximation to the nature of world politics is present within the mainstream of contemporary realist thought, even if some realists avoid its use.

Speaking of abstractions, this discussion has been rather abstract. To lend substance to the concept of system, we next examine two ways in which the concept of system has been used by realists: *system* as patterns of interactions, and *system* as anarchy plus the distribution of capabilities. In each case the intention of scholars has been to explain some aspect of international relations concerning such matters as instability, conflict, and war. In each case the state and state power have been a key focus of analysis and investigation.

System As Interactions

Two examples of viewing the international system as sets or patterns of interactions are to be found in the works of Rudolph J. Rummel and Charles A. McClelland. In his Dimensionality of Nations (DON) Project, Rummel attempts to explain and predict the behavior of states. In doing so he identifies recurrent patterns of behavior by using **factor analysis,** a statistical tool designed to identify patterns of variation in the data being analyzed. In one study, ninety-four **variables** falling into such categories as military, international conflict, international collaboration, colonialism, communication, and international organization were selected for factor analysis. The analysis involved eighty-two countries. According to Rummel, tentative findings included first, that conflict is not a necessary consequence of a nation's increased involvement in foreign affairs (which would seem to be counterintuitive, or contrary to what one might expect); and second, that the genesis of foreign conflict behavior lies outside the state, not internal to it (one answer to the questions raised in the discussion of the problem of levels of analysis). Such conflict behavior "is a *relational* phenomenon depending on the degree of economic, social, and political similarity between nations, the geographic distance between them, and their power parity." This latter point—that conflict is primarily relational—is the basis for Rummel's extensive work in what is termed *field theory.*[34]

Charles McClelland focuses on international transactions and interactions between states in his World Event/Interaction Survey (WEIS) project. The data base consists of the actions and responses of states over a number of years as reported in the press since 1966. Events are coded and placed in specific categories. Quantitative analyses of the data are meant to reveal patterns of behavior between and among states, the basis for prediction. Although the major focus is on conflict behavior and periods of high tension (particularly international crises), the data are not limited to this type of state action. The underlying assumption is that the past behavior of a state is a source for the prediction of its current and future behavior. The major results of the WEIS project have been reported in a number of articles.[35]

System As Anarchy and the Distribution of Capabilities

Many realist writers have emphasized anarchy and the distribution of capabilities, or power, among states as critical components of the international system. These so-called system-level, or **structural,** attributes are viewed as crucial because they act as constraints on decisionmakers. As we will see, the condition of international anarchy is seen by realists as contributing to the amount of distrust and conflict among states. Realists have also been concerned whether particular distributions of capabilities involving various balances of power make war between states more or less likely. We will first take up the concept of anarchy and related terms.

Anarchy.   The word *anarchy* brings forth images of violence, destruction, and chaos. For realists, however, anarchy simply refers to the absence of any authority above states. States are **sovereign.** They claim a right to be independent or autonomous from other states, and they claim a right to exercise complete authority over their own territories. Although states differ in terms of the power they possess or are able to exercise, none may claim the *right* to dominate another sovereign state.[36]

We wish to be clear on the term *anarchy* and the difference between **authority** and **power.** When we use the term *anarchy*, we are referring to the absence of any hierarchy of authority. There *is* hierarchy of power in international politics, but there is not a hierarchy of authority. Some states are clearly more powerful than others, but there is no recognized authority higher than that of any state.

Anarchy, so understood, is the defining characteristic of the environment within which sovereign states interact. Violence and war may be evident but so too are periods of relative peace and stability. This absence of any superordinate or central authority over states (such as a world government with authority to enforce rules and to maintain order) is fundamentally different from domestic societies where an authority exists to maintain order and act as an arbiter of disputes.

Realists argue that the absence of a central and overriding authority helps to explain why states come to rely on power, seeking to maintain or increase their power positions relative to other states. For one thing, the condition of anarchy is usually accompanied by a lack of trust among states in this environment. Each state faces a **self-help** situation in which it is dangerous to place the security of one's own country in the hands of another. What guarantee is there against betrayal, however solemn another state's promises may be to an ally? Consistent with the world described by Hobbes, there is really nothing to keep a supposed ally from reneging on a security agreement or any other international pact. There is no world governmental authority to enforce convenants or agreements among states. In such a world it is logical, rational, and prudent to look out for number one. Indeed, this was the same counsel reported by Thucydides when he noted Athenian advice to the Melians not to place their hope for survival in the hands of the Spartans and their allies.

Given international anarchy and the lack of trust in such a situation, states find themselves in what has been called a **security dilemma**.[37] The more one state arms to protect itself from other states, the more threatened these states become and the more prone they are to resort to arming themselves to protect their own national security interests. The dilemma is that even if a state is sincerely arming only for defensive purposes, it is rational in a self-help system to assume the worst in an adversary's intentions and keep pace in any arms buildup. How can one know for certain that a rival is arming strictly for defensive purposes? This is the stuff of arms races. Isn't it best to hedge one's bets by devoting more resources to match a potential adversary's arms buildup? Because a state may not have sufficient resources to be completely self-reliant, it may join an alliance in an attempt to deter aggression by any would-be adversaries.

Given an understanding of the anarchic condition of international politics, one can more easily grasp certain dynamics of arms races. All sides involved may sincerely desire peace, but the anarchical nature of international politics leads states to be suspicious of one another and engage in worst-case analyses of one another's intentions. This realist insight, it is argued, is just as applicable to understanding the ancient competition between Sparta and Athens as it is to understanding contemporary Soviet–American relations. It is a system-level explanation in that the emphasis is placed on the anarchic structure of international politics as a whole, not on the *internal* nature of a particular state. An example of an explanation that relies on internal factors is the claim that the Soviets keep building more and more weapons because of demands from its own military-industrial complex or because of the nature of a Soviet mentality that reflects global ambitions. *External* factors such as the anarchic structure of the system or the reactions of other states are ignored.

Finally, an anarchical, self-help system obviously makes cooperation among states difficult to achieve. How are states to act in such a world? Is it inevitable that they will be self-seeking, attempting to maximize their short-term individual or self-interests? Or is it possible that states can upgrade their common (perhaps enlightened) self-interests over both the short and long term? What is the rational thing to do? The informing image for some realists is provided by the allegory of the stag hunt, taken from the writings of the Geneva-born, eighteenth-century philosopher Jean Jacques Rousseau.[38]

	Individual interests: pursue the hare	Group/collective interests: pursue the stag
Short run	Serve immediate self-interest	May provide basis for possible future collaboration
Long run	No apparent basis for collaborative behavior	Serve long-term common interest

Figure 2–2   The Stag Hunt Fable: A Dilemma of Rational Choice

Each of five individuals in the state of nature—a world without government or any other form of social structure—has to decide (1) whether to collaborate in the hunting of a stag necessary to meet the hunger needs of all five or (2) to defect from the group to capture a hare. To choose the latter course of action would be to serve one's own self-interest at the expense of the group (see Figure 2.2).

If the individual prefers to serve the common interest (go after the stag), can he trust the others to do so? And if he can't trust the others, is it not rational for him to go for the hare and defect from the group before any of the others do? Or is it possible to develop the basis for collaboration on a continuing basis by all five?[39] Scholars who deal with **game theory** attempt to answer such questions. Game theory is an approach to determining rational choice or optimum strategy under conditions of uncertainty. As such, game theory has direct relevance to the study of foreign policy choice and to much scholarly work on **deterrence** as a means of avoiding war.

How one understands Rousseau's stag hunt fable has a great deal to do with how one sees states interacting in world politics. Some tend to see the state as serving only narrow self-interest. Pessimists point to the number, duration, and intensity of wars. Those of a more optimistic bent note that in many cases states live in peace and harmony for years, and there is, indeed, great potential for collaboration among states.

The Distribution of Capabilities: Balance of Power.   Unless one state or some sort of superordinate international authority comes to dominate the world, anarchy will continue to be a defining characteristic of the international system. Within this anarchical environment, however, various distributions of capabilities or power among states are possible. Anarchy plus the distribution of capabilities define for many realists the international system at any one time.

As we have seen, many realists begin with the security dilemma in an anarchic world. Where does order come from under such conditions? What keeps states from continually attacking one another? One answer is the development of international norms as codified in international law. Another answer offered by realists is that states find it expedient to band together and pool their capabilities whenever one state or group of states appears to be gathering a disproportionate amount of power, thus threatening to dominate the world, or even a portion of it.

This reasoning—the need to maintain a **balance of power** to avoid the triumph of a dominant power—is a realist concern dating back to the works of Thucydides. It is also found in a report of the British Foreign Office written before World War I:

> History shows that the danger threatening the independence of this or that nation has generally arisen, at least in part, out of the momentary predominance of a neighboring State at once militarily powerful, economically efficient, and ambitious to extend its frontiers or spread its influence.... The only check on the abuse of political predominance derived from such a position has always consisted in the opposition of an equally formidable rival, or a combination of several countries forming leagues of defense. The equilibrium established by such a grouping of forces is technically known as the balance of power, and it has become almost an historical truism to identify England's secular policy with the maintenance of this balance by throwing her weight now in this scale and now in that, but ever on the side opposed to the political dictatorship of the strongest single State or group at a given time.[40]

A **bipolar** balance of power (two states with relatively equal power) or a **multipolar** balance of power (three or more states engaging in checks and balances) are two realist categorizations of particular distributions of capabilities. Such power configurations have occurred in the aftermath of major European wars—the Peace of Westphalia in 1648 following the Thirty Years' War, the Congress of Vienna in 1815 following the defeat of Napoleon, and the settlements following both twentieth-century world wars. Although the post-World War I arrangements bought only twenty years of peace, the Congress of Vienna was more successful in establishing a basis for maintaining a balance of power without general or major war for almost a century. Assessing the efforts of the diplomats at Vienna and subsequent meetings, Henry Kissinger concluded: "Their goal was stability, not perfection, and the balance of power is the classic expression of the lesson of history that no order is safe without physical safeguards against aggression." In short, according to Kissinger, a "new international order came to be created with a sufficient awareness of the connection between power and morality; between security and legitimacy."[41]

Two questions are subject to debate among realist scholars: (1) Do balances of power automatically occur, or are they created by statesmen? and (2) Which balance of power—bipolar or multipolar—is more likely to maintain international stability?

As to the first question, Kissinger's view emphasizes **voluntarism**—the balance of power is a foreign policy creation of statesmen; it doesn't just occur automatically. Makers of foreign policy do not act as automatons, prisoners of the balance of power and severely constrained by it. Rather, they are its creators and those charged with maintaining it. They are free to exercise their judgment and their will as agents for their states in the conduct of foreign policy with the expectation that they can have some effect on outcomes.

In contrast to this voluntarist conception is that of Kenneth Waltz, who sees the balance of power as an attribute of the system of states that will occur whether it is willed or not.[42] Given the assumptions that the state is a rational and a unitary actor that will use its capabilities to accomplish its objectives, states inevitably interact and conflict in the competitive environment of international politics. The outcome of state actions and interactions is a tendency toward equilibrium, or balance of power. Balance of power from this point of view, then, is a systemic tendency that occurs whether or not states seek to establish such a balance. Indeed, states may be motivated to improve their own positions so as to dominate others, but such attempts will likely be countered by other states similarly motivated. Thus, a balance of power inevitably occurs. Balance-of-power theory so viewed can be used to account for arms races, alliances and counteralliances, and other forms of competitive behavior among states.

This image of the balance of power, therefore, refers to a recurrent phenomenon characteristic of international relations. It seems to matter little whether the states are democratic or authoritarian; the systemic tendency toward balance, or equilibrium, is always the same. It is as if states were billiard balls colliding with one another.[43] The faster and larger balls (the major powers) knock the smaller balls (the lesser powers) out of the way, although their own paths may also be deflected slightly by these collisions. These interactions, it is argued, tend toward international equilibrium or stability just as billiard balls eventually come to rest, at least until the balance is upset once again. But then the same tendency toward equilibrium repeats itself, only to be upset again. And so forth. The actors involved in this timeless drama remain the same: states. Actor combinations involving two or more states can be observed as the mechanical workings of the balance of power: multipolar prior to World War II, bipolar since that time (the United States and the Soviet Union) or, at least, in the years immediately following the war.

Thus, Kenneth Waltz observes that in international relations "the freedom of choice of any one state is limited by the actions of all the others." Moreover, he argues that "the balance of power is not so much imposed by statesmen on events as it is imposed by events on statesmen."[44] For Waltz, the statesman has much less freedom to maneuver, much less capability to affect the workings of international politics, than Kissinger would allow. In a sense, then, Kissinger and Waltz represent alternative ends of a spectrum of contemporary realists conversant with balance-of-power thinking. Realists such as Waltz who emphasize balance of power as a system tendency have been labelled (usually by their critics) as "structural realists" or "neorealists" because they have allegedly departed from a realist tradition that granted the statesman or policymaker greater freedom from constraint and thus greater ability to affect international events.[45]

Some critics of balance of power as a system tendency reject this mode of thinking precisely because of its mechanistic quality. One such critic, Ernst B. Haas, who finds little if any use in realist notions of balance of power, rejects "this formulation" because of its "system-dominant automaticity."[46] In other words, this mode of balance-of-power theory is too **deterministic;** individual policymakers can do little to affect events. Haas is even more explicit in later writings, criticizing determinists who

> see the components [of systems, i.e. states] as relatively unchangeable and arrange them in an eternal preprogrammed dance; the rules of the dance may be unknown to the actors and are specified by the theorist. The recurrent patterns discovered by him constitute a super-logic which predicts the future state of the system.[47]

The voluntarism–determinism debate is comparable in some ways to theological dispute over determinism and free will. As we use the term, *voluntarism* does not refer to freedom of choice only but to the ability of human beings to influence the course of events. How free are individuals to determine their own fates? How much effective choice do they have? How much are events *determined* by factors independent of human will exercised by statesmen? In the context of international relations, the question is whether states or their decision makers can affect their environment or whether their actions are severely constrained by other states interacting in a system of states. How much is free? How much is determined?

Kissinger's position is closer to the voluntarist pole, but he definitely would not argue that foreign policymakers are totally free of external constraints. Indeed, their ability to maneuver within these constraints is at least partly a function of their diplomatic skill. Similarly, Waltz would reject the idea that he is in any way a determinist. Nevertheless, his views are far removed from the purely voluntarist pole. The implication of his view of the balance of power is that individual decision makers and their states have much less freedom or capability to affect the course of events than others such as Kissinger would assert.

In some respects, the writings of Hans J. Morgenthau are an attempt to combine the two perspectives, thus inviting wrath by proponents of both. Morgenthau acknowledged the balance of power as a tendency within international politics while, at the same time, prescribing what statesmen should do to maintain the balance. He argued that "the balance of power and policies aiming at its preservation are not only inevitable but are an essential stabilizing factor in a society of sovereign nations."[48] Quite apart from the apparent determinism in this statement, Morgenthau assigned to diplomats not just the task of maintaining the balance of power; he also charged them to "create the conditions under which it will not be impossible from the outset to establish a world state."[49]

In short, for Morgenthau, escape from the balance of power and the voluntarist creation of a new world order remained possibilities worthy of pursuit. At the same time, his detractors have noted that, on the one hand, to argue that the balance of power is an inevitable system tendency and, on the other hand, to prescribe what should be done to maintain a balance or transform the system itself is to argue in contradictory terms. Be that as it may, Morgenthau's thinking represents a middle ground between realists who tend toward voluntarist or determinist poles.

Balance of Power and System Stability

We conclude this discussion of the realist's use of the system concept with reference to a long-standing realist debate: Is a bipolar or a multipolar balance of power more conducive to the stability of the international system? Stated another way, is war more likely to occur in a bipolar or a multipolar world?

The best-known statements on this matter are by Kenneth Waltz on the one hand and J. David Singer and Karl Deutsch on the other.[50] All three agree that the amount of uncertainty about the consequences of a particular action taken by a decision maker increases as the number of international actors increases. The logic of this assumption is that as the number increases, a decision maker has to deal with a greater quantity of information; more international actors mean more information is generated that has to be taken into account in the formulation of foreign policy. Therefore, all three authors agree that as an international system moves from being bipolar to multipolar, the amount of overall uncertainty in the system increases. So far, so good.

Where they part company is on the matter of whether an increase in the number of actors (and hence uncertainty) makes war more or less likely. Waltz argues that greater uncertainty makes it *more* likely that a decision maker will misjudge the intentions and actions of a potential foe. Hence, a multipolar system, given its association with higher levels of uncertainty, is less desirable than a bipolar system because multipolarity makes uncertainty and thus the probability of war greater. Singer and Deutsch, however, make the opposite argument. They believe a multipolar system is more conducive to stability because uncertainty breeds caution on the part of decision makers. Caution means following tried and true policies of the past, avoiding deviations.

Furthermore, they argue that "the increase in number of independent actors diminishes the share [of attention] that any nation can allocate to any other single actor."[51] This, it is argued, also reduces the probability of war because a state's attention is allocated to a larger number of actors.

Both arguments seem logical. But if *both* cannot be correct, it is still possible that *neither* one is correct. This is a proposition put forth by Bruce Bueno de Mesquita. For example, he challenges the assumption that uncertainty is greater in a multipolar world, arguing that "if the system's structure—be it bipolar or multipolar—does not change, there will be little uncertainty" because "learned patterns from prior behavior will aid decision makers to anticipate the likely consequences of similar behaviors under similar circumstances." Hence, "the level of systemic uncertainty, by itself, neither increases nor decreases the likelihood of war. Consequently, neither the number of blocs, nor the magnitude of change in the number of blocs in the system is expected to be associated with the likelihood of war."[52] Bueno de Mesquita goes on to discuss a number of other propositions dealing with such matters as the relationship between the increase in overlapping interests of states (détente) and war, and the relationship between the tightening and loosening of alliances and the probability of war. He found, for example, that since the early nineteenth century the amount of war tended to rise as commitments within a bloc became more tightknit. This was particularly true for the twentieth century. Bueno de Mesquita's work is an example of explicitly stating commonly held and sometimes conflicting assumptions and hypotheses about the causes of war and then subjecting them to formal empirical tests. In recent years research has focused less on the question of what distribution of power is most conducive to international stability and more on the consequences of changes in the relative power of states. This topic is addressed later in the chapter. (For a summary of empirical research on the causes of war, see the article by Singer in this volume.)

INTERDEPENDENCE

To this point we have discussed some of the intellectual precursors of realism and have then examined two concepts important to the realist analysis of world politics: power and system. In the next two sections, we discuss the realist view on two current concerns within the international relations discipline: interdependence and accounting for system change. As will become apparent in Chapter Three, the concept of interdependence is an important one to many scholars whom we would classify as pluralists. It is useful, therefore, to present the realist view of this concept, a view that is derived from the realist emphasis on power in the international system.

Interdependence and Vulnerability

To realists, interdependence is not necessarily such a good thing. Rather than being a symmetric relation between coequal parties—which is how many people view the term—interdependence is, realists argue, usually dominance–dependence, with the dependent party particularly vulnerable to the choices of the dominant party. Interdependence does not mean equality. Interdependence connotes some degree of vulnerability by one party to another. Indeed, interdependence as vulnerability is a source of power of one state over another. To reduce this vulnerability, realists have argued that it is better for the state to be independent or, at least, to minimize its dependency. For example, the state needing to import oil is vulnerable to an embargo or price rise engineered by the state or states exporting the commodity. To reduce this vulnerability would require reducing oil imports—by finding an alternative source, for example.

To realists, interdependence does not affect all states equally. Although the economies of most oil-importing countries were affected by the quadrupling of oil prices in 1973–1974, they were not all equally vulnerable. Vulnerability is in part a question of what alternatives are available. For example, as a matter of policy the United States has tried to increase domestic production, create a strategic oil reserve to be drawn down only in emergencies, find other foreign sources of oil, and substitute alternative forms of energy whenever feasible. Given these measures, the United States has been able to reduce somewhat its vulnerability to a new oil embargo. Not all oil-importing countries have been able to develop even this degree of protection against the oil embargo risk. In short, in any given issue area, not all states are equally vulnerable. Therefore, the realist is suspicious of such blanket statements as "the entire world is interdependent" to the extent that such claims are supposedly *equally* applicable to all states.

Realists thus tend to see interdependence as being between or among states. Therefore, the balance of power is a kind of interdependence. To be sure, some realists of a more eclectic sort acknowledge interdependence involving non-state actors such as multinational corporations and try to take them into account. But at the core of realist thought is the image of states interacting like billiard balls. This captures the essential meaning of interdependence for the realist, which is a fundamentally different view of interdependence from that held by either pluralists or globalists.

Interdependence and Economics

Economic factors, as we noted earlier, are important to realists to the extent that they reflect or affect national power or capabilities. Industrial countries that effectively combine technology with capital, skilled labor, and raw materials not only enjoy a higher standard of living but also tend to have more leverage in their relations with other states. In addition to trade, financial, and monetary influence that flows from a strong economy, military capabilities are usually greatest in states with advanced industrial economies. This is particularly true in modern military establishments that rely so heavily on technology and on a relatively large pool of skilled manpower.

As is clear from reading Machiavelli, the relation between socioeconomic and military capabilities was also acknowledged in earlier, preindustrial times. But the realist has tended to see the economy as subordinate to political choice. If grand strategy, alliance theory, and national and international security are the stuff of high politics, then trade, finance, monetary exchange, fishing rights, and other socioeconomic issues have traditionally been viewed by the realist as somewhat less important—low politics.

On the other hand, realists do understand that maintenance of access to oil and other natural resources is essential to national security. Some economic issues, for example, have been elevated to the status of high politics, as was true following the 1973 oil embargo and the subsequent rise in the real price of petroleum. Conceiving of world politics in terms of separate issue areas or, in the words of one realist, alternative "chessboards," is one example of increasing awareness among realists of the importance to the state of socioeconomic and other nonmilitary issues.[53] If a state wants to be more powerful, however, it avoids or minimizes economic dependency on other states just as it avoids political or military dependency on other states if this amounts to a reduction of its relative power position. Dependency *on* others is to be minimized, whereas dependency *of* others on one's own state may be desirable to the extent that it increases one's leverage over those other states.

Interdependence, Peace, and Hegemony

Interdependence, according to realists, may or may not enhance prospects for peace. Conflict, not cooperation, could just as easily result. Just as in households or community conflicts, one way to establish peace is to eliminate or minimize contact among opponents or potential adversaries. Separation from other units, if that were possible, would mean less contact and thus less conflict.[54]

Furthermore, some realists see leadership exercised by one state or another as conducive to stability even if this "leadership" becomes hegemonic. According to the theory of **hegemonic stability,** the hegemon, or dominant power, assumes leadership, perhaps for the entire globe, in dealing with a particular issue. Thus, Britain was seen as offering leadership in international monetary matters in the nineteenth and early twentieth centuries. The gold standard associated with the international exchange of money was managed from London by the Bank of England. After World War II, the leadership role was finally assumed by the United States.[55]

The hegemon influences states to cohere and establish the rules by which international relations are to be conducted in various issue areas, such as the exchange of money, trade, finance, health, communications, air transport, and navigation on the high seas. The term **regime** has been used to refer to each of these sets of rules and associated international organizations. The absence of hegemony, or leadership, may result in chaos and instability, as happened in the 1930s when the United States was unwilling to assume leadership of the world economy and Britain, given its weakened position, was unable to do so.[56] Competitive depreciation of currencies, erection of trade barriers, and a drastic reduction in the volume of trade were the outcome.

Although not all realists would subscribe to the view, stability is therefore seen by some as enhanced by a concentration of power in international politics; there is virtue in inequality among states. The hegemonic state or states benefit, but so too do other, less powerful states. By contrast, the decline of hegemony and the consequent fragmentation of power in international politics is said to produce disorder—a breakdown or unraveling of previously constructed international regimes. Leadership provided by hegemonic states is understood as facilitating achievement of collaboration among states.

In sum, the realist view of interdependence challenges many conventional ideas of the concept: (1) Interdependence is not necessarily a good thing for any one particular state if interdependence is defined in terms of vulnerability; (2) increasing interdependence may produce conflict as opposed to peace; and (3) in an interdependent world, there are certain virtues in having a hegemonic power capable of enforcing stability in a number of different issue areas.

CHANGE

Realists stress the continuity of international relations. Many of the insights of Thucydides are deemed to be as relevant today as they were 2,500 years ago. Balance of power involving states, whether viewed as a policy or a recurrent outcome, has existed at least since the fifteenth and sixteenth centuries. Although continuity is the watchword for realists, this does not mean that they are uninterested in change. For many theorists of international relations, understanding the evolution of the international system and predicting its future should be the preeminent research goals. The methods for discovering global patterns may vary. Some scholars have applied quantitative measures to historical data, as in the Correlates of War project.[57] Others have approached the issue of international political change by attempting to discern cycles of national power and their relation to the outbreak of war.

To illustrate how realists have recently dealt with the issue of change, we will briefly discuss the works of Robert Gilpin and George Modelski. As the title of his book suggests, Gilpin is interested in developing a framework for thinking about *War and Change in World Politics*. He believes "it is possible to identify recurrent patterns, common elements, and general tendencies in the major turning points in international history." International political change is the result of efforts of political actors "to change the international system in order to advance their own interests," however these interests may be defined (security, economic gain, ideological goals, etc.).[58] Gilpin lists five assumptions concerning the behavior of states that will guide his analysis. For example, the realist emphasis on the unified, rational actor state is revealed in the second assumption: "A state will attempt to change the international system if the expected benefits exceed the expected costs (i.e., if there is an expected net gain)."[59]

Various periods of history are marked by equilibrium (such as after the Congress of Vienna in 1815) or disequilibrium. As long as the system can adjust to the demands of its constituent states, stability is maintained. What accounts for change and the undermining of the status quo? The key factor "is the tendency in an international system for the powers of member states to change at different rates because of political, economic, and technological developments. In time, the differential growth in power of the various states in the system causes a fundamental redistribution of power in the system."[60] A state with ever-increasing power may determine that the costs involved in attempting to change the nature of the system are outweighed by the benefits if such an endeavor is successful. What has been the principal mechanism of change throughout history? War, because wars determine which states will govern the system. The peace settlement after the war codifies the new status quo. This equilibrium reflects the new distribution of power in the international system until eventually the differential growth in the power of states leads to another attempt to change the system.

George Modelski has argued that the global political system goes through distinct and identifiable historical cycles or recurrent patterns of behavior.[61] The global political system dates from about A.D. 1500, and over the years various world powers have helped to shape and maintain the system. According to Modelski, since A.D. 1500 four states have played dominant roles, each one corresponding to a "long cycle": Portugal (1500 to the end of the sixteenth century), the Netherlands (the seventeenth century), Great Britain (early eighteenth century to the Napoleonic Wars, and a second cycle from 1815 to 1945), and the United States (1945 to the present). As in the case of Gilpin's analysis, war tends to mark the end of one cycle and the beginning of another.

What produces these cycles? Two conditions are critical: (1) the urge of a power to create a global order, and (2) particular properties and weaknesses of the global system. Modelski notes that, as with long-term business cycles, world order is also subject to decay. The dominant power is inevitably faced with the growth of rival power centers, and attempts to maintain territorial control around the globe prove to be a costly task that drains the vitality and energy of the home country. Each cycle, therefore, exhibits a particular nation-state in an ascending and then a descending phase. As Modelski notes, following a major war one world power

> emerges from that conflict in an advantageous position and organizes the world even as the struggle still goes on and then formalizes its position in the global layer in the peace settlement. For the space of another generation that new power maintains basic order and is the mainspring of world institutions, often taking transnational forms. But the time comes when the energy that built this order begins to run down.... The prominent role of world power attracts competitors (other great powers) ... ; the system moves into multipolarity. Rivalries among the major powers grow fiercer and assume the characteristics of oligopolistic competition. Gradually, as order dissolves, the system moves toward its original point of departure, that of minimal order and a Babel of conflicting and mutually unintelligible voices.[62]

Modelski and Gilpin, therefore, both present a dynamic view of the international system. Patterns of behavior are evident throughout history. Periods of rapid change alternate with periods of relative stability. Given the emphasis on the importance of war in changing the structure of the system, are we currently experiencing a lull before some sort of global cataclysm? Both Gilpin and Modelski would undoubtedly find such a question too pessimistic. As Modelski notes, it is possible that the international system may be "propelled in a new direction. We have no means of predicting what that new direction might be except that it could be moved away from the present system that relies too heavily on the steady, if long-spaced-out, progression of global wars."[63]

There is a growing body of literature emphasizing how changes in the power positions of states—some of which are in an ascending phase and some in a descending trend relative to other states—contribute to the outbreak of war.[64]

REALISTS AND THEIR CRITICS: AN OVERVIEW

Realism: The Term Itself

What is perhaps most impressive about the realist image of international politics is its longevity. Although modifications, clarifications, additions, and methodological innovations have been made down through the years, the core elements have remained basically intact.

If realism represents a "realistic" image of international politics, what does that say about competing images? Are they by definition "unrealistic"? In debate and discourse, labels are important. A good example of this involves the interwar years during which realists were challenged by advocates of the League of Nations, world federalism, or peace through international law. Many of these individuals came to be known as "idealists" or "utopians."

The very labels attached to these competing images of world order obviously put the so-called idealists at a disadvantage. Realists could claim that they were dealing with the world as it actually functioned. The idealists, on the other hand, were supposedly more concerned with what *ought* to be. "Yes," a realist might say, "I, too, wish the world were a more harmonious place, but that unfortunately is not the case." Those persons who were placed in the idealist camp certainly did not choose this particular label for themselves. Who did? The realists. By so doing, the opposition was stripped of a certain amount of legitimacy. Idealism conjured up images of wooly-headed professors, unsophisticated peace advocates, and impractical, utopian schemes.

Realists would respond that *realism* should be taken at face value; it is an appropriate term precisely because its basic tenets in fact closely approximate the world as it is. This is nothing of which to be ashamed. The longevity of the realist tradition is not simply a function of the expropriation of a particular label but a result of realism's inherent descriptive, explanatory, and predictive strengths.

Another reason for the longevity of realism is that this particular image of the world most closely approximates the image held by practitioners of statecraft. Realism has always had a strong policy-prescriptive component, as we have already noted. Machiavelli's *The Prince,* for example, was expressly presented as a guide for the ruler. Nor is it mere coincidence that two of the best known American academics who held high positions in the U.S. foreign policy establishment in the 1970s, Henry A. Kissinger and Zbigniew Brzezinski, are both self-professed realists. The realist as academic speaks much the same language as the realist as statesman: power, force, national interest, and diplomacy.

It has been argued, however, that some realist writers help to perpetuate the very world they analyze. By describing the world in terms of violence, duplicity, and war, and then providing advice to statesmen as to how statesmen should act, such realists are justifying one particular conception of international relations. Realism becomes a self-fulfilling prophecy. Even more recent efforts to place realism on a stronger theoretical foundation (referred to as "structural realism" or "neorealism") that favors explanation over policy prescription have the same effect. Critics contend that such realists suffer from a lack of imagination and an inability to consider seriously alternative conceptions of world politics and how these might be achieved.

The realist response is that there is nothing inherently wrong with being policy-relevant and helping leaders navigate through dangerous waters. Advice based on wishful thinking and questionable assessments of international forces and trends could lead to disastrous policies, particularly if one is the lone "idealist" leader in a world of realists. Moreover, most criticism is understood to be based on a selective reading of realists, ignoring their genuine concern not only with the causes of war but also with how peace can be achieved or maintained. Finally, not all realists would claim to be particularly interested in providing advice to statesmen. They would rather use realist assumptions and insights to develop better theories of international politics. Being policy-relevant or ingratiating oneself with political leaders is not the goal for these realists who entertain the scholarly goal of explaining how the world functions.

The System and Determinism

As we have seen, the concept of system is critical to many realist writers. Whether the rather simple notion of anarchy or the more elaborate formulations devised by contemporary realist authors, the system is deemed important for its impact on international actors. It is charged, however, that recent realist writers portray the system as having a life of its own, seemingly independent of the wishes and actions of states. Statesmen are granted too little autonomy, too little room to maneuver, and the decision-making process is seemingly devoid of human volition. Leaders are pawns of a bloodless system that looms over them, a structure whose functioning they do not understand, the mechanics of which they only dimly perceive. Statesmen are faced with an endless array of constraints, few opportunities. It is as if they are engaged in a global game, a game called power politics, and they are unable to change the rules even if they so desire. In sum, critics claim there is a fatalistic, deterministic, and pessimistic undercurrent to much of the realist work.

Realists differ among themselves as to how much explanatory emphasis is to be given the international system. There is disagreement as to what extent the system functions as an **independent variable** in influencing state behavior. For some realists, the system is more than the aggregation of state interactions. Rather, it represents a structure that does indeed influence the behavior of states that are part of the system. It is these scholars who have drawn the most criticism, but they reject the charge that they are structural determinists who ignore actors operating at the unit, or state, level of analysis. One realist who argues that a systemic theory of international politics is composed of "the structure of the system and its interacting units," notes that

> if structure influences without determining, then one must ask how and to what extent the structure of a realm accounts for outcomes and how and to

what extent the units [i.e., states] account for outcomes. Structure has to be studied in its own right as do units.[65]

Another realist categorically states that "no new realist that I have read argues that political structure determines all behavior."[66] Realists therefore differ on the extent to which statesmen impose themselves on events, or vice versa. No realist is completely determinist or voluntarist. It is not a matter of either–or but varying assessments as to how strong are the constraints placed on statesmen and how much room leaders have to maneuver.[67]

Realists and the State

The state is the centerpiece of realist work. Few persons would disagree as to the importance of the state in international affairs. The criticism, however, is that realists are so obsessed with the state that they ignore other actors and other issues not directly related to the maintenance of state security. Other non-state actors—multinational corporations, banks, terrorists, and international organizations—are either excluded, downplayed, or trivialized in the realist perspective. Furthermore, given the national security prism through which realists view the world, other concerns such as the socioeconomic gap between rich and poor societies or international pollution rarely make the realist agenda. At best, such issues are dealt with in a derivative manner. A preoccupation with national security and the state by definition relegates other issues to secondary importance or bans them entirely from the realist agenda.

Realists counter that simply because non-state actors are not dealt with in depth does not mean that they are considered irrelevant. Political scientists, one realist notes, should avoid slipping "into thinking that what an author fails to concentrate his attention upon, he takes to be inconsequential."[68] Similarly, another realist has stated that to argue "that the state . . . is the principal actor in international relations does not deny the existence of other individual and collective actors."[69]

Second, realists contend that theories are constructed to answer certain questions and to explain certain types of international behavior and outcomes. As a result, they purposely limit the type of actors analyzed. A theory concerned with explaining state behavior naturally focuses on states, not multinational corporations or terrorist groups. Similarly, a concern with national security issues by definition makes it unlikely that global welfare issues will receive the same degree of attention.

Finally, it can be argued that focusing on the state is justified on normative grounds. Many scholars, for example, are concerned with how unbridled arms races and military spending (a trillion dollars worldwide) contribute to international tension, devastating regional wars, and socioeconomic deprivation.[70] Because it is almost exclusively states that spend this money to buy or produce military hardware, it makes sense to focus on them as the unit of analysis. Hence, far from being enamored of states, many realists are critical of these political entities that are deemed too important to be ignored.

Realists and the Balance of Power

Given the emphasis on the state and the concern with national security issues, we have seen how the concept of balance of power has played a dominant role in realist thought and theory. Although balance of power has been a constant theme in realist writings down through the centuries, it has also come in for a great deal of abuse. Balance of power has been criticized for creating definitional confusion. Hans Morgenthau, a realist himself, discerned at least four definitions: (1) a policy aimed at a certain state of affairs; (2) an objective or actual state of affairs; (3) an approximately equal distribution of power, as when a balance of power exists between the United States and the Soviet Union; and (4) any distribution of power including a preponderance of power, as when the balance of power shifts in favor of either superpower. One critic has found eight meanings of the term.[71] If the balance of power means so many different things, does it mean anything?

Balance of power has also been criticized for leading to war as opposed to preventing it, serving as a poor guide for statesmen, and functioning as a propaganda tool to justify defense spending and foreign adventures. Despite these constant attacks and continual reformulations of the meaning of the term, balance of power remains a crucial concept in the realist vocabulary.

At times it has appeared that the harshest critics of balance of power as a concept have been the realists themselves. All of these criticisms have been acknowledged and some deemed valid. Attempts have been made, however, to clear up misconceptions and misinterpretations of balance of power, placing it on a more solid conceptual footing. Having clarified the term, it is now thought to be theoretically useful, though even recent formulations are not without their critics.

Realism and Change

Given the realist view of the international system, the role of the state, and balance of power politics, critics suggest that very little possibility for the fundamental and peaceful transformation of international politics is left. Realists, claim the critics, at best offer analysis aimed at understanding how international stability is achieved but nothing approaching true peace. Realist stability reflects a world bristling with weapons, forever on the verge of violent conflict and war. Alternative world futures—scenarios representing a real alternative to the dismal

Hobbesian world—are rarely discussed or taken seriously. The timeless quality of international politics, its repetitious nature and cycles of war, and a world in which the strong do as they will and the weak as they must dominate the realist image. We are given little information, let alone any hope, say the critics, as to how meaningful and peaceful change can occur and help us escape from the security dilemma.

The issue of change, of course, is intimately connected to that of determinism. Although power politics and the state are central to all realist analyses, this does not mean that fundamental change is impossible, or that change is limited to war and the cyclical rise and fall of states. Robert Gilpin argues that

> the state is the principal actor in that the nature of the state and the patterns of relations among states are the most important determinants of the character of international relations at any given moment. This argument does not presume that states need always be the principal actors, nor does it presume that the nature of the state need always be the same and that the contemporary nation-state is the ultimate form of political organization.[72]

Another realist has held out the possiblity of diplomacy leading to a world state.[73] What separates realists from some other writers on the question of system change, however, is a belief that "if the nation-state is to disappear ... it will do so through age-old political processes and not as idealists would wish through a transcendence of politics itself."[74] Hence, realists claim that fundamental change *is* possible and is taken into consideration in their work. Once again, however, the strength of this view varies depending on the author under consideration.

Realism: The Entire Enterprise

Critics of realism have always felt that they have been faced with a difficult task because the image comes close to approaching an impregnable edifice seemingly unscathed by years of criticism. Indeed, scholars who at one time in their careers struggled to devise alternative approaches based on alternative images of international politics have in some instances given up the quest, become converts, or resigned themselves to modifying existing realist explanatory frameworks.

Critics are faced with several problems. First, as noted earlier, given realism's affinity to the real world of policy making, this particular image of the world is automatically imbued with a certain degree of attractiveness and legitimacy. It represents the world out there, not some ivory tower perspective on human events. Not only is the realist perspective the accepted wisdom of the western foreign policy establishments, but even in the Third World leaders more often than not speak the language of realism as a result of concern over the survival of their regimes and states. Within the halls of academe, realism also has great attractiveness; "peace studies" programs sometimes find it advantageous to change the title to "security and conflict studies" in order to generate student interest. Realism can be as seductive to the academic professional as it can be to the student.

Second, realism is also seductive in that it has been given an increasingly scientific face. Earlier criticisms of the realist literature were very often based on the contention that such concepts as balance of power had less to do with theory building and more to do with ideology and self-justification of one particular approach to conducting international relations. Much of the realist work was, therefore, considered "unscientific." But at least some realists have cast their hunches and insights in the form of **hypotheses,** testable either quantitatively or with nonquantitative indicators.[75] The work is better grounded scientifically and placed within the context of the **positivist** view of how we comprehend reality. The positivist approach to knowledge reigns supreme in the natural and social sciences. As a result, any image of international politics that can be presented in the cloak of positivism is immediately granted a certain stature.

Realism has a lot going for it: it has a venerable tradition, is often policy-relevant, addresses the big issues of war and peace, is intuitively plausible, and has more recently aspired to truly scientific status.

More recent formulations of realism, however, have actually been criticized for violating the realist tradition, particularly by ignoring the value sensitivity of the realist legacy as represented by E. H. Carr and Hans J. Morgenthau. In a sweeping attack on those he calls *neorealists,* Richard Ashley argues that this recent work presents a "self-enclosed, self-affirming" view of the world biased toward the existing state-centric order, subordinates all issues to a concern for control and survival of this state system, presents a historically homogeneous view of world history, trivializes alternative conceptions of world order, and dismisses the possibilities of fundamental change and peaceful transformation of the international system.[76] Neorealism, it is claimed, represents the new orthodoxy of the international relations discipline, and hence "students must prepare themselves to retell and carry forward yet another lore."[77] Neorealists reject these charges.

In conclusion, a comment is in order on criticism in general. One may wish to be wary of sweeping criticisms concerning an entire image, whether it be realist, pluralist, or globalist. It is not particularly difficult to find fault with the work of individual theorists, compile a list of their shortcomings, and then present the results as criticisms of the image as a whole. Such selectivity can be misleading. As this chapter illustrates, although realists may find common ground in terms of basic assumptions and key international actors, they also differ in a number of important respects such as methods they use, levels of analysis they choose, and what they assume about the ability of decision makers to influence international outcomes. That is why it is imperative for the serious student of the international relations literature to go to the original sources, evaluate the validity of such criticisms, and assess the value of each image as the basis for a mode of thinking about international relations.

NOTES

1. See Barbara W. Tuchman, *The March of Folly* (New York: Knopf, 1984).
2. Hans J. Morgenthau, *Politics Among Nations*, 4th ed. (New York: Knopf, 1966), p.5.
3. *Ibid.*, p.25.
4. See also George Modelski, "Kautilya: Foreign Policy and International System in the Ancient Hindu World," *American Political Science Review* 58 (September 1964): 549–60.
5. See John H. Finley's introduction to *The Complete Writings of Thucydides* (New York: Modern Library, 1951), pp. ix–x.
6. See Thucydides, *History of the Peloponnesian War*, trans. Rex Warner (Harmondsworth, England, and New York: Penguin Books, 1982), p.49. Cf. Finley, *Complete Writings*, p. 15.
7. See "The Melian Dialogue" in Thucydides, *History*, p. 402. The idea that "it has always been a rule that the weak should be subject to the strong" is discussed earlier in the same work in "The Debate at Sparta and Declaration of War 432," pp. 80–81.
8. In his lengthier work, *The Discourses*, Machiavelli's republican preferences are apparent. Given the audience for which he wrote *The Prince* (the Medicis), Machiavelli does not emphasize there this republican orientation as he does in *The Discourses*. For a discussion of Machiavelli's thought, see the introduction by Max Lerner in Niccolo Machiavelli, *The Prince and The Discourses* (New York: Modern Library, 1950), pp. xxv–xxvi.
9. The distinction between the ethics of "responsibility" and "ultimate ends" is drawn by Max Weber, "Politics As a Vocation," in *From Max Weber: Essays in Sociology*, eds. H. H. Gerth and C. Wright Mills, (New York: Oxford University Press, 1946, 1978), p. 120.
10. See Machiavelli, *The Prince*, Chapter XV, p. 56.
11. For example, Machiavelli argues in Chapter XVIII that the prince "should not deviate from what is good, if possible, but be able to do evil if constrained." Indeed, "it is well" for the prince "to seem merciful, faithful, humane, sincere, religious, and also to be so." *The Prince*, p. 65.
12. See William Ebenstein, *Great Political Thinkers: Plato to the Present*, 4th ed. (New York: Holt, Rinehart and Winston, 1969), p. 364.
13. Thomas Hobbes, *Leviathan*, edited by Michael Oakeshott (New York and London: Collier Macmillan, 1974). These classic citations are drawn from Book 1, Chapter 13.
14. *Ibid.*, Book 1, Chapter 15, p. 113.
15. *Ibid.*, Book 1, Chapter 13, p. 101.
16. One such realist is Hedley Bull. See his *The Anarchical Society: A Study of Order in World Politics* (New York: Columbia University Press, 1977).
17. Carl von Clausewitz, *On War*, ed. and trans. Michael Howard and Peter Paret (Princeton, NJ: Princeton University Press, 1976) p. 87. See also Peter

Paret, "The Genesis of *On War*," Michael Howard, "The Influence of Clausewitz," and Bernard Brodie, "The Continuing Relevance of *On War*" and "A Guide to the Reading of *On War*," all in *On War* pp. 3–58 and 641–711. For an extension of Clausewitzian ideas on the importance of societal factors, see Michael Howard, "The Forgotten Dimensions of Strategy," *Foreign Affairs*, 57, no. 5 (Summer 1979): 975–86.

18. Edward Hallett Carr, *The Twenty Years' Crisis, 1919–1939* (London: Macmillan and Co., 1962), p. ix.
19. *Ibid.*, pp. 111–12.
20. *Ibid.*, p. 112.
21. *Ibid.*, pp. 112–13.
22. *Ibid.*, p. 51.
23. *Ibid.*, p. 93.
24. Kenneth N. Waltz, *Man, the State and War* (New York: Columbia University Press, 1959).
25. J. David Singer, "The Level-of-Analysis Problem in International Relations," in *International Politics and Foreign Policy*, ed. James N. Rosenau (New York: Free Press, 1969), pp. 20–29.
26. The literature of arms races is extensive. For reviews, see Urs Luterbacher, "Arms Race Models: Where Do We Stand?" *European Journal of Political Research*, 3, no. 2 (June 1975): 199–217, and Kendall D. Moll and Gregory M. Luebbert, "Arms Races and Military Expenditure Models: A Review," *Journal of Conflict Resolution* 24, no. 1 (March 1980): 153–85. A preliminary test of an external model of arms races is Thomas R. Cusack and Michael D. Ward, "Military Spending in the United States, Soviet Union, and the People's Republic of China," *Journal of Conflict Resolution*, 25, no. 3 (September 1981): 429–69.
27. See, however, the series of books by Rudolph J. Rummel under the title *Understanding Conflict and War*. The first of the series is subtitled *The Dynamic Psychological Field* (Beverly Hills, CA: Sage Publications, 1975).
28. A. F. K. Organski, *World Politics*, 2d ed. (New York: Knopf, 1968), p. 104; Morgenthau, *Politics Among Nations*, p. 26; Karl Deutsch, *The Analysis of International Relations* (Englewood Cliffs, NJ: Prentice-Hall, 1967), p. 22.
29. Howard, "The Forgotten Dimensions of Strategy."
30. Organski, *World Politics*, p. 358; and J. David Singer, Stuart Bremer, and John Stuckey, "Capability Distribution, Uncertainty, and Major Power War, 1820–1965," in *Peace, War, and Numbers*, ed. Bruce Russett (Beverly Hills, CA: Sage Publications, 1972), pp. 21–27. See also Klaus Knorr, *Military Power and Potential* (Cambridge, MA: D. C. Heath, 1970).
31. Bruce Bueno de Mesquita, *The War Trap*. (New Haven, CT: Yale University Press, 1981), p. 153. J. David Singer and associates, *Explaining War: Selected Papers from the Correlates of War Project* (Beverly Hills, CA: Sage Publications, 1979).
32. See the discussion in Ernst B. Haas, "On Systems and International Regimes," *World Politics*, 27, no. 2 (January 1975), especially pp. 149–55. For examples of the use of the concept of system, see Morton Kaplan, *System and Process in International Politics* (New York: Wiley, 1957), and Richard Rosecrance, *Action and Reaction in World Politics* (Boston: Little, Brown, 1962).
33. For a discussion of a number of supposed fallacies, including reification, see

Marion J. Levy, Jr., " 'Does it Matter If He's Naked?' Bawled the Child," in *Contending Approaches to International Politics*, ed. Klaus Knorr and James N. Rosenau (Princeton, NJ: Princeton University Press, 1969), pp. 87–106.

34. Rudolph J. Rummel, "Some Dimensions in the Foreign Behavior of States," in *International Politics and Foreign Policy*, ed. James N. Rosenau, p. 612. A pioneering work on field theory is Quincy Wright, *The Study of International Relations* (New York: Appleton-Century-Crofts, 1955).

35. Charles A. McClelland and Gary D. Hoggard, "Conflict Patterns in the Interactions Among Nations," in *International Politics and Foreign Policy*, ed. James N. Rosenau, pp. 711–24. Also Charles A. McClelland, "Warnings in the International Events Flow: EFI and Roz as Threat Indicators," *International Interactions* 5, nos. 2 and 3 (1978): 135–204; "The Acute International Crisis," in *The International System: Theoretical Essays*, ed. Klaus Knorr and Sidney Verba (Princeton, NJ: Princeton University Press, 1961), pp. 77–92; "The Anticipation of International Crises: Prospects for Theory and Research," *International Studies Quarterly* 21, no. 1 (March 1977): 15–30. For another example of system as interaction, see K. J. Holsti, *International Politics: A Framework for Analysis*, 4th ed. (Englewood Cliffs, NJ: Prentice-Hall, 1983), p. 27.

36. See J. L. Brierly, *The Law of Nations: An Introduction to the International Law of Peace* (New York: Oxford University Press, 1963), p. 47.

37. See John H. Herz, "Idealist Internationalism and the Security Dilemma," *World Politics*, 5, no. 2 (January 1950): 157–80.

38. Kenneth N. Waltz develops the stag hunt allegory in his *Man, the State and War*, pp. 165–71. For a critique of Waltz's interpretation of Rousseau, see Stanley Hoffmann, "Rousseau on War and Peace," *American Political Science Review* 57, no. 2 (June 1963): 317–33. Cf. J. J. Rousseau, "A Discussion on the Origins of Inequality," in *The Social Contract and Discourses*, trans. G. D. H. Cole (New York: E. P. Dutton and Co., 1950), pp. 235–238.

39. A nonrealist, Ernst B. Haas, argues that such collaboration is indeed possible. Although collaboration is not an inevitable outcome, even "if the cooperative hunting of the stag is demonstrated to be impossible" a likely possibility would be for the hunters to "make informal rules regulating the separate or cooperative hunting of hares." See Haas, *Beyond the Nation-State* (Stanford, CA: Stanford University Press, 1964), pp. 69–71. An important work that has influenced the use of game theory in international relations is John von Neumann and Oskar Morgenstern, *Theory of Games and Economic Behavior* (Princeton, NJ: Princeton University Press, 1944, 1953). See also Martin Shubik, *Games for Society, Business, and War: Towards a Theory of Gaming* (New York: Elsevier, 1975); Barry R. Schlenker and Thomas V. Bonoma, "Fun and Games: The Validity of Games for the Study of Conflict," *Journal of Conflict Resolution* 22, no. 1 (March 1978): 1–28; Anatol Rapoport and A. M. Ghammah, *Prisoner's Dilemma* (Ann Arbor: University of Michigan Press, 1965). On bargaining, see Thomas C. Schelling, *The Strategy of Conflict* (Cambridge, MA: Harvard University Press, 1960). For a discussion of games such as stag hunt, prisoner's dilemma, deadlock, and chicken, see Robert Axelrod and Robert O. Keohane, "Achieving Cooperation Under Anarchy," *World Politics* 38, no. 1 (October 1985): 226–254.

40. See "Memorandum by Sir Eyre Crowe on the Present State of British Relations with France and Germany, January 1, 1907" in G. P. Gooch and H. Temperly, eds., *British Documents on the Origin of the War, 1898–1914* (London: H. M. Stationery Office, 1928), 5, no. 3, pp. 402–7 and 414–420. Reprinted in Fred A. Sondermann, David S. McClellan, and William C. Olson, eds., *The Theory and Practice of International Relations*, 5th ed. (Englewood Cliffs, NJ: Prentice-Hall, 1979), p. 120.

41. See Henry A. Kissinger, *A World Restored: The Politics of Conservatism in a Revolutionary Age* (New York: Grosset & Dunlap, 1964), pp. 317–18.

42. Kenneth Waltz, *Theory of International Politics* (Reading, MA: Addison-Wesley, 1979). The use of the term *voluntarism* differs somewhat from the technical use of the term by many philosophers. See Paul Edwards, ed., *Encyclopedia of Philosophy* 5, nos. 7 and 8 (New York: Free Press, 1972), pp. 270–72.

43. The billiard bill metaphor for the balance of power is generally attributed to Arnold Wolfers, "The Actors in International Politics," in *Theoretical Aspects of International Relations*, ed. William T. R. Fox, (Notre Dame, IN: Notre Dame University Press, 1959); pp. 83–106.

44. See Waltz, *Man, the State and War*, pp. 204, 209.

45. Richard K. Ashley, "The Poverty of Neorealism," *International Organization* 38, no. 2 (Spring 1984): 225–86.

46. See non-realist Ernst B. Haas, *Beyond the Nation-State*, p. 70.

47. See Ernst B. Haas, "On Systems and International Regimes," *World Politics* 27, no. 2 (January 1975), p. 151.

48. Morgenthau, *Politics Among Nations, p. 161.*

49. *Ibid.*, p. 519.

50. Kenneth N. Waltz, "The Stability of a Bipolar World," *Daedalus* 93 (Summer 1964): 881–909; Karl W. Deutsch and J. David Singer, "Multipolar Power Systems and International Stability," *World Politics* 16, no. 3 (April 1964): 390–406.

51. Deutsch and Singer, "Multipolar Power Systems," p. 400.

52. Bruce Bueno de Mesquita, "Systemic Polarization and the Occurrence and Duration of War," *Journal of Conflict Resolution* 22, no. 2 (June 1978): 245, 246. See also Michael D. Wallace, *War and Rank Among Nations* (Lexington, MA: D. C. Heath, 1973).

53. Stanley Hoffmann, "Weighing the Balance of Power," *Foreign Affairs* 50, no. 4 (July 1972): 618–43.

54. Steven L. Spiegel and Kenneth N. Waltz, eds. *Conflict in World Politics* (Cambridge, MA: Winthrop, 1971), pp. 454–74.

55. Robert O. Keohane, "The Theory of Hegemonic Stability and Changes in International Economic Regimes, 1967–1977," in Ole R. Holsti, Randolph M. Siverson, and Alexander L. George, eds., *Change in the International System* (Boulder, CO: Westview Press, 1980), pp. 131–62. For a critique and citations of the literature, see Arthur A. Stein, "The Hegemon's Dilemma: Great Britain, the United States, and the International Economic Order," *International Organization* 38, no. 2 (Spring 1984): 355–86.

56. Charles P. Kindleberger, *The World in Depression, 1929–1939* (Berkeley: University of California Press, 1973).

57. For works associated with the Correlates of War project, see "Suggested Readings" for this chapter under Singer's name.

58. Robert Gilpin, *War and Change in World Politics* (New York: Cambridge University Press, 1981), pp. 3, 10.
59. *Ibid.*, p. 10.
60. *Ibid.*, p. 13.
61. George Modelski, "The Long Cycle of Global Politics and the Nation-State," *Comparative Studies in Society and History* 20, no. 2 (April 1978): 214-35. Notice that Modelski does not describe the international system as being anarchic. Although a central authority is lacking, order and authority do exist. See his comments in "Long Cycles and the Strategy of the U.S. International Economic Policy," in *America in a Changing World Political Economy*, ed. William P. Avery and David P. Rapkin (White Plains, NY: Longman, 1982), p. 99.
62. Modelski, "The Long Cycle of Global Politics," p. 217. It is Modelski's emphasis on the primacy of political factors that places him within the context of the realist as opposed to globalist image.
63. *Ibid.*, p. 235.
64. Aside from Robert Gilpin and George Modelski, other authors who deal with power cycles include Charles F. Doran, *The Politics of Assimilation* (Baltimore: Johns Hopkins University Press, 1971); Charles F. Doran and Wes Parsons, "War and the Cycle of Relative Power," *American Political Science Review* 74, no. 4 (December 1980): 947-65; Mancur Olson, *The Rise and Decline of Nations* (New Haven, CT: Yale University Press, 1982); A. F. K. Organski and Jacek Kugler, *The War Ledger* (Chicago: University of Chicago Press, 1980); William Thompson, *Multiple Perspectives on the World System* (Beverly Hills, CA: Sage Publications, 1983).
65. See Kenneth N. Waltz, "Letter to the Editor," *International Organization* 36, no. 3 (Summer 1982): 680, which cites his *Theory of International Politics*, p. 78.
66. Robert G. Gilpin, "The Richness of the Tradition of Political Realism," *International Organization* 38, no. 2 (Spring 1984): 302.
67. In a review of Kenneth Waltz's *Theory of International Politics*, Richard Rosecrance suggests Waltz's work is heavily determinist. Rosecrance, "International Relations Theory Revisited," *International Organization* 35, no. 4 (Autumn 1981): 691-713. Waltz rejects this charge in his "Letter to the Editor," p. 680.
68. Waltz, "Letter to the Editor," p. 680.
69. Gilpin, "Richness of Political Realism," p. 300.
70. U.S. Arms Control and Disarmament Agency, *World Military Expenditures and Arms Transfers 1985* (Washington, DC: Government Printing Office, 1985), p. 3.
71. Morgenthau, *Politics Among Nations*, p. 161; and Ernst B. Haas, "The Balance of Power: Prescription, Concept or Propaganda?" *World Politics* 5, no. 2 (July 1953): 442-77.
72. Gilpin, "Richness of Political Realism," p. 300.
73. Morgenthau, *Politics Among Nations*, p. 548.
74. Gilpin, "Richness of Political Realism," p. 299; Morgenthau, *Politics Among Nations*, p. 9.
75. See, for example, P. Terrence Hopmann, Dina A. Zinnes, and J. David Singer, *Cumulation in International Relations Research* (Denver, CO: University of Denver, Graduate School of International Studies, 1981).

76. Richard K. Ashley is criticizing such authors as Kenneth Waltz, Robert Gilpin, Stephen Krasner, George Modelski, Robert Tucker, and Charles Kindleberger. See Ashley's "The Poverty of Neorealism," *International Organization* 38, no. 2 (Spring 1984): 225-86, p. 228. Also see Ashley, "Political Realism and Human Interests," *International Studies Quarterly* 25, no. 2 (June 1984): 204-35; Ashley, "Three Modes of Economism," *International Studies Quarterly* 27, no. 4 (December 1983): 463-96.

77. Ashley, "Poverty of Neorealism," p. 230. See also Robert Keohane, *Neorealism and Its Critics* (New York: Columbia University Press, 1986).

SUGGESTED READINGS

Aron, Raymond. *On War: Atomic Weapons and Global Diplomacy.* London: Secker and Warburg, 1958.

———. *Peace and War.* Garden City, NY: Doubleday, 1966.

Ashley, Richard K. "Political Realism and Human Interests." *International Studies Quarterly* 25, 2 (June 1981): 204-36.

———. "The Poverty of Neorealism." *International Organization* 38, 2 (Spring 1984): 225-86.

Baldwin, David A. "Power Analysis and World Politics." *World Politics* 31, 2 (January 1979): 161-194.

Brams, Steven J., Morton D. Davis, Philip D. Straffin, Jr. "The Geometry of the Arms Race." *International Studies Quarterly* 23, 4 (December 1979): 567-88.

Brodie, Bernard. *War and Politics.* New York: Macmillan, 1973.

Bueno de Mesquita, Bruce. "The Costs of War: A Rational Expectations Approach." *American Political Science Review* 77, 2 (June 1983): 347-57.

———. "Risk, Power Distributions, and the Likelihood of War." *International Studies Quarterly* 25, 4 (December 1981): 541-68.

———. *The War Trap.* New Haven, CT: Yale University Press, 1981.

———. "The War Trap Revisited: A Revised Expected Utility Model." *American Political Science Review* 79, 1 (March 1985): 156-173.

———. "Theories of International Conflict: An Analysis and an Appraisal." In *Handbook of Political Conflict,* edited by Ted R. Gurr. New York: Free Press, 1980.

Bull, Hedley. *The Anarchical Society: A Study of Order in World Politics.* New York: Columbia University Press, 1977.

Buzan, Barry, and R. J. Barry Jones, eds. *Change and the Study of International Relations.* London: Frances Pinter, 1981.

Claude, Inis, Jr. *Power and International Relations.* New York: Random House, 1962.

Doran, Charles F., and Wes Parsons. "War and the Cycle of Relative Power." *American Political Science Review* 74, 4 (December 1980): 946-65.

Duncan, George T., and Randolph M. Siverson. "Flexibility of Alliance Partner Choice in a Multipolar System." *International Studies Quarterly* 26, 4 (December 1982): 511-38.

Ferris, Wayne H. *The Power Capabilities of Nation-States: International Conflict and War.* Lexington, MA: D. C. Heath, 1973.

George, Alexander, David K. Hall, and William R. Simons. *The Limits of Coercive Diplomacy.* Boston, MA: Little, Brown, 1971.

George, Alexander, and Richard Smoke. *Deterrence in American Foreign Policy: Theory and Practice.* New York: Columbia University Press, 1974.

Gilpin, Robert G. "The Richness of the Tradition of Political Realism." *International Organization* 38, 2 (Spring 1984): 287–304.

———. *U.S. Power and the Multinational Corporation.* New York: Basic Books, 1975.

———. *War and Change in World Politics.* Cambridge: Cambridge University Press, 1981.

Haas, Ernst B. "The Balance of Power: Prescription, Concept or Propaganda?" *World Politics* 5, 4 (July 1953): 442–77.

Haas, Michael, ed. *International Systems: A Behavioral Approach.* New York: Chandler, 1974.

Hart, Jeffrey. "Three Approaches to the Measurement of Power in International Relations." *International Organization* 30, 2 (Spring 1976): 289–305.

Herz, John H. *International Politics in the Atomic Age.* New York: Columbia University Press, 1959.

———. *The Nation–State and the Crisis of World Politics.* New York: David McKay, 1976.

———. *Political Realism and Political Idealism.* Chicago: University of Chicago Press, 1951.

———. "Political Realism Revisited. " *International Studies Quarterly* 25, 2 (June 1981): 182–241.

Hoffmann, Stanley. *Contemporary Theory of International Relations.* Englewood Cliffs, NJ: Prentice-Hall, 1960.

———. "Obstinate or Obsolete? The Fate of the Nation–State and the Case of Western Europe." *Daedalus* 95 (Summer 1966): 862–915.

———. *Primacy or World Order.* New York: McGraw-Hill, 1978.

———. "Raymond Aron and the Theory of International Relations." *International Studies Quarterly* 29, 1 (March 1985): 13–27.

———. *The State of War.* New York: Praeger, 1965.

Howard, Michael E. *The Causes of War and Other Essays.* Cambridge, MA: Harvard University Press, 1983.

———. *War and the Liberal Conscience.* New Brunswick, NJ: Rutgers University Press, 1978.

Iklé, Fred C. *How Nations Negotiate.* New York: Harper & Row, 1964.

Jervis, Robert. "Cooperation Under the Security Dilemma." *World Politics,* 30 (January 1978): 167–86.

———. "Deterrence Theory Revisited." *World Politics* 31, 2 (January 1979): 289–324.

———. *The Illogic of American Nuclear Strategy.* Ithaca, NY: Cornell University Press, 1984.

Kaplan, Morton, ed. *New Approaches to International Relations.* New York: St. Martin's, 1968.

———. *System and Process in International Politics.* New York: John Wiley, 1957.

———. *Towards Professionalism in International Theory: Macrosystem Analysis.* New York: Free Press, 1979.

Kegley, Charles, W., Jr., and Gregory A. Raymond. "Alliance Norms and War." *International Studies Quarterly* 26, 4 (December 1982): 572–95.

Kennedy, Paul. *Strategy and Diplomacy, 1870–1945.* Winchester, MA: Allen & Unwin, 1984.

Keohane, Robert O. *After Hegemony: Cooperation and Discord in the World Political Economy.* Princeton, NJ: Princeton University Press, 1984.

———. ed. *Neorealism and Its Critics.* New York: Columbia University Press, 1986.

———. "The Theory of Hegemonic Stability and Changes in International Economic Regimes." In *Change in the International System,* edited by Ole Hosti, Randolph M. Siverson, and Alexander L. George. Boulder, CO: Westview Press, 1980.

———. "Theory of World Politics: Structural Realism and Beyond." In *Political Science: The State of the Discipline,* ed. Ada W. Finifter. Washington, DC: American Political Science Association, 1983.

Keohane, Robert O., and Joseph S. Nye. *Power and Interdependence: World Politics in Transition.* Boston, MA: Little, Brown, 1977.

Kissinger, Henry A. *A World Restored.* New York: Grosset & Dunlap, 1964.

———. *The Necessity for Choice.* New York: Harper & Row, 1961.

———. *Nuclear Weapons and Foreign Policy.* New York: Harper & Row, 1957.

Knorr, Klaus. *Military Power and Potential.* Lexington, MA: Lexington Books, 1970.

———. *On the Uses of Military Power.* Princeton, NJ: Princeton University Press, 1966.

———. *The Power of Nations: The Political Economy of International Relations.* New York: Basic Books, 1975.

Krasner, Stephen D. *Defending the National Interest.* Princeton, NJ: Princeton University Press, 1978.

———, ed. *International Regimes.* Ithaca, N.Y.: Cornell University Press, 1983.

———. "State Power and the Structure of International Trade." *World Politics* 28, 3 (April 1976): 317–48.

———. *Structural Conflict: The Third World Against Global Liberalism.* Berkeley: University of California Press, 1985.

Kratochwil, Friedrich. "On the Notion of Interest in International Relations." *International Organization* 36, 1 (Winter 1982): 1–30.

Levy, Jack S. "Historical Trends in Great Power War, 1495–1975." *International Studies Quarterly* 26, 2 (June 1982): 278–300.

———. "Misperception and the Causes of War." *World Politics* 36, 1 (October 1983): 76–99.

———. "Theories of General War." *World Politics* 37, 3 (April 1985): 344–74.

Liska, George. *Beyond Kissinger: Ways of Conservative Statecraft.* Baltimore: Johns Hopkins University Press, 1975.

———. *Nations in Alliance: The Limits of Interdependence.* Baltimore, MD: Johns Hopkins University Press, 1968.

Mackinder, Sir Halford, J. "The Round World and the Winning of the Peace." *Foreign Affairs* 21, 4 (July 1943): 595–605.

Majeski, Stephen J., and David J. Sylvan. "Simple Choices and Complex Calculations: A Critique of The War Trap." *Journal of Conflict Resolution* 28, 2 (June 1984): 316–40, and rejoinder by Bruce Bueno de Mesquita.

March, James G. "Bounded Rationality, Ambiguity, and the Engineering of Choice." *Bell Journal of Economics* 9, 2 (Autumn 1978): 587–608.

Modelski, George. *A Theory of Foreign Policy.* New York: Praeger, 1962.

————. "The Long Cycle of Global Politics and the Nation-State." *Comparative Studies in Society and History* 20, 2 (April 1978): 214-35.

————. "Long Cycles and the Strategy of U.S. Economic Policy." In *America in a Changing World Political Economy*, ed. William P. Avery and David P. Rapkin. New York: Longman, 1982.

————. *Principles of World Politics*. New York: Free Press, 1972.

Modelski, George, and Patrick M. Morgan. "Understanding Global War." *Journal of Conflict Resolution* 29, 2 (September 1985): 391-417.

Morgenthau, Hans J. *In Defense of the National Interest*. New York: Knopf, 1951.

————. *Politics Among Nations: The Struggle for Power and Peace*. 5th ed. New York: Knopf, 1978.

————. *Scientific Man vs. Power Politics*. Chicago: University of Chicago Press, 1946.

Moul, William B. "The Level of Analysis Problem Revisited." *Canadian Journal of Political Science* 6, 3 (September 1973): 494-513.

Osgood, Robert E. *Alliances and American Foreign Policy*. Baltimore, MD: Johns Hopkins University Press, 1968.

Osgood, Robert E., and Robert W. Tucker. *Force, Order and Justice*. Baltimore, MD: Johns Hopkins University Press, 1967.

Rapoport, Anatol. *Strategy and Conscience*. New York: Schocken Books, 1969.

Rapoport, Anatol, and A. M. Ghammah. *Prisoner's Dilemma*. Ann Arbor: University of Michigan Press, 1965.

Ray, James Lee. "Understanding Rummel." *Journal of Conflict Resolution* 26, 1 (March 1982): 161-87.

Richardson, Lewis F. *Arms and Insecurity*. Pittsburg, PA.: Boxwood, 1960.

Riker, William H. *A Theory of Political Coalitions*. New Haven, CT: Yale University Press, 1962.

Rogowski, Ronald. "Structure, Growth, and Power: Three Rationalist Accounts," *International Organization* 37, 4 (Autumn 1983): 713-38.

Rosecrance, Richard. *Action and Reaction in World Politics*. Boston, MA: Little, Brown, 1963.

————. *International Relations: Peace or War?* New York: McGraw-Hill, 1973.

————. "International Relations Theory Revisited." *International Organization* 35, 4 (Autumn 1981): 691-713. A review of Waltz, *Theory of International Politics* and Bull, *The Anarchical Society*. See also the Waltz--Rosecrance exchange in *International Organization* 36, 3 (Summer 1982): 679-85.

Ruggie, John Gerard. "Continuity and Transformation in the World Polity: Toward a Neorealist Synthesis." *World Politics* 35, 2 (January 1983): 261-85. A review of Waltz, *Theory of International Politics*.

Rummel, Rudolph. *Dimensions of Nations*. Beverly Hills, CA: Sage Publications, 1972.

————. *Field Theory Evolving*. Beverly Hills, CA: Sage Publications, 1977.

————. *Understanding Conflict and War*. Five volumes. Beverly Hills, CA: Sage Publications, 1975-1981.

Russett, Bruce M. *International Regions and the International System*. Chicago: Rand McNally, 1967.

————. "The Mysterious Case of Vanishing Hegemony." *International Organization* 39, 2 (Spring 1985): 207-231.

————, ed. *Peace, War, and Numbers.* Beverly Hills, CA: Sage Publications, 1972.

Schelling, Thomas S. *Arms and Influence.* New Haven, CT: Yale University Press, 1966.

————. *The Strategy of Conflict.* New York: Oxford University Press, 1960.

Schlenker, Barry R., and Thomas V. Bonoma. "Fun and Games: The Validity of Games for the Study of Conflict." *Journal of Conflict Resolution* 22 (March 1978): 9–13.

Sigal, Leon V. "The Logic of Deterrence in Theory and Practice." *International Organization* 33, 4 (Autumn 1979): 567–79.

Singer, J. David. "Accounting for International War: The State of the Discipline." *Journal of Peace Research* 18, 1 (1981): 1–18.

————, ed. *Correlates of War I: Research Origins and Rationale.* New York: Free Press, 1979.

————, ed. *Correlates of War II: Testing Some Balance-of-Power Models.* New York: Free Press, 1980.

————. "Confrontational Behavior and Escalation to War 1816–1980: A Research Plan." *Journal of Peace Research* 19, 1 (1982): 37–48.

————, ed. *Quantitative International Politics: Insights and Evidence.* New York: Free Press, 1968.

Singer, J. David, and Michael D. Wallace, eds. *To Augur Well: Early Warning Indicators in World Politics.* Beverly Hills, CA: Sage Publications, 1979.

Singer J. David, and Melvin Small. *The Wages of War 1816–1965: A Statistical Handbook.* New York: John Wiley, 1972.

Singer, J. David, and associates. *Explaining War: Selected Papers From the Correlates of War Project.* Beverly Hills, CA: Sage Publications, 1979.

Siverson, Randolph M., and Michael R. Tennefoss. "Power, Alliance, and the Escalation of International Conflict, 1815–1965." *American Political Science Review* 78, 4 (December 1984): 1057–69.

Snidal, Duncan. "The Limits of Hegemonic Stability Theory." *International Organization* 39, 4 (Autumn 1985): 579–614.

Stoessinger, John G. *Why Nations Go to War.* New York: St. Martin's, 1978.

Sylvan, David J. "The Newest Mercantilism." *International Organization* 35, 2 (Spring 1981): 375–93. A review article.

Tucker, Robert W. *The Inequality of Nations.* New York: Basic Books, 1977.

Wagner, R. Harrison. "War and Expected Utility Theory." *World Politics* 36, 3 (April 1984): 407–23. A review of Bueno de Mesquita, *The War Trap.*

————. "The Theory of Games and the Problem of International Cooperation." *American Political Science Review* 77, 2 (June 1983): 330–46.

Wallace, Michael P. "Arms Races and Escalation." *Journal of Conflict Resolution* 23, 1 (March 1979): 3–16.

Waltz, Kenneth N. *Foreign Policy and Democratic Politics.* Boston, MA: Little, Brown, 1967.

————. *Man, the State and War.* New York: Columbia University Press, 1959.

————. *Theory of International Politics.* Reading, MA: Addison-Wesley, 1979.

Wayman, Frank W., J. David Singer, and Gary Goertz. "Capabilities, Allocations, and Success in Militarized Disputes and Wars, 1816–1976." *International Studies Quarterly* 27, 4 (December 1983): 497–515.

Wight, Martin. *Power Politics.* New York: Holmes and Meier, 1978.

———. *Systems of States*. Edited by Hedley Bull. Leicester: Leicester University Press, 1977.

Wolfers, Arnold. *Discord and Collaboration*. Baltimore, MD: Johns Hopkins University Press, 1962.

Wright, Quincy. *A Study of War*. Chicago: University of Chicago Press, 1964.

———. *The Study of International Relations*. New York: Appleton-Century-Crofts, 1955.

Zinnes, Dina. "Empirical Evidence on the Outbreak of International Conflict." In *Handbook of Political Conflict*, ed. Ted R. Gurr. New York: Free Press, 1980.

Zinnes, Dina, and Francis W. Hoole, eds. *Quantitative International Politics: An Appraisal*. New York: Praeger, 1976.

The Melian Dialogue

Thucydides

This classic contains the essential ingredients of the realist perspective stated in perhaps its boldest and most extreme form. The Athenians have no interest in whether the demands they make on the Melians are just or moral. In a classic statement, the Athenians emphasize the over-riding importance of power: "The strong do what they have the power to do, and the weak accept what they have to accept." Other important concepts and notions such as honor, perception, neutrality, self-interest, alliances, balance of power, capabilities, and the uncertainty of power calculations are also discussed.

Next summer Alcibiades sailed to Argos with twenty ships and seized 300 Argive citizens who were still suspected of being pro-Spartan. These were put by the Athenians into the nearby islands under Athenian control.

The Athenians also made an expedition against the island of Melos. They had thirty of their own ships, six from Chios, and two from Lesbos; 1,200 hoplites, 300 archers, and twenty mounted archers, all from Athens; and about 1,500 hoplites from the allies and the islanders.

The Melians are a colony from Sparta. They had refused to join the Athenian empire like the other islanders, and at first had remained neutral without helping either side; but afterwards, when the Athenians had brought force to bear on them by laying waste their land, they had become open enemies of Athens.

Now the generals Cleomedes, the son of Lycomedes, and Tisias, the son of Tisimachus, encamped with the above force in Melian territory and, before doing any harm to the land, first of all sent representatives to negotiate. The Melians did not invite these representatives to speak before the people, but asked them to make the statement for which they

From Thucydides, *History of the Peloponnesian War,* translated by Rex Warner. Penguin Classics, 1954, pages 400–408. Reprinted by permission of Penguin Books Ltd.

had come in front of the governing body and the few. The Athenian representatives then spoke as follows:

"So we are not to speak before the people, no doubt in case the mass of the people should hear once and for all and without interruption an argument from us which is both persuasive and incontrovertible, and should so be led astray. This, we realize, is your motive in bringing us here to speak before the few. Now suppose that you who sit here should make assurance doubly sure. Suppose that you, too, should refrain from dealing with every point in detail in a set speech, and should instead interrupt us whenever we say something controversial and deal with that before going on to the next point? Tell us first whether you approve of this suggestion of ours."

The Council of the Melians replied as follows:

"No one can object to each of us putting forward our own views in a calm atmosphere. That is perfectly reasonable. What is scarcely consistent with such a proposal is the present threat, indeed the certainty, of your making war on us. We see that you have come prepared to judge the argument yourselves, and that the likely end of it all will be either war, if we prove that we are in the right, and so refuse to surrender, or else slavery."

Athenians: If you are going to spend the time in enumerating your suspicions about the future, or if you have met here for any other reason except to look the facts in the face and on the basis of these facts to consider how you can save your city from destruction, there is no point in our going on with this discussion. If, however, you will do as we suggest, then we will speak on.

Melians: It is natural and understandable that people who are placed as we are should have recourse to all kinds of arguments and different points of view. However, you are right in saying that we are met together here to discuss the safety of our country and, if you will have it so, the discussion shall proceed on the lines that you have laid down.

Athenians: Then we on our side will use no fine phrases saying, for example, that we have a right to our empire because we defeated the Persians, or that we have come against you now because of the injuries you have done us—a great mass of words that nobody would believe. And we ask you on your side not to imagine that you will influence us by saying that you, though a colony of Sparta, have not joined Sparta in the war, or that you have never done us any harm. Instead we recommend that you should try to get what it is possible for you to get, taking into consideration what we both really do think; since you know as well as we do that, when these matters are discussed by practical people, the standard of justice depends on the equality of power to compel and that in fact the strong do what they have the power to do and the weak accept what they have to accept.

Melians: Then in our view (since you force us to leave justice out of account and to confine ourselves to self-interest)—in our view it is at any rate useful that you should not destroy a principle that is to the general good of all men—namely, that in the case of all who fall into danger there should be such a thing as fair play and just dealing, and that such people should be allowed to use and to profit by arguments that fall short of a mathematical accuracy. And this is a principle which affects you as much as anybody, since your own fall would be visited by the most terrible vengeance and would be an example to the world.

Athenians: As for us, even assuming that our empire does come to an end, we are not despondent about what would happen next. One is not so much frightened of being conquered by a power which rules over others, as Sparta does (not that we are concerned with Sparta now), as of what would happen if a ruling power is attacked and defeated by its own subjects. So far as this point is concerned, you can leave it to us to face the risks involved. What we shall do now is to show you that it is for the good of our own empire that we are here and that it is for the preservation of your city that we shall say what we are going to say. We do not want any trouble in bringing you into our empire, and we want you to be spared for the good both of yourselves and of ourselves.

Melians: And how could it be just as good for us to be the slaves as for you to be the masters?

Athenians: You, by giving in, would save yourselves from disaster; we, by not destroying you, would be able to profit from you.

Melians: So you would not agree to our being neutral, friends instead of enemies, but allies of neither side?

Athenians: No, because it is not so much your hostility that injures us; it is rather the case that, if we were on friendly terms with you, our subjects would regard that as a sign of weakness in us, whereas your hatred is evidence of our power.

Melians: Is that your subjects' idea of fair play—that no distinction should be made between people who are quite unconnected with you and people who are mostly your own colonists or else rebels whom you have conquered?

Athenians: So far as right and wrong are concerned they think that there is no difference between the two, that those who still preserve their independence do so because they are strong, and that if we fail to attack them it is because we are afraid. So that by conquering you we shall increase not only the size but the security of our empire. We rule the sea and you are islanders, and weaker islanders too than the others; it is therefore particularly important that you should not escape.

Melians: But do you think there is no security for you in what we suggest? For here again, since you will not let us mention justice, but tell us to give in to your interests, we, too, must tell you what our interests are and, if yours and ours happen to coincide, we must try to persuade you of the fact. Is it not certain that you will make enemies of all states who are at present neutral, when they see what is happening here and naturally conclude that in course of time you will attack them too? Does not this mean that you are strengthening the enemies you have already and are forcing others to become your enemies even against their intentions and their inclinations?

Athenians: As a matter of fact we are not so much frightened of states on the continent. They have their liberty, and this means that it will be a long time before they begin to take precautions against us. We are more concerned about islanders like yourselves, who are still unsubdued, or subjects who have already become embittered by the constraint which our empire imposes on them. These are the people who are most likely to act in a reckless manner and to bring themselves and us, too, into the most obvious danger.

Melians: Then surely, if such hazards are taken by you to keep your empire and by your subjects to escape from it, we who are still free would show ourselves great cowards and weaklings if we failed to face everything that comes rather than submit to slavery.

Athenians: No, not if you are sensible. This is no fair fight, with honour on one side and shame on the other. It is rather a question of saving your lives and not resisting those who are far too strong for you.

Melians: Yet we know that in war fortune sometimes makes the odds more level than could be expected from the difference in numbers of the two sides. And if we surrender, then all our hope is lost at once, whereas, so long as we remain in action, there is still a hope that we may yet stand upright.

Athenians: Hope, that comforter in danger! If one already has solid advantages to fall back upon, one can indulge in hope. It may do harm, but will not destroy one. But hope is by nature an expensive commodity, and those who are risking their all on one cast find out what it means only when they are already ruined; it never fails them in the period when such a knowledge would enable them to take precautions. Do not let this happen to you, you who are weak and whose fate depends on a single movement of the scale. And do not be like those people who, as so commonly happens, miss the chance of saving themselves in a human and practical way, and, when every clear and distinct hope has left them in their adversity, turn to what is blind and vague, to prophecies and oracles and such things which by encouraging hope lead men to ruin.

Melians: It is difficult, and you may be sure that we know it, for us to oppose your power and fortune, unless the terms be equal. Nevertheless we trust that the gods will give us fortune as good as yours, because we are standing for what is right against what is wrong; and as for what we lack in power, we trust that it will be made up for by our alliance with the Spartans, who are bound, if for no other reason, then for honour's sake, and because we are their kinsmen, to come to our help. Our confidence, therefore, is not so entirely irrational as you think.

Athenians: So far as the favour of the gods is concerned, we think we have as much right to that as you have. Our aims and our actions are perfectly consistent with the beliefs men hold about the gods and with the principles which govern their own conduct. Our opinion of the gods and our knowledge of men lead us to conclude that it is a general and necessary law of nature to rule whatever one can. This is not a law that we made ourselves, nor were we the first to act upon it when it was made. We found it already in existence, and we shall leave it to exist forever among those who come after us. We are merely acting in accordance with it, and we know that you or anybody else with the same power as ours would be acting in precisely the same way. And therefore, so far as the gods are concerned, we see no good reason why we should fear to be at a disadvantage. But with regard to your views about Sparta and your confidence that she, out of a sense of honour, will come to your aid, we must say that we congratulate you on your simplicity but do not envy you your folly. In matters that concern themselves or their own constitution the Spartans are quite remarkably good; as for their relations with others, that is a long story, but it can be expressed shortly and clearly by saying that of all people we know the Spartans are most conspicuous for believing that what they like doing is honourable and what suits their interests is just. And this kind of attitude is not going to be of much help to you in your absurd quest for safety at the moment.

Melians: But this is the very point where we can feel most sure. Their own self-interest will make them refuse to betray their own colonists, the Melians, for that would mean losing the confidence of their friends among the Hellenes and doing good to their enemies.

Athenians: You seem to forget that if one follows one's self-interest one wants to be safe, whereas the path of justice and honour involves one in danger. And, where danger is concerned, the Spartans are not, as a rule, very venturesome.

Melians: But we think that they would even endanger themselves for our sake and count the risk more worth taking than in the case of others, because we are so close to the Peloponnese that they could operate more easily, and because they can depend on us more than on others, since we are of the same race and share the same feelings.

Athenians: Goodwill shown by the party that is asking for help does not mean security for the prospective ally. What is looked for is a positive preponderance of power in action. And the Spartans pay attention to this point even more than others do. Certainly they distrust their own native resources so much that when they attack a neighbour they bring a great army of allies with them. It is hardly likely therefore that, while we are in control of the sea, they will cross over to an island.

Melians: But they still might send others. The Cretan sea is a wide one, and it is harder for those who control it to intercept others than for those who want to slip through to do so safely. And even if they were to fail in this, they would turn against your own land and against those of your allies left unvisited by Brasidas. So, instead of troubling about a country which has nothing to do with you, you will find trouble nearer home, among your allies, and in your own country.

Athenians: It is a possibility, something that has in fact happened before. It may happen in your case, but you are well aware that the Athenians have never yet relinquished a single siege operation through fear of others. But we are somewhat shocked to find that, though you announced your intention of discussing how you could preserve yourselves, in all this talk you have said absolutely nothing which could justify a man in thinking that he could be preserved. Your chief points are concerned with what you hope may happen in the future, while your actual resources are too scanty to give you a chance of survival against the forces that are opposed to you at this moment. You will therefore be showing an extraordinary lack of common sense if, after you have asked us to retire from this meeting, you still fail to reach a conclusion wiser than anything you have mentioned so far. Do not be led astray by a false sense of honour—a thing which often brings men to ruin when they are faced with an obvious danger that somehow affects their pride. For in many cases men have still been able to see the dangers ahead of them, but this thing called dishonour, this word, by its own force of seduction, has drawn them into a state where they have surrendered to an idea, while in fact they have fallen voluntarily into irrevocable disaster, in dishonour that is all the more dishonourable because it has come to them from their own folly rather than their misfortune. You, if you take the right view, will be careful to avoid this. You will see that there is nothing disgraceful in giving way to the greatest city in Hellas when she is offering you such reasonable terms—alliance on a tribute-paying basis and liberty to enjoy your own property. And, when you are allowed to choose between war and safety, you will not be so insensitively arrogant as to make the wrong choice. This is the safe rule—to stand up to one's equals, to behave with deference towards one's superiors, and to treat one's inferiors with moderation. Think it over again, then, when we have withdrawn from the meeting, and let this be a point that constantly recurs to your minds—that you are discussing the fate of your country, that you have only one country, and that its future for good or ill depends on this one single decision which you are going to make.

The Athenians then withdrew from the discussion. The Melians, left to themselves, reached a conclusion which was much the same as they had indicated in their previous replies. Their answer was as follows:

"Our decision, Athenians, is just the same as it was at first. We are not prepared to give up in a short moment the liberty which our city has enjoyed from its foundation for 700 years. We put our trust in the fortune that the gods will send and which has saved us up to now, and in the help of men—that is, of the Spartans; and so we shall try to save ourselves. But we invite you to allow us to be friends of yours and enemies to neither side, to make a treaty which shall be agreeable to both you and us, and so to leave our country."

The Melians made this reply, and the Athenians, just as they were breaking off the discussion, said:

"Well, at any rate, judging from this decision of yours, you seem to us quite unique in your ability to consider the future as something more certain than what is before your eyes, and to see uncertainties as realities, simply because you would like them to be so. As you have staked most on and trusted most in Spartans, luck, and hopes, so in all these you will find yourselves most completely deluded."

The Athenian representatives then went back to the army, and the Athenian generals, finding that the Melians would not submit, immediately commenced hostilities and built a wall completely round the city of Melos, dividing the work out among the various states. Later they left behind a garrison of some of their own and some allied troops to blockade the place by land and sea, and with the greater part of their army returned home. The force left behind stayed on and continued with the siege.

About the same time the Argives invaded Phliasia and were ambushed by the Phliasians and the exiles from Argos, losing about eighty men.

Then, too, the Athenians at Pylos captured a great quantity of plunder from Spartan territory. Not even after this did the Spartans renounce the treaty and make war, but they issued a proclamation saying that any of their people who wished to do so were free to make raids on the Athenians. The Corinthians also made some attacks on the Athenians because of private quarrels of their own, but the rest of the Peloponnesians stayed quiet.

Meanwhile the Melians made a night attack and captured the part of the Athenian lines opposite the market-place. They killed some of the troops, and then, after bringing in corn and everything else useful that they could lay their hands on, retired again and made no further move, while the Athenians took measures to make their blockade more efficient in future. So the summer came to an end.

In the following winter the Spartans planned to invade the territory of Argos, but when the sacrifices for crossing the frontier turned out unfavourably, they gave up the expedition. The fact that they had intended to invade made the Argives suspect certain people in their city, some of whom they arrested, though others succeeded in escaping.

About this same time the Melians again captured another part of the Athenian lines where there were only a few of the garrison on guard. As a result of this, another force came out afterwards from Athens under the command of Philocrates, the son of Demeas. Siege operations were now carried on vigorously and, as there was also some treachery from inside, the Melians surrendered unconditionally to the Athenians, who put to death all the men of military age whom they took, and sold the women and children as slaves. Melos itself they took over for themselves, sending out later a colony of 500 men.

On Princes and the Security of Their States

Niccolo Machiavelli

In this selection from The Prince, *Machiavelli makes a number of his famous observations on how a prince should rule. Although a prince may not wish to be hated, Machiavelli argues "it is much safer to be feared than to be loved, if one must choose." Although the prince may be criticized for being cruel, this is acceptable to Machiavelli so long as the prince keeps his subjects united and loyal. These are the sorts of argument that have given Machiavellianism a negative connotation, but followers of Machiavelli would respond that the ultimate goal meant to justify particular policies is the security of the state, not just the security of an individual ruler.*

ON THINGS FOR WHICH MEN, AND PARTICULARLY PRINCES, ARE PRAISED OR BLAMED

We now have left to consider what should be the manners and attitudes of a prince toward his subjects and his friends. As I know that many have written on this subject I feel that I may be held presumptuous in what I have to say, if in my comments I do not follow the lines laid down by others. Since, however, it has been my intention to write something which may be of use to the understanding reader, it has seemed wiser to me to follow the real truth of the matter rather than what we imagine it to be. For imagination has created many principalities and republics that have never been seen or known to have any real existence, for how we live is so different from how we ought to live that he who studies what ought to be done rather than what is done will learn the way to his downfall rather than to his preservation. A man striving in every way to be good will meet his ruin among the great number who are not good. Hence it is necessary for a prince, if he wishes to remain in power, to learn how not to be good and to use his knowledge or refrain from using it as he may need.

Putting aside then the things imagined as pertaining to a prince and considering those that really do, I will say that all men, and particularly princes because of their prominence, when comment is made of them, are noted as having some characteristics deserving either praise or blame. One is accounted liberal, another stingy, to use a Tuscan term—

Reprinted from *The Prince* by Niccolo Machiavelli, translated and edited by Thomas G. Bergin. Reprinted by permission.

for in our speech avaricious (*avaro*) is applied to such as are desirous of acquiring by rapine whereas stingy (*misero*) is the term used for those who are reluctant to part with their own—one is considered bountiful, another rapacious; one cruel, another tenderhearted; one false to his word, another trustworthy; one effeminate and pussillanimous, another wild and spirited; one humane, another haughty; one lascivious, another chaste; one a man of integrity and another sly; one tough and another pliant; one serious and another frivolous; one religious and another skeptical, and so on. Everyone will agree, I know, that it would be a most praiseworthy thing if all the qualities accounted as good in the above enumeration were found in a Prince. But since they cannot be so possessed nor observed because of human conditions which do not allow of it, what is necessary for the prince is to be prudent enough to escape the infamy of such vices as would result in the loss of his state; as for the others which would not have that effect, he must guard himself from them as far as possible but if he cannot, he may overlook them as being of less importance. Further, he should have no concern about incurring the infamy of such vices without which the preservation of his state would be difficult. For, if the matter be well considered, it will be seen that some habits which appear virtuous, if adopted would signify ruin, and others that seem vices lead to security and the well-being of the prince.

CRUELTY AND CLEMENCY AND WHETHER IT IS BETTER TO BE LOVED OR FEARED

Now to continue with the list of characteristics. It should be the desire of every prince to be considered merciful and not cruel, yet he should take care not to make poor use of his clemency. Cesare Borgia was regarded as cruel, yet his cruelty reorganized Romagna and united it in peace and loyalty. Indeed, if we reflect, we shall see that this man was more merciful than the Florentines who, to avoid the charge of cruelty, allowed Pistoia to be destroyed.[1] A prince should care nothing for the accusation of cruelty so long as he keeps his subjects united and loyal; by making a very few examples he can be more truly merciful than those who through too much tender-heartedness allow disorders to arise whence come killings and rapine. For these offend an entire community, while the few executions ordered by the prince affect only a few individuals. For a new prince above all it is impossible not to earn a reputation for cruelty since new states are full of dangers. Virgil indeed has Dido apologize for the inhumanity of her rule because it is new, in the words:

Res dura et regni novitas me talia cogunt Moliri et late fines custode tueri.

Nevertheless a prince should not be too ready to listen to talebearers nor to act on suspicion, nor should he allow himself to be easily frightened.

He should proceed with a mixture of prudence and humanity in such a way as not to be made incautious by overconfidence nor yet intolerable by excessive mistrust.

Here the question arises; whether it is better to be loved than feared or feared than loved. The answer is that it would be desirable to be both but, since that is difficult, it is much safer to be feared than to be loved, if one must choose. For on men in general this observation may be made: they are ungrateful, fickle, and deceitful, eager to avoid dangers, and avid for gain, and while you are useful to them they are all with you, offering you their blood, their property, their lives, and their sons so long as danger is remote, as we noted above, but when it approaches they turn on you. Any prince, trusting only in their words and having no other preparations made, will fall to his ruin, for friendships that are bought at a price and not by greatness and nobility of soul are paid for indeed, but they are not owned and cannot be called upon in time of need. Men have less hesitation in offending a man who is loved than one who is feared, for love is held by a bond of obligation which, as men are wicked, is broken whenever personal advantage suggests it, but fear is accompanied by the dread of punishment which never relaxes.

Yet a prince should make himself feared in such a way that, if he does not thereby merit love, at least he may escape odium, for being feared and not hated may well go together. And indeed the prince may attain this end if he but respect the property and the women of his subjects and citizens. And if it should become necessary to seek the death of someone, he should find a proper justification and a public cause, and above all he should keep his hands off another's property, for men forget more readily the death of their father than the loss of their patrimony. Besides, pretexts for seizing property are never lacking, and when a prince begins to live by means of rapine he will always find some excuse for plundering others, and conversely pretexts for execution are rarer and are more quickly exhausted.

A prince at the head of his armies and with a vast number of soldiers under his command should give not the slightest heed if he is esteemed cruel, for without such a reputation he will not be able to keep his army united and ready for action. Among the marvelous things told of Hannibal is that, having a vast army under his command made up of all kinds and races of men and waging war far from his own country, he never allowed any dissension to arise either as between the troops and their leaders or among the troops themselves, and this both in times of good fortune and bad. This could only have come about through his most inhuman cruelty which, taken in conjunction with his great valor, kept him always an object of respect and terror in the eyes of his soldiers. And without the cruelty his other characteristics would not have achieved this effect. Thoughtless writers have admired his actions and at the same time deplored the cruelty which was the basis of them. As evidence of the truth of our statement that his other virtues would have been insufficient let us examine the case of Scipio, an extraordinary leader not only in his own day but for all recorded history. His army in Spain revolted and for no other reason than because of his kind-heartedness, which had allowed more license to his soldiery than military discipline properly permits. His policy was attacked in the Senate by Fabius Maximus, who called him a corrupter of the Roman arms. When the Locrians had been mishandled by one of his lieutenants, his easy-going nature prevented him from avenging them or disciplining his officer, and it was à propos of this incident that one of the senators remarked, wishing to find an excuse for him, that there were many men who knew better how to avoid error themselves than to correct it in others. This characteristic of Scipio would have clouded his fame and glory had he continued in authority, but as he lived under the government of the Senate, its harmful aspect was hidden and it reflected credit on him.

Hence, on the subject of being loved or feared I will conclude that since love depends on the subjects, but the prince has it in his own hands to create fear, a wise prince will rely on what is his own, remembering at the same time that he must avoid arousing hatred, as we have said.

NOTE

1. By unchecked rioting between opposing factions (1502).

Of the Natural Condition of Mankind

Thomas Hobbes

Hobbes analyzes why conflict and violence between individuals or states is to be expected. Although his focus in The Leviathan is on domestic societies, his observations are also relevant to international politics and have had a major impact on realism. In the absence of a sovereign or central, superordinate authority, the world described by Hobbes is a

From Thomas Hobbes, Leviathan, introduction by Richard S. Peters, New York: Macmillan/ Collier Books, 1962.

rather dismal one in which the life of the individual is "solitary, poor, nasty, brutish, and short" and "kings . . . because of their independency, are in continual jealousies, and in the state and posture of gladiators."

Men by Nature Equal. Nature hath made men so equal, in the faculties of the body, and mind; as that though there be found one man sometimes manifestly stronger in body, or of quicker mind than another; yet when all is reckoned together, the difference between man, and man, is not so considerable, as that one man can thereupon claim to himself any benefit, to which another may not pretend, as well as he. For as to the strength of body, the weakest has strength enough to kill the strongest, either by secret machination, or by confederacy with others, that are in the same danger with himself.

And as to the faculties of the mind, setting aside the arts grounded upon words, and especially that skill of proceeding upon general, and infallible rules, called science; which very few have, and but in few things; as being not a native faculty, born with us; nor attained, as prudence, while we look after somewhat else, I find yet a greater equality amongst men, than that of strength. For prudence, is but experience; which equal time, equally bestows on all men, in those things they equally apply themselves unto. That which may perhaps make such equality incredible, is but a vain conceit of one's own wisdom, which almost all men think they have in a greater degree, than the vulgar; that is, than all men but themselves, and a few others, whom by fame, or for concurring with themselves, they approve. For such is the nature of men, that howsoever thay may acknowledge many others to be more witty, or more eloquent, or more learned; yet they will hardly believe there be many so wise as themselves; for they see their own wit at hand, and other men's at a distance. But this proveth rather that men are in that point equal, than unequal. For there is not ordinarily a greater sign of the equal distribution of any thing, than that every man is contented with his share.

From Equality Proceeds Diffidence. From this equality of ability, ariseth equality of hope in the attaining of our ends. And therefore if any two men desire the same thing, which nevertheless they cannot both enjoy, they become enemies; and in the way to their end, which is principally their own conservation, and sometimes their delectation only, endeavour to destroy, or subdue one another. And from hence it comes to pass, that where an invader hath no more to fear, than another man's single power; if one plant, sow, build, or possess a convenient seat, others may probably be expected to come prepared with forces united, to dispossess, and deprive him, not only of the fruit of his labour, but also of his life, or liberty. And the invader again is in the like danger of another.

From Diffidence War. And from this diffidence of one another, there is no way for any man to secure himself, so reasonable, as anticipation; that is, by force, or wiles, to master the persons of all men he can, so long, till he see no other power great enough to endanger him: and this is no more than his own conservation requireth, and is generally allowed. Also because there be some, that taking pleasure in contemplating their own power in the acts of conquest, which they pursue farther than their security requires; if others, that otherwise would be glad to be at ease within modest bounds, should not by invasion increase their power, they would not be able, long time, by standing only on their defence, to subsist. And by consequence, such augmentation of dominion over men being necessary to a man's conservation, it ought to be allowed him.

Again, men have no pleasure, but on the contrary a great deal of grief, in keeping company, where there is no power able to overawe them all. For every man looketh that his companion should value him, at the same rate he sets upon himself: and upon all signs of contempt, or undervaluing, naturally endeavours, as far as he dares, (which amongst them that have no common power to keep them in quiet, is far enough to make them destroy each other), to extort a greater value from his contemners, by damage; and from others, by the example.

So that in the nature of man, we find three principal causes of quarrel. First, competition; secondly, diffidence; thirdly, glory.

The first, maketh men invade for gain; the second, for safety; and the third, for reputation. The first use violence, to make themselves masters of other men's persons, wives, children, and cattle; the second, to defend them; the third, for trifles, as a word, a smile, a different opinion, and any other sign of undervalue, either direct in their persons, or by reflection in their kindred, their friends, their nation, their profession, or their name.

Out of Civil States, There Is Always War of Every One Against Every One. Hereby it is manifest, that during the time men live without a common power to keep them all in awe, they are in that condition which is called war; and such a war, as is of every man, against every man. For WAR, consisteth not in battle only, or the act of fighting; but in a tract of time, wherein the will to contend by battle is sufficiently known: and therefore the notion of *time,* is to be considered in the nature of war; as it is in the nature of weather. For as the nature of foul weather, lieth not in a shower or two of rain; but in an inclination thereto of many days together: so the nature of war, consisteth not in actual fighting; but in the known disposition thereto, during all the time there is no assurance to the contrary. All other time is PEACE.

The Incommodities of Such a War. Whatsoever therefore is consequent to a time of war, where every man is enemy to every man; the same is consequent to the time, wherein men live without other security, than what their own strength, and their own invention shall furnish them withal. In such condition, there is no place for industry; because the fruit thereof is uncertain: and consequently no culture of the earth; no navigation, nor use of the commodities that may be imported by sea; no commodious building; no instruments of moving, and removing, such things as require much force; no knowledge of the face of the earth; no account of time; no arts; no letters; no society; and which is worst of all, continual fear, and danger of violent death; and the life of man, solitary, poor, nasty, brutish, and short.

It may seem strange to some man, that has not well weighed these things; that nature should thus dissociate, and render men apt to invade, and destroy one another: and he may therefore, not trusting to this inference, made from the passions, desire perhaps to have the same confirmed by experience. Let him therefore consider with himself, when taking a journey, he arms himself, and seeks to go well accompanied; when going to sleep, he locks his doors; when even in his house he locks his chests; and this when he knows there be laws, and public officers, armed, to revenge all injuries shall be done him; what opinion he has of his fellow-subjects, when he rides armed; of his fellow citizens, when he locks his doors; and of his children, and servants, when he locks his chests. Does he not there as much accuse mankind by his actions, as I do by my words? But neither of us accuse man's nature in it. The desires, and other passions of man, are in themselves no sin. No more are the actions, that proceed from those passions, till they know a law that forbids them: which till laws be made they cannot know: nor can any law be made, till they have agreed upon the person that shall make it.

It may peradventure be thought, there was never such a time, nor condition of war as this; and I believe it was never generally so, over all the world: but there are many places, where they live so now. For the savage people in many places of America, except the government of small families, the concord whereof dependeth on natural lust, have no government at all; and live at this day in the brutish manner, as I said before. Howsoever, it may be perceived what manner of life there would be, where there were no common power to fear, by the manner of life, which men that have formerly lived under a peaceful government, use to degenerate into, in a civil war.

But though there had never been any time, wherein particular men were in a condition of war one against another; yet in all times, kings, and persons of sovereign authority, because of their independency, are in continual jealousies, and in the state and posture of gladiators; having their weapons pointing, and their eyes fixed on one another; that is, their forts, garrisons, and guns upon the frontiers of their kingdoms; and continual spies upon their neighbours; which is a posture of war. But because they uphold thereby, the industry of their subjects; there does not follow from it, that misery, which accompanies the liberty of particular men.

In Such a War Nothing Is Unjust. To this war of every man, against every man, this also is consequent; that nothing can be unjust. The notions of right and wrong, justice and injustice have there no place. Where there is no common power, there is no law: where no law, no injustice. Force, and fraud, are in war the two cardinal virtues. Justice, and injustice are none of the faculties neither of the body, nor mind. If they were, they might be in a man that were alone in the world, as well as his senses, and passions. They are qualities, that relate to men in society, not in solitude. It is consequent also to the same condition, that there be no propriety, no dominion, no *mine* and *thine* distinct; but only that to be every man's, that he can get: and for so long, as he can keep it. And thus much for the ill condition, which man by mere nature is actually placed in; though with a possibility to come out of it, consisting partly in the passions, partly in his reason.

The Passions that Incline Men to Peace. The passions that incline men to peace, are fear of death; desire of such things as are necessary to commodious living; and a hope by their industry to obtain them. And reason suggesteth convenient articles of peace, upon which men may be drawn to agreement.

Does Order Exist in World Politics?

Hedley Bull

The late Professor Bull identifies three traditions of thought—Hobbesian (or realist), Kantian (or universalist), and Grotian (or internationalist). Bull's own work is a blend of the Hobbesian and Grotian traditions in that order in world politics rests, in his view, both on the balance of power and agreed-on rules or norms.

Order in world politics may one day take the form of the maintenance of elementary goals of social life in a single world society or great society of all mankind. . . . It cannot be seriously argued, however, that the society of all mankind is already a going concern. In the present phase we

From Hedley Bull, *The Anarchical Society,* © 1977, Columbia University Press. By permission of Columbia University Press and Macmillan Ltd.

are still accustomed to thinking of order in world politics as consisting of domestic order, or order within states, and international order, or order among them.

No one would deny that there exists within some states a high degree of domestic or municipal order. It is, however, often argued that international order does not exist, except as an aspiration, and that the history of international relations consists simply of disorder or strife. To many people the idea of international order suggests not anything that has occurred in the past, but simply a possible or desirable future state of international relations, about which we might speculate or which we might work to bring about. To those who take this view a study of international order suggests simply a design for a future world, in the tradition of Sully, Cruce, St. Pierre and other irenists or peace theorists.

This present study takes as its starting-point the proposition that, on the contrary, order is part of the historical record of international relations; and in particular, that modern states have formed, and continue to form, not only a system of states but also an international society. To establish this proposition I shall begin by showing first that there has always been present, throughout the history of the modern states system, an idea of international society, proclaimed by philosophers and publicists, and present in the rhetoric of the leaders of states. . . .

THE IDEA OF INTERNATIONAL SOCIETY

Throughout the history of the modern states system there have been three competing traditions of thought: the Hobbesian or realist tradition, which views international politics as a state of war; the Kantian or universalist tradition, which sees at work in international politics a potential community of mankind; and the Grotian or internationalist tradition, which views international politics as taking place within an international society.[1] Here I shall state what is essential to the Grotian or internationalist idea of international society, and what divides it from the Hobbesian or realist tradition on the one hand, and from the Kantian or universalist tradition on the other. Each of these traditional patterns of thought embodies a description of the nature of international politics and a set of prescriptions about international conduct.

The Hobbesian tradition describes international relations as a state of war of all against all, an arena of struggle in which each state is pitted against every other. International relations, on the Hobbesian view, represent pure conflict between states and resemble a game that is wholly distributive or zero-sum: the interests of each state exclude the interests of any other. The particular international activity that, on the Hobbesian view, is most typical of international activity as a whole, or best provides the clue to it, is war itself. Thus peace, on the Hobbesian view, is a period of recuperation from the last war and preparation for the next.

The Hobbesian prescription for international conduct is that the state is free to pursue its goals in relation to other states without moral or legal restrictions of any kind. Ideas of morality and law, on this view, are valid only in the context of a society, but international life is beyond the bounds of any society. If any moral or legal goals are to be pursued in international politics, these can only be the moral or legal goals of the state itself. Either it is held (as by Machiavelli) that the state conducts foreign policy in a kind of moral and legal vacuum, or it is held (as by Hegel and his successors) that moral behaviour for the state in foreign policy lies in its own self-assertion. The only rules or principles which, for those in the Hobbesian tradition, may be said to limit or circumscribe the behaviour of states in their relations with one another are rules of prudence or expediency. Thus agreements may be kept if it is expedient to keep them, but may be broken if it is not.

The Kantian or universalist tradition, at the other extreme, takes the essential nature of international politics to lie not in conflict among states, as on the Hobbesian view, but in the transnational social bonds that link the individual human beings who are the subjects or citizens of states. The dominant theme of international relations, on the Kantian view, is only apparently the relationship among states, and is really the relationship among all men in the community of mankind—which exists potentially, even if it does not exist actually, and which when it comes into being will sweep the system of states into limbo.[2]

Within the community of all mankind, on the universalist view, the interests of all men are one and the same; international politics, considered from this perspective, is not a purely distributive or zero-sum game, as the Hobbesians maintain, but a purely cooperative or non-zero-sum game. Conflicts of interest exist among the ruling cliques of states, but this is only at the superficial or transient level of the existing system of states; properly understood, the interests of all peoples are the same. The particular international activity which, on the Kantian view, most typifies international activity as a whole is the horizontal conflict of ideology that cuts across the boundaries of states and divides human society into two camps—the trustees of the immanent community of mankind and those who stand in its way, those who are of the true faith and the heretics, the liberators and the oppressed.

The Kantian or universalist view of international morality is that, in contrast to the Hobbesian conception,there are moral imperatives in the field of international relations limiting the action of states, but that these imperatives enjoin not coexistence and cooperation among states but rather the overthrow of the system of states and its replacement by a cosmopolitan society. The community of mankind, on the Kantian view, is not only the central reality in international politics, in the sense that the forces able to bring it into being are present; it is also the end or object of the highest moral endeavour. The rules that sustain coexistence and social intercourse among states should be ignored if the imperatives of this higher morality require it. Good faith with heretics has no meaning, except in terms of tactical convenience; between the elect and the damned, the liberators and the oppressed, the question of mutual acceptance of rights to sovereignty or independence does not arise.

What has been called the Grotian or internationalist tradition stands between the realist tradition and the universalist tradition. The Grotian tradition describes international politics in terms of a society of states or international society.[3] As against the Hobbesian tradition, the Grotians contend that states are not engaged in simple struggle, like gladiators in an arena, but are limited in their conflicts with one another by common rules and institutions. But as against the Kantian or universalist perspective the Grotians accept the Hobbesian premise that sovereigns or states are the principal reality in international politics; the immediate members of international society are states rather than individual human beings. International politics, in the Grotian understanding, expresses neither complete conflict of interest between states nor complete identity of interest; it resembles a game that is partly distributive but also partly productive. The particular international activity which, on the Grotian view, best typifies international activity as a whole is neither war between states, nor horizontal conflict cutting across the boundaries of states, but trade—or, more generally, economic and social intercourse between one country and another.

The Grotian prescription for international conduct is that all states, in their dealings with one another, are bound by the rules and institutions of the society they form. As against the view of the Hobbesians, states in the Grotian view are bound not only by rules of prudence or expediency but also by imperatives of morality and law. But, as against the view of the universalists, what these imperatives enjoin is not the overthrow of the system of states and its replacement by a universal community of mankind, but rather acceptance of the requirements of coexistence and cooperation in a society of states.

Each of these traditions embodies a great variety of doctrines about international politics, among which there exists only a loose connection. In different periods each pattern of thought appears in a different idiom and in relation to different issues and preoccupations. This is not the place to explore further the connections and distinctions within each tradition. Here we have only to take account of the fact that the Grotian idea of international society has always been present in thought about the states system. . . .

My contention is that the element of a society has always been present, and remains present, in the modern international system, although only as one of the elements in it, whose survival is sometimes precarious. The modern international system in fact reflects all three of the elements singled out, respectively, by the Hobbesian, the Kantian and the Grotian traditions: the element of war and struggle for power among states, the element of transnational solidarity and conflict, cutting across the divisions among states, and the element of cooperation and regulated inter-course among states. In different historical phases of the states system, in different geographical theatres of its operation, and in the policies of different states and statesmen, one of these three elements may predominate over the others. . . .

NOTES

1. This threefold division derives from Martin Wight. The best published account of it is his "Western Values in International Relations," in *Diplomatic Investigations,* ed. Herbert Butterfield and Martin Wight (London: Allen and Unwin, 1967). The division is further discussed in my "Martin Wight and the Theory of International Relations. The Second Martin Wight Memorial Lecture," *British Journal of International Studies,* 2, no. 2 (1976).
2. In Kant's own doctrine there is of course ambivalence as between the universalism of *The Idea of Universal History from a Cosmopolitan Point of View* (1784) and the position taken up in *Perpetual Peace* (1795), in which Kant accepts the substitute goal of a league of 'republican' states.
3. I have myself used the term 'Grotian' in two senses: (i) as here, to describe the broad doctrine that there is a society of states; (ii) to describe the solidarist form of this doctrine, which united Grotius himself and the twentieth–century neo–Grotians, in opposition to the pluralist conception of international society entertained by Vattel and later positivist writers. See "The Grotian Conception of International Society," in *Diplomatic Investigations.*

The Balance of Power in International Politics

Kenneth N. Waltz

The author discusses balance of power, attempting to clarify the concept.

The whole notion of balance of power, said John Bright one hundred years ago, is "a mischievous delusion which has come down to us from past times." The balance of power is an impossible thing like perpetual motion, a will-o'-the-wisp in pursuit of which Britain has expended thou-

From *Man, the State and War,* pages 198–210. © 1959 Columbia University Press. By permission.

sands of millions of pounds.[1] Not a will-o'-the-wisp, not a delusion, but a fact of political life, a descriptive, scientific law said Hume nearly one hundred years earlier and Morgenthau nearly one hundred years later.[2]

If the balance of power is a delusion, it is, as Bright says, one of long standing. In the fifth century B.C., Thucydides explained the policy of Tissaphernes, King of the Persians, as one of holding "the balance evenly between the two contending powers," Athens and Lacedaemon.[3] In the second century B.C., Polybius, in his explanation of the policies of Hiero,[4] makes brilliantly clear the effect of balance-of-power worries on the thinking of a statesman. When the Roman legions first arrived in Sicily to aid the Mamertines, Hiero, perceiving the relative strength of the Romans and concluding that their prospects were better than those of the Carthaginians, made proposals of peace and alliance to the Romans, which they accepted. Some years later, though still an ally of Rome, Hiero became alarmed at the extent of the Romans' success and sent assistance to Carthage. He was convinced, as Polybius explains it, that

> it was in his own interest for securing both his Sicilian dominions and his friendship with the Romans, that Carthage should be preserved, and that the stronger power should not be able to attain its ultimate object entirely without effort. In this he reasoned very wisely and sensibly, for such matters should never be neglected, and we should never contribute to the attainment by one state of a power so preponderant, that none dare dispute with it even for their acknowledged rights.[5]

Yet "balance of power" is sometimes a frightening, sometimes a bewildering, phrase. People differ on whether it is good or bad, on who has approved it and who has not, and even on whether or not it exists. William Graham Sumner, for example, lines himself up with the Founding Fathers—he is against the balance of power.[6] But Hamilton, who has always been considered one of the Founding Fathers, perceived and stated, in his usual clear style, that United States security if not dependent upon was certainly enhanced by the involvement of the European powers with each other.[7] Somewhat like Sumner, Frank Tannenbaum emphatically rejects balance-of-power doctrine and attributes the past successes of American foreign policy to the fact that we have, in our acts, renounced the balance of power in favor of the policies of the coordinate state. Balance-of-power policy is, in his opinion, so against all the traditions and institutions of the United States that our adopting it is inconceivable.[8] Alfred Vagts has concluded, however, after careful study of European and American diplomatic and military history, that the survival and well-being of the United States have always been closely tied to the functioning of a system of balance in Europe.[9]

Is the balance of power illusion or reality? Is it something pursued by the vicious and stupid, rejected by the pure and wise? Did the United States throughout its history extricate itself from dependence on the external politics of balance, or in saying now that it did are we behaving like the rich man who proclaims that money means nothing to him? These questions can be answered only by looking more closely at the logic of the balance of power, a logic that is intimately connected with the third image [or international level of analysis. Ed.].

A man attacked by would-be thieves on Main Street may fairly hope that the police will either thwart the attackers or recover the loot. The chances of getting away with the crime are sufficiently small to reduce such incidents well below the point at which the ordinary citizen begins to carry arms. States, however, do not enjoy even an imperfect guarantee of their security unless they set out to provide it for themselves. If security is something the state wants, then this desire, together with the conditions in which all states exist, imposes certain requirements on a foreign policy that pretends to be rational. The requirements are *imposed* by an automatic sanction: Departure from the rational model imperils the survival of the state.[10] The clue to the limitations of policy imposed by the condition of anarchy among states is contained in the maxim: "Everybody's strategy depends on everybody else's," a statement that appears in John McDonald's popularization of the game theory of John von Neumann and Oskar Morgenstern.[11] One who wants to win a simple card game, in fact any game with two or more players, must follow a strategy that takes into consideration the strategies of the other player(s). And if there are three or more players, he will, on occasion, have to form a coalition even though this may mean cooperating with his recent "enemy," one who still remains a potential enemy. Such a necessity arises most obviously where one man will win shortly unless his opponents help each other. There is, of course nothing automatic about the forming of the coalition. It may not be formed at all: because the two men we would expect to help each other are inveterate noncooperators, because they dislike each other too much to cooperate even for mutual advantage, because they are not intelligent enough to do so, or because the game is one in which it is difficult to perceive the proper moment for cooperation. But what would we say of one who under these conditions denounced the mere thought of coalition? Simply that he has either missed the point of the game or has decided that other things, contrary feelings or moral principles, are worth more than winning it.

Can the actions of states in international politics be considered in terms of this roughly sketched model? A considerable elaboration, requiring us to go beyond John McDonald's popularization to the original theory of von Neumann and Morgenstern, is necessary. A card game, such as poker, is a zero-sum game: my winnings plus your winnings are exactly equal to the losses of our opponent or opponents. In a zero-sum game, the problem is entirely one of distribution, not at all one of production. But the activities in which men and states are engaged seldom correspond to the zero-sum model. The problem may be one of production as well as distribution. The game, in the terminology of von Neumann and Morgenstern, becomes a general game. In a general game, "the advantage of one group of players need not be synonymous with the disadvantage of the others. In such a game moves—or rather changes in strategy—may exist which are advantageous to both groups. In other words, there may exist an opportunity for genuine increases of productivity, simultaneously in all sectors of society."[12] This is a situation in which we have not just a pie to divide but the problem of how much pie to make as well. Under these conditions the game can tend toward either of two extremes. (1) It may become a simple problem in maximization: all the players may cooperate to make the largest possible pie.[13] In international politics this corresponds to the hypothetical case in which all states band together with nature as their adversary. (2) All the players may be so intent on the question of how the pie already in existence should be divided that they forget about the possibility of increasing the amount each will have by working together to make more of it. Instead of a simple maximum problem, the game then reverts to a zero-sum or constant-sum game.[14] In international politics this corresponds roughly to the situation now prevailing, in which two sides have formed and the gain of one side is often considered to be the loss of the other. There is another possibility. It may be that nobody likes pie, or that everybody likes something else better. In this case the game is not played at all.

To what extent do states have a choice among these three alternatives? A game must have an object. In poker the object of each player is to win the largest possible amount of money. States have many objects. Some states may aim at the conquest of the world, other states may aim at a local hegemony, other states may aim at no hegemony at all but desire simply to be left alone. Common to the desires of all states is the wish for survival. Even the state that wants to conquer the world wants also, as a minimum, to continue its present existence. If all states wanted simply to survive, then none would need to maintain military forces for use in either defensive or offensive action. But whenever some states give the impression that survival does not exhaust their political ambitions, others are forced, logically, to look to their defenses. Many states may prefer to play a game in which all states cooperate in the attempt to solve problems of maximization. Others may prefer to play no game at all. The implication of game theory, which is also the implication of the third image, is, however, that the freedom of choice of any one state is limited by the actions of all others. And this limitation applies as much to the process of deciding which game to play as it does to the actual playing of the game!

Given a sufficient number of players engaged in a competitive game, von Neumann and Morgenstern demonstrate with convincing mathematical rigor the possible advantages of combinations among them.[15] The clever player will be on the watch for a chance to increase his gains or cut his losses by cooperating with another. Similarly in international politics, so long as the participants do not consider themselves players of a game in which all concentrate on production and none worries about distribution, states will ever be tempted to form coalitions for the simple reason that those who combine acquire an advantage over those who do not. If some states seek an advantage over others, they combine; if other states want to counteract this advantage, they in turn combine. If the advantage sought is measured in terms of power to destroy or damage another state, then the threatened state refrains from the effort to increase its strength only at the risk of its survival. Pursuing a balance-of-power policy is still a matter of choice, but the alternatives are those of probable suicide on the one hand and the active playing of the power-politics game on the other. The factors that distinguish international politics from other games are: (1) that the stakes of the game are considered to be of unusual importance and (2) that in international politics the use of force is not excluded as a means of influencing the outcome. The cardinal rule of the game is often taken to be: Do whatever you must in order to win it. If some states act on this rule, or are expected to act on it, other states must adjust their strategies accordingly. The opportunity and at times the necessity of using force distinguishes the balance of power in international politics from the balances of power that form inside the state. In both cases we can define power, following Hobbes, as the capacity to produce an intended effect. In domestic politics one of the possible capacities—the use of physical force—is ordinarily monopolized by the state. In international politics there is no authority effectively able to prohibit the use of force. The balance of power among states becomes a balance of all the capacities, including physical force, that states choose to use in pursuing their goals.

If there is an advantage in forming coalitions, then logically the players will pursue the advantage until all of them are divided into two blocs. Yet the game of power politics does not often eventuate in two blocs unalterably opposed and using whatever means come to hand in order to weaken each other. This is explained, still in terms of game theory, by the fact that all states are playing more than one game. The aim of game theory is "a set of rules for each participant which tell him how to behave in every situation which may conceivably arise."[16] But no set of rules can specify how important the game should be considered! If, for example, survival were the only goal of the United States it would be irrational for us to neglect any means of strengthening ourselves vis-à-vis possible attackers. If adopting a Spartan regimen would make us stronger, then clearly we should adopt it. However, at the same time that we play the game of power politics, a game that we are forced to play so long as survival remains a goal, we pursue a number of other goals—in a sense we play other games—such as the maximization of economic welfare or, in the most general terms, the maintenance of a way of life. The ideal strategy in international politics may, in terms of the other games the state is playing, cost too much. To say, then, that international politics is a game the general rules of which are disregarded at the peril of the player's very existence does not necessarily mean that every state must bend all its efforts toward securing its own survival. Clausewitz, for example, pointed out that he who uses force ruthlessly will gain an advantage if his opponent does not do likewise, but he noted as well that social institutions may moderate the extent and the savagery of the competition for power.[17] States may cooperate as well as compete, and even when competition becomes more important than cooperation their domestic aims may mitigate the external competition among them. Nevertheless, if survival is one of the ends of the state, the state that would ignore balance-of-power considerations while others do not is analogous to the player of games who refrains from joining a coalition—for what is a balance of power but a series of coalitions in which the momentarily disadvantaged combine and recombine to prevent the ascendancy (the winning of the game) of the opposing country or coalition?

The preceding analysis indicates that the balance of power among states has a firm basis in reality, that it is much more than a "delusion." The analysis also puts into perspective the frequent allegations that statesmen in pursuing balance-of-power policies often behave immorally. To most people there is nothing immoral about a game of cards, but there is definitely something immoral about cheating at cards. In cards, the code of morals is established by custom and enforced by the fact that anyone who cares to stop playing may do so. In international politics there are some rules of law to guide states both in peace and in war, but if it is found that some states break them, the others cannot simply quit playing the game. A state may then have to consider whether it would prefer to violate its code of behavior or abide by the code and risk its survival. Or, more accurately, the leaders of the state may have to choose between behaving *immorally* in international politics in order to preserve the state, on the one hand, and, on the other, abandoning their *moral* obligation to ensure their state's survival in order to follow preferred ways of acting in international politics. The conclusion? Moral behavior is one thing in a system that provides predictable amounts and types of security; another thing where such security is lacking. Kant, a philosopher never called immoral, recognized this as well as did Machiavelli, a philosopher often so described.[18] Those who call "power politicians" immoral simply because they play the game of power politics have transferred a definition of immorality from one social setting to another, and in the other it is not applicable without serious qualification.

Is the balance of power inevitable? Obviously not. But if it depends on a wish for state survival in a condition of anarchy among states, then it will disappear in its present form only when the wish or the condition disappears. The most ardent desire cannot bring about its abolition unless one or both of these factors are first modified.

A balance of power may exist because some countries consciously make it the end of their policies, or it may exist because of the quasi-automatic reactions of some states to the drive for ascendancy of other states. Even if the anti-balance-of-power people are in control of a state's policy, they will tend to act in ways that perpetuate or establish a balance. This need affect neither their verbal disavowal of balance-of-power politics nor the honesty of those disavowals. The last statement is well illustrated by the conclusion of one of the Tannenbaum articles previously cited.[19] Is the Atlantic Security Pact a power-substitute for a United Nations that has failed, he asks? No, he replies, for it is temporary, defensive, and "has nothing to do with the balance of power idea and less to do with dividing the world into spheres of interest between Russia and ourselves." In accordance with our traditions, the United States will organize as much of the world as possible on the basis of the coordinate state. We will not do this for the sake of the balance of power but in order to build a system of collective security for all who wish to join without having to sacrifice their independence or dignity. Then, if we have to fight, at least we will be fighting for what we believe worth defending. To pursue a balance-of-power settlement would, on the other hand, alienate others and destroy the only hope for an association of coordinate states organized to resist Russian efforts to dominate the world.

The lofty tone of Tannenbaum's description of our policy does not obscure the fact that the Western Defense Community was, in large part at least, motivated by fear of Soviet power and intentions and is intended to deter the Soviet Union from using that power in wars of aggression. For possible opponents to act with the possibility of a future war in mind is, in the light of history, no more difficult to understand than is baseball's yearly spring training. If Tannenbaum chooses to call this something other than balance-of-power politics, that is, of course, his privilege. It becomes apparent, however, that he objects more to the "realists" terminology than to the foreign policies they recommend. If Tannenbaum were Secretary of State his foreign policy would apparently differ little from Morgenthau's or Kennan's, the two men he considers his principal intellectual opponents.

In summary, then, it can be said that the balance of power is not so much imposed by statesmen on events as it is imposed by events on statesmen. It is not to be eliminated by declamation but, if it is to be eliminated at all, by altering the circumstances that produce it. The circumstances are simply the existence of a number of independent states that wish to remain independent. Freedom is implied in the word "independence" but so is the necessity of self-reliance. Competition takes a number of forms, but the units in all systems of competition tend to drive for favored positions. If the drive of some units appears to promise success, it is blocked by other units whose similar motives cause them in turn to counter and thrust. Where an effective law-enforcing authority exists, balance is measured in terms other than force.[20] Where there is nothing to prevent the use of force as a means of altering the forms and the results of competition, the capacity to use force tends to become the index by which the balance of power is measured. No system of balance functions automatically. A drive for hegemony by any one state may be successful despite the resistance of other states, or for some reason the other states may not resist; but under certain conditions, conditions that have often existed in international politics, systems of balance do develop. If a condition of balance becomes the conscious goal of states, then one would expect the balancing process to be one of greater precision and subtlety. In the midst of a large number of roughly equal states, competition is intense and the balancing process intricate. Thus among the Greek and Italian city-states and among the European nation-states, any state threatening to outstrip the others in power could expect that an attempt would be made to check it. And this was the case not because they enjoyed the process of checking each other, but because for each state its power in relation to other states is ultimately the key to its survival.

NOTES

1. John Bright, *Speeches,* edited by James E. Thorold Rogers (London: Macmillan and Co., 1869), pp. 233, 460–61, 468–69.
2. David Hume, "Of the Balance of Power," in *Essays Moral, Political, and Literary,* V. I, edited by T. H. Green and T. H. Grose (London: Longmans, Green and Co., 1875), pp. 348–56; and Hans J. Morgenthau, *In Defense of the National Interest* (New York: Alfred A. Knopf, 1951), pp. 32–33.
3. Thucydides, *History of the Peloponnesian War,* translated by B. Jowett, second edition (London: Oxford University Press, 1900), Book VIII, par. 57; cf. par. 87.
4. King of Syracuse, 270–216 B.C.
5. Polybius, *The Histories,* trans. by W. R. Paton (London: William Heinemann), V. I, 41, 225 (Book I, secs. 16, 83). The Hiero example is one used by Hume.
6. According to the Founding Fathers, he says, "There was to be no balance of power and 'reason of state' to cost the life and happiness of citizens." William Graham Sumner, "The Conquest of the United States by Spain," in *War and Other Essays,* edited by Albert G. Keller (New Haven: Yale University Press, 1911), p. 333.
7. Alexander Hamilton, "Americanus II," in *The Works of Alexander Hamilton,* edited by Henry Cabot Lodge (New York: G.P. Putnam's Sons, 1904), V, 88–94. Cf. *The Federalist* (New York: The Modern Library, 1941), Nos. 4–5 (Jay), 6–8 (Hamilton).
8. Frank Tannenbaum, "The American Tradition in Foreign Relations," *Foreign Affairs,* XXX (1951): 31–50; and "The Balance of Power versus the Co-ordinate State," *Political Science Quarterly,* LXVII (1952): 173–97.
9. Alfred Vaghts, "The United States and the Balance of Power," *Journal of Politics,* III (1941): 401–49.

10. For a variety of reasons the pressure to adopt the "correct" strategy may be resisted. Tacitus, speaking of the wars among the Germans, said: "May the nations retain and perpetuate, if not an affection for us, at least an animosity against each other! since, while the fate of the empire is thus urgent, fortune can bestow no higher benefit upon us, than the discord of our enemies." "A Treatise on the Situation, Manners, and Inhabitants of Germany," par. 33, in *The Works of Tacitus,* Oxford translation, revised, Vol. II (New York: Harper and Brothers, 1858). In the terms used here, the German tribes were not sufficiently interested in winning the game of power competition with Rome to give up the games they were playing with each other.

11. John McDonald, *Strategy in Poker, Business and War* (New York: W. W. Norton and Co., 1950), p. 52. The reference to game theory does not imply that there is available a technique by which international politics can be approached mathematically. Balance-of-power politics, however, can profitably be described using the concepts of von Neumann and Morgenstern—what can be explained without reference to their speculations can perhaps be made clearer by qualified comparisons between the behavior of players of games and participants in international politics. For references to some of the unsolved difficulties in game theory, see below, note 15. For an impressive attempt to apply game theory to strategy in international politics, see Morton A. Kaplan, *System and Process in International Politics* (New York: John Wiley and Sons, 1957), Part IV.

12. John von Neumann and Oskar Morgenstern, *Theory of Games and Economic Behavior* (Princeton, NJ: Princeton University Press, 1944), p. 540.

13. *Ibid.,* p. 517.

14. Strategically these are equivalents, *Ibid.,* p. 348.

15. The minimum numbers required are two or more for a general game, three or more for a zero-sum game. Game theory, however, cannot specify the distributions of gains or losses among the coalition partners. For comments on this and other limitations of game theory, see J. C. C. McKinsey, *Introduction to the Theory of Games* (New York: McGraw-Hill Book Co., 1952), especially Chapters 15–18; J. D. Williams, *The Compleat Strategyst* (New York: McGraw-Hill Book Co., 1954), pp. 20–24, 30–34, 213–14.

16. Von Neumann and Morgenstern, *Theory of Games and Economic Behavior,* p. 31.

17. Karl von Clausewitz, *On War,* translated by O. J. Matthijs Jolles (Washington, DC: Infantry Journal Press, 1950), p. 4.

18. Notice Kant's justification of preventive war: "Lesion of a less powerful country may be involved merely in the condition of a more powerful neighbor *prior* to any action at all; and in the State of Nature an attack under such circumstances would be warrantable." Immanuel Kant, *The Philosophy of Law,* translated by W. Hastie (Edinburgh: T. and T. Clark, 1887), sec. 56; cf. sec. 60.

19. Tannenbaum, "The Balance of Power versus the Co-ordinate State," pp. 195–97.

20. But a balancing process there will be nevertheless. That Tannenbaum realizes this makes his more recent articles on the balance of power all the more surprising. See his "The Balance of Power in Society," *Political Science Quarterly,* 61 (1946): 481–504.

Obscurities Enshrined: The Balance of Power As an Analytical Concept

Ernst B. Haas

Professor Haas severely criticizes balance-of-power thinking on a number of grounds, questioning its utility as an analytic concept, theory, or guide to statesmen. He concludes: "As for the balance of power in our age, let it rest in peace."

In examining the relevance of balance-of-power theorizing to Functionalism and integration, we must be very clear what form of balance-of-power theory is being scrutinized. In an earlier study, I culled from the historical literature on the balance of power no fewer than eight distinct verbal meanings of the expression, ranging from "distribution" of power to a complex notion that holds the balance to be a "guide" to policymakers, developing into a "system" of international relations when simultaneously used as a guide by all statesmen. However, in the huge majority of cases, those who used the term "balance of power" apparently sought to convey no more than the actions, conditions, and events that can be described by the terms "power politics" or "distribution of power."

Further, in probing the intentions of the writers, I identified four distinct aims. (1) *There is a descriptive intent,* in which the term could be used with any of eight verbal meanings isolated, merely in order to circumscribe factually a given international situation. Although, of course, theoretical assumptions enter the descriptive effort here, the overall purpose of the user remains the delineation of a state of affairs. (2) *Prescriptive intent* emerges when the "guide-and-system" or "universal law of history" meanings of the term are so used as to prescribe for governments the kind of action they ought to take. Here theoretical misconceptions can have more serious consequences. (3) *Propagandistic intent* is dominant when the various meanings associated with the balance of power are used loosely to justify publicly a given course of action involving the application of power. The term serves here as "ideology," as a legitimating device to cloak state action that may have been decided on for a variety of reasons having nothing to do with balancing. (4) Finally, *the intent may be conceptual or analytical:* the user applies the "guide-

and-system" meaning in order to gain clarity and accuracy in predicting the future course of events. This may or may not lead to prescription; it certainly includes description, but avoids propaganda rigorously.[1] It is this fourth usage that will concern us here.

We shall examine several contemporary versions of balance-of-power theorizing. We shall ask ourselves in each case whether the effort is free from the shortcomings of functional systems theory [discussed in Chapter Three of this book.-Ed.], whether it comprehends a sufficient range of environmental conditions for accuracy, whether it can help in explaining transitions to new dominating relationships, and whether it is free from the dangers of self-maintenance assumptions.

BALANCE OF POWER AS ETERNAL LAW

In a very sensitive demonstration that draws on the theory of the social contract, Kenneth Waltz argues that a systemic version of the balance of power today retains its explanatory superiority as compared with theories stressing the psychological nature of man or the internal political order of the states that make up international society.[2] Psychological and internal political considerations are not irrelevant; but, argues Waltz, they can be properly understood only if they are placed into the *system* in which they unroll, and that system is the international balance of power, as valid today as it always was—in the absence of a world state with universal law.

The informing image is Rousseau's fable of the stag hunt. A number of hungry hunters agree to stick together until they have shot a stag, a quarry large enough to sustain them all. They have difficulty in finding one. One hunter loses patience and, breaking his agreement with the others, leaves the group to shoot a hare he has seen. As a result the remaining members of the group are not strong enough to attain their original objectives. Is the deserter to be blamed for betraying the general good in favor of his particular short-run advantage? Rousseau answers that, in the state of nature, the short-run decision of the deserter to maximize his individual immediate advantage is rational and to be expected. Since nations live in the state of nature, war is rational and to be expected as long as it is to a nation's immediate advantage. According to Waltz, the system of international relations, which does not provide the security of community and law, imposes the superiority of the short-range rationality of the hare-hunter.

> But to emphasize the importance of political structure is not to say that the acts that bring about conflict and lead to the use of force are of no importance. It is the specific acts that are the immediate causes of war, the general structure that permits them to exist and wreak their disasters. To eliminate every vestige of selfishness, perversity, and stupidity in nations would serve

to establish perpetual peace, but to try directly to eliminate all the immediate causes of war without altering the structure of the "union of Europe" is utopian.[3]

Waltz then concludes that in international relations of the competitive type "the implication of game theory, which is also the implication of [Rousseau's] image, is . . . that the freedom of choice of any one state is limited by the actions of all the others."[4] Hence, irrespective of morality or governmental intent, as long as survival remains the basic state objective, the system as a whole will determine relationships—and the relationships will be those of power politics. More, power politics will take the form of countervailing coalitions and alliances; hence a "balance" of power describes the system, whether consciously willed by statesmen or automatically introduced by their instinctive reaction to challenges. And this would be equally true even if the leading statesmen, like Cobden, publicly adjured the balance of power and claimed to be acting on different grounds. "In summary, then, it can be said that the balance of power is not so much imposed by statesmen on events as it is imposed by events on statesmen."[5]

In the state of nature, irrespective of technology, communism, liberalism, space exploration, urbanization, economic development, alienation, or whatever other modern phenomena one may wish to add, the balance of power remains an eternal law permitting institutionally unregulated state behavior. We reject this formulation for the same reason that we reject all system-dominant automaticity. Obviously, any sound analysis has the right to insist that the categories found important in characterizing the conduct of a system need not be overtly recognized by the actors; the very purpose of analysis is to rise above these data and events, and induce conclusions from them at a higher level of abstraction. But this is very different from what we do have the right to demand: that the analytic categories must at all times *be consistent with* the perceptions and motives of the actors. We can assume nothing else if we argue that systems are made up of people, groups, and actions instead of pretending that the reverse is the case. Waltz's treatment of the balance of power as an analytic system, however, is not consistent with the perceptions and motives attributed to actors in an earlier portion of his argument. The balance is merely superimposed on the remainder.

The very image of the stag hunt can yield short-run and practical individual motives—understood and reciprocated, if not shared in identical terms, by others—which will erode the simple picture of power balanced against power. The Functional logic is wholly compatible with the stag-hunt image; in fact, in its reformulated version, it depends upon it.[6] If the cooperative hunting of the stag is demonstrated to be impossible, the hunters will make informal rules regulating the separate or cooperative hunting of hares. Obviously, as our reformulated separability doctrines argue, this is not inevitable. But neither is the unflinching balancing of power inevitable in the international state of nature—because, in Functional terms, there really is no state of nature at all. Functionalism calls attention to the variety of motives and relationships that flow from a technologically, economically, and socially diverse environment. The eternal law of the balance of power, as an analytic system, sees only physical survival. But a theory of integration sees much more than that.

BALANCE OF POWER AS A TEMPORAL, UNDIMENSIONAL SYSTEM

Taking as his point of departure Waltz's vision of an analytical system of the balance of power, Arthur Lee Burns set himself the task of stating the limits of the system and sketching the conditions of its transition into something quite new.[7] International relations, prior to the advent of nuclear weapons, was a "balance-of-power" system, in which the dominant relationships between the member states were those of an n-person non-zero-sum game, with the payoff consisting in the ability to remain in the game, i.e. to survive. Therefore, military potential, and especially military technology, is held to be the factor that determines the conduct of the actors, and thus shapes the system. "Relationships of alliance, of pressure or opposition . . . are the relations which constitute the international system."[8] The balance-of-power system will then follow the rules normally stated by those who use this image as a supreme analytical device: the maximization of security, switching of alliances, minimizing of uncertainty, etc. The system is unidimensional because it abstracts only military relationships; it is temporal because it is inherently unstable and cannot last. Unlike Waltz, therefore, Burns concluded that the balance of power as an analytical device is temporally limited in its usefulness. Why is this true?

A balance-of-power system is held to lead to the diminution of the number of its members because the contending blocs or states are perpetually in rivalry; they are therefore unwilling deliberately to build up the additional blocs mathematically necessary to maximize system stability. This, in turn, is held to be true because states and blocs are constantly undergoing changes that are assumed to heighten their sense of rivalry. One set of changes refers to the system itself, because wars reduce the number of participants. But, in addition, changes come about as a result of unsystemic developments of a demographic, industrial, and technological nature in certain member states. When these changes have created a situation in which warfare is certain to destroy completely the enemy's economy but is incapable of destroying his military apparatus, we have attained a "deterrent system," an entirely new species. The advent of nuclear weapons and missiles, therefore, has made the balance of power obsolete. We then have the system made familiar by those who associate global stability with the balance of terror, in which no bloc can move meaningfully.

Two things can be said about this formulation. Contrary to Burn's argument, the deterrent system is still, in analytical terms, a variant of the balance-of-power-system. It remains unidimensional and takes no account of environmental factors ("alternatives open to governments," in Burns's afterthoughts) other than the military. It therefore fails to satisfy one of the major needs a system must satisfy for our purposes. Furthermore, as Burns himself argues, the new system is also unstable because it can be upset by military innovations that reintroduce possibilities of local maneuver and limited war, thus giving small and unaligned states a new lease on life. Yet the deterrent system is also expected by Burns to increase the size and reduce the number of blocs in juxtaposition. Paradoxically, Burns closes with a backhanded encouragement to the Functional argument in expressing the hope that "the international republic of science might develop institutions and like-minded relationships cutting across state sovereignties and alliances, and thus create the elements of a concrete world community."[9]

In a sense, these thoughts symbolize the unsatisfactory character of all analysis couched in terms of balance-of-power systems. Consequences and causes are interchangeable. When systemic factors do not seem to yield acceptable consequences, the authors feel free to bring in considerations that their own initial assumptions of military or power primacy should lead them to discount. When it suits the argument, system feedback on the actors is stressed; when that seems to work hardships on history, actor feedback on the system is singled out instead. The poor empiricist is left rather bewildered in his search for guiding precepts that would propel him beyond simple empiricism.

The undimensional and temporal character of balance-of-power thinking has prompted a good deal of soul-searching among scholars addicted to this mode of analysis. Has the soul-searching resulted in any significant reformulations germane to our examination? John Herz, in confronting this question directly, has concluded that the "new" balance of power introduced by nuclear relationships is a mere quantitative—and hence highly dangerous—change over the "classical" power balance. But he also believes that the new balance obeys essentially the same systemic rules as the old, which can be rendered less dangerous for survival by strengthening certain features—such as the reliability of signals exchanged by opponents, the neutralization of territory, limited and symmetrical arms control—which were also allegedly part of the classical game. We must conclude that the analysis and prescription, no matter how appealing on policy grounds, introduce no theoretical refinement.[10]

Unidimensionality, however, is the very factor that stimulates Glenn Snyder to "update" the balance of power as an analytical concept. Taking Burns's two balancing systems as his point of departure, Snyder transfers them from the plane of analysis to the level of immediate existence: they coexist now as living superimposed systems. The balance of power refers to the military relationships of the nations at the level of conventional and limited war forces, and to the strategies associated with them; the balance of deterrence, on the other hand, refers to the relationships created by total nuclear striking capacity, a capacity to deter and destroy, rather than to defend.[11] Various concrete "balances" are possible, depending on the nature of the capabilities and forces confronting one another, but none "mean *matching* the enemy in offensive striking forces or having a slight margin of superiority over the enemy in such forces, as in the traditional concept of balance of power. . . . 'Balancing' means introducing into the enemy's risk calculus a prospect of cost which will be sufficient to offset his prospect of gain, *after* discounting the costs by some factor representing the enemy's doubts about one's willingness to inflict them."[12] Yet these two superimposed systems are said to possess a degree of equilibrium to the extent that the forces are invulnerable.

Now Snyder feels that the simple systemic superimposition of the two balances is analytically unsatisfactory, even if descriptively accurate, because it obscures the dependence of one systemic balance upon the other; it also neglects the credibility factor; finally, it fails to specify and predict the degree to which unequal local conventional forces depend on the expected behavior of global deterrent forces, and vice versa. Therefore, for Snyder a truly useful analytical balance-of-power theory must specify not only the balance of military capabilities, but also the "balance of intentions" of the antagonists and the "balance of persuasion" that characterizes their non-military relations. The new balance of power, he demonstrates, does not function in disregard of the intentions of statesmen. Whereas under classical conditions intent and motive could be ignored for analytical purposes, the risks involved in nuclear warfare make the assessment of motivation a vital and autonomous component of the balance.

No doubt we must be grateful that balance-of-power devotees have rediscovered the role of motivation. But does this shift to the motives of actors really help us? In his very eagerness to overcome the unidimensionality of military analysis, Snyder has destroyed the analytical appeal that balance-of-power theorizing has—without justification—exerted. How can one meaningfully speak of a "balance" of intentions or a "balance" of persuasion, as if these relationships were in some state of equilibrium? Certainly, the effect of persuasion must be understood and the intentions of governments ascertained. But does descriptive zeal here have anything to do with a conceptual construct suggesting balanced relationships of a systemic character? The quantitative nature of military considerations contributes to the attraction the "balance" concept has exerted; but we can hardly rescue the theory by adding two wholly different ranges of transaction and perception that make a sum of apples and pears.

BALANCE OF POWER AS MULTIDIMENSIONAL ANALYSIS

There remains another analytical formulation of the balance of power as system, a formulation at once multidimensional and temporal in conception. Military relationships cease to be the dominating consideration, and the historical limits of a world that can be analyzed in balance-of-power terms are made explicit. One such formulation is Morton Kaplan's, which we had occasion to describe in a different context.[13] We may take it as an ideal type of what international actors *should* have done all the time, and—Kaplan feels—*did* do frequently enough to permit the drawing up of the model. Whether they actually did so is a matter of historical dispute and empirical disagreement. Ultimate motives are assumed as constant; actors are either smart or stupid in their practical efforts to realize them, able to internalize the rules or to ignore them at their peril. It is this assumption that renders even this formulation of an analytical balance of power of dubious value to us. If we grant that environments have something to do with the prevalence of certain kinds of motives, we simply cannot hold the intentions of actors constant. Or if we do so, we commit ourselves to a series of assumptions that reduce the analytical relevance of the system.

Hoffmann avoids this difficulty by making the environment the point of departure for his historical mode of reasoning, and thereby commits himself to the actor and his motives as the chief analytical referent. But he, too, sees the eighteenth and nineteenth centuries as a concrete balance-of-power system. Furthermore, it was a stable system because the prevalent intentions, local conditions, and common tasks imposed a moderate style. What were the environmental properties singled out by Hoffmann? The balance was centered in the European core area, with an "uncivilized" frontier under European dominance to serve as a theater for expansive tendencies. (Apparently, the *function* of the colonial world for the *system* was to preserve the European balance.) The major states in the core were roughly equal in power, and the process of industrialization did not give any one of them a striking advantage. Value ties among elite groups persisted across national boundaries despite the growth of nationalism. The limited state was ascendant everywhere, and commercial values enjoyed a high degree of legitimacy.[14] Consequently, state objectives were similar enough to avoid running into serious collision and to yield the "common law of Europe" represented by the Concert system; they were identical enough to permit the growth of a large body of reciprocal obligations permitting ease of commercial intercourse and limiting the incidence of violence; and there were sufficient common commitments to technical tasks that could be performed only by autonomous bodies to result in the creation of the first "Functional" international organizations with their own "Functional" community-type law.[15]

But, alas, the system was temporal, soon to be defeated by the revolutionary system in which we now live. What happened to it? The environment began to be transformed asymmetrically so as to destroy homogeneously changing relationships. As history, this is undoubtedly true, and as analysis, it carries us further than if we were merely to note that the boundaries of the system were breached. As an analysis of the nineteenth century it represents an intelligent and fruitful use of the balance-of-power construct. But it helps us only up to a point. It specifies conditions and relationships resulting in certain organizational tasks. It abstracts from national policies the features which, since they were repeated many times, did tend to create the cumulative kinds of interactions that can justifiably be identified as a "system." What it does not do is tell us which of these features survive to make their appearance in the next system. The tone of Hoffmann's argument would militate against any survival at all, even though history would hardly validate such a conclusion.[16]

Where does that leave us with respect to the analytical usefulness of balance-of-power theorizing? We have rejected the dominant formulations that the literature has to offer because they are either overly system-oriented, or unidimensional, or both. We have accepted the version that stresses multidimensional environmental elements and preserves the creative role of the actors: but we have concluded that it does not carry us far enough along the road of reconciling systems theory with Functionalism. The endless efforts to accommodate the interrelations created by various kinds of nuclear deterrents within a concept of bipolarity—the feature that in fact has given the balance-of-power approach its undeserved new lease on life—are little more than *descriptions* of the *distribution* of military power at any one time. At best they are metaphors, not analysis.[17] Whatever the merits of these efforts may be on military grounds, the notion of "balance" is a superfluous terminological complication that pretends to give theoretical sophistication to a wholly legitimate descriptive attempt that needs no such aid. Let the balance of power be confined to the setting in which Hoffmann placed it, and let the theorists of deterrence labor in the workshop of missile hardware. As for the balance of power in our age, let it rest in peace. . . .

NOTES

1. For a full exposition of these verbal and contextual meanings, see Ernst B. Haas, "The Balance of Power: Prescription, Concept or Propaganda?" *World Politics* 5, no. 2 (1953). Descriptive intent must be judged on its factual accuracy; prescriptive intent is dangerous for policy, impossible in action, and irrelevant to serious theory; propagandistic intent is simply irrelevant to theory.
2. The following treatment will rest heavily on Kenneth N. Waltz, *Man, the State and War* (New York: Columbia University Press, 1959), Chapters 6 and 7.

3. *Ibid.,* pp. 184–85.
4. *Ibid.,* p. 204.
5. *Man, the State, and War,* p. 209. Lest Waltz's intentions be distorted, let it be repeated that he considers the balance of power to explain the indirect, the permissive, causes of war. But he grants that immediate and specific causes of given wars must be sought in individual motivation and the internal order of the nations involved (*ibid.,* pp. 232ff).
6. As Hoffmann shows, this formulation is very different from Rousseau's own conclusions.When Rousseau's occasional excursions into international politics are read together with his focused work on the desirable national polity, it appears that there is an inevitable hiatus between a good national order peopled by good citizens and a corrupt international order. Only if all states lived up to the formula of the *Contrat social* could this hiatus be transcended, a condition Rousseau himself did not expect to materialize. Therefore, even good states are exposed to perpetual international competition; the corrupt properties of the system aggravate—and may even destroy—the life of the virtuous units.

   On the other hand, Rousseau had no faith in the possibility of reforming international relations by restructuring national and international institutions. A league of ideal societies would undermine the normal working of the general will because it would take the place of the small polity that was held requisite for its operation. In other words, Rousseau's image was of the "all or nothing" variety that is incompatible with Functionalism. It is possible, however, that my reformulation of the stag-hunt would fit Kant's adaptation of the Rousseauan approach. Hoffmann, "Rousseau on War and Peace," *American Political Science Review,* LVII (1963), esp. 329–33.
7. Arthur L. Burns, "From Balance to Deterrence: A Theoretical Analysis," *World Politics,* Vol. IX (1957). I am citing from the reprinted version in James N. Rosenau, ed., *International Politics and Foreign Policy* (Glencoe, Ill.: The Free Press, 1961). As is his commendable wont, Burns later published another essay in which he scrutinized his earlier argument and found it unsatisfactory. After examining the argument I am about to summarize, he found that "it now seems to me very difficult indeed to construct a useful model for the regular workings of a particular international system: each Power enjoys quite a variety of alternatives, and the sort of considerations which I had thought conclusive for one alternative look less so when one reminds oneself of some of the others. And, turning from theory to history, it would not be easy, working only from a description of the European system after the Peace of Westphalia (1648), to predict its subsequent history until the Peace of Utrecht (1713)." He adds that "a truly general and rigorous theory of power politics is unobtainable. But piecemeal theoretical insights are possible; and those that we have owe much to hints and suggestions derived from both the informal varieties of game theory and bargaining theory." "Prospects for a General Theory of International Relations," *World Politics,* XIV (1961), 36 and 45.

   Consequently, I shall confine myself to stating and evaluating only that portion of the argument which deals with the recurring influence of the balance of power on contemporary theorizing, and which seems to retain its relevance in the minds of many scholars despite Burns's disavowal of his own formulation.

8. Burns, "From Balance to Deterrence," in Rosenau, *International Politics and Foreign Policy,* p. 351.
9. *Ibid.,* p. 364.
10. John H. Herz, "Balance System and Balance Policies in a Nuclear and Bipolar Age," *Journal of International Affairs,* XIV (1960), 35–48. Significantly, this issue is entitled "A New Balance of Power." Arthur Burns contributed an article avoiding the theoretical issue posed by balance-of-power analysis, and limiting himself to a discussion of balancing in factual-descriptive terms. If the word "balance" had been omitted from the discussion, the meaning would have remained the same. *Ibid.,* pp. 61–69.
11. This discussion is based on Glenn H. Snyder, "Balance of Power in the Missile Age," *ibid.,* pp. 21–34. The distinction between deterrence and defense is crucial and perceptive, and is developed by Snyder in *Deterrence and Defense* (Princeton: Princeton University Press, 1961).
12. In *Journal of International Affairs,* XIV (1960), 25–26 (italics in original).
13. Another such formulation is found in the work of George Liska, whose fine sense of the temporal aspects of systems and of their dependence on a multidimensional environment does not prevent him from seeing systems-dominance. See his *International Equilibrium* (Cambridge: Harvard University Press, 1957), and his *Nations in Alliance* (Baltimore: Johns Hopkins Press, 1962).
14. Stanley Hoffmann, "International Systems and International Law," *World Politics,* 14 (1961): 218.
15. Compare this explanation of the growth of international law with that provided by Morton A. Kaplan and Nicholas deB. Katzenbach, *The Political Foundations of International Law* (New York: Wiley, 1961), in which the characteristics of the system rather than the nature of the actors emerge as the crucial explanatory variable.
16. Adda B. Bozeman, using many of the same social and economic considerations in her historical account of international relations adduced by Hoffmann, comes to the opposite conclusion. She claims that the contemporary system of international law and organizations, in effect, represents the universal sway of the European-western system. Although her argument mistakes the nature of the United Nations and overstates the case considerably, it nevertheless points up the possibility of using this kind of historical demonstration toward a radically different conclusion. *Politics and Culture in International History* (Princeton: Princeton University Press, 1960), pp. 513–22.
17. With respect to the use of metaphors as a substitute for theory, Anatol Rapoport said: "Interpreted in a physical context, the metaphor 'conflict of forces' calls for some sort of equilibrium theory. Such a theory can be and has been developed purely metaphorically. The concepts of 'force,' 'pressure,' 'balance of power,' 'leverage,' 'stability,' 'instability,' are mostly terms borrowed from physics. Descriptions of conflict situations in these terms sound like descriptions of physical systems. But of course the analogy is a metaphorical not a logical one, i.e., the similarity is felt intuitively, not derived as a consequence of an isomorphism between the two situations. Therefore metaphorical models of conflict, although they may be valuable for a variety of reasons, cannot be expected to yield logically compelling theorems, let alone theorems translatable into predictions." "Various Meanings of Theory," reprinted in Rosenau, p. 51.

War and Change in World Politics

Robert Gilpin

Professor Gilpin outlines key factors to explain the rise and decline of states.

During the 1970s and early 1980s a series of dramatic events signaled that international relations were undergoing a significant upheaval. Long-established and seemingly stable sets of relationships and understandings were summarily cast aside. Political leaders, academic observers, and the celebrated "man in the street" were suddenly conscious of the fact that the energy crisis, dramatic events in the Middle East, and tensions in the Communist world were novel developments of a qualitatively different order from those of the preceding decade. These developments and many others in the political, economic, and military realms signaled far-reaching shifts in the international distribution of power, an unleashing of new sociopolitical forces, and the global realignment of diplomatic relations. Above all, these events and developments revealed that the relatively stable international system that the world had known since the end of World War II was entering a period of uncertain political changes.

Ours is not the first age in which a sudden concatenation of dramatic events has revealed underlying shifts in military power, economic interest, and political alignments. In the twentieth century, developments of comparable magnitude had already taken place in the decades preceding World War I and World War II. This awareness of the dangers inherent in periods of political instability and rapid change causes profound unease and apprehension. The fear grows that events may get out of hand and the world may once again plunge itself into a global conflagration. Scholars, journalists, and others turn to history for guidance, asking if the current pattern of events resembles the pattern of 1914 and 1939.[1]

These contemporary developments and their dangerous implications raise a number of questions regarding war and change in international relations: How and under what circumstances does change take place at the level of international relations? What are the roles of political, economic, and technological developments in producing change in international systems? Wherein lies the danger of intense military conflict during periods of rapid economic and political upheaval? And, most important of all, are answers that are derived from examination of the past valid for the contemporary world? In other words, to what extent

From Robert Gilpin, *War and Change in World Politics* (1981), pages 1–15 and 39–44. Reprinted by permission of Cambridge University Press.

have social, economic, and technological developments such as increasing economic interdependence of nations and the advent of nuclear weapons changed the role of war in the process of international political change? Is there any reason to hope that political change may be more benign in the future than it has been in the past?

The purpose of this book is to explore these issues. In this endeavor we shall seek to develop an understanding of international political change more systematic than the understanding that currently exists. We do not pretend to develop a general theory of international relations that will provide an overarching explanatory statement. Instead, we attempt to provide a framework for thinking about the problem of war and change in world politics. This intellectual framework is intended to be an analytical device that will help to order and explain human experience. It does not constitute a rigorous scientific explanation of political change. The ideas on international political change presented are generalizations based on observations of historical experience rather than a set of hypotheses that have been tested scientifically by historical evidence; they are proposed as a plausible account of how international political change occurs.[2]

To this end we isolate and analyze the more obvious regularities and patterns associated with changes in international systems. However, we make no claim to have discovered the "laws of change" that determine when political change will occur or what course it will take.[3] On the contrary, the position taken here is that major political changes are the consequences of the conjuncture of unique and unpredictable sets of developments. However, the claim is made that it is possible to identify recurrent patterns, common elements, and general tendencies in the major turning points in international history. As the distinguished economist W. Arthur Lewis put it, "The process of social change is much the same today as it was 2,000 years ago. . . . We can tell how change will occur if it occurs; what we cannot foresee is what change is going to occur."[4]

The conception of political change presented in this book, like almost all social science, is not predictive. Even economics is predictive only within a narrow range of issues.[5]

Most of the alleged theories in the field of political science and in the sub-field of international relations are in fact analytical, descriptive constructs; they provide at best a conceptual framework and a set of questions that help us to analyze and explain a type of phenomenon.[6] Thus, Kenneth Waltz, in his stimulating book, *Man, the State and War,* provided an explanation of war in general terms, but not the means for predicting any particular war.[7] In similar fashion, this study seeks to explain in general terms the nature of international political change.

The need for a better understanding of political change, especially international political change, was well set forth by Wilbert Moore in the latest edition of the *International Encyclopedia of the Social Sciences:*

"Paradoxically, as the rate of social change has accelerated in the real world of experience, the scientific disciplines dealing with man's actions and products have tended to emphasize orderly interdependence and static continuity."[8]

Moore's judgment concerning the inadequate treatment of political change by social scientists is borne out by analyses of international-relations textbooks and theoretical works. Although there are some recent outstanding exceptions,[9] few of these books have addressed the problem of political change in systematic fashion. As David Easton rightly commented, "students of political life have . . . been prone to forget that the really crucial problems of social research are concerned with the patterns of change."[10]

It is worth noting, as Joseph Schumpeter pointed out, that the natural development of any science is from static analysis to dynamic analysis.[11] Static theory is simpler, and its propositions are easier to prove. Unfortunately, until the statics of a field of inquiry are sufficiently well developed and one has a good grasp of repetitive processes and recurrent phenomena, it is difficult if not impossible to proceed to the study of dynamics. From this perspective, systematic study of international relations is a young field, and much of what passes for dynamics is in reality an effort to understand the statics of interactions of particular international systems: diplomatic bargaining, alliance behavior, crisis management, etc. The question whether or not our current understanding of these static aspects is sufficiently well advanced to aid in the development of a dynamic theory poses a serious challenge to the present enterprise.

A second factor that helps to explain the apparent neglect, until recent years, of the problem of political change is what K. J. Holsti called the decline of "grand theory."[12] The political realism of Hans Morgenthau, the systems theory of Morton Kaplan, and the neofunctionalism of Ernst Haas, as well as numerous other "grand theories," have one element in common: the search for a general theory of international politics. Each in its own way, with varying success, has sought, in the words of Morgenthau, "to reduce the facts of experience to mere specific instances of general propositions."[13] Yet none of these ambitious efforts to understand the issues (war, imperialism, and political change) has gained general acceptance. Instead, "the major preoccupations of theorists during the past decade have been to explore specific problems, to form hypotheses or generalizations explaining limited ranges of phenomena, and particularly, to obtain data to test those hypotheses."[14] In brief, the more recent emphasis on so-called middle-range theory, though valuable in itself, has had the unfortunate consequence of diverting attention away from more general theoretical problems.[15]

A third reason for neglect of the study of political change is the Western bias in the study of international relations. For a profession whose intellectual commitment is the understanding of the interactions of societies, international relations as a discipline is remarkably parochial and ethnocentric. It is essentially a study of the Western state system, and a sizable fraction of the existing literature is devoted to developments since the end of World War II. Thus the profession has emphasized recent developments within that particular state system. Although there are exceptions, the practitioners of this discipline have not been forced to come to terms with the dynamics of this, or any other, state system.[16] As Martin Wight suggested, international relations lacks a tradition of political theorizing. In large measure, of course, this is because of the paucity of reliable secondary studies of non-Western systems.[17] This situation in itself is a formidable obstacle to the development of a theory of international political change.

A fourth reason for neglect of the theoretical problem of political change is the widespread conviction of the futility of the task. Prevalent among historians, this view is also held by many social scientists.[18] The search for "laws of change" is held to be useless because of the uniqueness and complexity of historical events. Thus the search for generalizations or patterns in human affairs is regarded as a hopeless enterprise. Such a position, if taken at face value, denies the very possibility of a science or history of society; yet one should note its admonitions that there are no immutable laws of change and that although repetitive patterns may exist, social change is ultimately contingent on unique sets of historical events.

Finally, the development of a theory of political change has been inhibited by ideology and emotion. In part this is due to a conservative bias in Western social science. Most academic social scientists have a preference for stability or at least a preference for orderly change. The idea of radical changes that threaten accepted values and interests is not an appealing one. This issue is especially acute for the theorist of international political change, who must confront directly the fundamental problem of international relations: war. The inhibiting effect of this dreadful issue has been well put by John Burton in a sweeping indictment of contemporary international-relations scholarship:

> The chief failure of orthodoxy has been in relation to change. The outstanding feature of reality is the dynamic nature of International Relations. No general theory is appropriate which cannot take into consideration the rapidly changing technological, social and political environment in which nations are required to live in peace one with the other. But the only device of fundamental change which is possible in the context of power politics is that of war, for which reason war is recognized as a legitimate instrument of national policy. It is not surprising that International Relations has tended to be discussed in static terms, and that stability has tended to be interpreted in terms of the maintenance of the *status quo*. A dynamic approach to International Relations would immediately confront the analyst with no alternative but to acknowledge war as the only available mechanism for change.[19]

Burton's challenge to orthodox theory of international relations goes to the heart of the present study. In recent years theorists of international relations have tended to stress the moderating and stabilizing influences of contemporary developments on the behavior of states, especially the increasing economic interdependence among nations and the destructiveness of modern weapons. These important developments have encouraged many individuals to believe that peaceful evolution has replaced military conflict as the principal means of adjusting relations among nation-states in the contemporary world. This assumption has been accompanied by a belief that economic and welfare goals have triumphed over the traditional power and security objectives of states. Thus, many believe that the opportunity for peaceful economic intercourse and the constraints imposed by modern destructive warfare have served to decrease the probability of a major war.

In the present study we take a very different stance, a stance based on the assumption that the fundamental nature of international relations has not changed over the millennia. International relations continue to be a recurring struggle for wealth and power among independent actors in a state of anarchy. The classic history of Thucydides is as meaningful a guide to the behavior of states today as when it was written in the fifth century B.C. Yet important changes have taken place. One of the sub-themes of this book, in fact, is that modern statecraft and premodern statecraft differ in significant respects, a situation first appreciated by Montesquieu, Edward Gibbon, and other earlier writers on the subject. Nevertheless, we contend that the fundamentals have not been altered. For this reason, the insights of earliers writers and historical experience are considered relevant to an understanding of the ways in which international systems function and change in the contemporary era.

Thus, although there is obviously an important element of truth in the belief that contemporary economic and technological development have altered relations among states, events in Asia, Africa, and the Middle East in the 1970s and early 1980s force us once again to acknowledge the continuing unsolved problem of war and the role of war in the process of international political change. Even more than in the past, in the last decades of the twentieth century we need to understand the relationship of war and change in the international system. Only in this way can we hope to fashion a more peaceful alternative. As E. H. Carr reminded us, this is the basic task of the study of international relations: "To establish methods of peaceful change is . . . the fundamental problem of international morality and of international politics."[20] But if peace were the ultimate goal of statecraft, then the solution to the problem of peaceful change would be easy. Peace may always be had by surrender to the aggressor state. The real task for the peaceful state is to seek a peace that protects and guarantees its vital interests and its concept of international morality.

THE NATURE OF INTERNATIONAL POLITICAL CHANGE

An international system is established for the same reason that any social or political system is created; actors enter social relations and create social structures in order to advance particular sets of political, economic, or other types of interests. Because the interests of some of the actors may conflict with those of other actors, the particular interests that are most favored by these social arrangements tend to reflect the relative powers of the actors involved. That is, although social systems impose restraints on the behavior of all actors, the behaviors rewarded and punished by the system will coincide, at least initially, with the interests of the most powerful members of the social system. Over time, however, the interests of individual actors and the balance of power among the actors do change as a result of economic, technological, and other developments. As a consequence, those actors who benefit most from a change in the social system and who gain the power to effect such change will seek to alter the system in ways that favor their interests. The resulting changed system will reflect the new distribution of power and the interests of its new dominant members. Thus, a precondition for political change lies in a disjuncture between the existing social system and the redistribution of power toward those actors who would benefit most from a change in the system.

This conception of political change is based on the notion that the purpose or social function of any social system, including the international system, may be defined in terms of the benefits that various members derive from its operation.[21]

As is the case with domestic society, the nature of the international system determines whose interests are being served by the functioning of the system. Changes in the system imply changes in the distribution of benefits provided to and costs imposed on individual members of the system. Thus the study of international political change must focus on the international system and especially on the efforts of political actors to change the international system in order to advance their own interests. Whether these interests are security, economic gain, or ideological goals, the achievement of state objectives is dependent on the nature of the international system (i.e., the governance of the system, the rules of the system, the recognition of rights, etc.). As is the case in any social or political system, the process of international political change ultimately reflects the efforts of individuals or groups to transform institutions and systems in order to advance their interests. Because these interests and the powers of groups (or states) change, in time the political system will be changed in ways that will reflect these underlying shifts in interest and power. The elaboration of this approach for the understanding of international political change is the purpose of the subsequent discussion.

A FRAMEWORK FOR UNDERSTANDING INTERNATIONAL POLITICAL CHANGE

The conceptualization of international political change to be presented [here] rests on a set of assumptions regarding the behavior of states:

1. An international system is stable (i.e., in a state of equilibrium) if no state believes it profitable to attempt to change the system.
2. A state will attempt to change the international system if the expected benefits exceed the expected costs (i.e., if there is an expected net gain).
3. A state will seek to change the international system through territorial, political, and economic expansion until the marginal costs of further change are equal to or greater than the marginal benefits.
4. Once an equilibrium between the costs and benefits of further change and expansion is reached, the tendency is for the economic costs of maintaining the status quo to rise faster than the economic capacity to support the status quo.
5. If the disequilibrium in the international system is not resolved, then the system will be changed, and a new equilibrium reflecting the redistribution of power will be established.

Obviously these assumptions are abstractions from a highly complex political reality. They do not describe the actual decision processes of statesmen, but as in the case of economic theory, actors are assumed to behave as if they were guided by such a set of cost/benefit calculations. Moreover, these assumptions are not mutually exclusive; they do overlap. Assumptions 2 and 4 are mirror images of one another, assumption 2 referring to a revisionist state and assumption 4 referring to a status quo state.

On the basis of these assumptions, the conceptualization of international political change to be presented here seeks to comprehend a continuing historical process. Because history has no starts and stops, one must break into the flow of history at a particular point. The following analysis of political change begins with an international system in a state of equilibrium as shown in Figure 1. An international system is in a state of equilibrium if the more powerful states in the system are satisfied with the existing territorial, political, and economic arrangements. Although minor changes and adjustments may take place, an equilibrium condition is one in which no powerful state (or group) believes that a change in the system would yield additional benefits commensurate with the anticipated costs of bringing about a change in the system.[22] Although every state and group in the system could benefit from particular types of change, the costs involved will discourage attempts to seek a change in

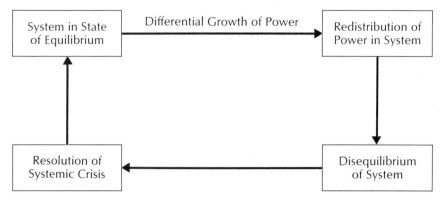

Figure 1. Diagram of international political change.

system. As one writer has put it, "a power equilibrium represents a stable political configuration provided there are no changes in returns to conquest."[23] Under these conditions, where no one has an incentive to change the system, the status quo may be said to be stable.

In the more traditional language of international relations, the international status quo is held to be a legitimate one, at least by the major states in the system. The meaning of legitimacy was defined by Henry Kissinger as follows:

> [Legitimacy] implies the acceptance of the framework of the international order by all major powers, at least to the extend that no state is so dissatisfied that, like Germany after the Treaty of Versailles, it expresses its dissatisfaction in a revolutionary foreign policy. A legitimate order does not make conflicts impossible, but it limits their scope. Wars may occur, but they will be fought *in the name of* the existing structure and the peace which follows will be justified as a better expression of the "legitimate," general consensus. Diplomacy in the classic sense, the adjustment of differences through negotiations, is possible only in "legitimate international orders."[24]

What this quotation suggests is that an international system or order exists in a condition of homeostatic or dynamic equilibrium. Like any other system, it is not completely at rest; changes at the level of interstate interactions are constantly taking place. In general, however, the conflicts, alliances, and diplomatic interactions among the actors in the system tend to preserve the defining characteristics of the system. Thus, as Kissinger demonstrated, the legitimate order or equilibrium created at the Congress of Vienna (1814) survived limited conflicts and diplomatic maneuvering until it finally collapsed in response to the profound economic, technological, and political upheavals of the latter part of the nineteenth century. This issue of legitimacy will be discussed later.

In every international system there are continual occurrences of political, economic, and technological changes that promise gains or threaten losses for one or another actor. In most cases these potential gains and losses are minor, and only incremental adjustments are necessary in order to take account of them. Such changes take place within the existing international system, producing a condition of homeostatic equilibrium. The relative stability of the system is, in fact, largely determined by its capacity to adjust to the demands of actors affected by changing political and environmental conditions. In every system, therefore, a process of disequilibrium and adjustment is constantly taking place. In the absence of large potential net benefits from change, the system continues to remain in a state of equilibrium.

If the interests and relative powers of the principal states in an international system remained constant over time, or if power relations changed in such a way as to maintain the same relative distribution of power, the system would continue indefinitely in a state of equilibrium. However, both domestic and international developments undermine the stability of the status quo. For example, shifts in domestic coalitions may necessitate redefinition of the "national interest." However, the most destabilizing factor is the tendency in an international system for the powers of member states to change at different rates because of political, economic, and technological developments. In time, the differential growth in power of the various states in the system causes a fundamental redistribution of power in the system.

The concept of power is one of the most troublesome in the field of international relations and, more generally, political science. Many weighty books have analyzed and elaborated the concept. In this book, power refers simply to the military, economic, and technological capabilities of states. This definition obviously leaves out important and intangible elements that affect the outcomes of political actions, such as public morale, qualities of leadership, and situational factors. It also excludes what E. H. Carr called "power over opinion."[25] These psychological and frequently incalculable aspects of power and international relations are more closely associated with the concept of prestige . . . .

As a consequence of the changing interests of individual states, and especially because of the differential growth in power among states, the international system moves from a condition of equilibrium to one of disequilibrium. Disequilibrium is a situation in which economic, political, and technological developments have increased considerably the potential benefits or decreased the potential costs to one or more states of seeking to change the international system. Forestalling one's losses or increasing one's gains becomes an incentive for one or more states to attempt to change the system. Thus there develops a disjuncture between the existing international system and the potential gains to particular states from a change in the international system.

The elements of this systemic disequilibrium are twofold. First, mili-

TABLE 1   Mechanisms of Control (Components of System)

Domestic	International
Government[a]	Dominance of great powers[b]
Authority	Hierarchy of prestige
Property rights	Division of territory
Law	Rules of the system
Domestic economy	International economy

[a]Based on distribution of power among domestic groups, coalitions, classes, etc.
[b]Based on distribution of power among states in the system.

tary, technological, or other changes have increased the benefits of territorial conquest or the benefits of changing the international system in other ways. Second, the differential growth in power among the states in the system has altered the cost of changing the system. This transformation of the benefits and/or the costs of changing the system produces an incongruity or disjuncture among the components of the system (Table 1). On the one hand, the hierarchy of prestige, the division of territory, the international division of labor, and the rules of the system remain basically unchanged; they continue to reflect primarily the interests of the existing dominant powers and the relative power distribution that prevailed at the time of the last systemic change. On the other hand, the international distribution of power has undergone a radical transformation that has weakened the foundations of the existing system. It is this disjuncture between the several components of the system and its implications for relative gains and losses among the various states in the system that cause international political change.

This disjuncture within the existing international system involving the potential benefits and losses to particular powerful actors from a change in the system leads to a crisis in the international system. Although resolution of a crisis through peaceful adjustment of the systemic disequilibrium is possible, the principal mechanism of change throughout history has been war, or what we shall call hegemonic war (i.e., a war that determines which state or states will be dominant and will govern the system). The peace settlement following such a hegemonic struggle reorders the political, territorial, and other bases of the system. Thus the cycle of change is completed in that hegemonic war and the peace settlement create a new status quo and equilibrium reflecting the redistribution of power in the system and the other components of the system.

NOTES

1. Miles Kahler, "Rumors of War: The 1914 Analogy," *Foreign Affairs,* 58 (1979–80), pp. 374–396.

2. However, in principle, these ideas are translatable into specific testable hypotheses. At least we would argue that this is possible for a substantial fraction of them. The carrying out of this task, or part of it, would require another volume.

3. The term "law" . . . is to be interpreted as a general tendency that may be counteracted by other developments. This conception of law is taken from Jean Baechler, *Les Origines du Capitalisme* (Paris: Editions Gallimard, 1971), English edition (Oxford: Basil Blackwell, 1975), p. 52.

4. W. Arthur Lewis, *The Theory of Economic Growth* (New York: Harper & Row, 1970), pp. 17–18.

5. F.S.C. Northrop, *The Logic of the Sciences and the Humanities* (New York: Macmillan, 1947), pp. 243–245.

6. Stanley Hoffmann (ed.), *Contemporary Theory in International Relations* (Englewood Cliffs, N.J.: Prentice-Hall, 1960), p. 40.

7. Kenneth N. Waltz, *Man, the State and War* (New York: Columbia University Press, 1959), p. 232.

8. Wilbert E. Moore, "Social Change" in *International Encyclopedia of the Social Sciences,* Vol. 14, ed. by David Sills (New York: Crowell Collier and Macmillan, 1968), p. 365.

9. Nazli Choucri and Robert C. North, *Nations in Conflict* (San Francisco: W. H. Freeman, 1975); Robert O. Keohane and Joseph S. Nye, *Power and Interdependence* (Boston: Little, Brown, 1977); Kenneth N. Waltz, *Theory of International Politics* (Reading, MA: Addison-Wesley, 1979).

10. David Easton, *The Political System* (New York: Alfred A. Knopf, 1953), p. 42. It is symptomatic of this continued general neglect that the *Handbook of Political Science* does not contain a section devoted to the problem of political change. Nor does the entry "political change" appear in its cumulative index. See Fred I. Greenstein and Nelson W. Polsby, eds., *Handbook of Political Science* (Reading, Mass.: Addison–Wesley, 1975).

11. Joseph Schumpeter, *History of Economic Analysis* (New York: Oxford University Press, 1954), p. 964.

12. K. J. Holsti, "Retreat from Utopia," *Canadian Journal of Political Science,* Vol. 4 (1971), pp. 165–177.

13. *Ibid.,* p. 167.

14. *Ibid.,* p. 171.

15. Several important books have recently indicated revival of interest in general theory. See Choucri and North, *Nations in Conflict;* Hedley Bull, *The Anarchical Society* (New York: Columbia University Press, 1977); Keohane and Nye, *Power and Interdependence;* Stanley Hoffmann, *Primacy or World Order* (New York: McGraw-Hill, 1978); Ralph Pettman, *State and Class* (London: Croom Helm, 1979); Kenneth N. Waltz, *Theory of International Politics* (Reading, Mass.: Addison–Wesley, 1979).Marxist scholars, of course, never lost interest in "grand theory."

16. Three recent exceptions are Evan Luard, *Types of International Society* (New York: Free Press, 1976); Robert G. Wesson, *The Imperial Order* (Berkeley: University of California Press, 1967); Martin Wight, *Systems of States,* ed. by Hedley Bull (Leicester: Leicester University Press, 1977).

17. Martin Wight, "Why Is There No International Theory?" in Herbert Butterfield and Martin Wight (eds.), *Diplomatic Investigations* (London: George Allen and Unwin, 1966), pp. 17–34.

18. Albert O. Hirschman, "The Search for Paradigms as a Hindrance to Under-standing," *World Politics,* Vol. 22 (1970), pp. 329–343.
19. John Burton, *International Relations: A General Theory* (Cambridge, MA: Cambridge University Press, 1965), pp. 71–72.
20. E. H. Carr, *The Twenty Years' Crisis* (London: Macmillan, 1951).
21. John Harsanyi, "Rational-Choice Models of Political Behavior vs. Function-alist and Conformist Theories," *World Politics,* Vol. 21 (1969), pp. 513–538.
22. R. L. Curry Jr, and L. L. Wade, *A Theory of Political Exchange* (Englewood Cliffs, N.J.: Prentice–Hall, 1968), p. 49, and Lance E. Davis and Douglass C. North, *Institutional Change and American Economic Growth* (Cambridge: Cambridge University Press, 1971), p. 40.
23. Trout Rader, *The Economics of Feudalism* (New York: Gordon and Breach, 1971), p. 50.
24. Henry A. Kissinger, *A World Restored* (Boston: Houghton Mifflin, 1957), pp. 1–2.
25. Carr, *Twenty Years' Crisis,* p. 132.

Theory of World Politics: Structural Realism and Beyond

Robert O. Keohane

The author surveys and critically evaluates the work of some contemporary realists whom he calls "structural realists."

For over 2000 years, what Hans J. Morgenthau dubbed "Political Realism" has constituted the principal tradition for the analysis of international relations in Europe and its offshoots in the New World (Morgenthau, 1966). Writers of the Italian Renaissance, balance of power theorists, and later adherents of the school of *Machtpolitik* all fit under a loose version of the Realist rubric. Periodic attacks on Realism have taken place; yet the very focus of these critiques seems only to reconfirm the centrality of Realist thinking in the international political thought of the West.[1]

Realism has been criticized frequently during the last few years, and demands for a "new paradigm" have been made. Joseph S. Nye and I called for a "world politics paradigm" a decade ago, and Richard Mans-

From *Political Science: The State of the Discipline,* ed. Ada W. Finifter (Washington, D.C.: American Political Science Association, 1983). Reprinted by permission of the APSA.

bach and John A. Vasquez have recently proposed a "new paradigm for global politics." In both these works, the new paradigm that was envisaged entailed adopting additional concepts—for instance, "transnational relations," or "issue phases" (Keohane & Nye, 1972, esp. pp. 379–386; Mansbach & Vasquez, 1981, Chapter 4). Yet for these concepts to be useful as part of a satisfactory general theory of world politics, a theory of state action—which is what Realism purports to provide—is necessary. Understanding the general principles of state action and the practices of governments is a necessary basis for attempts to refine theory or to extend the analysis to non-state actors. Approaches using new concepts may be able to supplement, enrich, or extend a basic theory of state action, but they cannot substitute for it.[2]

The fixation of critics and reformers on the Realist theory of state action reflects the importance of this research tradition. In my view, there is good reason for this. Realism is a necessary component in a coherent analysis of world politics because its focus on power, interests, and rationality is crucial to any understanding of the subject. Thus any approach to international relations has to incorporate, or at least come to grips with, key elements of Realist thinking. Even writers who are concerned principally with international institutions and rules, or analysts in the Marxist tradition, make use of some Realist premises. Since Realism builds on fundamental insights about world politics and state action, progress in the study of international relations requires that we seek to build on this core.

Yet as we shall see, Realism does not provide a satisfactory theory of world politics, if we require of an adequate theory that it provide a set of plausible and testable answers to questions about state behavior under specified conditions. Realism is particularly weak in accounting for change, especially where the sources of that change lie in the world political economy or in the domestic structures of states. Realism, viewed dogmatically as a set of answers, would be worse than useless. As a sophisticated framework of questions and initial hypotheses, however, it is extremely valuable.[3]

Since Realism constitutes the central tradition in the study of world politics, an analysis, like this one, of the current state of the field must evaluate the viability of Realism in the penultimate decade of the twentieth century. Doing this requires constructing a rather elaborate argument of my own, precluding a comprehensive review of the whole literature of international relations. I have therefore selected for discussion a relatively small number of works that fit my theme, ignoring entire areas of research, much of it innovative.[4] Within the sphere of work dealing with Realism and its limitations, I have focused attention on several especially interesting and valuable contributions. My intention is to point out promising lines of research rather than to engage in what Stanley Hoffmann once called a "wrecking operation" (Hoffmann, 1960, p. 171).

Since I have written on the subject of Realism in the past, I owe the reader an explanation of where I think my views have changed, and where I am only restating, in different ways, opinions that I have expressed before. This chapter deals more systematically and more sympathetically with Realism than does my previous work. Yet its fundamental argument is consistent with that of *Power and Interdependence*. In that book Nye and I relied on Realist theory as a basis for our structural models of international regime change (Keohane & Nye, 1977, pp. 42–46). We viewed our structural models as attempts to improve the ability of Realist or neo-Realist analysis to account for international regime change: we saw ourselves as adapting Realism, and attempting to go beyond it, rather than rejecting it.

Admittedly, Chapter 2 of *Power and Interdependence* characterized Realism as a descriptive ideal type rather than a research program in which explanatory theories could be embedded. Realist and Complex Interdependence ideal types were used to help specify the conditions under which overall structure explanations of change would or would not be valid; the term, "Realist," was used to refer to conditions under which states are the dominant actors, hierarchies of issues exist, and force is usable as an instrument of policy (Keohane & Nye, 1977, pp. 23–29). Taken as a full characterization of the Realist tradition this would have been unfair, and it seems to have led readers concerned with our view of Realism to focus excessively on Chapter 2 and too little on the attempt, which draws on what I here call structural realism, to account for regime change (Chapters 3–6).[5]

To provide criteria for the evaluation of theoretical work in international politics—Structural Realism, in particular—I employ the conception of a "scientific research programme" explicated in 1970 by the philosopher of science, Imre Lakatos (1970). Lakatos developed this concept as a tool for the comparative evaluation of scientific theories, and in response to what he regarded as the absence of standards for evaluation in Thomas Kuhn's (1962) notion of a paradigm.[6] Theories are embedded in research programs. These programs contain inviolable assumptions (the "hard core") and initial conditions, defining their scope. For Lakatos, they also include two other very important elements: auxiliary, or observational, hypotheses, and a "positive heuristic," which tells the scientist what sorts of additional hypotheses to entertain and how to go about conducting research. In short, a research program is a set of methodological rules telling us what paths of research to avoid and what paths to follow.

Consider a research program, with a set of observational hypotheses, a "hard core" of irrefutable assumptions, and a set of scope conditions. In the course of research, anomalies are bound to appear sooner or later: predictions of the theory will seem to be falsified. For Lakatos, the reaction of scientists developing the research program is to protect the hard core by constructing auxiliary hypotheses that will explain the anomalies. Yet any research program, good or bad, can invent such auxiliary hypotheses on an *ad hoc* basis. The key test for Lakatos of the value of a research program is whether these auxiliary hypotheses are "progressive," that is, whether their invention leads to the discovery of *new facts* (other than the anomalous facts that they were designed to explain). Progressive research programs display "continuous growth": their auxiliary hypotheses increase our capacity to understand reality (Lakatos, 1970, pp. 116-122, 132-138, 173-180).

Lakatos developed this conception to assess developments in the natural sciences, particularly physics. If we took literally the requirements that he laid down for "progressive" research programs, all actual theories of international politics—and perhaps all conceivable theories—would fail the test. Indeed, it has been argued that much of economics, including oligopoly theory (heavily relied upon by Structural Realists), fails to meet this standard (Latsis, 1976). Nevertheless, Lakatos's conception has the great merit of providing clear and sensible criteria for the evaluation of scientific traditions, and of asking penetrating questions that may help us to see Realism in a revealing light. Lakatos' questions are relevant, even if applying them without modification could lead to premature rejection not only of Realism, but of our whole field, or even the entire discipline of political science![7]

The stringency of Lakatos' standards suggests that we should supplement this test with a "softer," more interpretive one. That is, how much insight does Realism provide into contemporary world politics?

For this line of evaluation we can draw inspiration from Clifford Geertz's discussion of the role of theory in anthropology. Geertz argues that culture "is not a power, something to which social events, behaviors, institutions, or processes can be causally attributed; it is a context—something within which they can be intelligibly—that is, thickly—described" (1973, p. 14). The role of theory, he claims, is "not to codify abstract regularities but to make thick description possible, not to generalize across cases but to generalize within them" (*ibid.*, p. 26). This conception is the virtual antithesis of the standards erected by Lakatos, and could all too easily serve as a rationalization for the proliferation of atheoretical case studies. Nevertheless, culture as discussed by Geertz has something in common with the international system as discussed by students of world politics. It is difficult to generalize across systems. We are continually bedeviled by the paucity of comparable cases, particularly when making systemic statements—for example, about the operation of balances of power. Much of what students of world politcs do, and what Classical Realism in particular aspires to, is to make the actions of states understandable (despite obfuscatory statements by their spokesmen): that is, in Geertz's words, to provide "a context within which they can be intelligibly described." For example, Morgenthau's discussion of the concept of interest defined in terms of power, quoted at length below, reflects this objective more than the goal of arriving at testable generalizations.

This essay is divided into four major sections. The first of these seeks to establish the basis for a dual evaluation of Realism: as a source of interpretive insights into the operation of world politics, and as a scientific research program that enables the investigator to discover new facts. I examine the arguments of Thucydides and Morgenthau to extract the key assumptions of Classical Realism. Then I discuss recent work by Kenneth N. Waltz, whom I regard as the most systematic spokesman for contemporary Structural Realism.

Section II addresses the question of interpretation and puzzle-solving within the Realist tradition. How successful are Realist thinkers in making new contributions to our understanding of world politics? In Section III, I consider the shortcomings of Realism when judged by the standards that Lakatos establishes, or even when evaluated by less rigorous criteria, and begin to ask whether a modified version of Structural Realism could correct some of these faults. Section IV carries this theme further by attempting to outline how a multi-dimensional research program, including a modified structural theory, might be devised; what its limitations would be; and how it could be relevant, in particular, to problems of peaceful change.

The conclusion emphasizes the issue of peaceful change as both a theoretical and a practical problem. Realism raises the question of how peaceful change could be achieved, but does not resolve it. Understanding the conditions under which peaceful change would be facilitated remains, in my view, the most urgent task facing students of world politics.

I. STRUCTURAL REALISM AS RESEARCH PROGRAM

To explicate the research program of Realism, I begin with two classic works, one ancient, the other modern: *The Peloponnesian War,* by Thucydides, and *Politics Among Nations,* by Morgenthau.[8] The three most fundamental Realist assumptions are evident in these books: that the most important actors in world politics are territorially organized entities (city–states or modern states); that state behavior can be explained rationally; and that states seek power and calculate their interests in terms of power, relative to the nature of the international system that they face.

The Peloponnesian War was written in an attempt to explain the causes of the great war of the Fifth Century B.C. between the coalition led by Athens and its adversaries, led by Sparta. Thucydides assumes that to achieve this purpose, he must explain the behavior of the major city–states involved in the conflict. Likewise, Morgenthau assumes that the subject of a science of international politics is the behavior of states. Realism is "state-centric."[9]

Both authors also believed that observers of world politics could understand events by imagining themselves, as rational individuals, in authoritative positions, and reflecting on what they would do if faced with the problems encountered by the actual decision-makers. They both, therefore, employ the method of *rational reconstruction*. Thucydides admits that he does not have transcripts of all the major speeches given during the war, but he is undaunted:

> It was in all cases difficult to carry [the speeches] word for word in one's memory, so my habit has been to make the speakers say what was in my opinion demanded of them by the various occasions, of course adhering as closely as possible to the general sense of what they really said. (Thucydides, Book I, paragraph 23 [Chapter I, Modern Library edition. p. 14])

Morgenthau argues that in trying to understand foreign policy,

> We put ourselves in the position of a statesman who must meet a certain problem of foreign policy under certain circumstances, and we ask ourselves what the rational alternatives are from which a statesman may choose . . . and which of these rational alternatives this particular statesman, acting under these circumstances, is likely to choose. It is the testing of this rational hypothesis against the actual facts and their consequences that gives meaning to the facts of international politics and makes a theory of politics possible. (Morgenthau, 1966, p. 5)

In reconstructing state calculations, Thucydides and Morgenthau both assume that states will act to protect their power positions, perhaps even to the point of seeking to maximize their power. Thucydides seeks to go beneath the surface of events to the power realities that are fundamental to state action:

> The real cause [of the war] I consider to be the one which was formally most kept out of sight. The growth in the power of Athens, and the alarm which this inspired in Lacedemon, made war inevitable. (Thucydides, Book I paragraph 24, Chapter I, Modern Library Edition, p. 15)[10]

Morgenthau is even more blunt: "International politics, like all politics, is a struggle for power" (1966, p. 25, see also Morgenthau, 1946). Political Realism, he argues, understands international politics through the concept of "interest defined as power":

> We assume that statesmen think and act in terms of interest defined as power, and the evidence of history bears that assumption out. That assumption allows us to retrace and anticipate, as it were, the steps a statesman— past, present, or future—has taken or will take on the political scene. We look over his shoulder when he writes his dispatches; we listen in on his conversation with other statesmen; we read and anticipate his very thoughts. (1966, p. 5)

The three assumptions just reviewed define the hard core of the Classical Realist research program:

(1) The *state-centric assumption:* states are the most important actors in world politics;

(2) The *rationality assumption:* world politics can be analyzed as if states were unitary rational actors, carefully calculating costs of alternative courses of action and seeking to maximize their expected utility, although doing so under conditions of uncertainty and without necessarily having sufficient information about alternatives or resources (time or otherwise) to conduct a full review of all possible courses of action;[11]

(3) The *power assumption;* states seek power (both the ability to influence others and resources that can be used to exercise influence); and they calculate their interests in terms of power, whether as end or as necessary means to a variety to other ends.

More recently, Kenneth N. Waltz (1959) has attempted to reformulate and systematize Realism on the basis of what he called, in *Man, the State and War,* a "third image" perspective. This form of Realism does not rest on the presumed iniquity of the human race—original sin in one form or another—but on the nature of world politics as an anarchic realm:

> Each state pursues its own interests, however defined, in ways it judges best. Force is a means of achieving the external ends of states because there exists no consistent, reliable process of reconciling the conflicts of interests that inevitably arise among similar units in a condition of anarchy. (p. 238)[12]

Even well-intentioned statesmen find that they must use or threaten force to attain their objectives.

Since the actions of states are conceived of as resulting from the nature of international politics, the paramount theoretical task for Realists is to create a *systemic* explanation of international politics. In a systemic theory, as Waltz explains it, the propositions of the theory specify relationships between certain aspects of the system and actor behavior (1979, pp. 67–73). Waltz's third-image Realism, for instance, draws connections between the distribution of power in a system and the actions of states: small countries will behave differently from large ones, and in a balance of power system, alliances can be expected to shift in response to changes in power relationships. Any theory will, of course, take into account the attributes of actors, as well as features of the system itself. But the key distinguishing characteristic of a systemic theory is that *the internal attributes of actors are given by assumption rather than treated as variables.* Changes in actor behavior, and system outcomes, are explained not on the basis of variations in these actor characteristics, but on the basis of changes in the attributes of the system itself. A good example of such a systemic theory is microeconomic theory in its standard form. It posits the existence of business firms, with given utility functions (such as profit maximization), and attempts to explain their behavior on the basis of environmental factors such as the competitiveness of markets. It is systemic because its propositions about variations in behavior depend on variations in characteristics of the system, not of the units (Waltz, 1979, pp. 89–91, 93–95, 98).

To develop a systemic analysis, abstraction is necessary: one has to avoid being distracted by the details and vagaries of domestic politics and other variables at the level of the acting unit. To reconstruct a systemic research program, therefore, Structural Realists must devise a way to explain state behavior on the basis of systemic characteristics, and to account for outcomes in the same manner. This needs to be a coherent explanation, although it need not tell us everything we would like to know about world politics.

Waltz's formulation of Structural Realism as a systemic theory seeks to do this by developing a concept not explicitly used by Morgenthau or Thucydides: the *structure* of the international system. Two elements of international structure are constants: (1) the international system is anarchic rather than hierarchic, and (2) it is characterized by interaction among units with similar functions. These are such enduring background characteristics that they are constitutive of what we mean by "international politics."[14] The third element of structure, the distribution of capabilities across the states in the system, varies from system to system, and over time. Since it is a variable, this element—the distribution of "power"—takes on particular importance in the theory. The most significant capabilities are those of the most powerful actors. Structures "are defined not by all of the actors that flourish within them but by the major ones" (Waltz, 1979, p. 93).

According to Waltz, structure is the principal determinant of outcomes at the systems level: structure encourages certain actions and discourages others. It may also lead to unintended consequences, as the ability of states to obtain their objectives is constrained by the power of others (1979, pp. 104–111).

For Waltz, understanding the structure of an international system allows us to explain patterns of state behavior, since states determine their interests and strategies on the basis of calculations about their own positions in the system. The link between system structure and actor behavior is forged by the rationality assumption, which enables the theorist to predict that leaders will respond to the incentives and constraints imposed by their environments. Taking rationality as a constant permits one to attribute variations in state behavior to variations in characteristics of the international system. Otherwise, state behavior might have to be accounted for by variations in the calculating ability of states; in that case, the systemic focus of Structural Realism (and much of its explanatory power) would be lost. Thus the rationality assumption—as we will see in examining Waltz's balance of power theory—is essential to the theoretical claims of Structural Realism.[15]

The most parsimonious version of a structural theory would hold that any international system has a single structure of power. In such a conceptualization, power resources are homogeneous and fungible: they can be used to achieve results on any of a variety of issues without significant loss of efficacy. Power in politics becomes like money in economics: "in many respects, power and influence play the same role in international politics as money does in a market economy" (Wolfers, 1962, p. 105).

In its strong form, the Structural Realist research program is similar to that of micro-economics. Both use the rationality assumption to permit inferences about actor behavior to be made from system structure. The Realist definition of interests in terms of power and position is like the economist's assumption that firms seek to maximize profits: it provides the utility function of the actor. Through these assumptions, actor characteristics become constant rather than variable, and systemic theory becomes possible.[16] The additional assumption of power fungibility simplifies the theory further: on the basis of a *single* characteristic of the international system (overall power capabilities), *multiple* inferences can be drawn about actor behavior and outcomes. "Foreknowledge"—that aspiration of all theory—is thereby attained (Eckstein, 1975, pp. 88–89). As we will see below, pure Structural Realism provides an insufficient basis for explaining state interests and behavior, even when the rationality assumption is accepted; and the fungibility assumption is highly questionable. Yet the Structural Realist research program is an impressive intellectual achievement: an elegant, parsimonious, deductively rigorous instrument for scientific discovery. The anomalies that it generates are more interesting than its own predictions; but as Lakatos emphasizes, it is the exploration of anomalies that moves science forward.

Richard K. Ashley has recently argued that Structural Realism—which he calls "technical realism"—actually represents a regression from the classical Realism of Herz or Morgenthau.[17] In his view, contemporary Realist thinkers have forgotten the importance of subjective self-reflection, and the dialectic between subjectivity and objectivity, which are so important in the writings of "practical," or "classical" realists such as Thucydides and Morgenthau. Classical Realism for Ashley is interpretive: "a practical tradition of statesmen is the real subject whose language of experience the interpreter tries to make his own" (1981, p. 221). It is self-reflective and non-deterministic. It treats the concept of balance of power as a dialectical relation: not merely as an objective characterization of the international system but also as a collectively recognized orienting scheme for strategic action. Classical Realism encompasses the unity of opposites, and draws interpretive insight from recognizing the dialectical quality of human experience. Thus its proponents understand that the state system is problematic, and that "strategic artistry" is required to keep it in existence (Ashley, 1982, p. 22).

The problem with Classical Realism is that it is difficult to distinguish what Ashley praises as dialectical insight from a refusal to define concepts clearly and consistently, or to develop a systematic set of propositions that could be subjected to empirical tests. Structural Realism seeks to correct these flaws, and thus to construct a more rigorous theoretical framework for the study of world politics, while drawing on the concepts and insights of the older Realism. Structural Realism, as embodied particularly in the work of Waltz, is more systematic and logically more coherent than that of its Classical Realist predecessors. By its own standards, Structural Realism is, in Ashley's words, "a progressive scientific redemption of classical realism" (Ashley, 1982, p. 25). That is, it sees itself, and Classical Realism, as elements of a continuous research tradition.

Ashley complains that this form of Realism objectifies reality, and that in particular it regards the state as unproblematic. This leads, in his view, to some pernicious implications; that the interests expressed by dominant elites must be viewed as legitimate, that economic rationality is the highest form of thought, and that individuals are not responsible for the production of insecurity (1982, pp. 34–41). But Structural Realists need not make any of these claims. It is true that Structural Realism seeks to understand the limits of, and constraints on, human action in world politics. It emphasizes the strength of these constraints, and in that sense could be considered "conservative." But an analysis of constraints, far from implying an acceptance of the *status quo,* should be seen as a precondition to sensible attempts to change the world. To be self-reflective, human action must take place with an understanding of the context within which it occurs. Structural Realists can be criticized, as we will see, for paying insufficient attention to norms, institutions, and change. But this represents less a fault of Structural Realism as such than a failure of some of its advocates to transcend its categories. Structural Realism's focus on systemic constraints does not contradict Classical Realism's concern with action and choice. On the contrary, Classical Realism's emphasis on *praxis* helps us to understand the orgins of Structural Realism's search for systematic understanding, and—far from negating the importance of this search—makes it seem all the more important.

I have argued thus far that Structural Realism is at the center of contemporary international relations theory in the United States; that it constitutes an attempt to systematize Classical Realism; and that its degree of success as a theory can be legitimately evaluated in part according to standards such as those laid down by Lakatos, and in part through evaluation of its capacity to generate insightful interpretations of international political behavior. Two distinct tests, each reflecting one aspect of this dualistic evaluative standard, can be devised to evaluate Structural Realism as a research program for international relations:

(1) How "fruitful" is the Realist paradigm for puzzle-solving and interpretation of world politics (Toulmin, 1963)? That is, does current work in the Realist tradition make us see issues more clearly, or provide answers to formerly unsolved puzzles? Realism was designed to provide insights into such issues, and if it remains a live tradition, should continue to do so.

(2) Does Realism meet the standards of a scientific research program as enunciated by Lakatos? To answer this question, it is important to

remind ourselves that the hard core of a research program is irrefutable within the terms of the paradigm. When anomalies arise that appear to challenge Realist assumptions, the task of Realist analysts is to create auxiliary theories that defend them. These theories permit explanation of anomalies consistent with Realist assumptions. For Lakatos, the key question about a research program concerns whether the auxiliary hypotheses of Realism are "progressive." That is, do they generate new insights, or predict new facts? If not, they are merely exercises in "patching up" gaps or errors on an ad hoc basis, and the research program is degenerative.

Realism cannot be judged fairly on the basis of only one set of standards. Section II addresses the question of fruitfulness by examining works in the central area of Realist theory: the study of conflict, bargaining, and war. Section II then judges Realism by the more difficult test of Lakatos, which (as noted above) is better at asking trenchant questions than at defining a set of standards appropriate to social science. We will see that in one sense, Realism survives these tests, since it still appears as a good starting point for analysis. But it does not emerge either as a comprehensive theory or as a progressive research program in the sense employed by Lakatos. Furthermore, it has difficulty interpreting issues, and linkages among issues, outside of the security sphere: it can even be misleading when applied to these issues without sufficient qualification. It also has little to say about the crucially important question of peaceful change. The achievements of Realism, and the prospect that it can be modified further to make it even more useful, should help students of world politics to avoid unnecessary self-deprecation. Yet they certainly do not justify complacency.

II. PROGRESS WITHIN THE REALIST PARADIGM: THREE ACHIEVEMENTS

The fruitfulness of contemporary Realist analysis is best evaluated by considering some of the finest work in the genre. Poor scholarship can derive from even the best research program; only the most insightful work reveals the strengths as well as the limits of a theoretical approach. In this section I will consider three outstanding examples of works that begin, at least, from Realist concerns and assumptions: Waltz's construction of balance of power theory in *Theory of International Politics* (1979); the attempt by Glenn Snyder and Paul Diesing in *Conflict Among Nations* (1977) to apply formal game-theoretic models of bargaining to sixteen case studies of major-power crises during the seventy-five years between Fashoda and the Yom Kippur "alert crisis" of 1973; and Robert Gilpin's fine recent book, *War and Change in World Politics* (1981). These works are chosen to provide us with one systematic attempt to develop structural Realist theory, one study of bargaining in specific cases, and one effort to understand broad patterns of international political change. Other recent works could have been chosen instead, such as three books on international conflict and crisis published in 1980 or 1981 (Brecher, 1980; Bueno de Mesquita, 1981; Lebow, 1981), or the well-known works by Nazli Choucri and Robert C. North (1975) or by Alexander George and Richard Smoke (1974). But there are limits on what can be done in a single chapter of limited size.

Balance of Power Theory: Waltz

Waltz has explicated balance of power theory as a central element in his Structural Realist synthesis: "If there is any distinctively political theory of international politics, balance of power theory is it" (1979, p. 117). The realization that balances of power periodically form in world politics, is an old one, as are attempts to theorize about it. The puzzle that Waltz addresses is how to "cut through such confusion" as has existed about it: that is, in Kuhn's words, how to "achieve the anticipated in a new way" (1962, p. 36).

Waltz attacks this problem by using the concept of structure, which he has carefully developed earlier in the book, and which he also employs to account for the dreary persistence of patterns of international action (1979, pp. 66–72). Balance of power theory applies to "anarchic" realms, which are formally unorganized and in which, therefore, units have to worry about their survival: "Self-help is necessarily the principle of action in an anarchic order" (p. 111). In Waltz's system, states (which are similar to one another in function) are the relevant actors; they use external as well as internal means to achieve their goals. Relative capabilities are (as we saw above) the variable element of structure; as they change, we expect coalitional patterns or patterns of internal effort to be altered as well. From his assumptions, given the condition for the theory's operation (self-help), Waltz deduces "the expected outcome: namely, the formation of balances of power" (p. 118). His solution to the puzzle that he has set for himself is carefully formulated and ingenious.

Nevertheless, Waltz's theory of the balance of power encounters some difficulties. First, it is difficult for him to state precisely the conditions under which coalitions will change. He only forecasts that balances of power will periodically recur. Indeed, his theory is so general that it hardly meets the difficult tests that he himself establishes for theory. In Chapter 1 we are told that to test a theory, one must "devise a number of distinct and demanding tests" (1979, p. 13). But such tests are not proposed for balance of power theory: "Because only a loosely defined and inconstant condition of balance is predicted, it is difficult to say that any given distribution of power falsifies the theory" (p. 124). Thus rather than applying demanding tests, Waltz advises that we "should seek *confirmation* through observation of difficult cases" (p. 125, emphasis added). In other words, he counsels that we should search through history to find examples that conform to the predictions of the theory: he then proclaims that "these examples tend to confirm the theory" (p. 125). Two pages later, Waltz appears to change his view, admitting that "we can almost always find confirming cases if we look hard." We should correct for this by looking "for instances of states conforming to common international practices even though for internal reasons they would prefer not to" (p. 127). But Waltz is again making an error against which he warns us. He is not examining a universe of cases, in all of which states would prefer not to conform to "international practice," and asking how often they nevertheless do conform. Instead, he is looking only at the latter cases, chosen *because* they are consistent with his theory. Building grand theory that meets Popperian standards of scientific practice is inherently difficult; even the best scholars, such as Waltz, have trouble simultaneously saying what they want to say and abiding by their canons of scientific practice.

Waltz's theory is also ambiguous with respect to the status of three assumptions that are necessary to a strong form of Structural Realism. I have already mentioned the difficult problem of whether a structural theory must (implausibly) assume fungibility of power resources. Since this problem is less serious with respect to balance of power theory than in a broader context, I will not pursue it here, but will return to it in Section III. Yet Waltz is also, in his discussion of balances of power, unclear on the questions of rationality and interests.

Waltz argues that his assumptions do not include the rationality postulate: "The theory says simply that if some do relatively well, others will emulate them or fall by the wayside" (p. 118). This evolutionary principle, however, can hold only for systems with many actors, experiencing such severe pressure on resources that many will disappear over time. Waltz undermines this argument by pointing out later (p. 137) that "the death rate for states is remarkably low." Furthermore, he relies explicitly on the rationality principle to show that bipolar balances must be stable. "Internal balancing," he says, "is more reliable and precise than external balancing. States are less likely to misjudge their relative strengths than they are to misjudge the strength and reliability of opposing coalitions" (p. 168). I conclude that Waltz does rely on the rationality argument, despite his earlier statement to the contrary.

The other ambiguity in Waltz's balance of power theory has to do with the interests, or motivations, of states. Waltz recognizes that any theory of state behavior must ascribe (by assumption) some motivations to states, just as microeconomic theory ascribes motivations to firms. It is not reductionist to do so as long as these motivations are not taken as varying from state to state as a result of their internal characteristics. Waltz specifies such motivations: states "at a minimum, seek their own preservation, and at a maximum, drive for universal domination" (p. 118).

For his balance of power theory to work, Waltz needs to assume that states seek self-preservation, since if at least some major states did not do so, there would be no reason to expect that roughly equivalent coalitions (i.e., "balances of power") would regularly form. The desire for self-preservation makes states that are behind in a struggle for power try harder, according to Waltz, and leads states allied to a potential hegemon to switch coalitions in order to construct balances of power. Neither of these processes on which Waltz relies to maintain a balance—intensified effort by the weaker country in a bipolar system and coalition formation against potentially dominant states in a multipolar system—could operate reliably without this motivation.

The other aspect of Waltz's motivational assumption—that states "at a maximum, drive for universal domination," is reminiscent of the implication of Realists such as Morgenthau that states seek to "maximize power." For a third-image Realist theory such as Waltz's, such an assumption is unnecessary. Waltz's defense of it is that the balance of power depends on the possibility that force may be used. But this possibility is an attribute of the self-help international system, for Waltz, rather than a reflection of the actors' characteristics. That some states seek universal domination is not a necessary condition for force to be used.

This ambiguity in Waltz's analysis points toward a broader ambiguity in Realist thinking: *Balance of power theory is inconsistent with the assumption frequently made by Realists that states "maximize power,"* if power is taken to refer to tangible resources that can be used to induce other actors to do what they would not otherwise do, through the threat or infliction of deprivations.[18] States concerned with self-preservation do not seek to maximize their power when they are not in danger. On the contrary, they recognize a trade-off between aggrandizement and self-preservation; they realize that a relentless search for universal domination may jeopardize their own autonomy. Thus they moderate their efforts when their positions are secure. Conversely, they intensify their efforts when danger arises, which assumes that they were not maximizing them under more benign conditions.

One might have thought that Realists would readily recognize this point, yet they seem drawn against their better judgment to the "power maximization" or "universal domination" hypotheses. In part, this may be due to their anxiety to emphasize the significance of force in world politics. Yet there may be theoretical as well as rhetorical reasons for their ambivalence. The assumption of power maximization makes possible strong inferences about behavior that would be impossible if we assumed only that states "sometimes" or "often" sought to aggrandize themselves. In that case, we would have to ask about competing goals, some of which would be generated by the internal social, political, and economic characteristics of the countries concerned. Taking into account these competing goals relegates Structural Realism to the status of partial, incomplete theory.

Waltz's contribution to the study of world politics is conceptual. He helps us think more clearly about the role of systemic theory, the explanatory power of structural models, and how to account deductively for the recurrent formation of balances of power. He shows that the international system shapes state behavior as well as vice versa. These are major contributions. But Waltz does not point out "new ways of seeing" international relations that point toward major novelties. He reformulates and systematizes Realism, and thus develops what I have called Structural Realism, consistent with the fundamental assumptions of his classical predecessors.

Game Theory, Structure and Bargaining: Snyder and Diesing

Game theory has yielded some insights into issues of negotiations, crises, and limited war, most notably in the early work of Thomas Schelling (1960). Snyder and Diesing's contribution to this line of analysis, as they put it, is to "distinguish and analyze nine different kinds of bargaining situations, each one a unique combination of power and interest relations between the bargainers, each therefore having its own dynamics and problems" (1977, pp. 181–182). They employ their game-theoretic formulations of these nine situations, within an explicit structural context, to analyze sixteen historical cases.

This research design is consistent with the hard core of Realism. Attention is concentrated on the behavior of states. In the initial statement of the problem, the rationality assumption, in suitably modest form, is retained: each actor attempts "to maximize expected value across a given set of consistently ordered objectives given the information actually available to the actor or which he could reasonably acquire in the time available for decision" (p. 181). Interests are defined to a considerable extent in terms of power: that is, power factors are built into the game structure. In the game of "Protector," for instance, the more powerful state can afford to "go it alone" without its ally, and thus has an interest in doing so under certain conditions, whereas its weaker partner cannot (pp. 145–147). Faced with the game matrix, states, as rational actors, calculate their interests and act accordingly. The structure of world politics, as Waltz defines it, is reflected in the matrices and becomes the basis for action.

If structural Realism formed a sufficient basis for the understanding of international crises, we could fill in the entries in the matrices solely on the basis of states' positions in the international system, given our knowledge of the fact that they perform "similar functions," including the need to survive as autonomous entities. Interests would indeed be defined in terms of power. This would make game theory a powerful analytic tool, which could even help us predict certain outcomes. Where the game had no unique solution (because of strategic indeterminacy), complete predictability of outcomes could not be achieved, but our expectations about the range of likely action would have been narrowed.

Yet Snyder and Diesing find that even knowledge of the values and goals of top leaders could not permit them to determine the interests of about half the decision-making units in their cases. In the other cases, one needed to understand intragovernmental politics, even when one ignored the impact of wider domestic political factors (pp. 510–511). The "internal-external interaction" is a key to the understanding of crisis bargaining.

As Snyder and Diesing make their analytical framework more complex and move into detailed investigation of their cases, their focus shifts toward concern with cognition and with the effects on policy of ignorance, misperception, and misinformation. In my view, the most creative and insightful of their chapters use ideas developed largely by Robert Jervis (1976) to analyze information processing and decision-making. These chapters shift the focus of attention away from the systemic-level factors reflected in the game-theoretic matrices, toward problems of perception, personal bias, and group decision-making (Snyder & Diesing, 1977, Chapter IV and V).

Thus Snyder and Diesing begin with the hard core of Realism, but their most important contributions depend on their willingness to depart from these assumptions. They are dissatisfied with their initial game-theoretic classificatory scheme. They prefer to explore information processing and decision-making, without a firm deductive theory on which to base their arguments, rather than merely to elucidate neat logical typologies.

Is the work of Snyder and Diesing a triumph of Realism or a defeat? At this point in the argument, perhaps the most that can be said is that it indicates that work in the Realist tradition, analyzing conflict and bargaining with the concepts of interests and power, continues to be fruitful, but it does not give reason for much confidence that adhering strictly to Realist assumptions will lead to important advances in the field.

Cycles of Hegemony and War: Gilpin

In *War and Change in World Politics,* Gilpin uses Realist assumptions to reinterpret the last 2400 years of Western history. Gilpin assumes that states, as the principal actors in world politics, make cost-benefit calculations about alternative courses of action. For instance, states attempt to change the international system as the expected benefits of so doing exceed the costs. Thus, the rationality assumption is applied explicitly, in a strong form, although it is relaxed toward the end of the book (1981, pp. 77, 202). Furthermore, considerations of power, relative to the structure of the international system, are at the core of the calculations made by Gilpin's states: "the distribution of power among states constitutes the principal form of control in every international system" (p. 29). Thus Gilpin accepts the entire hard core of the classical Realist research program as I have defined it.[19]

Gilpin sees world history as an unending series of cycles: "The conclusion of one hegemonic war is the beginning of another cycle of growth, expansion, and eventual decline" (p. 210). As power is redistributed, power relations become inconsistent with the rules governing the system and, in particular, the hierarchy of prestige: war establishes the new hierarchy of prestige and "thereby determines which states will in effect govern the international system" (p. 33).

The view that the rules of a system, and the hierarchy of prestige, must be consistent with underlying power realities is a fundamental proposition of Realism, which follows from its three core assumptions. If states, as the central actors of international relations, calculate their interests in terms of power, they will seek international rules and institutions that are consistent with these interests by maintaining their power. Waltz's conception of structure helps to systematize this argument, but it is essentially static. What Gilpin adds is a proposed solution to the anomalies (for static Realism) that institutions and rules can become inconsistent with power realities over time, and that hegemonic states eventually decline. If, as Realists argue, "the strong do what they can and the weak suffer what they must" (Thucydides, Book V, paragraph 90 [Chapter XVII, Modern Library edition, p. 331]), why should hegemons ever lose their power? We know that rules do not always reinforce the power of the strong and that hegemons do sometimes lose their hold, but static Realist theory cannot explain this.

In his attempt to explain hegemonic decline, Gilpin formulates a "law of uneven growth":

> According to Realism, the fundamental cause of wars among states and changes in international systems is the uneven growth of power among states. Realist writers from Thucydides and MacKinder to present-day scholars have attributed the dynamics of international relations to the fact that the distribution of power in an international system shifts over a period of time: this shift results in profound changes in the relationships among states and eventually changes in the nature of the international system itself. (p. 94)

This law, however, restates the problem without resolving it. In accounting for this pattern, Gilpin relies on three sets of processes. One has to do with increasing, and then diminishing, marginal returns from empire. As empires grew, "the economic surplus had to increase faster than the cost of war" (p. 115). Yet sooner or later, diminishing returns set in: "the law of diminishing returns has universal applicability and causes the growth of every society to describe an S-shaped curve" (p. 159). Secondly, hegemonic states tend increasingly to consume more and invest less; Gilpin follows the lead of Carlo Cipolla in viewing this as a general pattern in history (Cipolla, 1970). Finally, hegemonic states decline because of a process of diffusion of technology to others. In *U.S. Power and the Multinational Corporation* (1975), Gilpin emphasized this process as contributing first to the decline of Britain, then in the 1970s to that of the United States. In *War and Change* he makes the argument more general:

> Through a process of diffusion to other states, the dominant power loses the advantage on which its political, military, or economic success has been based. Thus, by example, and frequently in more direct fashion, the dominant power helps to create challenging powers. (p. 176)

This third argument is systemic, and, therefore, fully consistent with Waltz's Structural Realism. The other two processes, however, reflect the operation of forces within the society, as well as international forces. A hegemonic power may suffer diminishing returns as a result of the expansion of its defense perimeter and the increased military costs that result (Gilpin, 1981, p. 191; Luttwak, 1976). But whether diminishing returns set in also depends on internal factors such as technological inventiveness of members of the society and the institutions that affect incentives for innovation (North, 1981). The tendency of hegemonic states to consume more and invest less is also, in part, a function of their dominant positions in the world system: they can force costs of adjustment to change onto others, at least for some time. But it would be hard to deny that the character of the society affects popular tastes for luxury, and, therefore, the tradeoffs between guns and butter that are made. Eighteenth Century Saxony and Prussia were different in this regard; so are contemporary America and Japan. In Gilpin's argument as in Snyder and Diesing's, the "external-internal interaction" becomes a crucial factor in explaining state action, and change.

Gilpin explicitly acknowledges his debt to Classical Realism: "In honesty, one must inquire whether or not twentieth-century students of international relations know anything that Thucydides and his fifth-century compatriots did not know about the behavior of states" (p. 227). For Gilpin as for Thucydides, changes in power lead to changes in relations among states: the *real* cause of the Peloponnesian War, for Thucydides, was the rise of the power of Athens and the fear this evoked in the Spartans and their allies. Gilpin has generalized the theory put forward by Thucydides to explain the Peloponnesian War, and has applied it to the whole course of world history:

> Disequilibrium replaces equilibrium, and the world moves toward a new round of hegemonic conflict. It has always been thus and always will be, until men either destroy themselves or learn to develop an effective mechanism of peaceful change. (p. 210)

This Thucydides–Gilpin theory is a systemic theory of change only in a limited sense. It explains the *reaction* to change systematically, in a rationalistic, equilibrium model. Yet at a more fundamental level, it does not account fully for the sources of change. As we saw above, although it is insightful about systemic factors leading to hegemonic decline, it also has to rely on internal processes to explain the observed effects. Furthermore, it does not account well for the rise of hegemons in the first place, or for the fact that certain contenders emerge rather than others.[20] Gilpin's systemic theory does not account for the extraordinary bursts of energy that occasionally catapult particular countries into dominant positions on the world scene. Why were the Athenians, in words that Thucydides attributes to Corinthian envoys to Sparta, "addicted to innovation," whereas the Spartans were allegedly characterized by a "total want of invention" (Thucydides, Book I, paragraph 70 [Chapter III, Modern Library edition, p. 40])? Like other structural theories, Gilpin's theory underpredicts outcomes. It contributes to our understanding but (as its author recognizes) does not explain change.

This is particularly true of peaceful change, which Gilpin identifies as a crucial issue: "The fundamental problem of international relations in the contemporary world is the problem of peaceful adjustment to the consequences of the uneven growth of power among states, just as it was in the past" (p. 230).

Gilpin's book, like much contemporary American work on international politics, is informed and propelled by concern with peaceful change under conditions of declining hegemony. Gilpin sympathetically discusses E. H. Carr's "defense of peaceful change as the solution to the problem of hegemonic war," written just before World War II (Gilpin, p. 206; Carr, 1939/1946). Yet peaceful change does not fit easily into Gilpin's analytical framework, since it falls, by and large, into the category of "interactions change," which does not entail alteration in the overall hierarchy of power and prestige in a system, and Gilpin deliberately avoids focusing on interactions change (p. 44). Yet after one puts down *War and Change*, the question of how institutions and rules can be developed *within* a given international system, to reduce the probability of war and promote peaceful change, looms even larger than it did before.

Thus Gilpin's sophisticated adaptation of Classical Realism turns us away from Realism. Classical Realism, with its philosophical roots in a tragic conception of the human condition, directs our attention in the twentieth century to the existential situation of modern humanity, doomed apparently to recurrent conflict in a world with weapons that could destroy life on our planet. But Realism, whether classical or structural, has little to say about how to deal with that situation since it offers few insights into the international rules and institutions that people invent to reduce risk and uncertainty in world affairs in the hope of ameliorating the security dilemma.[21] Morgenthau put his hopes in diplomacy (1966, chapter 32). This is a practical art far removed from the abstractions of structural Realism. But diplomacy takes place within a context of international rules, institutions, and practices, which affect the incentives of the actors (Keohane, 1982). Gilpin realizes this, and his gloomy argument—hardly alleviated by a more optimistic epilogue—helps us to understand their importance, although it does not contribute to an explanation of their creation or demise.

Conclusions

Realism, as developed through a long tradition dating from Thucydides, continues to provide the basis for valuable research in international relations. This point has been made by looking at writers who explicitly draw on the Realist tradition, and it can be reinforced by briefly examining some works of Marxist scholars. If they incorporate elements of Realism despite their general antipathy to its viewpoint, our conclusion that Realism reflects enduring realities of world politics will be reinforced.

For Marxists, the fundamental forces affecting world politics are those of class struggle and uneven development. International history is dynamic and dialectical rather than cyclical. The maneuvers of states, on which Realism focuses, reflect the stages of capitalist development and the contradictions of that development. Nevertheless, in analyzing the surface manifestations of world politics under capitalism, Marxists adopt similar categories to those of Realists. Power is crucial; world systems are periodically dominated by hegemonic powers wielding both economic and military resources.

Lenin defined imperialism differently than do the Realists, but he analyzed its operation in part as a Realist would, arguing that "there can be *no* other conceivable basis under capitalism for the division of spheres of influence, of interests, of colonies, etc. than a calculation of the *strength* of the participants in the division. . . . " (Lenin, 1916/1939, p. 119).

Immanuel Wallerstein provides another example of my point. He goes to some effort to stress that modern world history should be seen as the history of capitalism as a world system. Apart from "relatively minor accidents" provided by geography, peculiarities of history, or luck—which give one country an edge over others at crucial historical junctures—"it is the operations of the world-market forces which accentuate the differences, institutionalize them, and make them impossible to surmount over the long run" (1979, p. 21). Nevertheless, when his attention turns to particular epochs, Wallerstein emphasizes hegemony and the role of military force. Dutch economic hegemony in the seventeenth century was destroyed in quintessential Realist fashion, not by the operation of the world-market system, but by the force of British and French arms (Wallerstein, 1980, pp. 38–39).

The insights of Realism are enduring. They cross ideological lines. Its best contemporary exponents use Realism in insightful ways. Waltz has systematized the basic assumptions of Classical Realism in what I have called Structural Realism. Snyder and Diesing have employed this framework for the analysis of bargaining; Gilpin has used the classical arguments of Thucydides to explore problems of international change. For all of these writers, Realism fruitfully focuses attention on fundamental issues of power, interests, and rationality. But as we have seen many of the most interesting questions raised by these authors cannot be answered within the Realist framework.

III. EXPLANATIONS OF OUTCOMES FROM POWER: HYPOTHESES AND ANOMALIES

A Structural Realist theory of interests could be used both for explanation and for prescription. If we could deduce a state's interests from its position in the system, via the rationality assumption, its behavior could be explained on the basis of systemic analysis. Efforts to define the national interest on an a priori basis, however, or to use the concept for prediction and explanation, have been unsuccessful. We saw above that the inability to define interests independently of observed state behavior robbed Snyder and Diesing's game-theoretical matrices of predictive power. More generally, efforts to show that external considerations of power and position play a dominant role in determining the "national interest" have failed. Even an analyst as sympathetic to Realism as Stephen D. Krasner has concluded, in studying American foreign economic policy, that the United States was "capable of defining its own autonomous goals" in a non-logical manner (1978, p. 333). That is, the systemic constraints emphasized by Structural Realism were not binding on the American government during the first thirty years after the Second World War.

Sophisticated contemporary thinkers in the Realist tradition, such as Gilpin, Krasner, and Waltz, understand that interests cannot be derived, simply on the basis of rational calculation, from the external positions of states, and that this is particularly true for great powers, on which, ironically, Structural Realism focuses its principal attentions (Gilpin, 1975; Waltz, 1967). Realist analysis has to retreat to a "fall-back position": that, given state interests, whose origins are not predicted by the theory, patterns of outcomes in world politics will be determined by the overall distribution of power among states. This represents a major concession for systemically-oriented analysts, which it is important not to forget. Sensible Realists are highly cognizant of the role of domestic politics and of actor choices within the constraints and incentives provided by the system. Since systemic theory cannot predict state interests, it cannot support deterministic conclusions (Sprout & Sprout, 1971, pp. 73–77). This limitation makes it both less powerful as a theory, and less dangerous as an ideology.[22] Despite its importance, it cannot stand alone.

When realist theorists say that, given interests, patterns of outcomes will be determined by the overall distribution of power among states, they are using "power" to refer to resources that can be used to induce other actors to do what they would not otherwise do, in accordance with the desires of the power-wielder. "Outcomes" refer principally to two sets of patterns: (1) the results of conflicts, diplomatic or military, that take place between states; and (2) changes in the rules and institutions that regulate relations among governments in world politics. This section focuses on conflicts, since they pose the central puzzles that Realism seeks to explain. Section IV and the Conclusion consider explanations of changes in rules and institutions.

Recent quantitative work seems to confirm that power capabilities (measured not only in terms of economic resources but with political variables added) are rather good predictors of the outcomes of wars. Bueno de Mesquita finds, for example, that countries with what he calls positive "expected utility" (a measure that uses composite capabilities but adjusts them for distance, alliance relationships, and uncertainty) won 179 conflicts while losing only 54 between 1816 and 1974, for a success ratio of over 75% (1981, especially p. 151; Organski & Kugler, 1980, Chapter 2).

The question of the fungibility of power poses a more troublesome issue. As I have noted earlier (see footnote 19), Structural Realism is ambiguous on this point; the desire for parsimonious theory impels Realists toward a unitary notion of power as homogeneous and usable for a variety of purposes, but close examination of the complexities of world politics induces caution about such an approach. In his discussion of system structure, for instance, Waltz holds that "the units of an anarchic system are distinguished primarily by their greater or lesser capabilities for performing similar tasks," and that the distribution of capabilities across a system is the principal characteristic differentiating international-political structures from one another (1979, pp. 97, 99). Thus each international political system has one structure. Yet in emphasizing the continued role of military power, Waltz admits that military power is not perfectly fungible: "Differences in strength do matter, *although not for every conceivable purpose*"; "military power no longer brings political control, but then it never did" (1979, pp. 189, 191, emphasis added). This seems to imply that any given international system is likely to have *several* structures, differing by issue-areas and according to the resources that can be used to affect outcomes. Different sets of capabilities will qualify as "power resources" under different conditions. This leads to a much less parsimonious theory and a much more highly differentiated view of the world, in which what Nye and I called "issue-structure" theories play a major role, and in which military force, although still important, is no longer assumed to be at the top of a hierarchy of power resources (Keohane & Nye, 1977, chs. 3 and 6).

The status in a Structural Realist theory of the fungibility assumption affects both its power and the incidence of anomalies. A strong version of Structural Realism that assumed full fungibility of power across issues would predict that when issues arise between great powers and smaller states, the great powers should prevail. This has the advantage of generating a clear prediction and the liability of being wrong much of the time. Certainly it does not fit the American experience of the last two decades. The United States lost a war in Vietnam and was for more than a year unable to secure the return of its diplomats held hostage in Iran. Small allies such as Israel, heavily dependent on the United States have displayed considerable freedom of action. In the U.S.-Canadian relationship of the 1950s and 1960s, which was virtually free of threats of force, outcomes of conflicts as often favored the Canadian as the American position although this was not true for relations between Australia and the United States (Keohane & Nye, 1977, Chapter 7).

In view of power theory in social science, the existence of these anomalies is not surprising. As James G. March observes, "there appears to be general consensus that either potential power is different from actually exerted power or that actually exerted power is variable (1966, p. 57). That is, what March calls "basic force models," which rely, like Realist theory, on measurable indices of power, are inadequate tools for either prediction or explanation. They are often valuable in suggesting long-term trends and patterns, but they do not account well for specific outcomes: the more that is demanded of them, the less well they are likely to perform.

Lakatos's discussion of scientific research programs leads us to expect that, when confronted with anomalies, theorists will create auxiliary theories that preserve the credibility of their fundamental assumptions. Thus it is not surprising that Realists committed to the fungibility assumption have devised auxiliary hypotheses to protect its "hard core" against challenge. One of these is what David Baldwin calls the "conversion-process explanation" of unanticipated outcomes:

> The would-be wielder of power is described as lacking in skill and/or the "will" to use his power resources effectively: "The Arabs had the tanks but didn't know how to use them." "The Americans had the bombs but lacked the will to use them." (1979, pp. 163–164)

The conversion-process explanation is a classic auxiliary hypothesis, since it is designed to protect the assumption that power resources are homogeneous and fungible. If we were to accept the conversion-process account, we could continue to believe in a single structure of power, even if outcomes do not favor the "stronger" party. This line of argument encounters serious problems, however, when it tries to account for the discrepancy between anticipated and actual outcomes by the impact of intangible resources (such as intelligence, training, organization, foresight) not recognized until after the fact. The problem with this argument lies in its post hoc quality. It is theoretically degenerate in Lakatos's sense, since it does not add any explanatory power to structural Realist theory, but merely "explains away" uncomfortable facts.

Thus what March says about "force activation models" applies to

Structural Realist theories when the conversion-process explanation relies upon sources of power that can be observed only after the events to be explained have taken place:

> If we observe that power exists and is stable and if we observe that sometimes weak people seem to triumph over strong people, we are tempted to rely on an activation hypothesis to explain the discrepancy. But if we then try to use the activation hypothesis to predict the results of social-choice procedures, we discover that the data requirements of 'plausible' activation models are quite substantial. As a result, we retreat to what are essentially degenerate forms of the activation model—retaining some of the form but little of the substance. This puts us back where we started, looking for some device to explain our failures in prediction. (1966, p. 61).

A second auxiliary hypothesis designed to protect the fungibility assumption must be taken more seriously: that discrepancies between power resources and outcomes are explained by an asymmetry of motivation in favor of the objectively weaker party. Following this logic, John Harsanyi has proposed the notion of power "in a schedule sense," describing how various resources can be translated into social power. An actor with intense preferences on an issue may be willing to use more resources to attain a high probability of a favorable result, than an actor with more resources but lower intensity. As a result, outcomes may not accurately reflect underlying power resources (Harsanyi, 1962).

To use this insight progressively rather than in a degenerate way, Realist theory needs to develop indices of intensity of motivation that can be measured independently of the behavior that theorists are trying to explain. Russett, George, and Bueno de Mesquita are among the authors who have attempted, with some success, to do this (Russett, 1963; George et al., 1971; Bueno de Mesquita, 1981). Insofar as motivation is taken simply as a control, allowing us to test the impact of varying power configurations more successfully, Harsanyi's insights can be incorporated into structural Realist theory. If it became a key variable, however, the effect could be to transform a systemic theory into a decision-making one.

An alternative approach to relying on such auxiliary hypotheses is to relax the fungibility assumption itself. Failures of great powers to control smaller ones could be explained on the basis of independent evidence that in the relevant issue-areas, the states that are weaker on an overall basis have more power resources than their stronger partners, and that the use of power derived from one area of activity to affect outcomes in other areas (through "linkages") is difficult. Thus Saudi Arabia can be expected to have more impact on world energy issues than on questions of strategic arms control; Israel more influence over the creation of a Palestinian state than on the reconstruction of the international financial and debt regime.

Emphasizing the problematic nature of power fungibility might help to create more discriminating power models, but it will not resolve the inherent problems of power models, as identified by March and others. Furthermore, at the limit, to deny fungibility entirely risks a complete disintegration of predictive power. Baldwin comes close to this when he argues that what he calls the "policy-contingency framework" of an influence attempt must be specified before power explanations are employed. If we defined each issue as existing within a unique "policy-contingency framework," no generalizations would be possible. Waltz could reply, if he accepted Baldwin's view of power, that all of world politics should be considered a single policy-contingency framework, characterized by anarchy and self-help.[23] According to this argument, the parsimony gained by assuming the fungibility of power would compensate for the marginal mispredictions of such a theory.

This is a crucial theoretical issue, which should be addressed more explicitly by theorists of world politics. In my view, the dispute cannot be resolved a priori. The degree to which power resources have to be disaggregated in a structural theory depends both on the purposes of the theory and on the degree to which behavior on distinct issues is linked together through the exercise of influence by actors. The larger the domain of a theory, the less accuracy of detail we expect. Since balance of power theory seeks to explain large-scale patterns of state action over long periods of time, we could hardly expect the precision from it that we demand from theories whose domains have been narrowed.

This assertion suggests that grand systemic theory can be very useful as a basis for further theoretical development in international relations, even if the theory is lacking in precision, and it therefore comprises part of my defense of the Realist research program as a foundation on which scholars should build. Yet this argument needs immediate qualification.

Even if a large-scale theory can be developed and appropriately tested, its predictions will be rather gross. To achieve a more finely-tuned understanding of how resources affect behavior in particular situations, one needs to specify the policy-contingency framework more precisely. The domain of theory is narrowed to achieve greater precision. Thus the debate between advocates of parsimony and proponents of contextual subtlety resolves itself into a question of *stages,* rather than an either/or choice. We should seek parsimony first, then add complexity while monitoring the adverse effects that this has on the predictive power of our theory: its ability to make significant inferences on the basis of limited information.

To introduce greater complexity into an initially spare theoretical structure, the conception of an issue-area, developed many years ago by Robert A. Dahl (1961) and adapted for use in international relations by James N. Rosenau (1966), is a useful device. Having tentatively selected an area of activity to investigate, the analyst needs to delineate issue-areas at various levels of aggregation. Initial explanations should seek to account for the main features of behavior at a high level of aggregation—such as the international system as a whole—while subsequent hypotheses are designed to apply only to certain issue-areas.

In some cases, more specific issue-areas are "nested" within larger ones (Aggarwal, 1981; Snidal, 1981). For instance, North Atlantic fisheries issues constitute a sub-set of fisheries issues in general, which comprise part of the whole area of oceans policy, or "law of the sea." In other cases, specific issues may belong to two or more broader issues: the question of passage through straits, for example, involves questions of military security as well as the law of the sea.

Definitions of issue-areas depend on the beliefs of participants, as well as on the purposes of the investigator. In general, however definitions of issue-areas should be made on the basis of empirical judgments about the extent to which governments regard sets of issues as closely interdependent and treat them collectively. Decisions made on one issue must affect others in the issue-area, either through functional links or through regular patterns of bargaining. These relationships of interdependence among issues may change. Some issue-areas, such as international financial relations, have remained fairly closely linked for decades; others, such as oceans, have changed drastically over the past 35 years (Keohane & Nye, 1977, Chapter 4, especially pp. 64–65; Simon, 1969; Haas, 1980).

When a hierarchy of issue-areas has been identified, power-structure models employing more highly aggregated measures of power resources can be compared with models that disaggregate resources by issue-areas. How much accuracy is gained, and how much parsimony lost, by each step in the disaggregation process? In my view, a variegated analysis, which takes some specific "snapshots" by issue-area as well as looking at the broader picture, is superior to either monistic strategy, whether assuming perfect fungibility or none at all.

This approach represents an adaptation of Realism. It preserves the basic emphasis on power resources as a source of outcomes in general, but it unambiguously jettisons the assumption that power is fungible across all of world politics. Disaggregated power models are less parsimonious than more aggregated ones, and they remain open to the objections to power models articulated by March and others. But in one important sense disaggregation is progressive rather than degenerative. Disaggregated models call attention to linkages among issue-areas, and raise the question: under what conditions, and with what effects, will such linkages arise? Current research suggests that understanding linkages systematically, rather than merely describing them on an ad hoc basis, will add significantly to our comprehension of world politics (Oye, 1979, 1983; Stein, 1980; Tollison & Willett, 1979). It would seem worthwhile, in addition, for more empirical work to be done on this subject, since we know so little about when, and how, linkages are made.

Conclusions

Structural Realism is a good starting-point for explaining the outcomes of conflicts, since it directs attention to fundamental questions of interest and power within a logically coherent and parsimonious theoretical framework. Yet the ambitious attempt of Structural Realist theory to deduce national interests from system structure via the rationality postulate has been unsuccessful. Even if interests are taken as given, the attempt to predict outcomes from interests and power leads to ambiguities and incorrect predictions. The auxiliary theory attributing this failure to conversion-processes often entails unfalsifiable tautology rather than genuine explanation. Ambiguity prevails on the question of the fungibility of power: whether there is a single structure of the international system or several. Thus the research program of Realism reveals signs of degeneration. It certainly does not meet Lakatos' tough standards for progressiveness.

More attention to developing independent measures of intensity of motivation, and greater precision about the concept of power and its relationship to the context of action, may help to correct some of these faults. Careful disaggregation of power-resources by issue-area may help to improve the predictive capability of structural models, at the risk of reducing theoretical parsimony. As I argue in the next section, modified structural models, indebted to Realism although perhaps too different to be considered Realist themselves, may be valuable elements in a multi-level framework for understanding world politics.

Yet to some extent the difficulties encountered by Structural Realism reflect the inherent limitations of structural models which will not be corrected by mere modifications or the relaxation of assumptions. Domestic politics and decision-making, Snyder and Diesing's "internal-external interactions," and the workings of international institutions all play a role, along with international political structure, in affecting state behavior and outcomes. Merely to catalog these factors, however, is not to contribute to theory but rather to compound the descriptive anarchy that already afflicts the field, with too many independent variables, exogenously determined, chasing too few cases. As Waltz emphasizes, the role of unit-level forces can only be properly understood if we comprehend the structure of the international system within which they operate.

IV. BEYOND STRUCTURAL REALISM

Structural Realism helps us to understand world politics as in part a systemic phenomenon, and provides us with a logically coherent theory that establishes the context for state action. This theory, because it is relatively simple and clear, can be modified progressively to attain closer correspondence with reality. Realism's focus on interests and power is central to an understanding of how nations deal with each other. Its adherents have understood that a systemic theory of international relations must account for state behavior by examining the constraints and incentives provided by the system; for this purpose to be accomplished, an assumption of rationality (although not of perfect information) must be made. The rationality assumption allows inferences about state behavior to be drawn solely from knowledge of the structure of the system.

Unfortunately, such predictions are often wrong. The concept of power is difficult to measure validly a priori; interests are underspecified by examining the nature of the international system and the position of various states in it; the view of power resources implied by overall structure theories is overaggregated, exaggerating the extent to which power is like money. The problem that students of international politics face is how to construct theories that draw on Realism's strengths without partaking fully of its weaknesses.

To do this we need a multi-dimensional approach to world politics that incorporates several analytical frameworks or research programs. One of these should be that of Structural Realism, which has the virtues of parsimony and clarity, although the range of phenomena that it encompasses is limited. Another, in my view, should be a modified structural research program, which relaxes some of the assumptions of Structural Realism but retains enough of the hard core to generate a priori predictions on the basis of information about the international environment. Finally, we need better theories of domestic politics, decision-making, and information processing, so that the gap between the external and internal environments can be bridged in a systematic way, rather than by simply adding catalogs of exogenously determined foreign policy facts to theoretically more rigorous structural models. That is, we need more attention to the "internal-external interactions" discussed by Snyder and Diesing.

Too much work in this last category is being done for me to review it in detail here. Mention should be made, however, of some highlights. Peter J. Katzenstein, Peter Gourevitch, and others have done pioneering work on the relationship between domestic political structure and political coalitions, on the one hand, and foreign economic policies, on the other (Katzenstein, 1978; Gourevitch, 1978). This line of analysis, which draws heavily on the work of Alexander Gerschenkron (1962) and Barrington Moore (1966), argues that the different domestic structures characteristic of various advanced industrialized countries result from different historical patterns of development; in particular, whether development came early or late, and what the position of the country was in the international political system at the time of its economic development (Kurth, 1979). Thus it attempts to draw connections both between international and domestic levels of analysis, and across historical time. This research does not provide deductive explanatory models, and it does not account systematically for changes in established structures after the formative developmental period, but its concept of domestic structure brings order into the cacophony of domestic political and economic variables that could affect foreign policy, and therefore suggests the possibility of eventual integration of theories relying on international structure with those focusing on domestic structure.

Katzenstein and his associates focus on broad political, economic, and social patterns within countries, and their relationship to the international division of labor and the world political structure. Fruitful analysis can also be done at the more narrowly intragovernmental level, as Snyder and Diesing show. An emphasis on bureaucratic politics was particularly evident in the 1960s and early 1970s, although Robert J. Art has pointed out in detail a number of difficulties, weaknesses, and contradictions in this literature (1973). At the level of the individual decision-maker, insights can be gained by combining theories of cognitive psychology with a rich knowledge of diplomatic history, as in Jervis's work, as long as the investigator understands the systemic and domestic-structural context within which decision-makers operate.[24] This research program has made decided progress, from the simple-minded notions criticized by Waltz (1959) to the work of Alexander and Juliette George (1964), Alexander George (1980), Ole Holsti (1976) and Jervis (1976).[25]

Despite the importance of this work at the levels of domestic structure, intragovernmental politics, and individual cognition, the rest of my analysis will continue to focus on the concept of international political structure and its relevance to the study of world politics. I will argue that progress could be made by constructing a modified structural research program, retaining some of the parsimony characteristic of Structural Realism and its emphasis on the incentives and constraints of the world system, while adapting it to fit contemporary reality better. Like Realism, this research program would be based on microeconomic theory, particularly oligopoly theory. It would seek to explain actor behavior by specifying a priori utility functions for actors, using the rationality principle as a "trivial animating law" in Popper's sense (Latsis, 1976, p. 21), and deducing behavior from the constraints of the system as modeled in the theory.

Developing such a theory would only be worthwhile if there were something particularly satisfactory both about systemic explanations and about the structural forms of such explanations. I believe that this is the case, for two sets of reasons.

First, systemic theory is important because we must understand the context of action before we can understand the action itself. As Waltz (1979) has emphasized, theories of world politics that fail to incorporate a sophisticated understanding of the operation of the system—that is, how systemic attributes affect behavior—are bad theories. Theoretical analysis of the characteristics of an international system is as important for understanding foreign policy as understanding European history is for understanding the history of Germany.

Second, structural theory is important because it provides an irreplaceable *component* for a thorough analysis of action, by states or non-state actors, in world politics. A good structural theory generates testable implications about behavior on an a priori basis, and, therefore, comes closer than interpretive description to meeting the requirements for scientific knowledge of neo-positivist philosophers of science such as Lakatos. This does not mean, of course, that explanation and rich interpretation—Geertz's "thick description" (1973)—are in any way antithetical to one another. A good analysis of a given problem will include both.[26]

The assumptions of a modified structural research program can be compared to Realist assumptions as follows:

(1) The assumption that the principal actors in world politics are states would remain the same, although more emphasis would be placed on non-state actors, intergovernmental organizations , and transnational and transgovernmental relations than is the case in Realist analysis (Keohane & Nye, 1972).

(2) The rationality assumption would be retained, since without it, as we have seen, inferences from structure to behavior become impossible without heroic assumptions about evolutionary processes or other forces that compel actors to adapt their behavior to their environments. It should be kept in mind, however, as is made clear by sophisticated Realists, that the rationality postulate only assumes that actors make calculations "so as to maximize expected value across a given set of consistently ordered objectives" (Snyder & Diesing, 1977, p. 81). It does not assume perfect information, consideration of all possible alternatives, or unchanging actor preferences.

(3) The assumption that states seek power and calculate their interests accordingly, would be qualified severely. Power and influence would still be regarded as important state interests (as ends or necessary means), but the implication that the search for power constitutes an overriding interest in all cases, or that it always takes the same form, would be rejected. Under different systemic conditions states will define their self-interests differently. For instance, where survival is at stake efforts to maintain autonomy may take precedence over all other activities, but where the environment is relatively benign energies will also be directed to fulfilling other goals. Indeed, over the long run, whether an environment is malign or benign can alter the standard operating procedures and sense of identity of the actors themselves.[27]

In addition, this modified structural approach would explicitly modify the assumption of fungibility lurking behind unitary conceptions of "international structure." It would be assumed that the value of power resources for influencing behavior in world politics depends on the goals sought. Power resources that are well-suited to achieve certain purposes are less effective when used for other objectives. Thus power resources are differentially effective across issue-areas, and the usability of a given set of power resources depends on the "policy-contingency frameworks" within which it must be employed.

This research program would pay much more attention to the roles of institutions and rules than does Structural Realism. Indeed, a structural interpretation of the emergence of international rules and procedures, and of obedience to them by states, is one of the rewards that could be expected from this modified structural research program (Krasner, 1982; Keohane, 1982; Stein, 1982).

This research program would contain a valuable positive heuristic—a set of suggestions about what research should be done and what questions should initially be asked—which would include the following pieces of advice:

(1) When trying to explain a set of outcomes in world politics, always consider the hypothesis that the outcomes reflect underlying power resources, without being limited to it;

(2) When considering different patterns of outcomes in different relationships, or issue-areas, entertain the hypothesis that power resources are differently distributed in these issue-areas, and investigate ways in which these differences promote or constrain actor attempts to link issue-areas in order to use power-resources from one area to affect results in another;

(3) When considering how states define their self-interests, explore the effects of international structure on self-interests, as well as the effects of other international factors and of domestic structure.

Such a modified structural research program could begin to help generate theories that are more discriminating, with respect to the sources of power, than is Structural Realism. It would be less oriented toward reaffirming the orthodox verities of world politics and more inclined to explain variations in patterns of rules and institutions. Its concern with international institutions would facilitate insights into processes of peaceful change. This research program would not solve all of the problems of Realist theory, but it would be a valuable basis for interpreting contemporary world politics.

Yet this form of structural theory still has the weaknesses associated with power analysis. The essential problem is that from a purely systemic point of view, situations of strategic interdependence do not have determinate solutions. No matter how carefully power resources are defined, no power model will be able accurately to predict outcomes under such conditions.[28]

One way to alleviate this problem without moving immediately to the domestic level of analysis (and thus sacrificing the advantages of systemic theory), is to recognize that what it is rational for states to do, and what states' interests are, depend on the institutional context of action as well as on the underlying power realities and state position upon which Realist thought concentrates. Structural approaches should be seen as only a basis for further systemic analysis. They vary the power condition in the system, but they are silent on variations in the frequency of mutual interactions in the system or in the level of information.

The importance of these non-power factors is demonstrated by some recent work on cooperation. In particular, Robert Axelrod has shown that cooperation can emerge among egoists under conditions of strategic interdependence as modelled by the game of prisoners' dilemma. Such a result requires, however, that these egoists expect to continue to interact with each other for the indefinite future, and that these expectations of future interactions be given sufficient weight in their calculations (Axelrod, 1981). This argument reinforces the practical wisdom of diplomats and arms controllers, who assume that state strategies, and the degree of eventual cooperation, will depend significantly on expectations about the future. The "double-cross" strategy, for instance, is more attractive when it is expected to lead to a final, winning move, than when a continuing series of actions and reactions is anticipated.

High levels of uncertainty reduce the confidence with which expectations are held, and may therefore lead governments to discount the future heavily. As Axelrod shows, this can inhibit the evolution of cooperation through reciprocity. It can also reduce the ability of actors to make mutually beneficial agreements at any given time, quite apart from their expectations about whether future interactions will occur. That is, it can lead to a form of "political market failure" (Keohane, 1982).

Information that reduces uncertainty is therefore an important factor in world politics. But information is not a systemic constant. Some international systems are rich in institutions and processes that provide information to governments and other actors; in other systems, information is scarce or of low quality. Given a certain distribution of power (Waltz's "international structure"), variations in information may be important in influencing state behavior. If international institutions can evolve that improve the quality of information and reduce uncertainty, they may profoundly affect international political behavior even in the absence of changes either in international structure (defined in terms of the distribution of power) or in the preference functions of actors.

Taking information seriously at the systemic level could stimulate a new look at theories of information-processing within governments, such as those of Axelrod (1976), George (1980), Jervis (1976), and Holsti (1976). It could also help us, however, to understand a dimension of the concept of complex interdependence (Keohane & Nye, 1977) that has been largely ignored. Complex interdependence can be seen as a condition under which it is not only difficult to use conventional power resources for certain purposes, but under which information levels are relatively high due to the existence of multiple channels of contact among states. If we focus exclusively on questions of power, the most important feature of complex interdependence—almost its *only* important feature—is the ineffectiveness of military force and the constraints that this implies on fungibility of power across issue-areas. Sensitizing ourselves to the role of information, and information-provision, at the international level brings another aspect of complex interdependence—the presence of multiple channels of contact among societies—back into the picture. Actors behave differently in information-rich environments than in information-poor ones where uncertainty prevails.

This is not a subject that can be explored in depth here.[29] I raise it, however, to clarify the nature of the multi-dimensional network of theories and research programs that I advocate for the study of world politics. We need both spare, logically tight theories, such as Structural Realism, and rich interpretations, such as those of the historically-oriented students of domestic structure and foreign policy. But we also need something in-between: systemic theories that retain some of the parsimony of Structural Realism, but that are able to deal better with differentiations between issue-areas, with institutions, and with change. Such theories could be developed on the basis of variations in power (as in Structural Realism), but they could also focus on variations in other systemic characteristics, such as levels and quality of information.

CONCLUSION: WORLD POLITICS AND PEACEFUL CHANGE

As Gilpin points out, the problem of peaceful change is fundamental to world politics. Thermonuclear weapons have made it even more urgent than it was in the past. Realism demonstrates that peaceful change is more difficult to achieve in international politics than within well-ordered domestic societies, but it does not offer a theory of peaceful change.[30] Nor is such a theory available from other research traditions. The question remains for us to grapple with: Under what conditions will adaptations to shifts in power, in available technologies, or in fundamental economic relationships take place without severe economic disruption or warfare?

Recent work on "international regimes" has been addressed to this question, which is part of the broader issue of order in world politics (*International Organization*, Spring, 1982). Structural Realist approaches to understanding the origins and maintenance of international regimes are useful (Krasner, 1982), but since they ignore cognitive issues and questions of information, they comprise only part of the story (Haas, 1982).

Realism, furthermore, is better at telling us why we are in such trouble than how to get out of it. It argues that order can be created from anarchy by the exercise of superordinate power: periods of peace follow establishment of dominance in Gilpin's "hegemonic wars." Realism sometimes seems to imply, pessimistically, that order can *only* be created by hegemony. If the latter conclusion were correct, not only would the world economy soon become chaotic (barring a sudden resurgence of American power), but at some time in the foreseeable future, global nuclear war would ensue.

Complacency in the face of this prospect is morally unacceptable. No serious thinker could, therefore, be satisfied with Realism as the correct theory of world politics, even if the scientific status of the theory were stronger than it is. Our concern for humanity requires us to do what Gilpin does in the epilogue to *War and Change* (1981), where he holds out the hope of a "new and more stable international order" in the final decades of the twentieth century, despite his theory's contention that such a benign outcome is highly unlikely. Although Gilpin could be criticized for inconsistency, this would be beside the point: the conditions of terror under which we live compel us to search for a way out of the trap.

The need to find a way out of the trap means that international relations must be a policy science as well as a theoretical activity.[31] We should be seeking to link theory with practice, bringing insights from Structural Realism, modified structural theories, other systemic approaches, and actor-level analyses to bear on contemporary issues in a sophisticated way. This does not mean that the social scientist should adopt the policy-maker's framework, much less his normative values or blinders about the range of available alternatives. On the contrary, independent observers often do their most valuable work when they reject the normative or analytic framework of those in power, and the best theorists may be those who maintain their distance from those at the center of events. Nevertheless, foreign policy and world politics are too important to be left to bureaucrats, generals, and lawyers—or even to journalists and clergymen.

Realism helps us determine the strength of the trap, but does not give us much assistance in seeking to escape. If we are to promote peaceful change, we need to focus not only on basic long-term forces that determine the shape of world politics independently of the actions of particular decision-makers, but also on variables that to some extent can be manipulated by human action. Since international institutions, rules, and patterns of cooperation can affect calculations of interest, and can also be affected incrementally by contemporary political action, they provide a natural focus for scholarly attention as well as policy concern.[32] Unlike Realism, theories that attempt to explain rules, norms, and institutions help us to understand how to create patterns of cooperation that could be essential to our survival. We need to respond to the questions that Realism poses but fails to answer: How can order be created out of anarchy *without* superordinate power; how can peaceful change occur?

To be reminded of the significance of international relations as policy analysis, and the pressing problem of order, is to recall the tradition of Classical Realism. Classical Realism, as epitomized by the work of John Herz (1981), has recognized that no matter how deterministic our theoretical aspirations may be, there remains a human interest in autonomy and self-reflection. As Ashley puts it, the Realism of a thinker such as Herz is committed to an "emancipatory cognitive interest—an interest in securing freedom from unacknowledged constraints, relations of domination, and conditions of distorted communication and understanding that deny humans the capacity to make their future with full will and consciousness" (1981, p. 227).[33] We think about world politics not because it is aesthetically beautiful, because we believe that it is governed by simple, knowable laws, or because it provides rich, easily accessible data for the testing of empirical hypotheses. Were those concerns paramount, we would look elsewhere. We study world politics because we think it will determine the fate of the earth (Schell, 1982). Realism makes us aware of the odds against us. What we need to do now is to understand peaceful change by combining multi-dimensional scholarly analysis with more visionary ways of seeing the future.

NOTES

1. An unfortunate limitation of this chapter is that its scope is restricted to work published in English, principally in the United States. I recognize that this reflects the Americanocentrism of scholarship in the United States, and I regret it. But I am not sufficiently well-read in works published elsewhere to comment intelligently on them. For recent discussions of the distinctively American stamp that has been placed on the international relations field see Hoffmann (1977) and Lyons (1982).
2. Nye and I, in effect, conceded this in our later work, which was more cautious about the drawbacks of conventional "state-centric" theory. (See Keohane & Nye, 1977.)
3. For a discussion of "theory as a set of questions," see Hoffmann (1960, pp. 1–12).
4. Bruce Russett has written a parallel essay on "International Interactions and Processes: The Internal vs. External Debate Revisited." Professor Russett discusses the extensive literature on arms control and on dependency, neither of which I consider here.
5. Stanley J. Michalak, Jr. pointed out correctly that our characterization of Realism in *Power and Interdependence* was unfair when taken literally, although he also seems to me to have missed the Realist basis of our structural models. (See Michalak, 1979.)
6. It has often been noted that Kuhn's definition of a paradigm was vague: one sympathetic critic identified 21 distinct meanings of the term in Kuhn's relatively brief book (Masterman, 1970). But Lakatos particularly objected to what he regarded as Kuhn's relativism, which in his view interpreted major changes in science as the result of essentially irrational forces. (See Lakatos, 1970, p. 178.)
7. Lakatos' comments on Marxism and psychology were biting, and a colleague of his reports that he doubted the applicability of the methodology of scientific research programs to the social sciences. (See Latsis, 1976, p. 2.)

8. Robert Jervis and Ann Tickner have both reminded me that Morgenthau and John H. Herz, another major proponent of Realist views in the 1950s, later severely qualified their adherence to what has generally been taken as Realist doctrine. (See Herz, 1981, and Boyle, 1980, p. 218.) I am particularly grateful to Dr. Tickner for obtaining a copy of the relevant pages of the latter article for me.

9. For commentary on this assumption, see Keohane and Nye (1972), and Mansbach, Ferguson, and Lampert (1976). In *Power and Interdependence*, Nye and I were less critical than we had been earlier of the state-centric assumption. In view of the continued importance of governments in world affairs, for many purposes it seems justified on grounds of parsimony. Waltz's rather acerbic critique of our earlier position seems to me essentially correct. (See Waltz, 1979, p. 7.)

10. Emphasis added. Thucydides also follows this "positive heuristic" of looking for underlying power realities in discussions of the Athenian–Corcyrean alliance (Chapter II), the decision of the Lacedemonians to vote that Athens had broken the treaty between them (Chapter III), and Pericles' Funeral Oration (Chapter IV). In the Modern Library edition, the passages in question are on pp. 28, 49–50, and 83.

11. Bruce Bueno de Mesquita (1981, pp. 29–33) has an excellent discussion of the rationality assumption as used in the study of world politics.

12. As Waltz points out, Morgenthau's writings reflect the "first-image" Realist view that the evil inherent in man is at the root of war and conflict.

13. Sustained earlier critiques of the fungibility assumption can be found in Keohane and Nye (1977, pp. 49–52) and in Baldwin (1979).

14. In an illuminating recent review essay, John Gerard Ruggie has criticized Waltz's assumption that the second dimension of structure, referring to the degree of differentiation of units, can be regarded as a constant (undifferentiated units with similar functions) in world politics. Ruggie argues that "when the concept differentiation is properly defined, the second structural level of Waltz's model . . . serves to depict the kind of institutional transformation illustrated by the shift from the medieval to the modern international system." See Ruggie (1983, p. 279).

15. Waltz denies that he relies on the rationality assumption; but I argue in Section II that he requires it for his theory of the balance of power to hold.

16. For a brilliant discussion of this theoretical strategy in micro-economics, see Latsis (1976, especially pp. 16–23).

17. Since the principal purpose of Realist analysis in the hands of Waltz and others is to develop an explanation of international political reality, rather than to offer specific advice to those in power, the label, "technical realism," seems too narrow. It also carries a pejorative intent that I do not share. "Structural Realism" captures the focus on explanation through an examination of the structure of the international system. Capitalization is used to indicate that Realism is a specific school, and that it would be possible to be a realist—in the sense of examining reality as it really is—without subscribing to Realist assumptions. For a good discussion, see Krasner (1982).

18. This is the commonsense view of power, as discussed, for example, by Arnold Wolfers (1962, p. 103). As indicated in Section III, any such definition conceals a large number of conceptual problems.

19. My reading of Gilpin's argument on pp. 29–34 led me originally to believe

that he also accepted the notion that power is fungible, since he argues that hegemonic war creates a hierarchy of prestige in an international system, which is based on the hegemon's "demonstrated ability to enforce its will on other states" (p. 34), and which in turn determines governance of the international system (p. 33). This appears to imply that a single structure of power resources exists, usable for a wide variety of issues. But in letters sent to the author commenting on an earlier draft of this paper, both Gilpin and Waltz explicitly disavowed the assumption that power resources are necessarily fungible. In *War and Change*, Gilpin is very careful to disclaim the notion, which he ascribes to Political Realists but which I have not included in the hard core of Realism, that states seek to maximize their power: "Acquisition of power entails an opportunity cost to a society; some other desired good must be abandoned" (p. 51).

20. A similar issue is posed in Chapter 3 of Part II of *Lineages of the Absolutist State* (1974). Its author, Perry Anderson, addresses the puzzle of why it was Prussia, rather than Bavaria or Saxony, that eventually gained predominance in Germany. Despite his inclinations, Anderson has to rely on a variety of conjunctural, if not accidental, factors to account for the observed result.

21. For a lucid discussion of the security dilemma, see Jervis (1978).

22. The fact that sensitive Realists are aware of the limitations of Realism makes me less worried than Ashley about the policy consequences of Realist analysis.

23. Waltz does not accept Baldwin's (and Dahl's) definition of power in terms of causality, arguing that "power is one cause among others, from which it cannot be isolated." But this makes it impossible to falsify any power theory; one can always claim that other factors (not specified a priori) were at work. Waltz's discussion of power (1979, pp. 191–192) does not separate power-as-outcome properly from power-as-resources; it does not distinguish between resources that the observer can assess a priori from those only assessable post hoc; it does not relate probabilistic thinking properly to power theory; and it takes refuge in a notion of power as "affecting others more than they affect him," which would result (if taken literally) in the absurdity of attributing maximum power to the person or government that is least responsive to outside stimuli, regardless of its ability to achieve its purposes.

24. Jervis (1976, Chapter 1) has an excellent discussion of levels of analysis and the relationship between perceptual theories and other theories of international relations. Snyder and Diesing discuss similar issues in Chapter VI on "Crises and International Systems" (1977).

25. Waltz commented perceptively in *Man, the State and War* that contributions of behavioral scientists had often been "rendered ineffective by a failure to comprehend the significance of the political framework of international action" (1959, p. 78).

26. Thorough description—what Alexander George has called "process-tracing"—may be necessary to evaluate a structural explanation, since correlations are not reliable where only a small number of comparable cases is involved. (See George, 1979.)

27. I am indebted for this point to a conversation with Hayward Alker.

28. Latsis (1976) discusses the difference between "single-exit" and "multiple-exit" situations in his critique of oligopoly theory. What he calls the research

program of "situational determinism"—structural theory, in my terms—works well for single-exit situations, where only one sensible course of action is possible. (The building is burning down and there is only one way out: regardless of my personal characteristics, one can expect that I will leave through that exit.) It does not apply to multiple-exit situations, where more than one plausible choice can be made. (The building is burning, but I have to choose between trying the smoky stairs or jumping into a fireman's net: my choice may depend on deep-seated personal fears.) In foreign policy, the prevalence of multiple-exit situations reinforces the importance of decision-making analysis at the national level.

29. For a more detailed discussion of some aspects of this notion, and for citations to some of the literature in economics on which my thinking is based, see Keohane (1982). Discussions with Vinod Aggarwal have been important in formulating some of the points in the previous two paragraphs.

30. Morgenthau devotes a chapter of *Politics Among Nations* to peaceful change, but after a review of the reasons why legalistic approaches will not succeed, he eschews general statements for descriptions of a number of United Nations actions affecting peace and security. No theory of peaceful change is put forward. In *Politics Among Nations* Morgenthau put whatever faith he had in diplomacy. The chapter on peaceful change is Chapter 26 of the fourth edition (1966).

31. For a suggestive discussion of international relations as policy science, see George and Smoke (1974), Appendix, "Theory for Policy in International Relations," pp. 616–642.

32. Recall Weber's aphorism in "Politics as a Vocation": "Politics is the strong and slow boring of hard boards." Although much of Weber's work analyzed broad historical forces beyond the control of single individuals or groups, he remained acutely aware of "the truth that man would not have attained the possible unless time and again he had reached out for the impossible" (Gerth & Mills, 1958, p. 128). For a visionary, value-laden discourse on future international politics by a scholar "reaching out for the impossible," see North (1976, Chapter 7).

33. Ernst B. Haas, who has studied how political actors learn throughout his distinguished career, makes a similar point in a recent essay, where he espouses a "cognitive-evolutionary view" of change and argues that such a view "cannot settle for a concept of hegemony imposed by the analyst. . . . It makes fewer claims about basic directions, purposes, laws and trends than do other lines of thought. It is agnostic about the finality of social laws" (1982, pp. 242–243). The difference between Haas and me is that he seems to reject structural analysis in favor of an emphasis on cognitive evolution and learning, whereas I believe that modified structural analysis (more modest in its claims than Structural Realism) can provide a context within which analysis of cognition is politically more meaningful.

REFERENCES

Aggarwal, Vinod, *Hanging by a thread: International regime change in the textile apparel system, 1950–1979.* Unpublished doctoral dissertation, Stanford University, 1981.

Anderson, Perry. *Lineages of the absolutist state*. London: New Left Books, 1974.

Art, Robert J. Bureaucratic politics and American foreign policy: A critique. *Policy Sciences,* 1973, *4,* 467–490.

Ashley, Richard K. Political realism and human interest. *International Studies Quarterly,* 1981, *25,* 204–236.

Ashley, Richard K. Realistic dialectics: Toward a critical theory of world politics. Paper presented at the Annual Meeting of the American Political Science Association, Denver, Colorado, September 1982.

Axelrod, Robert (Ed.). *The structure of decision: The cognitive maps of political elites*. Princeton, N.J.: Princeton University Press, 1976.

Axelrod, Robert. The emergence of cooperation among egoists. *American Political Science Review,* 1981, *25,* 306–318.

Baldwin, David A. Power analysis and world politics: New trends versus old tendencies. *World Politics,* 1979, *31,* 161–194.

Boyle, Francis A. The irrelevance of international law: The schism between international law and international politics. *California Western International Law Journal,* 1980, *10.*

Brecher, Michael, with Geist, Benjamin. *Decisions in crisis: Israel 1967–1973.* Berkeley: University of California Press, 1980.

Bueno de Mesquita, Bruce. *The war trap.* New Haven: Yale University Press, 1981.

Carr, E. H. *The twenty years' crisis, 1919–1939* (1st ed.). London: Macmillan, 1946. (Originally published, 1939.)

Choucri, Nazli and North, Robert C. *Nations in conflict: National growth and international violence.* San Francisco: W. H. Freeman & Co., 1975.

Cipolla, Carlo. *The economic decline of empires.* London: Methuen, 1970.

Dahl, Robert A. *Who governs? Democracy and power in an American city.* New Haven: Yale University Press, 1961.

Eckstein, Harry. Case study and theory in political science. In Fred I. Greenstein & Nelson W. Polsby (Eds.), *Handbook of political science* (Vol. 7) *Strategies of inquiry.* Reading, MA: Addison-Wesley, 1975.

Geertz, Clifford. *The interpretation of cultures.* New York: Basic Books, 1973.

George, Alexander L. Case studies and theory development: The method of structured, focused comparison. In Paul Gordon Lauren (Ed.), *Diplomacy: New approaches in history, theory and policy.* New York: Free Press, 1979.

George, Alexander L. *Presidential decision making in foreign policy: The effective use of information and advice.* Boulder: Westview, 1980.

George, Alexander L. & George, Juliette. *Woodrow Wilson and Colonel House.* New York: Dover, 1964.

George, Alexander L., Hall, D. K. & Simons, W. E. *The limits of coercive diplomacy.* Boston: Little, Brown, 1971.

George, Alexander L. & Smoke, Richard. *Deterrence in American foreign policy.* New York: Columbia University Press, 1974.

Gerschenkron, Alexander. *Economic backwardness in historical perspective.* Cambridge: The Belknap Press of Harvard University Press, 1962.

Gerth, H. H., & Mills, G. Wright. *From Max Weber: Essays in Sociology:* New York: Oxford University Press, 1958.

Gilpin, Robert. *U.S. power and the multinational corporation.* New York: Basic Books, 1975.

Gilpin, Robert. *War and change in world politics.* New York: Cambridge University Press, 1981.

Gourevitch, Peter A. The second image reversed: The international sources of domestic politics. *International Organization,* 1978, *32,* 881–913.

Haas, Ernst B. Why collaborate? Issue-linkage and international regimes. *World Politics,* 1980, *32,* 357–405.

Haas, Ernst B. Words can hurt you: Or who said what to whom about regimes. *International Organization,* 1982, *36,* 207–244.

Harsanyi, John. Measurement of social power, opportunity costs, and the theory of two-person bargaining games. *Behavioral Sciences,* 1962, *7,* 67–80.

Herz, John H. Political realism revisited. *International Studies Quarterly,* 1981, *25,* 182–197.

Hoffmann, Stanley. *Contemporary theory in international relations.* Englewood Cliffs, N.J.: Prentice-Hall, 1960.

Hoffmann, Stanley. An American social science: International relations. *Daedalus,* Summer 1977, 41–60.

Holsti, Ole. Foreign policy viewed cognitively. In Robert Axelrod (Ed.), *The structure of decision: The cognitive maps of political elites.* Princeton, N.J.: Princeton University Press, 1976.

International organization, 1982, *36.* Special issue on international regimes edited by Stephen D. Krasner.

Jervis, Robert. *Perception and misperception in international politics.* Princeton, N.J.: Princeton University Press, 1976.

Jervis, Robert. Cooperation under the security dilemma. *World Politics,* 1978, *30,* 167–214.

Katzenstein, Peter J. *Between power and plenty: Foreign economic policies of advanced industrial states.* Madison: University of Wisconsin Press, 1978.

Keohane, Robert O. The demand for international regimes. *International Organization,* 1982, *36,* 325–356.

Keohane, Robert O., & Nye, Joseph (Eds.). *Transnational relations and world politics.* Cambridge, MA: Harvard University Press, 1972.

Keohane, Robert O., & Nye, Joseph. *Power and interdependence: World politics in transition.* Boston: Little, Brown, 1977.

Krasner, Stephen D. *Defending the national interest: Raw materials investments and U.S. foreign policy.* Princeton: Princeton University Press, 1978.

Krasner, Stephen D. Structural causes and regime consequences: Regimes as intervening variables. *International Organization,* 1982 *36,* 185–206.

Kuhn, Thomas S. *The structure of scientific revolutions.* Chicago: University of Chicago Press, 1962.

Kurth, James R. The political consequences of the product cycle: Industrial history and political outcomes. *International Organization,* 1979, *33,* 1–34.

Lakatos, Imre. Falsification and the methodology of scientific research programmes. In Imre Lakatos & Alan Musgrave (Eds.), *Criticism and the growth of knowledge.* Cambridge: Cambridge University Press, 1970.

Latsis, Spiro J. A research programme in economics. In Latsis (Ed.), *Method and approval in economics.* Cambridge: Cambridge University Press, *1976.*

Lebow, Richard Ned. *Between peace and war. The nature of international crisis.* Baltimore: Johns Hopkins University Press, 1981.

Lenin, V. I. *Imperialism: The highest stage of capitalism.* New York: International Publishers, 1939. (Originally written 1916.)

Luttwak, Edward. *The grand strategy of the Roman Empire—from the first century A.D. to the third.* Baltimore: Johns Hopkins University Press, 1976.

Lyons, Gene M. Expanding the study of international relations: The French connection. *World Politics,* 1982, *35,* 135–149.

Mansbach, Richard, Ferguson, Yale H. & Lampert, Donald E. *The Web of World Politics.* Englewood Cliffs, N.J.: Prentice Hall, 1976.

Mansbach, Richard & Vasquez, John A. *In Search of Theory: A New Paradigm for Global Politics.* New York: Columbia University Press, 1981.

March, James G. The power of power. In David Easton (Ed.), *Varieties of Political Theory.* New York: Prentice-Hall, 1966.

Masterman, Margaret. The nature of a paradigm. In Lakatos & Musgrave (Eds.), *Criticism and the Growth of Knowledge.* Cambridge: Cambridge University Press, 1970).

Michalak, Stanley J., Jr. Theoretical perspectives for understanding international interdependence. *World Politics,* 1979, *32,* 136–150.

Moore, Barrington, Jr. *Social Origins of Dictatorship and Democracy: Lord and Peasant in the Making of the Modern World.* Boston: Beacon Press, 1966.

Morgenthau, Hans J. *Scientific Man Versus Power Politics.* Chicago: University of Chicago Press, 1946.

Morgenthau, Hans J. *Politics Among Nations* (4th ed.). *New York: Knopf, 1966.* (Originally published, 1948).

North, Douglass C. *Structure and Change in Economic History.* New York: W. W. Norton, 1981.

North, Robert C. *The World That Could Be.* (The Portable Stanford: Stanford Alumni Association.) Palo Alto: Stanford University, 1976.

Organski, A. F. K., & Kugler, Jacek. *The War Ledger.* Chicago: University of Chicago Press, 1980.

Oye, Kenneth A. The domain of choice. In Kenneth A. Oye, Donald Rothchild, & Robert J. Lieber (Eds.), *Eagle Entangled: U.S. Foreign Policy in a Complex World.* New York: Longman, 1979, pp. 3–33.

Oye, Kenneth A. *Belief Systems, Bargaining and Breakdown: International Political Economy 1929–1934.* Unpublished doctoral dissertation, Harvard University, 1983.

Rosenau, James N. Pre-theories and theories of foreign policy. In R. Barry Farrell (Ed.). *Approaches to Comparative and International Politics.* Evanston: Northwestern University Press, 1966.

Ruggie, John Gerard. Continuity and transformation in the world polity: Toward a neo-realist synthesis. *World Politics,* 1983, *35,* 261–285.

Russett, Bruce M. The calculus of deterrence. *Journal of Conflict Resolution,* 1963, *7,* 97–109.

Schell, Jonathan. *The Fate of the Earth.* New York: Knopf, 1982.

Schelling, Thomas. *The Strategy of Conflict.* New York: Oxford University Press, 1960.

Simon, Herbert A. The architecture of complexity. In Simon (Ed.), *The Sciences of the Artificial.* Cambridge: MIT Press. 1969.

Snidal, Duncan. *Interdependence, Regimes, and International Cooperation.* Unpublished manuscript, University of Chicago, 1981.

Snyder, Glenn H. & Diesing, Paul. *Conflict Among Nations: Bargaining, Decision-Making and System Structure in International Crises.* Princeton, N.J.: Princeton University Press, 1977.

Sprout, Harold & Sprout, Margaret. *Toward a Politics of the Planet Earth.* New York: Van Nostrand Reinhold, 1971.

Stein, Arthur. The politics of linkage. *World Politics,* 1980, *33,* 62–81.

Stein, Arthur. Coordination and collaboration: Regimes in an anarchic world. *International Organization,* 1982, *36,* 299–324.

Thucydides. *The Peloponnesian War* (John H. Finley, Jr., trans). (Originally written c. 400 B.C.) New York: Modern Library, 1951.

Tollison, Robert D. & Willett, Thomas D. An economic theory of mutually advantageous issue linkage in international negotiations. *International Organization,* 1979, *33,* 425–450.

Toulmin, Stephen. *Foresight and Understanding: An Enquiry into the Aims of Science.* New York: Harper Torchbooks, 1963.

Wallerstein, Immanuel. The rise and future demise of the world capitalist system: Concepts for comparative analysis. In Wallerstein, *The Capitalist World-Economy.* Cambridge: Cambridge University Press, 1979. (This essay was originally printed in *Comparative Studies in Society and History,* 1974, *16.*)

Wallerstein, Immanuel. *The Modern World-System II: Mercantilism and the Consolidation of the European World-Economy, 1600–1750.* New York: Academic Press, 1980.

Waltz, Kenneth N. *Man, the State and War.* New York: Columbia University Press, 1959.

Waltz, Kenneth N. *Foreign Policy and Democratic Politics: The American and British Experience.* Boston: Little, Brown, 1967.

Waltz, Kenneth N. *Theory of International Politcs.* Reading, MA: Addison-Wesley, 1979, p. 7.

Wolfers, Arnold. *Discord and Collaboration: Essays on International Politics.* Baltimore: Johns Hopkins University Press, 1962.

Accounting for International War

J. David Singer

Professor Singer, himself a realist, summarizes much of the theoretical work done with formal hypothesis testing, causal modeling, and other statistical tools—methods he has long advocated. He concludes the article, however, by stating an ultimate purpose for conducting such

Reprinted from "Accounting for International War: The State of the Discipline," by J. David Singer, from *Journal of Peace Research,* No. 1, Vol. 18, 1981 by permission of Universitetsforlaget, Oslo.

research on war—"to put an end to one of the most destructive and dysfunctional activities known to human history."

In the early 1930s, when Quincy Wright in America and Lewis Richardson in England began their respective investigations into the causes of war, they were not only unaware of one another's work; they were, of necessity, equally unaware of the radical change that their studies would produce in the field of war and peace research. With perhaps the exception of Jean de Bloch—whose *Future of War* (1899) sought all too successfully to predict what warfare would look like on the basis of a systematic examination of previous wars—and Pitirim Sorokin (1937)—whose focus was on the relationship between long cycles in cultural patterns and fluctuations in war and revolution over several thousand years—Wright (1942) and Richardson (1941 and 1960a, b) mark the first traceable efforts to bring scientific method to bear on international conflict. While physical phenomena had been studied in an essentially scientific fashion for several centuries, and biological phenomena for nearly a century, social phenomena had remained largely the domain of theological speculation, moral imperative, and conventional folklore. But even as economics and sociology began to emerge as systematic sciences, followed in due course by the study of national political systems, international politics remained one of the most backward of disciplines.

This state of affairs was, and often still is, explained in terms of the intractability of the material; not only does much of the behavior occur in secret, but the material, structural, and cultural conditions associated with the international system are allegedly too spread out in time and in space to permit direct observation. But that explanation is incomplete. Political elites, it can be assumed, preferred things this way, partly because it made diplomatic bargaining easier and partly because political power brokers have typically shown an almost visceral reluctance to operate in the open. But if any event dramatically exposed the incompetence of these elites and the dangers of their secret diplomacy, it was World War I. While the most visible (and audible) result of this exposure was the Wilsonian call for "open covenants, openly arrived at," another message was received by Wright and Richardson.

As I interpret their prefatory remarks, each had begun to appreciate that another reason for secrecy was that the decision makers often did not "know what they were doing," that is, even after lengthy domestic debate over foreign or military policy, the elites made recurrently erroneous predictions as to the consequences of their actions. Further, these two scholars arrived at a judgment that was not only generous, but probably correct: that the problem lay not so much with the stupidity or ambition of the foreign policy elites, but more with their ignorance. In addition, they observed that this ignorance was not peculiar to the practitioners alone; the scholarly community was hardly better off.

Having arrived at these general conclusions, it was natural that they would then have some caustic observations on the absence of evidence, and the heavy reliance on "brilliant, witty political discussion" (Richardson, 1960a, p.v.). This British meteorologist and pacifist also noted that "many of those who are considered to be experts on foreign affairs do not base their opinions on historical facts, but on some sort of instinctive reasoning." But, as the subsequent research of each makes clear, they saw the need for something more than historical facts, as gathered and interpreted by the standard diplomatic historian or political analyst. If the behavior of governments in the international setting was to become less destructive, the knowledge base from which they worked would have to be greatly improved. That is, if decision makers could more accurately predict—on the basis of historically observed regularities and theoretical inferences therefrom—the consequences of their decisions, there might be a decline in the frequency and magnitude of war. Even if that knowledge base served only to help challenge and question the assumptions behind our decisions, the error rate might be reduced. Of course, while the acquisition and codification of such knowledge would be necessary, neither Wright nor Richardson thought that it would be sufficient; decision makers and attentive publics would also have to be able and willing to understand, evaluate, and apply that knowledge.

1. TYPOLOGIES AND TAXONOMIES

Given, then, the need for a more solid knowledge base in the emerging inter-disciplinary field of war/peace studies, where do we stand now? What kinds of knowledge have we acquired and how adequately has it been codified into theoretically coherent form? What are the dominant orientations, and what are the more promising of these? In order to address these questions, we need some sort of organizing framework, within which we can differentiate the several theoretical orientations as well as summarize our knowledge to date. The variety of frameworks is, of course, quite large, and people gravitate to one or another of them for all sorts of reasons, scientific or otherwise: nationality, social class, age, gender, education, personality, academic identity, foundation and governmental fashions, and even (!) on the basis of prior research findings.

1.1 A Familiar Typology

One of the more familiar ways of classifying—and often, selecting from among—the possible approaches, is to divide them into the standard categories of technological, economic, geographic, political, demographic, ideological, psychological, etc. As suggested, the advocates of any of these approaches often arrive at their position as a result of disciplinary affiliation, reflecting the oft-implicit premise that the academic discipline that one selects reflects one's "belief" that *its* major explanatory variables will account for virtually all sorts of social outcomes. Choosing such a typology and one of its approaches may, however, reflect nothing more than the conviction that one studies best those phenomena that one knows best, and that such partial models and their findings must eventually be integrated into those generated within the other social sciences.

But regardless of the motives and assumptions, we usually end up with a typology that helps to perpetuate and legitimize these parochial orientations and to encourage the appearance, disappearance, and reappearance of those "theories" that are all too typical of the no-growth, non-cumulative disciplines. Thus we find heavy, if not sole reliance on such factors as power discrepancies (Blainey, 1973), surplus capital (Lenin, 1939), business cycles (Secerov, 1919), demographic pressures (Organski, 1968), resource needs (Choucri & North, 1975), elite personalities (Stoessinger, 1978), national moods (Klingberg, 1952; McClelland, 1961), misperceptions (White, 1968), and so forth. These at least have the virtue of resting upon variables that show some *variation* across time and place. But other alleged models of a single-variable sort fail to even recognize that a phenomenon as irregularly (and infrequently) distributed across time and space as war cannot be explained on the basis of relatively *in*variant phenomena. Thus, it is difficult to take seriously such putative explanations as the human drive for power (Morgenthau, 1948) · or territory (Ardrey, 1966), the instinct of aggressiveness (Lorenz, 1967), or libidinous drive (Fornari, 1974).

In addition to the fact that most of the above orientations are rarely examined empirically, are seldom related to other explanations (Nelson & Olin, 1979; Silberner, 1946), ignore the multi-dimensional complexities of the war-inducing process, show insufficient variation in their "explanatory variables," and are overly responsive to current events, political pressures, and funding agency fads, they usually suffer from another fatal flaw. That is, they tend to overlook the critical distinction between international *conflict* and international *war*. While conflicts can arise out of an impressive range of social incompatibilities, the processes that lead to so frequent an event as conflicts are not necessarily those that lead to so infrequent an event as war. In a global system that is so poorly integrated in the structural or cultural sense, the relatively high frequency of serious international conflicts and military confrontations (about 225 involving the major powers alone since the Congress of Vienna) need not surprise us, whereas the relatively low frequency of war (fewer than 30 among those same powers in those 160-odd years) surely calls forth our curiosity.

Then there is the dinstinction between necessary conditions and sufficient ones (Deutsch & Senghass, 1971). Many conditions are *necessary* for modern war: the fact that humans can behave aggressively and that many of them do seek power or territory under the proper stimuli; the availability of transport and weapons technology; centralized decision authority; some sort of credible justification, and so forth. While these may well be certain necessary conditions, it is far from clear that any single factor is *sufficient* to carry a conflict across the threshold to war.

We need, therefore, a typology that: a) recognizes the qualitative differences among competition, rivalry, and dispute on the one hand, and sustained military combat on the other, and that b) also recognizes the complex interplay of necessary and/or sufficient conditions reflecting a wide range of material, structural, cultural, and behavioral phenomena. In addition, it should aid in integrating what we *have* discovered with what we *hope* to discover, and if possible, illuminate the research path that links the two. A discrete check list will not suffice; an integrated, but multitheoretical, framework would seem to be essential. Let us turn, then, to a scheme derived from the general systems literature that might possibly help us to organize what we know, and think we know, and to help stimulate the most appropriate next steps. This scheme has been laid out in considerable detail elsewhere, along with an elaborate epistemological rationale (Singer, 1971), but its bare outlines can be summarized here.

1.2 A General Systems Taxonomy

Since war is waged, contemplated, and conducted by and on behalf of human beings organized into a variety of social entities, and is not conducted by relationships or roles or system properties, it makes perfect sense to build our taxonomy around those entities, however transitory and/or amorphous they may turn out to be. All sorts of social groups can and do engage in sustained military combat, but since our concern here is with international war, we can confine ourselves to the most relevant sub-national, national, and extra-national groups, ranging at the sub-national level from the family and primary work group up through all sorts of secondary associations to political parties, government agencies, legislatures, cabinets, and armies.

When many such groups—at various levels of aggregation, and covering various functional sectors—are relatively unified and coordinated within a national territory, the resulting coalition may be called a national (or multi-national) state. The state or nation is the dominant unit of the international system, but for centuries before the emergence of that system, man was organized in many other types of social organization; and as other more effective groupings develop and attract the loyalty of their members, that pattern may be renewed, and it will be increasingly appropriate to refer to the *global,* rather than the *international* system. In any event, the nation is the major participant in international war, even though the probability of any such war, and its outcome, may well be influenced as much by the various sub-national and extra-national groupings with which the nation shares the world stage. There is an almost limitless range of levels of social aggregation at which the causes of war question might be addressed, but for the purposes of the discussion at hand, we will address only four of them: the international system (defined globally, regionally, or functionally, depending on the work being summarized); the inter-nation dyad; the single nation; and the decision making agency level. Social entities at any of these levels may be thought of as systems, embracing the attributes by which they are described, as well as the behaviors and interactions of the subsystems which make up the larger system; hence we distinguish here between the ecological and behavioral variables by which we seek to understand dynamic social phenomena.

Social entities from the individual up to the global system may be described in terms of three sets of attributes; ranged in order of tangibility and ease of operational measurement, they are material, structural, and cultural. *Material* attributes may be divided into three subsets, of minimal relevance to the individual human, but highly germane to any other entity: geographic, demographic, and technological. And by the *structural* attributes of a social system we mean the institutional and organizational phenomena by which economists, sociologists, and political scientists usually describe it. Structural properties may be of a relatively formal nature, embracing the types and powers of institutions that deal with legislative, administrative, judicial, banking, commercial, welfare, informational, and similar activities in the entity or system. But they also embrace such informal attributes as access to and influence over decision-making processes; the number and configuration of political parties and interest groups; the number and distribution of religious, linguistic, and ethnic aggregations; the social and geographical mobility of the population; the extent and configurations of pluralistic cross-cutting bonds; and the nature and stability of the resulting coalitions.

By the *cultural* attributes of a social entity, we mean strictly the distribution of the psychological properties of the individuals who comprise that particular system; this reductionist definition explicitly excludes any so-called emergent or organic properties of the system "as a whole," so as to avoid reification and any suggestion that social groups may have personalities, purposes, etc. The cultural dimension embraces the distribution of individual personality types, attitudes, and opinions, and extends to the way in which all three of these psychological attributes relate to the way things are, should be, and will be; these can be thought of, respectively, as perceptions, preferences, and predictions. We can, in turn, treat the distribution of personalities as national (or any other system's) character, that of attitudes as ideology, and that of opinion as cultural climate.

To summarize, the above set of dimensions should permit us to describe a nation or any social entity, compare it to itself at different points in time, and compare it to other entities at the same or different levels of analysis at the same or different point in time. To put it in All-port's suggestive language, these attributes permit us to deal with our objects of analysis in terms of their being and in terms of their becoming, and having done this, we can then move on to deal with their behaving and interacting.

While the distinction between behavior and inter-action (between/among actors) is self-evident, one of the inadequacies of the English language and the concepts conveyed by its vocabulary is that the word *relationship* carries so wide a variety of meanings, but it is used here in only two of its senses: that of comparison and that of connectedness. Thus, when we say that the political integration of system *X* is very high in relation to that of system *Y,* we are comparing the two systems on a particular set of attributes. The confusion, as well as the distinctions, between these two meanings is well illustrated by the notion of "social distance." Two systems may be close or distant in terms of their position on a given attribute scale, such as size, ethnic homogeneity, or structural complexity. They may also be close or distant in terms of their interdependence or their friendship, and there is absolutely no reason to expect that entities that are close in the sense of similarity will always be close in the sense of connectedness or interdependence as well, despite the frequency of this assumption (implicit or otherwise) in the social sciences.

Let me mention here two other sources of confusion. One is the relationship *(sic)* between relationships (in the sense of connections) among entities at one level of analysis and the structure of any system at the next higher level of aggregation; the other is the relationship between such relationships and interaction. To consider the first, many structural properties of a given system are inferred from observation of the relationships among its sub-systems. We are often told that a social system is more than the sum of its parts, but this bromide often leads us into all sorts of metaphysical pursuits, as we search for the emergent or organic properties of the system itself. I maintain that a system is nothing more than the sum of its parts, along with the relationships and interactions among them. This formulation is important not only because it helps eliminate much of the mysticism surrounding social entities, but because it quickly converts a difficult and costly process of observation and measurement into a relatively straightforward one: many structural attributes of a system may be inferred quite simply by observing the relationships among its component parts. And we can discover the cultural attributes of a system by observing the interactions among its components, but this requires a longer inferential leap, inasmuch as we must first be confident of the extent to which the behaviors comprising interaction actually reflect cultural perceptions, predictions, and preferences.

As to the other relationship—that between relationship and interaction—we note that the first may be thought of as a *condition:* the bonds and links that connect two or more social entities. While relationships are largely the consequence of interaction, and while we can often predict interaction *events* from observed relationships, the differentiation between relationship and interaction is critical to the empirical examination of many of our models and hypotheses.

1.3 Measuring the Incidence of International War

Before utilizing this scheme to examine the evidence as to which factors might cause, explain, lead to, make for, or account for fluctuations in the incidence of war, a brief digression is in order. Surprising as it may seem, scholars have been speculating on the causes of war for centuries before they tried to ascertain its empirical distribution, and even today many of our theoretical disagreements stem partly from the failure to identify our population of cases, and from differing conceptions and definitions of our outcome variable (Blechman & Kaplan, 1978; Bloomfield & Leiss, 1969; Bouthoul, 1951; Kende, 1971; Urlanis, 1960). But following on the work of Sorokin, Richardson, and Wright, the Correlates of War project at Michigan has assembled what seems to be the population of international (inter-state, imperial, and colonial) and civil wars involving one or more sovereign states any place in the world since the Congress of Vienna, and has presented the coding rules, resulting data, and summary statistics (Singer & Small, 1972).

In the handbook (Wages of War), we differentiate among four basic indicators of the incidence of war. The first is that of *frequency,* and is measured by the onset of sustained military hostilities between authorized armed forces of two or more sovereign national states culminating in at least 1,000 battle deaths. The second is *severity,* and is measured by the number of battle deaths resulting from a qualifying war; the third is *magnitude* measured in terms of nation-months of war; and the fourth is that of *intensity,* measured in battle deaths per nation-month or per capita. While frequency is measured only in the context of a given time and space domain, the other three indicators of the incidence of war can be applied to a given war as well as to all of the qualifying wars that occur in a specified time and space domain. In most, but not all of the studies summarized here, the Correlates of War data base and indicators have been used, and unless the choice of indicator makes an appreciable difference, the results will be reported in terms of the simplest indicator of war: its frequency.

Yet another consideration when seeking to account for the fluctuations in a given phenomenon is the extent to which they show a discernible regularity across time or space. While I would not accept the proposition that goodness of fit between a given distribution and one or another statistical model permits a legitimate inference as to the *processes that produced* that distribution, such regularities can certainly be suggestive (Horvath, 1968; Voevodsky, 1969; Weiss, 1963). Perhaps the most suggestive fit would be that of periodicity, on the assumption that a strong cyclical pattern might imply a degree of inexorability in international warfare. And, given the frequency with which cyclical patterns have been asserted, as well as the variety of inferences drawn from these putative patterns (Alcock, 1972; Davis et al., 1978; Denton & Phillips, 1968; Dewey, 1964), it may be worth reporting the results of a fairly systematic search for them. Simply put, we have found only the weakest trace of periodicity in the incidence of all international warfare over these 160 years, with a barely discernible cycle of 20-odd years (Singer & Small, 1972). More important, when we look at the war experiences of the more war-prone nations one at a time, virtually every conceivable technique fails to produce evidence for any kind of regularity (Singer & Cusack, 1981). Thus, it is perfectly true that there are peaks and troughs in the time plots of war at both the national and the systemic levels, but the time intervals between those peaks and/or troughs are of sufficiently random length to support the skeptical conclusions of Sorokin (1937, p. 359) and Richardson (1960a, pp. 129–30 and 140). I would not, however, want to foreclose further research into the question, especially from the war expansion and contagion perspective. That is, despite the diverse results—stemming from diverse domains, indicators, and techniques— the evidence for *addiction* to war on the part of the system or any nation seems weak. But a close reading of Davis, Duncan, and Siverson (1978) and Siverson and King (1980) suggests that more complex models of *diffusion and contagion*—via alliance bonds—might well stand against the empirical test.

If war itself does not appear and re-appear in a regular cyclical fashion, it is unlikely that it results to any important extent from *any other* single-factor cycle, be it commercial, agricultural, climatic, or demographic. Rather, if there are indeed cyclical phenomena at work, there must be *several* of them involved in this process (Hart, 1946; Sorokin, 1937), with their concatenations falling at relatively irregular intervals. While there seems to be no concentrated research effort in this direction at the moment, it certainly appears to be worth pursuing further, perhaps when more is known regarding the time–space distributions of some of the more promising explanatory variables. Let us, then, attempt a brief and admittedly selective survey of these latter as they impinge on the incidence of international war.

2. FINDINGS TO DATE ON THE INCIDENCE OF WAR

To reiterate a point that has already been noted, there is no substitute for a good theoretical model when laying out an empirical investigation, but when we are not nearly far enough along to even specify the key variables of such a model, we have little choice but to work within a multi-theoretical framework and get on with our more inductive efforts. The problem now is one of identifying the results of the inductive work to date, some (but not all) of which has been shaped by the proposed framework, and to see how far it permits us to summarize and synthesize these diverse findings. We will work with three of the levels of aggregation noted earlier, and within each, look at the extent to which the several classes of variables seem to be accounting historically for the incidence of war. And, reflecting my strong suspicion that variables of a systemic and dyadic sort will turn out to be more powerful than those at the national and the decision-making levels of aggregation, let me deal with the findings at these levels in that order.

While it is often a rule of thumb to look first at the phenomena that are closest—in space or time—to the outcome we seek to explain, there seem to be reasonable grounds for *not* doing so in the case of war. While these grounds are far from conventional and the evidence for them is sparse, space limitations permit only stark assertions here; for a more detailed justification, see Singer (1961 and 1976). First, I assume that there is a great deal of homogeneity in the intellectual style of foreign policy/national security decision makers from nation to nation and from decade to decade over the past century or so. Similarly, there seems to be a remarkable homogeneity in the decision rules that nations follow, especially when they are in conflict, again irrespective of such allegedly critical distinctions as regime type, national culture and ideology, and level of economic development (Rosenau, 1966). These two assumptions suggest that we will not find a great deal of variation at the decisional and national levels, and therefore should not expect the attributes of nations or their decision makers to be very powerful in explaining so varying an outcome as war/no war.

A second consideration that follows quite logically is that most of the variation in the behavior of nations in conflict will be accounted for, not by their internal attributes, but by variation in their environment. That environment can, in turn, be viewed as having two basic components; the dyadic relationship with another nation, and the regional or global systemic context in which the conflicting nation finds itself. From this, it follows that we might expect to find the dyadic relationship and the properties of the system to carry us further in accounting for the incidence of international war than would the attributes of the nations or their decision-making organizations (Zinnes, 1980a). Thus, we will begin with the systemic environment and examine some of the empirical evidence to date, and then move on to the effects of dyadic phenomena. But, to reiterate, the selection is intended to be more representative and suggestive than exhaustive.

2.1 Systemic Attributes

Despite the possible attractiveness of the above argument, few other investigators into the war/peace question have accepted it, and as a result, a fair fraction of research on the systemic conditions associated with war has emanated so far largely from the Michigan Correlates of

War project. Further, of the three types of systemic conditions—material, structural, and cultural—most of the reproducible evidence to date reflects the structural dimension (Sullivan, 1976). Unfortunately, there is little systematic work on such material attributes of the system as weapons technology, industrial development, resource limits, climate, or demographic patterns. Similarly, outside of some preliminary efforts by Kegley et al. (1979), Choi (1978), and Gantzel (1972) little effort has been invested in the search for systematic connections between cultural conditions and the incidence of war. On the other hand, researchers of a scientific bent have been as assiduous in their examination of structural correlates of war as their methodologically traditional colleagues, and it is to that literature that we now turn.

Perhaps the most plausible of the system's structural attributes in the war/peace context is that of the configurations generated by alliance bonds, with those generated by distributions of power following closely behind. Looking first at the structural characteristic known as bipolarity, we usually have in mind the extent to which the nations in a given geographical region, or in the major power sub-set (a functional "region"), or world-wide, are clustered into two clearly opposed coalitions. While there are several definitions of bipolarity and rather diverse operational indicators, it generally implies the degree of conformity to an "ideal" condition in which all the nations are—via military alliance—in one or another of two equally powerful coalitions with no alliance bonds between the polar blocs, and full bondedness *within* each. While such a set of conditions has never obtained, the reasoning is that even an approximation would so severely hamper the conflict-resolving efficacy of the pluralistic cross-cutting, multiple balancing mechanism of the system as to make conflict escalation and war much more likely (Deutsch & Singer, 1964; Waltz 1967; Rosecrance et al., 1974; Kaplan, 1957; Liska, 1956). But like all too many theoretical hunches in the world politics field, there is an equally plausible counter-argument: that so clearly bipolar a system structure would eliminate all ambiguity as to who is on whose side, or as to the possibility of military victory, that war would just never be considered. Rather, according to this orientation, war occurs when there is ambiguity, either because behavior becomes less predictable and governments stumble into war, or because governments have a "drive toward certainty," and war helps to clarify the picture.

In any event, the research findings to date only partially resolve the theoretical disagreements. In one of the first systematic analyses, Singer and Small (1968) found that the relationship between their indicators of polarity and war differed in the 19th and 20th centuries. In the earlier epoch, higher polarity levels tended to be followed by lower levels of international war, but in the period since 1900, fluctuations in the incidence of war were *positively* associated with the fluctuations in polarity. In a follow-up, Wallace (1973) used a somewhat different indicator of polarity and found a curvilinear association, with war levels generally associated with very high bipolarity scores or very low ones, suggesting—for the entire 1816–1965 period—that there may be an optimal level of three or four relatively discernible alliance clusters, with war levels quite low when those intermediate conditions obtain. In a third and more recent analysis of the question, Bueno de Mesquita (1978) found that fluctuations in war were accounted for less by the *level* of bipolarity in the system than by the direction and rate of change in the alliance configurations that might produce such bipolarity. That is, the amount of war in the system since the Congress of Vienna tended to rise when the "tightness" of alliance clusters was on the increase. Even more confusing are Levy's finding (1979) that bipolarity makes for maximum stability and unipolarity for maximum war, and Wayman's finding (1981) that cluster polarity exercises a different effect from power polarity. Perhaps Ostrom and Aldrich (1978, p. 765) summarize things best in reporting that 'our results have a distinctly negative flavor'.

As might be expected, there are several interesting extensions of the bipolarity–war hypothesis. The simplest is that since alliances involving one set of major powers will generally be in opposition to other majors, the greater the percentage of major powers in alliance, the greater the bipolarity of the system as a whole, and thus the greater (or lesser) will be the incidence of war in the ensuing years. Once again, the empirical findings are mixed; Singer and Small (1968) found that their alliance aggregation indicator, which was indeed highly correlated with their bipolarity index, predicted positively to the incidence of war in the 1900–1945 period, but negatively in the 1816–1899 period. Imposing more stringent analytical tests and slightly different indicators, Ostrom and Hoole (1978) turned up similar, but considerably weaker patterns.

A more complex version of this systemic hypothesis can be interpreted in two ways. One is that the concentration of military and industrial capabilities tends to follow the concentration of national coalitions and groupings (especially the majors), and that the concentration of these capabilities should have the same effect on the incidence of war as the concentration of the nations into a small number of tight polar groupings. While this isomorphism does occur from time to time, it is not constant enough to make this interpretation very compelling. Thus, one takes a more generalized view and treats both types of concentration as producing a high degree of *clarity* in the system's structure. And to the extent that the systemic environment is clear and unambiguous as to: a) who will fight on which side if a conflict escalates to war, and b) which side will probably win that war, the decision makers are thought to be less likely to either entertain the war option or to merely stumble into war.

Regardless of the theoretical interpretation, the empirical investigations lead once more to inconsistent results. And, as before, a major anomaly is the inter-century one. In the 19th century, high concentration of capabilities in the hands of a very few powers makes for increases in the incidence of war, while more equal distributions are associated with *low* levels of war (Singer, Bremer and Stuckey, 1972). But in the period 1900–1965, high concentrations lead to low levels of warfare and low concentrations are associated with higher levels of war. In a follow-up study, Champion and Stoll (1980) went a step further and: a) introduced an important control variable, classifying each major power as either "satisfied" or "dissatisfied" on the eve of each war as reflected in the historians' consensus; and b) calculated the concentrations in terms of *coalitions,* rather than concentrations in terms of the nations separately and individually. These modifications appreciably enhanced the post-dictive power of the capability distribution model across the full time period, suggesting that if the blocs have indeed been accurately identified and the powers accurately classified on the "satisfaction" dimension, this systemic factor may be of considerable importance. But as the authors remind us, the validity of these additional indicators remains to be more fully demonstrated. In an interesting variation on this theme, Cannizzo (1978) examined the effect of such capability configurations on the major powers individually, and found that these were far from uniform; concentrations and changes therein strongly affected France, Italy, and Austria–Hungary, for example, while having little impact on the war experiences of England, Japan, and Russia. Wayman (1980) found that wars occurring under conditions of high concentration are less severe than those occurring when capabilities are more evenly distributed.

Another factor—related to the others in the sense that it taps the structural clarity dimension—is that of status inconsistency, aggregated to the systemic level. In two of the earlier investigations, Wallace (1973a) and East (1972) found moderately clear associations between the incidence of international war and the extent to which the rank scores of the nations on the material capability and diplomatic importance dimensions were inconsistent with one another. That is, the more similar the systemic pecking orders on power and on prestige, the less war-prone the system was in the years following. On the other hand, the inquiries by Ray (1974) and Gochman (1980) produced more ambiguous results, perhaps due in part to the use of different indicators.

2.2 Dyadic Conditions

While there is a clear conceptual difference between the structural characteristics of a system and the relationships among the component units of the system, it is worth reiterating their empirical and conceptual connections. As noted earlier, most systemic properties rest upon, and can be inferred from, the links and bonds among the components, and while some scholars have sought their indicators of system structure in the triad (Harary, 1961), most of the data-based work has been restricted to the more manageable "two-body problem," to borrow from the vocabulary of physics. Following the distinction noted earlier, we will treat dyadic conditions of a relational sort first, and then turn to those of a comparative sort, resting not on the links, but on the similarities, between nations.

As to the former, we again find the familiar emphasis upon alliance bonds, followed by the bonds created via membership in discernible diplomatic clusters, trading blocs, and international organizations. First, we discover that, in general, nations with formal and long-standing alliance bonds experience a significantly higher frequency of war than do those without them (Small & Singer, 1966); on the other hand, Sabrosky (1980) found that nations that were allied to one another had a very low probability of going to war against one another. Neither case suggests anything as to the *intentions* of the alliance makers (Singer & Bueno de Mesquita, 1973). Looking at another type of bond, Skjelsbaek (1971) found that war opponents tended to decrease their shared inter-governmental organization memberships in the five-year period preceding the onset of war, and Singer and Wallace (1970) found that while most IGOs were founded *after* the termination of war, there was virtually no relationship between the number of them in the system and the amount of interstate war experienced in the subsequent five years. More surprisingly, Gochman (1980) found that militarized disputes between major trading partners were *more* likely to escalate to war than were disputes between states that did not heavily trade with each other.

Shifting from the role of dyadic bonds and associations in accounting for the incidence of war to that of similarities and differences, the ubiquitous dimension of power again captures most of our attention. The theoretical argument is rather direct: even though sub-military conflict seems to be no more likely between nations of very unequal strength than between those of approximate parity, this factor should become more critical as the war threshold is approached. The familiar dictum is that the weaker *dare* not fight and the stronger *need* not; the corollary is that one purpose of war is to ascertain which party is stronger when any doubt does exist.

While the evidence on this question is relatively consistent, the final word has hardly been said. For example, Garnham (1976a) found that equality in population reduced the likelihood of dyadic war, but that equality in geographical size or industrial base did not, in the 1816–1965 period. Controlling for geographical contiguity, however, both he (1976b) and Weede (1976), as well as Barringer (1972) and Wright (1965), found that nations that were approximately equal in material capabilities were significantly more likely to carry their disputes to war than were nations of discernible *dis*-parity. Further, Stoll and Champion (1977) found that serious disputes were more likely to escalate to war if the weak side was the initiator of the dispute; disputes initiated by the stronger side were less likely to end in war. Mihalka (1976) found that once military force was threatened or used, the greater the disparity in capabilities of the disputants, the less likely the dispute was to escalate to hostilities. More recently, Singer and his colleagues (1979a) found that while only 13% of all major power militarized disputes since 1816 escalated to war, that figure rose to 20% when the parties were approximately equal in military terms, and to 75% if such parity was combined with rapid military buildup during the three years prior to the dispute.

A second emphasis in this literature is more diffuse, but worth noting briefly, given the theoretical pervasiveness of its assumptions. That is, the more similar two nations are in terms of certain political or cultural attributes, the more friendly their relationship might be expected to be, and the more friendly they are, the less frequently or severely might they be expected to wage war against one another. Here, too, Richardson (1960a) was the first to look into the question systematically, and he found little historical evidence to support the classical view. For the period 1820–1949 and using his population of 300-odd wars and military disputes, he found that neither a common language nor a common religion had a depressing effect on the incidence of dyadic war (pp. 230–31). To the contrary, as he himself demonstrated (pp. 285–86) and as others have confirmed (Gleditsch and Singer, 1975), geographical contiguity is the confounding variable. That is, since geographical neighbors are not only more likely to be culturally similar but also to have more sources of conflict and to be more accessible to one another's armies, it follows that such similarities should actually be related to dyadic war in the *positive* direction (Gantzel, 1972).

These findings lead, in turn, to another of the more interesting paradoxes in research to date. Reference is to the effect of common boundaries, with the reasonable hypothesis that the greater the number of immediate neighbors a nation has, the more frequently it will be drawn into warfare against one or another of them. While Richardson's data (1960a, p. 177) tend to support this hypothesis, the findings of Starr and Most (1978) do not. Rather, they find an *inverse* relationship between a nation's war proneness and the number of immediate neighbors. Nor should these results be surprising, when we consider that the number of direct neighbors is physically a function of a land-locked nation's geographic size vis-à-vis that of its neighbors. The longer its boundaries, the greater the number of others that can border on it, and the smaller these latter are, the more numerous they can be. From this, it follows that the greater will be the discrepancy between its size (and strength, all else being equal) and theirs, and given the finding that war is more likely between equals, it again follows that the frequency of war *should* be lower.

2.3 National Attributes and Relationships

In an earlier section I indicated that national attributes seemed less crucial in accounting for war than either systemic or dyadic conditions, and before summarizing the evidence to date, let me expand on that assertion. Briefly put, the exigencies of survival in an international system of such inadequate organization and with so pervasively dysfunctional a culture require relatively uniform response. That is, for a national entity to adapt to and survive in such an environment, it must achieve a fair degree of political mobilization, military preparedness, and political centralization. Despite great differences in tradition and culture, or great apparent differences in political regime and economic arrangements, these external considerations tend to reinforce the essential domestic similarity of national states, regardless of their size, strength, level of economic development, etc.

To what extent does the empirical evidence to date support this alleged lack of cross-national variation in the attributes that might be associated with the incidence of war? On the one hand, certain of these attributes do seem to be related to the frequency and/or severity of national war experiences (Richardson, 1960a; Rummel, 1972), with overall military-industrial capabilities the most potent predictor. In a systematic examination of the relationship between a six-dimensional index of such capabilities and war proneness since the Congress of Vienna, Bremer (1980) found a very strong positive correlation between the strength of nations (including industrial development and military preparedness) and their tendency to go to war. Using a more restricted indicator, reflecting the size of the military establishment, and using more general indicators of foreign conflict, several studies further confirm this positive association with national strength (Naroll, 1974; Choucri and North, 1975; Small, 1978; Weede, 1970).

On the other hand, if we turn to more complex models that might link national characteristics to war proneness, the findings are considerably more ambiguous. Applying the sociological concept of status inconsistency to nations whose material capabilities are high and whose attributed diplomatic status scores are low (or vice-versa), neither Ray (1974) nor Gochman (1980) found any consistent pattern. Another domestic characteristic that has often been thought of as contributing to national war proneness is that of domestic instability. Yet no investigation identified much of an association until Wilkenfeld (1973) controlled for regime type, and found, for part of the post-World War II period, several clear associations. However, looking at regime type alone and examining the full 1816–1965 period, Small and Singer (1976) found that autocratic and democratic regimes were equally likely to both initiate wars and to become embroiled in them, but Haas (1965) found, at least for the twentieth century, that democratic regimes were less war prone than authoritarian ones. He also concludes in the same study that wealthy urbanized nations, especially during periods of social strain, are particularly susceptible to war involvement.

Shifting from attributes of an essentially internal sort to external relationships, the dimension most often examined is that of alliance bonds. In studies covering members of the interstate system since 1816, both Singer and Small (1966) and Siverson and King (1978) find a strong positive association between alliance involvement and war proneness; this is not to suggest that the relationship rests on the high reliability of alliance commitments (Sabrosky, 1980). And, given the well-known association between high capabilities and high alliance involvement, as well as that between capabilities and war proneness, this should come as no surprise. On a related dimension and picking up the geographical variables summarized earlier in the dyadic context, Richardson (1960a) found a positive relationship between the number of neighbors a nation had and the frequency of its wars from 1820 to 1945, and Wesley (1969), Weede (1970), Midlarsky (1975), and Starr and Most (1978) found relatively similar patterns for comparable spatial-temporal domains. Finally, Gleditsch and Singer (1975) examined the effect of a nation's mean distance from all other sovereign members of the system, and they, too, found a positive relationship; the more centrally located they were, the more war they experienced.

The tentative inference from this limited set of studies is that such basic geo-strategic factors as location and strength seem to be of importance, but that despite persuasive arguments to the contrary (Rosenau, 1966), domestic factors of a less material sort would appear to be rather negligible in accounting for the war proneness of individual nations.

2.4 Behavioral and Interactional Patterns

To this juncture, our focus has been on the extent to which the frequency and magnitude of war might be accounted for historically by the contextual and ecological variables: fluctuations in systemic, dyadic, or national conditions. Following the check list implied in the taxonomy, this leaves untouched the question of behavior itself: to what extent can we account for war by the actions and interactions of the nations? Given the emphasis on diplomatic and military behavior in the speculative literature on war, one might expect to find a respectable body of empirical work on the question. The fact that we do *not,* however, need not be very surprising. First of all, behavioral phenomena are more elusive and seem to be more difficult to observe and measure. Second, a good many researchers suspect that behavioral patterns are so heavily determined by the ecological conditions summarized above that these former will account for very little variation in our outcome. Third, and closely related, is the suspicion that we can treat ecological variables as surrogates of behavior, given their assumed covariation, and thus avoid all of the grief associated with the observation and measurement of behavior.

Be that as it may, there is a modest body of empirical work in which behavior patterns serve as predictors, and once again Richardson offers a convenient point of departure. Perhaps his most important contribution is found in the posthumous *Arms and Insecurity* (1960b), where he derives and then puts to the test a simple differential equation designed to capture the essence of an interactive arms race. Vis-à-vis the arms expenditure patterns preceding the two World Wars, the model offers a fairly good fit, and generally supports the notion that each protagonist's annual increase will be a function of the other's absolute expenditure in the previous year, controlling for a fatigue factor and an exacerbation factor.

These analyses have stimulated the development of a rich and diverse array of follow-up models, a fair number of which have been tested against various 19th and 20th century arms interaction processes. While it would require a major review article to summarize and interpret this body of research (Kurakawa, 1978; Luterbacher, 1974; Zinnes, 1980b) two general conclusions seem justified. One is that we have not yet been able to separate the effects of the domestic and foreign stimuli at the various stages of arms races, and the other is that we have yet to differentiate between the profiles or "signatures" of those that *have* ended in war and those that have not (Singer, 1970). But two important findings have resulted from Wallace's work in this area. In an earlier study (1971), he not only found that status inconsistency levels in the international system predicted system-wide increases in military expenditures, but also that these increases predicted in turn the incidence of war. In a later analysis (1979) Wallace found that if two nations started a military confrontation, their likelihood of crossing the war threshold was considerably lower if they were not in an arms race with one another, but much higher if they were.

An even more elusive problem arises when we shift from military expenditures and arms acquisition to less easily observed behavior such as the diplomatic moves and countermoves associated with the escalation of conflict. But a satisfactory coding and scaling scheme has been developed (Leng and Singer, 1977). In some preliminary analyses, Leng (1980) found that the use of threats had a higher probability of ending in war when met with a defiant counterthreat, whereas there is no clear association between the mere frequency of threats and the onset of war. In an earlier set of investigations, North et al. (1964) combined behavior and perception in order to examine their reciprocal effects in a number of crises, particularly that preceding World War I. In general, they found a propensity toward over-estimation of the adversary's intentions (compared with his actual behavior) and an under-estimation of his relative capabilities, the combination of which leads to escalatory behavior.

Not surprisingly, and despite the attention of diplomatic historians and traditional political scientists, the systematic examination of the relationship between behavioral phenomena and war has lagged discernibly behind that of the other three sets of factors discussed earlier. While the explanation lies partially in the observation and measurement problem noted above, this lag also reflects the reasonable idea that the more we first discover regarding the effects of the ecological conditions, the greater the theoretical mileage we will obtain from subsequent analyses of the behavioral and interactional phenomena.

3. CONCLUSION

While this summary hardly suggests that we are well on the way to understanding the causes of war and conditions of peace (to use Wright's phrase), some modest optimism would not be completely out of place. That is, despite the limited amount of research and the relative lack of convergence in our findings, there are two grounds for believing that we are no longer moving in non-cumulative circles. First, we are finally seeing systematic research that rests on reproducible evidence, and after several centuries of preoperational speculation, this is to be applauded. Second, despite the diversity of theoretical orientations, there seems to be a growing awareness that the resulting paradigms and investigations need not be incompatible.

On the one hand, my sense is that researchers in the war–peace sector are increasingly aware of the difference between explaining the *high* incidence of recurrent conflict and rivalry of a non-military sort, and explaining the low—but destructive—incidence of war. The range of models intended to address the former question is, admittedly, impressive in its diversity. But that, in my judgment, is a less critical problem; conflict is ubiquitous in all social systems and the problem is not to prevent it, but to reduce the frequency with which it becomes socially destructive. Thus, when we shift from conflict in general to war in particular, we find a diminished and more manageable array of theoretical models (Burton, 1962; Hoffmann, 1965; Holsti, 1972; Kaplan, 1957; Wallensteen, 1973; Midlarsky, 1975; Russett, 1974). And, on the other hand, a close scrutiny of these models shows a remarkable overlap, if not convergence. To illustrate, let me mention some of the emphases found in the literature most frequently: realpolitik, arms race, power transition, economic development, and imperialism. There are indeed those who insist that such models are not only inconsistent with one another logically and empirically, but also not even subject to comparative analysis and testing. There are even those who insist on a different epistemology and assert that the western scientific method is inappropriate to the examination of rival models and hypotheses. But my suspicion is that their numbers and influence are on the wane, and that a compelling theoretical convergence could encourage a more open-minded examination of the empirical evidence.

In order to move toward such a theoretical convergence, two prior steps would seem necessary. First, we need to identify the extent to which these competing models rest upon similar explanatory variables. Given the Babel-like discourse of theorizers and practitioners, this might appear to be impossible. But as systematic empirical work goes forward, one inexorable consequence is the translation of ideologically loaded verbalization into operationally defined variables, and the evidence to date is that devotees of rather diverse approaches can agree on (at least) the face validity of these indicators. Moreover, it looks as if a rather wide range of putatively explanatory concepts can be validly translated into identical indicators. Thus, "defining our terms" and operationalizing our variables may well reveal a considerable degree of convergence amongst theoretical models that have often been thought of as hopelessly divergent and incomparable.

Second, we need to recognize that at rock bottom the most important difference amongst the contending causes of war models is that of the foreign policy decision process. That is, each model assumes—often implicitly—a different class of decision makers in power, and each postulates a different set of decision rules. Thus, one strategy might be to conceive of the policy making process in terms of interest aggregation, with the decision makers seen as trying to respond to and balance a complex array of international incentives and constraints vis-à-vis an equally complex array of domestic interests, including their own. Once those assumptions and postulations have been teased out of the verbal models, our highly general paradigm might then be converted into operational versions of the several more specific models. Note that we have assumed, to this juncture, a high degree of homogeneity in decision makers and the rules they employ, but to move closer to a full explanation, that assumption would have to be relaxed.

These assumptions, however, should be put to the empirical/historical test directly, and this is why the research described in the body of this paper can be so valuable. It is one thing to observe and then classify the backgrounds and interest group affiliations of foreign policy elites in a wide range of nations across an appreciable span of time; while this research task is far from complete, it is clearly manageable. But the decision rules that they employ, and the utilities that they assign to various outcomes in the economic, diplomatic, and military sectors will remain forever beyond the range of *direct* observation. Thus, we have little choice but to rely on careful inference, and the most solid basis for inferring their decision criteria will be found in the sort of evidence discussed above, especially when embedded in computerized representations of the historical process (Alker and Brunner, 1969; Bremer, 1977). *Under which systemic, dyadic, and national conditions do which'foreign policy elites respond to which behavioral stimuli of which other nations in which specific fashion?* The more fully we can answer these empirical questions, the more reliably can we infer the decision rules that are at work. And the more we can check these inferences against those that are embedded in the rival models, the closer we can get to their confirmation and disconfirmation.

This brief overview leaves out a great deal of important detail, just as our survey of the evidence to date is far from complete; a more complete picture emerges in three volumes from the Michigan project: *Explaining War,* 1979; *Correlates of War I: Research Origins and Rationale,* 1979; and *Correlates of War II: Testing Some Realpolitik Models,* 1980. But these pages should serve to remind us that the causes-of-war question is not only a researchable one, soluble in principle. They also serve to remind us that the task is finally under way, and if the scientific talent and the necessary support can be mobilized, we may yet be in time to put an end to one of the most destructive and dysfunctional activities known to human history.

REFERENCES

Alcock, N. Z. 1972. *The War Disease*. Oakville, Canada: Canadian Peace Research Institute.

Alker, H., and Brunner, R. 1969. Simulating international conflict. *International Studies Quarterly*, 13/1: 70–110.

Ardrey, R. 1966. *The Territorial Imperative*. New York: Atheneum.

Barringer, R. E. 1972. *War: Patterns of Conflict*. Cambridge, Mass.: MIT Press.

Blainey, G. 1973. *The Causes of War*. New York: Free Press.

Blechman, B. M. and Kaplan, S. S. 1978. *Force Without War*. Washington, D.C.: Brookings Institute.

Bloch, I. 1899. *The Future of War*. New York: Doubleday & McClure.

Bloomfield, L. and Leiss, A. 1969. *Controlling Small Wars*. New York: Knopf.

Bouthoul, G. 1951. *Les Guerres: Eléments de Polémologie*. Paris: Payot.

Bremer, S. A., Singer, J. D. and Luterbacher, U. The population density and war proneness of European nations 1816–1965. *Comparative Political Studies*, 6/3: 329–348.

Bremer, S. A. 1977. *Simulated Worlds*. Princeton, N.J.: Princeton Univ. Press.

Bremer, S. A. 1980. National capabilities and war proneness. In *Correlates of War II: Testing Some Realpolitik Models*, ed. J. D. Singer. New York: Free Press.

Bueno de Mesquita, B. June 1978. Systemic polarization and the occurrence and duration of war. *Journal of Conflict Resolution*, 22/2: 241–267.

Bueno de Mesquita, B. 1981. *The War Trap*. New Haven, Conn.: Yale Univ. Press.

Burton, J. W. 1962. *Peace Theory*. New York: Knopf.

Cannizzo, C. 1978. Capability distribution and major power war experience, 1816–1965. *Orbis*, 21/4: 947–957.

Champion, M. and Stoll, R. Capability concentration, alliance bonding, and conflict among the major powers. In *Alliances and International Conflict*, ed. A. N. Sabrosky. Philadelphia: Foreign Policy Research Institute.

Choi, K. L. 1978. *An Empirical Investigation of the Relationship Between International Legal Norms Relevant to the Control of Violence and the Amount of International War*. Seoul, Korea: Department of Political Science and Diplomacy, mimeo.

Choucri, N. and North, R. C. 1975. *Nations in Conflict*. San Francisco: W. H. Freeman.

Davis, W., Duncan, G. and Siverson, R. 1978. The dynamics of warfare, 1816–1965. *American Journal of Political Science*, 22/4: 772–792.

Dedring, J. 1976. *Recent Advances in Peace and Conflict Research*. Beverly Hills: Sage.

Denton, F. H. and Phillips, W. 1968. Some patterns in the history of violence. *Journal of Conflict Resolution*, 12/2: 182–195.

Deutsch, K. W. and Singer, J. D. 1964. Multipolar power systems and international stability. *World Politics*, 16/3: 390–406.

Deutsch, K. W. and Senghaas, D. 1971. A framework for a theory of war and peace. In *Search for World Order*, ed. A. Lepawsky et al. New York: Appleton-Century. pp. 23–46.

Dewey, E. R. 1964. *The 177-Year Cycle in War, 600 B.C.–A.D. 1957*. Pittsburgh: Foundation for the Study of Cycles.

East, M. A. 1972. Status discrepancy and violence in the international system: An empirical analysis. In *The Analysis of International Politics*, ed. V. Davis et al. New York: Free Press. pp. 299–319.

Ferris, W. H. 1973. *The Power Capabilities of Nation States*. Lexington, Mass.: Lexington Books.

Fornari, F. 1974. *Psychoanalysis of War*. Garden City, N.Y.: Doubleday.

Galtung, J. 1964. A structural theory of aggression. *Journal of Peace Research*, 1/2: 95–119.

Gantzel, K. J. 1972. *System and Akteur: Beiträge zur Vergleichenden Kriegsursachenforschung*. Düsseldorf: Bertelsmann.

Garnham, D. 1976a. Dyadic International War, 1816–1965: the role of power parity and geographical proximity. *Western Political Quarterly*, 29/2: 231–242.

Garnham, D. 1976b. Power parity and lethal international violence 1969–1973. *Journal of Conflict Resolution*, 20/3: 379–394.

Garnham, D. 1979. The Causes of War: Systemic Findings. Milwaukee, Wisconsin: University of Wisconsin Department of Political Science.

Gleditsch, N. P. and Singer, J. D. 1975. Distance and international war 1816–1965. *Proceedings of the International Peace Research Association, fifth general conference*. Oslo, 481–506.

Gochman, C. S. 1980. Status, capabilities, and major power conflict. In *Correlates of War II: Testing Some Realpolitik Models*, ed. J. D. Singer, New York: Free Press.

Haas, M. 1965. Societal approaches to the study of war. *Journal of Peace Research*, 4: 307–323.

Harary, F. June 1961. A structural analysis of the situation in the Middle East in 1956. *Journal of Conflict Resolution*, 5/2: 167–78.

Hart, H. 1946. Depression, war, and logistic trends. *American Journal of Sociology*, 52: 112–122.

Hoffmann, S. 1965. *The State of War*. New York: Praeger.

Holsti, O. 1972. *Crisis, Escalation, War*. Montreal: McGill-Queens Univ. Press.

Horvath, W. J. Jan. 1968. A statistical model for the duration of wars and strikes. *Behavioral Science*, 13/1: 18–28.

Kaplan, M. A. 1957. *System and Process in International Politics*. New York: John Wiley.

Kegley, C. W., et al. (eds.). 1975. *International Events and the Comparative Analysis of Foreign Policy*, Columbia, South Carolina: University of South Carolina Press.

Kegley, C. W., Raymond, G. A., Choi, K. L. August 1979. Fluctuations in Legal Norms and Arbital Behavior, 1825–1970: indicators of major power conflict? Columbia, South Carolina: Department of Political Science.

Kegley, C. W. 1979. Measuring transformations in the global legal system. In *Law Making In The Global Community*, ed. M. G. Onuf. Princeton: Princeton University Press.

Kende, I. 1971. Twenty-five years of local wars. *Journal of Peace Research*, 8: 5–22.

Klingberg, F. L. 1952. The historical alternation of moods in American foreign policy. *World Politics,* 4/2: 239–273.

Kurokawa, S. 1978. *A simple model of arms races: Richardson's model revisited.* Prepared for delivery at the Hiroshima, Japan Conference of the Peace Science Society (International).

Leng, R. J. 1980. Influence strategies and interstate conflict. In *The Correlates of War II: Testing Some Realpolitik Models,* ed. J. D. Singer. New York: Free Press.

Leng, R. J. and Singer, J. D. 1977. Towards a multitheoretical typology of international behavior. In *Mathematical Approaches to International Relations,* ed. Bunge, Galtung & Malitza. Bucharest: Romanian Academy of Social & Political Sciences, 71–93.

Lenin, V. I. 1939. *Imperialism.* New York: International Publishers.

Levy, J. S. 1979. The polarity of the system and international stability. International Studies Association. Mimeo.

Liska, G. 1956. *International Equilibrium.* Cambridge: Harvard University Press.

Lorenz, K. 1967. *On Aggression.* New York: Bantam Books.

Luterbacher, U. 1974. *Dimensions Historiques de Modèles Dynamiques de Conflit.* Leiden: A. W. Sijthoff.

McClelland, D. 1961. *The Achieving Society.* New York: Free Press.

Midlarsky, M. I. 1975. *On War.* New York: Free Press.

Mihalka, M. 1976. *Interstate Conflict in the European State System, 1816–1970.* Unpublished Doctoral Dissertation. Ann Arbor, Mich.: University of Michigan.

Morgenthau, H. J. 1948. *Politics Among Nations.* New York: Alfred A. Knopf.

Naroll, R. 1974. *Military Deterrence in History.* Albany: State University of New York Press.

Nelson, K. L., Olin, S. C. 1979. *Why War?: Ideology, Theory and History.* Berkeley, Calif.: Univ. of California Press.

North, R. C., Brody, R. A., Holsti, O. R. 1964. Some empirical data on the conflict spiral. *Peace Research Society Papers,* 1: 1–14.

Ostrom, C., Aldrich, J. H. Nov. 1978. The relationship between size and stability in the major power international system. *American Journal of Political Science,* 22: 743–771.

Ostrom, C. and Hoole, F. June 1978. Alliances and war revisited: a research note. *International Studies Quarterly,* 22: 215–235.

Organski, A. F. K. 1968. *World Politics.* New York: Alfred Knopf.

Ray, J. L. 1974. Status inconsistency and war involvement in Europe, 1816–1970. *Peace Science Society Papers,* 23: 69–80.

Ray, J. L. 1980. The measurement of system structure. In *The Correlates of War II: Testing Some Realpolitik Models,* ed. J. D. Singer. New York: Free Press.

Richardson, L. F. 15. November 1941. Frequency of occurrence of wars and other total quarrels. *Nature,* 148/37–59.

Richardson, L. F. 1960a. *Statistics of Deadly Quarrels.* Pittsburgh: Boxwood.

Richardson, L. F. 1960b. *Arms and Insecurity.* Pittsburgh: Boxwood.

Rosecrance, R. et al. 1974. *Power, Balance of Power and Status in Nineteenth Century International Relations.* Beverly Hills, Calif.: Sage.

Rosenau, J. N. 1966. Pre-theories and theories of foreign policy. In *Approaches to Comparative and International Politics,* ed. R. B. Farrell. Evanston, Ill.: Northwestern Univ. Press.

Rummel, R. J. 1972. *The Dimensions of Nations.* Beverly Hills, Calif.: Sage.

Russett, B. M. 1974. *Power and Community in World Politics*. San Francisco: Freeman.

Sabrosky, A. D. 1980. Interstate alliances: their reliability and the expansion of war. In *Correlates of War II: Testing Some Realpolitik Models*, ed. J. D. Singer. New York: Free Press.

Secerov, S. 1919. *Economic Phenomena Before and After War*. London: Rutledge.

Silberner, E. 1946. *The Problem of War in Nineteenth Century Economic Thought*. Princeton, N.J.: Princeton Univ. Press.

Singer, J. D. October, 1961. The level-of-analysis problem in international relations. *World Politics*, 14/1: 77–92.

Singer, J. D. 1970. The outcome of arms races: A policy problem and a research approach. *Proceedings of the International Peace Research Association, Third General Conference*, 2: 137–46.

Singer, J. D. 1971. *A General Systems Taxonomy for Political Science*. Morristown, N.J.: General Learning Press.

Singer, J. D. 1976. The correlates of war project: Continuity, diversity and convergence. In *Quantitative International Politics: An Appraisal*, eds. F. Hoole and D. Zinnes, pp. 21–66. New York: Praeger.

Singer, J. D. ed. 1979. *Correlates of War I: Research Origins and Rationale*. New York: Free Press.

Singer, J. D. ed. 1979. *Explaining War*. Beverly Hills, Calif.: Sage.

Singer, J. D. 1979a. The Management of Serious International Disputes. Ann Arbor, Mich.: University of Michigan Department of Political Science.

Singer, J. D. ed. 1980. *Correlates of War II: Testing Some Realpolitik Models*. New York: Free Press.

Singer, J. D., Bremer, S. A. and Stuckey, J. 1972. Capability distribution, uncertainty and major power war, 1820–1965. In *Peace, War & Numbers*, ed. B. M. Russett. Beverly Hills, Calif.: Sage, 19–48.

Singer, J. D. and Bueno de Mesquita, B. 1973. Alliances, Capabilities, and War: A Review and Synthesis. *Political Science Annual*, IV, 237–280.

Singer, J. D. and Cusack, T. 1981. Periodicity, inexorability, and steersmanship in international war. In *From National Development to Global Community*, R. Merritt and B. M. Russett.

Singer, J. D. and Small, M. 1968. Alliance aggregation and the onset of war, 1815–1945. In *Quantitative International Politics: Insights and Evidence*, ed. J. D. Singer. New York: Free Press.

Singer, J. D. and Small, M. 1972. *The Wages of War: A Statistical Handbook, 1816–1965*. New York: John Wiley.

Singer, J. D. and Wallace, M. 1970. Intergovernmental organization and the preservation of peace, 1816–1964: Some bivariate relationships. *International Organization*, 24/3: 520–47.

Siverson, R. and King, J. 1980. Attributes of national alliance membership and war participation, 1815–1965. *American Jnl. of Political Science*, 24/1: 1–15.

Skjelsbaek, K. Shared membership in intergovernmental organizations and dyadic war, 1865–1964. *The United Nations: Problems & Prospects*. St. Louis, Mo.: University of Missouri Center for International Studies.

Small, M. 1978. Does size make a difference? In *Studien i Dansk Udenrigspolitik*, eds. N. Amstrup and I. Faurby. Aarhus, Denmark: Forlaget Politika.

Small, M., Singer, J. D. Summer, 1976. The war proneness of democratic regimes. *Jerusalem Journal of International Relations*, 1/4: 49–69.

Sorokin, Pitrim A. 1937. *Social and Cultural Dynamics: Fluctuations of Social Relationships, War and Revolution* vol. 3. New York: American Book.

Starr, H. and Most, B. Sept. 1978. A return journey. *Journal of Conflict Resolution,* 22/3: 441–468.

Stoessinger, J. G. 1978. *Why Nations Go to War.* New York: St. Martins.

Stoll, R. and Champion, M. November 1977. Predicting the escalation of serious disputes to international war: some preliminary findings. Philadelphia, Pa.: North American Peace Science Conference.

Sullivan, M. 1976. *International Relations: Theories and Evidence.* Englewood Cliffs, N.J.: Prentice-Hall.

Sullivan, M. 1978. The Causes of War: An Evaluation of the State of Theory. Tucson, Arizona: Univ. of Arizona, Department of Political Science.

Urlanis, B. T. 1960. *Wars and the Population of Europe.* Moscow, USSR: Government Publishing.

Voevodsky, J. July, 1969. Quantitative behavior of warring nations. *Journal of Psychology,* 72: 269–292.

Wallace, M. D. 1973. *War and Rank Among Nations.* Lexington, Mass.: Heath.

Wallace, M. D. 1973a. Alliance polarization, cross-cutting, and international war, 1815–1964. *Journal of Conflict Resolution,* 17: 4.

Wallace, M. 1979b. The role of arms races in the escalation of disputes into war: Some new evidence. *Journal of Conflict Resolution,* 23/1: 3–16.

Wallensteen, P. 1973. *Structure and War.* Stockholm, Sweden: Roben and Sjogren.

Waltz, K. 1967. International structure, national force, and the balance of world power. *Journal of International Affairs,* 21: 215–231.

Wayman, F. 1981. Bipolarity, multipolarity and the threat of war. In *Power, Pacts, and War,* ed. A. N. Sabrosky. Boulder, Colo: Greenwood Press.

Weede, E. 1970. Conflict behavior of nation states. *Journal of Peace Research,* 3: 229–236.

Weede, E. Sept. 1976. Overwhelming preponderance as a pacifying condition among contiguous Asian dyads, 1950–1969. *Journal of Conflict Resolution,* 20/3: 395–412.

Weiss, H. K. 1963. Stochastic models for the duration and magnitude of a deadly quarrel. *Operations Research,* 11/1: 101–121.

Wesley, J. P. 1969. Frequency of wars and geographic opportunity. In *Theory & Research on the Causes of War,* ed. D. G. Pruitt, R. C. Snyder.

White, R. K. 1968. *Nobody Wanted War.* Garden City, N.Y.: Doubleday.

Wilkenfeld, J. 1973. Domestic and foreign conflict. In *Conflict Behavior and Linkage Politics,* ed. J. Wilkenfeld, pp. 107–123. New York: McKay.

Wilkinson, D. 1980. *Deadly Quarrels.* Berkeley, Calif.: University of California Press.

Wright, Q. 1942. *A Study of War,* 2 vols. Chicago: University of Chicago. Revised edition, 1965.

Wright, Q. 1965. The escalation of international conflicts. *Journal of Conflict Resolution,* 9/4: 434–449.

Zinnes, D. 1980a. Empirical evidence on the outbreak of international violence. In *Handbook of Political Conflict,* ed. T. Gurr. New York: Free Press.

Zinnes, D. 1980b. 'Three Puzzles in Search of a Researcher.' Bloomington, Indiana, mimeo.

CHAPTER THREE

Pluralism: Decision Making, Transnationalism, and Interdependence

MAJOR ACTORS AND ASSUMPTIONS: A SUMMARY

The pluralist image of international relations is based on four key assumptions. First, *non-state actors* are important entities in world politics. International organizations, for example, may on certain issues be independent actors in their own right. They are more than simply forums within which states compete and cooperate with one another. The staff of a particular international organization may have a great deal of power in terms of agenda setting as well as in providing information on which the representatives of states base their demands. International organizations may also have an important role in implementing, monitoring, and adjudicating disputes arising from decisions made by constituent states of the organization. Over time, such functions may make the international organization indispensable to member states. Similarly, other nongovernmental, **transnational** organizations such as multinational corporations (MNCs) play important roles in world politics. Nor can one ignore the impact of such non-state actors as terrorist groups, arms dealers, and guerrilla movements.

Second, for the pluralist *the state is not a unitary actor*. It is composed of competing individuals, interests groups, and bureaucracies. Although it may be convenient for newspapers and governmental representatives to refer to "decisions taken by the United States," it is generally more accurate to speak of a decision made by a particular governmental coalition, bureaucracy, or even perhaps a single individual. The decision is not made by some abstract entity called "the United States" but by some combination of actors within the foreign policy establishment.

Different organizations, for example, may have different perspectives on a particular foreign policy issue. Competition, coalition building, and compromise will eventually result in a decision that is then announced in the name of the United States. Furthermore, this state decision may be the result of lobbying carried out by such nongovernmental actors as multinational corporations, or interest groups, or it may even be influenced by something as amorphous as public opinion. To the pluralist, the state cannot therefore be viewed as a unitary actor because to do so misses the multiplicity of actors comprising the entity termed *the state*, the interactions occurring among these actors, and the role of influences emanating from beyond the territorial boundaries of the state as well as from domestic sources—ideas and values, international and transnational organizations, interest groups, and public opinion.

Third, pluralists *challenge the realist assumption of the state as rational actor.* Given their fragmented view of the state, it is assumed that the clash of interests, bargaining, and need for compromise do not always make for a rational decision-making process. Misperception or bureaucratic politics may dominate decision-making, leading to poor decisions that are often *suboptimal* or less than the best in terms of objectives sought. Instead of leading their country, statesmen may be tempted to take their cue from public opinion polls, evincing more concern for their personal standing or power position than for the good of the country as a whole. Pressure resulting from a crisis situation may also make a mockery of the notion of a cool and calculating decision-making process.

Finally, for pluralists the *agenda of international politics is extensive.* Although national security concerns are important, the pluralist is also concerned with a number of economic, social, and ecological issues arising from the growth of **interdependence** among states and societies in the twentieth century. Certain pluralists, for example, emphasize trade, monetary, and energy issues and how these issues have come to be placed high on the international agenda. Other pluralists examine international attempts to deal with the world population problem and famine in parts of the **Third World.** Still others have studied the politics of international pollution and the degradation of the environment. The foreign affairs agendas of states are not exclusively preoccupied with national security issues, narrowly defined in terms of military matters. Economic and social issues can often have a direct bearing on the security and welfare of a particular regime or country. Because this is so, pluralists tend to reject the high versus low politics dichotomy accepted by most realists. Socioeconomic issues are often as important as military concerns.

INTELLECTUAL PRECURSORS AND INFLUENCES

In the case of realism, it was relatively easy to identify its intellectual precursors. At least two of these, Grotius and E. H. Carr, have also had significant impact on scholars associated with the pluralist image. In the case of pluralism, however, the impact of particular theorists has tended to be more indirect. This is because many of these writers have not been observers of international relations per se but have been economists, social scientists, theologians, or political scientists interested in domestic politics. Their one common denominator, however, has been an interest in the individual or group as the unit of analysis, as opposed to the unified state that is the focus of realist writings. Therefore, we have organized the discussion of the intellectual precursors of pluralism around two themes within which individual theorists are mentioned: **liberalism** as a political philosophy and **interest group liberalism** as an approach to the study of domestic politics.

Although some aspects of liberal thought have also influenced realist scholars, we focus here on those aspects of liberalism that lead to rejection of a view of the state as unitary and rational actor. That the state is (or should be) disaggregated into component parts or becomes the battleground for competing interests is a view found in liberalism as well as interest group liberalism. Within the international relations discipline, works on **decision making** and **transnationalism** best reflect this view of the disaggregated state and the importance of nonstate actors.

Liberalism

Liberalism is a tradition of political thought composed of a set of practical goals and ideals. For classical liberal theorists, the individual is the most important unit of analysis and the claimant of rights. The state is to play a minimal role in a liberal society, principally acting as arbiter in disputes between individuals and ensuring the maintenance of conditions under which individuals can enjoy their rights to the fullest. There are important differences among liberal theorists, but they do agree on the primacy of the individual in political life and on the role of the state as being limited to maintaining a stable political, social, and economic environment within which individuals can interact and pursue their chosen ends. This emphasis on the individual and the limited state is perhaps best exemplified in John Locke's *Second Treatise on Government*, published in England in 1689.[1]

Liberalism as an ideology came to dominate much of the political and economic thought in the eighteenth and nineteenth centuries, particularly in Great Britain and the United States. Liberal concerns for the individual were reinforced by Adam Smith's and David Ricardo's works in economics. They emphasized the important role of the individual entrepreneur who should be relatively unconstrained by a minimalist state—a major theme in early capitalist writings. David Hume's contribution to logic and the philosophy of science similarly stressed the importance of the individual as the unit of analysis. The nineteenth-century essays of such **utilitarians** as Jeremy Bentham viewed people as rational, calculating individuals capable of deciding what was best for themselves without much government interference. Liberalism reigned supreme, virtually unchallenged in the United States and Great Britain until the turn of the century. The spirit of liberalism and its emphasis on the individual pervaded all spheres of life and thought—scientific, political, economic, social, and religious.[2] The industrial revolution, however, eventually resulted in modifications of liberal doctrine, which although retaining an emphasis on the individual now allowed the state to be given a somewhat more activist role in order to mitigate the most harmful effects of unrestrained economic competition.

For liberals the minimal state was a possibility (and necessity) because it was assumed that there was an underlying harmony of interests among individuals. Just as the competiton of the marketplace would produce the best goods, so too would the marketplace of ideas produce sound political sense. It followed that liberals emphasized the positive role played by public opinion in providing guidance to state officials and producing good public policy, including foreign policy. The state, therefore, was not some unitary, solitary actor pursuing its own course independently of the public. To the contrary, it was composed of numerous persons representing a multitude of interests. Nor were decisions the sole province of those individuals acting in the name of the state. Decisions were supposed to be informed by the public opinion and political consensus arising out of the clash of ideas and interests.

This view of the domestic polity was carried over into the international realm. Liberals recognized that war was a defining characteristic of international politics. They also agreed with realists that the state of anarchy that characterized world (as opposed to domestic) politics contributed to suspicion and distrust among states, posing an obstacle to cooperation and peace. But just as it was assumed that there could be a harmony of interests among individuals within a given state, so too did liberal theorists argue that a harmony of interests among states was possible.

It was recognized that war had existed down through the centuries. What, then, had changed to allow for this more optimistic view of interstate relations? Liberals made at least four arguments. First, the expansion of the international economy made it more costly for states to go to war. As economic interdependence increased, there would be a disinclination to cut profitable economic ties. Second, the spread of democratic political systems meant that questions of war and peace were no longer confined to a small group of political and military elites as in the past. Instead, leaders would have to be concerned with domestic public opinion that could act as a brake on any moves toward international confrontation and the outbreak of hostilities. Third, the growing corpus of international law would contribute to the peaceful settlement of disputes. Finally, it was argued that western civilization had suffered enough from war and that leaders and citizens had learned how costly it was to wage it.

The German, or more precisely East Prussian, philosopher Immanuel Kant (1724-1804) observed that over the years it had become increasingly likely that *reason* would be a substitute for the use of force in world politics. He was guardedly optimistic that international law would grow stonger and come to play a larger role in regulating inter-state relations.[3] Since World War I, liberal thinking has particularly stressed the positive role international law can play in promoting peace and harmony in world politics. Collaborative action by international organizations that represents the consensus of their constitutent states works to mitigate the worst aspects of anarchy and to encourage cooperation.[4]

In sum, this brief overview of liberal thought highlights a number of concepts, arguments, and perspectives that directly or indirectly influence the pluralist image of international politics: the importance of the individual and societal **levels of analysis,** the disaggregated and non-unified state broken into its component parts, the intimate connection between international economics and politics, the role of public opinion, the importance of international law and organizations, and the ability of leaders to learn from past historical mistakes and disasters. Current scholars whom we would term pluralist have not been equally influenced by all strands of liberal thought as it has developed over the years. Some have been particularly influenced by the liberal view of the disaggregated state with an emphasis on the *individual* as the unit of analysis. Others have been less influenced by such methodological questions, but more by the optimistic elements of liberalism concerning the possibilities for peaceful change and harmony in the international system.

Interest Group Liberalism

The roots of the pluralist image of international politics also lie in the view held by many scholars of the domestic political order. This is particularly true of American academics who are prone to see international politics through domestic political lenses. Indeed, the pluralist image of international politics held by many American international relations scholars can be understood as a projection of American political processes onto the entire globe. International political processes are not all that different from, and may even be considered an extension of, those conducted within the boundaries of a given state. As a result, pluralists tend to reject the realist distinction between "international" and "domestic" politics. For the pluralist, one is an extension of the other. This perspective is quite evident in much of the literature on decision making and transnationalism that disaggregates the state-as-actor.

The majority (but certainly not all) of authors we would term pluralist is American. Each has either directly or indirectly been influenced by political scientists who are students of the American political system. We use the term **interest group liberalism** to describe the perspective of these latter individuals.

The connection to the discussion of eighteenth- and nineteenth-century liberal thought is apparent. One critic of interest group liberalism, for example, comments that from this perspective the domestic political "role of government is one of assuring access to the most effectively organized, and of ratifying the agreements and adjustments worked out among competing leaders and their claims."[5] He further notes the "zeal ... for the group and its belief in a natural harmony of group competition." In short, interest group liberalism defines both "the policy agenda and the public interest ... in terms of the organized interests in society."[6] All three observations are consistent with the liberal notions of (1) the state as neutral arbiter, (2) the potential for a natural harmony of interest (in this case groups instead of individuals), and (3) public concern for, and participation in, a policy process not restricted to elites.

In the image of politics held by adherents of interest group liberalism, conflict and competition among interest groups play an important role. There is a proliferation of interest groups. Individuals form interest groups in attempts to outmaneuver, end-run, or overwhelm opposing groups or coalitions. Viewed in this way, politics is a game but a game with very real stakes to be won or lost. Authoritative choices (or decisions) are made by government decisionmakers as the outcome of this process.

David Truman, whose writings are in the school of interest group liberalism, acknowledges his intellectual debt to Arthur F. Bentley, whose 1908 volume *The Process of Government* served as "the principal bench mark for my thinking."[7] Observing that "the outstanding characteristic of American politics" is the "multiplicity of co-ordinate or nearly co-ordinate points of access to governmental decisions," Truman describes the conflictual nature of American politics but comments that "overlapping membership among organized interest groups" provides what he calls "the principal balancing force in the politics of a multigroup society such as the United States."[8]

The writings of Harold Lasswell and Robert Dahl are also illustrative of this image of American politics. Dahl describes American politics as a "system in which all the active and legitimate groups in the population can make themselves heard at some crucial stage in the process of decision."[9] Noting that it is a decentralized system, he observes that "decisions are made by endless bargaining." Groups are central to the process. Rather than either majority rule or minority rule, Dahl argues that the term *minorities rule* is the more accurate.[10] Politically active groups—minorities—are the most influential.

Thus, the image of politics that interest group liberals hold is of a fragmented political system, one in which multiple actors compete. The image is shared by most American political scientists even though their views may differ greatly on other conceptual and normative matters. The scholars mentioned are not, of course, creators of this image of American politics. Certainly *The Federalist Papers*, especially the writings of James Madison and later those of the Frenchman Alexis de Tocqueville, expose one to a good dose of this view of American domestic politics.[11]

In sum, what the group is to the interest group liberal, the individual is to the liberal philosopher. What they have in common is agreement on the fragmented nature of the state and society and the potential for harmony to develop out of competition and conflict. The state is not an independent, coherent, autonomous actor separated or aloof from society. Its primary function is as arbiter of conflicting demands and claims, or as an arena for the expression of such interests. Furthermore, the focus of analysis is less on the state and more on the competition among individuals and groups.

DECISION MAKING

If states were the only important actors and all states simply responded to their environment according to the same rational logic, there would be no need to disaggregate the state-as-actor or to consider a multiplicity of domestic and international influences. Although it is possible to chart relations among states (as realists sometimes do) without ever looking "inside" the states, pluralists argue that a complete understanding of the *reasons* for these relations requires analysis of the decision-making process. In this section we first examine some early work on foreign policy decision making, and then we focus on scholarly literature that examines the role of individuals and bureaucracies in the formulation of foreign policy.

One of the first major attempts to develop a systematic decision-making approach to the study of international politics was made in the early 1950s by Richard C. Snyder and his colleagues.[12] Snyder stated that the focus of international relations research should be on the actions, reactions, and interactions of states. For him, the state is specifically its decision makers, and state action "is the action taken by those acting in the name of the state."[13] So far, realists would have little with which to disagree.

Snyder, however, emphasized that his analytical objective was to recreate the world as actual decision makers view it in order to explain behavior. This led him to discuss (1) subjective factors from the standpoint of decision makers—how they define the situation—not from the perspective of the analyst, and (2) potential sources of state action found in the decision makers' setting. The framework hence draws attention to numerous factors at different levels of analysis. Under the heading "internal setting," for example, domestic politics and public opinion are listed as potentially important elements in the formulation and execution of foreign policy. Nongovernmental factors and relations between countries (trade, family ties, shared values, mass media, migration, cultural exchanges) may also be important. Snyder therefore developed a decision-making framework consisting of numerous factors. It was up to the scholar to test them **empirically** by means of case studies. The relative importance of any one factor would vary from case to case.

This work is considered a pioneering effort, particularly given Snyder's claim that the foreign policy process could be studied scientifically. From the standpoint of the current state of the international relations discipline, such a perspective on decision making may seem passé, little more than an inventory of potentially relevant factors. For our purposes, it is important to point out that Snyder argued for the systematic consideration of a number of factors that may influence the decisions of flesh-and-blood policymakers. The framework explicity emphasizes **perception** on the part of decision makers and the role of nongovernmental influences on the foreign policy process. These factors are part of the domestic, international, and decision-making settings within which policymakers operate. Hence, a plurality of factors is given prominence. Despite its innovative nature, Snyder's framework failed to generate more than one major empirical case study.[14] What it did do, however, was to encourage a shift in analytic focus away from the **reified,** abstract state.

The 1960s witnessed a proliferation of studies that identified an almost unending inventory of factors that may influence the foreign policy process. But as James N. Rosenau, a long-time student of foreign policy, stated in 1966:

> the dynamics of the processes which culminate in the external behavior of societies remain obscure. To identify factors is not to trace their influence. To uncover processes that affect external behavior is not to explain how and why they are operative under certain circumstances and not under others. To recognize that foreign policy is shaped by internal as well as external factors is not to comprehend how the two intermix or to indicate the conditions under which one predominates the other.[15]

What was missing were attempts to develop general theories of foreign policy—theories that contained testable hypotheses aimed at explaining the external behavior of more than one country. Single case studies were the norm.

Comparative studies—examining the similarities and differences of various decision-making systems—were rare until the late 1960s. Spurred by the comparative analysis of political systems, students of international relations began to generate and test hypotheses concerning the foreign policy behavior of states. Although different levels of analysis and different **variables** were used, what these studies had in common was a commitment to discovering common patterns or processes in the foreign (and most recently defense) policies of states.[16]

The Individual and Small Groups

Scholars engaged in studying decision-making processes from a pluralist perspective emphasize, as we have noted, that entities known as the "United States" or "Canada" do not make decisions; decisions are made by individuals. Similarly, a particular bureaucratic entity termed the "State Department" or "Foreign Office" is composed of individuals. It is, therefore, not surprising that the study of individuals and small groups has been a primary focus of analysis for a number of scholars.

The study of individuals and their role in international relations or foreign policy has drawn heavily on the disciplines of **psychology** and **social psychology.** Some of the work can be termed **psychohistory** and has focused on how life experiences influence an individual's foreign policy behavior and orientation. Other work by such scholars as Alexander George and Ole Holsti has attempted to discern an individual's belief system or **operational code.**[17]

A number of research efforts have drawn on the psychology literature in an attempt to generalize about the circumstances under which certain psychological processes occur. What these approaches have in common is an emphasis on how **cognitive** distortions undermine the realist view of decision making as a rational process. But unlike much of the earlier work, many of these scholars have also studied political science and history in addition to psychology and social psychology. As a result, their insights into the role that perception plays in the foreign policy process or during crisis situations is deserving of further comment.

The work of Robert Jervis, to take one example, starts with some realist assumptions, but then it focuses on individuals and individual perceptions, a more pluralist view.[18] Jervis is concerned less with how emotions affect foreign policy decision making and more with how cognitive factors and a confusing international environment can result in a poor decision even if the individual is relatively unemotional and as intelligent as he or she can be in evaluating alternatives. Furthermore, Jervis takes into account how the **anarchic** nature of international politics contributes to this confusing environment by encouraging cognitive processes that make decision making more difficult. Jervis accepts the realist argument that the anarchic **structure** of the international system breeds suspicion and distrust. The lack of a single **sovereign** or authority makes it a self-help system, and it is not necessarily irrational or a sign of paranoia to be preoccupied with real, potential, or imagined threats.

Jervis devotes a great deal of time to applying psychological concepts to historical events. According to him his propositions are

> generalizations about how decision-makers perceive others' behavior and form judgments about their intentions. These patterns are explained by the general ways in which people draw inferences from ambiguous evidence and, in turn, help explain seemingly incomprehensible policies. They show how, why, and when highly intelligent and conscientious statesmen misperceive their environments in specified ways and reach inappropriate decisions.[19]

Jervis is interested in discerning how a decision maker comprehends a complex world filled with uncertainty. Each decision maker has a particular image of the world that has been shaped by his or her interpretations of historical events. Very often these events (such as wars and revolutions) occurred when the individual was young and impressionable. Lessons learned from history, when combined with personal experiences, contribute to the development of particular expectations and beliefs concerning how the world operates that will have a major impact on the decisions made by policymakers. Once formed, these images of reality are difficult to change. Cognitive consistency is the norm. Information that conflicts with the decision maker's image tends either to be dismissed, ignored, or interpreted in such a manner as to buttress a particular policy preference or course of action.

Jervis emphasizes how the striving for cognitive consistency can have a negative effect on decision-making processes, and other scholars focus on how psychological stress arising out of difficult, emotion-laden situations affects rational calculations. One example of this perspective is the work of Irving L. Janis.[20]

Janis has examined the tendency for social pressure to enforce conformity and consensus in cohesive decision-making groups. He calls this tendency **groupthink**, a "mode of thinking that people engage in when they are deeply involved in a cohesive in-group, when the members' strivings for unanimity override their motivation to realistically appraise alternative courses of action."[21] Indicators of groupthink include limiting discussions to only a few alternative courses of action, failing to reexamine initial decisions and possible courses of action initially rejected, and making little attempt to seek information from outside experts who may challenge a preferred policy. To make his case for the persuasiveness of concurrence seeking within a group and the resultant impact, Janis examines several foreign policy fiascos such as the Bay of Pigs invasion in 1961, the military unpreparedness of the United

States at Pearl Harbor in 1941, and the American decisions to escalate the Korean and Vietnam wars. He argues that in each case the pressure to conform to group norms interfered with critical, rational thinking.

A number of international relations scholars have been particularly interested in how psychological processes influence decision making during times of crisis—a situation between peace and war. The tendency for individuals to strive for cognitive consistency and for groups to enforce consensus among their members is particularly evident in crisis situations characterized by high stress, surprise, exhausting around-the-clock work schedules, and complex and ambiguous environments. As a result, there is a general erosion of cognitive capabilities. Tolerance for ambiguity is reduced, policy options are restricted, opposing actors and their motives are stereotyped. Compared to noncrisis situations, decisions are based even more on policymakers' predispositions, expectations, biases, and emotional states.[22]

In sum, scholarly work suggests that misperception can play a major role in crisis situations, perhaps contributing to the outbreak of war. Furthermore, it has been argued that not all decision makers operate with the same kind of rationality, making it difficult for leaders to judge what actions may deter an enemy.[23] The cumulative effect of such studies is to undermine the image of decision making as an essentially rational process. Nevertheless, scholars tend at the same time to exhort decision makers "to be more rational."[24]

No one would deny that the study of individuals is important if we wish to improve our understanding of international relations. The important question, however, is how much emphasis should be placed on the individual level of analysis as opposed to other levels. Recall Hans Morgenthau's observation in the previous chapter that in order to understand how a statesman reached a particular decision, we speculate how we would respond in similar circumstances. In other words, by keeping the decision-making environment constant, we could hypothesize that any rational individual would have acted in the same manner. Despite a diversity of backgrounds or temperaments, the structure of the situation encourages decision makers to respond in a similar fashion. What if, however, beliefs and perceptions *do* make a difference and individuals respond to common stimuli or the environment in divergent ways? If so, the individual as a focus of analysis *is* important.

This debate over the relative importance of the individual as opposed to the environment in explaining behavior is common to all the social sciences. It also touches on the matter of **determinism** versus **voluntarism.** If the international system is the key to understanding international relations, then other levels of analysis—individual, organizational, societal, or state—are by definition of less importance. If one accepts a more pluralistic view of international relations, however, then greater consideration and weight are given to the role of the individual. Individuals matter simply because their choices significantly affect the functioning of world politics.

Organizational Process and Bureaucratic Politics

Theorists who take an organizational or bureaucratic politics view of the foreign policymaking process offer a fragmented image as an alternative to the usual set of assumptions associated with the realists: that the state is the principal actor behaving in a rational and unitary manner.

Both unitary and rational assumptions are relaxed from the **organizational process** and **bureaucratic politics** perspectives. Graham Allison's organizational process model of foreign policy decision making, a view of bureaucracy that owes an intellectual debt to the German scholar Max Weber, sees organizational routines and procedures as determining at least some, and influencing other, foreign policy decisions and outcomes.[25] Organizational ethos and world view are also relevant considerations. In an often cited statement, Allison notes that where a given bureaucratic actor "stands" on a given issue is often determined by where he or she "sits"; one's view of alternative courses of action is highly colored by the perspective of the organization to which one belongs. Perceptions of what is the **optimal** or best course of action often vary from one bureaucratic actor to another, reflecting organizational biases that raise serious doubts concerning the rationality of the process as a whole. What assurance is there that optimal choices for the state as a whole will be made? Or is optimality, when achieved, purely accidental?

Allison's bureaucratic politics model of foreign policy decision making involves forming coalitions and countercoalitions among diverse bureaucratic actors in a competitive environment. The focus is on specific individuals in positions at the top of organizations and on the pulling and hauling among them. This is in contrast to the more routine, preprogrammed activity of the organizational process model. Hence, foreign policy decisions at times may be the result of which individual, or which coalition of individuals, can muster the most political power. What may be best for an individual and/or his bureaucracy in terms of increased prestige and relative standing within the government may lead to less than the best foreign policy for the state as a whole. Parochial personal and bureaucratic interests may reign over any expressed concern for the national interest.

Allison's work does not pose as direct a challenge to the unitary assumption about state behavior as does some of the other literature on decision making. Although multiple actors influenced by diverse organizational and individual interests compete to influence policy choices, in the final analysis these decisions are still made by certain authoritative individuals. Notwithstanding all the competition and airing of alternative views, the state still speaks ultimately with one voice.[26] At the same time, however, the Allison study did at least raise some questions concerning the unitary character of the state in *implementation* of policy. Decisions made were not always carried out as quickly as anticipated or in precisely the same fashion as intended. After all, policy involves both **decisions** and **actions.** Even if the decisions are unitary and the state speaks with one voice (which may not always be the case), if consequent actions are fragmented or otherwise inconsistent, then how unitary is the state after all?

Robert Keohane, Joseph Nye, and others took the pluralist image a major step forward when they argued in their earlier work that the state may not be able to confine these bureaucratic actors.[27] Organizations, whether private or governmental, may well transcend the boundaries of states, forming coalitions with their foreign counterparts. Such **transnational** actors may even be working at cross-purposes with governmental leaders in their home states who possess the formal authority to make binding decisions. For example, the British Foreign Office may see a given issue similarly to its American State Department counterpart. On the other hand, the British Defence Ministry and the U.S. Defense Department may share a common view contrary to that of both diplomatic organizations. Moreover, nongovernmental interest groups in both countries may also form coalitions supportive of one or another **transgovernmental** coalition.

To what extent, then, do coalitions of bureaucratic actors, multinational corporations, and other transnational actors circumvent the authoritative decision makers of states through formation of such coalitions? An interesting example of a transgovernmental coalition that had a significant, though unpublicized, impact during the October 1962 Cuban missile crisis involved redeployment of Canadian naval units for an "exercise" in the North Atlantic. This decision effectively relieved the U.S. Navy of at least a part of its patrolling responsibilities there, allowing American ships to be redeployed to the Caribbean as part of the naval blockade of Cuba. All of this was apparently established between American and Canadian military officers while the Diefenbaker government was still debating the question of Canadian policy in the crisis. Was this circumvention by the Canadian navy an exception, or is it commonplace for bureaucratic actors to form coalitions across national borders that in effect make policy? Pluralists would argue that it is more commonplace than most realists would suppose.

If it *is* typically the way foreign policy is made, then focus by realists on the state as principal actor would seem to be misdirected. More attention should be given to the entire range of transnational actors and their interactions. On the other hand, if the example used here is indeed an exception, then it is an exception that makes the rule. The state in most cases retains its hard shell, precluding circumvention by transnational bureaucratic actors.

TRANSNATIONALISM

We have referred to transnational actors in the context of foreign policy decision making. We now turn to a lengthier discussion of **transnationalism,** a phenomenon closely associated with the pluralist image of international relations. Whereas the literature on decision making has generally emphasized political processes within states, the literature on transnationalism emphasizes ties between societies that include much more than state-to-state relations. James Rosenau has offered a useful definition of transnationalism, viewing it as "the processes whereby international relations conducted by governments have been supplemented by relations among private individuals, groups, and societies that can and do have important consequences for the course of events."[28] We begin with the question of what accounts for the increase in transnational ties and actors in the twentieth century.

Modernization

Realists stress the timeless quality of international relations. The insights of Thucydides, for example, are deemed relevant to the modern age of nuclear weapons. The same basic forces are at work, constraining and disposing actors to respond to similar situations in similar fashion. A certain continuity in international affairs is assumed.

Although they do not reject the foregoing assumption, pluralists believe it to be overstated. For them, the nature of international relations has indeed changed over the years. There is a qualitative difference between the world of seventeenth-century diplomacy and its Europe-oriented system and the twentieth-century international system characterized by some 160 states. Modernization describes and explains this fundamental transformation of the international system. **Modernization** can be defined as the social, political, and economic prerequisites for, and consequences of, industrialization and technological development.[29] Proponents of this perspective point to the growth of scientific technology that allows for greater control over nature, the dramatic improvements in transportation and communication, the rise of mass consumption made posssible by the industrial revolution, the growth of global ties as a legacy of colonialism, and the extension of European diplomatic and political ideologies throughout the world. National autonomy, the traditional goal of statecraft, has become increasingly difficult as economic activities spill over borders.

The distinction between domestic and foreign policy becomes blurred as domestic policy becomes foreign policy and economic and foreign policies become politicized. For example, protectionist tariff barriers to save jobs and rescue ailing industries are weighed against international consequences to include retaliatory trade or financial measures taken by states adversely affected. Borders become porous as ideas, capital, people, technology, goods, and services move from one geographic point to another.[30] For selfish reasons, states find it in their best interest to cooperate with one another, creating modest yet important international organizations designed to facilitate the flow of mail or more ambitious endeavors aimed at ensuring international peace.

If the invoking image for the realist is that of states as billiard balls colliding with one another, for the pluralist it is a latticework or cobweb image. Instead of visualizing international relations as states and their interactions in an anarchic environment, some scholars argue that a cobweb image depicts a much more complex system composed not simply of states with geographic and political boundaries.[31] Also included would be the interactions and behavior of nonstate actors such as multinational corporations, terrorist groups, international banks, and international organizations such as the European Economic Community (EEC), the Organization of African Unity (OAU), the United Nations, and the North Atlantic Treaty Organization (NATO). The cobweb image would also depict such transactions as migration, tourism, communications, and trade flows. For pluralists, a cobweb image is much more apt in depicting the world than is the billiard ball image with its almost exclusive attention to the interactions of sovereign states. The state-centric model may perhaps have been appropriate in seventeenth- or eighteenth- century Europe, but the modernization process has so transformed societies that pluralists believe an alternative image of the world is required if one is to grasp the nature of world affairs in the twentieth century.

Integration

The impact of modernization on world politics, particularly the use of modern technology in the creation of weapons of mass destruction, is a phenomenon that drew the attention of certain international relations scholars in the period before and after World War II. One such scholar was David Mitrany.[32]

Mitrany was interested in investigating the possibility of how transnational ties might lead to international **integration,** the reduction of extreme nationalism, and hence increase the chances for a stable international peace. How might this come about?

Mitrany argued that by definition modern society has created a myriad of technical problems that can best be resolved by experts as opposed to politicians. This is true within states as well as between states. He believed that the proliferation of common problems logically requires collaborative responses from states. Hence, these essentially nonpolitical problems (economic, social, scientific) should be assigned to nonpolitical experts from the affected countries for resolution.

Mitrany reasoned that successful collaboration in one particular technical field or functional area would lead to further collaboration in other related fields. This process is what he termed **ramification.** Governments would recognize the common benefits to be gained by such cooperative endeavors and so would encourage or allow for a further expansion of collaborative tasks. In effect, Mitrany saw a way to sneak up on the authority of the **sovereign** state. As states and societies became increasingly integrated due to the expansion of collaboration in technical areas in which all parties gained, the cost of breaking these functional ties would be great and hence give leaders reason to pause before doing so. In particular, Mitrany emphasized how economic unification would contribute to the development of political integration. Hence, as opposed to a tendency among some realists to view international interactions as basically a **zero-sum game** (what one side wins the other loses), Mitrany instead argued that international interactions could be turned into a **variable** or **positive-sum game** in which all the players could benefit. For Mitrany, this was not an idealistic dream far removed from reality. Rather, he grounded his analysis in what he believed to be a realistic assessment of the likelihood of the need for international cooperation to deal with common problems deriving from a complex and modern world. As international integration based on cooperation in functional, nonpolitical areas developed, the chances for international peace would be enhanced, he felt.

The interest in Mitrany's **functionalist** theory—and integration in general—was spurred by the successful creation of the European Coal and Steel Community (ECSC) in 1952 and the European Economic Community (EEC) or Common Market, in the 1956 Treaty of Rome. The EEC seemed to hold out promise for the eventual political integration of Western Europe. Furthermore, the EEC's initial successes in the realm of economic integration increased interest in the more general question: Under what conditions is integration among states possible? Scholars noted that what was occurring in Western Europe did not match the Hobbesian image of states constantly prepared to go to war, an image that included little faith in the possibility of collaborative behavior among sovereign states. Hence, alternative perspectives were devised to explain international cooperation.

One of the best-known theorists of regional integration, Ernst Haas, defined integration as a *process* "whereby political actors in several distinct national settings are persuaded to shift their loyalties, expectations and political activities toward a new centre, whose institutions possess or demand jurisdiction over the preexisting national states."[33] Haas's conceptual approach to the study of political integration soon acquired the label **neofunctionalism**—an acknowledgment of the intellectual debt owed to Mitrany, but with significant differences. Where Haas parted company with Mitrany was in his rejection of the notion that one could separate technical tasks from politics or welfare from power. For integration to occur, Haas argued that it must be perceived by political elites to be in their self-interest. The assigning of tasks to an international organization—even if this involves a seemingly technical function such as supervising an international mail system—will be attained and sustained only if actors believe their own interests are best served by making a political commitment to an international organization.

What Haas attempted to do, therefore, was to stipulate the conditions and processes whereby individuals find it in their own rational self-interest to collaborate for mutual gain, which results in the potential for a peaceful transformation of international politics. To put it another way, Haas directed his efforts *not* toward understanding conflict among states faced with a security dilemma but toward understanding how states achieve collaborative behavior. In terms of Rousseau's stag hunt fable discussed in Chapter Two, Haas focused on ways to encourage the group to pursue the stag as opposed to assuming individuals will always defect in pursuit of the hare.

Early predictions of progress in regional integration did not occur, at least not to the extent anticipated. That stong, nationally oriented leaders would emerge (such as Charles DeGaulle in France) to block transfer of too much authority to regional institutions had not been anticipated. Beyond this strong-leader explanation for the slowing down of regional integration, however, a more fundamental evaluation of integration theory was offered by Haas himself.

Haas described the contemporary period as a "turbulent" one in which there are "confused and clashing perceptions of organizational actors which find themselves in a setting of great social complexity." Moreover,

> the number of actors is very large. Each pursues a variety of objectives which are mutually incompatible; but each is also unsure of the trade-offs between the objectives. Each actor is tied into a network of interdependencies with other actors that are as confused as the first. Yet some of the objectives sought by each cannot be obtained without cooperation from others.[34]

There is also uncertainty or outright confusion on means–ends relationships—what the causes of international problems are or what their solutions might be in areas such as the environment, energy, industrial policy, research and development, and technology transfer. Indeed, the approach for dealing with a problem in one area may have negative implications in another. For example, in substituting coal or nuclear power for petroleum as principal sources of energy, there may be a trade-off in terms of an adverse impact on the environment.

Haas argued, therefore, that gaining control over such complexity is emerging as the major political task during the last part of the twentieth century. Significantly, states may be led to seek nonregional solutions to these problems, whatever may be the effect of such solutions on the objectives of regional integration. Haas concluded that his earlier "theory of regional integration ought to be subordinated to a general theory of interdependence."[35]

Despite its predictive shortcomings, the literature on integration has provided important insights on the nature of world politics and has contributed to the development of the pluralist image of international relations.

First, the literature of regional integration downplays the state as the unit of analysis. Transactions—economic, social, and technical—have also been the focus of attention as have interest groups, transnational nonstate actors, and public opinion.

Second, the neofunctionalist literature in particular has disaggregated the nation-state, examining such component parts as bureaucracies and elites. The latter are viewed as flesh-and-blood individuals with conflicting perspectives, opinions subject to change, and decision-making power.

Third, integration theorists pose the question of what other forms of political organization—aside from the territorially based nation-state—are possible. How can they be attained?

Finally, integration theorists have analyzed the conditions under which international cooperation is facilitated. The realist emphasis on state competition and international anarchy, it has been argued, provides few clues on this matter, but cooperation is just as much a defining characteristic of international relations as is conflict. Military and security affairs do not monopolize the agenda of international politics. Economic, social, and welfare issues also deserve attention, and integration theorists have addressed these topics.

Interdependence and Regimes

The concept of interdependence is discussed by proponents of all three images of international relations, but the pluralists take it to heart because it captures much of the essence of their view of world politics. **Interdependence** is to many pluralists what **balance of power** is to realists and what **dependency** is to many globalists. The idea of international interdependence is certainly not new, and its basic notion—that two or more units are dependent on one another—is easy to grasp. In recent years, however, the term has been developed to give it some analytical utility and conceptual content useful for the development of international relations theory. Pluralists have argued that the term provides a more accurate grasp of the current nature of world politics than does the concept of balance of power.

Interdependence means different things to different people. As discussed in Chapter Two, realists tend to see it as the **vulnerability** of one state to another, a view that suggests that interdependence is to be avoided or at least minimized. A common view among pluralists, by contrast, is that interdependence involves "reciprocal effects among countries or among actors in different countries."[36] There is sensitivity in Country B to what is going on in or emanating from Country A.

Although there are costs associated with interdependence as **sensitivity**, benefits to either or both parties may outweigh these costs.[37] Thus, interdependence is not necessarily only a matter of country B's vulnerability to Country A. Pluralists do not exclude consideration of interdependence as vulnerability, but instead they focus on the multiple channels that connect societies, including interstate, transgovernmental, and transnational relations. There is a decided absence of hierarchy among issues such that socioeconomic issues may be as or more important than security issues. Moreover, when such complex interdependence exists, military force tends to have less utility in the resolution of conflicts.[38]

To the pluralist, interdependence may have benign implications and may be worth seeking; this is the influence of the liberal view of international relations. Whether the issues are trade, finance, communications, environmental pollution, or transfer of technology, the pluralist sees at least the opportunity for building good relations among the interdependent units. Managing interdependent relations may even involve construction of sets of rules and associated institutions or international organizations to govern interactions in these issue areas—so-called **international regimes.** The term *regime* is borrowed from domestic politics where it refers typically to an existing governmental order (democratic, authoritarian, or otherwise) or to a set of rules and institutions established to govern relations among individuals, groups, or classes within a state. In its international context, given the absence of a superordinate or overarching central authority, these rules are voluntarily established by states to provide some degree of order in international relations. Thus, there is a strong Grotian strain in pluralist thought, particularly when talk turns to managing interdependence through the construction of regimes.[39]

There are, after all, costs associated with interdependence that make it very political. Choices have to be made. Given the uneven or **asymmetric** distribution of benefits and costs associated with interdependence, these relations have to be managed if major conflicts are to be avoided. Regimes may be the vehicles for accommodating differences and upgrading the common interest. Consistent with Rousseau's stag hunt fable discussed in Chapter Two, the actors agree to collaborate in hunting the stag rather than serving only narrowly defined, short-term self-interest. Differences arise among actors, but at least a possibility for their peaceful resolution remains.

This is anything but **determinist** thinking. **Voluntarism** is central in this mode of thought. Individual statesmen can, if they are willing, shape the world order. They have to deal with power and they understand that political choices have to be made among competing alternatives if international regimes for the management of interdependence are to be maintained in such fields as money, trade, postal service, telecommunication, fishing, and environmental protection.

SYSTEM

Pluralists do not always employ the concept of **system,** although it is common currency in the literature. To the extent that pluralists use the terminology, systems tend to be open.[40] This means that the system is open to both external influences and effective choice by actors within the system. The actors, or component units, of the system can have some effect on outcomes. It is not the system that determines what the actors will do as if the actors were automatons. Or, to put it another way, statesmen impose themselves on events, not the reverse.

There is a good deal of indeterminancy in most pluralist formulations. Outcomes depend on combinations of actors that outmaneuver or overwhelm opposing coalitions. The result is authoritative decisions and actions or, in a word, **policy.** Of course, all this freedom, or indeterminacy, also has its costs. Pluralist theories of politics tend to have less predictive power. One can have a fairly clear understanding of the complexity associated with political processes seen through pluralist lenses without having too much insight as to the outcome that will ultimately be achieved. On the other hand, predictions offered by balance of power theorists in the realist school often are at a very high level of generality that is somewhat removed from day-to-day events.

Pluralists use the term *system* in at least three different ways. First, for some pluralists the international system is merely the sum of the foreign policies of all states. Governmental actions are the principal focus. This is the view accepted by some realists as well. As we have seen, however, pluralists also tend to emphasize the role of specific bureaucracies and pressure groups in the formulation of foreign policy. They have direct impact on the final decision.

Second, other pluralists view the system as the sum of foreign policies plus the activities of non-state actors. Non-state actors include multinational corporations, terrorist groups, international banks, and transnational interest groups such as the Red Cross.

Third, certain pluralists include all the foregoing elements in their definition of a system but add other types of transactions such as ideas, values, communications, trade patterns, and financial flows. This most fully approximates the cobweb image mentioned earlier.[41]

What all these views have in common, however, is a belief in the difficulty (if not impossibility) of insulating the foreign policy process from domestic and international forces. Not only is foreign policy influenced by such factors as public opinion, lobbying, and the policies and performances of allies and foes; it is also influenced by the individual and bureaucratic infighting that occurs within and among most governmental institutions. Government and society in general are penetrated in innumerable ways, making the notion of the impermeable nation–state a myth.[42]

The focus for the pluralist thus tends to be on various parts of the political process and on particular issues. Islands of theory are constructed rather than building such general theory as is offered by realist proponents of balance of power theory.[43] As we have seen, a number of pluralists focus on perception and decision-making processes of small groups. Others have studied regional integration, the impact of domestic and bureaucratic politics on foreign policy, and the roles played by transnational actors in world politics.

Unfortunately for the pluralist, however, these theoretical parts have tended to be nonadditive. To attempt merely to combine islands of theory (referred to by some theorists as **microtheories**) does not necessarily result in a **general theory.** A pluralist does not start with the system and work down to assess its impact on component units, as many realists do. Instead, one creeps up on the system by trying to put its parts together in some coherent fashion, which is not an easy task.[44]

On the other hand, interdependence has been a key concept entertained by theorists seeking to integrate pluralist thought by establishing some common denominator. There have been a number of attempts to measure interdependence as a systemic property or attribute.[45] As one might expect, findings on whether interdependence is rising, declining, or holding relatively constant depend heavily on the analyst's definition of the concept and on its **operationalization**—how it is measured through quantification or even by the use of non quantitative indicators. Even if agreement were reached on these definitional and measurement problems, there remains considerable disagreement on such questions as whether increasing interdependence is more or less conducive to peace and world prosperity.[46]

Perhaps not surprisingly, the most fruitful issues for the pluralist approach have been the nonsecurity ones—those dealing with social, cultural, economic, technological, and related subjects. This has certainly been the case in **systemic** studies of interdependence and the construction and maintenance of international regimes.

CHANGE

It should be apparent by now that, compared to realists, pluralists place much greater emphasis on the possibilities of change, particularly peaceful change. This is quite evident in the literature on integration and regimes in which policymakers learn from their experiences in international collaboration. There is also a possibility, but by no means an inevitability, that sovereign state members of international organizations may choose to transfer some authority to these institutions. To the extent that a given state cannot address adequately problems that confront a larger number of states, it may be in the state's interest to effect such transfers of authority. Whether such transfers would be permanent or whether such international institutions would acquire supranational authority that could be exercised over states is not clear. Were either to occur, it would be a fundamental **transformation** of world politics as we now understand it. States, assuming they would continue to exist, would no longer perform the large number of functions they now do. Again, such an outcome is not understood by pluralists as being inevitable or necessarily even desirable. Indeed, the question of alternative futures or alternative world orders continues to be addressed by pluralists of different persuasions.[47] There is, in any event, no single vision of the future that has currency among contemporary pluralists. Where pluralists differ from most realists, however, is that their image of world politics allows for a greater possibility of change. Their states and statesmen are not so constrained by the existing international system and balances of power within that system.

Similarly, much of the work on decision making emphasizes **feedback** processes—actors monitoring responses to actions they have taken so that future policies can be adjusted if necessary. The emphasis on choice in much of the pluralist work reveals a philosophical commitment to voluntarism, a belief that people can control or at least have some impact on their individual and collective destinies. Hence, the international system is viewed as being open and subject to directed change. For pluralists interested in transnational ties and interdependence, understanding the dynamics of system change is one of the most important tasks of scholars. It is not enough to describe particular types of systems (bipolar or multipolar, for example). Instead, efforts need to be directed toward understanding why and how the international system is changing and what this means in terms of war, peace, and stability.[48]

PLURALISTS AND THEIR CRITICS: AN OVERVIEW

The comments in this section are relatively brief but not because works based on the pluralist image lack their critics. Much of the criticism has already been discussed in Chapter Two and earlier in this chapter, however.

Anarchy

Pluralists generally tend to downplay the role of **anarchy** and the **security dilemma** in explaining international relations. It has been argued by realists, however, that no analysis of world politics is complete unless the anarchical structure of the system is taken into account. How is it possible to assess realistically the possibilities for cooperation and peace between states unless the role of anarchy in creating suspicion and distrust is considered? The realist would contend that if one ignores or reduces the importance of such considerations, thinking can quickly become **utopian** with little relation to reality. In addition, by emphasizing misperception and the role of bureaucratic politics, there is a danger in thinking that all conflicts result from essentially nonrational forces and that somehow better communication would reduce the amount of conflict in the international system. By contrast, realists argue that states often have fundamentally different interests that conflict, and the notions of "slipping into war" and "the war nobody wanted" are overused and misleading.[49]

A pluralist response is that placing so much emphasis on the security dilemma loads the dice against any change from the status quo. To see the world as nothing more than competition and conflict born of mistrust among states is itself a distortion of reality, or even a self-fulfilling prophecy. One's acts, if born of suspicion and distrust, will tend to produce similar responses in others, thus confirming one's initial suspicions.

Furthermore, the history of world politics is a history not only of conflict but also of collaboration. To study instances of when the security dilemma has been overcome is just as important as studying instances when it has contributed to the onset of war. Finally, to argue that misperception, bureaucratic politics, or domestic pressures may contribute to the onset of war is not to argue that states do not have conflicting national interests as well. Historical studies have shown time and again, however, that such factors as misperception are often critical in explaining the outbreak of wars.

Theory Building

Realists have argued that by describing the world in greater and greater detail, descriptive accuracy increases at the expense of developing a parsimonious theory of international relations. In other words, theories should be as simple as possible, not more complicated than what they are supposed to explain. Understanding increases by moving *away* from the real world, not by moving closer to it. At first, this statement might seem counterintuitive or different from what one might expect. But ambitious theories aim at producing valid generalizations by viewing the forest as a whole, not individual trees. By faithfully cataloguing the complexity of the world, critics argue that pluralists are in danger of remaining in the realm of merely describing things as opposed to explaining why things happen the way they do.

In response, pluralists claim that before theories of international relations can be constructed, we need an accurate image of international relations. The pluralist image, it is argued, more accurately captures the nature of world politics. Yes, it is admitted, the pluralist image is not as neat and streamlined as the realist image. It consists of a number of different actors and influences that make for complexity, but theories of international relations should aspire to deal with such complexity and not pretend that it doesn't exist. How adequate are theories that fail to deal with and explain many of the changes that have occurred in the nature of world politics over the past century?

Voluntarism

If realists have been criticized for being excessively pessimistic concerning the human condition and the ability of individuals to control international events and forces, pluralists can be criticized for their heavy reliance on the assumption of voluntarism or effective free will. Some pluralist writings leave one with the impression that international harmony can be achieved if only leaders *really* wanted it—that it is a simple matter of human volition, a mere matter of desiring cooperation as opposed to competition. Hence, the transformation of the nature of world politics is seen to be desirable as well as attainable. Either "bad leaders" or "bad governments" stand in the way; if they could be changed or removed, the world would be a better place. Once again the influence of the liberal philosophy is evident, and once again the realist evaluation would be that this view of international change and how it can be achieved ignores constraints placed on *all* leaders and states by the anarchical nature of the international system and the balance of power. Moreover, some realists would argue that people are indeed aggressive with a proclivity toward warlike behavior; it is part of human nature to behave so.

The emphasis on voluntarism is not always acknowledged by pluralist writings. Nor is it necessarily a function of a philosophical commitment to a belief in free will that can influence outcomes. It could also derive from the fact that the focus of analysis for many pluralists happens to be government bureaucracies or individual actors. By studying real individuals within real organizations, world politics takes on a human face.

Pluralists would claim that they are well aware of constraints imposed on the actions of individuals or groups. For example, studies of individual leaders may *not* emphasize voluntarism but, rather, psychological constraints resulting from life experiences. There remains, however, an array of possible options available to decision makers and the ability to make real choices among these competing alternatives. After all, to the pluralist, both opportunities and constraints are associated with foreign policy choice. Too often, history is interpreted as if certain events were inevitable, that a particular war was the result of a number of trends inexorably coming together.

Ethnocentrism

A final criticism of the pluralist school is that many scholars tend to view the world through the lenses of the American political system. If American government and processes are understood to conform to a pluralist image, then the same image is imposed on the rest of the world where it may bear little relation to reality. Thus, even the making of Soviet foreign policy in the politburo and state apparatus is said to involve the same construction of coalitions, end running, and similar tactics observed in American politics. This view is hotly disputed by those who think the analogy between American and Soviet decision-making processes is overdrawn.[50]

Acknowledging cultural, societal, and other differences, the pluralist who argues that bureaucracies, interest groups, and transnational actors are important to understanding international relations would deny that this image is merely American ethonocentrism imposed on the globe. It is, instead, a fairly accurate description of world politics. The actors and processes studied by pluralists are not confined to the states of the West but are found in and among political systems around the globe.

NOTES

1. John Locke, "An Essay Concerning the True, Original, Extent and End of Civil Government: Second Treatise on Government," in *Social Contract*, introduction by Sir Ernest Barker (London: Oxford University Press, 1962).
2. William Ebenstein, *Great Political Thinkers: Plato to the Present*, 4th ed. (New York: Holt, Rinehart & Winston, 1969) p. 63. Realists have also been influenced by liberalism, particularly by the emphasis on the rational individual pursuing his or her self-interest.
3. Immanuel Kant, *Idea of a Universal History of a Cosmological Plan* (Hanover, NH: The Sociological Press, 1972), and *Perpetual Peace*, trans. Lewis W. Beck (Indianapolis, IN: Bobbs-Merrill, 1957). Kant's emphasis on learning seems to have influenced modern works on regional and international integration.
4. On the liberal view of international relations, see Kenneth N. Waltz, *Man, the State and War* (New York: Columbia University Press, 1959), pp. 95–123. See also Michael Howard, *War and the Liberal Conscience* (Oxford: Oxford University Press, 1957).
5. Theodore J. Lowi, *The End of Liberalism: Ideology, Policy, and the Crisis of Public Authority* (New York: W. W. Norton, 1969), p. 71.
6. *Ibid.*, pp. 48, 71.
7. See David Truman, *The Governmental Process* (New York: Knopf, 1959), p. ix.
8. *Ibid.*, pp. 519, 520.
9. Robert A. Dahl, *A Preface to Democratic Theory* (Chicago: University of Chicago Press, 1963), p. 137. Also see Harold D. Lasswell, *Politics: Who Gets What, When, How* (New York: McGraw-Hill, 1936), pp. 233–50. Reprinted in Dwaine Marvick, ed., *Harold D. Lasswell on Political Sociology* (Chicago: University of Chicago Press, 1977), pp. 108–13.
10. Dahl, *A Preface to Democratic Theory*, p. 128
11. Alexis de Tocqueville, *Democracy in America*, ed. Phillips Bradley (New York: Vintage Books, 1954).

12. Richard C. Snyder, H. W. Bruck, and Burton Sapin, *Foreign Policy Decision Making: An Approach to the Study of International Politics* (New York: Free Press, 1962). The work was originally published in 1954. Other important early works include: Joseph Frankel, "Towards a Decision-Making Model in Foreign Policy," *Political Studies* 7 (1959): 1-11, and Karl W. Deutsch, "Mass Communications and the Loss of Freedom in National Decision-Making: A Possible Research Approach to Interstate Conflicts," *Journal of Conflict Resolution* 1 (1957): 200-211.
13. Snyder, Bruck, and Sapin, p.65.
14. Glen D. Paige, *The Korean Decision* (New York: Free Press, 1968).
15. James N. Rosenau, "Pre-Theories and Theories of Foreign Policy," in *The Scientific Study of Foreign Policy*, by James N. Rosenau, 2d ed., rev. and enl. (New York: Nichols, 1980), p. 118.
16. Maurice A. East, Stephen A. Salmore, and Charles F. Hermann, eds., *Why Nations Act: Theoretical Perspectives for Comparative Foreign Policy Studies* (Beverly Hills, CA: Sage Publications, 1978); Patrick J. McGowan and Howard B. Shapiro, *The Comparative Study of Foreign Policy* (Beverly Hills, CA: Sage Publications, 1973); Jonathan Wilkenfeld, Gerald W. Hopple, Paul J. Rossa, and Stephen J. Andriole, *Foreign Policy Behavior: The Interstate Behavior Analysis Model* (Beverly Hills, CA: Sage Publications, 1980); Wolfram F. Hanrieder, ed., *Comparative Foreign Policy: Theoretical Essays* (New York: David McKay, 1971); James N. Rosenau, ed., *Comparing Foreign Policies: Theories, Findings, and Methods* (Beverly Hills, CA: Sage Publications, 1974); and Douglas J. Murray and Paul R. Viotti, eds., *The Defense Policies of Nations: A Comparative Study* (Baltimore, MD: Johns Hopkins University Press, 1982).
17. H. N. Hirsch, "Clio on the Couch," *World Politics* 32, no. 3 (April 1980): 406-24; Alexander George, "The Operational Code: A Neglected Approach to the Study of Political Leaders and Decision-Making," *International Studies Quarterly* 13, no. 2 (June 1969): 190-220; Robert Axelrod, ed., *The Structure of Decision* (Princeton, N.J.: Princeton University Press, 1976); Harvey Starr, "The Kissinger Years: Studying Individuals and Foreign Policy," *International Studies Quarterly* 24, no. 4 (December 1980): 465-96; and Ole Holsti, "The Operational Code Approach to the Study of Political Leaders," *Canadian Journal of Political Science* 3, no. 1 (March 1970): 123-57.
18. Robert Jervis, *Perception and Misperception in International Politics* (Princeton, NJ: Princeton University Press, 1976), p. 29. See also Jervis, *The Logic of Images in International Relations* (Princeton, NJ: Princeton University Press, 1970); "Cooperation Under the Security Dilemma," *World Politics* 30, no. 2 (January 1978): 167-214; "Deterrence Theory Revisited," *World Politics* 31, no. 2 (January 1979): 289-324.
19. Jervis, *Perception and Misperception*, p. 9.
20. Irving L. Janis, *Victims of Groupthink* (Boston, MA: Houghton Mifflin, 1972). See also Janis and Leon Mann, *Decision Making: A Psychological Analysis of Conflict, Choice, and Commitment* (New York: Free Press, 1977).
21. Janis, *Victims of Groupthink*, p. 9
22. On crises, see Ole Holsti, *Crisis, Escalation, War* (Montreal and London: McGill-Queen's University Press, 1972); Ole Holsti, "Historians, Social Scientists, and Crisis Management," *Journal of Conflict Resolution* 24, no. 4

(December 1980): 665-82. An important recent work is Richard Ned Lebow, *Between Peace and War: The Nature of International Crisis* (Baltimore, MD: Johns Hopkins University Press, 1981). See also Alexander L. George "Adaptation to Stress in Political Decision Making," *Coping and Adaptation,* ed. G. Coelho, D. Hamburg, and J. Adams (New York: Basic Books, 1974).

23. Alexander L. George and Richard Smoke, *Deterrence in American Foreign Policy: Theory and Practice* (New York: Columbia University Press, 1974), p. 505.

24. Miriam Steiner, "The Search for Order in a Disorderly World: Worldviews and Prescriptive Decision Paradigms," *International Organization* 37, no. 3 (Summer 1983): 373-413.

25. See Graham Allison, "Conceptual Models and the Cuban Missile Crisis," *American Political Science Review* 63 (September 1969): 689-718. See also Allison, *Essence of Decision* (Boston, MA: Little, Brown, 1971); Graham Allison and Morton H. Halperin, "Bureaucratic Politics: A Paradigm and Some Policy Implications," in *Theory and Policy in International Relations,* ed. Raymond Tanter and Richard H. Ullman (Princeton, NJ: Princeton University Press, 1972), pp. 40-79; Halperin with Priscilla Clapp and Arnold Kanter, *Bureaucratic Politics and Foreign Policy* (Washington, The Brookings Institution, 1974). See Weber's classic "Parliament and Government in a Reconstructed Germany," in *Economy and Society,* vol. 2, Appendix 2, ed. Guenther Roth and Claus Wittich (New York: Bedminster Press, 1968), pp. 1381-1469.

26. For realist critiques of Allison's work, see Stephen D. Krasner, "Are Bureaucracies Important? (or Allison's Wonderland)," *Foreign Policy* 7 (Summer 1972): 159-79; and Robert J. Art, "Bureaucratic Politics and American Foreign Policy: A Critique," *Policy Sciences* 4, no. 4 (December 1973): 467-90.

27. See Robert Keohane and Joseph Nye, eds., *Transnational Relations and World Politics* (Cambridge, MA: Harvard University Press, 1972) and their later *Power and Interdependence: World Politics in Transition* (Boston, MA: Little, Brown, 1977). In the latter work an attempt is made to blend pluralist and realist approaches.

28. James N. Rosenau, *The Study of Global Interdependence: Essays on the Transnationalisation of World Affairs* (New York: Nichols, 1980), p. 1.

29. For a detailed treatment of the impact of modernization on international relations that resulted from the global spread of the effects of the industrial revolution, see Edward L. Morse, *Modernization and the Transformation of International Relations* (New York: Free Press, 1976). See also John H. Kautsky, *The Political Consequences of Modernization* (New York: John Wiley & Sons, 1972); and C. E. Black, *The Dynamics of Modernization* (New York: Harper & Row, 1966).

30. For a defense of the concept of the "hard shell" of the state, see Stanley Hoffmann's realist perspective in his "Obstinate or Obsolete? The Fate of the Nation-State and the Case of Western Europe," *Daedalus* 3 (Summer 1966): 862-915. See also Samuel P. Huntington's argument that the state retains control over access to its territory by transnational actors in his "Transnational Organizations in World Politics," *World Politics* 26, no. 3 (April 1973): 333-68.

31. See Ernst B. Haas for the latticework metaphor in his "The Study of Regional Integration: Reflections on the Joy and Anguish of Pretheorizing," in *Regional Intergration: Theory and Research*, ed. Leon N. Lindberg and Stuart A. Scheingold (Cambridge, MA: Harvard University Press, 1971) pp. 30–31. For the cobweb image, see Ernst Haas, *Tangle of Hopes: American Commitments and World Order* (Englewood Cliffs, NJ: Prentice-Hall, 1969), Chapter 1; and John W. Burton, *World Society* (Cambridge: Cambridge University Press, 1972).

32. See David Mitrany, *A Working Peace System* (Chicago: Quadrangle Books, 1966). See also Mitrany, "The Functional Approach to World Organization," *International Affairs* 24, no. 3 (July 1948): 350–63, and the discussion in Ernst B. Haas, *Beyond the Nation-State* (Stanford, CA: Stanford University Press, 1964), Chapter 1.

33. Ernst B. Haas, *The Uniting of Europe* (Stanford, CA: Stanford University Press, 1958), p. 16. See also the influential work by Karl W. Deutsch and associates, *Political Community and the North Atlantic Area* (Princeton, NJ: Princeton University Press, 1957), p. 5.

34. See Ernst B. Haas, "Turbulent Fields and the Theory of Regional Integration," *International Organization* 30, no. 2 (Spring 1976): 179. This article is a summary of a much more detailed treatment in a monograph by Haas, *The Obsolescence of Regional Integration Theory* (Berkeley: University of California Institute of International Studies, 1975). For antecedents of this argument, see his earlier "Study of Regional Integration."

35. Haas, "Turbulent Fields and Regional Integration," p. 199.

36. Keohane and Nye, *Power and Interdependence*, p. 8.

37. *Ibid.*, p. 9. Alex Inkeles differentiates between "inter-connectedness" or the effect of international transaction flows and "interdependence," which involves some degree of cost for the parties. Alex Inkeles, "The Emerging Social Structure of the World," *World Politics* 27, no. 4 (July 1975): 467–95.

38. See Keohane and Nye, *Power and Interdependence*, pp. 24–29.

39. See Stephen Krasner, ed., "International Regimes," special issue of *International Organization* 36, no. 2 (Spring 1982); Oran R. Young, "International Regimes: Problems of Concept Formation," *World Politics* 32, no. 3 (April 1980): 331–56; Ernst Haas, Mary Pat Williams and Don Babai, *Scientists and World Order: The Uses of Technical Knowledge in International Organizations* (Berkeley: University of California Press, 1977); Anthony J. Dolman, *Resources, Regimes, and World Order* (New York: Pergamon Press, 1981); John Gerard Ruggie, "International Organization: A State of the Art on an Art of the State" (Paper presented at the 1985 Annual Meeting of the American Political Science Association, New Orleans, August 29–September 1, 1985).

40. See Ernst B. Haas, "On Systems and International Regimes," *World Politics*, 27, no. 2 (January 1975): 152–53.

41. One approach to understanding transaction and communications flows in the international system is through the construction of cybernetic models. For example, see Karl W. Deutsch, *The Nerves of Government* (New York: Free Press, 1964).

42. See James N. Rosenau, ed., *Linkage Politics: Essays on the Covergence of National and International Systems* (New York: Free Press, 1969) and an earlier piece by Fred A. Sondermann, "The Linkage between Foreign Policy

and International Politics" in *International Politics and Foreign Policy*, ed. James N. Rosenau (New York, Free Press, 1961), pp. 8-17.

43. See Harold Guetzkow, "Long Range Research in International Relations," in *International Politics and Foreign Policy*, ed. James N. Rosenau (New York: Free Press, 1961), pp. 55-56.
44. This evocative idea of creeping up on the nation-state is from Ernst Haas.
45. See Richard Rosecrance and associates "Whither Interdependence?" *International Organization* 31, no. 3 (Summer 1977): 425-71; Mary Ann Tetreault, "Measuring Interdependence," *International Organization* 34, no. 3 (Summer 1980): 429-43; and rejoinder by Rosecrance and William Gutowitz, followed by Tetreault's response in *International Organization*, 35, no. 3 (Summer 1981): 553-60.
46. For an antidote to the conventional wisdom that the effects of increased interdependence are benign and therefore desirable, see the realist critique of interdependence in Kenneth N. Waltz, "The Myth of National Interdependence, in *The International Corporation*, ed. Charles P. Kindleberger (Cambridge, MA: MIT Press, 1970), pp. 205-23.
47. For an example, see Richard A. Falk, *A Study of Future Worlds* (New York: Free Press, 1975).
48. See Ole R. Holsti, Randolph M. Siverson, and Alexander L. George, *Change in the International System* (Boulder, CO: Westview Press, 1980).
49. See Christopher Layne, "1914 Revisited: A Reply to Miles Kahler," *Orbis* 14, no. 4 (Winter 1981): 719-50.
50. For example, see the debate between a pluralist and a more unitary conception of high-level Soviet politics in Roman Kolkowicz, "Interest Groups in Soviet Politics: The Case of the Military," *Comparative Politics* 2, no. 3 (April 1970): 445-72; William E. Odom, "The Part Connection," *Problems of Communism* 22, no. 5 (September-October 1973): 12-26; Karen Dawisha, "The Limits of the Bureaucratic Politics Model: Observations on the Soviet Case," *Studies in Comparative Communism* 13, no. 4 (Winter 1980): 300-46; Robert M. Cutler, "The Formation of Soviet Foreign Policy: Organizational and Cognitive Perspectives," *World Politics* 33, no. 3 (April 1982): 418-36.

SUGGESTED READINGS

Allison, Graham. *Essence of Decision: Explaining the Cuban Missile Crisis*. Boston: Little, Brown, 1971.

Allison, Graham, and Morton H. Halperin. "Bureaucratic Politics: A Paradigm and Some Policy Implications." *World Politics 24*, supplement (Spring 1972): 40-79.

Axelrod, Robert. *Framework for a General Theory of Cognition and Choice*. Berkeley, CA: Institute of International Studies, 1972.

———, ed. *Structure of Decision: The Cognitive Maps of Political Elites*. Princeton, NJ: Princeton University Press, 1976.

Baldwin, David A. "Interdependence and Power: A Conceptual Analysis." *International Organization* 34, 4 (Autumn 1980): 471-506.

Banks, Michael, ed. *Conflict in World Society*. New York: St. Martin's Press, 1984.

Bergsten, C. Fred, and Lawrence B. Krause, eds. *World Politics and International Economics.* Washington DC: Brookings Institution, 1975.

Betts, Richard K. "Analysis, War, and Decision: Why Intelligence Failures Are Inevitable." *World Politics* 31, 1 (October 1978): 61–89.

Brecher, Michael. "Research Findings and Theory-Building on Foreign Policy Behavior." In *Sage International Yearbook of Foreign Policy Studies II.* Beverly Hills and London: Sage Publications, 1974.

———. "State Behavior in International Crisis." *Journal of Conflict Resolution* 23 (September 1979): 446–80.

———, ed. *Studies in Crisis Behavior.* New Brunswick, NJ: Transaction Books, 1979.

Brecher, Michael, and Jonathan Wilkenfeld. "Crisis in World Politics." *World Politics* 34, 3 (April 1982): 380–417.

Brown, Lester B. *World Without Borders: The Interdependence of Nations.* New York: Foreign Policy Association, Headline Series, 1972.

Brown, Seyom. *New Forces in World Politics.* Washington, DC: Brookings Institution, 1974.

Burton, John W. *Systems, States, Diplomacy and Rules.* New York: Cambridge University Press, 1968.

———. *World Society.* New York: Cambridge University Press, 1972.

Caldwell, Dan. "Bureaucratic Foreign Policy-Making." *American Behavioral Scientist* 21, 1 (September–October 1977): 87–110.

Cooper, Richard N. *The Economics of Interdependence.* New York: McGraw-Hill, 1968.

De Rivera, Joseph. *The Psychological Dimension of Foreign Policy.* Columbus, OH: C. E. Merrill, 1968.

Deutsch, Karl W. and associates. *Political Community and the North Atlantic Area.* Princeton, NJ: Princeton University Press, 1957.

Etzioni, Amitai. *Political Unification.* New York: Holt, Rinehart & Winston, 1965.

Galtung, Johan. "A Structural Theory of Integration." *Journal of Peace Research* 5 (1968): 375–95.

George, Alexander. "The Operational Code: A Neglected Approach to the Study of Political Leaders and Decision-Making." *International Studies Quarterly* 13, 2 (June 1969): 190–222.

George, Alexander, and Richard Smoke. *Deterrence in American Foreign Policy: Theory and Practice.* New York: Columbia University Press, 1974.

Gourevitch, Peter. "The Second Image Reversed: The International Sources of Domestic Politics." *International Organization* 32, 4 (Autumn, 1978): 881–911.

Guetzkow, Harold, and associates, *Simulation in International Relations: Developments for Research and Teaching.* Englewood Cliffs, NJ: Prentice-Hall, 1963.

Haas, Ernst B. *Beyond the Nation-State.* Stanford, CA: Stanford University Press, 1964).

———. "Is There a Hole in the Whole? Knowledge, Technology, Interdependence, and the Construction of International Regimes." *International Organization* 29, 3 (Summer 1975): 827–76.

———. *Tangle of Hopes: American Commitments and World Order.* Englewood Cliffs, NJ: Prentice-Hall, 1969.

―――. "Turbulent Fields and the Theory of Regional Integration." *International Organization* 30, 2 (Spring 1976): 173–212.

―――. "Why Collaborate? Issue-Linkage and International Regimes." *World Politics* 32, 3 (April 1980): 357–405.

Haas, Ernst, B., Mary Pat Williams, and Don Babai. *Scientists and World Order: The Uses of Technical Knowledge in International Organizations.* Berkeley: University of California Press, 1977.

Halperin, Morton H. *Bureaucratic Politics and Foreign Policy.* Washington, DC: Brookings Institution, 1974.

Hermann, Charles F. ed. *International Crises: Insights from Behavioral Research.* New York: Free Press, 1972.

Hermann, Margaret G. "Explaining Foreign Policy Behavior Using the Personal Characteristics of Political Leaders." *International Studies Quarterly* 24, 1 (March 1980): 7–46.

Herz, John. "The Territorial State Revisited: Reflections on the Future of the Nation–State." *Polity* 1, 1 (Fall 1968): 11–34.

Holsti, Kal J. "A New International Politics? Diplomacy in Complex Interdependence." *International Organization* 32, 2 (Spring 1978): 513–30. A review of Nye and Keohane, *Power and Interdependence.*

Holsti, Ole R. *Crisis, Escalation, War.* Montreal: McGill-Queen's University Press, 1972.

Holsti, Ole R., Randolph M. Siverson, and Alexander L. George. *Change in the International System.* Boulder, CO: Westview Press, 1980.

Holsti, Ole R., P. Terrence Hopmann, and John D. Sullivan *Unity and Disintegration in International Alliances.* New York: John Wiley, 1973.

Janis, Irving L. *Victims of Groupthink.* Boston: Houghton Mifflin, 1972.

Janis, Irving L., and Leon Mann. *Decision Making: A Psychological Analysis of Conflict, Choice, and Commitment.* New York: Free Press, 1977.

Jervis, Robert. "Deterrence and Perception." *International Security* 7, 3 (Winter 1982/83): 3–30.

―――. *The Logic of Images in International Relations.* Princeton, NJ: Princeton University Press, 1970.

―――. *Perception and Misperception in International Politics.* Princeton, NJ: Princeton University Press, 1976.

Katzenstein, Peter. "International Interdependence: Some Long-Term Trends and Recent Changes." *International Organization* 29, 4 (Autumn 1975): 1021–34.

Keohane, Robert O. and Joseph S. Nye, Jr. *Power and Interdependence: World Politics in Transition.* Boston: Little, Brown, 1977.

―――. "Transgovernmental Relations and International Organization." *World Politics* 27, 1 (October 1974): 39–62.

―――, eds. *Transnational Relations and World Politics.* Cambridge, MA: Harvard University Press, 1971.

Kinder, Donald R., and Janet A. Weiss. "In Lieu of Rationality: Psychological Perspectives on Foreign Policy Decisionmaking." *Journal of Conflict Resolution* 22 (December 1978): 707–35.

Krasner, Stephen D., ed. *International Regimes.* London and Ithaca, N.Y.: Cornell University Press, 1983.

Lebow, Richard Ned. *Between Peace and War: The Nature of International Crisis.* Baltimore, MD: Johns Hopkins University Press, 1981.

Leonard, H. Jeffrey. "Multinational Corporations and Politics in Developing Countries." *World Politics* 32, 3 (April 1980): 454-83.

Levy, Jack F. "Misperception and the Causes of War." *World Politics* 36, 1 (October 1983): 76-99.

Lindberg, Leon N., and Stuart A. Scheingold, eds. *Regional Integration: Theory and Research.* Cambridge, MA: Harvard University Press, 1971.

McGowan, Patrick J., and Howard B. Shapiro. *The Comparative Study of Foreign Policy.* Beverly Hills, CA: Sage Publications, 1973.

Mansbach, Richard W., Yale H. Ferguson, and Donald F. Lampert. *The Web of World Politics.* Englewood Cliffs, NJ: Prentice-Hall, 1976.

Mansbach, Richard W., and John A. Vasquez. *In Search of Theory: A New Paradigm for Global Politics.* New York: Columbia University Press, 1981.

Michalak, Stanley J. "Theoretical Perspectives for Understanding International Interdependence." *World Politics* 32, 1 (October 1979): 136-50. A review of Keohane and Nye, *Power and Interdependence.*

Mitrany, David. *A Working Peace System.* Chicago: Quadrangle Books, 1966.

———. *The Functional Theory of Politics.* London: St. Martin's Press, 1975.

Modelski, George, ed. *Transnational Corporations and World Order.* San Franciso: W. H. Freeman and Co., 1979.

Morse, Edward L. *Modernization and the Transformation of International Relations.* New York: Free Press, 1976.

———. "The Politics of Interdependence." *International Organization* 23 (1969): 311-26.

Nau, Henry R. "From Integration to Interdependence: Gains, Losses, and Continuing Gaps." *International Organization* 33, 1 (Winter 1979): 119-47. A review article.

Northedge, F. S. "Transnationalism: The American Illusion." *Millennium* 5 (Spring 1976): 21-27.

Nye, Joseph S. *Peace in Parts: Integration and Conflict in Regional Organization.* Boston, MA: Little, Brown, 1971.

Pirages, Dennis. *The New Context For International Relations: Global Ecopolitics.* North Scituate, MA: Duxbury Press, 1978.

Rosecrance, Richard R., and associates, "Whither Interdependence?" *International Organization* 31, 3 (Summer 1977): 425-72.

Rosecrance, Richard, and Arthur Stein. "Interdependence: Myth or Reality?" *World Politics* 26, 1 (October 1973): 1-27.

Rosenau, James N. "A Pre-Theory Revisited: World Politics in an Era of Cascading Interdependence." *International Studies Quarterly* 28, 3 (September 1984): 245-305.

———, ed. *Comparing Foreign Policies: Theories, Findings, and Methods.* Beverly Hills, CA: Sage Publications, 1974.

———, ed. *In Search of Global Patterns.* New York: Free Press, 1976.

———, ed. *International Politics and Foreign Policy,* rev. ed. New York: Free Press, 1969.

———, ed. *Linkage Politics.* New York: Free Press, 1969.

———. "Order and Disorder in the Study of World Politics." In *Globalism Versus Realism: International Relations' Third Debate,* ed. Ray Maghroori and Bennett Ramberg. Boulder, CO: Westview Press, 1982, pp. 1-7.

———. "Pre-Theories and Theories of Foreign Policy." In *The Scientific Study* of Foreign Policy, ed. James N. Rosenau. 2d ed. rev. and enl. New York: Nichols, 1980.

———. The Study of Global Interdependence: Essays on the Transnationalisation of World Affairs. New York: Nichols, 1980.

———. The Study of Political Adaptation. London: Frances Pinter, 1981.

Rourke, Francis. Bureaucracy and Foreign Policy. Baltimore: Johns Hopkins University Press, 1972.

Ruggie, John Gerard, ed. The Antinomies of Interdependence. New York: Columbia University Press, 1983.

Singer, J. David. Human Behavior and International Politics: Contributions from the Social-Psychological Sciences. Chicago: Rand McNally, 1965.

Snyder, Glenn H., and Paul Diesing. Conflict Among Nations: Bargaining, Decision Making, and System Structure in International Crisis. Princeton, NJ: Princeton University Press, 1977.

Snyder, Jack L. "Rationality at the Brink: The Role of Cognitive Processes in Failures of Deterrence." World Politics 30, 3 (April 1978): 345-65.

Snyder, Richard C., H. W. Bruck, and Burton Sapin. Decisionmaking as an Approach to the Study of International Politics. Princeton, NJ: Princeton University Press, 1954.

Spero, Joan E. The Politics of International Economic Relations, 2d ed. New York: St. Martin's Press, 1981.

Stech, Frank J. Estimating Intentions in Military and Political Intelligence. Boulder, CO: Westview Press, 1985.

Steinbruner, John D. The Cybernetic Theory of Decision: New Dimensions of Political Analysis. Princeton, NJ: Princeton University Press, 1974.

Strange, Susan. "The Study of Transnational Relations." International Affairs 52, 3 (July, 1976): 333-45.

Sylvan, David A., and Steve Chan, eds. Foreign Policy Decision Making: Perception, Cognition, and Artificial Intelligence. New York: Praeger, 1984.

Taylor, Philip. Nonstate Actors in International Politics. Boulder, CO: Westview Press, 1984.

Vernon, Raymond. Sovereignty at Bay: The Multinational Spread of U.S. Enterprises. New York: Basic Books, 1971.

———. "Sovereignty at Bay Ten Years After." International Organization 35, 3 (Summer 1981): 517-29.

Ward, Michael Don, ed. Theories, Models, and Simulations in International Relations. Boulder, CO: Westview Press, 1985.

Wright, Quincy. A Study of War. Chicago: University of Chicago Press, 1964.

Young, Oran R. "International Regimes: Problems of Concept Formation." World Politics 32 (April 1980): 331-56.

Young, Robert A., ed. "International Crisis: Progress and Prospects for Applied Forecasting and Management." International Studies Quarterly 21, 1 (March 1977). A special issue.

Perception and Misperception in International Politics

Robert Jervis

Professor Jervis discusses the relations among different levels of analysis used by students of international relations. He also makes a case for the importance of understanding individual perception (and misperception) in the study of foreign policy and world politics.

DO PERCEPTIONS MATTER?

Before discussing the causes and consequences of the ways in which decision-makers draw inferences from the world, we must ask a preliminary question: do the decision-makers' perceptions matter? This is an empirical question. Logic permits us to distinguish between the "psychological milieu" (the world as the actor sees it) and the "operational milieu" (the world in which the policy will be carried out) and to argue that policies and decisions must be mediated by statesmen's goals, calculations, and perceptions.[1] But it does not follow from this that we must deal with these intervening variables in order to understand and predict behavior. This is not an uncommon claim:

> One may describe particular events, conditions, and interactions between states without necessarily probing the nature and outcome of the processes through which state action evolves. However, and the qualification is crucial, if one wishes to probe the "why" questions underlying the events, conditions, and interaction patterns which rest upon state action, then decision-making analysis is certainly necessary. We would go so far as to say *that the "why" questions cannot be answered without analysis of decision-making.*[2]

But theory and explanation need not fill in all the links between cause and effect. Indeed, this is impossible. One can always ask for the links between the links. High density theories have no privileged status; they are not automatically illuminating or fruitful.[3] It is true that re-creating a decision-maker's goals, calculations, and perceptions is a satisfying method of explaining his behavior because the scholar, sharing as he does the decision-maker's characteristics of being a thinking, goal-seeking person, can easily say: "If that is the way the statesman saw the situation, it is no wonder that he acted as he did." But the comfort we feel with this form of explanation should not blind us to the fact that, unless there are significant variations in the ways people see the world that affect how they act, we need not explore decision-making in order to explain foreign policy. Most case studies assume that the details presented significantly affected the outcomes. This may not be true, however. "Pleikus are streetcars," McGeorge Bundy said in explaining that the Viet Cong attack on the American installation in February 1965 had affected only the timing of the American bombing of North Vietnam.[4] If you are waiting for one, it will come along. The specifics of the triggering event cannot explain the outcome because so many probable events could have substituted for it. To understand the American policy of bombing the North we should not examine the attack on Pleiku. Had it not occurred, something else would have happened that would have permitted the same response. Logic alone cannot tell us that a similar claim about the decision-making process is invalid: the way people perceive others and make decisions only marginally influences outcomes. So we must seek empirical evidence on the question: do the important explanatory variables in international relations involve decision-making? In terms of perceptions this can be separated into two subsidiary questions: "are important differences in policy preferences traceable to differences in decision-makers' perceptions of their environments?" and "are there important differences between reality and shared or common perceptions?"[5]

These questions raise the familiar level of analysis problem. Although it has been much debated, agreement is lacking not only on the substantive dispute but even on the number of levels. Arnold Wolfers proposes two, Kenneth Waltz three, and James Rosenau five.[6] To fill in the sequence, we will discuss four. One is the level of decision-making, the second is the level of the bureaucracy, the third is that of the nature of the state and the workings of domestic politics, and the fourth focuses on the international environment.[7] Which level one focuses on is not arbitrary and is not a matter of taste—it is the product of beliefs (or often hunches) about the nature of the variables that influence the phenomena that concern one. To restate the first question in terms of the level of analysis problem, we need not adopt a decision-making approach if all states behave the same way in the same objective situation, if all states of the same kind (i.e., with the same internal characteristics and politics) behave the same way in the same objective situation, or if state behavior is determined by bureaucratic routines and interests.

Although the empirical questions are central here, we should also note that the level of analysis problem has important moral implications. When all people would respond the same way to a given situation, it is hard to praise or blame the decision-maker. Thus, those accused of war crimes will argue that their behavior did not differ from others who found themselves in the same circumstances. And the prosecution will charge, as it did against Tojo and his colleagues, that, "These defendants were not automatons; they were not replaceable cogs in a machine. . . . It was theirs to choose whether their nation would lead an honored life . . . or . . . would become a symbol of evil throughout the world. They made their choice. For this choice they must bear the guilt." Similarly, if all nations follow similar courses of action, one cannot argue that some deserve to be branded as immorally aggressive. Thus in 1918 Bethmann-Hollweg rebutted those who blamed Germany for the war by pointing to the "general disposition towards war in the world . . . how else explain the senseless and impassioned zeal which allowed countries like Italy, Rumania and even America, not originally involved in the war, no rest until they too had immersed themselves in the bloodbath?"[8]

The three non-decision-making levels assert the importance of various aspects of the objective situation or the actor's role.[9] They say that if we know enough about the setting—international, national, or bureaucratic—we can explain and predict the actor's behavior. An interesting sidelight is that if other actors believed that the setting is crucial they would not need to scrutinize the details of the state's recent behavior or try to understand the goals and beliefs held by the state's decision-makers.[10] It would be fruitless and pointless to ask what the state's intentions are if its behavior is determined by the situation in which it finds itself. Instead, observers would try to predict how the context will change because this will tell them what the state's response will be. Decision-makers could then freely employ their powers of vicarious identification and simply ask themselves how they would act if they were in the other's shoes. They would not have to worry about the possibility that the other might have values and beliefs that differed from theirs. It is interesting, although not decisive, to note that decision-makers rarely feel confident about using this method. They usually believe both that others may not behave as they would and that the decision-makers within the other state differ among themselves. So they generally seek a great deal of information about the views of each significant person in the other country.

Of course it is unlikely that there is a single answer to the question of which level is most important. Rather than one level containing the variables that are most significant for all problems, the importance of each level may vary from one issue area to another.[11] Furthermore, which level of analysis is the most important may be determined by how rich and detailed an answer we are seeking. The environment may influence the general outline of the state's policy but not its specific responses. Thus is can be argued that, while decision-making analysis is needed to explain why World War I broke out in August 1914, the external situation would have led the states to fight sooner or later. Or the importance of variables at each level may vary with the stages of a decision. For example, domestic politics may dictate that a given event be made the occasion for a change in policy; bargaining within the bureaucracy may explain what options are presented to the national leaders; the decision-maker's predisposition could account for the choice that was made; and the interests and routines of the bureaucracies could explain the way the decision was implemented. And the same variable may have different effects at different stages of the decision-making process—for example, conflicts among subordinates may increase the variety of information and the number of opportunities for decision that the top decision-maker gets, but may simultaneously decrease his ability to see that his decisions are faithfully implemented.

The importance of variables at one level can also vary with the state of variables at other levels. Rosenau suggests that the international environment is more important in determining the policy of small states than it is of large ones and Stanley Hoffmann argues that nuclear weapons and bipolarity have reversed this relationship.[12] More generally, the importance of the other levels decreases if the variables in one level are in extreme states.[13] Thus, maneuvering within the bureaucracy may be more important when the top decision-makers are inexperienced or preoccupied with other matters.[14] And Wolfers argues that states tend to behave the same way when they are faced with extreme danger or extreme opportunity, but that when environmental constraints are less severe there will be differences in behavior that must be explained at the decision-making level. More complex interactions among the levels are also possible. For example, the effect of internal instability on expansionism could vary with the opportunities for success in war. Unstable states may be more prone to aggression than stable ones when the chances of victory are high but might be more cautious than others when their leaders perceive a significant probability of defeat or even of temporary setback. Or the stability of the regime might influence its propensity for aggression, but the nature of the regime (e.g., whether it is democratic or dictatorial) might be more important in explaining how it makes peace.

To deal with all these questions would require another book. Here all I will try to do is to outline the kinds of evidence necessary to establish the validity of simple propositions about the importance of the various levels. In doing so, I will sketch the most extreme arguments for the importance of each level. It is obvious that the questions and arguments could be rephrased in more subtle terms but since I am concerned with the kinds of evidence that the propositions call for the gain in analytical clarity is worth the sacrifice involved in ignoring more complete explanations that combine a multitude of variables at many levels.

The International Environment

To argue that the international environment determines a state's behavior is to assert that all states react similarly to the same objective external situation. Changes in a state's domestic regime, its bureaucratic structure, and the personalities and opinions of its leaders do not lead to changes of policies. Changes in the external situation, however, do alter behavior, even when variables on the other levels remain constant. To test these claims, we would need good measures of all the variables, especially the nature of the objective situation and the state's policies.[15] Even if we had such indicators, we would have to cope with the paucity of the most desired kinds of comparisons. This is easily understood by glancing at the similar issue in the study of individual behavior—the debate over the relative importance of situation and role versus idiosyncratic variables in determining individual behavior.[16] Because so many people of widely differing backgrounds, personalities, and opinions fill the same role and because the same person fills many different roles, we can try to determine the relative impact of situational and idiosyncratic variables by examining how a person's behavior varies as his role changes and how people of widely differing characteristics perform in similar situations.

It is much harder to make the analogous comparisons in international relations. In only a few international systems do we find many cases in which states play, either simultaneously or consecutively, several roles and in which each role is filled by states that are otherwise quite different. This would occur in a long-lasting system where there were frequent changes in the relations among the actors. Thus each state might at one time be a neutral, a "holder of the balance," a state with aggressive designs, a defender faced by a state whose intentions are difficult to determine, and so on. To a limited degree this test is possible in a balance-of-power system. But it is not available for most other systems, for example the one prevailing since World War II. Most nations have not changed roles, and indeed cannot do so because of such permanent factors as size and geography. The United States can never play the role of a second-ranking state caught between two blocs of greater powers. France can never be the leader of one of two dominant blocs. And while the United States and France may have played roles similar to these in the past, the extensive differences in the situation mean that any differences in response that might be found would not show that roles are unimportant.

Compulsion in Extreme Circumstances.   It is worthwhile to look at cases of the kind that are supposed to show most strongly the influence of external conditions. If there are differences of behavior here, the argument for not ignoring the other levels of analysis will apply a fortiori to a wider domain of cases. Arnold Wolfers argues that, the greater the external compulsion, the greater the homogeneity of behavior and therefore the less the need to study decision-making. In a well-known passage he says: "Imagine a number of individuals, varying widely in their predispositions, who find themselves inside a house on fire. It would be perfectly realistic to expect that these individuals, with rare exceptions, would feel compelled to run toward the exits. . . . Surely, therefore, for an explanation of the rush for the exits, there is no need to analyze the individual decisions that produced it."[17]

But the case is not as clear as this analogy suggests. If a situation were so compelling that all people would act alike, decision-makers would not hesitate nor feel torn among several alternative policies, nor would there be significant debates within the decision-making elite. In fact, key decisions that are easily reached, such as those involving the Truman Doctrine and Marshall Plan, stand out because they are so rare. For despite the implication of Wolfers' proposition that we know when we are faced by extreme danger, just as we can tell when the house is on fire, in fact this question is often bitterly contested. (To say that once decision-makers perceive the fire they will head for the exits leads us back to decision-making analysis.) For Churchill, the house was burning soon after Hitler took power in Germany; for Chamberlain, this was the case only after March 1939; and for others there never was a fire at all. To some decision-makers, the Soviet Union is a threat to which the United States is compelled to respond. To others the threat passed years ago. Again, to a growing number of scholars it never existed. Similarly, American statesmen saw a much greater threat from communism in both Europe and Southeast Asia than did the leaders of our allies. Decision-makers may even agree that their state's existence is threatened but disagree about the source of the threat. This was true, for example, in the United States around the turn of the nineteenth century, when the Federalists believed France so much a menace that they favored war with her. At the same time, the Republicans believed England an equal menace. (It should be noted that this disagreement was rooted as much in differences in values and interests as in divergent empirical analyses of the situation.)

In extreme cases we can specify with some certainty an indicator of the "fire" that all decision-makers will recognize—for example a large armed attack—and we can be relatively certain that the state will react.

But even then the objective situation will not determine all aspects of the state's response. There are apt to be several exits from the burning house. Will the state limit the extent of its involvement? What will its war aims be? While the United States may have had no choice but to declare war on Japan after Pearl Harbor, the major decisons that followed were less compelled and require further explanation. For example: the United States decided not to concentrate its energies on the country that had attacked it but to fight Germany first; the war was to be fought with few considerations for the shape of the postwar world; and no compromise with the enemies would be accepted (had the Japanese realized this would be the case, they almost certainly would not have attacked).

Even if all states and all statesmen responded similarly to similar high threats, we have to explain how the threat arose—i.e., why the adversary was so aggressive. In some cases we may be able to do this by reference to the other's objective situation, for example by focusing on the anarchic nature of the international system and the resulting security dilemma. . . . But when this analysis is insufficient, the state (and later scholars) must examine variables at other levels of analysis to establish some of the most important facts about the objective situation that the state faces.

Finally, one cannot prove that the external environment determines the response by simply showing that the decision-makers believed this to be the case. It is not enough to say with Kecskemeti that "In tense war situations, the decision-maker is likely to feel that he is acting from necessity rather than from deliberate choice." Nor is it sufficient to cite Holsti's finding that the decision-makers on both sides in July 1914 felt that when "Mr. Acheson was advised not to favor the production of the first thermonuclear bomb, he is reported to have declared that its production was a matter of necessity and not of choice: in other words, that he was experiencing 'compulsion.'"[18] The subjective feeling of determinacy is interesting and may lead decison-makers unnecessarily to restrict their search for alternatives, but it does not show that other decision-makers in the same situation would have felt the same compulsion and acted in the same way. Indeed the theory of cognitive dissonance . . . and other theories of irrational cognitive consistency . . . lead us to expect that decision-makers may avoid psychological conflict by thinking that they had no choice but to act as they did. This also means that, when scholars claim that a situation permitted no policy other than the one that was adopted, it may be that at least part of the reason why the circumstances appear overwhelming in retrospect is that they were claimed to be so by the decision-makers.

These arguments are, of course, far from conclusive. The necessary comparisons have merely been mentioned, not made. But, as we have seen, there are many points at which people can disagree about what the objective situation is or what policies will best cope with it, and there is little evidence for the existence of the homogeneity of behavior that would allow us to ignore everything except the international setting.

Domestic Determinants

Even if all states do not behave similarly in similar situations, the details of decision-making and images may not be significant. Instead, the state may be the appropriate level of analysis—i.e., variations in decision-makers' policies may be accounted for by variations in social and economic structure and domestic politics of the states they are serving. Wilsonian and Marxist theories are examples of this position. Other theories at this level of analysis argue for the importance of a state's geographical position, its traditions, its national style, or the consequences, often unintended, of domestic conflicts. Extreme formulations hold that the state's internal system determines its foreign policy, while weaker versions claim that foreign policies are a product of both domestic politics and international circumstances.

The forms of the assertions correspond to those discussed in the previous section. States wtih the same critical internal attributes behave the same way in similar situations—and often behave the same way in the face of significant variations in the environment—and this behavior is different from that displayed by other states with different attributes even when the setting is the same. The latter claim denies the overriding importance of the international environment.Thus while Cold War revisionists stress the importance of America's domestic political and economic needs, others reply that American actions were heavily influenced by external constraints and that her behavior was not peculiarly American or perculiarly capitalist but rather was typical of any great power in such a situation.[19] Because we are concerned with examining the importance of decision-making, we will not treat this part of the argument that deals with conflicts between claims for two other levels of analysis.

If states of the same type behave in the same way, then changes in a state's leadership will not produce significant changes in foreign policy, and we need not examine the images, values, and calculations of individual decision-makers. Unfortunately, claims about continuity in a state's foreign policy are notoriously difficult to judge. We might try to see whether we could deduce changes in the identities of the state's decision-makers from the course of its foreign policy. Could we tell when Democrats replaced Republicans or Conservatives replaced Labour governments? Scholars used to agree that Stalin's death led to major foreign policy changes, but now even this is in doubt.[20] Before taking office, decision-makers often claim they will introduce new policies. But these promises are often neglected. Eisenhower's foreign policy more closely resembled that of his predecessor than it did his campaign rhetoric.

Gladstone pledged himself to avoid immoral and wasteful imperialism, and, although he successfully extricated Britain from some entanglements, he was eventually drawn into commitments similar to those made by Disraeli. And while in 1937 Clement Atlee said that "the foreign policy of a Government is the reflection of its internal policy," when his party took power the foreign secretary declared that "Revolutions do not change geography, and revolutions do not change geographical needs."[21]

Many arguments about the wisdom of policies can be understood in terms of claims about the autonomy of the decision-making level. Those who praise Bismarck's diplomacy claim that, had he continued in office, he would have been able to maintain German security by avoiding the errors of severing Germany's ties to Russia, being forced to rely on Austria, and recklessly antagonizing several powerful countries. The rejoinder is that the dynamics of German domestic society and of the international system would have destroyed Bismarck's handiwork no matter who was in power. The glittering skill of Bismarck's diplomacy could not alter the underlying forces at work. Debates about the origins of the Cold War must deal with the similar question of whether Roosevelt's death changed American policy. Most traditional accounts argue that F. D. R. was coming to an anti-Soviet position and would have acted much as Truman did. This view is shared by those revisionists who look to the American political and economic system for the roots of foreign policy but is disputed by those who see the Cold Was as avoidable. Similarly, those who defend President Kennedy but opposed the war in Vietnam argue that he would not have acted as Johnson did. Those who either favored the war or opposed not only it but also most recent American foreign policies argue that the policies of these—and other—presidents were consistent. While those who supported the war see the determinants as international and those who criticize the general lines of America's postwar policy see the causes as domestic, both argue that few significant differences can be traced to the identity of the president.

These questions are so difficult to resolve partly because the situation facing the new government always differs from that which confronted the old. Kennedy was never forced to choose between defeat in Vietnam and fighting a major war. F. D. R. did not live to see Russia consolidate her hold over East Europe. The questions must then be hypothetical, and the comparisions that underlie our judgments are often strained. This problem can be avoided by using alternative comparisions—by examining the views of members of the elite to see whether they favor the policy that was adopted.[22] Of course disagreement with a policy does not prove that a person would have acted on his views were he in office. His opposition might be rooted in his role in the government, lack of information, freedom from the pressures that accompany holding power, or the belief that opposition is politically expedient. But when these explanations are not satisfactory, internal elite disagreement reveals the limits of the impact of both domestic politics and the international situation.

The Bureaucracy

Even if state behavior cannot be explained by the state's internal politics and external environment, we still may not need to examine the perceptions and calculations of the top decision-makers. The workings of the bureaucracy may determine policy. It is not enough for proponents of this position to show that the state's course of action appears inconsistent and lacks value integration. Such inadequacies can be the product of individual decision-making. As we will show later, normal human behavior often does not fit even a loose definition of rationality. Individuals as well as organizations fail to coordinate their actions and to develop carefully designed strategies. The fact that people must reach decisions in the face of the burdens of multiple goals and highly ambiguous information means that policies are often contradictory, incoherent, and badly suited to the information at hand. Unless we understand this, puzzling state behavior will automatically be seen as the product of either internal bargaining or the autonomous operation of different parts of the government. Thus if we did not know better it would be tempting to argue that the contradictory and erratic behavior displayed by Richard Nixon in Watergate and related matters shows that "Nixon" is not a single individual at all, but rather a title for the set of behaviors that are produced by the interaction of conflicting entities, each pursuing its own narrow interests in ignorance of or indifference to any wider goal of the "general Nixon interest." Similarly, if we were to insist that theories of individual behavior apply only when the actor is following a coherent path guided by his self-interest, we would have to say that Spiro Agnew was an uncoordinated bureaucracy rather than a person because he simultaneously accepted kickbacks and sought the presidency.

Because incoherent policy is insufficient evidence for the importance of bureaucracies, the "pure" theories of this type must make two basic assertions. First, bureaucrats' policy preferences are determined by their positions in the government: "Where you stand is determined by where you sit." The external environment and the nature of the state and domestic politics have only limited and indirect impact on these preferences. Of course if the concept of bureaucratic interest is to be more useful than the concept of national interest, we must be able to specify in advance what the bureaucratic position will be.[23] Even if we cannot do this, it would still be significant if everyone in each unit of the government had the same position on a given issue. If, on the other hand, there is a good deal of disagreement within the organization about the goals to be sought or the means that are appropriate, then we would have to apply decision-making analysis to the bureaucratic level, and so this approach would lose much of its distinctiveness. More importantly, if people in different units share the same policy preferences or if preferences are distributed at random throughout the government, then the first assertion would be undermined.

The second basic claim of theories on this level of analysis is that the state's policies are formed by bureaucratic bargains and routines. Bureaucratic actions either determine the statesman's decision or else implement it in a way that renders the decision largely irrelevant to what is actually done. This point is vital because, even if bureaucrats' policy preferences were linked to their positions within the government, this would be relatively unimportant unless these preferences explain policy outcomes.[24] But we should note at the start that even if this were true we would have to explore the sources of power of parts of the bureaucracy. If we find, for example, that the military often prevails in conflicts with the organization in charge of arms control, this may be because over a period of years the state's leaders have supported the former more than the latter. Sometimes we can go back some years to find a decisive action that set the guidelines for both the policy and the distribution of power within the bureaucracy. In less dramatic cases the relative strengths of interests represent the standing decision of the decision-makers—and often of wider publics—and their choices among competing policies and values. To the extent that this distribution of power is both important and accounted for by factors outside the bureaucracy, an explanation of specific outcomes in terms of bureaucratic maneuvering will be superficial at best.

Are policy preferences determined by one's role within the government? With the important exception of questions of military hardware and doctrine, the evidence is limited and ambiguous. It is not hard to find examples of units taking consistent and unified stands and political appointees adopting their units' views and thus expressing different opinions depending upon their positions in the government. "General Marshall, while Chief of Staff, opposed the State Department's idea of using aid to promote reforms in the Chinese government. Then, when he became Secretary of State, he defended this very idea against challenges voiced by the new chiefs of Staff." In "1910, Winston Churchill, as Home Secretary, led the attack upon the demand of McKenna, First Lord of the Admiralty, for more ships; by 1913 they had exchanged offices and each, with equal conviction, maintained the opposite view." When Samuel Hoare was secretary of state for air, he strongly fought against naval control of the Fleet Air Arm; when he later served as first lord of the Admiralty he took the opposite position. When Théophile Delcassé was the minister of colonies in France before the turn of the century, he supported an expedition to the Nile that would give France a lever to use against Britain. As foreign secretary, he sought to recall the adventure.[25]

But not all policy disagreements are traceable to roles. Organizational perspectives and loyalties are less important when issues are unusual rather than routine, necessitate relatively quick decisions, and involve important and generally shared values. Beliefs about the most important issues of foreign policy—those involving war and peace—are usually unrelated to roles. When we look at the major decisions of American foreign policy—those that set the terms for future debates and established the general framework within which policy was then conducted—it does not seem to be true, at least for the top decision-makers, that "where you sit determines where you stand."

In several important cases what is most striking is the degree of unanimity. In the spring of 1947 there was general agreement within the government that massive aid for Europe was needed. Three years later most officials felt that foreign policy considerations argued for large-scale rearmament, although there was a disagreement—which was not tightly connected with bureaucratic interests—over whether domestic political and economic constraints made such a policy feasible. Once the Korean War removed this opposition, government officials were again in general agreement. In other important cases there are basic disputes, but the key to them is not divergent bureaucratic interests. Doves and hawks on Vietnam were to be found in all parts of the American government. Views on whether to take a hard line toward Japan before World War II, and specifically on the crucial issue of embargoing oil and other vital raw materials, were only loosely related to organizational affiliations. The advice that Truman received at the start of the Berlin blockade and the Korean War and most of the differences that emerged in the discussions during the Cuban missile crisis were not predictable by the participants' roles.

In the missile crisis none of the leading officials espoused views that were linked to his position within the government. The Republican secretary of the treasury was concerned about the effects of a "soft" response on the fortunes of the Democratic party in the coming elections; the secretary of defense at first argued that the missiles did not present a major military threat; the secretary of state did not take a strong position and did not pay special attention to the political consequences of various moves; and the attorney general opposed an air strike. (It should also be noted that his view carried great weight not because of his governmental position or independent political resources, but because he was thought to speak for the president.)

The other claim—that policies can be explained by bureaucratic maneuvering—could be supported in either of two ways. First, it could be shown that different parts of the government carry out, or fail to carry out, policies in ways that are consistent with their preferences and routines rather than with the decisions of the national leaders. But the other possible linkage in the second point—the argument that authoritative decisions can be explained by the interaction of bureaucratic stands—raises difficulties that go deeper than the temporary absence of evidence. To verify this claim we must be able to specify the expected relationship between the variety of bureaucratic positions on the one hand and policy outcomes on the other. It is not enough to show that the outcome can be seen as a compromise among views that have been advocated by various parts of the government. Almost any decision could fit this description. The theory must provide generalizations that tell us more exactly what the outcome will be. If the goals of different parts of the bureaucracy are complementary, then presumably each agency will give up its position on the part of the program it cares least about in order to gain a larger voice on those issues that are more important to it. Presumably the success of an organization in conflicts with others is related to its strength (determined independently of outcomes), although as we noted this raises further questions. Still another likely pattern is that the symbols will be given to one side in a bureaucratic conflict and the substance to the other. But much more detail is needed. Furthermore, these generalizations must not involve the values and beliefs that vary with the identity of the top decision-makers, and they must be able to explain how policies change. The latter task poses great problems since bureaucratic structures and interests often remain constant over periods in which policies shift.

Although the paucity of research on this level makes conclusions especially tentative, it is hard to see how any of the major decisions of American foreign policy in recent years could meet this test. The Marshall Plan, the establishment of NATO, the crucial decisions in Korea, the rearmament that followed, the decision to integrate West Germany into West Europe, the New Look in defense, American policy in the Suez crisis, Kennedy's attempt to increase conventional forces in Europe, the major decisions to fight and later withdraw from Vietnam, and crucial choices in the Cuban missile crisis cannot be explained as the outcome of intrabureaucratic conflict. That these decisions combined major elements of positions held within the bureaucracy is hardly surprising because different parts of the bureaucracy serve and represent divergent values that the president seeks to further. Thus what seems to be a clash of bureaucratic interests and stands can often be more fruitfully viewed as a clash among values that are widely held in both the society and the decision-makers' own minds. What embarrasses the theories under consideration here is that, while the decisions listed above did embody some of the preferences that had been articulated by parts of the bureaucracy, they did not combine them in a way that can be predicted by rules of bureaucratic politics. Or, to put the argument more exactly, until we have a theory that specifies how policy is formed out of conflicting bureaucratic perspectives and preferences, we cannot tell whether any given outcome can be explained by this level of analysis. As things stand now, there is no way to explore the extent to which bureaucratic factors cause the outcome because we have no grounds for claiming that a different constellation of bureaucratic interests and forces would have produced a different result or that the outcome would have been different were there no bureaucracies at all.

PERCEPTIONS, REALITY, AND A TWO-STEP MODEL

Our discussion thus far leads to the conclusion that it is often impossible to explain crucial decisions and policies without reference to the decision-makers' beliefs about the world and their images of others. That is to say, these cognitions are part of the proximate cause of the relevant behavior and other levels of analysis cannot immediately tell us what they will be. And even if we found that people in the same situation— be it international, domestic, or bureaucratic—behave in the same way, it is useful to examine decision-making if there are constant differences between the decision-makers' perceptions and reality. In this case all people might react in the same way to the same situation, but this behavior would puzzle an observer because it was self-defeating, based on incorrect beliefs about the world, or generally lacking in a high degree of rationality.[26] Many of the propositions advanced in here fit in this category: they are generalizations about how decision-makers perceive others' behavior and form judgments about their intentions. These patterns are explained by the general ways in which people draw inferences from ambiguous evidence and, in turn, help explain many seemingly incomprehensible policies. They show how, why, and when highly intelligent and conscientious statesmen misperceive their environments in specified ways and reach inappropriate decisions.

Other propositions deal with cases in which an analysis of decision-making is necessary because people in the same situations behave differently. This is often the case because people differ in their perceptions of the world in general and of other actors in particular. Sometimes it will be useful to ask who, if anyone, was right; but often it will be more fruitful to ask why people differed and how they came to see the world as they did.

The exploration of the images actors hold and the development of the two kinds of propositions discussed above should be seen in the context of a mediated or two-step model.[27] Rather than trying to explain foreign policies as the direct consequence of variables at the three levels of analysis previously discussed, we will examine the actor's perceptions as one of the immediate causes of his behavior. Thus Britain and France felt that their security was endangered by Germany before both world wars. They may have been mistaken in the first case and correct in the second, but both cases can be grouped together in discussing the immediate causes of their responses.

Our understanding of the actor's images and beliefs affects the further question that we ask about that event and the behavior that we expect of the actor in other cases. For example, when it was believed that most American decision-makers had thought that escalation would bring a quick victory in Vietnam, the interesting questions concerned the reasons for the error and the ways by which successive small steps increased the stakes of the conflict. If the decision-makers believed that victory was cheap, it is not surprising that they acted as they did. But by revealing that the decision-makers had a relatively accurate view of the chances of success, the Pentagon Papers and related commentaries have shown that the crucial question is why saving Vietnam was considered important enough to justify the high expected price. This then leads us to look at this and other American actions in terms of beliefs about "domino effects" rather than directing our attention to commitments that develop inadvertently and "quagmires" that trap unwary statesmen. Similarly, the question about Russian behavior raised by the Cuban missile crisis probably is not "What Soviet calculus and risk-taking propensity could explain this bold and dangerous step?" but rather "How could they have so badly misestimated the probable American response?"[28] And previous Soviet behavior can be re-examined to see if it could be explained by similar misperceptions. . . . Actors as well as scholars must engage in these kinds of analyses.

Of course perceptions, and more specifically perceptions of other actors, are not the only decision-making variables that are important. That two actors have the same perceptions does not guarantee that they will adopt the same response. But their responses will often be the same, and, when they are not, it is usually relatively easy to find the causes of the differences. Although people with different images of an adversary may agree on the appropriate response, just as people may favor the same policy for different reasons, this agreement is apt to be short-lived. . . . The roots of many important disputes about policies lie in differing perceptions. And in the frequent cases when the actors do not realize this, they will misunderstand their disagreement and engage in a debate that is unenlightening.

Images, however, are not first causes, and so we will try to find the causes both of common misperceptions and of differences in perceptions. Thus the second step in the model involves relating the images held, if not to reality, then at least to the information available to the actor. How, for example, do statesmen come to develop their images of other actors? What evidence do they pay most attention to? What makes them perceive threat? Under what conditions do they think that the other, although hostile, has only limited objectives? What differentiates legitimate inducements from bribes? What kinds of behavior are most apt to change an established image?

This is not to claim that we will be able to explain nearly all state behavior. Propositions about both the causes and the effects of images can only be probabilistic. There are too many variables at work to claim more. In the cases in which we are interested, decision-makers are faced with a large number of competing values, highly complex situations, and very ambiguous information. The possibilities and reasons for misperceptions and disagreements are legion. For these reasons, generalizations in this area are difficult to develop, exceptions are common, and in many instances the outcomes will be influenced by factors that, from the standpoint of most theories, must be considered accidental. Important perceptual predispositions can be discovered, but often they will not be controlling.

NOTES

1. See especially the following works by Harold and Margaret Sprout: *Man–Milieu Relationship Hypotheses in the Context of International Politics* (Princeton, N.J.: Center of International Studies, 1956); *The Ecological Perspective on Human Affairs* (Princeton, N.J.: Princeton University Press, 1965); and *An Ecological Paradigm for the Study of International Politics* (Princeton, N.J.: Center of International Studies, Princeton University, Research Monograph No. 30, March, 1968).

2. "Decision-Making As an Approach to the Study of International Politics," in Richard Snyder, H. W. Bruck, and Burton Sapin, eds., *Foreign Policy Decision-Making* (New York: Free Press, 1962), p. 33. For a similar argument see Fred Greenstein, "The Impact of Personality on Politics: An Attempt to Clear Away Underbrush," *American Political Science Review 61* (September 1967), 631–33. This is related to the debate about the significance of developmental sequences. For differing views on this question see Herbert Hyman, *Survey Design and Analysis* (Glencoe, Ill.: Free Press, 1955), pp. 254–63, and Travis Hirschi and Hanan Selvin, *Delinquency Research* (New York: Free Press, 1967), pp. 82–85. (The latter book [republished in paperback as *Principles of Survey Analysis*] has much broader relevance than its title indicates and is extremely valuable not only for its explanation of the use of survey research data but for its treatment of general questions of theory, causation, and evidence.)

   This issue is also related to the broader debate between what Maurice Natanson has called the "Two distinctively opposed philosophic attitudes . . . underlying the social sciences: . . . [the] 'objective' and 'subjective' *Weltanschauungen.*" ("Foreword" in Natanson, ed., *Philosophy of the Social Sciences* [New York: Random House, 1963], p. viii.) This reader is a good introduction to the arguments.

3. Hirschi and Selvin, *Delinquency Research,* p. 38. As Abraham Kaplan puts it, "I would not wish to say that something has been explained only when we have traced the microconnections with their antecedents, or even only when we can believe that such conditions exist." ("Noncausal Explanation," in Daniel Lerner, ed. *Cause and Effect* [New York: Free Press, 1965], p. 146.)

4. Quoted in Townsend Hoopes, *The Limits of Intervention* (New York: McKay, 1969), p. 30.

5. The question of the existence and nature of reality need not be treated here in its profound sense. For our purposes the consensus of later observers usually provides an adequate operational definition of reality.

6. Arnold Wolfers, "The Actors in International Politics," in *Discord and Collaboration* (Baltimore, Md: Johns Hopkins Press, 1962), pp. 3–24; Kenneth Waltz, *Man, the State and War* (New York: Columbia University Press, 1959); James Rosenau, "Pre-Theories and Theories of Foreign Policy," in R. Barry Farrell, ed., *Approaches to Comparative and International Politics* (Evanston, Ill.: Northwestern University Press, 1966), pp. 29–92.

7. We refer to the international environment rather than the international system because we are not dealing with systems theories. Our concern is with explaining specific foreign policies rather than finding general patterns of interaction.

8. Quoted in Robert Butow, *Tojo and the Coming of the War* (Princeton, N.J.: Princeton University Press, 1961), p. 506; quoted in Egmont Zechlin, "Cabinet versus Economic Warfare in Germany," in H. W. Koch, ed., *The Origins of the First World War* (London: Macmillan & Co., 1972), p. 165.

9. See K. J. Holsti, "National Role Conceptions in the Study of Foreign Policy," *International Studies Quarterly* 14 (September 1970), 233–309.

10. It is interesting to note that in interpersonal perception people tend to overestimate the degree to which the other's behavior is determined by his personality and underestimate the impact of the external situation. See, for example, Gustav Ichheiser, *Appearances and Realities* (San Francisco: Jossey-Bass, 1970), pp. 49–59. But when the person explains his own behavior, he will attribute his actions to the requirements of the situation, not to his own predispositions. See Edward Jones and Richard Nisbett, *The Actor and the Observer: Divergent Perceptions of the Causes of Behavior* (New York: General Learning Press, 1971).

11. Two recent articles explore the utility of the concept of issue areas in foreign-policy research, but they are not concerned with the level of analysis problem. See Thomas Brewer, "Issue and Context Variations in Foreign Policy," *Journal of Conflict Resolution* 17 (March 1973), 89–114, and William Zimmerman, "Issue Area and Foreign-Policy Process," *American Political Science Review* 67 (December 1973), 1204–12.

12. James Rosenau, "Pre-Theories and Theories of Foreign Policy," pp. 47–48; Stanley Hoffmann, "Restraints and Choices in American Foreign Policy," *Daedalus* (Fall 1962), 692–94.

13. Most of the propositions in Greenstein, "The Impact of Personality on Politics," about the conditions under which personality is most important can be subsumed under this heading.

14. Thus the famous remark by a cabinet officer that you have to obey the president only when he repeats an order for the third time.

15. An excellent discussion of the evidence on this point derived from quantitative studies is Dina Zinnes, "Some Evidence Relevant to the Man–Milieu Hypothesis," in James Rosenau, Vincent Davis, and Maurice East, eds., *The Analysis of International Politics* (New York: Free Press, 1972), pp. 209–51. But these studies have limited utility for the questions being asked here because they do not provide adequate measures of the similarity of the objective situation and the similarity of the state's responses. This is also true

for the growing body of literature that examines these questions using event-scaling techniques. For a study that copes with these problems relatively well and finds that differences in perceptions among decision-makers decrease as tension increases, see Ole Holsti, "Individual Differences in 'Definition of the Situation,'" *Journal of Conflict Resolution* 14 (September 1970), 303–10.

16. For a general discussion, see Herbert Blumer, "Society as Symbolic Interaction," in Arnold Rose, ed., *Human Behavior and Social Processes* (Boston: Houghton Mifflin, 1962), pp. 180–91. For an inventory of findings see Kenneth Terhune, "Personality in Cooperation and Conflict," in Paul Swingle, ed., *The Structure of Conflict* (New York: Academic Press, 1970), pp. 193–234. This subject has received much attention from psychologists in the past few years. For a review of the literature and an excellent argument, see Daryl Bem and Andrea Allen, "On Predicting Some of the People Some of the Time," *Psychological Review* 81 (1974), 506–20.

17. Wolfers, *Discord and Collaboration,* p. 13.

18. Paul Kecskemeti, *Strategic Surrender* (New York: Atheneum, 1964), pp. 19–20; Ole Holsti, "The 1914 Case," *The American Political Science Review* 59 (June 1965), 365–78; Wolfers, *Discord and Collaboration,* p. 14.

19. See, for example, Charles Maier, "Revisionism and the Interpretation of Cold War Origins," *Perspectives in American History* 4 (1970), 313–47; Robert Tucker, *The Radical Left and American Foreign Policy* (Baltimore, Md.: Johns Hopkins Press, 1971); James Richardson, "Cold-War Revisionism: A Critique," *World Politics* 24 (July 1972), 579–612; and Ole Holsti, "The Study of International Politics Makes Strange Bedfellows: Theories of the Radical Right and the Radical Left," *American Political Science Review* 68 (March 1974), 217–42. Comparisons with the reactions of European statesmen would also shed light on the question of whether there was anything peculiarly American in the United States' perceptions.

20. Marshall Shulman, *Stalin's Foreign Policy Reappraised* (Cambridge, Mass.: Harvard University Press, 1963).

21. Michael Gordon, *Conflict and Consensus in Labour's Foreign Policy, 1914–1965* (Stanford: Stanford University Press, 1969), p. 6; M. A. Fitzsimons, *The Foreign Policy of the British Labour Government, 1945–1951* (Notre Dame, Ind.: University of Notre Dame Press, 1953), p. 26.

22. In this group we include potential leaders who could come to power without drastic changes in the state's internal political system. Dissent from those outside this group does not undermine the arguments for the importance of the nature of the state, and, indeed, if such people have been rejected as possible powerholders because of their foreign policy views, this would demonstrate the importance of this level of analysis rather than showing the autonomy of the decision-making level.

23. Most light is shed on this subject by the writings of Philip Selznick. See his *TVA and the Grassroots* (Berkeley and Los Angeles: University of California Press, 1947) and *Leadership in Administration* (Evanston, Ill.: Row, Peterson, 1957). Also see Morton Halperin, "Why Bureaucrats Play Games," *Foreign Policy,* No. 2 (Spring 1971), 74–88, and *Bureaucratic Politics and Foreign Policy* (Washington: Brookings Institution, 1974), pp. 26–62.

24. During the Second World War the British set up an intelligence section to try to recreate the German perspective. They did well at predicting the positions taken by various parts of the German bureaucracy but could never ade-

quately predict when Hitler would side with a particular faction or impose his own solution. (Donald McLachlan, *Room* 39 [New York: Atheneum, 1968], pp. 252-58.

25. Ernest May, "The Development of Political-Military Consultation in the United States," in Aaron Wildavsky, ed., *The Presidency* (Boston: Little, Brown, 1969), p. 668; Patrick Gordon Walker, *The Cabinet* (New York: Basic Books, 1970), p. 67; W. J. Reader, *Architect of Airpower: The Life of the First Viscount Weir* (London: Collins, 1968), p. 270; Roger Brown, *Fashoda Reconsidered* (Baltimore, Md.: Johns Hopkins Press, 1970), pp. 24-32, 85.

26. The knowledge gained by studying how people view the world and process incoming information can lead to the discovery of patterns in state behavior that would not be apparent to an observer who had ignored decision-making. We may be able to say, for example, that two kinds of situations, although not seeming alike to later scholars, will appear to be similar to contemporary decision-makers and will be seen to call for similar responses. Thus, once we have examined a number of cases, detected common deviations, and isolated their causes, we could apply this knowledge to theories that do not call for intensive analysis of decision-making.

27. See Charles Osgood, "Behavior Theory and the Social Sciences," in Roland Young, ed., *Approaches to the Study of Politics* (Evanston, Ill.: Northwestern University Press, 1958), pp. 217-44. For a recent discussion and application, see Richard Jessor and Shirley Jessor, "The Perceived Environment in Behavioral Science," *American Behavioral Scientist* 16 (July/August 1973), 801-27. In an interesting critique, Robert Gorman asks "Must we look into the perception of the decision-maker at the time the decision was being made by centering our political analysis on the decision-maker himself? Or, should we concentrate on the social organization of which the decision-maker is a part and the social environment in which both the organization and the individual function? If we accept the first choice, then social factors assume a secondary, instrumental purpose. If we choose the second framework, the perceptions of the decision-maker would seem to be *logically* dependent on external rules, and investigation into the nature of individual perception would be absurd. If we combine the two, as the decision-making theorists seem to have done, we are left with a theory in which each premise is negated by the existence of the other, and the general theory itself is left to flounder in a formalistic but meaningless syncretism." ("On the Inadequacies of Non-Philosophical Political Science: A Critical Analysis of Decision-Making Theory," *International Studies Quarterly* 14 [December 1970], 408.) The use of a two-step model avoids this contradiction.

28. Daniel Ellsberg, "The Quagmire Myth and the Stalemate Machine," in *Papers on the War* (New York: Simon and Schuster, 1972), pp. 42-135; Leslie Gelb, "Vietnam: The System Worked," *Foreign Policy* No. 3 (Summer 1971), 140-67; Klaus Knorr, "Failures in National Intelligence Estimates: The Case of the Cuban Missiles," *World Politics* 16 (April 1967), 455-67. Theodore Draper fails to see the significance of these kinds of questions in explaining the American intervention in the Dominican Republic. ("The Dominican Intervention Reconsidered," *Political Science Quarterly* 86 [March 1971], 26-28.) To take an example from another field, the fact that young people in less politicized homes share fewer of their parents' political views than do those in more highly politicized families is not to be explained by the former group

having less desire to adopt their parents' beliefs, but by their lack of knowledge about what their parents believe. (Richard Niemi, *How Family Members Perceive Each Other* [New Haven: Yale University Press, 1974], pp. 200–201.)

Theories of Crisis Decision Making

Ole R. Holsti

The author reviews theoretical work done on crisis decision making, especially the World War I (1914) and the Cuban missile crisis (1962) cases.

In memoirs written some years before he assumed the presidency, Richard Nixon wrote of crises as "mountaintop experiences" in which he often performed at his best: "Only then [in crises] does he discover all the latent strengths he never knew he had and which otherwise would have remained dormant."[1] He added:

> It has been my experience that, more often than not, taking a break is actually an escape from the tough, grinding discipline that is absolutely necessary for superior performance. Many times I have found that my best ideas have come when I thought I could not work for another minute and when I literally had to drive myself to finish the task before a deadline. Sleepless nights, to the extent that the body can take them, can stimulate creative mental activity.[2]

Others have appraised the effects of crisis on decision making in a similar vein, suggesting, for example, that "a decision maker may, in a crisis, be able to invent or work out easily and quickly what seems in normal times to both the 'academic' scholar and the layman to be hypothetical, unreal, complex or otherwise difficult."[3] More important, theories of nuclear deterrence presuppose rational and predictable decision processes, even during intense and protracted international crises. They assume that threats and ultimata will enhance calculation, control, and caution while inhibiting recklessness and risk-taking.[4] Deterrence theories, in short, tend to be sanguine about the ability of policy makers to be creative when the situation requires it—and never is that requirement greater than during an intense international crisis.

These observations appear to confirm the conventional wisdom that in crisis decision making necessity is indeed the mother of invention. Is there any reason to question the universal validity of that view? Fortunately, scenarios of inadequate decision making resulting in a nuclear war are thus far limited to novels and movies, but otherwise the evidence is less than totally reassuring. The recollections of those who have experienced intense and protracted crises suggest they may be marked at times by great skill in policy making, and at others by decision processes and outcomes that fail to meet even the most permissive standards of rationality. Some recall the "sense of elation that comes with crises,"[5] whereas others admit to serious shortcomings in their own performance during such situations. Indeed, although the definitive history of the Watergate episode remains to be written, available evidence suggests that Nixon's performance during the culminating crisis of his presidency was at best erratic, certainly falling far short of his own self-diagnosis as described above.

But anecdotes do not provide a sufficient basis for addressing the question: How do policy makers respond to the challenges and demands of crises? Do they tend to approach such situations with high motivation, a keen sense of purpose, extraordinary energy, and an enhanced capacity for creativity? Or, is their capacity for coping with complex problems sometimes impaired, perhaps to the point suggested by Richard Neustadt's phrase, "the paranoid reaction characteristic of crisis behavior"?[6]

This article will address these questions by describing and analyzing several major theories of crisis decision making. It will begin with a discussion of the various definitions of the much abused term, "crisis," and review theoretical models of behavior during crisis. This will be followed by the presentation of several hypotheses concerning some of the effects of intense and protracted crisis on decision making, utilizing recent evidence from several social sciences, especially the field of psychology. Some of these hypotheses of crisis-induced stress will then be examined in the light of evidence from two classic case studies in diplomatic history: the 1914 crisis leading to the outbreak of World War I and, more briefly, the Cuban missile crisis of 1962. Finally, the conclusion will discuss some of the advantages and disadvantages of interdisciplinary research for psychologists, political scientists, and diplomatic historians.

CRISIS: DEFINITIONS, DESCRIPTIVE THEORIES, AND PRESCRIPTIVE THEORIES

One of the first requirements in establishing any viable body of theory is that of providing workable definitions. In this regard, theories of crisis behavior have been plagued with the fact that "crisis" is a much over-used term that has become burdened with a wide range of meanings, some of them quite imprecise. In common usage it is victim of the age of hyperbole, becoming a synonym for virtually every problem of even moderate difficulty. Even in foreign policy research and diplomatic history, diversity is more in evidence than uniformity. As one of the pioneers in crisis research, Charles McClelland, observes:

> So many studies of crisis have been published in the last fifteen years from so many different angles of inquiry that it is more difficult than it once was to be sure about the denotations and connotations of the term. Not only is there a heavy popular usage of the word in ordinary discourse but also there are indications that historical change has brought about an expansion of the variety of situations that are called readily by the crisis name.[7]

In order to resolve this problem, scholars have been working to establish an acceptable definition of a crisis. These efforts fall into two very broad groups. Common to the first is a systematic perspective in which crisis represents a significant change in the quantity, quality, or intensity of interactions among nations. As McClelland describes this approach, it "looks on the whole configuration of parties participating back and forth" and observes changes in the patterns of interaction.[8] Special attention is given to any significant step-level change or turning point. This might be a dramatic increase in the number of border incidents, verbal challenges, or physical threats. After a crisis, the number and type of these exchanges may return to a more "normal" state. Accordingly, one way to identify crises analytically in diplomatic history is through a *post hoc* search for changed interaction patterns between nations.[9]

A second approach to defining a crisis—the decision-making perspective—focuses on the human participants themselves rather than the system. Here, a situation is a crisis when it is so defined by those who are responsible for coping with it. It is thus possible that in a confrontation between nations X and Y, decision makers in the former will believe themselves to be facing a crisis, whereas those in the latter will not. Although differences may be found among those who adopt a decision-making approach to crisis, one definition developed by Charles Hermann has gained a number of adherents: A crisis is a situation characterized by *surprise,* a *high threat* to important values, and *short decision time.*[10] This definition is not without its critics, but most of them tend to disagree only with one or another of the three criteria, usually either surprise,[11] or short decision time.[12] Nevertheless, the Hermann definition offers some important advantages to both theorists and historians, not the least of which is the existence of at least some evidence linking each of the defining criteria with some consequences for decision making.

Most of the extensive literature on crisis extends far beyond this initial problem of definition and concentrates its attention on actual behavior during crisis situations. This proceeds from a wide variety of theoretical and empirical perspectives. It can perhaps be understood best by following the approach of Hermann and Brady, and systematically identifying four rather distinct, *descriptive* theories.[13]

The first of these is the *organizational response* model. It is directed at decision-making groups and the bureaucratic organizations which may shape and constrain policy choices in crisis. Studies at the level of the decision-making group reveal that the concomitants of crisis—for example, smaller groups or greater cohesion—can have both positive and negative consequences for the quality of decision processes. Leadership skills often determine whether, for example, group cohesion becomes a vehicle for constructive cooperation, or whether it takes on a more pathological form such as "groupthink."[14] Organizational theorists have often regarded crises as occasions in which greater than normal rationality prevails because decisions are made at the top of organizational hierarchies by persons less constrained by narrow parochial views.[15] Moreover, limited time reduces opportunities to adopt bargaining and incremental strategies that may reduce the quality of decisions.[16] But others have shown that not even in crisis situations is decision making free of the organizational processes and bureaucratic politics that may constrain rational choice.[17]

A second approach may be found in the *hostile interaction* model, which examines the antecedents and consequences of interactions among nations in crises, with special attention to the role of perceptions in exacerbating, sustaining, or mitigating the pattern of relations between contending parties. According to this model, those involved in a crisis perceive accurately any hostility directed toward them, and they respond in kind. Thus, crisis is viewed as an occasion that is likely to trigger a "conflict spiral." Stated somewhat differently, this conception of crisis highlights the processes by which hostility breeds more hostility, and it focuses less attention on the means by which such a pattern of interactions may be arrested.[18]

The *cost calculation* model emphasizes the strategic and tactical choices associated with maximizing gains and minimizing losses in crisis management. Crises that pose significant threats to such central goals as national existence are likely to engender greater caution in decision makers, as well as more vigorous efforts to reach peaceful settlements. Conversely, in crises posing threats of lesser magnitude, policy makers will feel less constrained and, therefore, they may be more willing to resort to high-risk strategies and tactics; for example, they may undertake actions that convey irrationality or loss of control in an effort to force concessions from the adversary. Thus, the hostile interaction and cost calculation models differ in some significant ways, especially with respect to the prospects for attenuating escalation in a crisis.[19]

The *individual stress* model focuses upon the impact of crisis-induced stress on certain aspects of cognitive performance that are critical in decision making. Theories and research at the individual level generally emphasize the negative effects of intense and protracted crises on decision processes and outcomes. It should be noted, however, that this model is not merely a variant of a frustration–aggression theory. As will be evident in later sections of this chapter that deal with the individual stress model in much more detail, the probable consequences of intense and protracted stress are by no means confined to or even most clearly manifested by the release of aggressive impulses.

Other theories address themselves to the *consequences* of crisis. These are also marked by diversity. Among those with a systemic perspective, crisis has been viewed both as a prelude to war[20] and as a surrogate for war that offers a means of effectuating needed change.[21] There are also competing views on the consequences of *multiple* crises. The first, suggested by Quincy Wright, among others, states that the more frequent the crises, the greater the likelihood that war will result. "If p_1, p_2, p_3, etc., indicate the probability of war in successive crises in the relations of two states and P indicates the probability of war for n crises, then $P = 1 - (1 - p_1) (1 - p_2) (1 - p_3) \ldots (1 - p_n)$. . . . Even though p is very small, as n approaches infinity the probability of war approaches certainty."[22] This might be labeled the "actuarial" view of crises. An insurance company typically charges a higher premium for the person who drives thirty thousand miles a year than for one who logs only a quarter of that distance, on the theory that greater exposure to the highways will increase the probability of a claim. The Wright formulation assumes that each crisis can be thought of as a discrete event and that there is little or no learning from [one] episode to another; that is, the participants can be thought of as beginning each time with a "crisis management tabula rasa." Thus, the cumulative probability of crises leading to war increases with each incidence of such an event.

An alternative position denies that decision makers begin with a blank slate at the onset of each crisis. Because the participants learn from their experiences, crises become "routinized." "Outputs received from occurrences and situations in the international environment and from sequences of international interaction are processed by the advanced modernizing social organizations according to their perceived characteristics: if these outputs are recognized as familiar and expected experiences met repeatedly in the remembered past, they will be treated in a highly routine fashion."[23] The participants gain experience in ways of coping with environment and adversaries and, although threats and challenges may continue to characterize relations between parties, uncertainty is reduced. Thus, "repeated exposure to acute crises may reduce the probabilities of an outbreak of general war."[24]

Finally, *prescriptive theories*—that is, theories that emphasize how to achieve one's purposes—of crisis management span an equally broad range. For present purposes, it may be sufficient to identify some basic features of two rather different perspectives. This is done merely for the purpose of illustration, and it should not be construed as an adequate treatment of the various positions or of all aspects of crisis management.

One position holds that the primary task of crisis management is to communicate one's interests and demands as unambiguously as possible, in order to prevent miscalculation on the part of adversaries. With a clear exposition of one's interests, the adversary will either avoid further provocation (ending the crisis) or demonstrate a calculated willingness to escalate the conflict (and thus reveal no interest in resolving it except on one's own terms). Strategies of crisis management include "burning one's bridges" and other forms of seemingly irrational behavior that are intended to convey to adversaries an unambiguous message of one's resolve and commitment.[25]

A rather different theory of crisis management places emphasis not only on protecting one's primary interests, but also on avoiding actions that might drive an opponent into a mutually undesirable process of escalation. Those in the group described in the previous paragraph believe that the primary danger of crisis management is that unwise concessions will mislead a thoroughly rational opponent into making further demands (the "appeasement model"); the opposing view is that an overly rigid policy may lead the adversary, whose rationality is not without limits under circumstances of crisis-induced stress, to strike back in ways that are disadvantageous to both sides.[26]

Perhaps this cursory review of a larger literature is sufficient to establish the point that even if there are fewer than a hundred flowers contending for the attention of those undertaking crisis studies, consensus remains an elusive goal rather than an established condition. Stated somewhat differently, the diplomatic historian who ventures into neighboring disciplines with expectations of finding broad agreement on key concepts that are linked together in well-established theories, and solidly buttressed by empirical evidence, is likely to be somewhat disappointed.

Lest this appraisal paint an overly pessimistic picture, it is also worth pointing to some signs of genuine progress toward the goals of cumulative knowledge. There is a convergence around, and refinements of, certain key terms and definitions (e.g., Hermann's definition of crisis) in the literature. There is also a growing willingness to undertake comparative studies in which a single crisis is viewed from several, rather than from a single, theoretical perspective,[27] or in which two or more crises are examined in a systematic and rigorous comparative manner.[28] Moreover, there is evidence that the crisis literature that has been heavily skewed toward studies of postwar crises involving one or more of the superpowers, is now being significantly broadened by research which includes both pre- and post-1945 cases as well as small- and middle-range powers.[29] Finally, the concept of crisis itself is being subjected to cross-cultural comparisons in order to understand the involvement of more than one decision system in the anticipation, avoidance, control, and termination of international crises.[30] These several developments suggest promising prospects for policy makers, political scientists, and diplomatic historians concerned with crisis behaviors.

CRISIS, STRESS, AND DECISION MAKING: SOME EVIDENCE FROM PSYCHOLOGY

One of the more interesting bodies of theory on crisis behavior is that concentrating upon individual stress. This approach, as indicated previously, focuses upon the impact of crisis-induced stress on certain aspects of cognitive performance that are critical in decision making. In assessing the potential impact of crisis on cognitive performance, it is important to do so against realistic standards. Cognitive limits on rationality include, as suggested by evidence from psychology, limits on the individual's capacity to receive, process, and assimilate information about the situation; an inability to generate the entire set of policy alternatives; fragmentary knowledge about the consequences of each option; and an inability to order preferences for all possible consequences on a single utility scale.[31] Because these constraints exist in all but the most trivial decision-making situations, it is not instructive to assess the impact on crises against a standard of synoptic rationality. A more modest and useful set of criteria might include an individual's ability to do the following:

Identify adequately the objectives to be fulfilled;

Survey the major alternative courses of action;

Estimate the probable costs and risks, as well as the positive consequences, of various alternatives (and, as a corollary, distinguish the possible from the probable);

Search for new information relevant to assessment of the options;

Maintain an open mind to new information, even that which calls into question the validity of preferred courses of action (and as corollaries, discriminate between relevant and irrelevant information, resist premature cognitive closure, and tolerate ambiguity);

Assess the situation from the perspective of other parties;

Resist both defensive procrastination and premature decision;

Make adjustments to meet real changes in the situation (and, as a corollary, distinguish real from apparent changes).[32]

A vast body of theory and evidence suggests that intense and protracted crises tend to erode rather than enhance these cognitive abilities. Figure 1—a series of hypotheses linking the defining attributes of crisis, first to stress and then to selected aspects of cognitive and decision-making performance—is a variant of the individual stress model described earlier.[33] These propositions are presented not as iron laws but as an

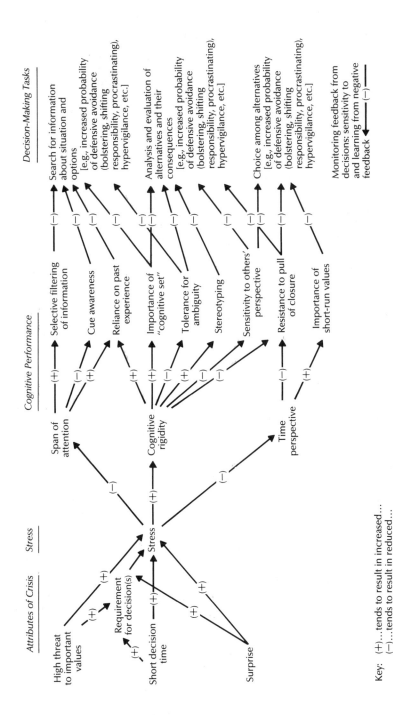

Key: (+)...tends to result in increased...
     (−)...tends to result in reduced...

Figure 1. Individual Decision Making in Crisis: Some Hypotheses alternative to the view that crisis heightens propensities toward rational and calculated decision processes. The remainder of this section summarizes briefly some of the relevant psychological evidence.

An important aspect of crises is that they are characterized by high stress for the individuals and organizations involved. That a severe threat to important values is stress inducing requires little elaboration. The element of surprise is also a contributing factor; there is evidence that unanticipated and novel situations are generally viewed as more threatening.[34] Finally, crises are often marked by almost around-the-clock work schedules, owing to the severity of the situation (high threat), the absence of established routines for dealing with them (surprise), and the absence of extended decision time. Lack of rest and diversion, combined with excessively long working hours, are likely to magnify the stresses in the situation. Moreover, crisis decisions are rarely if ever analogous to the familiar multiple-choice question, in which the full range of options is neatly outlined. The theoretical universe of choices usually exceeds by a substantial margin the number that can or will be considered. Especially in unanticipated situations for which there are no established SOPs (standard operating procedures) or decision rules, it is necessary to search out and perhaps create alternatives. Thus, the decision process itself may be a significant source of stress, arising, for example, from efforts to cope with cognitive constraints on rationality, role factors, small group dynamics, and bureaucratic politics.[35]

Some degree of stress is an integral and necessary precondition for individual or organizational problem solving; in its absence there is no motivation to act. Low levels of stress alert us to the existence of a situation requiring our attention, increase our vigilance and our preparedness to cope with it. Increasing stress to moderate levels may heighten our propensity and ability to find a satisfactory solution to the problem. Indeed, for some elementary tasks a rather high degree of stress may enhance performance, at least for limited periods of time. If the problem is qualitatively simple and performance is measured by quantitative criteria, stress can increase output. Our primary concern, however, is not with the effects of crisis on persons engaged in manual or routine tasks, but with its consequences on the performance of officials in leadership positions during major international crises. These are nearly always marked by complexity and ambiguity, and they usually demand responses which are judged by qualitative rather than quantitative criteria. It is precisely these qualitative aspects of performance that are most likely to suffer under high stress.[36]

Experimental findings generally indicate a curvilinear relationship, most easily described as an "inverted U," between stress and the performance of individual and groups. A moderate level of anxiety can be beneficial, but at higher levels it disrupts decision processes.[37] Observational evidence from related field research (e.g., studies of natural disasters, or performance in combat and other dangerous circumstances) also suggests that intense and protracted stress often erodes rather than enhances the ability of individuals to cope with complex problems.[38] To summarize, in situations of high stress, "there is a narrowing of the cognitive organization at the moment; the individual loses broader perspective, he is no longer able to 'see' essential aspects of the situation and his behavior becomes, consequently, less adaptive."[39]

At this point we shall consider in more detail some potential consequences of stress for cognitive rigidity, span of attention, and time perspectives.

Cognitive Rigidity. Charles Lindblom suggests that "a serious emergency or crisis often transforms a policy analyst's perceptions (and sometimes galvanizes his energies) with the result that he gets a new grasp on his problem."[40] But there is also evidence that the effects of stress on cognitive performance are often less benign. Persons experiencing intense stress tend to suffer increased cognitive rigidity, and erosion of general cognitive abilities, including creativity and the ability to cope with complexity. As a consequence, the range of perceived policy options may be narrow. The decision maker is likely to establish a dominant percept through which to interpret information, and to maintain it tenaciously in the face of information that might seem to call for a reappraisal.[41] Often this percept is a familiar one transferred from previous situations (e.g., "lessons of history"), even though it may be inappropriate for the circumstances at hand,[42] and it is more likely to be characterized by stereotypes than by subtlety as the complexity of the psychological field is reduced.[43] To change one's beliefs and theories each time some discrepant information is received is neither possible nor wise, but it is at least useful to be aware that evidence about an unfolding situation may be consistent with more than a single explanation.[44] A finding of special relevance for crisis decision making is that tolerance for ambiguity is reduced when there is high stress. Under these conditions individuals made decisions before adequate information was available, with the result that they performed much less capably than persons working under normal conditions. The combination of stress and uncertainty leads some persons to feel that "the worst would be better than this."[45] Finally, caricatures of motivational structures may develop: the anxious become more anxious, the energetic become more energetic, the repressors become more repressive, and so on.[46] The effects of stress on perception have been summarized as follows:

> Perceptual behavior is disrupted, becomes less well controlled than under normal conditions, and hence is less adaptive. The major dimensions of perceptual function are affected: selection of percepts from a complex field becomes less adequate and sense is less well differentiated from nonsense; there is maladaptive accentuation in the direction of aggression and escape; untested hypotheses are fixated recklessly.[47]

As a result of these effects of stress, search for information and policy options may be adversely affected in several ways. Other actors and their motives are likely to be stereotyped, for example, and the situation itself may be defined in overly simple, one-dimensional terms—such as, that it is a zero-sum situation, or that everything is related to everything else.[48] The ability to invent nonobvious solutions to complex problems may also be impaired. Finally, complex problems are more likely to be defined by "what is already in" (the decision maker's beliefs, expectations, cognitive and emotional predispositions), and less by the "objective" attributes of the situation.[49]

The inception of a crisis usually results in a sharply increased pace of individual and bureaucratic activity and, concomitantly, an increasing volume of communication. Conversely, information overload in a decision-making situation may itself be a source of serious stress.[50] One way of coping with this phenomenon is to *narrow one's span of attention* to a few aspects of the decision-making task.[51] This may be a functional strategy if it permits the executive to eliminate trivial distractions, filter out irrelevant information, and develop an agenda of priorities. However, a number of costs may offset or even outweigh these benefits.

An experimental study of complex situations revealed that increased information loads resulted in fewer strategic integrated decisions and more unintegrated and simple retaliatory decisions.[52] As the volume of information directed at policy makers rises, the search for information within the communication system will tend to become less thorough, and selectivity in what is read, believed, and retained takes on increasing importance. In ambiguous situations or in circumstances of information overload, one may also be more likely to screen information and to respond in terms of personal predispositions.[53] Unpleasant information and that which does not support preferences and expectations may fall by the wayside, unless it is of such an unambiguous nature that it cannot be disregarded. "All Presidents, at least in modern times," writes Sorensen, "have complained about their reading pile, and few have been able to cope with it. There is a temptation, consequently, to cut out all that is unpleasant."[54] Thus, more communication may in fact result in less useful and valid information being available to policy makers.

Time perspectives are also likely to be affected by high stress. For example, the ability to judge time is impaired in situations which increase anxiety.[55] Thus, there appears to be a two-way relationship between time and stress. On the one hand, short decision time, a defining characteristic of crisis, is likely to increase the stress under which the executive must operate. On the other hand, increasing levels of stress tend to heighten the salience of time and to distort judgements about it. It has been found in "real life" crisis situations, as well as experimentally, that as danger increases there is a significant overestimation of how fast time is passing.[56]

Perceived time pressure may affect decision making in several ways. A number of studies indicate that some time pressure can enhance creativity as well the rate of performance, but most of the evidence suggests that beyond a moderate level it has adverse effects. Because complex tasks requiring feats of memory and inference suffer more from time pressure,[57] its effects on the most important decisions—which are usually marked by complexity—are likely to be particularly harmful. In such situations there is a tendency to fix upon a single approach, to continue using it whether or not it proves effective, and to hang on to familiar solutions, applying them even to problems that may be substantially different.[58]

Experimental research has often shown a curvilinear relationship between time pressure and performance. Under severe time pressure, normal subjects produce errors similar to those committed by schizophrenics. Another study revealed that, although a moderate increase in time pressure can increase the productivity of groups, an increase from low to high pressure has an adverse effect. Increasing the number of decisions required in a given period of time by a factor of five led to a fifteenfold rise in decision errors. There is, in addition, evidence that time pressure increases the propensity to rely upon stereotypes, disrupts both individual and group problem solving, narrows the focus of attention, and impedes the use of available information. Finally, both experimental and historical evidence indicates that high stress tends to result in a shorter time perspective and, as consequence, reduced resistance to premature closure.[59]

When decision time is short, the ability to estimate the range of possible consequences arising from a particular policy choice is likely to be impaired. Both experimental and field research indicate that severe stress is likely to give rise to a single-minded concern for the present and immediate future at the sacrifice of attention to longer range considerations.[60] The uncertainties attending severe crisis make it exceptionally difficult to follow outcomes from a sequence of actions and responses very far into the future. Increasing stress also tends to narrow the focus of attention, thereby further limiting perceptions of time to the more immediate future. During the Korean War, for instance, it was observed that combat troops "cannot exercise complex functions involving the scanning of a large number of factors or long-term foresight because the stress is too massive and time too short for anything but the immediately relevant."[61]

This brief overview of evidence is suggestive rather than exhaustive. Moreover, the emphasis has been on processes rather than on decision outputs and, just as we cannot assume that "good" processes will ensure high-quality decisions, we cannot assume that erratic processes will always result in low-quality decisions. But even if Figure 1 describes only some potential tendencies rather than unvarying responses to crisis, there is sufficient evidence to call into question the universal validity of the premise that we always rise to the occasion in crisis, drawing if necessary upon hidden reservoirs of strength. The evidence cited here suggests that among the more probable casualties of crises and the accompanying high stress are the very abilities that distinguish men from other species: to establish logical links between present actions and future goals; to search effectively for relevant policy options; to create appropriate responses to unexpected events; to communicate complex ideas; to deal effectively with abstractions; to perceive not only blacks and whites, but also to distinguish them from the many subtle shades of gray that fall in between; to distinguish valid analogies from false ones, and sense from nonsense; and, perhaps most important of all, to enter into the frame of references of others. With respect to these precious cognitive abilities, the law of supply and demand seems to operate in a perverse manner; as crisis increases the need for them, it also appears to diminish the supply.

Suggestive as these models and theories of crisis decision making may be, they cannot substitute for evidence from actual foreign policy crisis. Abstract and theoretical work must be examined and analyzed in terms of specific evidence—in this case, evidence from diplomatic history. Toward this end, the next two sections will utilize the "focused comparison" approach[62]—in which case studies aim not at a full historical description but at developing or testing explicit propositions of theoretical or policy relevance—and will explore several very specific aspects of individual stress in crisis decision making from the 1914 and Cuban missile crises.

DECISION MAKING IN THE 1914 CRISIS

The assassination of Archduke Franz Ferdinand on June 28, 1914, set off a chain of events that, within six weeks, brought all of the major powers of Europe into war. Soon after Prince von Bülow asked German Chancellor Bethmann Hollweg how the war had come about. "At last I said to him: 'Well, tell me, at least, how it all happened,' He raised his long, thin arms to heaven and answered in a dull exhausted voice: 'Oh—If I only knew.'" Another colleague wrote that "since the Russian mobilization the Chancellor gave one the impression of a drowning man."[63] Are these merely the self-serving recollections of war criminals or of fools whose incompetence visited upon the world a war of unparalleled devastation? If the answer is an affirmative one, the 1914 case is of little interest to the student of crisis, and the prescription is relatively simple—keep war criminals and fools out of high office.

But perhaps the answer to "how it all happened" is not quite so simple. The proposition to be explored in this section is that the individual stress model may help to explain the disastrous events of 1914. It should be made clear at the outset that what follows is an illustration and not an attempt at a full-scale explanation.[64] It does not deal with the state of military technology, European alliance commitments, the balance of power, contingency plans of foreign and war offices, historical enmities, economic competition, or imperial ambitions and rivalries. All of these were important in 1914 and nothing in the analysis that follows is intended to deny their relevance. Nevertheless, these were also important in 1911, in 1908, and in other years that featured confrontations among the major powers. But, unless we adopt a deterministic view—as is implied, for example, by the popular metaphor of the assassination as a lighted match thrown into a keg of powder—it is appropriate to consider not only the European context in 1914, but also the decision processes. The focus here is on two aspects of Figure 1—perceptions of time pressure and of policy options.

Perceptions of Time Pressure

To examine the effects of deepening crisis on perceptions of time pressure, techniques of content analysis were employed.[65] All documents written by high-ranking foreign policy officials were coded for evidence of time pressure as a factor in policy decisions. The resulting 167 statements are classified according to date and nation and specific issue (Table 1). Statements of concern about decision time increased steadily (except in the case of Austria–Hungary), not only in absolute frequency, but even in relation to the total number of policy themes. Perceptions of time pressure were also associated with increasing stress, with correlations ranging from .16 to .82.

During the earliest period of the 1914 crisis approximately two-thirds of the references to time focused on the desirability or necessity of early action by Austria–Hungary against Serbia. Count Alexander Hoyos, Chief of the Cabinet of the Austro-Hungarian Foreign Ministry, for example, wrote on July 7 that "from a military standpoint . . . it would be much more favorable to start the war now than later since the balance of power would weigh against us in the future."[66] The view that time was working against the Dual Monarchy was supported, for Germany was exerting considerable pressure on its ally not to postpone a showdown. Gottlieb von Jagow, German Foreign Minister, wrote on July 15: "We are concerned at present with the preeminent political question, perhaps the last opportunity of giving the Greater-Serbia menace its death blow under comparatively favorable circumstances."[67] In contrast, the view in London, Paris, and St. Petersburg was initially one of relative lack of concern. There is no evidence that leaders in the capitals of the Entente nations felt themselves under any pressure of time to react to this latest episode of instability in the Balkans.

Time perceptions from July 21 through July 28 focused predominantly on the necessity of delaying the course of events in the Balkans. Once the content of the Austrian ultimatum became known, the forty-eight-hour time limit within which the Serbian government had to draft a reply became an immediate subject of concern. Some European officials recognized that the conflict in the Balkans might well engulf all

TABLE 1 Perception of Time Pressure: The 1914 Crisis

Period	Total Themes	Perceptions of Time Pressure in the Documents of:						% Themes with Time Perceptions
		Austria-Hungary	Germany	Great Britain	France	Russia	Total	
June 27–July 20	1,031	13	9	0	0	0	22	2.1
July 21–28	1,658	3	11	18	13	8	53	3.2
July 29–August 2	1,910	0	35	12	13	3	63	3.3
August 3–4	479	0	14	12	3	0	29	6.1
June 27–August 4	5,078	16	69	42	29	11	167	3.3
Correlation (gamma) between stress and perceptions of time pressure		.16	.33	.61	.68	.82		

Period	A	B	C	D	E	Total
June 27–July 20	15	1	0	2	4	22
July 21–28	11	29	10	2	1	53
July 29–August 2	1	8	29	16	9	63
August 3–4	0	0	2	22	5	29
June 27–August 4	27	38	41	42	19	167

Codes for relevance of time:
   A—As a factor in Austro-Hungarian action toward Serbia
   B—As a factor in localization of conflict between Austria–Hungary and Serbia
   C—As a factor in mobilization
   D—As a factor in alliance and other political commitments
   E—Other

Europe if existing alliance commitments were honored. Whereas both German and Austro-Hungarian leaders had frequently expressed the desirability of moving swiftly against Serbia, those in London, Paris, St. Petersburg, and Belgrade were especially concerned with the necessity of gaining the time which might be used to work out a peaceful settlement of Vienna's demands on Serbia. Although they were far from united on the details of policy, the single common theme in their proposals was the fear that precipitate action could lead only to war. Typical of diplomatic messages during this period was the assertion that "the immediate danger was that in a few hours Austria might march into Serbia and Russian Slav opinion demand that Russia should march to help Serbia; it would be very desirable to get Austria not to precipitate military action and so to gain more time."[68] By July 29 it was apparent that war between Austria–Hungary and Serbia could not be prevented. At the same time, it was increasingly evident that a chain reaction was in danger of being set off.

As late as August 1 many European leaders continued to express the belief that if time permitted the concert powers to be reconvened, general war might be avoided. British Foreign Secretary Grey wrote, for example: "I still believe that if only a little respite in time can be gained before any Great Power begins war it might be possible to secure peace."[69] By this time, however, the pressure of time had taken a different meaning for many decision makers. A major concern was that one's nation not be caught unprepared for the war which might break out.

The situation, as perceived by leaders in the major capitals of Europe, posed a terrible dilemma. It was widely recognized that more time would be required if a general European war were to be averted; above all, a moratorium on military operations was necessary. It was equally evident that military preparations could become the justification for similar actions by others. The German ambassador in St. Petersburg warned the Russian foreign minister that "the danger of every preparatory military measure lay in the counter measures of the other side."[70] But, increasingly, these considerations were overshadowed by the fear of disastrous consequences if a potential adversary gained even a momentary head start in mobilizing its armed forces. As early as July 24, the French minister of war, apprehensive about the outcome of the crisis in the Balkans, asserted that, for France, "first military precautions could not be delayed."[71] Although no *official* mobilization orders except those of Austria–Hungary and Serbia were issued until July 29, rumors and suspicions of undercover preparations were not wholly without foundation. On July 25 the Russian government decided to set into motion all of the preparations preliminary to mobilization. Despite a badly divided Cabinet, even the British were undertaking a number of important military preparations. Winston Churchill, First Lord of the Admiralty, for example, mobilized the British navy contrary to a decision of the Cabinet.

In the early hours of the morning of July 30, the Kaiser wrote on the margin of a message from the Czar: " . . . the Czar—as is openly admitted by him here—instituted 'mil[itary] measures which have *now come into force*' against Austria and us and as a matter of fact five days ago. Thus it is almost *a week ahead of us.* And these measures are for a *defense* against *Austria,* which is *in no way* attacking him!!! I can not agree to any more mediation, since the Czar who requested it has at the same time secretly mobilized behind my back. It is only a maneuver, in order to hold us back and to increase the start they have already got. My work is at an end!"[72] Later, the Kaiser added, "In view of the colossal war preparations of Russia now discovered, this is all too late, I fear. Begin! Now!"[73] On July 30, German Chancellor Bethmann Hollweg was also concerned with the disadvantages of delay: " . . . the military preparations of our neighbors, especially in the east, will force us to a speedy decision, unless we do not wish to expose ourselves to the danger of surprise."[74]

On the same day René Viviani, French premier, urged Russia to avoid provocative measures that might provide Germany with a pretext for a total or partial mobilization of its own forces. Nevertheless, the Russians decided in favor of general mobilization, German warnings notwithstanding. "In these conditions," according to Foreign Minister Sazonov, "Russia can only hasten its armaments and face the imminence of war and that it counts upon the assistance of its ally France; Russia considers it desirable that England join Russia and France without losing time."[75] In response to what was perceived as a mounting threat against its eastern frontiers, the German Empire proclaimed a "state of threatening danger of war" on July 31, dispatching a twelve-hour ultimatum to Russia demanding a cessation of military preparations along the border. Berlin then ordered mobilization on August 1. "We could not sit back quietly and wait to see whether a more commonsense view would gain the upper hand at Petersburg, while at the same time the Russian mobilization was proceeding at such speed, that, if the worst came, we should be left completely outstripped in a military sense."[76]

The French government simultaneously ordered general mobilization on August 1. General Joffre had earlier argued that "it is absolutely necessary that the government know that from this evening on, any delay of twenty-four hours applied to the calling up of reserves and to the sending of the telegram ordering covering troops will result in a backward movement of our troops, that is to say an initial abandonment of a part of our territory, either 15 or 20 kilometers every day of delay."[77] Although official British naval mobilization was delayed until August 2, many officials in London had advocated such action considerably earlier. Winston Churchill was perhaps the most energetic proponent of early military preparations.[78] Others included Arthur Nicolson, Permanent Under Secretary for Foreign Affairs, who said on July 31: "It seems to me most essential, whatever our future course may be in regard to intervention, that we should at once give orders for mobilization of the army.... Mobilization is a precautionary measure—and to my mind essential." Three days later he added that "we ought to mobilize today so that our expeditionary force may be on its way during the next week. Should we waver now we shall rue the day later."[79]

Thus, ten days after the full-scale mobilizations by Serbia and Austria–Hungary on July 25, each of the major European countries had called up its armed forces. As each mobilization was ordered, it was defended as a necessary reaction to a previous decision within the other coalition. And with each mobilization came assurances that it was a defensive measure, although in 1914 a decision to mobilize was commonly regarded as tantamount to an act of war. In the rush to mobilize no one wanted to be beaten to the draw, even though there was sometimes an awareness of the logical end of military measures and countermeasures.

In some cases the escalation of military actions and counteractions was sustained almost by accident, or by the failure to perceive the effects of one's own acts. The mobilization of the Russian Baltic fleet provides a good example. "On 25 July, when the Czar looked over the minutes and resolutions of the Council of Ministers of the 24th, he not only approved them by adding 'agreed,' but, where it was the question of mobilizing the districts of Kiev, Moscow, Odessa and Kazan and the Black Sea fleet, he inserted in his own hand 'and Baltic' without any of his Ministers drawing his attention to the fact that the mobilization of the Baltic fleet constituted an act of hostility toward Germany."[80] Although the Russian Baltic fleet was no match for the powerful German navy, the Kaiser apparently felt genuinely threatened. In response to Bethmann Hollweg's plea that the German fleet be left in Norway, he wrote: "There is a Russian Fleet! In the Baltic there are now five Russian torpedo boat flotillas engaged in practice cruises, which as a whole or in part can be at the Belts within sixteen hours and close them. Port Arthur should be a lesson! My Fleet has orders to sail for Kiel, and to Kiel it is going to sail!"[81]

This inquiry into time pressures associated with the 1914 crisis supports the hypothesis that one reaction to decisional stress is hypervigilance. Concern for time increased as the crisis deepened, and it is also clear that time pressures were related to the central rather than peripheral issues in the crisis. When there was a conflict between the need to delay action in order to seek nonmilitary means of resolving the crisis and the perceived needs of military preparedness, the latter consideration prevailed, in large part because so many officials throughout Europe felt that the costs of falling behind the adversary's timetable would be catastrophic. Many decisions during the crisis were undertaken in great haste, and the processes by which they were made were at times highly erratic. For example, the initial Russian decision for a general mobilization was followed shortly by an order for only a partial callup of forces, and then by another reversal to the original decision. In the meanwhile, when it became clear that the conflict between Serbia and Austria–Hungary might lead to a general European war, a series of highly contradictory messages was dispatched from Berlin to Vienna. Demands for restraint in some of them were offset by a telegram from Moltke stating that Austria–Hungary should immediately mobilize against Russia, and that Germany would soon follow suit.

Policy Options

One way of coping with decision stress is a form of bolstering, attributing to the adversary sole responsibility for choices and outcomes, while absolving oneself, owing to the absence of real alternatives. Data from the 1914 crisis provide some striking support for the proposition that, in a crisis situation, decision makers will tend to perceive the range of their own alternatives to be more restricted than those of their opponents. That is, they will perceive their own decision making to be characterized by *necessity* and *closed* options, whereas those of the adversary are characterized by *open* choices (Table 2).

The 1914 documents are filled with such words as "must," "compelled," "obliged," "unable," "driven," "impossible," and "helpless," but these rarely occur except when the author is referring to the policies of his own nation. To students of strategy the assertions of the Kaiser, the Czar, and others that they were helpless once they had set their military machines into motion may appear to be a "real life" application of the tactics of *commitment,* "a device to leave the last clear chance to decide

TABLE 2   Perceptions of Alternatives (Choice, Necessity, Closed): Top-Ranking Decision Makers During 1914 Crisis

	GERMANY Own Nation	Allies	Opponents
CHOICE	10	7	25
NECESSITY	110	20	2
CLOSED	20	2	0
% Choice	7.1%	24.1%	92.6%
	AUSTRIA-HUNGARY Own Nation	Allies	Opponents
CHOICE	13	1	1
NECESSITY	80	2	1
CLOSED	7	1	0
% Choice	13.0%	25.0%	50.0%
	GREAT BRITAIN Own Nation	Allies	Opponents
CHOICE	7	21	21
NECESSITY	20	8	2
CLOSED	23	2	0
% Choice	14.0%	67.7%	91.3%
	FRANCE Own Nation	Allies	Opponents
CHOICE	1	6	12
NECESSITY	13	4	2
CLOSED	5	2	2
% Choice	5.3%	50.0%	75.0%
	RUSSIA Own Nation	Allies	Opponents
CHOICE	7	4	6
NECESSITY	20	3	2
CLOSED	7	3	0
% Choice	20.6%	40.0%	75.0%

NOTE:
Choice: Decision maker perceives that more than one course of action is open.
Necessity: Decision maker perceives only one possible course of action in a given situation.
Closed: Decision maker perceives that some course of action is not possible.

the outcome with the other party, in a manner that he fully appreciates; it is to relinquish further initiative, having rigged the incentives so that the other party must choose in one's favor."[82] This explanation may be valid for messages that were intended for wide circulation among officials in allied or enemy countries. On the other hand, the most "private" documents—those intended only for circulation within the various foreign offices—do not differ materially from the entire set of documents in respect to the findings reported here. The clearest evidence in support of this assertion is to be found in the Kaiser's marginal notations and in the various minutes of Eyre Crowe, Assistant Under-Secretary of State, in the British Foreign Office.

Even a cursory survey of the diplomatic documents reveals that, with the exception of Austria–Hungary, European leaders consistently perceived fewer options open to themselves than to their adversaries. Edward Grey, for example, who took the most active role in seeking mediation, wrote on July 24 that "we can do nothing for moderation unless Germany is prepared *pari passu* to do the same."[83] Until the final hours of the crisis, leaders in Berlin were opposed to mediation of the local conflict, in part because previous conferences called to settle international crises (such as Algeciras in 1906) had, in the eyes of the Kaiser and others, denied them the diplomatic victories to which they were entitled. According to Bethmann Hollweg, "We cannot mediate in the conflict between Austria and Serbia but possibly later between Austria and Russia."[84] Nor were the Russians inclined to mediation because, in the words of Sazonov, "we have assumed from the beginning a posture which we cannot change."[85]

But the same leaders who expressed varying degrees of inability to cope with the situation in the Balkans tended to perceive more freedom of action for members of the opposing alliance. After the outbreak of war between Serbia and Austria–Hungary, Grey wrote: "The whole idea of mediation or mediating influence was ready to be put into operation by any method that Germany could suggest if mine was not acceptable. In fact, mediation was ready to come into operation by any method that Germany thought possible if only Germany would 'press the button' in the interests of peace."[86]

The tendency to perceive one's own alternatives to be more restricted than those of the adversary is also evident in the reaction to the events leading up to general war. The reaction of German decision makers was typical. On the one hand, they asserted repeatedly that *they* had no choice but to take vigorous military measures against the threat to the east. "Then I must mobilize too! . . . He [Nicholas] expressly stated in his first telegram that he would be presumably forced to take measures that would lead to a European war. Thus he takes the responsibility upon himself."[87] On the other hand, they credited Russia with complete freedom to take the actions necessary to prevent war: "The responsibility for the disaster which is now threatening the whole civilized world will not be laid at my door. In this moment it still lies in your [Nicholas] power to avert it."[88] And Wilhelm, like the Czar, finally asserted that he had lost control of his own military and that only the actions of the adversary could stop further escalation: "On technical grounds my mobilization which had already been proclaimed this afternoon must proceed against two fronts, east and west as prepared. This cannot be countermanded because I am sorry your [George V] telegram came so late."[89] The same theme of a single option open to oneself, coupled with perceptions that the initiative for peace rested with the enemy, is evident in the French and Austrian statements regarding their own mobilizations.

An increasing sense of helplessness and resignation to the irresistible course of events is evident in many of the documents. On the day of the Serbian reply to the Austro-Hungarian ultimatum, Paul Cambon, French ambassador in London, stated that he saw "no way of halting the march of events."[90] In contrast to Edward Grey, who maintained the hope that the European powers would find a way to prevent a general war, Arthur Nicolson asserted on July 29, "I am of the opinion that the resources of diplomacy are, for the present, exhausted."[91] At the same time, in St. Petersburg, Sazonov wrote of the "inevitability of war" while in Berlin, the Kaiser, in one of the most vitriolic of his marginal notes, concluded that "we have proved ourselves helpless."[92]

Significantly contributing to the belief that options were severely restricted was the rigidity of the various mobilization plans. Austria–Hungary and Russia had more than one plan for mobilization, but once any one of them was set in motion, it could be altered only with great effort. The Russians could order either a general mobilization against both Germany and Austria–Hungary, or a partial one directed only at the latter. But, as Russian generals were to argue vehemently during the crucial days at the end of July, a partial mobilization would preclude a general one for months to come, leaving Russia completely at the mercy of Germany. According to General Dobrorolski, "The whole plan of mobilization is worked out ahead to its end in all its detail. When the moment has been chosen, one has only to press the button, and the whole state begins to function automatically with the precision of a clock's mechanism. . . . Once the moment has been fixed, everything is settled; there is no going back; it determines mechanically the beginning of war."[93]

France and Germany each had but a single plan for calling up their armed forces and, in the case of Germany, political leaders were ill informed about the rigidity of mobilization and war plans. The Kaiser's last-minute attempt to reverse the Schlieffen plan—to attack only in the East—shattered Moltke, Chief of the German General Staff, who replied: "That is impossible, Your Majesty. An army of a million cannot be improvised. It would be nothing but a rabble of undisciplined armed men, without a commissariat. . . . It is utterly impossible to advance except according to plan; strong in the west, weak in the east."[94]

Finally, all of the mobilization plans existed only on paper; except for the Russo-Japanese War, no major European power had mobilized since 1878. This fact rendered the plans all the more rigid and made military leaders responsible for carrying them out less likely to accept any last-minute modifications. It may also have added to the widely believed dictum that one did not mobilize for any purpose other than war.

Just as European leaders tended to perceive fewer alternatives open to themselves than to their adversaries, so they regarded their allies to be in a similar position vis-à-vis their enemies. On the one hand, German documents are replete with explanation that Austria was pursuing the *only* policy open to her and thus Germany could not play a moderating role in Vienna, although only four months earlier Wilhelm had stated that if Vienna gets into a war against the Slavs through "great stupidity," it would "leave us [Germany] quite cold."[95] On the other hand, the Kaiser appealed to England, apparently convinced that the latter could perform the very role which he felt was impossible for Germany—restraining the most belligerent member of the coalition. "Instead of making proposals for conferences, His Majesty the King should order France and Russia, frankly and plainly, at one and the same time—they were HIS ALLIES— to DESIST at once from the mobilization, remain NEUTRAL and await Austria's proposals, which I should immediately transmit as soon as I was informed of them. . . . I could do nothing more direct; it was for him to take hold now and prove the honesty of English love of peace."[96] The assumption of British freedom to determine the policy of her allies, coupled with restrictions on German policy, is nowhere as clear as in one of the Kaiser's marginal notes: "He [Grey] knows perfectly well, that if he were to say one single serious sharp warning word at Paris and Petersburg, and were to warn them to remain neutral, both would become quiet at once. But he takes care not to speak the word, and threatens us instead! Common cur! England *alone* bears the responsibility for peace and war, and not we any longer."[97]

This approach to the problem of allies was not confined to Berlin. Adducing arguments that were strikingly similar to those used by the Kaiser, British leaders denied their ability or willingness to dictate a policy of moderation in Paris or St. Petersburg. Nicolson wrote on July 29: "I do not think that Berlin quite understands that Russia cannot and will not stand quietly by while Austria administers a severe chastisement to Serbia. She does not consider that Serbia deserves it, and she could not, in view of that feeling and of her position in the Slav world, consent to it."[98] Grey assessed the requirements of his French ally in similar terms: "France did not wish to join in the war that seemed about to break out, but she was obliged to join in it, because of her alliance."[99] At the same time, however, he believed that Germany could constrain the cause of her ally: "But none of us could influence Austria in this direction unless Germany would propose and participate in such action in Vienna."[100] On July 28 Nicholas had appealed to his counterpart in Berlin: "To try and avoid such a calamity as a European war, I beg you in the name of our old friendship to do what you can to *stop* your allies from *going too far.*"[101]

The few attempts made to restrain the militant members of each alliance were either halfhearted or too late. Typical was the advice of Sir Eyre Crowe, who had written on July 25: "The moment has passed when it might have been possible to enlist French support in an effort to hold back Russia. It is clear that France and Russia are decided to accept the challenge thrown to them." He expressed the opinion that it would be both impolitic and dangerous to try to change their minds.[102] Similarly, a last-minute German attempt to hold Austria in check failed. At 2:55 A.M., July 30, Bethmann Hollweg concluded a telegram to Vienna: "Under these circumstances we must urgently and impressively suggest to the consideration of the Vienna Cabinet that acceptance of mediation on the mentioned honorable conditions. The responsibility for the consequences that would otherwise follow would be an uncommonly heavy one both for Austria and for us."[103] A few minutes later, however, Moltke sent a wire to Vienna urging immediate mobilization against Russia, promising Germany's full support for such an action—even if it led to general war.[104]

DECISION MAKING DURING THE MISSILE CRISIS[105]

A single U–2 American surveillance plane took off on October 14, 1962, for a reconnaissance flight over Cuba. Immediately upon returning, its high-altitude cameras were unloaded. After intensive study of the developed films, intelligence analysts uncovered unmistakable evidence of two medium-range ballistic missile (MRBM) sites in areas previously photographed and found to be empty. Overflights three days later confirmed these reports and revealed nine sites—36 launch positions—six for the 1,100-mile MRBM and three for 2,200-mile intermediate-range ballistic missiles (IRBM) in various states of readiness. Thus began the most serious international crisis of the nuclear era, a confrontation during which President Kennedy estimated that the chances of a nuclear war between the United States and the Soviet Union were one in three.

The 1914 and Cuban situations were similar in a number of respects and differed in many others. The similarity of present interest is that both episodes conform to the definition of crisis used here. Despite widespread rumors of Soviet missile installations in Cuba, photographic evidence of their presence was a surprise to virtually all officials in Washington, including the President; the rate of construction on the missile sites made it evident that any decision to prevent their completion could not long be delayed; and, with the exception of Secretary of Defense Robert McNamara, all who joined the American decision group interpreted the Soviet move as a serious threat to national security. As one participant in these discussions put it: "Everyone round the table recognized that we were in a major crisis. We didn't know, that day, if the country would come through it with Washington intact."[106]

The most significant difference between these two events is that the 1914 crisis led to a world war, whereas the Cuban confrontation was resolved without recourse to violence. Thus, the situation that confronted national leaders in the two crises shared a number of attributes (surprise, high threat, short decision time), but the decisions they made led to significantly different results: peaceful settlement versus a world war. In an attempt to explain the different outcomes, the remainder of this section examines several aspects of the decision-making process in 1962, again with special attention to time pressure and the search for and appraisal of alternatives.

Perceptions of Time Pressure

Several sources of time pressure impinged on the President and his advisers during the missile crisis. Initially, there was the need to formulate a policy before the Soviets were alerted by the stepped-up U-2 flights to the fact that their launching installations had been discovered. Conversely, once developments in Cuba became public knowledge, there would be no further time for deliberation and debate on the proper response.

An overriding concern throughout the period was the knowledge that construction on the missile sites was continuing at a rapid pace. The first photographic evidence of construction activities in Cuba indicated that they would be operational within a week to ten days. American officials perceived that their task would become immeasurably more difficult once construction on the launching sites was completed: "For all of us know that, once the missile sites under construction became operational, and capable of responding to any apparent threat or command with a nuclear volley, the President's options would be dramatically changed."[107] Thus, the situation did not compel a reflex-like response— at least, as it was defined by the President. But in relation to the task at hand decision time was indeed short, and all firsthand accounts of decision making during the Cuban crisis, especially that of Robert Kennedy, are replete with indications of time pressure.

Despite the sense of urgency created by these deadlines, the President and his advisers sought to reduce the probability that either side would respond by a "spasm reaction." Efforts were made to delay taking overt actions as long as the situation permitted. Equally important, discussions in Washington revealed a sensitivity for the time pressures under which the adversary was operating. There was a concern that Premier Khrushchev not be rushed into an irrevocable decision; it was agreed among members of the decision group that "we should slow down the escalation of the crisis to give Khrushchev time to consider his next move."[108] Measures designed to increase Soviet decision time included the President's management of the naval quarantine. He ordered American ships to delay intercepting Soviet vessels until the last possible moment, *and had the order transmitted in the clear.* The Soviets, who were certain to intercept the message, would thus learn that they had additional time in which to formulate a response to the blockade. This ploy also revealed a sophisticated understanding of the social psychology of communication; information from a distrusted source is more likely to be believed if it is obtained through the recipient's own efforts. The Soviet decision on October 25 to slow down the westward progress of their ships in mid-Atlantic can also be interpreted as an effort to lengthen decision time.

A comparison of the 1914 and 1962 crises points to the importance of a subjective rather than an objective definition of decision time. Owing to vast differences in military capabilities, time was objectively of far greater importance in 1962 than in 1914. Hence, Soviet and American leaders were no less aware of time pressures and of the potential costs of delaying action than were their counterparts in 1914. But they also perceived the dangers of acting in haste, and they were successful in mitigating the most severe dangers attending such pressures. They resisted the pressures for premature decisions and took a number of actions which avoided putting their adversaries in a position of having to respond in haste. President Kennedy later acknowledged that the ability to delay a decision after receipt of the photographic evidence of missile sites was crucial to the *content* of American policy: "If we had had to act on Wednesday [October 17], in the first 24 hours, I don't think probably we would have chosen as prudently as we finally did, the quarantine against the use of offensive weapons."[109]

Policy Options

During the missile crisis, the search for alternatives was intimately related to time pressures; in the words of Arthur Schlesinger, "The deadline defined the strategy."[110] Pressures of time notwithstanding, American policy makers made efforts to prevent premature foreclosure of options. McGeorge Bundy noted that upon receiving the first news of the photographic evidence, "his [Kennedy's] first reaction was that we must make sure, and were we making sure, and would there be evidence on which he could decide that this was in fact really the case."[111] As late as October 18, a series of alternatives was being considered pending more accurate information, and while the decision to institute a blockade was being hammered out, open discussion of the alternatives was encouraged. The President recalled that "though at the beginning there was a much sharper division . . . this was very valuable, because the people involved had particular responsibilities of their own."[112] Another participant in the crisis decision group asserted that President Kennedy, aware that discussion of alternatives in the National Security Council would be more frank in his absence, encouraged the group to hold preliminary meetings without him. Thus, the eventual decision was reached by relatively open and frank discussion.

Six alternative responses emerged from the initial discussions between the President's advisers. Ultimately, the choice narrowed down to the blockade and the air strike. Initially, the option of a sudden air strike against the missile sites had strong support among most of the conferees, including that of the President. An informal vote is reported to have revealed an 11–6 majority in favor of the blockade.[113] The United States Air Force could not guarantee, however, that an air strike would be 100 percent effective. The blockade did not necessarily guarantee success; on the other hand, it did not rule out further measures. After much shifting of positions, the blockade option was selected, partly on the reasoning that "the course we finally adopted had the advantage of permitting other steps, if this one was unsuccessful. In other words, we were starting, in a sense, at a minimum place."[114]

The desire to avoid killing Soviet troops also weighed heavily against the air strike option. The blockade shifted the immediate burden of decision concerning the use of violence to Premier Khrushchev and, should the blockade have proved unsuccessful, it did not preclude later employment of a "much more massive action."[115] By adopting that strategy, no irrevocable decisions on the use of violence had been made and multiple options remained for possible future actions by the United States. At the same time, Soviet leaders were given the time and the opportunity to assess their own choices. Thus, unlike several of the key foreign policy officials in the 1914 crisis, those in October 1962 seemed to perceive a close relationship between their own actions and the options of their adversaries. According to Theodore Sorensen, "We discussed what the Soviet reaction would be to any possible move by the United States, what our reaction with them would have to be to that Soviet reaction, and so on, trying to follow each of those roads to their ultimate conclusion."[116]

American decision makers also displayed a sensitivity for the position and perspective of the adversary, trying to insure that a number of options other than total war or total surrender were available to Soviet leaders. An important advantage of the blockade over other strategies was that it appeared to avoid placing Soviet leaders in that situation. An air strike on the missile bases or invasion of the island would have left Soviet leaders only the alternatives of capitulating to the United States or of counterattacking. In that case, the latter might have seemed the less distasteful course. In disagreeing with General Curtis LeMay's optimistic assessment of the likely Soviet response to air raids on the missile installations, the President asserted, "They, no more than we, can let these things go by without doing something,"[117] A blockade, on the other hand, gave the Soviet government a choice between turning back the weapons-bearing ships or running the blockade.

By October 26 it seemed clear that, Khrushchev's earlier threats to the contrary notwithstanding, Soviet ships would not challenge the blockade. Despite the advent of negotiations, however, it was far from certain that the Soviet missiles would be removed from Cuba; indeed, there was ample evidence of an accelerated pace of construction on the launching sites in Cuba that, it was then believed, would be completed by October 30. Thus, the question of further steps to be taken in case the blockade proved insufficient to force withdrawal of all offensive missiles again confronted American leaders. Among the options considered were: tightening the blockade to include all commodities other than food and medicine, increased low-level flights over Cuba for purposes of reconnaissance and harassment, action within Cuba, an air strike, and an invasion. In the meanwhile, the President's brother delivered an ultimatum to the Soviet ambassador, and both direct and indirect bargaining resulted in a settlement.[118] Just before "the most serious meeting ever to take place at the White House"[119] was to have started, Premier Khrushchev agreed to withdraw all offensive missiles from Cuba in exchange for President Kennedy's pledge not to invade Cuba.

Time pressure and the search for alternatives are key elements in crisis decision making. Data from 1914 indicate that these factors did in fact vary as crisis-induced stress increased, and these changes apparently had serious consequences for critical policy decisions. A more impressionistic analysis of the Cuban confrontation suggests that the ability of American decision makers to mitigate some of the adverse consequences of crisis contributed to its eventual peaceful resolution. In many respects, President Kennedy's behavior during the Cuban crisis appeared consciously designed to avert repetition of the 1914 disaster. Indeed, he frequently referred to the decision processes leading up to World War I as a source of negative lessons. Having read Barbara Tuchman's *The Guns of August,* for example, the President said: "I am not going to follow a course which will allow anyone to write a comparable book about this time, *The Missiles of October.* If anybody is around to write after this, they are going to understand that we made every effort to find peace and every effort to give our adversary room to move. I am not going to push the Russians an inch beyond what is necessary."[120] Even when discussing the Cuban missile crisis some weeks after its conclusion, he asserted, "Well now, if you look at the history of this century where World War I really came through a series of misjudgments of the intentions of others . . . it's very difficult to always make judgments here about what the effect will be of our decisions on other countries."[121] Yet the ability of American and Soviet leaders to avoid a nuclear Armageddon in October 1962, is not assurance that even great skill in crisis management will always yield a peaceful solution. As President Kennedy said some months later, referring to the missile crisis, "You can't have too many of those."[122]

CONCLUSION

The approach described here suffers from some clear limitations that should be addressed explicitly. Several objections might be raised about the relevance of the individual stress model of crisis decision making.[123] Does it adequately take into account the executive's prior experience in coping with crises? Will not experience, when combined with selective recruitment and promotion, weed out those who cannot stand "the heat in the kitchen" well before they reach top leadership positions? It is true that individuals differ in abilities to cope with crises and stress. The peak, breaking point and slope of the "inverted U" curve may vary not only according to the complexity of the task, but also across individuals. Thus, the point at which increasing stress begins to hamper cognitive performance, and the rate at which it does so, is not the same for all persons. But only the most optimistic will assume that the correlation between the importance of the executive's role and ability to cope with crisis-induced stress approaches unity. Richard Nixon's behavior during the Watergate episode is a grim reminder to the contrary. Perhaps even more sobering is Robert Kennedy's recollection of the Cuban missile crisis: "That kind of [crisis-induced] pressure does strange things to a human being, even to brilliant, self confident, experienced men. For some it brings out characteristics and strengths that perhaps they never knew they had, and for others the pressure is too overwhelming."[124]

A second possible objection is that, whereas the emphasis here has been on the individual's cognitive performance under conditions of crisis-induced stress, foreign policy leaders rarely need to face crises alone. They can instead draw upon support and resources from both advisory groups and the larger organizations of which they are a part. This point is valid, but on further examination it is not wholly comforting. There is some evidence that during crises advisory groups may be vulnerable to such malfunctions as "groupthink."[125] For various reasons, including preceived needs for secrecy, easier coordination, and the like, decision-making groups tend to become smaller during crises. There may be, moreover, a tendency to consult others less as the pressure of time increases, as well as to rely more heavily upon those who support the prevailing "wisdom."[126] Finally, leaders differ not only in their "executive styles" (note, for example, the strikingly different problem-solving styles exhibited by presidents Coolidge, Franklin Roosevelt, and Nixon), but also in their abilities to employ advisory groups effectively—that is, in ways that may help them to counteract some of the potentially adverse consequences of crisis. Even the same executive may demonstrate great skill during one crisis and equal ineptitude in another instance. John F. Kennedy's use of advisers during the missile crisis and the Bay of Pigs fiasco are illustrative in this respect.

Some more specific limitations can also be identified. Certainly, the two cases are not representative of all crises in any statistical sense. Thus, the results described here should be viewed as illustrative rather than definitive. Moreover, the analysis focused on very limited aspects of crises, to the exclusion of many other potentially fruitful comparisons. The results suggest that the individual stress model identifies some important elements of crises decision making, but the present analysis has not even fully explored the hypotheses identified in Figure 1. In any case, the rather different findings for the 1914 and 1962 crises raise a series of additional questions—about the necessary and sufficient conditions for avoiding decision-making malfunctions—that have barely been touched upon here. The individual stress model focuses on a few aspects of crisis and consciously excludes others. By posing some questions and not others, we have limited the range of answers. Every model or theoretical perspective does so, with some inevitable losses and, it is to be hoped, at least some commensurate gains. The proper question to ask, then, is not whether this approach serves as a complete model for all crises—the answer is unquestionably negative—but whether it directs our attention to important phenomena that might otherwise remain beyond our purview.

Variants of the individual stress model of crisis decision making have been employed in other studies and, not surprisingly, the pattern of findings is mixed. Lentner's study of State Department officials revealed that only about a third of the respondents felt a reduction in perceived alternatives as a result of crisis.[127] In their impressive study of a dozen international crises—including Fashoda (1898), Bosnia (1908–1909), Munich (1938), Iran (1945–1946), and Berlin (1948–1949)—Snyder and Diesing found no evidence of adverse consequences arising from high stress.[128] Yet they did report that misperception, miscalculation, and other cognitive malfunctions were common occurrences during the crises. Because their research was not designed to test for either the existence or consequences of crisis-induced stress, perhaps it is premature to count this study as definitive evidence against the propositions advanced here. On the other hand, drawing on his research on Israeli behavior during the crises of 1956, 1967, and 1970, Brecher found strong support for the hypotheses that time will be perceived as more salient, that decision makers will become more concerned with the immediate rather than the distant future, and that they will perceive the range of alternatives open to themselves to be narrow.[129] The individual stress model also received strong support in a study designed to test the effects of crisis-induced stress on information processing; in this respect, the convergence of findings from historical and experimental research adds an important element of confidence in the validity of the results and the underlying theory.[130]

These mixed results are not surprising, nor should they occasion premature conclusions about lack of significant research progress or the future of this approach for diplomatic history, theory, or even policy. Other studies could be cited in support of and against the individual stress model, but this does not appear to be the more fruitful way of proceeding. Sustained interest in the effects of crisis-induced stress does not depend on finding that *every* crisis from the historical past resulted in substandard decision-making performance, any more than concern for the consequences of smoking must await evidence that all smokers develop lung cancer. The much more interesting and important questions emerge precisely at the point of recognizing that the dangers and opportunities inherent in crises can give rise to various patterns of coping. At that point our attention is directed to a series of further questions—for example, what are the decision-making structures, personal attributes of leaders, strategies of crisis management, and other variables that are associated with more or less successful coping—that have barely been touched upon in this chapter. It is at this point that we can perhaps begin to appreciate the value of interdisciplinary approaches for the study of crises decision making.

NOTES

1. Richard M. Nixon, *Six Crises* (New York: Doubleday, 1962), p. xvi.
2. Ibid., p. 105.
3. Herman Kahn, *On Escalation: Metaphors and Scenarios* (New York: Praeger, 1965), p. 38.
4. The literature on deterrence is enormous. Recent and indispensable are Alexander L. George and Richard Smoke, *Deterrence in American Foreign Policy: Theory and Practice* (New York: Columbia University Press, 1974); and Patrick M. Morgan, *Deterrence: A Conceptual Analysis* (Beverly Hills: Sage, 1977). For more discussion, see Paul Gordon Lauren's chapter in this book [*Diplomacy: New Approaches in History, Theory, and Policy*] on bargaining theories.
5. Chris Argyris, *Some Causes of Organizational Ineffectiveness within the Department of State* (Washington, D.C.: Center for International Systems Research, Department of State Publication 8180, 1967), p. 42.
6. Richard E. Neustadt, *Alliance Politics* (New York: Columbia University Press, 1970), p. 116.
7. Charles A. McClelland, quoted in Michael Brecher, "Toward a Theory of International Crisis Behavior," *International Studies Quarterly* 21 (March 1977): 40.
8. Charles A. McClelland, quoted in Charles F. Hermann (ed.), *International Crises: Insights from Behavioral Research* (New York: Free Press, 1972), p. 6.

9. See Leo Hazelwood, John Hayes, and James Brownell, Jr., "Planning for Problems in Crisis Management," *International Studies Quarterly* 21 (March 1977): 78.

10. Charles F. Hermann, "Some Consequences of Crisis Which Limit the Viability of Organizations," *Administrative Science Quarterly* 8 (June 1963): 61–82. This definition has achieved moderately wide acceptance among students of foreign policy crises. For further discussions of the term, see Charles F. Hermann, *Crises in Foreign Policy: A Simulation Analysis* (Indianapolis: Bobbs–Merrill, 1969); Charles F. Hermann, "International Crisis as a Situational Variable," in James N. Rosenau (ed.), *International Politics and Foreign Policy* (New York: Free Press, 1969 ed.), pp. 409–421; James A. Robinson, "Crisis: An Appraisal of Concepts and Theories," in Hermann, *International Crises;* Kent Miller and Ira Iscoe, "The Concept of Crisis: Current Status and Mental Health Implications," *Human Organization* 22 (Fall 1963): 195–201; Glenn H. Snyder and Paul Diesing, *Conflict Among Nations: Bargaining, Decision Making and System in International Crises* (Princeton: Princeton University Press, 1977); Richard W. Parker, "An Examination of Basic and Applied International Crisis Research," *International Studies Quarterly* 21 (March 1977): 225–246; Raymond Tanter, "Crisis Management: A Critical Review of Academic Literature," *Jerusalem Journal of International Relations* 2 (Fall 1975): 71–101; and Richard G. Head, Frisco W. Short, and Robert C. McFarlane, *Crisis Resolution: Presidential Decision Making in the Mayagüez and Korean Confrontations* (Boulder, Colo.: Westview Press, 1978).

11. Brecher, "Toward a Theory of International Crisis Behavior," pp. 42–44.

12. Snyder and Diesing, *Conflict Among Nations,* pp. 6–21.

13. Charles F. Hermann and Linda P. Brady, "Alternative Models of International Crisis Behavior," in Hermann, *International Crises,* pp. 281–303. For another typology, see Parker, "An Examination of Basic and Applied International Crisis Research."

14. Irving Janis, *Victims of Groupthink: A Psychological Study of Foreign-Policy Decisions and Fiascoes* (Boston: Houghton Mifflin, 1972).

15. Sidney Verba, "Assumptions of Rationality and Non-rationality in Models of the International System," *World Politics* 14 (October 1961): 93–117.

16. H. O. Wilensky, *Organizational Intelligence* (New York: Basic Books, 1967).

17. See Samuel Williamson's chapter in this book [Lauren, *Diplomacy*], as well as Graham T. Allison, "Conceptual Models and the Cuban Missile Crisis," *American Political Science Review* 63 (1969): 689–718; Graham T. Allison, *Essence of Decision: Explaining the Cuban Missile Crisis* (Boston: Little, Brown, 1971); Graham T. Allison and Morton H. Halperin, "Bureaucratic Politics: A Paradigm and Some Policy Implications," *World Politics* 24 (1972, special supplement): 40–79; and Leon V. Sigal, "The 'Rational Policy' Model and the Formosa Straits Crises," *International Studies Quarterly* 14 (June 1970): 121–156.

18. See, for example, Dina A. Zinnes, Joseph L. Zinnes, and Robert D. McClure, "Hostility in Diplomatic Communication: A Study of the 1914 Crisis," in Hermann, *International Crises,* pp. 139–162; and David C. Schwartz, "Decision-Making in Historical and Simulated Crises," in Hermann, *International Crises,* pp. 167–184.

19. See, for example, Snyder and Diesing, *Conflict Among Nations;* Charles A. McClelland, "The Beginning, Duration and Abatement of International Crisis: Comparisons in Two Conflict Arenas," in Hermann, *International Crises,* pp. 83–105; and Glenn H. Snyder, "Crisis Bargaining," in Hermann, *International Crises,* pp. 217–256.

20. Quincy Wright, *A Study of War* (Chicago: University of Chicago Press, 1965 ed.), p. 1272; and Lewis F. Richardson, *Statistics of Deadly Quarrels* (Pittsburgh: Boxwood Press, 1960).

21. Charles A. McClelland, "The Acute International Crisis," *World Politics* 14 (October 1961); Kenneth Waltz, "The Stability of a Bipolar World," *Daedalus* 93 (Summer 1964): 883–884; and Coral Bell, *Conventions of Crisis: A Study in Diplomatic Management* (London: Oxford University Press, 1971), pp. 115–116.

22. Wright, *A Study of War,* p. 1272.

23. McClelland, "The Acute International Crisis," p. 199.

24. Ibid., p. 200. However, constant exposure to crises, especially simultaneous crises, may well result in a setting that is not conducive to rational decision making. On this point, see Wilensky, *Organizational Intelligence.*

25. Thomas C. Schelling, *The Strategy of Conflict* (New York: Oxford University Press, 1963) is a classic study. Less subtle and far more ideological are: Robert Strausz-Hupé et al., *Protracted Conflict* (New York: Harper and Brothers, 1959); as well as the many articles published in the journal *Orbis* by William Kintner, Stefan T. Possony, Chester C. Ward, and others.

26. See, for example, Morgan, *Deterrence;* Philip Green, *Deadly Logic* (Columbus: Ohio State University Press, 1966); Barry R. Schneider, "Danger and Opportunity," unpublished Ph.D. dissertation, Columbia University 1972; and Jack L. Snyder, "Rationality at the Brink: The Role of Cognitive Processes in Failures of Deterrence," *World Politics* 30 (April 1978): 345–365. Useful discussions of various views on these issues may be found in Aaron Wildavsky, "Practical Consequences of the Theoretical Study of Defence Policy," *Public Administration Review* 25 (March 1965): 90–103; Snyder and Diesing, *Conflict Among Nations,* pp. 297–310; and Thomas C. Wiegele, "Models of Stress and Disturbances in Elite Political Behaviors: Psychological Variables and Political Decision-Making," in Robert S. Robins (ed.), *Psychopathology and Political Leadership* (New Orleans: Tulane Studies in Political Science, 1977).

27. Allison, *Essence of Decision;* John D. Steinbruner, *The Cybernetic Theory of Decision* (Princeton: Princeton University Press, 1974); James M. McCormick, "Evaluating Models of Crisis Behavior: Some Evidence from the Middle East," *International Studies Quarterly* 19 (March 1975): 17–45; Raymond Tanter, *Modelling and Managing International Conflicts: The Berlin Crisis* (Beverly Hills: Sage, 1974); Janice Stein and Raymond Tanter, *Crisis Decision Making: Rationality and Israel's Choices;* and R. G. Trotter, "The Cuban Missile Crisis: An Analysis of Policy Formulation in Terms of Current Decision Making Theory," unpublished Ph.D. dissertation, University of Pennsylvania, 1971.

28. Alexander L. George, David Hall, and William Simons, *The Limits of Coercive Diplomacy* (Boston: Little, Brown, 1971); Head, Short, and McFarlane, *Crisis Resolution;* Richard Smoke, *War: Controlling Escalation* (Cambridge:

Harvard University Press, 1977); Thomas Halper, *Foreign Policy Crises: Appearance and Reality In Decision-Making* (Columbus: Merrill, 1971); Holsti, *Crisis, Escalation, War* (Montreal: McGill-Queens University Press, 1972); Glenn D. Paige, "Comparative Case Analysis of Crisis Decisions: Korea and Cuba," in Hermann, *International Crises,* pp. 41–55; Oran Young, *The Politics of Force: Bargaining During International Crises* (Princeton: Princeton University Press, 1968); Lawrence S. Falkowski, *Presidents, Secretaries of State, and Crises in U.S. Foreign Relations: A Model and Predictive Analysis* (Boulder, Colo.: Westview Press, 1978); and Phil Williams, *Crisis Management* (New York: Wiley, 1977).

29. Snyder and Diesing, *Conflict Among Nations.* See also the major crisis research project directed by Michael Brecher, most recently described in his "Toward a Theory of International Crisis Behavior."

30. Davis B. Bobrow, Steve Chan, and John A. Kringen, "Understanding How Others Treat Crisis: A Multimethod Approach," *International Studies Quarterly* 21 (March 1977): 199–223. Assessments of how much progress has in fact been made in crisis research vary widely. Compare, in this respect, the optimistic appraisals of Charles A. McClelland, "The Anticipation of International Crises: Prospects for Theory and Research," *International Studies Quarterly* 21 (March 1977): 15–38, and Robert A. Young, "Perspectives on International Crisis: Introduction," *International Studies Quarterly* 21 (March 1977): 3–14; with the much more critical views expressed in James A. Robinson, "Crises: An Appraisal of Concepts and Theories," in Hermann, *International Crises;* and Gerald W. Hopple and Paul J. Rossa, "International Crisis Analysis: An Assessment of Theory and Research," University of Maryland, Cross-National Crisis Indicators Project, Research Report No. 5, April 1978.

31. Herbert Simon, *Organizations* (New York: Wiley, 1958), p. 138.

32. Somewhat different lists appear in Morgan, *Deterrence,* pp. 102–103; and in Irving Janis and Leon Mann, *Decision-Making* (New York: Free Press, 1977).

33. Figure 1 is an expanded version of a diagram that initially appeared in Ole R. Holsti and Alexander L. George, "The Effects of Stress on the Performance of Foreign Policy-Makers," in Cornelius P. Cotter (ed.), *Political Science Annual* (Indianapolis: Bobbs–Merrill, 1975), VI: 284.

34. Sheldon J. Korchin and Seymour Levine, "Anxiety and Verbal Learning," *Journal of Abnormal and Social Psychology* 54 (March 1957): 234–240.

35. For a further elaboration of this point, see Alexander L. George, *Toward A More Soundly Based Foreign Policy: Making Better Use of Information,* Appendix D, vol. 2, *Report of the Commission on the Organization of the Government for the Conduct of Foreign Policy* (Washington, D.C.: Government Printing Office, 1975), especially pp. 17–53.

36. Alfred Lowe, "Individual Differences in Reaction to Failure: Modes of Coping with Anxiety and Interference Proneness," *Journal of Abnormal and Social Psychology* 62 (May 1961): 303–308; and Sara B. Kiesler, "Stress, Affiliation and Performance," *Journal of Experimental Research in Personality* 1 (December 1966): 227–235.

37. Sheldon J. Korchin et al., "Visual Discrimination and the Decision Process in Anxiety," *AMA Archive of Neurology and Psychiatry* 78 (1957): 424–438; Robert E. Murphy, "Effects of Threat of Shock, Distraction, and Task Design

on Performance," *Journal of Experimental Psychology* 58 (August 1959): 134–141; Harold M. Schroeder, Michael J. Driver, and Siegfried Streufert, *Human Information Processing* (New York: Holt, Rinehart and Winston, 1967); and C. R. Anderson, "Coping Behavior as Intervening Mechanisms in the Inverted-U Stress-Performance Relationship," *Journal of Applied Psychology* 60 (February 1976): 30–34.

38. R. R. Grinker and J. P. Spiegel, *Men Under Stress* (New York: McGraw–Hill, 1945); E. Paul Torrance, "A Theory of Leadership and Interpersonal Behavior Under Stress," in Luigi Petrullo and Bernard M. Bass (eds.), *Leadership and Interpersonal Behavior* (New York: Holt, Rinehart, and Winston, 1961), pp. 100–117; George W. Baker and Dwight W. Chapman (eds.), *Man and Society in Disaster* (New York: Basic Books, 1962); and A. D. Baddeley, "Selective Attention and Performance in Dangerous Environments," *British Journal of Psychology* 63 (1972): 537–546.

39. Sheldon J. Korchin, "Anxiety and Cognition," in Constance Sheerer (ed.), *Cognition: Theory, Research, Promise* (New York: Harper & Row, 1964), p. 63.

40. Charles E. Lindblom, *The Policy-Making Process* (Englewood Cliffs, N.J.: Prentice–Hall, 1968), p. 22.

41. Fredric Bertram Nalven, "Defense Preference and Perceptual Decision-Making," Ph.D. dissertation, Boston University, Boston, 1961, abstracted in Paul Wasserman and Fred S. Silander, *Decision-Making: An Annotated Bibliography, Supplement, 1958–1963* (Ithaca, N.Y.: Cornell University Press, 1964), p. 78.

42. Melvin Manis, *Cognitive Processes* (Belmont, Calif.: Wadsworth, 1966), pp. 97–102; and F. P. Kilpatrick, "Problems of Perception in Extreme Situations," in Robert R. Evans (ed.), *Readings in Collective Behavior* (Chicago: Rand McNally, 1969), pp. 168, 171. For relevant historical evidence on this point, see Ernest R. May, *"Lessons" of the Past: The Use and Misuse of History in American Foreign Policy* (New York: Oxford University Press, 1973); and Robert Jervis, *Perception and Misperception in International Politics* (Princeton: Princeton University Press, 1976).

43. Ralph K. White and Ronald Lippitt, *Autocracy and Democracy: An Experimental Inquiry* (New York: Harper and Brothers, 1960), p. 171.

44. Robert Jervis, "Hypotheses on Misperception," *World Politics* 20 (April 1968): 454–479; and Robert Jervis, *Perception and Misperception*.

45. C. D. Smock, "The Influence of Psychological Stress on the 'Intolerance of Ambiguity,'" *Journal of Abnormal and Social Psychology* 50 (March 1955): 177–182.

46. Thomas Milburn, "The Management of Crisis," in Hermann, *International Crisis*, p. 265.

47. Leo Postman and Jerome S. Bruner, "Perception under Stress," *Psychological Review* 55 (1948): 322.

48. Milburn, "The Management of Crisis."

49. Jerome Bruner, cited in Louis C. Gawthrop, *Bureaucratic Behavior in the Executive Branch* (New York: Free Press, 1969), p. 113.

50. James G. Miller, "Information Input Overload and Psychopathology," *American Journal of Psychiatry* 116 (February 1960): 695–704; James G. Miller, "Information Input Overload," *Self Organizing Systems* (1962, n.p.); Harry B. Williams, "Some Functions of Communication in Crisis Behavior,"

Human Organization 16 (Summer 1957): 15–19; Charles F. Hermann, "Some Consequences of Crisis Which Limit the Viability of Organizations"; and Holsti, Crisis, Escalation, War, pp. 82–118.

51. Baddeley, "Selective Attention and Performance in Dangerous Environments."

52. George A. Miller, "The Magical Number Seven Plus or Minus Two: Some Limits on our Capacity for Processing Information," Psychological Review 63 (March 1956): 81–97.

53. Karl E. Weick, "Processes of Ramification Among Cognitive Links," in Robert P. Abelson et al. (eds.), Theories of Cognitive Consistency (Chicago: Rand McNally, 1968), pp. 516–517; and Jerome E. Singer, "Consistency as a Stimulus Processing Mechanism," in the same volume, pp. 337–342.

54. Theodore C. Sorensen, Decision-Making in the White House (New York: Columbia University Press, 1964), p. 38.

55. Samuel I. Cohen and A. G. Mezey, "The Effects of Anxiety on Time Judgment and Time Experience in Normal Persons," Journal of Neurology, Neurosurgery and Psychiatry 24 (August 1961): 266–268.

56. Harry B. Williams and Jeannette F. Rayner, "Emergency Medical Services in Disaster," Medical Annals of the District of Columbia 25 (1956); Jonas Langer, Seymour Wapner, and Heinz Werner, "The Effects of Danger Upon the Experience of Time," American Journal of Psychology 74 (March 1961): 94–97. See also John Cohen, "Psychological Time," Scientific American (November 1964): 116–124.

57. Jerome Bruner, Jacequeline J. Goodnow, and George A. Austin, A Study of Thinking (New York: Wiley, 1956), p. 147.

58. Abraham S. Luchins, "Mechanization in Problem-Solving," Psychological Monographs 54 (1942): whole no. 248; Steinbruner, The Cybernetic Theory of Decision.

59. George Usdansky and Loren J. Chapman, "Schizophrenic-like Response in Normal Subjects under Time Pressures," Journal of Abnormal and Social Psychology 60 (January 1960): 143–146; Pauline N. Pepinsky and Willian B. Pavlik, "The Effects of Task Complexity and Time Pressure Upon Team Productivity," Journal of Applied Psychology 44 (February 1960): 34–38; N. H. Mackworth and J. F. Mackworth, "Visual Search for Successive Decisions," British Journal of Psychology 49 (August 1958): 210–221; Herbert G. Birch, "Motivational Factors in Insightful Problem-Solving," Journal of Comparative Psychology 38 (October 1945): 295–317; Bruner et al., A Study of Thinking; Peter Dubno, "Decision Time Characteristics of Leaders and Group Problem Solving Behavior," Journal of Social Psychology 59 (April 1963): 259–282; F. E. Horvath, "Psychological Stress: A Review of Definitions and Experimental Research," General Systems Yearbook 4 (1959): 203–230; and Donald R. Hoffeld and S. Carolyn Kent, "Decision Time and Information Use in Choice Situations," Psychological Reports 12 (February 1963): 68–70.

60. Robert J. Albers, "Anxiety and Time Perspectives," Dissertation Abstracts 26 (February 1966): 4848; and James D. Thompson and Robert W. Hawkes, "Disaster, Community Organization, and Administrative Process," in George Baker and Dwight Chapman (eds.), Man and Society in Disaster (New York; Basic Books, 1962).

61. Korchin, "Anxiety and Cognition," p. 63.

62. See the discussion in Alexander L. George's chapter in this book [Lauren, *Diplomacy*]; George and Smoke, *Deterrence in American Foreign Policy*, pp. 94–97; Sidney Verba, "Some Dilemmas in Comparative Research," *World Politics* 20 (October 1967): 111–127; Bruce M. Russett, "International Behavior Research: Case Studies and Cumulation," in Michael Haas and Henry Kariel (eds.), *Approaches to the Study of Political Science* (Scranton, Pa.: Chandler, 1970); Smoke, *War: Controlling Escalation*; James N. Rosenau, "Moral Fervor, Systematic Analysis, and Scientific Consciousness in Foreign Policy Research," in Austen Ranney (ed.), *Political Science and Public Policy* (Chicago: Markham, 1968); and Glenn D. Paige, *The Korean Decision: June 24–30, 1950* (New York: Free Press, 1968), pp. 3–18. The latter study is also an important contribution to the study of crisis decision making.

63. Prince Bernhard von Bülow, *Memoirs of Prince von Bülow*, 3 vols. (Boston: Little, Brown, 1932), III: 166; and Alfred von Tirpitz, *My Memoirs* (London: Hurst and Blackett, 1919), p. 280.

64. Further discussions of the 1914 crisis may be found in chapters by Robert Jervis and Samuel Williamson in this book. [Lauren, *Diplomacy*]

65. A detailed discussion of the methods of content analysis used with the 1914 data has appeared in Holsti, *Crisis, Escalation, War*, and very briefly in Melvin Small's chapter in this book. [Lauren, *Diplomacy*]

66. Quoted in Luigi Albertini, *Origins of the War of 1914*, 2 vols. (New York: Oxford University Press, 1953), II: 122.

67. Max Montgelas and Walter Schücking (eds.), *Outbreak of the World War, German Documents Collected by Karl Kautsky* (New York: Oxford University Press, 1924), #48. [Hereafter this source will be cited as Germany.]

68. Great Britain, Foreign Office, *British Documents on the Origins of the War, 1898–1914*, 11 vols., ed. G. P. Gooch and Harold Temperely, vol. 11, *Foreign Office Documents June 28th–August 4th, 1914*, collected by J. W. Headlam–Morely (London: His Majesty's Stationery Office, 1926), #99. [Hereafter cited as Great Britain.]

69. Great Britain, #411.

70. Germany, #343.

71. France, Commission de Publication des documents relatifs aux origines de la guerre, 1914, *Documents Diplomatiques Français (1871–1914)*, 3rd series, vols. 10, 11 (Paris: Imprimerie nationale, 1936), #32. [Hereafter cited as France.]

72. Germany, #390.

73. Germany, #433.

74. Germany, #451.

75. France, #305.

76. Germany, #529.

77. France, #401.

78. Winston S. Churchill, *The World Crisis, 1911–1914* (New York: Scribner's, 1928), p. 211.

79. Great Britain, #368, 446.

80. Albertini, *Origins of the War in 1914*, II: 558.

81. Germany, #221.

82. Schelling, *The Strategy of Conflict*, pp. 137–138.

83. Great Britain, #103.

84. Germany, #247.
85. Russian, Komissiia po izdaiiu dokumentov epokhi imperializma, *Mezhdun-arodyne otnosheniia v epokhe imperializma;* dokument 12 arkhivov tsarkogo i vremennogo pravitel'stv 1878–1917, gg. 3d series, vols. 4, 5, (Moscow and Leningrad: Gosudarstvennoe sotsial'no-ekonomicheskoe izdatal'stvo, 1931, 1934), #118. [Hereafter cited as Russia.]
86. Great Britain, #263.
87. Germany, #399.
88. Germany, #480.
89. Germany, #575.
90. France, #38.
91. Great Britain, #252.
92. Russia, #221; Germany, #401.
93. Quoted in Sidney B. Fay, *The Origins of the World War* (New York: Mac-millan, 1930 ed.), II: 481.
94. Moltke, *Erinnerungen,* quoted in Virginia Cowles, *The Kaiser* (New York: Harper & Row, 1964), pp. 343–346.
95. Quoted in Fay, *The Origins of the World War,* II: 207.
96. Germany, #474.
97. Germany, #368.
98. Great Britain, #264.
99. Great Britain, #447.
100. Great Britain, #99.
101. Russia, #170.
102. Great Britain, #101.
103. Germany, #395.
104. Quoted in Fay, *The Origins of the World War,* II: 509.
105. The literature on the missile crisis is immense, including memoirs of partic-ipants, polemics, descriptive accounts, and explicitly comparative or theo-retical studies. Of the latter genre, some of the most interesting are George, Hall, and Simons, *The Limits of Coercive Diplomacy;* George and Smoke, *Deterrence in American Foreign Policy;* Allison, *The Essence of Decision;* Roberta Wohlstetter, "Cuba and Pearl Harbor," *Foreign Affairs* 43 (July 1965): 691–707; Snyder and Diesing, *Conflict Among Nations;* Paige, "Com-parative Case Analysis of Crisis Decision: Korea and Cuba"; Young, *The Pol-itics of Force;* Snyder, "Rationality at the Brink"; and Albert and Roberta Wohlstetter, *Controlling the Risks in Cuba,* Adelphi Paper No. 17 (London: International Institute for Strategic Studies, 1965).
106. Douglas Dillon, quoted in Elie Abel, *The Missile Crisis* (Philadelphia: Lippin-cott, 1966), p. 48.
107. Theodore Soresen, *Decision-Making in the White House* (New York: Colum-bia University Press, 1963), p. 31.
108. National Broadcasting Company, "Cuba: The Missile Crisis" (mimeo. tran-script, February 9, 1964), p. 12.
109. Columbia Broadcasting System, "Conversation with President Kennedy" (mimeo. transcript, December 17, 1963), pp. 2–3.
110. Arthur M. Schlesinger, Jr., *A Thousand Days* (New York: Houghton Mifflin, 1965), p. 804.
111. NBC, "Cuba," p. 14.
112. CBS, "Conversation with President Kennedy," p. 4.

113. Schlesinger, *A Thousand Days,* p. 808.
114. CBS, "Conversation with President Kennedy," p. 4.
115. Ibid.
116. NBC, "Cuba," p. 17.
117. Quoted in Snyder and Diesing, *Conflict Among Nations,* p. 301.
118. The important role of the ultimatum in settlement of the missile crisis is discussed in more detail by George, Hall, and Simons, *The Limits of Coercive Diplomacy.*
119. NBC, "Cuba," p. 42.
120. Robert F. Kennedy, *Thirteen Days* (New York: Norton, 1969), p. 127.
121. CBS, "Conversation with President Kennedy," p. 3.
122. Theodore Soresen, *Kennedy* (New York: Harper & Row, 1965), p. 726.
123. Interesting alternative explanations for the outcome in 1914, for example, may be found in Bruce M. Russett, "Cause, Surprise, and No Escape," *Journal of Politics* 24 (February 1962): 3–22; and Lancelot L. Farrar, Jr., "The Limits of Choice: July 1914 Reconsidered," *Journal of Conflict Resolution* 16 (March 1972): 1–24. Other approaches to crisis decision making that have not received attention here include those that emphasize aspects of personality; see, for example, Falkowski, *Presidents, Secretaries of State, and Crisis in U.S. Foreign Relations;* James David Barber, *The Presidential Character* (Englewood Cliffs, N.J.: Prentice–Hall, 1972); and Thomas M. Mongar, "Personality and Decision-Making: John F. Kennedy in Four Crisis Decisions," *Canadian Journal of Political Science* 2 (June 1962): 200–225. The psychobiological effects of crisis are discussed in Wiegele, "Modes of Stress," and in the same author's "Decision Making in an International Crisis: Some Biological Factors," *International Studies Quarterly* 17 (September 1973): 295–335.
124. Robert F. Kennedy, "Thirteen Days: The Story About How the World Almost Ended," *McCall's* (November 1968): 148.
125. Janis, *Victims of Groupthink;* and Roland L. Frye and Thomas M. Stritch, "Effects of Timed vs. Non-timed Discussion Upon Measures of Influence and Change in Small Groups," *Journal of Social Psychology* 63 (June 1964): 139–143.
126. Dean G. Pruitt, "Problem Solving in the Department of State" (unpublished paper, Northwestern University, 1961).
127. Howard H. Lentner, "The Concept of Crisis as Viewed by the U.S. Department of State," in Hermann, *International Crisis,* pp. 112–135.
128. Snyder and Diesing, *Conflict Among Nations.*
129. Michael Brecher, "Research Findings and Theory-Building in Foreign Policy Behavior," in Patrick J. McGowan (ed.), *Sage International Yearbook of Foreign Policy Studies* (Beverly Hills: Sage, 1974), II: 71.
130. Peter Suedfeld and Philip Tetlock, "Integrative Complexity of Communications in International Crisis," *Journal of Conflict Resolution* 21 (March 1977): 169–186.

Conceptual Models and the Cuban Missile Crisis

Graham T. Allison

The author presents three models of the foreign policy decision-making process. The first (the rational actor model) tends to dominate the realist perspective. The organizational process and bureaucratic politics models, reflecting what we call a pluralist perspective, raise questions concerning the appropriateness of relying exclusively on the rational actor model to explain foreign policy choices.

The Cuban missile crisis is a seminal event. For thirteen days of October 1962, there was a higher probability that more human lives would end suddenly than ever before in history. Had the worst occurred, the death of 100 million Americans, over 100 million Russians, and millions of Europeans as well would make previous natural calamities and inhumanities appear insignificant. Given the probability of disaster—which President Kennedy estimated as "between 1 out of 3 and even"—our escape seems awesome.[1] This event symbolizes a central, if only partially thinkable, fact about our existence. That such consequences could follow from the choices and actions of national governments obliges students of government as well as participants in governance to think hard about these problems.

Improved understanding of this crisis depends in part on more information and more probing analyses of available evidence. To contribute to these efforts is part of the purpose of this study. But here the missile crisis serves primarily as grist for a more general investigation. This study proceeds from the premise that marked improvement in our understanding of such events depends critically on more self-consciousness about what observers bring to the analysis. What each analyst sees and judges to be important is a function not only of the evidence about what happened but also of the "conceptual lenses" through which he looks at the evidence. The principal purpose of this essay is to explore some of the fundamental assumptions and categories employed by analysts in thinking about problems of governmental behavior, especially in foreign and military affairs.

*A longer version of this paper was presented at the Annual Meeting of the American Political Science Association, September, 1968 (reproduced by the Rand Corporation, P–3919). The paper is part of a larger study, *Essence of Decision: Explaining the Cuban Missile Crisis* (Boston: Little, Brown and Co., 1971). For support in various stages of this work I am indebted to the Institute of Politics in the John F. Kennedy School of Government and the Center for International Affairs, both at Harvard University, the Rand Corporation, and the Council on Foreign Relations. For critical stimulation and advice I am especially grateful to Richard E. Neustadt, Thomas C. Schelling, Andrew W. Marshall, and Elisabeth K. Allison.

The general argument can be summarized in three propositions:

1. Analysts think about problems of foreign and military policy in terms of largely implicit conceptual models that have significant consequences for the content of their thought.[2]

Though the present product of foreign policy analysis is neither systematic nor powerful, if one carefully examines explanations produced by analysts, a number of fundamental similarities emerge. Explanations produced by particular analysts display quite regular, predictable features. This predictability suggests a substructure. These regularities reflect an analyst's assumptions about the character of puzzles, the categories in which problems should be considered, the types of evidence that are relevant, and the determinants of occurrences. The first proposition is that clusters of such related assumptions constitute basic frames of reference or conceptual models in terms of which analysts both ask and answer the question: What happened? Why did the event happen? What will happen?[3] Such assumptions are central to the activities of explanation and prediction, for in attempting to explain a particular event, the analyst cannot simply describe the full state of the world leading up to that event. The logic of explanation requires that he single out the relevant, important determinants of the occurrence.[4] Moreover, as the logic of prediction underscores, the analyst must summarize the various determinants as they bear on the event in question. Conceptual models both fix the mesh of the nets that the analyst drags through the material in order to explain a particular action or decision and direct him to cast his net in select ponds, at certain depths, in order to catch the fish he is after.

2. Most analysts explain (and predict) the behavior of national governments in terms of various forms of one basic conceptual model, here entitled the Rational Policy Model (Model 1).[5]

In terms of this conceptual model, analysts attempt to understand happenings as the more or less purposive acts of unified national governments. For these analysts, the point of an explanation is to show how the nation or government could have chosen the action in question, given the strategic problem that it faced. For example, in confronting the problem posed by the Soviet installation of missiles in Cuba, rational policy model analysts attempt to show how this was a reasonable act from the point of view of the Soviet Union, given Soviet strategic objectives.

3. Two "alternative" conceptual models, here labeled an Organizational Process Model (Model II) and a Bureaucratic Politics Model (Model III) provide a base for improved explanation and prediction.

Although the standard frame of reference has proved useful for many purposes, there is powerful evidence that it must be supplemented, if not supplanted, by frames of reference which focus upon the large organizations and political actors involved in the policy process. Model I's implication that important events have important causes, i.e., that monoliths perform large actions for big reasons, must be balanced by an appreciation of the facts (a) that monoliths are black boxes covering various gears and levers in a highly differentiated decision-making structure, and (b) that large acts are the consequences of innumerable and often conflicting smaller actions by individuals at various levels of bureaucratic organizations in the service of a variety of only partially compatible conceptions of national goals, organizational goals, and political objectives. Recent developments in the field of organization theory provide the foundation for the second model. According to this organizational process model, what Model I categorizes as "acts" and "choices" are instead *outputs* of large organizations functioning according to certain regular patterns of behavior. Faced with the problem of Soviet missiles in Cuba, a Model II analyst identifies the relevant organizations and displays the patterns of organizational behavior from which this action emerged. The third model focuses on the internal politics of a government. Happenings in foreign affairs are understood, according to the bureaucratic politics model, neither as choices nor as outputs. Instead, what happens is categorized as *outcomes* of various overlapping bargaining games among players arranged hierarchically in the national government. In confronting the problem posed by Soviet missiles in Cuba, a Model III analyst displays the perceptions, motivations, positions, power, and maneuvers of principal players from which the outcome emerged.[6]

A central metaphor illuminates differences among these models. Foreign policy has often been compared to moves, sequences of moves, and games of chess. If one were limited to observations on a screen upon which moves in the chess game were projected without information as to how the pieces came to be moved, he would assume—as Model I does—that an individual chess player was moving the pieces with reference to plans and maneuvers toward the goal of winning the game. But a pattern of moves can be imagined that would lead the serious observer, after watching several games, to consider the hypothesis that the chess player was not a single individual but rather a loose alliance of semi-independent organizations, each of which moved its set of pieces according to standard operating procedures. For example, movement of separate sets of pieces might proceed in turn, each according to a routine, the king's rook, bishop, and their pawns repeatedly attacking the opponent according to a fixed plan. Furthermore, it is conceivable that the pattern of play would suggest to an observer that a number of distinct players, with distinct objectives but shared power over the pieces, were determining the moves as the resultant of collegial bargaining. For example, the black rook's move might contribute to the loss of a black knight with no comparable gain for the black team, but with the black rook becoming the principal guardian of the "palace" on that side of the board.

The space available does not permit full development and support of such a general argument.[7] Rather, the sections that follow simply sketch each conceptual model, articulate it as an analytic paradigm, and apply it to produce an explanation. But each model is applied to the same event: the U.S. blockade of Cuba during the missile crisis. These "alternative explanations" of the same happening illustrate differences among the models—*at work*.[8] A crisis decision, by a small group of men in the context of ultimate threat, this is a case of the rational policy model *par excellence*. The dimensions and factors that Models II and III uncover in this case are therefore particularly suggestive. The concluding section of this paper suggests how the three models may be related and how they can be extended to generate predictions.

Model I: Rational Policy

Rational Policy Model Illustrated

Where is the pinch of the puzzle raised by the *New York Times* over Soviet deployment of an antiballistic missile system?[9] The question, as the *Times* states it, concerns the Soviet Union's objective in allocating such large sums of money for this weapon system while at the same time seeming to pursue a policy of increasing détente. In former President Johnson's words, "the paradox is that this [Soviet deployment of an antiballistic missile system] should be happening at a time when there is abundant evidence that our mutual antagonism is beginning to ease."[10] This question troubles people primarily because Soviet antiballistic missile deployment, and evidence of Soviet actions towards détente, when juxtaposed in our implicit model, produce a question. With reference to what objective could the Soviet government have rationally chosen the simultaneous pursuit of these two courses of action? This question arises only when the analyst attempts to structure events as purposive choices of consistent actors.

How do analysts attempt to explain the Soviet emplacement of missiles in Cuba? The most widely cited explanation of this occurrence has been produced by two RAND Sovietologists, Arnold Horelick and Myron Rush.[11] They conclude that "the introduction of strategic missiles into Cuba was motivated chiefly by the Soviet leaders' desire to overcome . . . the existing large margin of U.S. strategic superiority."[12] How do they reach this conclusion? In Sherlock Holmes style, they seize several salient characteristics of this action and use these features as criteria against which to test alternative hypotheses about Soviet objectives. For example, the size of the Soviet deployment, and the simultaneous emplacement of more expensive, more visible intermediate range missiles as well as medium range missiles, it is argued, exclude an explanation of the action in terms of Cuban defense—since that objective could have been secured with a much smaller number of medium range missiles alone. Their explanation presents an argument for one objective that permits interpretation of the details of Soviet behavior as a value-maximizing choice.

How do analysts account for the coming of the First World War? According to Hans Morgenthau, "the first World War had its origin exclusively in the fear of a disturbance of the European balance of power."[13] In the period preceding World War I, the Triple Alliance precariously balanced the Triple Entente. If either power combination could gain a decisive advantage in the Balkans, it would achieve a decisive advantage in the balance of power. "It was this fear," Morgenthau asserts, "that motivated Austria in July 1914 to settle its accounts with Serbia once and for all, and that induced Germany to support Austria unconditionally. It was the same fear that brought Russia to the support of Serbia, and France to the support of Russia."[14] How is Morgenthau able to resolve this problem so confidently? By imposing on the data a "rational outline."[15] The value of this method, according to Morgenthau, is that "it provides for rational discipline in action and creates astounding continuity in foreign policy which makes American, British, or Russian foreign policy appear as an intelligent, rational continuum . . . regardless of the different motives, preferences, and intellectual and moral qualities of successive statesmen."[16]

Stanley Hoffmann's essay, "Restraints and Choices in American Foreign Policy" concentrates, characteristically, on "deep forces": the international system, ideology, and national character—which constitute restraints, limits, and blinders.[17] Only secondarily does he consider decisions. But when explaining particular occurrences, though emphasizing relevant constraints, he focuses on the choices of nations. American behavior in Southeast Asia is explained as a reasonable choice of "downgrading this particular alliance (SEATO) in favor of direct U.S. involvement," given the constraint: "one is bound by one's commitments; one is committed by one's mistakes."[18] More frequently, Hoffmann uncovers confusion or contradiction in the nation's choice. For example, U.S. policy towards underdeveloped countries is explained as "schizophrenic."[19] The method employed by Hoffmann in producing these explanations as rational (or irrational) decisions, he terms "imaginative reconstruction."[20]

Deterrence is the cardinal problem of the contemporary strategic literature. Thomas Schelling's *Strategy of Conflict* formulates a number of propositions focused upon the dynamics of deterrence in the nuclear age. One of the major propositions concerns the stability of the balance of terror: in a situation of mutual deterrence, the probability of nuclear war is reduced not by the "balance" (the sheer equality of the situation) but rather by the *stability* of the balance, i.e., the fact that neither opponent in striking first can destroy the other's ability to strike back.[21] How does Schelling support this proposition? Confidence in the contention stems not from an inductive canvass of a large number of previous cases, but rather from two calculations. In a situation of "balance" but vulnerability, there are values for which a rational opponent could choose to strike first, e.g., to destroy enemy capabilities to retaliate. In a "stable balance" where no matter who strikes first, each has an assured capability to retaliate with unacceptable damage, no rational agent could choose such a course of action (since that choice is effectively equivalent to choosing mutual homicide). Whereas most contemporary strategic thinking is driven *implicitly* by the motor upon which this calculation depends, Schelling explicitly recognizes that strategic theory does assume a model. The foundation of a theory of strategy is, he asserts: "the assumption of rational behavior—not just of intelligent behavior, but of behavior motivated by conscious calculation of advantages, calculation that in turn is based on an explicit and internally consistent value system."[22]

What is striking about these examples from the literature of foreign policy and international relations are the similarities among analysts of various styles when they are called upon to produce explanations. Each assumes that what must be explained is an action, i.e., the realization of some purpose or intention. Each assumes that the actor is the national government. Each assumes that the action is chosen as a calculated response to a strategic problem. For each, explanation consists of showing what goal the government was pursuing in committing the act and how this action was a reasonable choice, given the nation's objectives. This set of assumptions characterizes the rational policy model. The assertion that Model I is the standard frame of reference implies no denial of highly visible differences among the interests of Sovietologists, diplomatic historians, international relations theorists, and strategists. Indeed, in most respects, differences among the work of Hans Morgenthau, Stanley Hoffmann, and Thomas Schelling could not be more pointed. Appreciation of the extent to which each relies predominantly on Model I, however, reveals basic similarities among Morgenthau's method of "rational reenactment," Hoffmann's "imaginative reconstruction," and Schelling's "vicarious problem solving;" family resemblances among Morgenthau's "rational statesman," Hoffmann's "roulette player," and Schelling's "game theorist."[23]

Most contemporary analysts (as well as laymen) proceed predominantly—albeit most often implicitly—in terms of this model when attempting to explain happenings in foreign affairs. Indeed, that occurrences in foreign affairs are the *acts* of *nations* seems so fundamental to thinking about such problems that this underlying model has rarely been recognized: to explain an occurrence in foreign policy simply means to show how the government could have rationally chosen that action.[24] These brief examples illustrate five uses of the model. To prove that most analysts think largely in terms of the rational policy model is not possible. In this limited space it is not even possible to illustrate the range of employment of the framework. Rather, my purpose is to convey to the reader a grasp of the model and a challenge: let the reader examine the literature with which he is most familiar and make his judgment.

The general characterization can be sharpened by articulating the rational policy model as an "analytic paradigm" in the technical sense developed by Robert K. Merton for sociological analyses.[25] Systematic statement of basic assumptions, concepts, and propositions employed by Model I analysts highlights the distinctive thrust of this style of analysis. To articulate a largely implicit framework is of necessity to caricature. But caricature can be instructive.

Rational Policy Paradigm

I. Basic Unit of Analysis: Policy As National Choice

Happenings in foreign affairs are conceived as actions chosen by the nation or national government.[26] Governments select the action that will maximize strategic goals and objectives. These "solutions" to strategic problems are the fundamental categories in terms of which the analyst perceives what is to be explained.

II. Organizing Concepts

A. *National Actor.* The nation or government, conceived as a rational, unitary decisionmaker, is the agent. This actor has one set of specified goals (the equivalent of a consistent utility function), one set of perceived options, and a single estimate of the consequences that follow from each alternative.
B. *The Problem.* Action is chosen in response to the strategic problem which the nation faces. Threats and opportunities arising in the "international strategic market place" move the nation to act.
C. *Static Selection.* The sum of activity of representatives of the government relevant to a problem constitutes what the nation has chosen as its "solution." Thus the action is conceived as a steady-state choice among alternative outcomes (rather than, for example, a large number of partial choices in a dynamic stream).
D. *Action as Rational Choice.* The components include:
    1. *Goals and Objectives.* National security and national interests are the principal categories in which strategic goals are conceived. Nations seek security and a range of further objectives. (Analysts rarely translate strategic goals and objectives into an explicit utility function; nevertheless, analysts do focus on major goals and objectives and trade off side effects in an intuitive fashion.)
    2. *Options.* Various courses of action relevant to a strategic problem provide the spectrum of options.
    3. *Consequences.* Enactment of each alternative course of action will produce a series of consequences. The relevant consequences constitute benefits and costs in terms of strategic goals and objectives.

4. *Choice.* Rational choice is value-maximizing. The rational agent selects the alternative whose consequences rank highest in terms of his goals and objectives.

III. Dominant Inference Pattern

This paradigm leads analysts to rely on the following pattern of inference: if a nation performed a particular action, that nation must have had ends towards which the action constituted an optimal means. The rational policy model's explanatory power stems from this inference pattern. Puzzlement is relieved by revealing the purposive pattern within which the occurrence can be located as a value-maximizing means.

IV. General Propositions

The disgrace of political science is the infrequency with which propositions of any generality are formulated and tested. "Paradigmatic analysis" argues for explicitness about the terms in which analysis proceeds, and seriousness about the logic of explanation. Simply to illustrate the kind of propositions on which analysts who employ this model rely, the formulation includes several.

The basic assumption of value-maximizing behavior produces propositions central to most explanations. The general principle can be formulated as follows: the likelihood of any particular action results from a combination of the nation's (1) relevant values and objectives, (2) perceived alternative courses of action, (3) estimates of various sets of consequences (which will follow from each alternative), and (4) net valuation of each set of consequences. This yields two propositions.

A. An increase in the cost of an alternative, i.e., a reduction in the value of the set of consequences which will follow from that action, or a reduction in the probability of attaining fixed consequences, reduces the likelihood of that alternative being chosen.
B. A decrease in the costs of an alternative, i.e., an increase in the value of the set of consequences which will follow from that alternative, or an increase in the probability of attaining fixed consequences, increases the likelihood of that action being chosen.[27]

V. Specific Propositions

A. *Deterrence.* The likelihood of any particular attack results from the factors specified in the general proposition. Combined with factual assertions, this general proposition yields the propositions of the sub-theory of deterrence.
1. A stable nuclear balance reduces the likelihood of nuclear attack. This proposition is derived from the general proposition plus the asserted fact that a second-strike capability affects the potential attacker's calculations by increasing the likelihood and the costs of one particular set of consequences which might follow from attack—namely, retaliation.

2. A stable nuclear balance increases the probability of limited war. This proposition is derived from the general proposition plus the asserted fact that though increasing the costs of a nuclear exchange, a stable nuclear balance nevertheless produces a more significant reduction in the probability that such consequences would be chosen in response to a limited war. Thus this set of consequences weighs less heavily in the calculus.

B. *Soviet Force Posture.* The Soviet Union chooses its force posture (i.e., its weapons and their deployment) as a value-maximizing means of implementing Soviet strategic objectives and military doctrine. A proposition of this sort underlies Secretary of Defense Laird's inference from the fact of 200 SS–9s (large intercontinental missiles) to the assertion that "the Soviets are going for a first-strike capability, and there's no question about it."[28]

Variants of the Rational Policy Model

This paradigm exhibits the characteristics of the most refined version of the rational model. The modern literature of strategy employs a model of this sort. Problems and pressures in the "international strategic marketplace" yield probabilities of occurrence. The international actor, which could be any national actor, is simply a value-maximizing mechanism for getting from the strategic problem to the logical solution. But the explanations and predictions produced by most analysts of foreign affairs depend primarily on variants of this "pure" model. The point of each is the same: to place the action within a value-maximizing framework, given certain constraints. Nevertheless, it may be helpful to identify several variants, each of which might be exhibited similarly as a paradigm. The first focuses upon the national actor and his choice in a particular situation, leading analysts to further constrain the goals, alternatives, and consequences considered. Thus, (1) national propensities or personality traits reflected in an "operational code," (2) concern with certain objectives, or (3) special principles of action, narrow the "goals" or "alternatives" or "consequences" of the paradigm. For example, the Soviet deployment of ABMs is sometimes explained by reference to the Soviet's "defense-mindedness." Or a particular Soviet action is explained as an instance of a special rule of action in the Bolshevik operational code.[29] A second, related, cluster of variants focuses on the individual leader or leadership group as the actor whose preference function is maximized and whose personal (or group) characteristics are allowed to modify the alternatives, consequences, and rules of choice. Explanations of the U.S. involvement in Vietnam as a natural consequence of the Kennedy–Johnson Administration's axioms of foreign policy rely on this variant. A third, more complex variant of the basic model recognizes the existence of several actors within a government, for example, Hawks and Doves or military and civilians, but attempts to explain (or predict) an occurrence by reference to the objectives of the victorious actor. Thus, for example, some revisionist histories of the Cold War recognize the forces of light and the forces of darkness within the U.S. government, but explain American actions as a result of goals and perceptions of the victorious forces of darkness.

Each of these forms of the basic paradigm constitutes a formalization of what analysts typically rely upon implicitly. In the transition from implicit conceptual model to explicit paradigm much of the richness of the best employments of this model has been lost. But the purpose in raising loose, implicit conceptual models to an explicit level is to reveal the basic logic of analysts' activity. Perhaps some of the remaining artificiality that surrounds the statement of the paradigm can be erased by noting a number of the standard additions and modifications employed by analysts who proceed *predominantly* within the rational policy model. First, in the course of a document, analysts shift from one variant of the basic model to another, occasionally appropriating in an *ad hoc* fashion aspects of a situation which are logically incompatible with the basic model. Second, in the course of explaining a number of occurrences, analysts sometimes pause over a particular event about which they have a great deal of information and unfold it in such detail that an impression of randomness is created. Third, having employed other assumptions and categories in deriving an explanation or prediction, analysts will present their product in a neat, convincing rational policy model package. (This accommodation is a favorite of members of the intelligence community whose association with the details of a process is considerable, but who feel that by putting an occurrence in a larger rational framework, it will be more comprehensible to their audience.) Fourth, in attempting to offer an explanation—particularly in cases where a prediction derived from the basic model has failed—the notion of a "mistake" is invoked. Thus, the failure in the prediction of a "missile gap" is written off as a Soviet mistake in not taking advantage of their opportunity. Both these and other modifications permit Model I analysts considerably more variety than the paradigm might suggest. But such accommodations are essentially appendages to the basic logic of these analyses.

The U.S. Blockade of Cuba: A First Cut[30]

The U.S. response to the Soviet Union's emplacement of missiles in Cuba must be understood in strategic terms as simple value-maximizing escalation. American nuclear superiority could be counted on to paralyze Soviet nuclear power; Soviet transgression of the nuclear threshold in response to an American use of lower levels of violence would be wildly irrational since it would mean virtual destruction of the Soviet Communist system and Russian nation. American local superiority was overwhelming: it could be initiated at a low level while threatening with high credibility an ascending sequence of steps short of the nuclear threshold. All that was required was for the United States to bring to bear its strategic and local superiority in such a way that American determination to see the missiles removed would be demonstrated, while at the same time allowing Moscow time and room to retreat without humiliation. The naval blockade—euphemistically named a "quarantine" in order to circumvent the niceties of international law—did just that.

The U.S. government's selection of the blockade followed this logic. Apprised of the presence of Soviet missiles in Cuba, the President assembled an Executive Committee (ExCom) of the National Security Council and directed them to "set aside all other tasks to make a prompt and intense survey of the dangers and all possible courses of action."[31] This group functioned as "fifteen individuals on our own, representing the President and not different departments."[32] As one of the participants recalls, "The remarkable aspect of those meetings was a sense of complete equality."[33] Most of the time during the week that followed was spent canvassing all the possible tracks and weighing the arguments for and against each. Six major categories of action were considered.

1. Do nothing. U.S. vulnerability to Soviet missiles was no new thing. Since the U.S. already lived under the gun of missiles based in Russia, a Soviet capability to strike from Cuba too made little real difference. The real danger stemmed from the possibility of U.S. over-reaction. The U.S. should announce the Soviet action in a calm, casual manner thereby deflating whatever political capital Khrushchev hoped to make of the missiles.

This argument fails on two counts. First, it grossly underestimates the military importance of the Soviet move. Not only would the Soviet Union's missile capability be doubled and the U.S. early warning system outflanked. The Soviet Union would have an opportunity to reverse the strategic balance by further installations, and indeed, in the longer run, to invest in cheaper, shorter-range rather than more expensive longer-range missiles. Second, the political importance of this move was undeniable. The Soviet Union's act challenged the American President's most solemn warning. If the U.S. failed to respond, no American commitment would be credible.

2. Diplomatic pressures. Several forms were considered: an appeal to the U.N. or O.A.S. for an inspection team, a secret approach to Khrushchev, and a direct approach to Khrushchev, perhaps at a summit meeting. The United States would demand that the missiles be removed, but the final settlement might include neutralization of Cuba, U.S. withdrawal from the Guantanamo base, and withdrawal of U.S. Jupiter missiles from Turkey or Italy.

Each form of the diplomatic approach had its own drawbacks. To arraign the Soviet Union before the U.N. Security Council held little promise since the Russians could veto any proposed action. While the diplomats argued, the missiles would become operational. To send a secret emissary to Khrushchev demanding that the missiles be withdrawn would be to pose untenable alternatives. On the one hand, this would invite Khrushchev to seize the diplomatic initiative, perhaps committing himself to strategic retaliation in response to an attack on Cuba. On the other hand, this would tender an ultimatum that no great power could accept. To confront Khrushchev at a summit would guarantee demands for U.S. concessions, and the analogy between U.S. missiles in Turkey and Russian missiles in Cuba could not be erased.

But why not trade U.S. Jupiters in Turkey and Italy, which the President had previously ordered withdrawn, for the missiles in Cuba? The U.S. had chosen to withdraw these missiles in order to replace them with superior, less vulnerable Mediterranean Polaris submarines. But the middle of the crisis was no time for concessions. The offer of such a deal might suggest to the Soviets that the West would yield and thus tempt them to demand more. It would certainly confirm European suspicions about American willingness to sacrifice European interests when the chips were down. Finally, the basic issue should be kept clear. As the President stated in reply to Bertrand Russell, "I think your attention might well be directed to the burglars rather than to those who have caught the burglars."[34]

3. A secret approach to Castro. The crisis provided an opportunity to separate Cuba and Soviet Communism by offering Castro the alternatives, "split or fall." But Soviet troops transported, constructed, guarded, and controlled the missiles. Their removal would thus depend on a Soviet decision.

4. Invasion. The United States could take this occasion not only to remove the missiles but also to rid itself of Castro. A Navy exercise had long been scheduled in which Marines, ferried from Florida in naval vessels, would liberate the imaginary island of Vieques.[35] Why not simply shift the point of disembarkment? (The Pentagon's foresight in planning this operation would be an appropriate antidote to the CIA's Bay of Pigs!)

Preparations were made for an invasion, but as a last resort, American troops would be forced to confront 20,000 Soviets in the first Cold War case of direct contact between the troops of the super powers. Such brinksmanship courted nuclear disaster, practically guaranteeing an equivalent Soviet move against Berlin.

5. Surgical air strike. The missile sites should be removed by a clean, swift conventional attack. This was the effective counter-action which the attempted deception deserved. A surgical strike would remove the missiles and thus eliminate both the danger that the missiles might become operational and the fear that the Soviets would discover the American discovery and act first.

The initial attractiveness of this alternative was dulled by several difficulties. First, could the strike really be "surgical"? The Air Force could not guarantee destruction of all the missiles.[36] Some might be fired during the attack; some might not have been identified. In order to assure destruction of Soviet and Cuban means of retaliating, what was required was not a surgical but rather a massive attack—of at least 500 sorties. Second, a surprise air attack would of course kill Russians at the missile sites. Pressures on the Soviet Union to retaliate would be so strong that an attack on Berlin or Turkey was highly probable. Third, the key problem with this program was that of advance warning. Could the President of the United States, with his memory of Pearl Harbor and his vision of future U.S. responsibility, order a "Pearl Harbor in reverse"? For 175 years, unannounced Sunday morning attacks had been an anathema to our tradition.[37]

6. Blockade. Indirect military action in the form of a blockade became more attractive as the ExCom dissected the other alternatives. An embargo on military shipments to Cuba enforced by a naval blockade was not without flaws, however. Could the U.S. blockade Cuba without inviting Soviet reprisal in Berlin? The likely solution to joint blockades would be the lifting of both blockades, restoring the new *status quo,* and allowing the Soviets additional time to complete the missiles. Second, the possible consequences of the blockade resembled the drawbacks which disqualified the air strike. If Soviet ships did not stop, the United States would be forced to fire the first shot, inviting retaliation. Third, a blockade would deny the traditional freedom of the seas demanded by several of our close allies and might be held illegal, in violation of the U.N. Charter and international law, unless the United States could obtain a two-thirds vote in the O.A.S. Finally, how could a blockade be related to the problem, namely, some 75 missiles on the island of Cuba, approaching operational readiness daily? A blockade offered the Soviets a spectrum of delaying tactics with which to buy time to complete the missile installations. Was a *fait accompli* not required?

In spite of these enormous difficulties the blockade had comparative advantages: (1) It was a middle course between inaction and attack, aggressive enough to communicate firmness of intention, but nevertheless not so precipitous as a strike. (2) It placed on Khrushchev the burden of choice concerning the next step. He could avoid a direct military clash by keeping his ships away. His was the last clear chance. (3) No possible military confrontation could be more acceptable to the U.S. than a naval engagement in the Caribbean. (4) This move permitted the U.S., by flexing its conventional muscle, to exploit the threat of subsequent non-nuclear steps in each of which the U.S. would have significant superiority.

Particular arguments about advantages and disadvantages were powerful. The explanation of the American choice of the blockade lies in a more general principle, however. As President Kennedy stated in drawing the moral of the crisis:

> Above all, while defending our own vital interests, nuclear powers must avert those confrontations which bring an adversary to a choice of either a humiliating retreat or a nuclear war. To adopt that kind of course in the nuclear age

would be evidence only of the bankruptcy of our policy—of a collective death wish for the world.[38]

The blockade was the United States' only real option.

MODEL II: ORGANIZATIONAL PROCESS

For some purposes, governmental behavior can be usefully summarized as action chosen by a unitary, rational decisionmaker: centrally controlled, completely informed, and value maximizing. But this simplification must not be allowed to conceal the fact that a "government" consists of a conglomerate of semi-feudal, loosely allied organizations, each with a substantial life of its own. Government leaders do sit formally, and to some extent in fact, on top of this conglomerate. But governments perceive problems through organizational sensors. Governments define alternatives and estimate consequences as organizations process information. Governments act as these organizations enact routines. Government behavior can therefore be understood according to a second conceptual model, less as deliberate choices of leaders and more as *outputs* of large organizations functioning according to standard patterns of behavior.

To be responsive to a broad spectrum of problems, governments consist of large organizations among which primary responsibility for particular areas is divided. Each organization attends to a special set of problems and acts in quasi-independence on these problems. But few important problems fall exclusively within the domain of a single organization. Thus government behavior relevant to any important problem reflects the independent output of several organizations, partially coordinated by government leaders. Government leaders can substantially disturb, but not substantially control, the behavior of these organizations.

To perform complex routines, the behavior of large numbers of individuals must be coordinated. Coordination requires standard operating procedures: rules according to which things are done. Assured capability for reliable performance of action that depends upon the behavior of hundreds of persons requires established "programs." Indeed, if the eleven members of a football team are to perform adequately on any particular down, each player must not "do what he thinks needs to be done" or "do what the quarterback tells him to do." Rather, each player must perform the maneuvers specified by a previously established play which the quarterback has simply called in this situation.

At any given time, a government consists of *existing* organizations, each with a *fixed* set of standard operating procedures and programs. The behavior of these organizations—and consequently of the government—relevant to an issue in any particular instance is, therefore, determined primarily by routines established in these organizations prior to that instance. But organizations do change. Learning occurs gradually, over time. Dramatic organizational change occurs in response to major crises. Both learning and change are influenced by existing organizational capabilities.

Borrowed from studies of organizations, these loosely formulated propositions amount simply to *tendencies*. Each must be hedged by modifiers like "other things being equal" and "under certain conditions." In particular instances, tendencies hold—more or less. In specific situations, the relevant question is: more or less? But this is as it should be. For, on the one hand, "organizations" are no more homogeneous a class than "solids." When scientists tried to generalize about "solids," they achieved similar results. Solids tend to expand when heated, but some do and some don't. More adequate categorization of the various elements now lumped under the rubric "organizations" is thus required. On the other hand, the behavior of particular organizations seems considerably more complex than the behavior of solids. Additional information about a particular organization is required for further specification of the tendency statements. In spite of these two caveats, the characterization of government action as organizational output differs distinctly from Model I. Attempts to understand problems of foreign affairs in terms of this frame of reference should produce quite different explanations.[39]

Organizational Process Paradigm[40]

I. Basic Unit of Analysis: Policy As Organizational Output

The happenings of international politics are, in three critical senses, outputs of organizational processes. First, the actual occurrences are organizational outputs. For example, Chinese entry into the Korean War—that is, the fact that Chinese soldiers were firing at U.N. soldiers south of the Yalu in 1950—is an organizational action: the action of men who are soldiers in platoons which are in companies, which in turn are in armies, responding as privates to lieutenants who are responsible to captains and so on to the commander, moving into Korea, advancing against enemy troops, and firing according to fixed routines of the Chinese Army. Government leaders' decisions trigger organizational routines. Government leaders can trim the edges of this output and exercise some choice in combining outputs. But the mass of behavior is determined by previously established procedures. Second, existing organizational routines for employing present physical capabilities constitute the effective options open to government leaders confronted with any problem. Only the existence of men, equipped and trained as armies and capable of being transported to North Korea, made entry into the Korean War a live option for the Chinese leaders. The fact that fixed programs (equipment, men, and routines which exist at the particular time) exhaust the range of buttons that leaders can push is not always perceived by these leaders. But in every case it is critical for an understanding of what is actually done. Third, organizational outputs structure the situation within the narrow constraints of which leaders must contribute their "decision" concerning an issue. Outputs raise the problem, provide the information, and make the initial moves that color the face of the issue that is turned to the leaders. As Theodore Sorensen has observed: "Presidents rarely, if ever, make decisions—particularly in foreign affairs—in the sense of writing their conclusions on a clean slate. . . . The basic decisions, which confine their choices, have all too often been previously made."[41] If one understands the structure of the situation and the face of the issue—which are determined by the organizational outputs—the formal choice of the leaders is frequently anti-climactic.

II. Organizing Concepts

A. *Organizational Actors.* The actor is not a monolithic "nation" or "government" but rather a constellation of loosely allied organizations on top of which government leaders sit. This constellation acts only as component organizations perform routines.[42]

B. *Factored Problems and Fractionated Power.* Surveillance of the multiple facets of foreign affairs requires that problems be cut up and parcelled out to various organizations. To avoid paralysis, primary power must accompany primary responsibility. But if organizations are permitted to do anything, a large part of what they do will be determined within the organization. Thus each organization perceives problems, processes information, and performs a range of actions in quasi-independence (within broad guidelines of national policy). Factored problems and fractionated power are two edges of the same sword. Factoring permits more specialized attention to particular facets of problems than would be possible if government leaders tried to cope with these problems by themselves. But this additional attention must be paid for in the coin of discretion for *what* an organization attends to, and *how* organizational responses are programmed.

C. *Parochial Priorities, Perceptions, and Issues.* Primary responsibility for a narrow set of problems encourages organizational parochialism. These tendencies are enhanced by a number of additional factors: (1) selective information available to the organization, (2) recruitment of personnel into the organization, (3) tenure of individuals in the organization, (4) small group pressures within the organization, and (5) distribution of rewards by the organization. Clients (e.g., interest groups), government allies (e.g., Congressional committees), and extra-national counterparts (e.g., the British Ministry of Defense for the Department of Defense, ISA, or the British Foreign Office for the Department of State, EUR) galvanize this parochialism. Thus organizations develop relatively stable propensities concerning operational priorities, perceptions, and issues.

D. *Action as Organizational Output.* The preeminent feature of organizational activity is its programmed character: the extent to which behavior in any particular case is an enactment of preestablished routines. In producing outputs, the activity of each organization is characterized by:

1. *Goals: Constraints Defining Acceptable Performance.* The operational goals of an organization are seldom revealed by formal mandates. Rather, each organization's operational goals emerge as a set of constraints defining acceptable performance. Central among these constraints is organizational health, defined usually in terms of bodies assigned and dollars appropriated. The set of constraints emerges from a mix of expectations and demands of other organizations in the government, statutory authority, demands from citizens and special interest groups, and bargaining within the organization. These constraints represent a quasi-resolution of conflict—the constraints are relatively stable, so there is some resolution. But conflict among alternative goals is always latent; hence, it is a quasi-resolution. Typically, the constraints are formulated as imperatives to avoid roughly specified discomforts and disasters.[43]

2. *Sequential Attention to Goals.* The existence of conflict among operational constraints is resolved by the device of sequential attention. As a problem arises, the subunits of the organization most concerned with that problem deal with it in terms of the constraints they take to be most important. When the next problem arises, another cluster of subunits deals with it, focusing on a different set of constraints.

3. *Standard Operating Procedures.* Organizations perform their "higher" functions, such as attending to problem areas, monitoring information, and preparing relevant responses for likely contingencies, by doing "lower" tasks, for example, preparing budgets, producing reports, and developing hardware. Reliable performance of these tasks requires standard operating procedures (hereafter SOPs). Since procedures are "standard" they do not change quickly or easily. Without these standard procedures, it would not be possible to perform certain concerted tasks. But because of standard procedures, organizational behavior in particular instances often appears unduly formalized, sluggish, or inappropriate.

4. *Programs and Repertoires.* Organizations must be capable of performing actions in which the behavior of large numbers of individuals is carefully coordinated. Assured performance requires clusters of rehearsed SOPs for producing specific actions, e.g., fighting enemy units or answering an embassy's cable. Each cluster comprises a "program" (in the terms both of drama and computers) which the organization has available for dealing with a situation. The list of programs relevant to a type of activity, e.g., fighting, constitutes an organizational repertoire. The number of programs in a repertoire is always quite limited. When properly triggered, organizations execute programs; programs cannot be substantially changed in a particular situation. The more complex the action and the greater the number of individuals involved, the more important are programs and repertoires as determinants of organizational behavior.

5. *Uncertainty Avoidance.* Organizations do not attempt to estimate the probability distribution of future occurrences. Rather, organizations avoid uncertainty. By arranging a *negotiated environment,* organizations regularize the reactions of other actors with whom they have to deal. The primary environment, relations with other organizations that comprise the government, is stabilized by such arrangements as agreed budgetary splits, accepted areas of responsibility, and established conventional practices. The secondary environment, relations with the international world, is stablized between allies by the establishment of contracts (alliances) and "club relations" (U.S. State and U.K. Foreign Office or U.S. Treasury and U.K. Treasury). Between enemies, contracts and accepted conventional practices perform a similar function, for example, the rules of the "precarious status quo" which President Kennedy referred to in the missile crisis. Where the international environment cannot be negotiated, organizations deal with remaining uncertainties by establishing a set of *standard scenarios* that constitute the contingencies for which they prepare. For example, the standard scenario for Tactical Air Command of the U.S. Air Force involves combat with enemy aircraft. Planes are designed and pilots trained to meet this problem. That these preparations are less relevant to more probable contingencies, e.g., provision of close-in ground support in limited wars like Vietnam, has had little impact on the scenario.

6. *Problem-directed Search.* Where situations cannot be construed as standard, organizations engage in search. The style of search and the solution are largely determined by existing routines. Organizational search for alternative courses of action is problem-oriented: it focuses on the atypical discomfort that must be avoided. It is simple-minded: the neighborhood of the symptom is searched first; then, the neighborhood of the current alternative. Patterns of search reveal biases which in turn reflect such factors as specialized training or experience and patterns of communications.

7. *Organizational Learning and Change.* The parameters of organizational behavior mostly persist. In response to non-standard problems, organizations search and routines evolve, assimilating new situations. Thus learning and change follow in large part from existing procedures. But marked changes in organizations do sometimes occur. Conditions in which dramatic changes are more likely include: (1) Periods of budgetary feast. Typically, organizations devour budgetary feasts by purchasing additional items on the existing shopping list. Nevertheless, if committed to change, leaders who control the budget can use extra funds to effect changes. (2) Periods of prolonged budgetary famine. Though a single year's famine typically results in few changes in organizational structure but a loss of effectiveness in performing some programs, prolonged famine forces major retrenchment. (3) Dramatic performance failures. Dramatic change occurs (mostly) in response to major disasters. Confronted with an undeniable failure of procedures and repertoires, authorities out-

side the organization demand change, existing personnel are less resistant to change, and critical members of the organization are replaced by individuals committed to change.

E. *Central Coordination and Control.* Action requires decentralization of responsibility and power. But problems lap over the jurisdictions of several organizations. Thus the necessity for decentralization runs headlong into the requirement for coordination. (Advocates of one horn or the other of this dilemma—responsive action entails decentralized power vs. coordinated action requires central control—account for a considerable part of the persistent demand for government reorganization.) Both the necessity for coordination and the centrality of foreign policy to national welfare guarantee the involvement of government leaders in the procedures of the organizations among which problems are divided and power shared. Each organization's propensities and routines can be disturbed by government leaders' intervention. Central direction and persistent control of organizational activity, however, is not possible. The relation among organizations, and between organizations and the government leaders depends critically on a number of structural variables including: (1) the nature of the job, (2) the measures and information available to government leaders, (3) the system of rewards and punishments for organizational members, and (4) the procedures by which human and material resources get committed. For example, to the extent that rewards and punishments for the members of an organization are distributed by higher authorities, these authorities can exercise some control by specifying criteria in terms of which organizational output is to be evaluated. These criteria become constraints within which organizational activity proceeds. But constraint is a crude instrument of control.

Intervention by government leaders does sometimes change the activity of an organization in an intended direction. But instances are fewer than might be expected. As Franklin Roosevelt, the master manipulator of government organizations, remarked:

> The Treasury is so large and far-flung and ingrained in its practices that I find it is almost impossible to get the action and results I want. . . . But the Treasury is not to be compared with the State Department. You should go through the experience of trying to get any changes in the thinking, policy, and action of the career diplomats and then you'd know what a real problem was. But the Treasury and the State Department put together are nothing compared with the Na-a-vy. . . . To change anything in the Na-a-vy is like punching a feather bed. You punch it with your right and you punch it with your left until you are finally exhausted, and then you find the damn bed just as it was before you started punching.[41]

John Kennedy's experience seems to have been similar: "The State Department," he asserted, "is a bowl full of jelly."[45] And lest the McNamara revolution in the Defense Department seem too striking a counter-example, the Navy's recent rejection of McNamara's major intervention in Naval weapons procurement, the F–111B, should be studied as an antidote.

F. *Decisions of Government Leaders.* Organizational persistence does not exclude shifts in governmental behavior. For government leaders sit atop the conglomerate of organizations. Many important issues of governmental action require that these leaders decide what organizations will play out which programs where. Thus stability in the parochialisms and SOPs of individual organizations is consistent with some important shifts in the behavior of governments. The range of these shifts is defined by existing organizational programs.

III. Dominant Inference Pattern

If a nation performs an action of this type today, its organizational components must yesterday have been performing (or have had established routines for performing) an action only marginally different from this action. At any specific point in time, a government consists of an established conglomerate of organizations, each with existing goals, programs, and repertoires. The characteristics of a government's action in any instance follows from those established routines, and from the choice of government leaders—on the basis of information and estimates provided by existing routines—among existing programs. The best explanation of an organization's behavior at t is $t - 1$; the prediction of $t + 1$ is t. Model II's explanatory power is achieved by uncovering the organizational routines and repertoires that produced the outputs that comprise the puzzling occurrence.

IV. General Propositions

A number of general propositions have been stated above. In order to illustrate clearly the type of proposition employed by Model II analysts, this section formulates several more precisely.

A. *Organizational Action.* Activity according to SOPs and programs does not constitute far-sighted, flexible adaptation to "the issue" (as it is conceived by the analyst.) Detail and nuance of actions by organizations are determined predominantly by organizational routines, not government leaders' directions.

1. SOPs constitute routines for dealing with *standard* situations. Routines allow large numbers of ordinary individuals to deal with numerous instances, day after day, without considerable thought, by responding to basic stimuli. But this regularized capability for adequate performance is purchased at the price of standardization. If the SOPs are appropriate, average performance, i.e., performance averaged over the range of cases, is better than it would be if each instance were approached individually (given fixed talent, timing, and resource constraints). But specific instances, particularly critical instances that typically do not have "standard" characteristics, are often handled sluggishly or inappropriately.

2. A program, i.e., a complex action chosen from a short list of programs in a repertoire, is rarely tailored to the specific situation in which it is executed. Rather, the program is (at best) the most appropriate of the programs in a previously developed repertoire.

3. Since repertoires are developed by parochial organizations for standard scenarios defined by that organization, programs available for dealing with a particular situation are often ill-suited.

B. *Limited Flexibility and Incremental Change.* Major lines of organizational action are straight, i.e., behavior at one time is marginally different from that behavior at $t - 1$. Simple-minded predictions work best: Behavior at $t + 1$ will be marginally different from behavior at the present time.

1. Organizational budgets change incrementally—both with respect to totals and with respect to intra-organizational splits. Though organizations could divide the money available each year by carving up the pie anew (in the light of changes in objectives or environment), in practice, organizations take last year's budget as a base and adjust incrementally. Predictions that require large budgetary shifts in a single year between organizations or between units within an organization should be hedged.

2. Once undertaken, an organizational investment is not dropped at the point where "objective" costs outweigh benefits. Organizational stakes in adopted projects carry them quite beyond the loss point.

C. *Administrative Feasibility.* Adequate explanation, analysis, and prediction must include administrative feasibility as a major dimension. A considerable gap separates what leaders choose (or might rationally have chosen) and what organizations implement.

1. Organizations are blunt instruments. Projects that require several organizations to act with high degrees of precision and coordination are not likely to succeed.

2. Projects that demand that existing organizational units depart from their accustomed functions and perform previously unprogrammed tasks are rarely accomplished in their designed form.

3. Government leaders can expect that each organization will do its "part" in terms of what the organization knows how to do.

4. Government leaders can expect incomplete and distorted information from each organization concerning its part of the problem.

5. Where an assigned piece of a problem is contrary to the existing goals of an organization, resistance to implementation of that piece will be encountered.

V. Specific Propositions

1. *Deterrence.* The probability of nuclear attack is less sensitive to balance and imbalance, or stability and instability (as these concepts are employed by Model I strategists) than it is to a number of organizational factors. Except for the special case in which the Soviet Union acquires a credible capability to destroy the U.S. with a disarming blow, U.S. supe-

riority or inferiority affects the probability of a nuclear attack less than do a number of organizational factors.

First, if a nuclear attack occurs, it will result from organizational activity: the firing of rockets by members of a missile group. The enemy's *control system*, i.e., physical mechanisms and standard procedures which determine who can launch rockets when, is critical. Second, the enemy's programs for bringing his strategic forces to *alert status* determine probabilities of accidental firing and momentum. At the outbreak of World War I, if the Russian Tsar had understood the organizational processes which his order of full mobilization triggered, he would have realized that he had chosen war. Third, organizational repertoires fix the range of effective choice open to enemy leaders. The menu available to Tsar Nicholas in 1914 has two entrees: full mobilization and no mobilization. Partial mobilization was not an organizational option. Fourth, since organizational routines set the chessboard, the training and deployment of troops and nuclear weapons is crucial. Given that the outbreak of hostilities in Berlin is more probable than most scenarios for nuclear war, facts about deployment, training, and tactical nuclear equipment of Soviet troops stationed in East Germany—which will influence the face of the issue seen by Soviet leaders at the outbreak of hostilities and the manner in which choice is implemented—are as critical as the question of "balance."

2. *Soviet Force Posture.* Soviet force posture, i.e., the fact that certain weapons rather than others are procured and deployed, is determined by organizational factors such as the goals and procedures of existing military services and the goals and processes of research and design labs, within budgetary constraints that emerge from the government leader's choices. The frailty of the Soviet Air Force within the Soviet military establishment seems to have been a crucial element in the Soviet failure to acquire a large bomber force in the 1950s (thereby faulting American intelligence predictions of a "bomber gap"). The fact that missiles were controlled until 1960 in the Soviet Union by the Soviet Ground Forces, whose goals and procedures reflected no interest in an intercontinental mission, was not irrelevant to the slow Soviet buildup of ICBMs (thereby faulting U.S. intelligence predictions of a "missile gap"). These organizational factors (Soviet Ground Forces' control of missiles and that service's fixation with European scenarios) make the Soviet deployment of so many MRBMs that European targets could be destroyed three times over, more understandable. Recent weapon developmemts, e.g., the testing of a Fractional Orbital Bombardment System (FOBS) and multiple warheads for the SS–9, very likely reflect the activity and interests of a cluster of Soviet research and development organizations, rather than a decision by Soviet leaders to acquire a first strike weapon system. Careful attention to the organizational components of the Soviet military establishment (Strategic Rocket Forces, Navy, Air Force, Ground Forces, and National Air Defense), the missions and weapons systems to which each

component is wedded (an independent weapon system assists survival as an independent service), and existing budgetary splits (which probably are relatively stable in the Soviet Union as they tend to be everywhere) offer potential improvements in medium and longer term predictions.

The U.S. Blockade of Cuba: A Second Cut

Organizational Intelligence. At 7:00 P.M. on October 22, 1962, President Kennedy disclosed the American discovery of the presence of Soviet strategic missiles in Cuba, declared a "strict quarantine on all offensive military equipment under shipment to Cuba," and demanded that "Chairman Khrushchev halt and eliminate this clandestine, reckless, and provocative threat to world peace."[46] This decision was reached at the pinnacle of the U.S. Government after a critical week of deliberation. What initiated that precious week were photographs of Soviet missile sites in Cuba taken on October 14. These pictures might not have been taken until a week later. In that case, the President speculated, "I don't think probably we would have chosen as prudently as we finally did."[47] U.S. leaders might have received this information three weeks earlier— if a U-2 had flown over San Cristobal in the last week of September.[48] What determined the context in which American leaders came to choose the blockade was the discovery of missiles on October 14.

There has been considerable debate over alleged American "intelligence failures" in the Cuban missile crisis.[49] But what both critics and defenders have neglected is the fact that the discovery took place on October 14, rather than three weeks earlier or a week later, as a consequence of the established routines and procedures of the organizations which constitute the U.S. intelligence community. These organizations were neither more nor less successful than they had been the previous month or were to be in the months to follow.[50]

The notorious "September estimate," approved by the United States Intelligence Board (USIB) on September 19, concluded that the Soviet Union would not introduce offensive missiles into Cuba.[51] No U-2 flight was directed over the western end of Cuba (after September 5) before October 4.[52] No U-2 flew over the western end of Cuba until the flight that discovered the Soviet missiles on October 14.[53] Can these "failures" be accounted for in organizational terms?

On September 19 when USIB met to consider the question of Cuba, the "system" contained the following information: (1) shipping intelligence had noted the arrival in Cuba of two large-hatch Soviet lumber ships, which were riding high in the water; (2) refugee reports of countless sightings of missiles, but also a report that Castro's private pilot, after a night of drinking in Havana, had boasted: "We will fight to the death and perhaps we can win because we have everything, including atomic weapons"; (3) a sighting by a CIA agent of the rear profile of a strategic missile; (4) U–2 photos produced by flights of August 29, September 5 and 17 showing the construction of a number of SAM sites and other defensive missiles.[54] Not all of this information was on the desk of the estimators, however. Shipping intelligence experts noted the fact that large-hatch ships were riding high in the water and spelled out the inference: the ships must be carrying "space consuming" cargo.[55] These facts were carefully included in the catalogue of intelligence concerning shipping. For experts sensitive to the Soviets' shortage of ships, however, these facts carried no special signal. The refugee report of Castro's private pilot's remark had been received at Opa Locka, Florida, along with vast reams of inaccurate reports generated by the refugee community. This report and a thousand others had to be checked and compared before being sent to Washington. The two weeks required for initial processing could have been shortened by a large increase in resources, but the yield of this source was already quite marginal. The CIA agent's sighting of the rear profile of a strategic missile had occurred on September 12: transmission time from agent sighting to arrival in Washington typically took 9 to 12 days. Shortening this transmission time would impose severe cost in terms of danger to sub-agents, agents, and communication networks.

On the information available, the intelligence chiefs who predicted that the Soviet Union would not introduce offensive missiles into Cuba made a reasonable and defensible judgment.[56] Moreover, in the light of the fact that these organizations were gathering intelligence not only about Cuba but about potential occurrences in all parts of the world, the informational base available to the estimators involved nothing out of the ordinary. Nor, from an organizational perspective, is there anything startling about the gradual accumulation of evidence that led to the formulation of the hypothesis that the Soviets were installing missiles in Cuba and the decision on October 4 to direct a special flight over western Cuba.

The ten-day delay between that decision and the flight is another organizational story.[57] At the October 4 meeting, the Defense Department took the opportunity to raise an issue important to its concerns. Given the increased danger that a U–2 would be downed, it would be better if the pilot were an officer in uniform rather than a CIA agent. Thus the Air Force should assume responsibility for U–2 flights over Cuba. To the contrary, the CIA argued that this was an intelligence operation and thus within the CIA's jurisdiction. Moreover, CIA U–2's had been modified in certain ways which gave them advantages over Air Force U–2's in averting Soviet SAM's. Five days passed while the State Department pressed for less risky alternatives such as drones and the Air Force (in Department of Defense guise) and CIA engaged in territorial disputes. On October 9 a flight plan over San Cristobal was approved by COMOR, but to the CIA's dismay, Air Force pilots rather than CIA agents would take charge of the mission. At this point details become sketchy, but several members of the intelligence community have speculated that an Air Force pilot in an Air Force U–2 attempted a high altitude overflight on October 9 that "flamed out", i.e., lost power, and thus had to descend in order to restart its engine. A second round between Air Force and CIA followed, as a result of which Air Force pilots were trained to fly CIA U–2's. A successful overflight took place on October 14.

This ten-day delay constitutes some form of "failure." In the face of well-founded suspicions concerning offensive Soviet missiles in Cuba that posed a critical threat to the United States' most vital interest, squabbling between organizations whose job it is to produce this information seems entirely inappropriate. But for each of these organizations, the question involved the issue: *"Whose* job was it to be?" Moreover, the issue was not simply, which organization would control U–2 flights over Cuba, but rather the broader issue of ownership of U–2 intelligence activities—a very long standing territorial dispute. Thus though this delay was in one sense a "failure," it was also a nearly inevitable consequence of two facts: many jobs do not fall neatly into precisely defined organizational jurisdictions; and vigorous organizations are imperialistic.

Organizational Options. Deliberations of leaders in ExCom meetings produced broad outlines of alternatives. Details of these alternatives and blueprints for their implementation had to be specified by the organizations that would perform these tasks. These organizational outputs answered the question: What, specifically, *could* be done?

Discussion in the ExCom quickly narrowed the live options to two: an air strike and a blockade. The choice of the blockade instead of the air strike turned on two points: (1) the argument from morality and tradition that the United States could not perpetrate a "Pearl Harbor in reverse"; (2) the belief that a "surgical" air strike was impossible.[58] Whether the United States *might* strike first was a question not of capability but of morality. Whether the United States *could* perform the surgical strike was a factual question concerning capabilities. The majority of the members of the ExCom, including the President, initially preferred the air strike.[59] What effectively foreclosed this option, however, was the fact that the air strike they wanted could not be chosen with high confidence of success.[60] After having tentatively chosen the course of prudence—given that the surgical air strike was not an option—Kennedy reconsidered. On Sunday morning, October 21, he called the Air Force experts to a special meeting in his living quarters where he probed once more for the option of a *"surgical"* air strike.[61] General Walter C. Sweeny, Commander of Tactical Air Forces, asserted again that the Air Force could guarantee no higher than ninety percent effectiveness in a surgical air strike.[62] That "fact" was false.

The air strike alternative provides a classic case of military estimates. One of the alternatives outlined by the ExCom was named "air strike." Specification of the details of this alternative was delegated to the Air Force. Starting from an existing plan for massive U.S. military action against Cuba (prepared for contingencies like a response to a Soviet Berlin grab), Air Force estimators produced an attack to guarantee success.[63] This plan called for extensive bombardment of all missile sites, storage depots, airports, and in deference to the Navy, the artillery batteries opposite the naval base at Guantanamo.[64] Members of the ExCom repeatedly expressed bewilderment at military estimates of the number of sorties required, likely casualties, and collateral damage. But the "surgical" air strike that the political leaders had in mind was never carefully examined during the first week of the crisis. Rather, this option was simply excluded on the grounds that since the Soviet MRBM's in Cuba were classified "mobile" in U.S. manuals, extensive bombing was required. During the second week of the crisis, careful examination revealed that the missiles were mobile, in the sense that small houses are mobile: that is, they could be moved and reassembled in 6 days. After the missiles were reclassified "movable" and detailed plans for surgical air strikes specified, this action was added to the list of live options for the end of the second week.

Organizational Implementation. ExCom members separated several types of blockade: offensive weapons only, all armaments, and all strategic goods including POL (petroleum, oil and lubricants). But the "details" of the operation were left to the Navy. Before the President announced the blockade on Monday evening, the first stage of the Navy's blueprint was in motion, and a problem loomed on the horizon.[65] The Navy had a detailed plan for the blockade. The President had several less precise but equally determined notions concerning what should be done, when and how. For the Navy the issue was one of effective implementation of the Navy's blockade—without the meddling and interference of political leaders. For the President, the problem was to pace and manage events in such a way that the Soviet leaders would have time to see, think, and blink.

A careful reading of available sources uncovers an instructive incident. On Tuesday, the British Ambassador, Ormsby–Gore, after having attended a briefing on the details of the blockade, suggested to the President that the plan for intercepting Soviet ships far out of reach of Cuban jets did not facilitate Khrushchev's hard decision.[66] Why not make the interception much closer to Cuba and thus give the Russian leader more time? According to the public account and the recollection of a number of individuals involved, Kennedy "agreed immediately, called McNamara, and over emotional Navy protest, issued the appropriate instructions."[67] As Sorensen records, "in a sharp clash with the Navy, he made certain his will prevailed."[68] The Navy's plan for the blockade was thus changed by drawing the blockade much closer to Cuba.

A serious organizational orientation makes one suspicious of this account. More careful examination of the available evidence confirms these suspicions, though alternative accounts must be somewhat speculative. According to the public chronology, a quarantine drawn close to

Cuba became effective on Wednesday morning, the first Soviet ship was contacted on Thursday morning, and the first boarding of a ship occurred on Friday. According to the statement by the Department of Defense, boarding of the *Marcula* by a party from the *John R. Pierce* "took place at 7:50 A.M., E.D.T., 180 miles northeast of Nassau."[69] The *Marcula* had been trailed since about 10:30 the previous evening.[70] Simple calculations suggest that the *Pierce* must have been stationed along the Navy's original arc which extended 500 miles out to sea from Cape Magsi, Cuba's eastern most tip.[71] The blockade line was *not* moved as the President ordered, and the accounts report.

What happened is not entirely clear. One can be certain, however, that Soviet ships passed through the line along which American destroyers had posted themselves before the official "first contact" with the Soviet ship. On October 26 a Soviet tanker arrived in Havana and was honored by a dockside rally for "running the blockade." Photographs of this vessel show the name *Vinnitsa* on the side of the vessel in Cyrillic letters.[72] But according to the official U.S. position, the first tanker to pass through the blockade was the *Bucharest,* which was hailed by the Navy on the morning of October 25. Again simple mathematical calculation excludes the possibility of the *Bucharest* and the *Vinnitsa* were the same ship. It seems probable that the Navy's resistance to the President's order that the blockade be drawn in closer to Cuba forced him to allow one or several Soviet ships to pass through the blockade after it was officially operative.[73]

This attempt to leash the Navy's blockade had a price. On Wednesday morning, October 24, what the President had been awaiting occurred. The 18 dry cargo ships heading towards the quarantine stopped dead in the water. This was the occasion of Dean Rusk's remark, "We are eyeball to eyeball and I think the other fellow just blinked."[74] But the Navy had another interpretation. The ships had simply stopped to pick up Soviet submarine escorts. The President became quite concerned lest the Navy—already riled because of Presidential meddling in its affairs—blunder into an incident. Sensing the President's fears, McNamara became suspicious of the Navy's procedures and routines for making the first interception. Calling on the Chief of Naval Operations in the Navy's inner sactum, the Navy Flag Plot, McNamara put his questions harshly.[75] Who would make the first interception? Were Russian-speaking officers on board? How would submarines be dealt with? At one point McNamara asked Anderson what he would do if a Soviet ship's captain refused to answer questions about his cargo. Picking up the Manual of Navy Regulations the Navy man waved it in McNamara's face and shouted, "It's all in there." To which McNamara replied, "I don't give a damn what John Paul Jones would have done; I want to know what you are going to do now."[76] The encounter ended on Anderson's remark: "Now, Mr. Secretary, if you and your Deputy will go back to your office the Navy will run the blockade."[77]

MODEL III: BUREAUCRATIC POLITICS

The leaders who sit on top of organizations are not a monolithic group. Rather, each is, in his own right, a player in a central, competitive game. The name of the game is bureaucratic politics: bargaining along regularized channels among players positioned hierarchically within the government. Government behavior can thus be understood according to the third conceptual model not as organizational outputs, but as outcomes of bargaining games. In contrast with Model I, the bureaucratic politics model sees no unitary actor but rather many actors as players, who focus not on a single strategic issue but on many diverse intra-national problems as well, in terms of no consistent set of strategic objectives but rather according to various conceptions of national, organizational, and personal goals, making government decisions not by rational choice but by the pulling and hauling that is politics.

The apparatus of each national government constitutes a complex arena for the intra-national game. Political leaders at the top of this apparatus plus the men who occupy positions on top of the critical organizations form the circle of central players. Ascendancy to this circle assures some independent standing. The necessary decentralization of decisions required for action on the broad range of foreign policy problems guarantees that each player has considerable discretion. Thus power is shared.

The nature of problems of foreign policy permits fundamental disagreement among reasonable men concerning what ought to be done. Analyses yield conflicting recommendations. Separate responsibilities laid on the shoulders of individual personalities encourage differences in perceptions and priorities. But the issues are of first order importance. What the nation does really matters. A wrong choice could mean irreparable damage. Thus responsible men are obliged to fight for what they are convinced is right.

Men share power. Men differ concerning what must be done. The differences matter. This milieu necessitates that policy be resolved by politics. What the nation does is sometimes the result of the triumph of one group over others. More often, however, different groups pulling in different directions yield a resultant distinct from what anyone intended. What moves the chess pieces is not simply the reasons which support a course of action, nor the routines of organizations which enact an alternative, but the power and skill of proponents and opponents of the action in question.

This characterization captures the thrust of the bureaucratic politics orientation. If problems of foreign policy arose as discreet issues, and decisions were determined one game at a time, this account would suffice. But most "issues," e.g., Vietnam or the proliferation of nuclear weapons, emerge piecemeal, over time, one lump in one context, a second in another. Hundreds of issues compete for players' attention every day. Each player is forced to fix upon his issues for that day, fight them on their own terms, and rush on to the next. Thus the character of emerging issues and the pace at which the game is played converge to yield government "decisions" and "actions" as collages. Choices by one player, outcomes of minor games, outcomes of central games, and "foul-ups"—these pieces, when stuck to the same canvas, constitute government behavior relevant to an issue.

The concept of national security policy as political outcome contradicts both public imagery and academic orthodoxy. Issues vital to national security, it is said, are too important to be settled by political games. They must be "above" politics. To accuse someone of "playing politics with national security" is a most serious charge. What public conviction demands, the academic penchant for intellectual elegance reinforces. Internal politics is messy; moreover, according to prevailing doctrine, politicking lacks intellectual content. As such, it constitutes gossip for journalists rather than a subject for serious investigation. Occasional memoirs, anecdotes in historical accounts, and several detailed case studies to the contrary, most of the literature of foreign policy avoids bureaucratic politics. The gap between academic literature and the experience of participants in government is nowhere wider than at this point.

Bureaucratic Politics Paradigm[78]

I. Basic Unit of Analysis: Policy As Political Outcome

The decisions and actions of governments are essentially intra-national political outcomes: outcomes in the sense that what happens is not chosen as a solution to a problem but rather results from compromise, coalition, competition, and confusion among government officials who see different faces of an issue; political in the sense that the activity from which the outcomes emerge is best characterized as bargaining. Following Wittgenstein's use of the concept of a "game," national behavior in international affairs can be conceived as outcomes of intricate and subtle, simultaneous, overlapping games among players located in positions, the hierarchical arrangement of which constitutes the government.[79] These games proceed neither at random nor at leisure. Regular channels structure the game. Deadlines force issues to the attention of busy players. The moves in the chess game are thus to be explained in terms of the bargaining among players with separate and unequal power over particular pieces and with separable objectives in distinguishable subgames.

II. Organizing Concepts

A. *Players in Positions.* The actor is neither a unitary nation, nor a conglomerate of organizations, but rather a number of individual players.

Groups of these players constitute the agent for particular government decisions and actions. Players are men in jobs.

Individuals become players in the national security policy game by occupying a critical position in an administration. For example, in the U.S. government the players include "Chiefs": the President, Secretaries of State, Defense, and Treasury, Director of the CIA, Joint Chiefs of Staff, and, since 1961, the Special Assistant for National Security Affairs;[80] "Staffers": the immediate staff of each Chief; "Indians": the political appointees and permanent government officials within each of the departments and agencies; and "Ad Hoc Players": actors in the wider government game (especially "Congressional Influentials"), members of the press, spokesmen for important interest groups (especially the "bipartisan foreign policy establishment" in and out of Congress), and surrogates for each of these groups. Other members of the Congress, press, interest groups, and public form concentric circles around the central arena—circles which demarcate the permissive limits within which the game is played.

Positions define what players both may and must do. The advantages and handicaps with which each player can enter and play in various games stems from his position. So does a cluster of obligations for the performance of certain tasks. The two sides of this coin are illustrated by the position of the modern Secretary of State. First, in form and usually in fact, he is the primary repository of political judgment on the political-military issues that are the stuff of contemporary foreign policy; consequently, he is a senior personal advisor to the President. Second, he is the colleague of the President's other senior advisers on the problems of foreign policy, the Secretaries of Defense and Treasury, and the Special Assistant for National Security Affairs. Third, he is the ranking U.S. diplomat for serious negotiation. Fourth, he serves as an Administration voice to Congress, the country, and the world. Finally, he is "Mr. State Department" or "Mr. Foreign Office," "leader of officials, spokesman for their causes, guardian of their interests, judge of their disputes, superintendent of their work, master of their careers."[81] But he is not first one, and then the other. All of these obligations are his simultaneously. His performance in one affects his credit and power in the others. The perspective stemming from the daily work which he must oversee—the cable traffic by which his department maintains relations with other foreign offices—conflicts with the President's requirement that he serve as a generalist and coordinator of contrasting perspectives. The necessity that he be close to the President restricts the extent to which, and the force with which, he can front for his department. When he defers to the Secretary of Defense rather than fighting for his department's position— as he often must—he strains the loyalty of his officialdom. The Secretary's resolution of these conflicts depends not only upon the position, but also upon the player who occupies the position.

For players are also people. Men's metabolisms differ. The core of the bureaucratic politics mix is personality. How each man manages to stand the heat in his kitchen, each player's basic operating style, and the complementarity or contradiction among personalities and styles in the inner circles are irreducible pieces of the policy blend. Moreover, each person comes to his position with baggage in tow, including sensitivities to certain issues, commitments to various programs, and personal standing and debts with groups in the society.

B. *Parochial Priorities, Perceptions and Issues.* Answers to the questions: "What is the issue?" and "What must be done?" are colored by the position from which the questions are considered. For the factors which encourage organizational parochialism also influence the players who occupy positions on top of (or within) these organizations. To motivate members of his organization, a player must be sensitive to the organization's orientation. The games into which the player can enter and the advantages with which he plays enhance these pressures. Thus propensities of perception stemming from position permit reliable prediction about a player's stances in many cases. But these propensities are filtered through the baggage which players bring to positions. Sensitivity to both the pressures and the baggage is thus required for many predictions.

C. *Interests, Stakes, and Power.* Games are played to determine outcomes. But outcomes advance and impede each player's conception of the national interest, specific programs to which he is committed, the welfare of his friends, and his personal interests. These overlapping interests constitute the stakes for which games are played. Each player's ability to play successfully depends upon his power. Power, i.e., effective influence on policy outcomes, is an elusive blend of at least three elements: bargaining advantages (drawn from formal authority and obligations, institutional backing, constituents, expertise, and status), skill and will in using bargaining advantages, and other players' perceptions of the first two ingredients. Power wisely invested yields an enhanced reputation for effectiveness. Unsuccessful investment depletes both the stock of capital and the reputation. Thus each player must pick the issues on which he can play with a reasonable probability of success. But no player's power is sufficient to guarantee satisfactory outcomes. Each player's needs and fears run to many other players. What ensues is the most intricate and subtle of games known to man.

D. *The Problem and the Problems.* "Solutions" to strategic problems are not derived by detached analysts focusing cooly on *the* problem. Instead, deadlines and events raise issues in games, and demand decisions of busy players in contexts that influence the face the issue wears. The problems for the players are both narrower and broader than *the* strategic problem. For each player focuses not on the total strategic problem but rather on the decision that must be made now. But each decision has critical consequences not only for the strategic problem but for each player's organizational, reputational, and personal stakes. Thus the gap between the problems the player was solving and the problem upon which the analyst focuses is often very wide.

E. *Action-Channels.* Bargaining games do not proceed randomly. Action-channels, i.e., regularized ways of producing action concerning types of issues, structure the game by pre-selecting the major players, determining their points of entrance into the game, and distributing particular advantages and disadvantages for each game. Most critically, channels determine "who's got the action," that is, which department's Indians actually do whatever is chosen. Weapon procurement decisions are made within the annual budgeting process; embassies' demands for action cables are answered according to routines of consultation and clearance from State to Defense and White House; requests for instructions from military groups (concerning assistance all the time, concerning operations during war) are composed by the military in consultation with the Office of the Secretary of Defense, State, and White House; crisis responses are debated among White House, State, Defense, CIA, and Ad Hoc players; major political speeches, especially by the President but also by other Chiefs, are cleared through established channels.

F. *Action As Politics.* Government decisions are made and government actions emerge neither as the calculated choice of a unified group, nor as a formal summary of leaders' preferences. Rather the context of shared power but separate judgments concerning important choices, determines that politics is the mechanism of choice. Note the *environment* in which the game is played: inordinate uncertainty about what must be done, the necessity that something be done, and crucial consequences of whatever is done. These features force responsible men to become active players. The *pace of the game*—hundreds of issues, numerous games, and multiple channels—compels players to fight to "get other's attention," to make them "see the facts," to assure that they "take the time to think seriously about the broader issue." The *structure of the game*—power shared by individuals with separate responsibilities—validates each player's feeling that "others don't see my problem," and "others must be persuaded to look at the issue from a less parochial perspective." The *rules of the game*—he who hesitates loses his chance to play at that point, and he who is uncertain about his recommendation is overpowered by others who are sure—pressures players to come down on one side of a 51–49 issue and play. The *rewards of the game*—effectiveness, i.e., impact on outcomes, as the immediate measure of performance—encourages hard play. Thus, most players come to fight to "make the government do what is right." The strategies and tactics employed are quite similar to those formalized by theorists of international relations.

G. *Streams of Outcomes.* Important government decisions or actions emerge as collages composed of individual acts, outcomes of minor and major games, and foul-ups. Outcomes which could never have been chosen by an actor and would never have emerged from bargaining in a single game over the issue are fabricated piece by piece. Understanding of the outcome requires that it be disaggregated.

III. Dominant Inference Pattern

If a nation performed an action, that action was the *outcome* of bargaining among individuals and groups within the government. That outcome included *results* achieved by groups committed to a decision or action, *resultants* which emerged from bargaining among groups with quite different positions and *foul-ups*. Model III's explanatory power is achieved by revealing the pulling and hauling of various players, with different perceptions and priorities, focusing on separate problems, which yielded the outcomes that constitute the action in question.

IV. General Propositions

1. *Action and Intention.* Action does not presuppose intention. The sum of behavior of representatives of a government relevant to an issue was rarely intended by any individual or group. Rather separate individuals with different intentions contributed pieces which compose an outcome distinct from what anyone would have chosen.
2. *Where you stand depends on where you sit.*[82] Horizontally, the diverse demands upon each player shape his priorities, perceptions, and issues. For large classes of issues, e.g., budgets and procurement decisions, the stance of a particular player can be predicted with high reliability from information concerning his seat. In the notorious B–36 controversy, no one was surprised by Admiral Radford's testimony that "the B–36 under any theory of war, is a bad gamble with national security," as opposed to Air Force Secretary Symington's claim that "a B–36 with an A-bomb can destroy distant objectives which might require ground armies years to take."[83]
3. *Chiefs and Indians.* The aphorism "where you stand depends on where you sit" has vertical as well as horizontal application. Vertically, the demands upon the President, Chiefs, Staffers, and Indians are quite distinct.

The foreign policy issues with which the President can deal are limited primarily by his crowded schedule: the necessity of dealing first with what comes next. His problem is to probe the special face worn by issues that come to his attention, to preserve his leeway until time has clarified the uncertainties, and to assess the relevant risks.

Foreign policy Chiefs deal most often with the hottest issue *de jour*, though they can get the attention of the President and other members of the government for other issues which they judge important. What they cannot guarantee is that "the President will pay the price" or that "the others will get on board." They must build a coalition of the relevant powers that be. They must "give the President confidence" in the right course of action.

Most problems are framed, alternatives specified, and proposals pushed, however, by Indians. Indians fight with Indians of other departments; for example, struggles between International Security Affairs of the Department of Defense and Political-Military of the State Department are a microcosm of the action at higher levels. But the Indian's major problem is how to get the *attention* of Chiefs, how to get an issue decided, how to get the government "to do what is right."

In policy making then, the issue looking *down* is options: how to preserve my leeway until time clarifies uncertainties. The issue looking *sideways* is commitment: how to get others committed to my coalition. The issue looking *upwards* is confidence: how to give the boss confidence in doing what must be done. To paraphrase one of Neustadt's assertions which can be applied down the length of the ladder, the essence of a responsible official's task is to induce others to see that what needs to be done is what their own appraisal of their own responsibilities requires them to do in their own interest.

V. Specific Propositions

a. *Deterrence.* The probability of nuclear attack depends primarily on the probability of attack emerging as an outcome of the bureaucratic politics of the attacking government. First, which players can decide to launch an attack? Whether the effective power over action is controlled by an individual, a minor game, or the central game is critical. Second, though Model I's confidence in nuclear deterrence stems from an assertion that, in the end, governments will not commit suicide, Model III recalls historical precedents. Admiral Yamamoto, who designed the Japanese attack on Pearl Harbor, estimated accurately: "In the first six months to a year of war against the U.S. and England I will run wild, and I will show you an uninterrupted succession of victories; I must also tell you that, should the war be prolonged for two or three years, I have no confidence in our ultimate victory."[84] But Japan attacked. Thus, three questions might be considered. One: could any member of the government solve his problem by attack? What patterns of bargaining could yield attack as an outcome? The major difference between a stable balance of terror and a questionable balance may simply be that in the first case most members of the government appreciate fully the consequences of attack and are thus on guard against the emergence of this outcome. Two: what stream of outcomes might lead to an attack? At what point in that stream is the potential attacker's politics? If members of the U.S. government had been sensitive to the stream of decisions from which the Japanese attack on Pearl Harbor emerged, they would have been aware of a considerable probability of that attack. Three: how might miscalculation and confusion generate foul-ups that yield attack as an outcome? For example, in a crisis or after the beginning of conventional war, what happens to the information available to, and the effective power of, members of the central game.

The U.S. Blockade of Cuba: A Third Cut

The Politics of Discovery. A series of overlapping bargaining games determined both the *date* of discovery of the Soviet missiles and the *impact* of this discovery on the Administration. An explanation of the politics of the discovery is consequently a considerable piece of the explanation of the U.S. blockade.

Cuba was the Kennedy Administration's "political Achilles' heel."[85] The months preceding the crisis were also months before the Congressional elections, and the Republican Senatorial and Congressional Campaign Committee had announced that Cuba would be "the dominant issue of the 1962 campaign."[86] What the administration billed as a "more positive and indirect approach of isolating Castro from developing, democratic Latin America," Senators Keating, Goldwater, Capehart, Thurmond, and others attacked as a "do-nothing" policy.[87] In statements on the floor of the House and Senate, campaign speeches across the country, and interviews and articles carried by national news media, Cuba—particularly the Soviet program of increased arms aid—served as a stick for stirring the domestic political scene.[88]

These attacks drew blood. Prudence demanded a vigorous reaction. The President decided to meet the issue head-on. The Administration mounted a forceful campaign of denial designed to discredit critics' claims. The President himself manned the front line of this offensive, though almost all Administration officials participated. In his news conference on August 19, President Kennedy attacked as "irresponsible" calls for an invasion of Cuba, stressing rather "the totality of our obligations" and promising to "watch what happens in Cuba with the closest attention."[89] On September 4, he issued a strong statement denying any provocative Soviet action in Cuba.[90] On September 13 he lashed out at "loose talk" calling for an invasion of Cuba.[91] The day before the flight of the U–2 which discovered the missiles, he campaigned in Capehart's Indiana against those "self-appointed generals and admirals who want to send someone else's sons to war."[92]

On Sunday, October 14, just as a U–2 was taking the first pictures of Soviet missiles, McGeorge Bundy was asserting:

> I *know* that there is no present evidence, and I think that there is no present likelihood that the Cuban government and the Soviet government would, in combination, attempt to install a major offensive capability.[93]

In this campaign to puncture the critics' charges, the Administration discovered that the public needed positive slogans. Thus, Kennedy fell into a tenuous semantic distinction between "offensive" and "defensive" weapons. This distinction originated in his September 4 statement that there was no evidence of "offensive ground to ground missiles" and warned "were it to be otherwise, the gravest issues would arise."[94] His September 13 statement turned on this distinction between "defensive" and "offensive" weapons and announced a firm commitment to action if the Soviet Union attempted to introduce the latter into Cuba.[95] Congressional committees elicited from administration officials testimony which read this distinction and the President's commitment into the *Congressional Record*.[96]

What the President least wanted to hear, the CIA was most hesitant to say plainly. On August 22 John McCone met privately with the President and voiced suspicions that the Soviets were preparing to introduce offensive missiles into Cuba.[97] Kennedy heard this as what it was: the suspicion of a hawk. McCone left Washington for a month's honeymoon on the Riviera. Fretting at Cap Ferrat, he bombarded his deputy, General Marshall Carter, with telegrams, but Carter, knowing that McCone had informed the President of his suspicions and received a cold reception, was reluctant to distribute these telegrams outside the CIA.[98] On September 9 a U–2 "on loan" to the Chinese Nationalists was downed over mainland China.[99] The Committee on Overhead Reconnaissance (COMOR) convened on September 10 with a sense of urgency.[100] Loss of another U–2 might incite world opinion to demand cancellation of U–2 flights. The President's campaign against those who asserted that the Soviets were acting provocatively in Cuba had begun. To risk downing a U–2 over Cuba was to risk chopping off the limb on which the President was sitting. That meeting decided to shy away from the western end of Cuba (where SAMs were becoming operational) and modify the flight pattern of the U–2s in order to reduce the probability that a U–2 would be lost.[101] USIB's unanimous approval of the September estimate reflects similar sensitivities. On September 13 the President had asserted that there were no Soviet offensive missiles in Cuba and committed his Administration to act if offensive missiles were discovered. Before Congressional committees, Administration officials were denying that there was any evidence whatever of offensive missiles in Cuba. The implications of a National Intelligence estimate which concluded that the Soviets were introducing offensive missiles into Cuba were not lost on the men who constituted America's highest intelligence assembly.

The October 4 COMOR decision to direct a flight over the western end of Cuba in effect "overturned" the September estimate, but without officially raising that issue. The decision represented McCone's victory for which he had lobbied with the President before the September 10 decision, in telegrams before the September 19 estimate, and in person after his return to Washington. Though the politics of the intelligence community is closely guarded, several pieces of the story can be told.[102] By September 27, Colonel Wright and others in DIA believed that the Soviet Union was placing missiles in the San Cristobal area.[103] This area was marked suspicious by the CIA on September 29 and certified top priority on October 3. By October 4 McCone had the evidence required to raise the issue officially. The members of COMOR heard McCone's argument, but were reluctant to make the hard decision he demanded.

The significant probability that a U–2 would be downed made overflight of western Cuba a matter of real concern.[104]

The Politics of Issues. The U–2 photographs presented incontrovertible evidence of Soviet offensive missiles in Cuba. This revelation fell upon politicized players in a complex context. As one high official recalled, Khrushchev had caught us "with our pants down." What each of the central participants saw, and what each did to cover both his own and the Administration's nakedness, created the spectrum of issues and answers.

At approximately 9:00 A.M., Tuesday morning, October 16, McGeorge Bundy went to the President's living quarters with the message: "Mr. President, there is now hard photographic evidence that the Russians have offensive missiles in Cuba."[105] Much has been made of Kennedy's "expression of surprise,"[106] but "surprise" fails to capture the character of his initial reaction. Rather, it was one of startled anger, most adequately conveyed by the exclamation: "He can't do that to *me!*"[107] In terms of the President's attention and priorities at that moment, Khrushchev had chosen the most unhelpful act of all. Kennedy had staked his full Presidential authority on the assertion that the Soviets would not place offensive weapons in Cuba. Moreover, Khrushchev had assured the President through the most direct and personal channels that he was aware of the President's domestic political problem and that nothing would be done to exacerbate this problem. The Chairman had *lied* to the President. Kennedy's initial reaction entailed action. The missiles must be removed.[108] The alternatives of "doing nothing" or "taking a diplomatic approach" could not have been less relevant to *his* problem.

These two tracks—doing nothing and taking a diplomatic approach—were the solutions advocated by two of his principal advisors. For Secretary of Defense McNamara, the missiles raised the spectre of nuclear war. He first framed the issue as a straightforward strategic problem. To understand the issue, one had to grasp two obvious but difficult points. First, the missiles represented an inevitable occurrence: narrowing of the missile gap. It simply happened sooner rather than later. Second, the United States could accept this occurrence since its consequences were minor: "seven-to-one missile 'superiority,' one-to-one missile 'equality,' one-to-seven missile 'inferiority'—the three postures are identical." McNamara's statement of this argument at the first meeting of the ExCom was summed up in the phrase, "a missile is a missile."[109] "It makes no great difference," he maintained, "whether you are killed by a missile from the Soviet Union or Cuba."[110] The implication was clear. The United State should not initiate a crisis with the Soviet Union, risking a significant probability of nuclear war over an occurrence which had such small strategic implications.

The perceptions of McGeorge Bundy, the President's Assistant for National Security Affairs, are the most difficult of all to reconstruct. There is no question that he initially argued for a diplomatic track.[111] But was Bundy laboring under his acknowledged burden of responsibility in Cuba I? Or was he playing the role of devil's advocate in order to make the President probe his own initial reaction and consider other options?

The President's brother, Robert Kennedy, saw most clearly the political wall against which Khrushchev had backed the President. But he, like McNamara, saw the prospect of nuclear doom. Was Khrushchev going to force the President to an insane act? At the first meeting of the ExCom, he scribbled a note, "Now I know how Tojo felt when he was planning Pearl Harbor."[112] From the outset he searched for an alternative that would prevent the air strike.

The initial reaction of Theodore Sorensen, the President's Special Counsel and "alter ego," fell somewhere between that of the President and his brother. Like the President, Sorensen felt the poignancy of betrayal. If the President had been the architect of the policy which the missiles punctured, Sorensen was the draftsman. Khrushchev's deceitful move demanded a strong counter-move. But like Robert Kennedy, Sorensen feared lest the shock and disgrace lead to disaster.

To the Joint Chiefs of Staff the issue was clear. *Now* was the time to do the job for which they had prepared contingency plans. Cuba I had been badly done; Cuba II would not be. The missiles provided the *occasion* to deal with the issue: cleansing the Western Hemisphere of Castro's Communism. As the President recalled on the day the crisis ended, "An invasion would have been a mistake—a wrong use of our power. But the military are mad. They wanted to do this. It's lucky for us that we have McNamara over there."[113]

McCone's perceptions flowed from his confirmed prediction. As the Cassandra of the incident, he argued forcefully that the Soviets had installed the missiles in a daring political probe which the United States must meet with force. The time for an air strike was now.[114]

The Politics of Choice. The process by which the blockade emerged is a story of the most subtle and intricate probing, pulling, and hauling; leading, guiding, and spurring. Reconstruction of this process can only be tentative. Initially the President and most of his advisers wanted the clean, surgical air strike. On the first day of the crisis, when informing Stevenson of the missiles, the President mentioned only two alternatives: "I suppose the alternatives are to go in by air and wipe them out, or to take other steps to render them inoperable."[115] At the end of the week a sizeable minority still favored an air strike. As Robert Kennedy recalled: "The fourteen people involved were very significant. . . . If six of them had been President of the U.S., I think that the world might have been blown up."[116] What prevented the air strike was a fortuitous coincidence of a number of factors—the absence of any one of which might have permitted that option to prevail.

First, McNamara's vision of holocaust set him firmly against the air strike. His initial attempt to frame the issue in strategic terms struck Kennedy as particularly inappropriate. Once McNamara realized that the name of the game was a strong response, however, he and his deputy Gilpatric chose the blockade as a fallback. When the Secretary of Defense—whose department had the action, whose reputation in the Cabinet was unequaled, in whom the President demonstrated full confidence—marshalled the arguments for the blockade and refused to be moved, the blockade became a formidable alternative.

Second, Robert Kennedy—the President's closest confidant—was unwilling to see his brother become a "Tojo." His arguments against the air strike on moral grounds struck a chord in the President. Moreover, once his brother had stated these arguments so forcefully, the President could not have chosen his initially preferred course without, in effect, agreeing to become what RFK had condemned.

The President learned of the missiles on Tuesday morning. On Wednesday morning, in order to mask our discovery from the Russians, the President flew to Connecticut to keep a campaign commitment, leaving RFK as the unofficial chairman of the group. By the time the President returned on Wednesday evening, a critical third piece had been added to the picture. McNamara had presented his argument for the blockade. Robert Kennedy and Sorensen had joined McNamara. A powerful coalition of the advisors in whom the President had the greatest confidence, and with whom his style was most compatible, had emerged.

Fourth, the coalition that had formed behind the President's initial preference gave him reason to pause. *Who* supported the air strike—the Chiefs, McCone, Rusk, Nitze, and Acheson—as much as *how* they supported it, counted. Fifth, a piece of inaccurate information, which no one probed, permitted the blockade advocates to fuel (potential) uncertainties in the President's mind. When the President returned to Washington Wednesday evening, RFK and Sorensen met him at the airport. Sorensen gave the President a four-page memorandum outlining the areas of agreement and disagreement. The strongest argument was that the air strike simply could not be surgical.[117] After a day of prodding and questioning, the Air Force had asserted that it could not guarantee the success of a surgical air strike limited to the missiles alone.

Thursday evening, the President convened the ExCom at the White House. He declared his tentative choice of the blockade and directed that preparations be made to put it into effect by Monday morning.[118] Though he raised a question about the possibility of a surgical air strike subsequently, he seems to have accepted the experts' opinion that this was no live option.[119] (Acceptance of this estimate suggests that he may have learned the lesson of the Bay of Pigs—"Never rely on experts"— less well than he supposed.)[120] But this information was incorrect. That no one probed this estimate during the first week of the crisis poses an interesting question for further investigation.

A coalition, including the President, thus emerged from the President's initial decision that something had to be done; McNamara, Robert Kennedy, and Sorensen's resistance to the air strike; incompatibility between the President and the air strike advocates; and an inaccurate piece of information.[121]

CONCLUSION

This essay has obviously bitten off more than it has chewed. For further developments and synthesis of these arguments the reader is referred to the larger study.[122] In spite of the limits of space, however, it would be inappropriate to stop without spelling out several implications of the argument and addressing the questions of relations among the models and extensions of them to activity beyond explanation.

At a minimum, the intended implications of the argument presented here are four. First, formulation of alternative frames of reference and demonstration that different analysts, relying predominantly on different models, produce quite different explanations should encourage the analyst's self-consciousness about the nets he employs. The effect of these "spectacles" in sensitizing him to particular aspects of what is going on—framing the puzzle in one way rather than another, encouraging him to examine the problem in terms of certain categories rather than others, directing him to particular kinds of evidence, and relieving puzzlement by one procedure rather than another—must be recognized and explored.

Second, the argument implies a position on the problem of "the state of the art." While accepting the commonplace characterization of the present condition of foreign policy analysis—personalistic, non-cumulative, and sometimes insightful—this essay rejects both the counsel of despair's justification of this condition as a consequence of the character of the enterprise, and the "new frontiersmen's" demand for a priori theorizing on the frontiers and ad hoc appropriation of "new techniques."[123] What is required as a first step is non-casual examination of the present product: inspection of existing explanations, articulation of the conceptual models employed in producing them, formulation of the propositions relied upon, specification of the logic of the various intellectual enterprises, and reflection on the questions being asked. Though it is difficult to overemphasize the need for more systematic processing of more data, these preliminary matters of formulating questions with clarity and sensitivity to categories and assumptions so that fruitful acquisition of large quantities of data is possible are still a major hurdle in considering most important problems.

Third, the preliminary, partial paradigms presented here provide a basis for serious reexamination of many problems of foreign and military policy. Model II and Model III cuts at problems typically treated in Model I terms can permit significant improvements in explanation and prediction.[124] Full Model II and III analyses require large amounts of information. But even in cases where the information base is severely limited, improvements are possible. Consider the problem of predicting Soviet strategic forces. In the mid-1950s, Model I style calculations led to predictions that the Soviets would rapidly deploy large numbers of long-range bombers. From a Model II perspective, both the frailty of the Air Force within the Soviet military establishment and the budgetary implications of such a buildup, would have led analysts to hedge this prediction. Moreover, Model II would have pointed to a sure, visible indicator of such a buildup: noisy struggles among the Services over major budgetary shifts. In the late 1950s and early 1960s, Model I calculations led to the prediction of immediate, massive Soviet deployment of ICBMs. Again, a Model II cut would have reduced this number because, in the earlier period, strategic rockets were controlled by the Soviet Ground Forces rather than an independent Service, and in the later period, this would have necessitated massive shifts in budgetary splits. Today, Model I considerations lead many analysts both to recommend that an agreement not to deploy ABMs be a major American objective in upcoming strategic negotiations with the USSR, and to predict success. From a Model II vantage point, the existence of an ongoing Soviet ABM program, the strength of the organization (National Air Defense) that controls ABMs, and the fact that an agreement to stop ABM deployment would force the virtual dismantling of this organization, make a viable agreement of this sort much less likely. A Model III cut suggests that (a) there must be significant differences among perceptions and priorities of Soviet leaders over strategic negotiations, (b) any agreement will affect some players' power bases, and (c) agreements that do not require extensive cuts in the sources of some major players' power will prove easier to negotiate and more viable.

Fourth, the present formulation of paradigms is simply an initial step. As such it leaves a long list of critical questions unanswered. Given any action, an imaginative analyst should always be able to construct some rationale for the government's choice. By imposing, and relaxing, constraints on the parameters of rational choice (as in variants of Model I) analysts can construct a large number of accounts of any act as a rational choice. But does a statement of reasons why a rational actor would choose an action constitute an explanation of the *occurrence* of that action? How can Model I analysis be forced to make more systematic contributions to the question of the determinants of occurrences? Model II's explanation of t in terms of $t - 1$ is explanation. The world is contiguous. But governments sometimes make sharp departures. Can an organizational process model be modified to suggest where change is likely? Attention to organizational change should afford greater understanding of why particular problems and SOPs are maintained by identifiable types of organizations and also how a manager can improve organizational performance. Model III tells a fascinating "story." But its complexity is enormous, the information requirements are often overwhelming, and many of the details of the bargaining may be superfluous. How can such a model be made parsimonious? The three models are obviously not exclusive alternatives. Indeed, the paradigms highlight the partial emphasis of the framework—what each emphasizes and what it leaves out. Each concentrates on one class of variables, in effect, relegating other important factors to a *ceteris parabus* clause. Model I concentrates on "market factors": pressures and incentives created by the "international strategic marketplace." Models II and III focus on the internal mechanism of the government that chooses in this environment. But can these relations be more fully specified? Adequate synthesis would require a typology of decisions and actions, some of which are more amenable to treatment in terms of one model and some to another. Government behavior is but one cluster of factors relevant to occurrences in foreign affairs. Most students of foreign policy adopt this focus (at least when explaining and predicting). Nevertheless, the dimensions of the chess board, the character of the pieces, and the rules of the game—factors considered by international systems theorists—constitute the context in which the pieces are moved. Can the major variables in the full function of determinants of foreign policy outcomes be identified?

Both the outline of a partial, *ad hoc* working synthesis of the models, and a sketch of their uses in activities other than explanation can be suggested by generating predictions in terms of each. Strategic surrender is an important problem of international relations and diplomatic history. War termination is a new, developing area of the strategic literature. Both of these interests lead scholars to address a central question: *Why* do nations surrender *when?* Whether implicit in explanations or more explicit in analysis, diplomatic historians and strategists rely upon propositions which can be turned forward to produce predictions. Thus at the risk of being timely—and in error—the present situation (August, 1968) offers an interesting test case: Why will North Vietnam surrender when?[125]

In a nutshell, analysis according to Model I asserts: nations quit when costs outweigh the benefits. North Vietnam will surrender when she realizes "that continued fighting can only generate additional costs without hope of compensating gains, this expectation being largely the consequence of the previous application of force by the dominant side."[126] U.S. actions can increase or decrease Hanoi's strategic costs. Bombing North Vietnam increases the pain and thus increases the probability of surrender. This proposition and prediction are not without meaning. That—"other things being equal"—nations are more likely to surrender when the strategic cost–benefit balance is negative, is true. Nations rarely surrender when they are winning. The proposition specifies a range within which nations surrender. But over this broad range, the relevant question is: why do nations surrender?

Models II and III focus upon the government machine through which this fact about the international strategic marketplace must be filtered to produce a surrender. These analysts are considerably less sanguine about the possibility of surrender *at the point* that the cost–benefit calculus turns negative. Never in history (i.e., in none of the five cases I have examined) have nations surrendered at that point. Surrender occurs sometime thereafter. *When* depends on process of organizations and politics of players within these governments—as they are affected by the opposing government. Moreover, the effects of the victorious power's action upon the surrendering nation cannot be adequately summarized as increasing or decreasing strategic costs. Imposing additional costs by bombing a nation may increase the probability of surrender. But it also may reduce it. An appreciation of the impact of the acts of one nation upon another thus requires some understanding of the machine which is being influenced. For more precise prediction, Models II and III require considerably more information about the organizations and politics of North Vietnam than is publicly available. On the basis of the limited public information, however, these models can be suggestive.

Model II examines two sub-problems. First, to have lost is not sufficient. The government must know that the strategic cost–benefit calculus is negative. But neither the categories, nor the indicators, of strategic costs and benefits are clear. And the sources of information about both are organizations whose parochial priorities and perceptions do not facilitate accurate information or estimation. Military evaluation of military performance, military estimates of factors like "enemy morale," and military predictions concerning when "the tide will turn" or "the corner will have been turned" are typically distorted. In cases of highly decentralized guerrilla operations, like Vietnam, these problems are exacerbated. Thus strategic costs will be underestimated. Only highly *visible* costs can have direct impact on leaders without being filtered through organizational channels. Second, since organizations define the details of options and execute actions, surrender (and negotiation) is likely to entail considerable bungling in the early stages. No organization can define options or prepare programs for this treasonous act. Thus, early overtures will be uncoordinated with the acts of other organizations, e.g., the fighting forces, creating contradictory "signals" to the victor.

Model III suggests that surrender will not come at the point that strategic costs outweigh benefits, but that it will not wait until the leadership group concludes that the war is lost. Rather the problem is better understood in terms of four additional propositions. First, strong advocates of the war effort, whose careers are closely identified with the war, rarely come to the conclusion that costs outweigh benefits. Second, quite often from the outset of a war, a number of members of the government (particularly those whose responsibility sensitize them to problems other than war, e.g., economic planners or intelligence experts) are convinced that the war effort is futile. Third, surrender is likely to come as the result of a political shift that enhances the effective power of the latter group (and adds swing members to it). Fourth, the course of the war, particularly actions of the victor, can influence the advantages and disadvantages of players in the loser's government. Thus, North Vietnam will surrender not when its leaders have a change of heart, but when Hanoi has a change of leaders (or a change of effective power within the central circle). How U.S. bombing (or pause), threats, promises, or action in the South affect the game in Hanoi is subtle but nonetheless crucial.

That these three models could be applied to the surrender of governments other than North Vietnam should be obvious. But that exercise is left for the reader.

NOTES

1. Theodore Sorensen, *Kennedy* (New York, 1965), p. 705.
2. In attempting to understand problems of foreign affairs, analysts engage in a number of related, but logically separable enterprises: (a) description, (b) explanation, (c) prediction, (d) evaluation, and (e) recommendation. This essay focuses primarily on explanation (and by implication, prediction).
3. In arguing that explanations proceed in terms of implicit conceptual models, this essay makes no claim that foreign policy analysts have developed any satisfactory, empirically tested theory. In this essay, the use of the term "model" without qualifiers should be read "conceptual scheme."
4. For the purpose of this argument we shall accept Carl G. Hempel's characterization of the logic of explanation: an explanation "answers the question, '*Why* did the explanadum-phenomenon occur?' by showing that the phenomenon resulted from particular circumstances, specified in C_1, C_2, . . . C_k, in accordance with laws L_1, L_2, . . . L_r. By pointing this out, the argument shows that, given the particular circumstances and the laws in question, the occurrence of the phenomenon was to be *expected*; and it is in this sense that the explanation enables us to understand why the phenomenon occurred." *Aspects of Scientific Explanation* (New York, 1965), p. 337. While various patterns of explanation can be distinguished (*viz.,* Ernest Nagel, *The Structure of Science: Problems in the Logic of Scientific Explanation,* New York, 1961), satisfactory scientific explanations exhibit this basic logic. Consequently prediction is the converse of explanation.
5. Earlier drafts of this argument have aroused heated arguments concerning proper names for these models. To choose names for ordinary language is to court confusion, as well as familiarity. Perhaps it is best to think of these models as I, II, and III.
6. In strict terms, the "outcomes" which these three models attempt to explain are essentially actions of national governments, i.e., the sum of activities of all individuals employed by a government relevant to an issue. These models focus not on a state of affairs, i.e., a full description of the

world, but upon national decision and implementation. This distinction is stated clearly by Harold and Margaret Sprout, "Environmental Factors on the Study of International Politics," in James Rossenau (ed.), *International Politics and Foreign Policy* (Glencoe, Illinois, 1961), p. 116. This restriction excludes explanations offered principally in terms of international systems theories. Nevertheless, this restriction is not severe, since few interesting explanations of occurrences in foreign policy have been produced at that level of analysis. According to David Singer, "The nation state—our primary actor in international relations . . . is clearly the traditional focus among Western students and is the one which dominates all of the texts employed in English-speaking colleges and universities." David Singer, "The Level-of-Analysis Problem in International Relations," Klaus Knorr and Sidney Verba (eds.), *The International System* (Princeton, 1961). Similarly, Richard Brody's review of contemporary trends in the study of international relations finds that "scholars have come increasingly in focus on acts of nations. That is, they all focus on the behavior of nations in some respect. Having an interest in accounting for the behavior of nations in common, the prospects for a common frame of reference are enhanced."

7. For further development and support of these arguments see the author's larger study, *Essence of Decision: Explaining the Cuban Missile Crisis* (Boston: Little, Brown and Co., 1971). In its abbreviated form, the argument must, at some points, appear overly stark. The limits of space have forced the omission of many reservations and refinements.

8. Each of the three "case snapshots" displays the work of a conceptual model as it is applied to explain the U.S. blockade of Cuba. But these three cuts are primarily exercises in hypothesis generation rather than hypothesis testing. Especially when separated from the larger study, these accounts may be misleading. The sources for these accounts include the full public record plus a large number of interviews with participants in the crisis.

9. *New York Times,* February 18, 1967.

10. *Ibid.*

11. Arnold Horelick and Myron Rush, *Strategic Power and Soviet Foreign Policy* (Chicago, 1965). Based on A. Horelick, "The Cuban Missile Crisis: An Analysis of Soviet Calculations and Behavior," *World Politics* (April, 1964).

12. Horelick and Rush, *Strategic Power and Soviet Foreign Policy,* p. 154.

13. Hans Morgenthau, *Politics Among Nations* (3rd ed.; New York, 1960), p. 191.

14. *Ibid.,* p. 192.

15. *Ibid.,* p. 5.

16. *Ibid.,* pp. 5–6.

17. Stanley Hoffmann, *Daedalus* (Fall, 1962); reprinted in *The State of War* (New York, 1965).

18. *Ibid.,* p. 171.

19. *Ibid.,* p. 189.

20. Following Robert MacIver; see Stanley Hoffmann, *Contemporary Theory in International Relations* (Englewood Cliffs, 1960), pp. 178–179.

21. Thomas Schelling, *The Strategy of Conflict,* (New York, 1960), p. 232. This proposition was formulated earlier by A. Wohlstetter, "The Delicate Balance of Terror," *Foreign Affairs* (January, 1959).

22. Schelling, *op. cit.,* p. 4.

23. See Morgenthau, *op. cit.,* p. 5; Hoffmann, *Contemporary Theory,* pp. 178–179; Hoffmann, "Roulette in the Cellar," *The State of War;* Schelling, *op. cit.*

24. The larger study examines several exceptions to this generalization. Sidney Verba's excellent essay "Assumptions of Rationality and Non-Rationality in Models of the International System" is less an exception than it is an approach to a somewhat different problem. Verba focuses upon models of rationality and irrationality of *individual* statements: in Knorr and Verba, *The International System.*

25. Robert K. Merton, *Social Theory and Social Structures* (Revised and Enlarged Edition; New York, 1957), pp. 12–16. Considerably weaker than a satisfactory theoretical model, paradigms nevertheless represent a short step in that direction from looser, implicit conceptual models. Neither the concepts nor the relations among the variables are sufficiently specified to yield propositions deductively. "Paradigmatic Analysis" nevertheless has considerable promise for clarifying and codifying styles of analysis in political science. Each of the paradigms stated here can be represented rigorously in mathematical terms. For example, Model I lends itself to mathematical formulation along the lines of Herbert Simon's "Behaviorial Theory of Rationality," *Models of Man* (New York, 1957). But this does not solve the most difficult problem of "measurement and estimation."

26. Though a variant of this model could easily be stochastic, this paradigm is stated in non-probabilistic terms. In contemporary strategy, a stochastic version of this model is sometimes used for predictions; but it is almost impossible to find an explanation of an occurrence in foreign affairs that is consistently probabilistic.

   Analogies between Model I and the concept of explanation developed by R. G. Collingwood, William Dray, and other "revisionists" among philosophers concerned with the critical philosophy of history are not accidental. For a summary of the "revisionist position" see Maurice Mandelbaum, "Historical Explanation: The Problem of Covering Laws," *History and Theory* (1960).

27. This model is an analogue of the theory of the rational entrepreneur which has been developed extensively in economic theories of the firm and the consumer. These two propositions specify the "substitution effect." Refinement of this model and specification of additional general propositions by translating from the economic theory is straightforward.

28. *New York Times,* March 22, 1969.

29. See Nathan Leites, *A Study of Bolshevism* (Glencoe, Illinois, 1953).

30. As stated in the introduction, this "case snapshot" presents, without editorial commentary, a Model I analyst's explanation of the U.S. blockade. The purpose is to illustrate a strong, characteristic rational policy model account. This account is (roughly) consistent with prevailing explanations of these events.

31. Theodore Sorensen, *op. cit.,* p. 675.

32. *Ibid.,* p. 679.

33. *Ibid.,* p. 679.

34. Elie Abel, *The Missile Crisis* (New York, 1966), p. 144.

35. *Ibid.,* p. 102.

36. Sorensen, *op. cit.,* p. 684.

37. *Ibid.*, p. 685. Though this was the formulation of the argument, the facts are not strictly accurate. Our tradition against surprise attack was rather younger than 175 years. For example, President Theodore Roosevelt applauded Japan's attack on Russia in 1904.

38. *New York Times,* June, 1963.

39. The influence of organizational studies upon the present literature of foreign affairs is minimal. Specialists in international politics are not students of organization theory. Organization theory has only recently begun to study organizations as decisionmakers and has not yet produced behavioral studies of national security organizations from a decision-making perspective. It seems unlikely, however, that these gaps will remain unfilled much longer. Considerable progress has been made in the study of the business firm as an organization. Scholars have begun applying these insights to government organizations, and interest in an organizational perspective is spreading among institutions and individuals concerned with actual government operations. The "decisionmaking" approach represented by Richard Snyder, R. Bruck, and B. Sapin, *Foreign Policy Decision-Making* (Glencoe, Illinois, 1962), incorporates a number of insights from organization theory.

40. The formulation of this paradigm is indebted both to the orientation and insights of Herbert Simon and to the behavioral model of the firm stated by Richard Cyert and James March, *A Behaviorial Theory of the Firm* (Englewood Cliffs, 1963). Here, however, one is forced to grapple with the less routine, less quantified functions of the less differentiated elements in government organizations.

41. Theordore Sorensen, "You Get to Walk to Work," *New York Times Magazine,* March 19, 1967.

42. Organizations are not monolithic. The proper level of disaggregation depends upon the objectives of a piece of analysis. This paradigm is formulated with reference to the major organizations that constitute the U.S. government. Generalization to the major components of each department and agency should be relatively straightforward.

43. The stability of these constraints is dependent on such factors as rules for promotion and reward, budgeting and accounting procedures, and mundane operating procedures.

44. Marriner Eccles, *Beckoning Frontiers* (New York, 1951), p. 336.

45. Arthur Schlesinger, *A Thousand Days,* (Boston, 1965), p. 406.

46. U.S. Department of State, *Bulletin,* XLVII, pp. 715–720.

47. Schlesinger, *op. cit.,* p. 803.

48. Theodore Sorensen, *Kennedy,* p. 675.

49. See U.S. Congress, Senate, Committee on Armed Services, Preparedness Investigation Subcommittee, *Interim Report on Cuban Military Build-up,* 88th Congress, 1st Session, 1963, p.2; Hanson Baldwin, "Growing Risks of Bureaucratic Intelligence," *The Reporter* (August 15, 1963), 48–50; Roberta Wohlstetter, "Cuba and Pearl Harbor," *Foreign Affairs* (July, 1965), 706.

50. U.S. Congress, House of Representaives, Committee on Appropriations, Subcommittee on Department of Defense, Appropriations, *Hearings,* 88th Congress, 1st Session, 1963, 25ff.

51. R. Hilsman, *To Move a Nation* (New York, 1967), pp. 172–173.

52. Department of Defense Appropriations, *Hearings,* p. 67.

53. *Ibid.,* pp. 66–67.

54. For (1) Hilsman, *op. cit.,* p. 186; (2) Abel, *op. cit.,* p. 24; (3) Department of

Defense Appropriations, *Hearings*, p. 67; Abel, *op. cit.*, p. 24; (4) Department of Defense Appropriations, *Hearings*, pp. 1–30.

55. The facts here are not entirely clear. This assertion is based on information from (1) "Department of Defense Briefing by the Honorable R. S. McNamara, Secretary of Defense, State Department Auditorium, 5:00 P.M., February 6, 1963." A verbatim transcript of a presentation actually made by General Carroll's assistant, John Hughes; and (2) Hilsman's statement, *op. cit.*, p. 186. But see R. Wohlstetter's interpretation, "Cuba and Pearl Harbor," 700.

56. See Hilsman, *op. cit.*, pp. 172–174.

57. Abel, *op. cit.*, pp. 26 ff; Weintal and Bartlett, *Facing the Brink* (New York, 1967), pp. 62 ff; *Cuban Military Build-up;* J. Daniel and J. Hubbell, *Strike in the West* (New York, 1963), pp. 15 ff.

58. Schlesinger, *op. cit.*, p. 804.

59. Sorensen, *Kennedy,* p. 684.

60. *Ibid.,* pp. 684 ff.

61. *Ibid.,* pp. 694–697.

62. *Ibid.,* p. 697; Abel, *op. cit.*, pp. 100–101.

63. Sorensen, *Kennedy,* p. 669.

64. Hilsman, *op. cit.*, p. 204.

65. See Abel, *op. cit.*, pp. 97 ff.

66. Schlesinger, *op. cit.*, p. 818.

67. *Ibid.*

68. Sorensen, *Kennedy,* p. 710.

69. *New York Times,* October 27, 1962.

70. Abel, *op. cit.*, p. 171.

71. For the location of the original arc see Abel, *op. cit.*, p. 141.

72. *Facts on File,* Vol. XXII, 1962, p. 376, published by Facts on File, Inc., New York, yearly.

73. This hypothesis would account for the mystery surrounding Kennedy's explosion at the leak of the stopping of the *Bucharest.* See Hilsman, *op. cit.*, p. 45.

74. Abel, *op. cit.*, p. 153.

75. See *ibid.,* pp. 154 ff.

76. *Ibid.,* p. 156.

77. *Ibid.*

78. This paradigm relies upon the small group of analysts who have begun to fill the gap. My primary source is the model implicit in the work of Richard E. Neustadt, though his concentration on presidential action has been generalized to a concern with policy as the outcome of political bargaining among a number of independent players, the President amounting to no more than a "superpower" among many lesser but considerable powers. As Warner Schilling argues, the substantive problems are of such inordinate difficulty that uncertainties and differences with regard to goals, alternatives, and consequences are inevitable. This necessitates what Roger Hilsman describes as the process of conflict and consensus building. The techniques employed in this process often resemble those used in legislative assemblies, though Samuel Huntington's characterization of the process as "legislative" overemphasizes the equality of participants as opposed to the hierarchy which structures the game. Moreover, whereas for Huntington, foreign policy (in contrast to military policy) is set by the executive, this

paradigm maintains that the activities which he describes as legislative are characteristics of the process by which foreign policy is made.

79. The theatrical metaphor of stage, roles, and actors is more common than this metaphor of games, positions, and players. Nevertheless, the rigidity connoted by the concept of "role" both in the theatrical sense of actors reciting fixed lines and in the sociological sense of fixed responses to specified social situations makes the concept of games, positions, and players more useful for this analysis of active participants in the determination of national policy. Objections to the terminology on the grounds that "game" connotes non-serious play overlook the concept's application to most serious problems both in Wittgenstein's philosophy and in contemporary game theory. Game theory typically treats more precisely structured games, but Wittgenstein's examination of the "language game" wherein men use words to communicate is quite analogous to this analysis of the less specified game of bureaucratic politics. See Ludwig Wittgenstein, *Philosophical Investigations*, and Thomas Schelling, "What is Game Theory?" in James Charlesworth, *Contemporary Political Analysis*.

80. Inclusion of the President's Special Assistant for National Security Affairs in the tier of "Chiefs" rather than among the "Staffers" involves a debatable choice. In fact he is both super-staffer and near-chief. His position has no statutory authority. He is especially dependent upon good relations with the President and the Secretaries of Defense and State. Nevertheless, he stands astride a genuine action-channel. The decision to include this position among the Chiefs reflects my judgment that the Bundy function is becoming institutionalized.

81. Richard E. Neustadt, Testimony, United States Senate, Committee on Government Operations, Subcommittee on National Security Staffing, *Administration of National Security*, March 26, 1963, pp. 82–83.

82. This aphorism was stated first, I think, by Don K. Price.

83. Paul Y. Hammond, "Super Carriers and B–36 Bombers," in Harold Stein (ed.), *American Civil-Military Decisions* (Birmingham, 1963).

84. Roberta Wohlstetter, *Pearl Harbor* (Stanford, 1962), p. 350.

85. Sorensen, *Kennedy*, p. 670.

86. *Ibid.*

87. *Ibid.*, pp. 670ff.

88. *New York Times*, August, September, 1962.

89. *New York Times*, August 20, 1962.

90. *New York Times*, September 5, 1962.

91. *New York Times*, September 14, 1962.

92. *New York Times*, October 14, 1962.

93. Cited by Abel, *op. cit.*, p. 13.

94. *New York Times*, September 5, 1962.

95. *New York Times*, September 14, 1962.

96. Senate Foreign Relations Committee; Senate Armed Services Committee; House Committee on Appropriations; House Select Committee on Export Control.

97. Abel, *op. cit.*, pp. 17–18. According to McCone, he told Kennedy, "The only construction I can put on the material going into Cuba is that the Russians are preparing to introduce offensive missiles." See also Weintal and Bartlett, *op. cit.*, pp. 60–61.

98. Abel, *op. cit.,* p. 23.
99. *New York Times,* September 10, 1962.
100. See Abel, *op. cit.,* pp. 25–26; and Hilsman, *op. cit.,* p. 174.
101. Department of Defense Appropriation, *Hearings,* 69.
102. A basic, but somewhat contradictory, account of parts of this story emerges in the Department of Defense Appropriations, *Hearings,* 1–70.
103. Department of Defense Appropriations, *Hearings,* 71.
104. The details of the 10 days between the October 4 decision and the October 14 flight must be held in abeyance.
105. Abel, *op. cit.,* p. 44.
106. *Ibid.,* pp. 44ff.
107. See Richard Neustadt, "Afterword," *Presidential Power* (New York, 1964).
108. Sorensen, *Kennedy,* p. 676; Schlesinger, *op. cit.,* p. 801.
109. Hilsman, *op. cit.,* p. 195.
110. *Ibid.*
111. Weintal and Bartlett, *op. cit.,* p. 67; Abel, *op. cit.,* p. 53.
112. Schlesinger, *op. cit.,* p. 803.
113. *Ibid.,* p. 831.
114. Abel, *op. cit.,* p. 186.
115. *Ibid.,* p. 49.
116. Interview, quoted by Ronald Steel, *New York Review of Books,* March 13, 1969, p.22.
117. Sorensen, *Kennedy,* p. 686.
118. *Ibid.,* p. 691.
119. *Ibid.,* pp. 691–692.
120. Schlesinger, *op. cit.,* p. 296.
121. Space will not permit an account of the path from this coalition to the formal government decision on Saturday and action on Monday.
122. *Essence of Decision.*
123. Thus my position is quite distinct from both poles in the recent "great debate" about international relations. While many "traditionalists" of the sort Kaplan attacks adopt the first posture and many "scientists" of the sort attacked by Bull adopt the second, this third posture is relatively neutral with respect to whatever is in substantive dispute. See Hedley Bull, "International Theory: The Case for a Classical Approach," *World Politics* (April, 1966); and Morton Kaplan, "The New Great Debate: Traditionalism vs. Science in International Relations," *World Politics* (October, 1966).
124. A number of problems are now being examined in these terms both in the Bureaucracy Study Group on Bureaucracy and Policy of the Institute of Politics at Harvard University and at the Rand Corporation.
125. In response to several readers' recommendations, what follows is reproduced *verbatim* from the paper delivered at the September, 1968 Association meetings (Rand P–3919). The decision is heavily indebted to Ernest R. May.
126. Richard Snyder, *Deterrence and Defense* (Princeton, 1961), p. 11. For a more general presentation of this position see Paul Kecskemeti, *Strategic Surrender* (New York, 1964).

The Transformation of Foreign Policies

Edward L. Morse

As the title suggests, Professor Morse examines how foreign policy making has been transformed by the modernization process. He argues that the increasing interdependence caused by modernization has made the formulation and implementation of foreign policy decisions more difficult.

Foreign policy has been radically transformed by the revolutionary processes of modernization not only in the societies composing the Atlantic region, but wherever high levels of modernization exist. There is a quality about modernization that dissolves the effects of what have generally been considered the major determinants of foreign policy, whether these determinants are based on ideology and type of political system (democratic versus totalitarian foreign policies, for example), or power and capability (great-power versus small-power policies). Wherever modernized societies exist, their foreign policies are more similar to each other than they are to the foreign policies of nonmodernized societies, regardless of the scale of the society or its type of government.

Both the international and the domestic settings in which foreign policies are formulated and conducted are subjected to continual and revolutionary transformation once high levels of modernization exist. Internationally, modernization is accompanied by increased levels and types of interdependencies among national societies. Domestically, it is associated with increased centralization of governmental institutions and governmental decision-making as well as with increased priorities for domestic rather than for external needs.

As a result of these transformations, three general sets of conditions have developed. First, the ideal and classical distinctions between foreign and domestic affairs have broken down, even though the myths associated with sovereignty and the state have not. Second, the distinction between "high policies" (those associated with security and the continued existence of the state) and "low policies" (those pertaining to the wealth and welfare of the citizens) has become less important as low policies have assumed an increasingly large role in any society. Third, although there have been significant developments in the instrumentalities of political control, the actual ability to control events either internal

Edward L. Morse, "The Transformation of Foreign Policies: Modernization, Interdependence, and Externalization," *World Politics*, 22, no. 3 (April 1970). Copyright © 1970 by Princeton University Press. Reprinted by permission of Princeton University Press.

or external to modernized societies—even those that are Great Powers—has decreased with the growth of interdependence, and is likely to decrease further.

MODERNIZATION AND FOREIGN POLICY

The notion that modernization has a revolutionary effect on foreign policy is not a new one. Comte and Spencer, for example, among other optimistic observers of industrialization in the nineteenth century, tried to demonstrate the irrationality of war as an instrument of policy in the relations among highly developed countries. On the other hand, Hobson, Lenin, and others who surveyed industrialization and linked it to the "new imperialism" of the late nineteenth century found that what they understood as modernization would lead to conflict among the same societies.

The view of modernization that underlies the concept of foreign policy in this essay owes little to such theories of economic determinism and little to the normative biases held by those writers. Moreover, it is not concerned with what happens in a society, and, consequently, to the foreign policy of its government, during the various phases of modernization. Rather, it acknowledges that the development of levels associated with "high modernization" carries with it implications for foreign policy. Once high mass-consumption levels are reached in a society and once high levels of interdependence among modernized societies exist, several common features of foreign policy appear that can be discussed in general terms and that pertain to democratic and nondemocratic political systems alike.

The implications of modernization for foreign policy can be derived from many of the definitions of modernization that have been formulated. I have chosen to follow Levy's definition because of its power in isolating those societies in which I am interested. It is based on two variables: "the uses of inanimate sources of power and the use of tools to multiply the effect of effort."[1] Each of these variables is conceived as a continuum, so that "a society will be considered more or less modernized to the extent that its members use inanimate sources of power and/or tools to multiply the effects of their efforts."[2] Accordingly, "Among the members of relatively modernized societies, uses of inanimate sources of power not only predominate, but they predominate in such a way that it is almost impossible to envisage any considerable departure in the direction of the uses of animate sources of power without the most far-reaching changes of the entire system. The multiplication of effort by application of tools is high and the rate is probably increasing exponentially."[3]

Only a few such societies have existed in history, and they all reached high levels of modernization during the nineteenth or twentieth centuries. Those for which the generalizations in this essay are germane include the fourteen societies identified by Russett and others as "high mass-consumption" societies.[4] They are all modern democracies. There is no logical reason to assume, however, that the foreign policies of non-democratic modernized societies would not also be subsumed by these generalizations.

The general characteristics of modernized societies include the growth of knowledge about and control over the physical environment; increased political centralization, accompanied by the growth of specialized bureaucratic organizations and by the politicization of the masses; the production of economic surpluses and wealth generalized over an entire population; urbanization; and the psychological adjustment to change and the fleeting, rather than acceptance of the static and permanent.[5]

The achievement of high levels of modernization has also been associated with the growth of nationalism and the idealization of the nation–state as the basic political unit. The consolidation of the nation–state, however, is the central political enigma of contemporary international affairs, for modernization has also been accompanied by transnational structures that cannot be subjected to the control of isolated national political bodies. These structures exist in the military field, where security in the nuclear age has everywhere become increasingly a function of activities pursued outside the state's borders. They also exist in the economic field, where the welfare not only of the members of various societies, but of the societies themselves, increasingly relies upon the maintenance of stable commercial and monetary arrangements that are independent of any single national government.

The confrontation of the political structures that have developed along the lines of the nation–state with these transnational activities is one of the most significant features of contemporary international politics. Modernization has resulted in the integration of individual national societies, which face problems that can be solved in isolation with decreasing reliability. In other words, modernization has transformed not only the domestic setting in which foreign policy is formulated; by creating high levels of interdependence among the diverse national societies, it has also transformed the general structures of international society.

Foreign and Domestic Politics

The fundamental distinction that breaks down under modernization is between foreign and domestic policies, at least in ideal terms. This distinction is much more characteristic of the foreign policies of nonmodernized societies in both ideal and actual terms than it is of modernized states. In modernized societies, it is difficult to maintain because both predominantly political and predominantly nonpolitical interactions take place across societies at high levels, and because transnational phenomena are so significant that either territorial and political or the jurisdictional boundaries are extremely difficult to define. The whole constellation of activities associated with modernization blurs the distinction so that an observer must analyze carefully any interaction in order to ascertain in what ways it pertains to foreign and domestic affairs.

Foreign policies can be analytically distinguished from domestic policies. Foreign policies are, at a minimum, manifestly oriented to some actual or potential sphere external to a political system, i.e., to some sphere outside the jurisdiction or control of the polity. Domestic policies, on the contrary, are oriented to some sphere within the jurisdiction and control of the polity. Foreign policies may be addressed principally to some domestic interest group, but as long as they carry some minimum intention and recognition of an external orientation they are considered foreign policies.

Classical distinctions between foreign and domestic policies are more normatively based and break down once societies become fairly modernized. Two sorts of classical distinctions exist. One, which underlies the Rankean tradition of the primacy of foreign policy, stresses the special significance foreign policies carry that other policies do not. This significance is the concern of foreign policy with the existence and security of a society: "The position of a state in the world depends on the degree of independence it has attained. It is obliged, therefore, to organize all its internal resources for the purpose of self-preservation. This is the supreme law of the state."[6]

The other tradition is the democratic one, which also is normative and which stresses the primacy of domestic over foreign affairs. Unlike the Rankean tradition, associated originally with monarchic foreign policies and later with totalitarian ones, this tradition stresses the pacific nature of policy, its formulation by representative legislative groups, and the control of external events by open rather than closed-door diplomacy. In this sense, democracies were thought to suffer severe disabilities in the conduct of foreign affairs.

In either case, there is an assumption that there exists an ontological divorce between foreign and domestic affairs that carries with it in political analysis normative tendencies to stress one of the two while ignoring the other. Foreign policy has been thought to differ from domestic policy in its ends (the national interest as opposed to particular interests), its means (any means that can be invoked to achieve the ends, as opposed to domestically "legitimate" means), and its target of operation (a decentralized, anarchic milieu over which the state in question maintains little control, as opposed to a centralized domestic order in which the state has a monopoly of the instruments of social order). Whether the substance of the distinction stresses domestic or foreign affairs, the separation of the two has a strong empirical foundation. Levels of interdependence among all nonmodernized societies were generally so low that governments could take independent actions either domestically or abroad with fairly little likelihood that much spillover between them would take place. The instruments used to implement either domestic or foreign policies had effects on either that were in normal times negligible. The "externalities" generated by either domestic or foreign policies did not significantly alter policies in the other field.

This is not to say that domestic factors did not affect foreign policy at all, nor that the general international setting did not affect the substance of policies. What it does suggest is that the normative distinction between foreign and domestic activities was quite well matched by actual conditions. The degrees to which they did not coincide led to debates about ways to improve the efficacy of foreign or domestic policies, or about their goals. But the degree of divergence was not so great as to call the distinction into question.

Regardless of how the distinction is made, it breaks down once societies become fairly modernized. This does not mean, as Friedrich has argued, that "foreign and domestic policy in developed Western systems constitutes today a seamless web."[7] Distinctions along the analytic lines I have suggested above still obtain, and governments still formulate policies with a predominant external or internal orientation. But foreign and other policies formulated under modern conditions affect each other in ways that are not salient in nonmodernized or premodernized societies and that derive from both the domestic and international interdependencies associated with modernization. They also derive from the increased scope of governmental activities under modern conditions. Before the Western societies became highly modernized, for example, the major part of government expenditures was devoted to foreign affairs, which was the central concern of government. As the role of the government in the economy and in domestic social life increases, concern for foreign affairs must decrease relative to concern for domestic affairs.[8] In addition, as a result of growing international interdependencies, the external and internal consequences of domestic and foreign policies become more significant, and consequences that are not intended and that may or may not be recognized tend also to increase. Therefore, undesirable policy-consequences also increase. This is true, for example, in terms of allocations of resources, regardless of the multiplier effect.

One example of the growing interdependence of foreign and domestic affairs in all modernized societies is related to the emphasis on a favorable balance of payments position. A requisite of favorable trade and services balance may be the restraint of domestic economic growth and the maintenance of economic stability at home in order to prevent domestic prices (and wages) from rising. At the same time, domestic growth is required to meet demands for raised living standards. But, in order to foster growth and meet demands for increased wages, a favorable balance of trade may have to be sacrificed.

The linkages between domestic and foreign policies constitute the basic characteristic of the breakdown in the distinction between foreign and domestic affairs in the modernized, interdependent international system. This statement does not imply that foreign and domestic policies are indistinguishable; for with regard to articulated goals and problems of implementation, they remain separate. Rather, it is suggestive of the ways in which foreign policies are transformed by the processes of modernization and the development of high levels of interdependence. These processes have put an end to the normative distinctions asserting the primacy of the one or the other. They also overshadow the empirical distinction according to which foreign policies vary in type with the political institutions in which they are formulated.

The Dynamics of Foreign Policies in Modernized Societies

Foreign policies, like other sorts of policies, can be analyzed in terms of their substance, or *content,* the *processes* by which they are formulated, and their *outcomes.* Each of these three dimensions is transformed under the impact of modernization.

First, in terms of content, the ideal pattern of foreign policies, with its emphasis on the "high policy" function of security and defense, or, alternatively, on expansion of some attribute of the state, has been widened into if not replaced by a new pattern. Either there is a broadening of the spectrum of policy goals to include goals of wealth and welfare in addition to those of power and position associated with high policies, or these older ideal patterns are completely overshadowed by the advent of "low policies."[9] What is distinctive and new about these policies is that they are primarily non-conflictual. Like the relations of which they are a part, some are merely fleeting and casual. Others are explicitly cooperative and pertain to the production of international collective goods,[10] which require compatible efforts on the part of official and non-official groups in diverse societies. In the case of highly modernized societies, their chief trait is that they *are seen as* economic goods. They arise from growth in international trade and the concomitant necessity to regulate trade imbalances, to produce additional liquidity, to finance trade, and to create all the other regulative devices that go along with trade practices. They also pertain to the transformation of alliance structures in a nuclear world.

Although many of these goods are measurable in economic terms, they are not to be considered in the domain of international economics. On the contrary, one of the central features of politics among modernized societies is that the politics of wealth and welfare have overshadowed the politics of power and position, which in the relations among modernized societies are played out in economic terms. Trade rounds in GATT and reform measures in the IMF are the essence of international politics today. The purely political and purely economic cannot be seen as empirically separable.

Moreover, since the salient feature of this relation is an economic one, it has the additional characteristic that it is eminently commensurable, thus fostering theorizing about international political relations. One of the traditional difficulties associated with theorizing about international politics was that traditional national foreign objectives tended to be incommensurable. These goals were, in general, transcendental, by which I mean that they were never completely identified with empirical states of affairs. Such goals as "security," "grandeur," or "power" are characteristic transcendental national goals.[11] In the case of highly modernized societies, there arises an additional spectrum of goals that are empirical or at least almost completely transferable to empirical ones. These goals generally refer to qualities associated with wealth and welfare.

Second, with respect ot the processes by which foreign policies are formulated, it is modernization rather than democratization that has transformed foreign policy decision-making from cabinet-style, closed decision-making, to open politics, both domestically and in international negotiations. The locus of foreign policy decision-making, with rare exception, has remained fundamentally administrative, with the legislature in a democracy becoming a place where foreign policy debates, as opposed to decisions, occur.

Third, and last, the problem of implementing and controlling foreign policies is also transformed under modernization. In one sense, as indicated by the definition I have proposed concerning foreign policies, the problem of controlling events external to a state is the pre-eminent problem for foreign policy wherever there exist political units without any overarching political authority structures. There was a time when great powers were separated from other powers by the degree to which their governments could control events external to them as well as by the domestic effects of their external activities. Today that distinction is made either on the basis of destructive power alone, or with regard to nonmilitary areas. Because of the added complexity of the problems of control under modernized conditions, or at least in contemporary international society, no state can now be said to be a great power in the old sense of the term.

In addition, however, what is special about foreign policies as they are conducted in modern states today is the scale of the problem of control. The loss of control both domestically and in terms of foreign affairs, at a time when interdependencies among modernized societies are rising, will prove to be the central problem of international politics in the coming years. This central problem has several implications, not the least important of which is the future of the nation–state and the kinds of functional equivalents that can be devised to substitute for the state in those areas where the state can no longer be effective.

A. The Transformation of Policy Objectives. Preoccupation with high policies and traditional foreign policy objectives and instrumentalities has drawn the attention of scholars away from the changes in policy goals that have accompanied modernization, and specifically from the increased salience of low policies and the merging of goals of power and goals of plenty.

Most general discussions of foreign policy objectives focus on the goals of high policies, which in the past were generally conceived as ultimate ends and were transcendental. The classical goals of statecraft that Wolfers has defined as goals of "self-extension" or goals of "self-preservation" were such transcendental goals,[12] as were the goals known as "imperialism," "security," "prestige," and the ideal or postulated "position" or "role" of a state in the international system. For example, some transcendental goal of security may be identified with stature in the international system, or with a certain set of role-premises such as "mediator" or "balancer."

I suggested with regard to transcendental goals that the classical goals of power and security have been expanded to, or superseded by, goals of wealth and welfare. This change has been accompanied by a change in the empirical referents used to identify transcendental goals. Transcendental goals always have some empirical referent, but they are only partly and never wholly identified with them. For example, power, or prestige, has been associated, in part, with increased population and with accretions of territory. What is interesting about the empirical referents of transcendental goals is that "they change; new ones are created; old ones pass out of existence; and their relations . . . are shuffled."[13]

Here, the old identification of power and security with territory and population has been changed to an identification of welfare with economic growth. "Territorial conquest," as Klaus Knorr has written, "by force of arms has lost the perennial attraction it possessed throughout mankind's violent history."[14]

Two general transformations associated with high levels of modernization are responsible for this change. One pertains to the classical instruments of policy, armaments and weapons, and the changes brought about in external goals by the development of nuclear weapons and their delivery systems. The other is related to more general transformations of domestic society.

The effects of nuclear weapons on national external goals have received far greater attention than have the effects of the transformation of domestic society. This one-sided attention is a result of the preoccupation with high policies and serves to obscure more radical changes in policy objectives. It is also related to the assumption that even with the development of nuclear weapons systems *plus ça change, plus c'est la même chose,* or that neither military nor economic interdependence has grown in recent years, but that they may even have diminished considerably.[15] The development of nuclear weapons has had a crosscutting effect. On the one hand, it makes the territorial state incapable of providing defense and security, by creating the first truly global international system unified by the possibility of generating unacceptable levels of human destruction. On the other hand, nuclear weapons are also said to reaffirm the viability of the nation–state as a political unit, by providing its absolute defense by deterrence.[16]

In any case, the key to the obsolescence of territorial goals that accompanied the development of nuclear weapons is the increased cost of territorial accretion. No modernized state can afford it. It is therefore no accident that major territorial disputes have disappeared from relations among the highly modernized states and now can occur where there is no danger that nuclear weapons will be used and, therefore, accompany nation-building efforts only in the nonmodernized societies. Modernized societies are involved in major territorial disputes only when these disputes also involve a nonmodernized society as well, as in the case of the Sino-Soviet border. Territoriality decreases in importance even further as alliances become less useful. Requisites for American security, once consisting of territorial bases encircling the Soviet bloc, have changed tremendously with the hardening of missiles and the development of Polaris and Poseidon submarines.

Though the transformation of policy goals accompanying modernization is striking with reference to the ideal identification of power with territory and population, it is less apparent when power is identified with wealth, as it was by the mercantilist doctrine, which underlies classical notions of power politics.[17] The pursuit of both was thought to involve zero-sum conditions. Power, like wealth, was thought to be a universal constant. One state's gain was another's loss. Actual transformations associated with modernization and involving both domestic economic growth and international interdependence have changed these notions as well. The conditions giving verisimilitude to the zero-sum conception of power and wealth changed with rapid domestic economic growth and with the development of economic and other international interdependencies, as well as with the politicization of large groups in modernized societies that make increased demands upon government.

Rapid domestic economic growth, one of the prime indices of modernization, has a profound effect on both the relative priority of domestic and foreign goals and on the substance of each. Once economic growth sets in as a continuous, dynamic process, the value of accretion of territory and population dwindles and the "domestic savings and investment and advancement of education, science, and technology are [seen as] the most profitable means and the most secure avenues to the attainment of wealth and welfare."[18] The logic of economic growth, in other words, turns men's minds away from the external goals associated with the ruling groups of early modern Europe and toward the further development of domestic wealth by domestic means and under conditions of peace.[19]

Domestic economic growth, like the creation of nuclear weapons, offers only a partial explanation of the transformation of foreign policy goals. In addition, the salience of low policies and the expansion of conflictual, zero-sum relations to cooperative strategies result also from transnational structures associated with modernization and the interdependencies that have developed among the modernized states. Low policies, in this sense, derive from the interactions of citizens in various states and from the actions of governments in the interests of their citizens or their responses to private group behavior in order to assure general stability and the achievement of other goals. These goals are themselves undermined by the scope of nongovernmental transnational and international interchanges and may also be predominantly domestic and pertain to welfare and social services.

Another aspect of the increased salience of low policies pertains to the interests of governments in building new transnational structures in order to achieve both international and domestic goals. For example, one of the motivations for creating a common market in Europe has been the increased wealth it would bring to the citizens of each member-state as a result of increased levels of trade. It is for this reason that one principal characteristic of foreign policies under modernized conditions is that they approach the pole of cooperation rather than the pole of conflict. Conflictual or political activities, therefore, take place within the context of predominantly cooperative arrangements. Plays for power or position among these modernized states occur in the non-zero-sum worlds of the IMF and NATO rather than in predominantly conflictual arenas.

The low policies, in short, have become central to international politics among the modernized states and involve the building up of international collective goods in defense and NATO, and in international wealth-and-welfare organizations such as GATT and the EEC. It is within the parameters set by the need for cooperation that interplays of power and position can occur.

The collectivization of objectives in such matters as monetary and trade policies, which assume increased importance along with domestic welfare, has also set severe restrictions upon the traditional objective of independence. Since the modernized world is a highly interdependent one, both because of the existence of transnational politics and other phenomena in communications and trade, and because of policies, intentionally fostered by governments that increase interdependence, the ideal view of independence has been challenged. No amount of political will can recreate a world where independence can be obtained, except at costs that no government is willing to incur. This was as true for Gaullist France as it is for the United States.

Two of the chief characteristics of foreign policies conducted under modernized conditions are, then, (1) their predominantly cooperative rather than conflictual nature; and (2) the change in goals from power and position to wealth and welfare—or, at least, the addition of these new goals to the more classical ones. Both factors are accompanied by the loss of autonomy of any society in international affairs.

B. Increased Domestic Demands and the Allocation of Resources. It is a paradox at the heart of foreign policies in all modernized societies that increased demands on their governments result in a short-term problem of resource allocation, with the result that predominantly external goals decrease in priority relative to predominantly domestic goals. At the same time, however, increased "inward-looking" has been offset by the increased sensitivity of domestic conditions to international events as a result of international interdependence, and by absolute increases in international activities taken on by the citizens of all modernized societies.

One of the distinctive features of all modernized governments, democratic and authoritarian alike, is that they have assumed great multifunctionality. Both ideally and actually, they are not merely regulative agencies in a "night-watchman" state, but are and are seen as creators and redistributors of wealth. Increasing demands on governments have helped to create the modern social-service state and themselves result from the increased politicization of citizens in modernized societies. A government is impaled upon the "dilemma of rising demands and insufficient resources"[20] when its domestic demands are greater than its resources and when at the same time it must maintain even existing levels of commitments abroad. The demands may arise from the politicized poor who want a greater share in economic prosperity, the military for new weapons systems, the need for maintenance of public order in societies increasingly sensitive to labor and minority group disruption, etc. These are added to the "rising cost and widening scope of activities required to keep mature urban societies viable."[21] One inexorable result of these increased demands on governments is the curtailment of external commitments, or the decreased relative priority of external goals. Such curtailments add a dimension to the costs of independence.

It may well be that the multiplier-effect generated by the allocation of resources to external commitments produces greater goods domestically than would allocations directly meeting the increased demands.

However, with increased politicization it is more likely that any external allocation will be highly visible, as the case of United States expenditures in Vietnam, or French expenditures on a striking force, indicates. It will, therefore, be viewed as a squandering of the domestic wealth. This is all the more likely in modern democracies where such allocations afford groups in opposition to the government an opportunity to raise questions concerning them. In the contemporary world, with instantaneous communication across boundaries, demands for increased services in one society also stem from their existence elsewhere.

There are several ways that the dilemma can be met, and each of these has external effects, whether they are indirect or direct, intended or not. The Sprouts have summarized a number of the indirect effects as follows:

First, efforts may be made to *expand the economy*. . . .

Second, the rulers may prudentially *revise their order of priorities*. . . .

Third, the rulers may . . . *divert public attention* to other values. . . .

Fourth, the men in power may try to *change the opinions of dissenters*. . . .

Fifth, . . . the rulers may try to *silence dissent and opposition*. . . .[22]

In addition, these resources can be secured by various kinds of external activities involving cooperation and compatible efforts with other governments. One of the goals of the EEC, for example, is a rational division of labor in order to make available a greater pool of resources to each of the member-states in return for its giving up some degrees of domestic and external autonomy. This pooling of resources serves to create the international goods of which I spoke earlier and also serves to increase interdependence among societies, further limiting the freedom of any modern state to pursue a traditional policy of independence.

In the end, there is a decreased relative priority of external commitments made for military purposes, although other external commitments of an economic or legal nature may be made in their place. This does not imply what others have drawn as conclusions, that modern states are more "satisfied" than other states.[23] The organismic analogy is no more helpful in this case than it was in the case of appeasement policy.

C. Changes in the Processes of Foreign Policy-Making. Like other processes of policy-making, those associated with foreign policy change under modernization. Cabinet-style decision-making gives way to administrative politics as the information that must be gathered for policy-making increases, as the number of states and functional areas that must be dealt with increases, and as personnel standards become professionalized. Despite the predictions made at the turn of the century by the ideologues of democracy, policy-making has not been "democratized" so much as it has been "bureaucratized." At the same time, great losses of control from the top have occurred and have been well documented.

The major transformation brought about by changes in the policy-making process has been the decreased relevance of rationality models for understanding policy and the increased importance of the bureaucratic model.[24] Policy-making in modern bureaucracies undermines the ability of a political leader to pursue rationally any explicit external goals. Rather, interest-group politics assume greater importance and foreign policy becomes more and more a reflection of what occurs in the bureaucracies upon which leadership depends for information and position papers.

Policy-making in modern bureaucracies, with regard to foreign as well as domestic affairs, involves both lateral bargaining among the members of various adminstrative units and vertical or hierarchical bargaining among members of various strata in a single organization.[25] The single spokesman in foreign affairs, long prescribed as a necessity for security, is made impossible by the characteristics of modern bureaucracies. Plurality in the number of foreign policy voices accompanies the increased significance of routine, daily decision-making in low-policy areas that contrasts with the more unified and consistent nature of decision-making in crises and in high politics. With such increases in routine, control at the top becomes more difficult. The several aspects of control of routine can be summarized under two headings, the organizational problem and the problem of size.

Modern governments are organized predominantly along functional domestic lines into such departments as agriculture, labor, and education. The domestic-foreign distinction that seemed to fit the nineteenth-century model of governmental organization conflicts dramatically with the needs of even the predominantly domestic organizational structures of modernized governments. Here, the distinctive feature is that each domestic function has external dimensions: most of the predominantly domestic departments and ministries of modern governments have some kind of international bureau. The proliferation of these international bureaus severely undercuts the ability of one foreign ministry or department to control the external policies of its government, thus severely restricting the coordination of foreign policies. The problem is all the more serious insofar as the distinction between high policies and low policies in foreign affairs has become increasingly blurred.

One way this problem is dealt with is by the formation of committees that cross-cut several cabinet organizations, serving to coordinate both information and decision-making at several levels. Each American administration since World War II has tried to reorganize foreign policy decision-making to counter the disability, but no permanent decision-making structures have been devised. Other governments tackle the problem by forming *ad hoc* interministerial committees to meet specific problems.

In addition to decreased control as a result of "domestic orientation" in modern governments, there is the added difficulty of coordinating a large bureaucracy dealing predominantly with foreign affairs. At the turn of the last century, one of the problems of control stemmed from the lack of coordination between foreign ministries and ministries of the armed forces. Thus, for example, French armed forces often freely occupied underdeveloped areas in Africa and Southeast Asia without the knowledge of the foreign minister. Today the problem of size presents no less formidable an information gap at the top of large bureaucracies. With more information available than ever, its channeling to the right person has become an organizational problem no foreign ministry has mastered.

Modernization, then—usually associated with the rationalization of political structures that foster increased control over the events in a society as well as over the environment in which men live—also creates certain disabilities that impede rational and efficient foreign policies. But modernization has also exacerbated another problem of control that has always been central to international politics—the control of events external to a state. This problem, which originates in the political organization of international society, is the one to which I now turn.

D. Modern Foreign Policies and Problems of Control. The problem of control in international affairs arises from the condition of international society, which, conceived as a collection of nominally sovereign political units, has no overarching structure of political authority. The difficulty of coordination and control of events external to a society, always the major problem of international stability, is compounded by the development of interdependencies among modernized societies, for interdependence erodes the autonomy of a government to act *both* externally and internally, though the juridical status of sovereign states has not been significantly altered.

With the development of high levels of interdependence, all kinds of catastrophes, from nuclear holocaust to inflation or depression, can also become worldwide once a chain of events is begun. These disasters could be logical consequences of benefits derived from international collective goods.

One reason why modern governments have lost control over their foreign relations is that there has been an increasing number of international interactions, especially among the populations of pluralistic societies, in nongovernmental contexts. This increase was one of the first changes modernization brought in the foreign policies of states. It first became noticeable at the turn of the century with the rise of the "new imperialism" characterized by the rapidly increased mobility of people, of money, and of military equipment. It is associated today with the multinational corporation and with other new units of international activity that have varying degrees of autonomy abroad and whose external operations frequently act at cross-purposes with the foreign policy goals of their governments. They also contribute a large portion of any state's balance-of-payments accounts and therefore affect the monetary stability not only of a single state, but of the system of states in general.

The difference between interactions of transnational and intergovernmental systems is summarized in Karl Kaiser's ideal-typical models. A "transnational society subsystem," according to Kaiser, is one in which "relations between national systems are handled and decided upon by nongovernmental elites and pursued directly between social, economic, and political forces in the participating societies."[26] Intergovernmental transactions are those in which "relations between national systems are handled and decided upon by elites located in governmental institutions."[27] Examples of the former are exchanges of material, capital, population, and ideas among societies, independent of governmental actions; examples of the latter are traditional alliances and new regional or global organizational activities.

These transnational interactions break down both the control of foreign affairs by a government and the distinction between foreign and domestic affairs. They may bring about situations in which governments are forced to take action, often with their freedom of choice of action restricted. This has been the case especially with regard to the stability of currencies and the development of new forms of crisis management in the monetary field in the last decade.

As transnational interactions increase, the possibilities of effecting decision-making in a purely national setting, in isolation or national encapsulation, become less likely and control is a more difficult problem, especially because knowledge of the effects of interdependencies is still limited.

A second aspect of the problem of control stems from the decreasing number of instrumentalities relative to the number of goals associated with any government. An optimum policy situation is one where the number of instruments available for use exceeds the number of goals. In principle, an infinite number of policy mixes exist, in that one instrument can substitute for another and "it will always be possible to find one among the infinity of solutions . . . for which welfare, however defined, is a maximum."[28] This is not only the most efficient situation, but it is also the fairest, for it allows any pressure to be "distributed more evenly over the various social groups."[29] When, however, the number of instruments is smaller than the number of goals, there is no clear solution on grounds of efficiency or fairness.

It is precisely this situation that occurs with the breakdown of the domestic-foreign distinction and with increases in international interdependence. As long as the two spheres remain more or less distinct, policies in either area can be implemented with different sets of instrumentalities. As soon as the separation is eroded, the spillover of effects from one sphere to the other results in the reduction of the number of usable instrumentalities.

This is true for two reasons. First, since policy instruments have recognizable effects both internally and externally, it is more and more frequently the case that any one instrument can be used for either domestic or external purposes. However, domestic wage increases can be used for the purpose of establishing higher general levels of living. At the same time, the propensity to consume imported goods increases directly with wage increases and depresses any balance-of-payments surplus—a situation that is worsened by the positive effect of wage increases on prices and the subsequent negative effect on exports.

Second, what is optimally desired is that objectives be consistent. "If they are not consistent, no number of policy instruments will suffice to reach the objectives."[30] As long as domestic and foreign affairs were separated, consistency was a problem only within each sphere. With interdependence, not only must domestic and foreign goals be compatible with each other, but so must the goals of a set of societies if welfare effects are to spread optimally. Consistency then becomes more difficult because of the economic nature of the objectives and the diversity of political units in international society.

Together with increased international transactions associated with growing interdependence, there have also developed rising levels of transactions internal to modernized states as well as higher levels of national integration. It is often concluded that the increases in national cohesiveness that accompany modernization counteract international interdependence.[31] Actually the reverse is true.

There is a fairly simple relation between rising levels of transactions internal to one state and increased interdependence among states. As *internal* interdependencies increase and as governmental organizations are institutionalized, even if international transactions remain constant (and they do not) *international* interdependencies also increase. This is true because sensitivity to transnational activities increases the domestic implications of international transactions. For example, as the levels of interdependence within a state rise, the same order of trade has increased implications for domestic employment, fiscal, monetary, and welfare policies.[32] It is precisely this element of interdependence that is fundamental and that Deutsch and other theorists have overlooked.

The three-fold increase in the number of sovereign, if not autonomous, political entities since World War II disproportionately increases the problem of coordination and "mutual adjustment," just as it increases the size of a bureaucracy needed to gather information and to coordinate action. This increase presents a kind of change that is usually destabilizing for a social system. It compounds the problems accompanying the development of transnational society discussed above, by increasing the number of interactions among governments and between governments and transnational nongovernmental organizations.

The present diversity in type of state actor is unparalleled in history. This variety can be viewed along five different dimensions, and each dimension adds to the complexity of coordination because each represents a set of conditions that must be handled in a separate way. Moreover, the greater the diversity of approaches incorporated in handling each set of conditions, the greater is the problem of consistency in foreign policy objectives and instrumentalities.

First, there is tremendous diversity and "unevenness of development among national societies in response to the revolution of modernization."[33] This unevenness of development has been increasing recently, rather than narrowing. Second, there is great variety in the "power" of states. Third, there is increased diversity in the alignment of states. Fourth, states are differentiated according to whether they are interactionist or isolationist. Finally, governments differ along dimensions characterizing their internal organization, ranging from highly pluralistic to highly authoritarian. Accordingly, diplomatic initiatives and responses to such governments must take into account the particular context of governmental structures in other societies and this too hinders overall foreign policy consistency.

In addition to diversity of state units, there have arisen a variety of new kinds of nonstate units with impressive economic wherewithal, with which governments must interact at least indirectly and often directly and actively. The existence of these units has challenged the state-centric theory of international politics, for they have formed transnational links among societies. Their importance varies with the state and unit in question, and depends upon a variety of elements that have not yet been spelled out. In general, the effect on foreign policy of the nonstate units is one about which we know very little.

These additional units can be summarized under four headings, with great variety in each. First, there are international organizations of states. Second, there are international organizations of nongovernmental interest groups, including political parties, unions, and business organizations. Third, there are transnational or multinational corporations, some of which rival states in their economic power if their net sales are viewed as roughly equivalent to the G.N.P. of national economies.[34] Fourth, there are other transnational groupings, such as the Vatican and United Jewish Appeal, which deal in large transfers of capital across state lines and often to governments.

These new organizations serve both as evidence of interdependence and as important agencies furthering it. Either they have grown up as reflections of interdependence or they have been specifically established for the purpose of controlling its effects. Since both kinds of organized entities are of wide-ranging diversity, and since they differ from the formal sovereign states, they have remained anomalous for international politics theory. Like all organizations, they have political aspects in all senses of the term, but they are not predominantly political organizations. Moreover, they are of such complexity and diversity that the coordination and control of their activities by formal sovereign political entities has become difficult.

CONCLUSIONS

The transformations in all three aspects of foreign policies—in their contents, the processes associated with policy formation, and the control of policy effects—offer the citizens of any modernized society opportunities for increased wealth and welfare that were unthinkable in any system with much lower levels of interdependence. They also increase the chances of instability for international society as a whole; for interdependence has increased far in advance of either the instruments capable of controlling it or of available knowledge of its effects. There are, however, two aspects of modernization and foreign policy that, in conclusion, must be highlighted.

First, the various changes discussed above pertain to all modernized societies and are affected very little by ideology or by particular sets of political institutions. To be sure, it may make some difference whether institutions are democratic or nondemocratic in particular instances. In the long run, however, the general influences that have transformed foreign policies are ubiquitous.

Second, these changes are likely to be dispersed throughout the international system far ahead of other aspects of modernity. They are, therefore, likely to characterize the foreign policies of some less modernized societies before these societies become relatively modernized— or even if they do not become modernized. The speed with which modernity spreads will, therefore, only increase the problems of control and will make more urgent the need for establishing new mechanisms of international order.

NOTES

1. Marion J. Levy, Jr., *Modernization and the Structure of Societies* (Princeton 1966), II.
2. *Ibid.*
3. *Ibid.*, 85.
4. See Bruce M. Russett and others, *World Handbook of Political and Social Indicators* (New Haven 1964), 298. These fourteen societies are the Netherlands, West Germany, France, Denmark, Norway, the United Kingdom, Belgium, New Zealand, Australia, Sweden, Luxembourg, Switzerland, Canada, and the United States.

5. These five characteristics are adopted from Cyril E. Black, *The Dynamics of Modernization: A Study in Comparative History* (New York 1967), 9–34.
6. Leopold von Ranke, "A Dialogue on Politics," reprinted in Theodore H. Von Laue, *Leopold Ranke: The Formative Years* (Princeton 1950), 168.
7. Carl J. Friedrich, "Intranational Politics and Foreign Policy in Developed (Western) Societies," in R. Barry Farrell, ed., *Approaches to Comparative and International Politics* (Evanston 1966), 97.
8. See Russett and others, *World Handbook of Political and Social Indicators,* 308–309.
9. Stanley Hoffmann offers another argument on "low policies" and "high policies" in his essay "Obstinate or Obsolete? The Fate of the Nation–State and the Case of Western Europe," *Daedalus,* xcv (Summer 1966), 862–915. Hoffmann feels that nuclear stalemate has served to reinforce the attributes of the nation–state by stabilizing the structure of postwar international society, and that low policies do not generate the spillover expected of them by prophets of international integration. Although Hoffmann is quite right in saying that the integrationists overestimated the potential of economic exigencies for creating international integration, his denial of any effect of low policies is overstated.
10. In definitions of public goods, the emphasis is usually placed on one society rather than on a group of societies. The focus is then on nonexclusivity or the incapacity of a single organization or government to prevent any individual members from receiving its benefits. See Mancur Olson, Jr., *The Logic of Collective Action: Public Goods and the Theory of Groups* (Cambridge, Mass. 1965). It is also true, however, that incentives exist for cooperation within a group, based on the lure of greater benefits.
11. For a discussion of the transfer of action referents from transcendental to empirical ones, see Marion J. Levy, Jr., "Rapid Social Change and Some Implications for Modernization," *International Conference on the Problems of Modernization in Asia,* June 28–July 7, 1965 (Seoul 1965), 657–58.
12. Arnold Wolfers, *Discord and Collaboration: Essays on International Politics* (Baltimore 1962), 91–102. Wolfers adds a third category "self-abnegation," which fits a logical but not an empirical gap.
13. Levy, "Rapid Social Change," 657.
14. Klaus Knorr, *On the Uses of Military Power in the Nuclear Age* (Princeton 1966), 21.
15. This is the argument in Robert E. Osgood and Robert W. Tucker, *Force, Order, and Justice* (Baltimore 1967), 325.
16. A balanced analysis of both schools of thought can be found in Pierre Hassner, "The Nation–State in the Nuclear Age," *Survey,* lxvii (April 1968), 3–27.
17. See Jacob Viner, "Power versus Plenty as Objectives of Foreign Policy in the Seventeenth and Eighteenth Centuries," *World Politics,* 1 (October 1948), 1–20.
18. Knorr, *On the Uses of Military Power,* 22.
19. Recent economic thought on the relation between war and economic growth falls into a great tradition of non-Marxist economic-political theory. For a history of these writings, see Edmund Silberner, *La guerre et la paix dans l'histoire des doctrines économiques* (Paris 1957).

20. Harold and Margaret Sprout, "The Dilemma of Rising Demands and Insufficient Resources," *World Politics,* xx (July 1968), 660–93.
21. *Ibid.,* 685.
22. *Ibid.,* 690–91.
23. See, for example, the organismic metaphors, and their rationalization, in Karl W. Deutsch, *The Nerves of Government* (Glencoe 1963).
24. An important explication of these models is found in Graham T. Allison, "Conceptual Models and the Cuban Missile Crisis," *American Political Science Review,* LXIII (September 1969), 689–718.
25. See Paul Y. Hammond, "Foreign Policy-Making and Adminstrative Politics," *World Politics,* XVII (July 1965), 656–71.
26. Karl Kaiser, "The Interaction of Regional Subsystems: Some Preliminary Notes on Recurrent Patterns and the Role of Superpowers," *World Politics,* XXI (October 1968), 91. Also see his article, "Transnationalepolitik: Zu einer Theorie der multinationalen Politik," *Politische Vierteljahresschrift* (1969), 80–109.
27. *Ibid.,* 92.
28. Jan Tinbergen, *On the Theory of Economic Policy,* 2nd ed. (Amsterdam 1963), 37–38.
29. *Ibid.,* 41.
30. Richard N. Cooper, *The Economics of Interdependence: Economic Policy in the Atlantic Community* (New York 1968), 155.
31. See the works of Karl W. Deutsch, including Deutsch and others, *France, Germany, and the Western Alliance: A Study of Elite Attitudes on European Integration and World Politics* (New York 1967); and "The Impact of Communications upon International Relations Theory," in Abdul A. Said, ed., *Theory of International Relations: the Crisis of Relevance* (Englewood Cliffs 1968), 74–92.
32. For an elaboration of this point, see Richard Cooper, *Economics of Interdependence,* 10.
33. Manfred Halpern, "The Revolution of Modernization in National and International Society," in Carl J. Friedrich, ed., *Revolution* (New York 1966), 195.
34. General Motors, for example, with global net sales of $20.2 billion, would rank as the eighteenth most important state in such a ranking. See *War/Peace Reports* (October 1968), 10.

World Society

*Professor Burton contrasts the realist model of the international system
with what he terms the* cobweb model—*a pluralist image. He argues
that the term is descriptively a more accurate image of the world society
and that it does a better job in capturing the multitude of political, economic, social, and technological interactions.*

It will be seen that the history of thought about world society includes a
steady movement away from relations between states to broader
considerations. . . .

"INTERNATIONAL RELATIONS" OR "WORLD SOCIETY"

It is because of the past preoccupation with relations between nations
that "International Relations" is the title that is usually given to the discipline concerned with the study of world politics and world society. It
is an unfortunate title for our present purposes. States sometimes comprise different national groups, such as English, Irish, Scots and Welsh in
the state of the United Kingdom. If we were concerned only with relations among the 150 or so independent political units of today, "interstate" would be a more appropriate term than "inter-national" relations.
The general idea that most of us have of world society is one that is based
on maps of the world which emphasize state boundaries, on historical
studies which concentrate on relations among governments. We are
familiar with a set of national symbols, customs and institutions that make
us feel different from peoples in other states. For this reason we think
about world affairs as though they were confined to relations between
states. But the study of world society is not confined to relations among
states or state authorities. There are important religious, language, scientific, commercial and other relationships in addition to a variety of formal non-governmental institutions that are world-wide.

This is not just a matter of choosing between different words. We are
choosing an approach when we choose to speak of world society and
not inter-national relations. The study of world society is a much wider
study than the relations of units within it. It is, of course, possible and
useful to study inter-state trading relations and inter-governmental insti-

From John W. Burton, *World Society* (1972). Reprinted by permission of Cambridge University Press.

tutions of various kinds. It is also possible and useful to make comparative studies of the ways in which different governments behave and how their different institutions function. But these studies based on states cannot give us that understanding we seek of world society, and in particular its processes and trends. Obviously, any separation of domestic politics and world politics is arbitrary and probably misleading. For example, these state studies cannot tell us much about the nature of conflict among communities that originates within states and spills over into world society. The political and social life of people within states, which is always altering with changed thinking and new technologies, influences relations among states. This is clear where there are sudden and fundamental changes such as have taken place this century in Russia and in China. Less dramatic internal political and social changes are altering relations among states year by year. Indeed, it is because this is so that the more powerful states such as the United States of America and the Union of Soviet Socialist Republics endeavour to influence these changes in other states.

State boundaries are significant, but they are just one type of boundary which affects the behaviour of world society. There are local muncipal boundaries such as those of the Greater London Council, which include more people than do many states, and in which administrative functions are carried out such as those that occur within small states. At the other end of the scale there are boundaries that include several states, such as those of the European Common Market and the Organization of African Unity. There are also non-geographical boundaries to be taken into account. These are based on functions, for example, the boundaries that separate the work of the World Health Organization from the Food and Agricultural Organization. These cut across geographical or state boundaries. The world geographical map depicting states cannot show these—but they exist and an image of world society is not complete without them.

If states controlled all world activities even to the limited extent that they control the activities of an inter-state institution like the World Health Organization, then one could extend the idea of inter-state relations to include all activities in world society. But there are many transactions in addition to those initiated and regulated by governments within states that cut across state boundaries. Indeed, new ideas and philosophies cut across state boundaries sometimes despite attempts by governments to prevent this happening. There is now one world of science. No state can affort to cut itself off from scientific and technological developments. It is not possible to import just a selection of scientific thoughts. From our own studies we know how knowledge in one subject relates to knowledge in another. Natural science and political thought cannot be separated because the one employs the methodologies and thinking of the other, and developments in the one field lead to developments in the other. Technological inventions change political and social life wherever they occur. The working life of a factory worker in a developed socialist country is little different from the life of a factory worker in another industrialized country. Similarly, administrations and cultures tend to converge with the spread of ideas, and this will occur even more rapidly when television is received as radio is now.

If we employ the term "world society" instead of "international relations," if we approach our study in this global way instead of the more traditional "national" way, we will tend to have a wider focus, to ask questions that are more fundamental and important to civilization, and be able to assess better the relevance of our own national behaviour to the wider world environment. . . .

THE BILLIARD BALL MODEL

Over the ages there have been many models or abstractions used to bring to focus different aspects of world society. At one time, when the fortunes of a nation appeared to fluctuate for no apparent reason, this could be explained by reference to the swing of a pendulum—a simple mechanical device of which everyone was aware. Even today, when conditions responsible for change are not known precisely, we are prepared to refer to a run of unfavourable events as though there were some mysterious influences determining them. In earlier times "fate" seemed to be a sufficient explanation of events.

It is only a few hundred years since it would have been absurd to think of a world society. There was a European society, and going back much further there were Mediterranean and Chinese societies or civilizations. We know how small feudal holdings, almost tribal areas, gradually coming together, led to the establishment of provinces and nation–states. We know of the growth of empires after exploration from Europe, the movement towards independent states, and the increasing relative power of a few main states. As a consequence, we tend to have in mind a world society comprising states, small and large, each pursuing its "national interest." We are aware, too, of international institutions like the United Nations and its agencies, and perhaps we entertain the hope that one day there will be some world body with powers sufficient to regulate the power of states. Some such general notion of a world society of great and small states is in the back of our minds when we read of the events that unfold day by day. We interpret events in the light of this notion. Each event seems to confirm it: Soviet intervention in Czechoslovakia, United States intervention in Latin American countries and in Vietnam, the defence of spheres of influences by both of these great powers with navies, aircraft and forces deployed well outside their territorial boundaries.

This conventional image of a world composed of nation–states which are of different size and power has been termed the *"billiard-ball"* model. Each state is represented by a government and is seen as an entity—a sovereign, independent unit. What takes place within the boundaries of each is not the concern of the others—this is a matter of "domestic jurisdiction," to use the words of the United Nations Charter. The interactions or contacts are like those of different sized billiard balls. Only the hard exteriors touch, and heavier or faster moving ones push others out of the way. The points of contact are governments: it is only governments that are interacting.

This was a model that described conditions when city–states were ruled by feudal lords, when each was independent and virtually isolated from the rest of the world, when negotiation was through leaders, when the main concern was self-defence. It is a model that depicts some of the features of the contemporary world. There are direct diplomatic contacts between governments on many major matters. This same simple model of large and small balls interacting can take into account some of the internal happenings of states that affect relations with others. A new industry in one state affects an industry in another. There are internal political processes in the affected state that might result in tariff protection: the plight of the affected industry is referred to the chamber of manufacturers, to the local member of parliament, to the minister, to the cabinet, and the government might then consult with the government of the other country. The relationship is government to government, and this fits into the idea of world society being composed of sovereign states.

It is this image which leads us to focus our attention on diplomatic relations, on governments as the main actors in world affairs, on their relative power, and on the personal characteristics of their leaders. But with this model in mind our attention is directed away from other relationships. How important are diplomats and governments in the scheme of things? To what extent is the making of policy the free decision of governments, and to what extent do governments reflect the needs and interests of others conducting their own transactions across state boundaries?

Perhaps this general notion was a realistic one many years ago; but there have been some developments in world society, which have become apparent especially since the Second World War, that are forcing us to revise our picture. For example, there is a persistent increase in the number of states, a reduction in the size of political units, and an increase in the size of economic units and the degree of interdependence. The significance of state boundaries is altering as a consequence. There are changing values or priorities in objectives, restrictions on the freedom of action of powerful states, and accentuated racial and class conflict. With education and communication there is an assimilation of ideologies leading to greater similarities between political parties within each state, and between states. These are only some of the main trends.

They are interacting and not precisely defined ones. Each one of us could make his own personal list.

On the presence of one trend there will be agreement. Communications of all kinds have become quicker and more frequent between different geographical points. A great many consequences flow from this. Exchanges are promoted between persons with common and competing interests and objectives. There is a "one world" of science, of ideas, of trade and commerce that is only marginally affected by the barriers of mountains, seas and state boundaries. Values are shared, and objectives never previously entertained are known to be practical. The peasant worker of Asia knows that other people have a higher living standard and work their own land. Peoples who do not govern themselves know that others have revolted and won independence. Asians and Africans know that non-discrimination, equality of opportunity and human dignity are values that can be attained. Communications have brought peoples into contact, and made them aware of possibilities.

Industrial technology is another undisputed influence on world society. Political units or states are not always adequate as industrial units, and specialization has led to the production of aeroplanes and other complex manufactures being spread over many countries. The oil industry knows no state boundaries, and companies make agreements with governments of different ideological outlooks. International or transnational corporations are developing, and they are not responsible to anyone but themselves. The billiard-ball model cannot depict these developments.

Another remarkable change is in values. We now know that people hold some values even higher than material gains: independence, freedom of expression, and a sense of participation in making decisions that affect them. There are psychological and sociological explanations and these we must discuss. We know that values are influencing world society and the policies of states vary greatly. Probably many of these values have always been held: the serf always wanted freedom of expression and freedom from hunger. The significant difference is that now there are opportunities to demand values. Education and communications have made people aware of what is possible, and political institutions and political organizations have helped to make demands effective. The development of the ideal of "welfare state" has had profound effects upon the policies of states, and therefore upon world society. Once a ruler could decide upon a foreign adventure and command the service of princes and their subjects, and raise taxes to fight wars, with few political restraints imposed upon him. In the modern welfare state defence expenditure must compete with expenditure on education and other social services, and welfare generally. Even the most wealthy states find that there are political restraints on the degree to which they can sacrifice welfare needs in order to exercise their military and economic power in other countries. . . .

THE COBWEB MODEL

The conventional map of the world is a physical one: it shows geographical relationships, over which are sometimes drawn political boundaries. It does not tell us much about processes or behaviour. The same proportional space and importance are given to seas and deserts as are given to ports and cities. There do exist diagrammatic maps that tell us where populations are concentrated, where resources are to be found, how many newspapers are read and other information such as this. But even these do not give us much information about behaviour, or more particularly, about transactions and links that exist. We are familiar with maps of the world showing air and shipping routes. What we really need to have, either in map form or conceptually, is an image of world society that shows behaviour by showing these linkages. If we could superimpose on successive sheets of transparent paper air-passenger movements per week, telegraphic flows, ethnic and language relations, movements of scholars, technical advisers, migration, tourism, and all other transactions, we would begin to build up a picture of relationships which would help to explain behaviour in world society far better than traditional maps. Maps were designed to show people how to get from point A to point B. They are useful for this purpose. But they have been used for purposes other than this. They have had the effect of creating in our minds this geographical image of world society. What we need is a map or concept that tells us something about behaviour. The difference is like the difference between a set of photos of a car showing its headlamps and other details, and the type of diagram an electrical engineer would draw showing the wiring links within the electrical system. We cannot understand a car by looking at. Its processes need to be analysed, and then we can understand it, and remedy any failures.

If we had been brought up with such maps on the wall, if we were not so consciously aware of states whenever we looked at a map of the world, and best of all, if we had never seen an ordinary map of the world, we would think far more in terms of world society and far less in terms of a system of states. We would approach closer to a realistic model of world society.

An easy way to think about this second model is by use of the concept of "system." A system exists when there are relationships or transactions between units of the same set. There is a system of states, and there are also transactions between businessmen, traders, research workers, television stations, drug peddlers, students and others. There are systems or linkages such as those created by amateur radio enthusiasts, by peoples with the same ideological or religious outlooks, by scientists exchanging papers and meeting together, by people behaving in their different ways. It is the total of these which we need to see as a behavioural map of the world. In this model contacts are not only at the boundaries of sovereign states, but between points within each.

We have gone to a great deal of trouble and expense over the years to map rivers and mountains, sea depths and ocean currents; but we have not as yet been sufficiently interested in social and political studies to map the behaviour of men. In most cases we do not even have the basic information required. When we look at the ordinary physical map we have to impose on it our own personal knowledge. For example, we may know where populations are massed, and where there are deserts. We have our own ideas, usually inaccurate, about which populations are friendly, aggressive, backward, developed, black, white, yellow, and perhaps we have a vague idea which are Muslim, Hindu, Christian and Buddhist. We have some idea where different commodities are produced, where trade flows, and which are the most used shipping and air lanes. We rely on our personal knowledge. There are some physical maps which superimpose accurately some of this information for us, and even some diagrammatical "maps" or graphs which show comparative figures, such as percentages of total world wheat produced in various countries. The few maps of this kind that do exist are helpful. They give us a new perspective on the world, and help us to see at a glance what otherwise can be understood only by looking at statistics.

We still have difficulty in conceptualizing world society, first because these "maps" are inadequate, and second because by their nature they are misleading. They are inadequate not only in the sense that data are available which have not been presented in this form, and in the sense that relevant data have never been obtained. They are inadequate in terms of their analytical content. A population figure for a country, even an average population per square mile, does not tell us those things about distribution which would make a glance at a map meaningful. In theory it should be possible to put a dot wherever anyone is; in practice it is possible to do this by taking 10,000 people as a unit. Then we would have the rudimentary basis of a human behavioural map. A next step would be to differentiate between race, language and other differences in more and more detail in a series of superimposed maps. A further step would be to examine relationships between these sets or different groups of people. Take, for example, Malaysia. There are many differents sets: Malays, Chinese, anti-communist and pro-communist Malays and Chinese, traditionally-oriented and religious Muslims and other Malays, Chinese businessmen, and so on. Each of these sets has its own values and interests, and therefore its own external sympathies. Some Chinese look to China, and others to Taiwan, some Malays are nationalist and some look to Indonesia and other Muslim countries for support in any possible confrontation with Chinese. These sets can be represented by interlocking circles: one person can be Chinese by birth, regard himself as a Malay nationalist, a businessman, British educated and oriented and anti-communist. He must be placed in an area in which the circles representing all these sets overlap.

If we considered neighbouring Indonesia in the same way, we would find similar sets. Putting the two alongside each other it would at once become clear that any alliance between the two would be seen as a threat to some sets in each. Chinese, for example, would see such an alliance as a Malayan threat to them. We could reasonably assume, just by looking at these sets, that attempts to establish regional arrangements would lead to increased internal tension and conflict within each political unit. Just by analysing existing data we could come to some important hypotheses about behaviour. We are just beginning to do this—despite the urgent need to solve the problems of world society.

Even though our existing data were fully used in these ways, we would still not have a map of human behaviour. These are data based on state statistics: state populations, state trade, state classifications. We are interested in transactions across state boundaries of which states have little knowledge, and certainly no statistics—the sympathies Jewish people have for one another, the transmission of values attached to participation in decision-making, the way in which people of the same tribe or ethnic group identify with each other across state boundaries, and the flow of ideas. We are also interested in the direction of flow: there are state statistics giving the flow of mail across state boundaries, but not the direction of these flows. . . .

We would begin to get nearer to such a concept of world society if we were to map it without reference to political boundaries, and indeed, without reference to any physical boundaries. We are not particularly concerned with boundaries, except insofar as they affect behaviour by reducing transactions and communications among people. We are concerned with behaviour—boundaries or no boundaries. If we were to start with a clean sheet of paper and plot people in various sets, their transport and communications, we would, in fact, create a map some of which would be recognizable as parts of the physical map of the world. One difference would be that seas and deserts would look the same. We could build on this additional information, perhaps by a series of transparent sheets, and finally superimpose political boundaries.

Communications are a good starting point because they are an important means of transactions or links between people. It is communications or links between units that create systems. A useful map of the world could be drawn by plotting on a blank piece of paper all post offices. In some cases the system links would form clusters recognizable as a country. In others, for example, some areas of the Middle East, it would immediately seem that there were as many or more transactions across boundaries as within. If we could map all movements and communications in world society we would find some ethnic groups communicating across state boundaries as though they did not exist, as for example, between Somalia and Kenya, and between many Western European countries. This would give us a picture of some important aspects of behaviour which a physical map cannot give. Conceptually we could extend this to include all transactions and links, even those we cannot quantify and map, such as ideological sympathies, and the hidden transactions of international corporations and international institutions of all kinds. In practice there are so many direct communications or systems that a world map which represented them would look like a mass of cobwebs superimposed on one another, strands converging at some points more than others, and being concentrated between some points more than between others. The boundaries of states would be hidden from view.

Which is the more representative model of the world—the world of continents, islands and states or the world of transactions? This is not a superficial question. There are two different models or images presented. If we adopt the nation–state one we will use the language of relations between states and their relevant power, and have one set of solutions to problems of conflict and world organization. If we adopt the transactions one we will use a different language to describe world society, and have a different set of solutions to world problems. For example, we will be greatly concerned with political and social conditions within states because it is these which, in this model, determine relationships in world society, including relations between states.

Let us dwell on this a little more. The model we have at the back of our minds determines our interpretation of events, our theories and our policies. For example, the billiard-ball model is a power model—world society is seen to be organized by the relative power of each unit. There are matters of domestic jurisdiction of no concern to others, not even the United Nations. There are legal political entities that have a right to protect themselves and to expect assistance from others, including the United Nations, if they are threatened, even though they have no popular support—no legitimized status. Collective security is the means of preventing "aggression." Economic development is the means to social and political stability.

The model depicting transactions invites a different approach to world problems. The source of conflict between states is in internal politics, in failures by states to adjust to altering conditions, in the struggle of states to preserve their institutions, and in the conflict between states and systems that cut across state boundaries. Conflict cannot be prevented by external coercion, or by great power threats. Communal conflict—race, religious, ideological—invites sympathies across state boundaries and promotes international conflict. The role of authorities is to assist in the making of adjustments to altering conditions so that conflict between interests within the state, and the wider world system, does not occur. Development and stability must rest on internal conditions or political organization, that is, a high degree of participation so that authorities are strongly legitimized. In accordance with this model, a form of world government cannot rest on collective security, and must be based on the transactions inherent in functional organizations that are, by their nature, universal in potential membership. Viable political units can be very small, provided there is a high level of transactions with the wider environment. Communications, and not power, are the main organizing influence in world society.

There is an important practical question raised here. An image of world society that comprises separate state entities, each potentially hostile to others, leads understandably to defensive policies. Is the image a realistic one, or are the conflicts that occur and seem to validate the image merely the consequences of our having this image? An image of world society that depicts transactions, controlled and regulated by local state and international authorities, with a view to securing the maximum benefits from interdependence without loss of security, leads reasonably to integrative policies. Is the image a realistic one, or are the functional arrangements, world corporations and other evidences that seem to validate the image merely the consequence of our having this image? It is possible that the cobweb image is the realistic one, except insofar as lack of confidence has created the one comprising separate and fearful entities. Thus created it becomes part of our perceived reality. . . .

International Interdependence and Integration

Robert O. Keohane and Joseph S. Nye

The authors treat two concepts that are important to the pluralist perspective: interdependence and integration.

During the 1940s and 1950s, and to a considerable extent thereafter, political scientists have tended to describe world politics as a Hobbesian situation in which independent units called nation–states are locked into patterns of fundamental conflict. Some "Realists," such as Morgenthau and Niebuhr, have ascribed international conflict largely to characteristics of human nature. As Morgenthau puts it, "the selfishness of man has limits; his will to power has none."[1] Others have put less stress on human characteristics and more on the nature of the international system as a condition of what Waltz describes as "international anarchy."[2] The exis-

Robert Keohane and Joseph S. Nye, Jr., from Fred I. Greenstein & Nelson W. Polsby, HANDBOOK OF POLITICAL SCIENCE ©, 1975, Addison–Wesley, Reading, Massachusetts. Pgs. 363–377.

tence of powerful and antagonistic states creates a "security dilemma" for statesmen who must "compete for ever more power in order to find more security, an effort which proves self-defeating because complete security remains ultimately unobtainable."[3] Regardless of differences in explanation, however, there has been substantial agreement among many leading analysts about the crucial importance of conflict and war in the international arena. The title of a volume by a well-known student of the subject, *International Relations: Peace or War?*, summarizes the point.[4]

There was never complete agreement on any particular version of this approach to world politics. Robert W. Tucker, Arnold Wolfers, and I. L. Claude all challenged Morgenthau's analysis, often with devastating effect.[5] Yet global patterns of world politics, particularly during the height of the cold war, seemed to confirm the broad outlines of force- and security-oriented definitions of the subject matter of the field. States were paramount, and their conflicts seemed to threaten not only world peace, but also human existence. International relations was seen essentially as a state of war in the Hobbesian sense:

> For *war* consists not in battle only, or the act of fighting, but in a tract of time wherein the will to contend by battle is sufficiently known; and therefore the notion of *time* is to be considered in the nature of war as it is in the nature of weather. For as the nature of foul weather lies not in a shower or two of rain but in an inclination thereto of many days together, so the nature of war consists not in actual fighting but in the known disposition thereto during all the time there is no assurance to the contrary. All other time is *peace*.[6]

Yet even during the most bitter years of East–West conflict, interstate relations in Western Europe were characterized by unprecedented cooperation, which rapidly went beyond wary diplomatic coexistence— beyond, that is, the traditional "state of war." The European unity movement flourished in the 1950s, first in the European Coal and Steel Community (ECSC), then in the European Economic Community (EEC) or Common Market. Obviously, this change occurred in the context of a bipolar strategic balance and was encouraged both by United States support and Soviet hostility. Nonetheless, the growth of common institutions was spectacular in comparison with previous patterns or developments elsewhere, and despite the absence of supranational government, it would clearly have been misleading to characterize relations in Western Europe as "international anarchy," or to have interpreted those relations in terms of security or possible violent conflict.

The importance of European events, for contemporary world politics as well as for theories of international relations, led several scholars to examine the developments taking place on the continent. In the mid-1950s, the pioneering work of Karl W. Deutsch and his associates[7] and of Ernst B. Haas,[8] focused attention on "regional integration" as an appropriate concept for describing the process that was taking place. As thinking about regional integration developed over the years, it led scholars quite far from the Realists' assumptions about men and states. The movement toward European unity could not be explained as merely a new form of alliance, thus reflecting the hoary principles of the balance of power.[9] It represented a response to opportunity and an expression of hope as much as a response to threat and an expression of fear. To students of European developments, it did not seem helpful to posit war-threatening conflict as the key to understanding the human or international condition. On the contrary, whether there would be progress toward more cooperative association or movement toward intense conflict or dissociation was seen as conditional on a multiplicity of factors. Detailed arguments were therefore developed about the conditions under which the European integration process would persist, speed up, slow down, or reverse itself. The arguments were further elaborated as scholars made efforts to understand regional integration efforts in other parts of the globe such as Latin America and Africa.[10]

The analysis of integration processes tended also to undermine another basic tenet of conventional analysis: that students of world politics should limit their focus to nation–states and their interactions. The "cybernetic" approach pioneered by Deutsch focused largely on transactions among societies and on changes in public attitudes within societies; Haas's "neofunctionalism" stressed the interests of elites and institutions and the extent to which they altered their behavior through learning.[11] Neither took the nation–state as the basic unit of analysis, nor did they rely on traditional notions of "national interest," although both were criticized on this account.[12] Transnational interactions not controlled by central foreign-policy organs of governments were no longer ignored. To the contrary, they were regarded as often being of crucial importance to the integration process.

Students of regional integration eventually developed a complex and ingenious set of notions and distinctions about the processes they were attempting to explain. . . . In the mid-1960s, "integrationists" were a distinct cluster in the matrix of scholars concerned with international relations.[13] Yet the slowdown in European integration during the 1960s, and the failure of the dominant paradigms to explain this adequately, tended to throw doubt on the general validity of "integration theory." At the same time the middling success of regional integration attempts elsewhere produced more evidence about the conditions in which integration would *not* take place than about the process of integration itself. Theoretical progress along the lines of comparative politics was stymied by the infeasibility of testing integration theory in a systematic and comparative manner. To borrow a phrase from the literature, integration theory became "encapsulated."

Despite these difficulties in developing adequate theories, the literature on regional integration is important for the ideas it stimulated about studying world politics. Students of integration raised a number of issues that are highly relevant to understanding the politics of interdependence outside the regional context as well as within. Conversely, analyzing poltical integration in terms of interdependence may help to place "integration theory" in its proper context: not as a separate and arcane set of notions applicable only to Europe and perhaps a few other areas, but as a highly important part of the literature on world politics—and one which traditionally inclined writers ignore only at their intellectual peril.

Due to the ambiguity of words such as "integration" and "interdependence" as used in the literature, it seems desirable at the outset to define several dimensions of integration and interdependence and to discuss how these relate to one another. . . .

INTERDEPENDENCE AND INTEGRATION

Considerable confusion continues to persist among scholars about the uses of the term "integration." Some scholars define it as a process, others as a terminal condition—the "condition of being integrated"—and still others as a combination of the two. In practice, scholars often use the word interchangeably, so that the reader may have difficulty knowing what is being referred to at any given time. The dictionary definition is of a process or condition of "forming parts into a whole." But what is the relevant whole? And in what units should we measure the process of formation? Galtung stresses the creation of new actors.[14] Deutsch defines integration in terms of turning "previously separate units into components of a coherent system."[15] Elsewhere, however, he stresses the condition of security community.[16] For Haas integration is "a process for the creation of political communities defined in institutional or attitudinal terms," but

> the study of regional integration is concerned with explaining how and why states cease to be wholly sovereign, how and why they voluntarily mingle, merge, and mix with their neighbors so as to lose the factual attributes of sovereignty while acquiring new techniques for resolving conflict between themselves. Regional cooperation, organization, systems, and subsystems may help describe steps on the way; but they should not be confused with the resulting *condition* [italics added.][17]

Some writers interested in comparing regions to inquire which region has the higher level of integration have avoided definitions in terms of process or final condition—thus adding a third definition, implicitly, of integration as any level of association ascertained by specified measures.[18]

Since we intend in this chapter to compare the concepts of "integration" and "interdependence," we will define integration in this third way, as any level of association between actors, on one dimension or another. We will then be able to speak not only of various types of integration, such as economic, social, and policy integration, but of various levels of integration as well.

This definition places "integration" on the same analytical level as "interdependence," which is a term not so closely associated with teleological or process-oriented theory. Interdependence has normally been defined simply as a condition. Thus Oran Young uses the concept "interdependence" to refer to

> the extent to which events occurring in any given part or within any given component unit of a world system affect (either physically or perceptually) events taking place in each of the other parts or component units of the system.[19]

Depending on the type of system involved, it is clear that there can be various types of interdependence, as well as various levels of it. As with integration, relations may take place in a variety of issue-areas and may be more or less intense.

"Integration" and "interdependence" both carry evaluative overtones that have affected the way analysts have used the terms, sometimes with detrimental effects on conceptual clarity. Students of integration have oriented their work heavily toward the analysis of *peaceful* change. Indeed, in Haas's view,

> the main reason for studying . . . regional integration . . . is normative: the units and actions provide a living laboratory for observing the peaceful creation of possible new types of human communities at a very high level of organization and of the processes that may lead to such conditions.[20]

This distinguishes it from "previous systematic studies of political unification because it limits itself to noncoercive efforts." Not all scholars share this view. Nonetheless, it does tend to be the prevailing usage.

Similarly, rhetorical uses of "interdependence" frequently carry highly positive and egalitarian overtones. Interdependence is taken to be a characteristic of mutually beneficial relationships. In some cases, however, an interdependent relationship may have such negative consequences that both parties would be quite happy to cease contact with one another entirely, forgoing any benefits that such contact may bring. A tense and rapidly escalating arms race constitutes an example of "negative interdependence" of this type. Yet even within relationships that are beneficial to all parties involved, interdependence may be highly asymmetrical: one actor may depend on another to a much greater extent than applies vice versa. Such asymmetrical relations are quite common in contemporary world politics, particularly between developed and less-developed countries, or between the United States and most other states. Asymmetry is politically important. Being less dependent than other actors in an interdependent system can be an important source of power.

Marxist writers on economic imperialism have been much more aware of this than more traditional analysts.[21] Theorists interested in dependence (*dependencia*) have also stressed asymmetries of interdependent relations, particularly between developed "center" countries and those of the underdeveloped "periphery."[22]

It is important to remember that interdependence by no means implies equality. Interdependent relationships are more or less asymmetrical depending on the characteristics of issue-areas and the attitudes and interests of elites, as well as on the aggregate levels of power of the states involved. Thus we use the term "interdependence" to imply some degree of mutual effect: it is up to the investigator to determine the intensity of a particular relationship and its degree of asymmetry.

Quite apart from the sometime connotations of peace and equality that they carry, both "integration" and "interdependence" are such vague and ill-defined concepts that without further analysis hopeless confusion quickly results. Our first step will therefore be to distinguish types of integration and interdependence that are insofar as possible comparable. We will consider economic integration and interdependence, social integration and interdependence, and policy integration and interdependence. We will also refer to other frequently used notions of integration that can be classified under the broad rubric of "political integration."[23]

Economic Integration and Interdependence

It is important to clarify at the outset that neither economic integration nor interdependence is equivalent to, or perfectly measured by, the volume of economic transactions between the units with which the analyst is concerned. Absolute volumes of transactions in the context of growing world trade and production may mean little; relative volumes (as measured by an index of relative acceptance, or RA)[24] may also lead to interpretive distortions.[25] More significantly, volumes of transactions may not necessarily indicate the extent to which units are affected by events occurring outside (interdependence) or the extent to which a true regional transnational economy is in existence (integration). It is more enlightening in our judgment to define one aspect of economic interdependence, at any rate, as "the *sensitivity* of economic transactions between two or more nations to economic developments within those nations." As Cooper points out,

> this approach means that two countries with much mutual trade would still experience a low degree of interdependence if the value of the trade were not sensitive to price and income developments in the two countries; on the

other hand, two countries would be highly interdependent if their transactions were greatly sensitive to economic developments, even if their mutual trade were initially at a low level.[26]

This definition is closer to the intuitive meaning of interdependence than is a definition in terms of transactions volume. Furthermore, it can also be used as a definition of economic integration, consistent with economists' usage.[27] Thus at this level, "integration" and "interdependence" can be regarded as conceptually interchangeable terms. They differ only in the connotation that integration often takes place within an institutional framework.[28]

This definition is superior in our opinion to definitions that rely on the degree of formal suppression of national economic discrimination, as developed in particular by Bela Balassa.[29] Balassa set forth five categories ranging from "free trade area" at the low end of the spectrum to "total economic integration," as depicted in Table 1. These categories, however, are formal rather than behavioral. They do not measure the extent to which actual flows follow the suppression of formal discriminatory barriers, or the extent to which mutual sensitivity increases as a result. They can be useful in describing policies followed by states, at least on a formal level; but they do not indicate the significance of those politics for economic interdependence or effective levels of economic integration. This is true at the global as well as the regional level. As Cooper argues,

the integration of the pre-1914 world economy was something of an illusion. While the pre-1914 world was integrated in the sense that government-

TABLE 1   Balassa's Categories of Economic Integration

	No Tariff or Quotas	Common External Tariffs	Free Flow of Factors	Harmonization of Economic Policies	Unification of Policies, Political Institutions
1. Free trade area	X				
2. Customs union	X	X			
3. Common market	X	X	X		
4. Economic union	X	X	X	X	
5. Total economic integration	X	X	X	X	X

imposed barriers to the movement of goods, capital and people [i.e., Balassa's indicators of economic integration] were minimal, those imposed by nature were much greater and economic integration was not high in the sense used here: quick responsiveness to differential earning opportunities resulting in a sharp reduction in differences in factor rewards.[30]

Sensitivity is not the only dimension of interdependence. This form of interdependence is created by interaction within a framework that is established and generally taken for granted by the participants. Thus, under the fixed-exchange rate system of the late 1960s, European governments were dependent on (that is, sensitive to) changes in American monetary policy, and the United States was similarly dependent on European decisions to continue to hold dollars without demanding that they be exchanged for gold.

These sensitivities, however, depended on the rules of the system at the time: United States sensitivity to European decisions to continue to hold dollars could be drastically reduced by the simple act of unilaterally changing the rules, refusing any longer to redeem dollars for gold. A further question about interdependence therefore needs to be asked: Which actors in the system are most and least vulnerable to changes in the rules (as in the monetary system) or to a drastic reduction in the level of transactions in the system?[31] In vulnerability terms, the less dependent actor is not necessarily the one with less sensitivity to changes in transactions taking place within an established structure, but the one that would incur relatively lower costs from the termination or drastic alteration of the relationship.

Vulnerability interdependence has no direct parallel in the various definitions of economic integration. Nevertheless, power relations among a number of actors in a regional grouping or any other set of economic transactions are likely to be strongly affected by the differential costs to them of dissolution.[32] For this reason, vulnerability interdependence is particularly relevant for the analysis of the *structure* of relations in a common market or in an issue-area. In a sense, it asks which actors are the "definers of the *ceteris paribus* clause," or in game-theory terms, which actors can restructure the payoff matrix.[33] Since the relative power of actors is as important within the context of an integration process as elsewhere in politics, careful analysis of patterns of vulnerability interdependence, and asymmetries in those patterns, should be a necessary element of sophisticated explanations of behavior in regional or other economic transactions.

Social Integration and Interdependence

On an analogous basis to that of economic interdependence and levels of economic integration, one can define social interdependence, and levels of social integration, in terms of the sensitivity of societies to changes taking place in other societies. As the present authors have argued elsewhere,

> by facilitating the flow of ideas modern communications have also increased intersocietal sensitivity. Certainly there have been indirect "contagions" of ideas in earlier periods such as the European revolutions of 1848 or Latin American university reforms in 1917. . . . Today, however, television has created a "window on the West" in the living rooms of the elites of the third world. Widely separate elites, whether functionally similar social groups, students, military officers, or racial minorities, become more rapidly aware of each other's activities.[34]

It is clear that such sensitivities can be deliberately fostered or discouraged but rarely completely controlled by governments. Eastern European governments, for example, have not been able to keep younger generations from imitating aspects of Western youth culture. Within Western Europe, younger people tend to be particularly subject to "contagions" from other societies.[35]

Unfortunately, good indicators of social sensitivity have not been developed, and scholars have generally attempted to rely on levels of transactions, either in absolute terms or on a relative basis as expressed by the index of relative acceptance discussed above. Donald Puchala, for instance, has used absolute figures on mail, trade, tourism, and student exchanges, coupled with indices of relative acceptance of trade and mail to demonstrate that the EEC countries have become a distinct transactions network.[36] These data, although they reveal a good deal about transactions, say little about sensitivities.

Sensitivities of societies to one another could be explored, however, by an analysis of the diffusion of innovation in social patterns and of popular opinions and perceptions. Subjects for analysis could range from matters of cultural tastes and clothing styles to issues of labor-union organization, university governance, or social policies of governments. [One] study, for instance, has examined the diffusion of social-security arrangements from one society to another since the 1880s.[37] Some suggestive work has been done on policy diffusion, intranationally as well as crossnationally, that could provide a base for efforts to explore issues of social integration in this way.[38] By being closely tied intuitively to concepts of interdependence and integration, data on diffusion patterns would be likely to be of greater theoretical value than much of the transactions data that has been gathered so far.

Policy Integration and Interdependence

For political scientists, economic and social integration and interdependence are most interesting when they are perceived and acted upon, or even facilitated, by governments. Students of political integration have therefore concentrated much of their attention on "the evolution over time of a collective decision-making system among nations"[39] or what Nye[40] has elsewhere called "policy integration." This dimension excludes other aspects of political integration such as the construction of common institutions or the development of a sense of community. Instead, it focuses on the extent to which policies are coordinated with one another. Policy interdependence refers to the extent to which decisions taken by actors in one part of a system affect (intentionally or unintentionally) other actors' policy decisions elsewhere in the system. Policy integration can be regarded as an attempt to reduce adverse costs of policy interdependence by deliberately coordinating policy and thus changing the nature of policy interdependence without necessarily reducing its level. This by no means implies that conflict does not exist. Indeed, conflict or the serious threat of conflict may be critical in stimulating attempts at policy integration.

Policy interdependence may be indirect: governmental policies may affect one another without direct contacts between the governments themselves or deliberate attempts by governments to manipulate each other's behavior. Central bank policies toward interest rates in major Western countries during the 1960s would have affected each other even in the absence of consultation. Changes in Japanese tax policies toward their automobile companies could well affect exports of cars to the United States, and therefore U.S. trade and monetary policy. New antipollution standards for automobiles in California may affect economic policy in Japan. The ineffectiveness of American policy attempts to stop heroin use in the 1960s, and the increases in heroin shipments to the United States during that decade, affected French society and therefore French policies toward narcotics; conversely, the weakness of French law enforcement earlier had contributed to the American problem and to changes in American policy.[41] In all of these cases, we can speak of "indirect policy dependence." The effects of policies can be transmitted through transnational interactions between societies. As government policies extend "downward," deeper into society, and as transnational transactions multiply "horizontally," it can be expected that indirect policy interdependence will continue to increase, particularly among developed, market-economy countries.

Policy interdependence may also be direct. Governments may take action deliberately designed to affect others' policies, may threaten to do so, or may be in such a situation that such actions or threats are continual possibilities. The governments of the United States and the Soviet Union are directly interdependent strategically. Either could destroy the other's society, and leaders of both governments are aware of this situation. The United States, Japan, and Western Europe are interdependent economically. When the United States attempted in 1971 to persuade or force other governments to revalue their currencies, it was taking advantage of the high degree of dependence of other governments on American decisions. Most international negotiations involve the manipulation and management of direct policy interdependencies for national advantage—or sometimes for the advantage of subnational or transnational groups.

Insofar as governments are aware of the processes at work, indirect policy interdependence is likely to lead to direct policy interdependence. Seeing other governments' policies as one source of their troubles, leaders of states are likely to attempt to influence those policies. Possible results short of war include arms races and trade wars, as well as myriads of lesser conflicts. In a situation of high policy interdependence, the threats both to state autonomy and to joint welfare may very well lead to concerted attempts by groups of governments to coordinate policy, as a means to increase welfare *as well as,* on frequent occasions, to regain control of the situation from nongovernmental actors.[42] In the 1960s and early 1970s, for instance, governments faced the problem of coping with private monetary speculation, which threatened the structure of fixed exchange rates to which all governments subscribed. Their collaborations represented attempts to gain control over speculators while preserving what were then perceived as the general benefits of fixed exchange rates.[43]

In a developed and institutionalized system of policy integration, two distinguishing characteristics are present: on the one hand, the expectation that some agreement will eventually be reached; and on the other, a system of decision rules, formal and informal, that determine how the decision will be reached and that legitimize particular nonviolent means of influence while proscribing the use of force. These rules may be more or less institutionalized and may conform more or less closely to typical national democratic procedures. A formal voting scheme, for instance, is not a necessary prerequisite for a high level of policy integration. On the basis of their knowledge of various regional integration schemes, students have sometimes attempted to score them according to the degree to which joint decisions are taken, differentiating by issue-area.[44] Yet policy integration as defined here is by no means limited to the regional context, although the highest levels of it in the contemporary world are found in the European Community. NATO, the International Monetary Fund (IMF), the General Agreement on Tariffs and Trade (GATT), and the Organization for Economic Cooperation and Development (OECD) all represent focal points for varying degrees of policy integration by governments.

One of the most striking features of regional cooperation in Europe has been the way in which policy integration has reinforced economic and social integration, which have then provided new imperatives for further policy integration. This self-reinforcing process is much less evident on the global scale. There, the potential for policy disintegration is more often realized. Nevertheless, whatever the setbacks in particular areas, increased policy interdependence provides continual new opportunities for integrative as well as disintegrative responses. For the national policymaker, it implies decreased efficacy of purely national policies in

TABLE 2   A Summary of Usages: Integration and Interdependence

---

A. These dimensions of interdependence and integration are defined in virtually interchangeable ways, so that the only difference is in the connotations:
   1. Economic-sensitivity interdependence/economic integration:
   2. Social interdependence/social integration.
B. These dimensions of interdependence and integration are not interchangeable:
   1. Policy integration is one means of coping with the effects of indirect and direct policy interdependence, and may also increase policy interdependence.
   2. Economic interdependence in the sense of "vulnerability interdependence" is not developed explicitly in the integration literature, although the problem of the extent to which various actors are capable of changing the structure of the situation or "rules of the game" is sometimes discussed.

---

solving problems, whether these have to do with economic growth, balance of payments equilibrium, maintenance of national control of industry, protection of the environment, or efforts to control the use of harmful narcotics. Insofar as these goals are not shared widely in the world, or measures taken to achieve objectives in one state conflict with measures elsewhere, conflicts over policy are likely to arise. Leaders may in some circumstances attempt to insulate their societies from effects emanating from outside, as in the case of Burma. But where the costs of avoiding policy interdependence appear too high, it may seem more sensible, rather than changing its *level*, to alter its *form:* that is, to institute a joint decision-making procedure. Attempts to develop patterns of policy integration can therefore be regarded as ways to cope with policy interdependence—which may, on occasion, involve increasing it.

Table 2 summarizes the comparisons we have drawn between these principal aspects of interdependence and integration.

Institutional and Attitudinal Integration

Two other prominent usages of the term "political integration" deserve brief mention here, although they find no close parallel in the notion of interdependence.

The most common of these usages is that of political integration as "institutional integration," that is, the extent to which common institutions have been developing for a region. Thus one may hear Europeans or Central Americans complain that "economic integration has not led to political integration," by which they usually mean that political institutions have not developed as a result of closer economic ties. Other terms sometimes employed, such as "supranationality," "confederation," and "federation" indicate a similar institutional orientation. Yet institutions are usually sought not for their own sake but for the effects they are likely to have on social and economic conditions, usually through effects on governmental policies. A focus on policy integration therefore concentrates more directly on the critical outcomes that affect people's lives, and the analyst following this approach is less likely than the institutionally oriented observer to be misled into equating the political significance of an integration process with its degree of formal institutionalization.

Another common dimension of political integration, "attitudinal integration," can be defined in terms of the extent to which people share a sense of common identity and/or mutual obligation. This is how theorists of comparative politics tend to use the word "integration,"[45] and it is related to Deutsch's concept of security community as the extent to which a set of people holds reliable expectations of nonviolent relations among themselves. Disputes are rife among theorists about the importance of attitudinal integration for explaining other aspects of the phenomenon, such as institutional or policy integration.[46]

These usages of "political integration," which are often lumped together with joint policy formation, provide one reason for the frequent confusions that surround that term. We saw above that economic integration and interdependence, social integration and interdependence, and policy integration and interdependence, all had something to do with the sensitivities of one unit in a set to events taking place in another, as a result of transactions between them. Institutional integration refers, however, to structures; and attitudinal integration focuses on the compatibility of attitudes at a given time, rather than to sensitivities of attitudes of one set of people to those of another set. These usages of "integration" therefore refer not only to different substantive dimensions of the phenomenon, but to different types of processes as well. This is why they have no exact parallel in usages of the term "interdependence," which always refers to the effects (sensitivity or vulnerability) of patterns of transactions, whether actual or anticipated.

Evaluations of Integration and Interdependence

It should be clear from the foregoing discussion that integration and interdependence are both complex enough concepts that simply evaluating as "good" or "bad" the phenomena to which they refer will be extremely misleading. Their effects on conflict are difficult enough to evaluate. Efforts to increase policy *integration,* in particular, have usually taken place within the context of peaceful relations among states, and may well contribute to the development of such relations, although the patterns of causality are surely mutual. Violent conflicts between states have taken place within regions where integration schemes were in effect—notably, in Central America and East Africa in 1969 and 1972 respectively. Nevertheless, one's overall judgment of the effects of policy integration on peace—regionally or on a broader scope—must, on the evidence available, be positive.[47]

For policy *interdependence*, however, it is difficult indeed to argue persuasively that higher levels of interdependence necessarily promote world concord. Following Rousseau, Waltz has argued the opposite:

> It is hard to get a war going unless the potential participants are somehow closely linked. Interdependent states whose relations remain unregulated must experience conflict and will occasionally fall into violence. If regulation is hard to come by, as it is in the relations of states, then it would seem to follow that a lessening of interdependence is desirable.[48]

Waltz's contention that some degree of interdependence is necessary for conflict is irrefutable, but the conclusion that a lessening of interdependence is desirable does not follow unless we know the relative costs of attaining effective regulation as opposed to those of reducing interdependence. Theories of political integration focus precisely on the question of the attainability of regulation and that a high level of policy interdependence may therefore be tolerable. It would seem that neither the blanket proposition that "interdependence leads to peace," nor the opposite statement, would be well sustained in a systematic, empirical inquiry. Interdependence at some level is obviously a necessary condition for war; but that is quite uninteresting, since it does not tell us anything in particular about thresholds or conditions beyond the minimum requirement. Nevertheless, the proposition that higher levels of policy interdependence do not necessarily imply more peaceful relations seems incontestable.

Quite apart from the effects of integration and interdependence on conflict, it is not true that increases in levels of either are necessarily beneficial. Too often one finds an implicit assumption that integration (and less often interdependence) is a good thing *per se*. This is wrong for a variety of reasons:

1. Where many values are involved, integration and interdependence may enhance some while diminishing others. Many Canadians, for example, argue that increased levels of economic integration and interdependence with the United States have contributed to increased Canadian material welfare but decreased Canadian political and cultural autonomy.[49] In Eastern Europe, a high degree of regional trade has been achieved by forgoing greater welfare gains from trade with the rest of the world.[50]

2. Economic integration and interdependence have distributional effects, and may look different from the periphery than from the center of any unit. What is good for the whole is not necessarily good for each of the parts. The unification of Italy had a deleterious effect upon Southern Italy; the famous gold standard contributed to high levels of economic interdependence in the nineteenth century but accentuated instability in the periphery of the world economy. In the con-

temporary world, some U.S. workers complain about the effects on their welfare of high levels of interdependence. The British government worries about the effects on British growth rates of monetary union with their partners in the European Community.

3. Social integration and interdependence may introduce changes in societies that are undesired at least by many of the inhabitants. Importation of new patterns of life, whether involving the use of Coca-Cola, automobiles, or drugs, may drastically alter established social patterns and lead to more or less serious problems. Although to some these changes may represent progress, others view them negatively. Mass immigration—for example, into Switzerland during the 1960s—can be viewed as so threatening that special measures are taken to prevent it even at some economic cost.

4. As noted above, policy interdependence may create foci for conflict, although insofar as cleavages tend to be crosscutting, conflicts may be less intense, if more frequent. Yet even if patterns of policy integration are developed, serious normative problems may arise. Two of the most significant of these are:

   a. Costs to democratic control. Insofar as decisions become more responsive to the wishes of external actors within a complex communications network, it may be increasingly difficult for traditional democratic means of internal control to be effective. It may be unclear to domestic interests even how a given decision was made, much less how to influence it effectively.[51]

   b. Costs to third parties, and of conflict with third parties. Integration schemes are often designed purposefully to exclude outsiders, or some outsiders, from their benefits. If external interests are hurt, not only may their welfare, and perhaps world welfare, be damaged (for instance, through trade-diversion effects), but retaliation on their part could lead to further costs. The difficult relations between the United States and the European Community in the early years of the 1970s attest to that.

What this discussion suggests is that more explicit attention should be paid in the future to the normatively relevant consequences of regional integration and international interdependence. As Stuart A. Scheingold has argued,

> to date, the students of integration have been mainly describing, analyzing, and measuring the integration process. . . . What has been missing from all this work is some attention to the difference it makes whether or not such regional entities are created.[52]

The literature on integration and interdependence has frequently failed to challenge normative assumptions implying that integration is desirable *per se*. The attempt by students of the subject to correct for this by distinguishing clearly between questions of "more or less" and those of "better or worse" is laudable as far as it goes. But at some point, serious consideration of the normative issues should be reintroduced, on the basis of empirical findings that are as unbiased as possible. "The normative political theory of integration and interdependence" is a topic that could usefully benefit from substantial serious attention. . . .

NOTES

1. Hans J. Morgenthau, *Scientific Man Versus Power Politics* (Chicago: University of Chicago Press, 1946), p. 193.
2. Kenneth N. Waltz, *Man, the State and War* (New York: Columbia University Press, 1959).
3. John Herz, *International Politics in the Atomic Age* (New York: Columbia University Press, 1959).
4. Richard Rosecrance, *International Relations* (New York: McGraw-Hill, 1973).
5. Robert W. Tucker, "Professor Morgenthau's Theory of Political Realism," *American Political Science Review,* vol. 46 (1952), pp. 214–24; Arnold Wolfers, *Discord and Collaboration* (Baltimore: Johns Hopkins University Press, 1962); and Inis L. Claude, Jr., *Power and International Relations* (New York: Random House, 1962).
6. Thomas Hobbes, *Leviathan,* first published 1651, ed. by Michael Oakeshott (Oxford: Basil Blackwell, n.d.), Part I, ch. 13, p. 82.
7. Karl W. Deutsch and associates, *Political Community and the North Atlantic Area* (Princeton, NJ: Princeton University Press, 1957).
8. Ernst B. Haas, *The Uniting of Europe* (Stanford, CA: Stanford University Press, 1958).
9. George Liska, *Europe Ascendant* (Baltimore: Johns Hopkins University Press, 1964).
10. A collection of articles by leading scholars is Leon N. Lindberg and Stuart A. Scheingold (eds.), *Regional Integration* (Cambridge, MA: Harvard University Press, 1971). For a critique of that volume, see Roger D. Hansen, "European Integration," *International Organization,* vol. 27 (1973), pp. 225–54.
11. Peter J. Katzenstein, "Hare and Tortoise: The Race Toward Integration," *International Organization,* vol. 25, pp. 290–97.
12. Stanley Hoffmann, *State of War* (New York: Praeger, 1965).
13. Bruce M. Russett, "Methodological and Theoretical Schools in International Relations," in Norman Palmer (ed.), *A Design for International Relations Research* (Philadelphia: American Academy of Political and Social Science, 1970).
14. Johan Galtung, "A Structural Theory of Integration," *Journal of Peace Research,* vol. 5 (1968), pp. 375–95.
15. Karl W. Deutsch, *The Analysis of International Relations* (Englewood Cliffs, NJ: Prentice–Hall, 1971), p. 158.
16. Deutsch, *Political Community.*
17. Ernst B. Haas, "The Study of Regional Integration" in Lindberg and Scheingold, p. 6.
18. Joseph S. Nye, Jr., "Comparative Regional Integration," *International Organization,* vol. 22 (1968), pp. 855–80.
19. Oran R. Young, "Interdependencies in World Politics," *International Journal,* vol. 24 (1969), pp. 726–50.

20. Haas, "Study of Regional Integration," p. 4.
21. Harry Magdoff, *The Age of Imperialism* (New York: Monthly Review Press, 1969), and Arghiri Emmanuel, *Unequal Exchange* (New York: Monthly Review Press, 1972).
22. Andre Gunder Frank, *Capitalism and Underdevelopment in Latin America* (New York: Monthly Review Press, 1969); Johan Galtung, "A Structural Theory of Imperialism," *Journal of Peace Research,* vol. 8 (1971), pp. 81–117.
23. Joseph S. Nye, *Peace in Parts* (Boston: Little, Brown, 1971).
24. The formula for the index of relative acceptance (RA) is $RA = (A - E)/E$, where A equals actual values of transactions and E equals expected values on a basis of a null model based on the assumption of complete indifference between actors.
25. Richard W. Chadwick, "A Brief Critique of Transaction Data and Analysis" *International Organization,* vol. 26 (1972), pp. 681–85; Hansen, "European Integration"; and Barry B. Hughes, "Transaction Analysis," *International Organization,* vol. 25 (1971).
26. Richard N. Cooper, "Economic Interdependence and Foreign Policies in the Seventies," *World Politics,* vol. 24 (1972), pp. 159–81.
27. Robert D. Tollison and Thomas D. Willett, "International Integration and the Interdependence of Economic Variables," *International Organization,* vol. 27 (1973), pp. 255–72. Cooper does not distinguish between the two terms and appears to regard them as synonyms. The reader who looks up "integration, economic" in Cooper's index is referred to the listing of "interdependence" under "economic policy."
28. Factor price equalization is not the only measure of economic sensitivity, and students of integration have found it important to devise supplementary measurements to take into account nontrade contributions to mutual sensitivity, such as shared services among members of a regional arrangement.
29. Bela Belassa, *The Theory of Economic Integration* (London: Allen & Unwin, 1961).
30. Richard N. Cooper, *The Economics of Interdependence* (New York: McGraw–Hill, 1968), p. 152.
31. Kenneth N. Waltz, "The Myth of National Interdependence," in Charles Kindleberger (ed.), *The International Corporation* (Cambridge, MA: MIT Press, 1970).
32. Leon N. Lindberg, "Decision Making and Integration in the European Community," in *International Political Communities* (Garden City, NY: Anchor Books, 1966).
33. Anthony Lanyi, "Political Aspects of Exchange Rate Systems," in Richard Merritt (ed.), *Communications in International Politics* (Urbana, IL: University of Illinois Press, 1971).
34. Robert O. Keohane and Joseph S. Nye, Jr., *Transnational Relations and World Politics* (Cambridge, MA: Harvard University Press, 1971), p. 376.
35. Anthony Sampson, *Anatomy of Europe* (New York: Harper & Row, 1969), and Ronald Inglehart, "An End to European Integration?" *American Political Science Review,* vol. 61 (1967), pp. 91–105.
36. Donald J. Puchala, "International Transactions and Regional Integration," in Lindberg and Scheingold, *Regional Integration.*
37. David Collier and Richard E. Messick, "Functional Prerequisites Versus Diffusion," unpublished paper presented at the Midwest Political Science Association, Chicago, 1973.

38. Jack L. Walker, "The Diffusion of Innovations Among the American States," *American Political Science Review,* vol. 63 (1969), pp. 880–99; Robert D. Putnam, "Toward Explaining Military Intervention in Latin American Politics," *World Politics,* vol. 20 (1967), pp. 83–110; and Manus Midlarsky, "Mathematical Models of Instability and a Theory of Diffusion," *International Studies Quarterly,* vol. 14 (1970), pp. 60–84.

39. Leon N. Lindberg and Stuart A. Scheingold, *Europe's Would-Be Polity* (Englewood Cliffs, NJ: Prentice–Hall, 1970).

40. Nye, *Peace in Parts.*

41. Lester R. Brown, *The Interdependence of Nations* (New York: Foreign Policy Association, 1972).

42. John Ruggie has presented an interesting formal analysis of governmental reactions to interdependence, based on the assumption that joint decision making for the performance of joint tasks implies a sacrifice of governmental autonomy for the sake of benefits from collective action. Yet in situations where governmental autonomy has already been diminished as a result of indirect policy interdependence, coordinative procedures may very well not reduce autonomy further and may even increase it.

43. Lawrence B. Krause (ed.), "Private International Finance" in Keohane and Nye, *Transnational Relations.*

44. Leon N. Lindberg, "The European Community as a Political System," *Journal of Common Market Studies,* vol. 5 (1967), pp. 344–87 and Nye, "Comparative Regional Integration."

45. Claude Ake, *A Theory of Political Integration* (Homewood, IL: Dorsey Press, 1967.

45. For a further discussion, see Nye, *Peace in Parts.*

47. *Ibid.*

48. Waltz, "The Myth of National Interdependence," p. 205.

49. *International Organization,* Fall 1974.

50. Frederic L. Pryor, *The Communist Foreign Trade System* (Cambridge, MA: MIT Press, 1963).

51. Karl Kaiser, "Transnational Relations As a Threat to the Democratic Process" in Keohane and Nye, *Transnational Relations;* see also Keohane and Nye, "Transgovernmental Relations and International Organization," *World Politics,* vol. 27 (1974), pp. 39–62.

52. Stuart A. Scheingold, "Domestic and International Consequences of Regional Integration" in Lindberg and Scheingold, *Regional Integration,* p. 374.

Realism and Complex Interdependence

Robert O. Keohane and Joseph S. Nye

The authors contrast the realist perspective on international relations with the complex interdependence perspective on world politics associated with the pluralist image.

INTERDEPENDENCE IN WORLD POLITICS

We live in an era of interdependence. This vague phrase expresses a poorly understood but widespread feeling that the very nature of world politics is changing. The power of nations—that age-old touchstone of analysts and statesmen—has become more elusive: "calculations of power are even more delicate and deceptive than in previous ages."[1] Henry Kissinger, though deeply rooted in the classical tradition, has stated that "the traditional agenda of international affairs—the balance among major powers, the security of nations—no longer defines our perils or our possibilities. . . . Now we are entering a new era. Old international patterns are crumbling; old slogans are uninstructive; old solutions are unavailing. The world has become interdependent in economics, in communications, in human aspirations."[2]

How profound are the changes? A modernist school sees telecommunications and jet travel as creating a "global village" and believes that burgeoning social and economic transactions are creating a "world without borders."[3] To greater or lesser extent, a number of scholars see our era as one in which the territorial state, which has been dominant in world politics for the four centuries since feudal times ended, is being eclipsed by nonterritorial actors such as multinational corporations, transnational social movements, and international organizations. As one economist put it, "the state is about through as an economic unit."[4]

Traditionalists call these assertions unfounded "globaloney." They point to the continuity in world politics. Military interdependence has always existed, and military power is still important in world politics— witness nuclear deterrence; the Vietnam, Middle East, and India–Pakistan wars, and Soviet influence in Eastern Europe or American influence in the Caribbean. Moreover, as the Soviet Union has shown, authoritarian states can, to a considerable extent, control telecommunications and

From Robert O. Keohane and Joseph S. Nye, Jr., *Power and Interdependence: World Politics in Transition,* pp. 3–5, 8–11, 23–37. Copyright © 1977 by Little, Brown and Company (Inc.). Reprinted by permission.

social transactions that they consider disruptive. Even poor and weak countries have been able to nationalize multinational corporations, and the prevalence of nationalism casts doubt on the proposition that the nation–state is fading away.

Neither the modernists nor the traditionalist have an adequate framework for understanding the politics of global interdependence.[5] Modernists point correctly to the fundamental changes now taking place, but they often assume without sufficient analysis that advances in technology and increases in social and economic transactions will lead to a new world in which states, and their control of force, will no longer be important.[6] Traditionalists are adept at showing flaws in the modernist vision by pointing out how military interdependence continues, but find it very difficult accurately to interpret today's multidimensional economic, social, and ecological interdependence.

Our task . . . is not to argue either the modernist or traditionalist position. Because our era is marked by both continuity and change, this would be fruitless. Rather, our task is to provide a means of distilling and blending the wisdom in both positions by developing a coherent theoretical framework for the political analysis of interdependence. We shall develop several different but potentially complementary models, or intellectual tools, for grasping the reality of interdependence in contemporary world politics. Equally important, we shall attempt to explore the *conditions* under which each model will be most likely to produce accurate predictions and satisfactory explanations. Contemporary world politics is not a seamless web; it is a tapestry of diverse relationships. In such a world, one model cannot explain all situations. The secret of understanding lies in knowing which approach or combination of approaches to use in analyzing a situation. There will never be a substitute for careful analysis of actual situations.

Yet theory is inescapable; all empirical or practical analysis rests on it. Pragmatic policymakers might think that they need pay no more heed to theoretical disputes over the nature of world politics than they pay to medieval scholastic disputes over how many angels can dance on the head of a pin. Academic pens, however, leave marks in the minds of statesmen with profound results for policy. Not only are "practical men who believe themselves to be quite exempt from any intellectual influences" unconscious captives of conceptions created by "some academic scribbler of a few years back," but increasingly the scribblers have been playing a direct role in forming foreign policy.[7] Inappropriate images and ill-conceived perceptions of world politics can lead directly to inappropriate or even disastrous national policies.

Rationale and rationalization, systematic presentation and symbolism, become so intertwined that it is difficult, even for policymakers themselves, to disentangle reality from rhetoric. Traditionally, classical theories of world politics have portrayed a potential "state of war" in which states' behavior was dominated by the constant danger of military conflict. During the Cold War, especially the first decade after World War II, this conception, labeled "political realism" by its proponents, became widely accepted by students and practitioners of international relations in Europe and the United States.[8] During the 1960s, many otherwise keen observers who accepted realist approaches were slow to perceive the development of new issues that did not center on military–security concerns.[9] The same dominant image in the late 1970s or 1980s would be likely to lead to even more unrealistic expectations. Yet to exchange it for an equally simple view—for instance, that military force is obsolete and economic interdependence benign—would condemn one to equally grave, though different, errors. . . .

INTERDEPENDENCE AS AN ANALYTIC CONCEPT

In common parlance, *dependence* means a state of being determined or significantly affected by external forces. *Interdependence,* most simply defined, means *mutual* dependence. Interdependence in world politics refers to situations characterized by reciprocal effects among countries or among actors in different countries.

These effects often result from international transactions—flows of money, goods, people, and messages across international boundaries. Such transactions have increased dramatically since World War II: "Recent decades reveal a general tendency for many forms of human interconnectedness across national boundaries to be doubling every ten years."[10] Yet this interconnectedness is not the same as interdependence. The effects of transactions on interdependence will depend on the constraints, or costs, associated with them. A country that imports all of its oil is likely to be more dependent on a continual flow of petroleum than a country importing furs, jewelry, and perfume (even of equivalent monetary value) will be on uninterrupted access to these luxury goods. Where there are reciprocal (although not necessarily symmetrical) costly effects of transactions, there is interdependence. Where interactions do not have significant costly effects, there is simply interconnectedness. The distinction is vital if we are to understand the *politics* of interdependence.

Costly effects may be imposed directly and intentionally by another actor—as in Soviet-American strategic interdependence, which derives from the mutual threat of nuclear destruction. But some costly effects do not come directly or intentionally from other actors. For example, collective action may be necessary to prevent disaster for an alliance (the members of which are interdependent), for an international economic system (which may face chaos because of the absence of coordination, rather than through the malevolence of any actor), or for an ecological system threatened by a gradual increase of industrial effluents .

We do not limit the term *interdependence* to situations of mutual benefit. Such a definition would assume that the concept is only useful analytically where the modernist view of the world prevails: where threats of military force are few and levels of conflict are low. It would exclude from interdependence cases of mutual dependence, such as the strategic interdependence between the United States and the Soviet Union. Furthermore, it would make it very ambiguous whether relations between industrialized countries and less developed countries should be considered interdependent or not. Their inclusion would depend on an inherently subjective judgment about whether the relationships were "mutually beneficial."

Because we wish to avoid sterile arguments about whether a given set of relationships is characterized by interdependence or not, and because we seek to use the concept of interdependence to integrate rather than further to divide modernist and traditional approaches, we choose a broader definition. Our perspective implies that interdependent relationships will always involve costs, since interdependence restricts autonomy; but it is impossible to specify a priori whether the benefits of a relationship will exceed the costs. This will depend on the values of the actors as well as on the nature of the relationship. Nothing guarantees that relationships that we designate as "interdependent" will be characterized by mutual benefit.

Two different perspectives can be adopted for analyzing the costs and benefits of an interdependent relationship. The first focuses on the joint gains or joint losses to the parties involved. The other stresses *relative* gains and distributional issues. Classical economists adopted the first approach in formulating their powerful insight about comparative advantage: that undistorted international trade will provide overall net benefits. Unfortunately, an exclusive focus on joint gain may obscure the second key issue: how those gains are divided. Many of the crucial political issues of interdependence revolve around the old question of politics, "who gets what?"

It is important to guard against the assumption that measures that increase joint gain from a relationship will somehow be free of distributional conflict. Governments and nongovernmental organizations will strive to increase their shares of gains from transactions, even when they both profit enormously from the relationship. Oil-exporting governments and multinational oil companies, for instance, share an interest in high prices for petroleum; but they have also been in conflict over shares of the profits involved.

We must therefore be cautious about the prospect that rising interdependence is creating a brave new world of cooperation to replace the bad old world of international conflict. As every parent of small children knows, baking a larger pie does not stop disputes over the size of the slices. An optimistic approach would overlook the uses of economic and even ecological interdependence in competitive international politics.

The difference between traditional international politics and the politics of economic and ecological interdependence is *not* the difference between a world of "zero-sum" (where one side's gain is the other side's loss) and "nonzero-sum" games. Military interdependence need not be zero-sum. Indeed, military allies actively seek interdependence to provide enhanced security for all. Even balance of power situations need not be zero-sum. If one side seeks to upset the status quo, then its gain is at the expense of the other. But if most or all participants want a stable status quo, they can jointly gain by preserving the balance of power among them. Conversely, the politics of economic and ecological interdependence involve competition even when large net benefits can be expected from cooperation. There are important continuities, as well as marked differences, between the traditional politics of military security and the politics of economic and ecological interdependence.

We must also be careful not to define interdependence entirely in terms of situations of *evenly balanced* mutual dependence. It is *asymmetries* in dependence that are most likely to provide sources of influence for actors in their dealings with one another. Less dependent actors can often use the interdependent relationship as a source of power in bargaining over an issue and perhaps to affect other issues. At the other extreme from pure symmetry is pure dependence (sometimes disguised by calling the situation interdependence); but it too is rare. Most cases lie between these two extremes. And that is where the heart of the political bargaining process of interdependence lies. . . .

REALISM AND COMPLEX INTERDEPENDENCE

One's assumptions about world politics profoundly affect what one sees and how one constructs theories to explain events. We believe that the assumptions of political realists, whose theories dominated the postwar period, are often an inadequate basis for analyzing the politics of interdependence. The realist assumptions about world politics can be seen as defining an extreme set of conditions or *ideal type*. One could also imagine very different conditions. In this article, we shall construct another ideal type, the opposite of realism. We call it *complex interdependence*. After establishing the differences between realism and complex interdependence, we shall argue that complex interdependence sometimes comes closer to reality than does realism. When it does, traditional explanations of change in international regimes become questionable and the search for new explanatory models becomes more urgent.

For political realists, international politics, like all other politics, is a struggle for power but, unlike domestic politics, a struggle dominated by organized violence. In the words of the most influential postwar textbook, "All history shows that nations active in international politics are continuously preparing for, actively involved in, or recovering from organized violence in the form of war."[11] Three assumptions are integral to the realist vision. First, states as coherent units are the dominant actors in world politics. This is a double assumption: states are predominant; and they act as coherent units. Second, realists assume that force is a usable and effective instrument of policy. Other instruments may also be employed, but using or threatening force is the most effective means of wielding power. Third, partly because of their second assumption, realists assume a hierarchy of issues in world politics, headed by questions of military security: the "high politics" of military security dominates the "low politics" of economic and social affairs.

These realist assumptions define an ideal type of world politics. They allow us to imagine a world in which politics is continually characterized by active or potential conflict among states, with the use of force possible at any time. Each state attempts to defend its territory and interests from real or perceived threats. Political integration among states is slight and lasts only as long as it serves the national interests of the most powerful states. Transnational actors either do not exist or are politically unimportant. Only the adept exercise of force or the threat of force permits states to survive, and only while statesmen succeed in adjusting their interests, as in a well-functioning balance of power, is the system stable.

Each of the realist assumptions can be challenged. If we challenge them all simultaneously, we can imagine a world in which actors other than states participate directly in world politics, in which a clear hierarchy of issues does not exist, and in which force is an ineffective instrument of policy. Under these conditions—which we call the characteristics of complex interdependence—one would expect world politics to be very different than under realist conditions.

We will explore these differences in the next section of this chapter. We do not argue, however, that complex interdependence faithfully reflects world political reality. Quite the contrary: both it and the realist portrait are ideal types. Most situations will fall somewhere between these two extremes. Sometimes, realist assumptions will be accurate, or largely accurate, but frequently complex interdependence will provide a better portrayal of reality. Before one decides what explanatory model to apply to a situation or problem, one will need to understand the degree to which realist or complex interdependence assumptions correspond to the situation.

THE CHARACTERISTICS OF COMPLEX INTERDEPENDENCE

Complex interdependence has three main characteristics:

1. *Multiple channels* connect societies, including: informal ties between governmental elites as well as formal foreign office arrangements; informal ties among nongovernmental elites (face-to-face and through telecommunications); and transnational organizations (such

as multinational banks or corporations). These channels can be summarized as interstate, transgovernmental, and transnational relations. *Interstate* relations are the normal channels assumed by realists. *Transgovernmental* applies when we relax the realist assumption that states act coherently as units; *transnational* applies when we relax the assumption that states are the only units.

2. The agenda of interstate relationships consists of multiple issues that are not arranged in a clear or consistent hierarchy. This *absence of hierarchy among issues* means, among other things, that military security does not consistently dominate the agenda. Many issues arise from what used to be considered domestic policy, and the distinction between domestic and foreign issues becomes blurred. These issues are considered in several government departments (not just foreign offices), and at several levels. Inadequate policy coordination on these issues involves significant costs. Different issues generate different coalitions, both within governments and across them, and involve different degrees of conflict. Politics does not stop at the waters' edge.

3. Military force is not used by governments toward other governments within the region, or on the issues, when complex interdependence prevails. It may, however, be important in these governments' relations with governments outside that region, or on other issues. Military force could, for instance, be irrelevant to resolving disagreements on economic issues among members of an alliance, yet at the same time be very important for that alliance's political and military relations with a rival bloc. For the former relationships this condition of complex interdependence would be met; for the latter, it would not.

Traditional theories of international politics implicitly or explicitly deny the accuracy of these three assumptions. Traditionalists are therefore tempted also to deny the relevance of criticisms based on the complex interdependence ideal type. We believe, however, that our three conditions are fairly well approximated on some global issues of economic and ecological interdependence and that they come close to characterizing the entire relationship between some countries. One of our purposes here is to prove that contention. . . .

Multiple Channels

A visit to any major airport is a dramatic way to confirm the existence of multiple channels of contact among advanced industrial countries; there is a voluminous literature to prove it.[12] Bureaucrats from different countries deal directly with one another at meetings and on the telephone as well as in writing. Similarly, nongovernmental elites frequently get together in the normal course of business, in organizations such as the Trilateral Commission, and in conferences sponsored by private foundations.

In addition, multinational firms and banks affect both domestic and interstate relations. The limits on private firms, or the closeness of ties between government and business, vary considerably from one society to another; but the participation of large and dynamic organizations, not controlled entirely by governments, has become a normal part of foreign as well as domestic relations.

These actors are important not only because of their activities in pursuit of their own interests, but also because they act as transmission belts, making government policies in various countries more sensitive to one another. As the scope of governments' domestic activities has broadened, and as corporations, banks, and (to a lesser extent) trade unions have made decisions that transcend national boundaries, the domestic policies of different countries impinge on one another more and more. Transnational communications reinforce these effects. Thus, foreign economic policies touch more domestic economic activity than in the past, blurring the lines between domestic and foreign policy and increasing the number of issues relevant to foreign policy. Parallel developments in issues of environmental regulation and control over technology reinforce this trend.

Absence of Hierarchy Among Issues

Foreign affairs agendas—that is, sets of issues relevant to foreign policy with which governments are concerned—have become larger and more diverse. No longer can all issues be subordinated to military security. As Secretary of State Kissinger described the situation in 1975,

> progress in dealing with the traditional agenda is no longer enough. A new and unprecedented kind of issue has emerged. The problems of energy, resources, environment, population, the uses of space and the seas now rank with questions of military security, ideology and territorial rivalry which have traditionally made up the diplomatic agenda.[13]

Kissinger's list, which could be expanded, illustrates how governments' policies, even those previously considered merely domestic, impinge on one another. The extensive consultative arrangements developed by the OECD, as well as the GATT, IMF, and the European Community, indicate how characteristic the overlap of domestic and foreign policy is among developed pluralist countries. The organization within nine major departments of the United States government (Agriculture, Commerce, Defense, Health, Education and Welfare, Interior, Justice, Labor, State, and Treasury) and many other agencies reflects their extensive international commitments. The multiple, overlapping issues that result make a nightmare of governmental organization.[14]

When there are multiple issues on the agenda, many of which threaten the interests of domestic groups but do not clearly threaten the nation as a whole, the problems of formulating a coherent and consistent foreign policy increase. In 1975 energy was a foreign policy problem, but specific remedies, such as a tax on gasoline and automobiles, involved domestic legislation opposed by auto workers and companies alike. As one commentator observed "virtually every time Congress has set a national policy that changed the way people live . . . the action came after a consensus had developed, bit by bit, over the years, that a problem existed and that there was one best way to solve it."[15] Opportunities for delay, for special protection, for inconsistency and incoherence abound when international politics requires aligning the domestic policies of pluralist democratic countries.

Minor Role of Military Force

Political scientists have traditionally emphasized the role of military force in international politics. Force dominates other means of power: *if* there are no constraints on one's choice of instruments (a hypothetical situation that has only been approximated in the two world wars), the state with superior military force will prevail. If the security dilemma for all states were extremely acute, military force, supported by economic and other resources, would clearly be the dominant source of power. Survival is the primary goal of all states, and in the worst situations, force is ultimately necessary to guarantee survival. Thus military force is always a central component of national power.

Yet particularly among industrialized, pluralist countries, the perceived margin of safety has widened: fears of attack in general have declined, and fears of attacks *by one another* are virtually nonexistent. France has abandoned the *tous azimuts* (defense in all directions) strategy that President de Gaulle advocated (it was not taken entirely seriously even at the time). Canada's last war plans for fighting the United States were abandoned half a century ago. Britain and Germany no longer feel threatened by each other. Intense relationships of mutual influence exist between these countries, but in most of them force is irrelevant or unimportant as an instrument of policy.

Moreover, force is often not an appropriate way of achieving other goals (such as economic and ecological welfare) that are becoming more important. It is not impossible to imagine dramatic conflict or revolutionary change in which the use or threat of military force over an economic issue or among advanced industrial countries might become plausible. Then realist assumptions would again be a reliable guide to events. But in most situations, the effects of military force are both costly and uncertain.[16]

Even when the direct use of force is barred among a group of countries, however, military power can still be used politically. Each superpower continues to use the threat of force to deter attacks by the other superpower on itself or its allies; its deterrence ability thus serves an indirect, protective role, which it can use in bargaining on other issues with its allies. This bargaining tool is particularly important for the United States, whose allies are concerned about potential Soviet threats and which has fewer other means of influence over its allies than does the Soviet Union over its Eastern European partners. The United States has, accordingly, taken advantage of the Europeans' (particularly the Germans') desire for its protection and linked the issue of troop levels in Europe to trade and monetary negotiations. Thus, although the first-order effect of deterrent force is essentially negative—to deny effective offensive power to a superpower opponent—a state can use that force positively—to gain political influence.

Thus, even for countries whose relations approximate complex interdependence, two serious qualifications remain: (1) drastic social and political change could cause force again to become an important direct instrument of policy; and (2) even when elites' interests are complementary, a country that uses military force to protect another may have significant political influence over the other country.

In North–South relations, or relations among Third World countries, as well as in East–West relations, force is often important. Military power helps the Soviet Union to dominate Eastern Europe economically as well as politically. The threat of open or covert American military intervention has helped to limit revolutionary changes in the Caribbean, especially in Guatemala in 1954 and in the Dominican Republic in 1965. Secretary of State Kissinger, in January 1975, issued a veiled warning to members of the Organization of Petroleum Exporting Countries (OPEC) that the United States might use force against them "where there is some actual strangulation of the industrialized world."[17]

Even in these rather conflictual situations, however, the recourse to force seems less likely now than at most times during the century before 1945. The destructiveness of nuclear weapons makes any attack against a nuclear power dangerous. Nuclear weapons are mostly used as a deterrent. Threats of nuclear action against much weaker countries may occasionally be efficacious, but they are equally or more likely to solidify relations between one's adversaries. The limited usefulness of conventional force to control socially mobilized populations has been shown by the United States failure in Vietnam as well as by the rapid decline of colonialism in Africa. Furthermore, employing force on one issue against an independent state with which one has a variety of relationships is likely to rupture mutually profitable relations on other issues. In other words, the use of force often has costly effects on nonsecurity goals. And finally, in Western democracies, popular opposition to prolonged military conflicts is very high.[18]

It is clear that these constraints bear unequally on various countries, or on the same countries in different situations. Risks of nuclear escalation affect everyone, but domestic opinion is far less constraining for communist states, or for authoritarian regional powers, than for the United States, Europe, or Japan. Even authoritarian countries may be reluctant to use force to obtain economic objectives when such use might be ineffective and disrupt other relationships. Both the difficulty of controlling socially mobilized populations with foreign troops and the changing technology of weaponry may actually enhance the ability of certain countries, or nonstate groups, to use terrorism as a political weapon without effective fear of reprisal.

The fact that the changing role of force has uneven effects does not make the change less important, but it does make matters more complex. This complexity is compounded by differences in the usability of force among issue areas. When an issue arouses little interest or passion, force may be unthinkable. In such instances, complex interdependence may be a valuable concept for analyzing the political process. But if that issue becomes a matter of life and death—as some people thought oil might become—the use or threat of force could become decisive again. Realist assumptions would then be more relevant.

It is thus important to determine the applicability of realism or of complex interdependence to each situation. Without this determination, further analysis is likely to be confused. Our purpose in developing an alternative to the realist description of world politics is to encourage a differentiated approach that distinguishes among dimensions and areas of world politics—not (as some modernist observers do) to replace one oversimplification with another.

THE POLITICAL PROCESSES OF COMPLEX INTERDEPENDENCE

The three main characteristics of complex interdependence give rise to distinctive political processes, which translate power resources into power as control of outcomes. As we argued earlier, something is usually lost or added in the translation. Under conditions of complex interdependence the translation will be different than under realist conditions, and our predictions about outcomes will need to be adjusted accordingly.

In the realist world, military security will be the dominant goal of states. It will even affect issues that are not directly involved with military power or territorial defense. Nonmilitary problems will not only be subordinated to military ones; they will be studied for their politico-military implications. Balance of payments issues, for instance, will be considered at least as much in the light of their implications for world power generally as for their purely financial ramifications. McGeorge Bundy conformed to realist expectations when he argued in 1964 that devaluation of the dollar should be seriously considered if necessary to fight the war in Vietnam.[19] To some extent, so did former Treasury Secretary Henry

Fowler when he contended in 1971 that the United States needed a trade surplus of $4 billion to $6 billion in order to lead in Western defense.[20]

In a world of complex interdependence, however, one expects some officials, particularly at lower levels, to emphasize the *variety* of state goals that must be pursued. In the absence of a clear hierarchy of issues, goals will vary by issue, and may not be closely related. Each bureaucracy will pursue its own concerns; and although several agencies may reach compromises on issues that affect them all, they will find that a consistent pattern of policy is difficult to maintain. Moreover, transnational actors will introduce different goals into various groups of issues.

Linkage Strategies

Goals will therefore vary by issue area under complex interdependence, but so will the distribution of power and the typical political processes. Traditional analysis focuses on *the* international system, and leads us to anticipate similar political processes on a variety of issues. Militarily and economically strong states will dominate a variety of organizations and a variety of issues, by linking their own policies on some issues to other states' policies on other issues. By using their overall dominance to prevail on their weak issues, the strongest states will, in the traditional model, ensure a congruence between the overall structure of military and economic power and the pattern of outcomes on any one issue area. Thus world politics can be treated as a seamless web.

Under complex interdependence, such congruence is less likely to occur. As military force is devalued, militarily strong states will find it more difficult to use their overall dominance to control outcomes on issues in which they are weak. And since the distribution of power resources in trade, shipping, or oil, for example, may be quite different, patterns of outcomes and distinctive political processes are likely to vary from one set of issues to another. If force were readily applicable, and military security were the highest foreign policy goal, these variations in the issue structures of power would not matter very much. The linkages drawn from them to military issues would ensure consistent dominance by the overall strongest states. But when military force is largely immobilized, strong states will find that linkage is less effective. They may still attempt such links, but in the absence of a hierarchy of issues, their success will be problematic.

Dominant states may try to secure much the same result by using overall economic power to affect results on other issues. If only economic objectives are at stake, they may succeed: money, after all, is fungible. But economic objectives have political implications, and economic linkage by the strong is limited by domestic, transnational, and transgovernmental actors who resist having their interests traded off. Furthermore, the international actors may be different on different issues, and the international organizations in which negotiations take place are often quite separate. Thus it is difficult, for example, to imagine a militarily or economically strong state linking concessions on monetary policy to reciprocal concessions in oceans policy. On the other hand, poor weak states are not similarly inhibited from linking unrelated issues, partly because their domestic interests are less complex. Linkage of unrelated issues is often a means of extracting concessions or side payments from rich and powerful states. And unlike powerful states whose instrument for linkage (military force) is often too costly to use, the linkage instrument used by poor, weak states—international organization—is available and inexpensive.

Thus as the utility of force declines, and as issues become more equal in importance, the distribution of power within each issue will become more important. If linkages become less effective on the whole, outcomes of political bargaining will increasingly vary by issue area.

The differentiation among issue areas in complex interdependence means that linkages among issues will become more problematic and will tend to reduce rather than reinforce international hierarchy. Linkage strategies, and defense against them, will pose critical strategic choices for states. Should issues be considered separately or as a package? If linkages are to be drawn, which issues should be linked, and on which of the linked issues should concessions be made? How far can one push a linkage before it becomes counterproductive? For instance, should one seek formal agreements or informal, but less politically sensitive, understandings? The fact that world politics under complex interdependence is not a seamless web leads us to expect that efforts to stitch seams together advantageously, as reflected in linkage strategies, will, very often, determine the shape of the fabric.

The negligible role of force leads us to expect states to rely more on other instruments in order to wield power. For the reasons we have already discussed, less vulnerable states will try to use asymmetrical interdependence in particular groups of issues as a source of power; they will also try to use international organizations and transnational actors and flows. States will approach economic interdependence in terms of power as well as its effects on citizens' welfare, although welfare considerations will limit their attempts to maximize power. Most economic and ecological interdependence involves the possibility of joint gains, or joint losses. Mutual awareness of potential gains and losses and the danger of worsening each actor's position through overly rigorous struggles over the distribution of the gains can limit the use of asymmetrical interdependence.

Agenda Setting

Our second assumption of complex interdependence, the lack of clear hierarchy among multiple issues, leads us to expect that the politics of agenda formation and control will become more important. Traditional analyses lead statesmen to focus on politico-military issues and to pay little attention to the broader politics of agenda formation. Statesmen assume that the agenda will be set by shifts in the balance of power, actual or anticipated, and by perceived threats to the security of states. Other issues will only be very important when they seem to affect security and military power. In these cases, agendas will be influenced strongly by considerations of the overall balance of power.

Yet, today, some nonmilitary issues are emphasized in interstate relations at one time, whereas others of seemingly equal importance are neglected or quietly handled at a technical level. International monetary politics, problems of commodity terms of trade, oil, food, and multinational corporations have all been important during the last decade; but not all have been high on interstate agendas throughout that period.

Traditional analysts of international politics have paid little attention to agenda formation: to how issues come to receive sustained attention by high officials. The traditional orientation toward military and security affairs implies that the crucial problems of foreign policy are imposed on states by the actions or threats of other states. These are high politics as opposed to the low politics of economic affairs. Yet, as the complexity of actors and issues in world politics increases, the utility of force declines and the line between domestic policy and foreign policy becomes blurred; as the conditions of complex interdependence are more closely approximated, the politics of agenda formation becomes more subtle and differentiated.

Under complex interdependence we can expect the agenda to be affected by the international and domestic problems created by economic growth and increasing sensitivity interdependence. Discontented domestic groups will politicize issues and force more issues once considered domestic onto the interstate agenda. Shifts in the distribution of power resources within sets of issues will also affect agendas. During the early 1970s the increased power of oil-producing governments over the transnational corporations and the consumer countries dramatically altered the policy agenda. Moreover, agendas for one group of issues may change as a result of linkages from other groups in which power resources are changing; for example, the broader agenda of North–South trade issues changed after the OPEC price rises and the oil embargo of 1973–74. Even if capabilities among states do not change, agendas may be affected by shifts in the importance of transnational actors. The publicity surrounding multinational corporations in the early 1970s, coupled with their rapid growth over the past twenty years, put the regulation of such corporations higher on both the United Nations agenda and national agendas.

Politicization—agitation and controversy over an issue that tend to raise it to the top of the agenda—can have many sources, as we have seen. Governments whose strength is increasing may politicize issues, by linking them to other issues. An international regime that is becoming ineffective or is not serving important issues may cause increasing politicization, as dissatisfied governments press for change. Politicization, however, can also come from below. Domestic groups may become upset enough to raise a dormant issue, or to interfere with interstate bargaining at high levels. In 1974 the American secretary of state's tacit linkage of a Soviet-American trade pact with progress in détente was upset by the success of domestic American groups working through Congress to link a trade agreement with Soviet policies on emigration.

The technical characteristics and institutional setting in which issues are raised will strongly affect politicization patterns. In the United States, congressional attention is an effective instrument of politicization. Generally, we expect transnational economic organizations and transgovernmental networks of bureaucrats to seek to avoid politicization. Domestically based groups (such as trade unions) and domestically oriented bureaucracies will tend to use politicization (particularly congressional attention) against their transnationally mobile competitors. At the international level, we expect states and actors to "shop among forums" and struggle to get issues raised in international organizations that will maximize their advantage by broadening or narrowing the agenda.

Transnational and Transgovernmental Relations

Our third condition of complex interdependence, multiple channels of contact among societies, further blurs the distinction between domestic and international politics. The availability of partners in political coalitions is not necessarily limited by national boundaries as traditional analysis assumes. The nearer a situation is to complex interdependence, the more we expect the outcomes of political bargaining to be affected by transnational relations. Multinational corporations may be significant both as independent actors and as instruments manipulated by governments. The attitudes and policy stands of domestic groups are likely to be affected by communications, organized or not, between them and their counterparts abroad.

Thus the existence of multiple channels of contact leads us to expect limits, beyond those normally found in domestic politics, on the ability of statesmen to calculate the manipulation of interdependence or follow a consistent strategy of linkage. Statesmen must consider differential as well as aggregate effects of interdependence strategies and their likely implications for politicization and agenda control. Transactions among societies—economic and social transactions more than security ones— affect groups differently. Opportunities and costs from increased transnational ties may be greater for certain groups—for instance, American workers in the textile or shoe industries—than for others. Some organizations or groups may interact directly with actors in other societies or with other governments to increase their benefits from a network of interaction. Some actors may therefore be less vulnerable as well as less sensitive to changes elsewhere in the network than are others, and this will affect patterns of political action.

The multiple channels of contact found in complex interdependence are not limited to nongovernmental actors. Contacts between governmental bureaucracies charged with similar tasks may not only alter their perspectives but lead to transgovernmental coalitions on particular policy questions. To improve their chances of success, government agencies attempt to bring actors from other governments into their own decision-making processes as allies. Agencies of powerful states such as the United States have used such coalitions to penetrate weaker governments in such countries as Turkey and Chile. They have also been used to help agencies of other governments penetrate the United States bureaucracy.[21] Transgovernmental politics frequently characterizes Canadian-American relations, often to the advantage of Canadian interests.

The existence of transgovermental policy networks leads to a different interpretation of one of the standard propositions about international politics—that states act in their own interest. Under complex interdependence, this conventional wisdom begs two important questions: which self and which interest? A government agency may pursue its own interests under the guise of the national interest; and recurrent interactions can change official perceptions of their interests. As a careful study of the politics of United States trade policy has documented, concentrating only on pressures of various interests for decisions leads to an overly mechanistic view of a continuous process and neglects the important role of communications in slowly changing perceptions of self-interest.[22]

The ambiguity of the national interest raises serious problems for the top political leaders of governments. As bureaucracies contact each other directly across national borders (without going through foreign offices), centralized control becomes more difficult. There is less assurance that the state will be united when dealing with foreign governments or that its components will interpret national interests similarly when negotiating with foreigners. The state may prove to be multifaceted, even schizophrenic. National interests will be defined differently on different issues, at different times and by different governmental units. States that are better placed to maintain their coherence (because of a centralized political tradition such as France's) will be better able to manipulate uneven interdependence than fragmented states that at first glance seem to have more resources in an issue area.

Role of International Organizations

Finally, the existence of multiple channels leads one to predict a different and significant role for international organizations in world politics. Realists in the tradition of Hans J. Morgenthau have portrayed a world in which states, acting from self-interest, struggle for "power and peace." Security issues are dominant; war threatens. In such a world, one may assume that international institutions will have a minor role, limited by the rare congruence of such interests. International organizations are then clearly peripheral to world politics. But in a world of multiple issues imperfectly linked, in which coalitions are formed transnationally and transgovernmentally, the potential role of international institutions in political bargaining is greatly increased. In particular, they help set the international agenda, and act as catalysts for coalition-formation and as arenas for political initiatives and linkage by weak states.

Governments must organize themselves to cope with the flow of business generated by international organizations. By defining the salient issues, and deciding which issues can be grouped together, organizations may help to determine governmental priorities and the nature of inter-departmental committees and other arrangements within governments. The 1972 Stockholm Environment Conference strengthened the position of environmental agencies in various governments. The 1974 World Food Conference focused the attention of important parts of the United States government on prevention of food shortages. The September 1975 United Nations special session on proposals for a New International Economic Order generated an intragovernmental debate about policies toward the Third World in general. The International Monetary Fund and the General Agreement on Tariffs and Trade have focused governmental activity on money and trade instead of on private direct investment, which has no comparable international organization.

By bringing officials together, international organizations help to acti-vate potential coalitions in world politics. It is quite obvious that inter-national organizations have been very important in bringing together representatives of less developed countries, most of which do not main-tain embassies in one another's capitals. Third World strategies of soli-darity among poor countries have been developed in and for a series of international conferences, mostly under the auspices of the United Nations.[23] International organizations also allow agencies of govern-ments, which might not otherwise come into contact, to turn potential or tacit coalitions into explicit transgovernmental coalitions characterized by direct communications. In some cases, international secretariats deliberately promote this process by forming coalitions with groups of governments, or with units of governments, as well as with nongovern-mental organizations having similar interests.[24]

International organizations are frequently congenial institutions for weak states. The one-state-one-vote norm of the United Nations system favors coalitions of the small and powerless. Secretariats are often responsive to Third World demands. Furthermore, the substantive norms of most international organizations, as they have developed over the years, stress social and economic equity as well as the equality of states.

Past resolutions expressing Third World positions, sometimes agreed to with reservations by industrialized countries, are used to legitimize other demands. These agreements are rarely binding, but up to a point the norms of the institution make opposition look more harshly self-interested and less defensible.

International organizations also allow small and weak states to pursue linkage strategies. In the discussions on a New International Economic Order, Third World states insisted on linking oil price and availability to other questions on which they had traditionally been unable to achieve their objectives. Small and weak states have also followed a strategy of linkage in the series of Law of the Sea conferences sponsored by the United Nations.

Complex interdependence therefore yields different political patterns than does the realist conception of the world. (Table 1 summarizes these differences.) Thus, one would expect traditional theories to fail to explain

TABLE 1   Political Processes Under Conditions of Realism and Complex Interdependence

	Realism	Complex Interdependence
Goals of actors	Military security will be the dominant goal.	Goals of states will vary by issue area. Transgovernmental politics will make goals difficult to define. Transnational actors will pursue their own goals.
Instruments of state policy	Military force will be most effective, although economic and other instruments will also be used.	Power resources specific to issue areas will be most relevant. Manipulation of interdependence, international organizations, and transnational actors will be major instruments.
Agenda formation	Potential shifts in the balance of power and security threats will set the agenda in high politics and will strongly influence other agendas.	Agenda will be affected by changes in the distribution of power resources within issue areas; the status of international regimes; changes in the importance of transnational actors; linkages from other issues and politicization as a result of rising sensitivity interdependence.
Linkages of issues	Linkages will reduce differences in outcomes among issue areas and reinforce international hierarchy.	Linkages by strong states will be more difficult to make since force will be ineffective. Linkages by weak states through international organizations will erode rather than reinforce hierarchy.
Roles of international organizations	Roles are minor, limited by state power and the importance of military force.	Organizations will set agendas, induce coalition-formation, and act as arenas for political action by weak states. Ability to choose the organizational forum for an issue and to mobilize votes will be an important political resource.

international regime change in situations of complex interdependence. But, for a situation that approximates realist conditions, traditional theories should be appropriate.

NOTES

1. Stanley Hoffmann, "Notes on the Elusiveness of Modern Power," *International Journal* 30: (Spring 1975):184.
2. "A New National Partnership," speech by Secretary of State Henry A. Kissinger at Los Angeles, January 24, 1975. News release, Department of State, Bureau of Public Affairs, Office of Media Services, p. 1.
3. See, for example, Lester R. Brown, *World Without Borders: The Interdependence of Nations* (New York: Foreign Policy Association, Headline Series, 1972).
4. Charles Kindleberger, *American Business Abroad* (New Haven: Yale University Press, 1969), p. 207.
5. The terms are derived from Stanley Hoffmann, "Choices," *Foreign Policy* 12 (Fall 1973): 6.
6. For instance, see Robert Angell, *Peace on the March: Transnational Participation* (New York: Van Nostrand, 1969).
7. John Maynard Keynes, *The General Theory of Employment, Interest and Money* (London: Macmillan, 1957), p. 383.
8. For the classic contemporary formulation of political realism, see the works of Hans J. Morgenthau, particularly *Politics Among Nations: The Struggle for Power and Peace* (New York: Knopf, 1948 and subsequent editions). See also Morgenthau, "Another 'Great Debate': The National Interest of the United States," *American Political Science Review* 46 (December 1952): 961–88; and Morgenthau, *Scientific Man Versus Power Politics* (Chicago: University of Chicago Press, 1946). A different but equally impressive statement of a "realist" position can be found in E. H. Carr, *The Twenty Years' Crisis, 1919–1939,* 2nd ed. (London: Macmillan, 1946). Carr, however, emphasizes economic sources of power more strongly.
9. In *The Troubled Partnership* (New York: McGraw-Hill for the Council on Foreign Relations, 1965) Henry A. Kissinger discussed alliance problems with hardly a reference to economic issues, although economic issues were beginning seriously to divide the NATO allies.
10. Alex Inkeles, "The Emerging Social Structure of the World," *World Politics* 27 (July 1975): 479.
11. Hans J. Morgenthau, *Politics Among Nations: The Struggle for Power and Peace,* 4th ed. (New York: Knopf, 1967), p. 36.
12. See Inkeles, "The Emerging Social Structure of the World;" Richard Rosecrance and Arthur Stein, "Interdependence: Myth or Reality," *World Politics* 26, no. 1 (October 1973); Peter J, Katzenstein, "International Interdependence: Some Long-Term Trends and Recent Changes," *International Organization* 29, no. 4 (Fall 1975); Edward L. Morse, "Transnational Economic Processes," in Robert O. Keohane and Joseph S. Nye, Jr. (eds.), *Transnational Relations and World Politics* (Cambridge, Mass.: Harvard University Press, 1972).

13. Henry A. Kissinger, "A New National Partnership," *Department of State Bulletin,* February 17, 1975, p. 199.
14. See the report of the Commission on the Organization of the Government for the Conduct of Foreign Policy (Murphy Commission) (Washington, D.C.: U.S. Government Printing Office, 1975), and the studies prepared for that report. See also Raymond Hopkins, "The International Role of 'Domestic' Bureaucracy," *International Organization* 30, no. 3 (Summer 1976).
15. *New York Times,* May 22, 1975.
16. For a valuable discussion, see Klaus Knorr, *The Power of Nations: The Political Economy of International Relations* (New York: Basic Books, 1975).
17. *Business Week,* January 13, 1975.
18. Stanley Hoffmann, "The Acceptability of Military Force," and Laurence Martin, "The Utility of Military Force," in *Force in Modern Societies: Its Place in International Politics* (Adelphi Paper, International Institute for Strategic Studies, 1973). See also Knorr, *The Power of Nations.*
19. Henry Brandon, *The Retreat of American Power* (New York: Doubleday, 1974), p. 218.
20. *International Implications of the New Economic Policy,* U.S. Congress, House of Representatives, Committee on Foreign Affairs, Subcommittee on Foreign Economic Policy, Hearings, September 16, 1971.
21. For a more detailed discussion, see Robert O. Keohane and Joseph S. Nye, Jr., "Transgovernmental Relations and International Organizations," *World Politics 27,* no. 1 (October 1974): 39–62.
22. Raymond Bauer, Ithiel de Sola Pool, and Lewis Dexter, *American Business and Foreign Policy* (New York: Atherton, 1963), chap. 35, esp. pp. 472–75.
23. Branislav Gosovic and John Gerard Ruggie, "On the Creation of a New International Economic Order: Issue Linkage and the Seventh Special Session of the UN General Assembly," *International Organization* 30, no. 2 (Spring 1976): 309–46.
24. Robert W. Cox, "The Executive Head," *International Organization* 23, no. 2 (Spring 1969): 205–30.

CHAPTER FOUR

Globalism: Dependency and the World Capitalist System

MAJOR ACTORS AND ASSUMPTIONS: A SUMMARY

We have seen that realists organize their work around the basic question: How can stability be maintained in an anarchic world? Many pluralists ask how peaceful change can be promoted in a world that is increasingly interdependent politically, militarily, socially, and economically. Our third and final image of international relations, globalism, tends to concentrate on the broad question of why so many **Third World** states in Latin America, Africa, and Asia have been unable to develop. For some globalists this question is part of a larger effort to develop a theory of world capitalist development.

We have avoided the label **Marxism** because there are both Marxists and non-Marxists who work within what we have chosen to call the globalist image. Indeed, some globalists decidedly avoid Marxian modes of analysis. We acknowledge that in adopting the term *globalism* we have appropriated a word sometimes used by pluralists or realists to describe their images of the world. One could, perhaps, find another word as yet unclaimed. But we think globalism is particularly apt for those who see the **world capitalist system** as their starting point or who focus on **dependency** relations within a global political economy. As already noted in Chapter One, we are not alone in using the term *globalism* in this context.

Globalists are guided by four key assumptions. First, it is necessary to understand the *global context within which states and other entities interact*. Globalists argue that to explain behavior at any and all **levels of analysis**—the individual, bureaucratic, societal, and between states or between societies—one must first understand the overall structure of the global system within which such behavior takes place. As with some realists, globalists believe that the starting point of analysis should be the international system. To a large extent, the behavior of individual actors is explained by a system that provides constraints and opportunities.

Second, globalists stress the importance of *historical analysis* in comprehending the international system. Only by tracing the historical evolution of the system is it possible to understand its current structure. The key historical factor and defining characteristic of the system as a whole is **capitalism.** This particular economic system works to the benefit of some individuals, states, and societies but at the expense of others. Even socialist states must operate within a capitalist world economy that significantly constrains their options.

Third, globalists assume that particular *mechanisms of domination* exist that keep Third World states from developing and that contribute to worldwide **uneven development.** To understand these mechanisms requires an examination of dependency relations between the northern industrialized states (Europe and North America) and their poorer neighbors in the southern hemisphere (Africa, Latin America, Asia).

Finally, globalists assume that *economic factors* are absolutely critical in explaining the evolution and functioning of the world capitalist system and the relegation of Third World states to a subordinate position.

The globalist approach would seen to share certain commonalities with the other two perspectives. As noted, globalists and realists both place greater emphasis on the importance of the systems level, or world as a whole, in affecting actors' behavior than do the pluralists. But they differ as to how they characterize the systems level component. Globalists tend to focus on the capitalist mode of production and realists on the distribution of aggregate power.

Globalists and pluralists share at least three commonalities that can be viewed as criticisms of the realist perspective. First, both stress an approach to international relations grounded in **political economy.** The distinction of high politics versus low politics is rejected—if not totally reversed for certain globalists—in terms of the relative importance of economic as compared to political-military factors. For the globalist, various manifestations of political and military power generally reflect the driving force of underlying economic factors. Politics depends on economics; it is not an autonomous realm.

Second, both the globalists and pluralists are much more attuned to events, processes, institutions, and actors operating both within and between states; the impermeable billiard ball (the unitary rational actor) is broken down into its component parts. Both approaches tend to range up and down the levels of analysis and focus on a greater variety of actors, but the globalists place a much greater emphasis on the context (i.e., the capitalist nature of the international system) within which these actors operate than do the pluralists.

Third, both the globalists and those pluralists who write in the **transnationalist** tradition emphasize socioeconomic or welfare issues. A number of pluralists have a normative commitment to peaceful change. International relations do not have to be viewed and played as a **zero-sum game** with winners and losers but as a **positive-sum game** in which the restructuring of interstate relations is achieved through bargaining and compromise, allowing all parties to gain. Although the globalists are also concerned with the welfare of **less developed countries (LDCs),** they are not so optimistic about the possibility of peaceful change. The hierarchical nature of world politics with South subordinated to North and the economic dictates of the world capitalist system make it unlikely that the northern industrialized states will make any meaningful concessions to the Third World. Change, peaceful or revolutionary, is problematic. In sum, there are major differences between globalists and pluralists.

Although the globalists are primarily concerned with the question of why LDCs cannot develop, answering such a query is difficult. How and why did capitalism develop in Western Europe? How did it expand outward to other continents? How has capitalism changed over the centuries in terms of its international manifestations? What are the specific mechanisms of dependency that allow for the maintenance of exploitative relations? What is the relationship between the elites of the wealthy **center** countries (the **First World**) and the elites of the poorer **periphery**? Is it possible for an LDC to break out of a dependent situation? Answers to such questions are addressed in this chapter.

INTELLECTUAL PRECURSORS AND INFLUENCES

Karl Marx

Either directly or indirectly, all globalists have been influenced by the works of Karl Marx (1818–1883). This is certainly not to suggest that all globalists are Marxists any more than all Marxists accept without qualification the sum total of Marx's efforts. It is simply to acknowledge that they owe an intellectual debt to him in terms of their methods of analysis and certain critical insights into the functioning, development, and expansion of the capitalist mode of production. To appreciate Marx as scholar, one does not have to ascribe to the views of Marx as revolutionary.

Karl Marx's work concerns mankind's historical growth process and movement toward final self-realization and fulfillment in a society he called *communist.* For Marx, history was not so much the story of the rise and fall of particular city–states, empires, and nation–states as it was the story of **class conflict** generated by economic modernization. Having evolved out of a **feudal** system, capitalism reigned supreme in nineteenth century Europe. Marx argued that capitalism—which involves market exchanges, labor as a commodity, and the **means of production** held in private hands—produced particular political, social, and cultural effects. Marx's discussion and analysis of capitalism have influenced globalists in at least three ways.

First, Marx was concerned with exploitation of the many by the few. He may have recognized the historically progressive role played by capitalists (the **proletarian revolution** would not be possible until after the establishment of a capitalist system), but his personal sympathies were with the downtrodden.

Second, according to Marx, capitalism exhibited certain law-like qualities in terms of its development and expansion. He viewed capitalism as part of a world historical process unfolding **dialectically,** an economic system riddled with clashing contradictions or internal tensions that could be resolved only by transformation into a socialist mode of production.

Finally, Marx insisted that a society must be studied in its totality, not piecemeal. An analyst must be aware of how various parts of society were interrelated, including those aspects not so apparent to the casual observer.[1]

This perspective has deeply influenced the globalists, some of whom earlier in their careers had little use for history and were preoccupied almost exclusively with such **units of analysis** as states or individuals. As two leading globalists have argued: "If there is one thing which distinguishes a world-system perspective from any other, it is its insistence that the unit of analysis is a *world*-system defined in terms of *economic* processes and links, and not any units defined in terms of juridical, political, cultural, geographical, or other criteria."[2] Although such units of analysis are not ignored by the gloabalists, they take on connotations different from those of the realist or pluralist. The state, for example, is not viewed in terms of its being a **sovereign** entity preoccupied with security concerns. Rather, it derives its significance from the role it plays in actively aiding or hindering the capitalist accumulation process. Any one particular stage is not viewed in isolation but in terms of how it fits into the overall global capitalist system.

In sum, Marx has influenced contemporary scholars working within the globalist image by virtue of his emphasis on exploitation, discernible historical patterns of capitalist development and expansion, and the importance of understanding the "big picture" and then asking how individual parts fit into the whole.

Hobson and Imperialism

Marx's observations on capitalism in the nineteenth century have since been modified and generalized to cover the entire globe under various theories of **imperialism.** Imperialism assumes an international, hierarchical division of labor between rich and poor regions of the world, but the relation is not one of mutually beneficial **comparative advantage**. Rather, it is one of exploitation.

Ironically, perhaps one of the most significant theories of imperialism was devised by a non-Marxist, the English economist John A. Hobson (1858–1940). Near the turn of the century Hobson noted that capitalist societies were faced with three basic interrelated problems: overproduction, underconsumption by workers and other classes, and oversavings on the part of capitalists. As the capitalist owners of industry continued to exploit workers and pay the lowest possible wages, profits mounted and goods began to pile up. But who was to purchase the excess goods? Given the low wages, not the mass of the working class, because members of this class did not have sufficient purchasing power. The efficiency of the capitalist mode of production resulted, however, in the relentless production of more and more goods the society was unable to consume.

What could capitalists have done with excess goods and profits, and how could they have resolved the problem of underconsumption? Redistribute wealth? Highly unlikely. Because capitalist European and North American powers were experiencing overproduction and domestic underconsumption, investment opportunities in other developed countries remained limited.

The solution reached by capitalists was to invest in what are now known as Third World countries. The result was imperialism: "the endeavor of the great controllers of industry to broaden the channel for the flow of their surplus wealth by seeking foreign markets and foreign investments to take off the goods and capital they cannot sell or use at home." Hobson argued against the "fallacy of the supposed inevitability of imperial expansion." He stated that it is "not inherent in the nature of things that we should spend our natural resources on militarism, war, and risky, unscrupulous diplomacy, in order to find markets for our goods and surplus capital."[3] Hobson hence rejected the **determinism** so often found in the work of Marxist scholars who write on imperialism.

For Hobson, imperialism did not benefit the home country as a whole. Instead, selected groups such as industrialists, financiers, and the individuals who staffed the colonial empires profited. Furthermore, because the flag followed trade, large military expenditures were required to protect the imperialist system. The drive for capitalist profits by securing overseas territories led to competition and rivalry among European powers. Hence, imperialism was to Hobson a major cause of war, and Hobson suggested that capitalists might indeed profit from such conflicts.

Lenin

V. I. Lenin's (1870–1924) *Imperialism: The Highest Stage of Capitalism* is his most important theoretical work of interest to those in the globalist school. Writing in the midst of World War I (1916), Lenin was interested in developing a theory that explained the necessity for capitalist exploitation of lesser developed countries and the causes of war among advanced capitalist states. He drew heavily upon the works of Hobson and the German Social Democrat, Rudolph Hilferding (1877–1941).

From Hobson, Lenin accepted the key argument that underconsumption and overproduction caused capitalists to scramble for foreign markets beyond Europe and to engage in colonialism. From Hilferding, Lenin took the notion that imperialist policies reflected the existence of monopoly and finance capital, or the highest stage of capitalism. In other words, capitalism had developed such that oligopolies and monopolies controlled the key sectors of the economy, squeezing out or taking over smaller firms and milking domestic markets dry. The result was a need to look elsewhere for investment opportunities. This logically entailed the creation of overseas markets. As markets expanded, they required more economic inputs such as raw materials which encouraged the further spread of imperialism to secure such resources.

Marx had seen that rates of profits would decline because of overproduction and underconsumption and that greater misery for the working class would result because more and more people would be out of jobs or receive even less in wages. **Proletarian,** or working-class, consciousness would grow, leading ultimately to revolution in all capitalist countries. For Lenin, imperialism explained why Marx's prediction of proletarian revolution in Europe had failed to come about. Economic contradictions inherent in the capitalist mode of production still existed, but imperialism allowed capitalists a breathing space. Imperialism provided the European working class a taste or small portion of the spoils derived from the exploitation of overseas territories—new markets, cheap labor, and natural resources. By buying off the European working class in the short term, imperialism delayed the inevitable revolution. But an important trade-off was involved. Domestic stability was achieved at the cost of wars among the capitalist powers that resulted from the continual struggle for overseas markets. Once the globe had been effectively divided up, further expansion could come about only at the expense of a capitalist rival.

For Lenin, imperialism was therefore driven by *economic forces,* and it was *inevitable* that such exploitation and eventual conflict would occur. Hence, he disagreed with Hobson and later theorists (e.g., Joseph Schumpeter) who argued that other factors such as primitive or irrational instincts or an enjoyment of struggle and conquest also played a role in explaining imperialist policies. He also disagreed with writers who argued that imperialism was simply the chosen policy of capitalists and hence was subject to change. Lenin rejected this line of thinking. For him, imperialism was not a matter of choice but inevitability. The capitalists could not save themselves. Imperialism was the direct result of the attainment of monopoly capital, the highest stage of capitalism, and it was driven by its own internal dynamics. The resulting competition among states, reflecting the domination of capitalist class interests, unavoidably led to world wars such as the one being experienced at the time of Lenin's writing.

Although Lenin's theory of imperialism has been subject to a great deal of **empirical** and **conceptual** criticism over the years, Lenin was writing not just as a theorist but also as a revolutionary whose writings were designed to mobilize support for a socialist revolution. He is a prime example of a writer blending theory and practice. In combination with his works on the importance of revolutionary organization, Lenin's *Imperialism* has had a great deal of influence on revolutionaries throughout the Third World.

Strictly as a theorist, Lenin has particularly influenced the globalist literature with his emphasis on the global nature of capitalism and its inherent exploitativeness that primarily benefits the **bourgeoisie** in advanced capitalist states at the expense of poorer countries. Although there is arguably a good deal of determinism in his theory of imperialism, his work as a revolutionary (like that of Marx) reflected considerable voluntarism in practice.[4] The actions of revolutionaries were at the very least to serve as catalysts to the worldwide proletarian revolution whenever the *objective* conditions of working class exploitation were ripe or had reached their revolutionary stage.[5]

Luxemburg and Revolution vs. Reform

Not to be seduced by the appeal of peaceful, gradual change or reformism, Rosa Luxemburg (1870–1919) expressed deep commitment to revolution as the only effective means of transforming society. She wrote as a critic of Eduard Bernstein's late nineteenth-century German Social Democratic Party politics of **reformism.** She saw reformism as an abandonment of Marxist principles, however helpful such policies might appear to be for the workers in the short run. Luxemburg argued vociferously the necessity for revolution to effect "removal of obstacles that a privileged minority places in the path of social progress."[6] By contrast, she believed that reformism involves compromise with the bourgeoisie, strengthening the hand of the capitalist class: "Only the hammer blow of revolution, that is to say, the conquest of political power by the proletariat," or working class, "can break down this wall" of opposition posed by capitalists to "socialist society."[7] She also described the negative impact of imperialism on colonies.[8]

The issue of whether the kinds of changes anticipated by many globalists can be achieved by reformist tactics or whether they can be achieved only through revolutionary violence remains a matter for dispute. Many globalists are reform-minded, non-Marxists. Globalists who claim to be Marxists are divided. There are reform-minded Marxists in the tradition of Eduard Bernstein who are opposed by those who see revolution as the only effective means to change the existing world order. Even the latter disagree: When will the revolution occur, or when should it occur? Does one wait until objective conditions are ripe, or does one take some affirmative action to move the process along? Are revolutions inevitable, or must they be made? How much is the result of voluntary action, and how much is determined by "historical inevitabilities"? The one point on which these theorists tend to agree is the desirability of change from the present unjust order.[9]

DEPENDENCY THEORISTS

ECLA and UNCTAD Arguments

Some of the more provocative work in the globalist tradition has been produced by Latin Americanists representing various branches of the social sciences. They have come to be known collectively as **dependency** theorists, and they now include North American and European scholars as well as Latin Americans. Several of these writers were associated in the 1960s with the Economic Commission on Latin America (ECLA) and the United Nations Conference on Trade and Development (UNCTAD). They were concerned with the important problem of explaining why Latin America and other Third World regions were not developing as anticipated. North American social science models had predicted an economic takeoff for LDCs.[10] What had gone wrong? What explained economic stagnation, **balance of payments** difficulties, and deteriorating **terms of trade?** Why wasn't the North American–Western European experience being repeated?

One response came from mainstream **modernization** writers. This modernization literature attempted to answer these questions by exploring the difficulties of LDCs in moving from "traditional" to "modern" societies. The tradition–modernity dichotomy has been used in one form or another by social scientists as a tool of analysis since the mid-nineteenth century. The ethos and organization of a traditional society, it is argued, are both a cause and an expression of underdevelopment. The cultural values of a traditional society are postulated to be a hindrance to modernization. The LDCs are wedded to their pasts, reflecting a lack of entrepreneurial spirit that was found in European society during the rise of capitalism in the sixteenth century.[11]

This view of development and underdevelopment as the outcomes of *internal* processes has been criticized on a number of grounds. Two important criticisms are, first, that the modernization writers assume that the tradition–modernity dichotomy is universally applicable. But is the Latin American experience really so similar to the European experience? Are there really no significant historical differences between Africa and the West? Second, the modernization literature usually neglects a state's or society's external environment, particularly international political and economic factors. Instead, modernization writers have tended to focus on state or society, generally ignoring the state's or society's place in the world capitalist order. Is there any society, even in the European historical experience, that is immune to outside influences? Very unlikely, respond the dependency theorists, who place particular emphasis on Latin America's colonial heritage and a historical legacy of exploitation.

The focus of the ECLA and UNCTAD economists was initially quite narrow. They examined the unequal terms of trade between LDCs that exported raw materials and northern industrialized countries that exported finished manufactured goods. They questioned the supposed benefits of free trade. The ECLA at one point favored the diversification of exports, advising that LDCs produce goods instead of importing them. This policy did not result in the anticipated amount of success and in fact increased the influence of foreign multinational corporations brought in to facilitate domestic production.

Did all countries fail to experience economic growth? No, some economies did grow, but growth tended to occur in an LDC only when the developed countries had a need for a particular raw material or agricultural product. Because many LDCs are dependent on only a few of these commodities for their foreign exchange earnings, a drastic decline in the demand for one of them (perhaps caused by a recession in North America) would have a calamitous impact on a LDC's economy. Or, alternatively, a bumper crop in several LDCs heavily dependent on one particular export (such as coffee or sugar) would also cause prices to fall.

The volatility of prices for minerals and agricultural products and the generally downward tendency of those prices contrast sharply with more stable and gradually increasing prices for manufactured items produced by industrial countries. Thus, the terms of trade are thought to be stacked against those Third World states that export farm products or natural resources.

Radical Critiques

Writers in ECLA and UNCTAD (e.g., Argentine economist Raul Prebisch), although critical of the more conservative views of development, nevertheless tended to restrict their analyses to economic dimensions and to cast their arguments in terms of nationalism and the need for state-guided capitalism.[12] Other writers, however, more boldly emphasized political and social factors within the context of a capitalist economic system that bind Latin America to North America. Development, it was argued, is not autonomous. If it occurs at all, it is reflexive—subject to the vagaries and ups and downs of the world's advanced economies. Choices for Latin American countries are restricted or constrained as a result of the dictates of capitalism but also as a result of supporting political, social, and cultural relations that result in a structure of domination. This multifaceted web of dependency reinforces unequal exchange between the northern and southern parts of the hemisphere. Opportunities for LDCs are few and far between because LDCs are allocated a subordinate role in world capitalism.

That various states and societies produce those things of which they are relatively the most efficient producers or sell those items in which they have a comparative advantage is seen by dependency theorists as a "one-way advantage." Economic exploitation of LDCs by the industrialized states is not an accident or simply an additional means by which these states enrich themselves. Rather, economic exploitation is an integral part of the capitalist system and is required to keep it functioning.

The result is a situation of dependency, succinctly defined as a "situation in which a certain number of countries have their economy conditioned by the development and expansion of another . . . , placing the dependent countries in a backward position exploited by the dominant countries."[13] The modernization experience of a particular society should not be seen in isolation, "but as part of the development of an internationalist capitalist system, whose dynamic has a determining influence on the local processes." As a result, underdevelopment is not "a moment in the evolution of a society which has been economically, politically and culturally antonomous and isolated."[14] Instead, Latin American and other Third World countries are attempting to develop under historical conditions quite different from those of the northern industrialized states.

Some globalists use Marxist terminology and Leninist insights to explain this situation of dependency. More important than relations between states are transnational class coalitions linking elites in industrially developed countries (the center) with their counterparts in the South (or periphery). This version of class analysis emphasizes how transnational ties within the global bourgeois or capitalist class work to the disadvantage of workers and peasants in the periphery. The multinational corporation (MNC) and international banks, therefore, are viewed from a much different perspective than that of the realist or pluralist. To the pluralist, MNCs and international banks appear merely as other, potentially benign, actors. To the realist, they tend to be of secondary importance because of the emphasis on the state-as-actor. To the globalist, however, they are central players in establishing and maintaining dependency relations. To globalists of Marxist persuasion, MNCs and banks are agents *par excellence* of the international bourgeoisie. They represent two of the critical means by which Third World states are maintained in their subordinate position within the world capitalist economy.

Domestic Forces

Dependency theorists deal not only with external factors (such as foreign states, multinational corporations, international banks, multilateral lending institutions, foreign control of technology, and an international bourgeoisie). They also deal increasingly with internal constraints on development (such as patterns of land tenure, social structures, class alliances, and the role of the state). These internal factors tend to reinforce instruments of foreign domination. It is argued, for example, that the inability to break out of a dependent situation is often strengthened by citizens of a Latin American country who accrue selfish benefits at the expense of the country as a whole. This so-called **comprador class,** or national bourgeoisie, aids in the exploitation of its own society. Allied with foreign capitalists, its self-serving policies encourage the expansion of social and economic inequality, which may take the form of an ever-widening rural-urban gap. Although limited development may occur in a few urban centers, the countryside stagnates and is viewed only as a provider of cheap labor and raw materials. These exploiters, therefore, have more in common with the elites of the center countries than they do with their fellow citizens of the periphery.

Such arguments are rather sweeping in scope. The importance of internal dimensions, however, will vary depending on the particular country under examination. Class coalitions, for example, will differ and may relate to external actors in a variety of ways. As two noted dependency theorists have stated:

> We conceive the relationship between external and internal forces as forming a complex whole whose structural links are not based on mere external forms of exploitation and coercion, but are rooted in coincidence of interests between local dominant classes and international ones.[15]

In some cases this "coincidence of interests" might even involve portions of the working class.

As a result of the interplay of external and internal factors, the nature of the development or underdevelopment of a society will vary. Changes in the international economy will affect LDCs in different ways. Dependency theorists, therefore, do *not* claim that economic stagnation in LDCs is always and inevitably the norm. They argue, however, that development benefits some at the expense of others, increases social inequalities, and leads to greater foreign control over Third World economies.

THE WORLD CAPITALIST SYSTEM

The dependency theorists pointed the way for scholars who write from what is known as the world capitalist system perspective. This perspective is truly globalist and differs from dependency in two ways.

First, advocates of the world capitalist system perspective not only are concerned with the lack of Third World development but also wish to understand the economic, political, and social development of regions throughout the *entire* world. Developed and underdeveloped states, winners and losers, are all examined in attempts to explain the global existence of uneven development.

Second, the goal is to understand the fate of various parts of the world at various times in history within the larger context of a developing world political economy. Latin America, for example, is not unique. Its experience is an integral part of the world capitalist system. Third World underdevelopment and exploitation are central to maintaining the present structure of dominance in the world capitalist system. The first priority, therefore, is to understand this global system from a historical perspective. Only then can the fates of particular societies or regions of the globe be understood.

The writings of Immanuel Wallerstein represent the most ambitious of the globalist work and have been the catalyst for an extensive amount of subsequent research. In attempting to understand the origins and dynamics of the modern world economy and the existence of worldwide uneven development, he aspires to no less than a historically based theory of global development, which he terms *world-system theory.*[16]

Wallerstein begins by analyzing the emergence of capitalism in Europe, tracing its development into a world capitalist system that contains a **core,** a **periphery,** and a **semi-periphery.** The core areas historically have engaged in the most advanced economic activities: banking, manufacturing, technologically advanced agriculture, and ship building. The periphery has provided raw materials such as minerals and timber to fuel the core's economic expansion. Unskilled labor is repressed, and the peripheral countries are denied advanced technology in those areas that might make them more competitive with core states. The semi-periphery is involved in a mix of production activities, some associated with core areas and others with peripheral areas. The semi-periphery also serves a number of other functions such as being an outlet for investment when wages in core economies become too high. Over time, particular regions of the world may gravitate between core, peripheral, and semi-peripheral status.

Class structure varies in each zone depending on how the dominant class relates to the world economy. Contrary to the liberal economic notion of specialization based on comparative advantage, this division of labor *requires* as well as *increases* inequality between regions. States in the periphery are weak in that they are unable to control their fates, whereas states in the core are economically, politically, and militarily dominant. The basic function of the state is to ensure the continuation of the capitalist mode of production.

Wallerstein's explanatory goals are breathtaking in scope, and his debt to Marx and other globalist intellectual precursors is evident. He deals with such topics as the cause of war among states and factors leading to the rise and fall of core powers. These issues are discussed in the context of the creation and expansion of capitalism as a historical world system. The focus is first and foremost on economic processes and how they in turn influence political and security considerations.

System

Wallerstein and other globalists insist that in order to understand the development of global economic, political, and social processes, we must keep our eye on the development of capitalism. Capitalism is a system-wide, or global, phenomenon. We should not concentrate on individual states and national economies and then extrapolate from their experiences. Instead, we should examine capitalism as an integrated, historically expanding system that transcends any particular political or geographic boundaries. By first understanding capitalism as a truly integrated world system, we then can better understand the fate of particular countries. This emphasis on the system as the key to understanding may sound familiar. It should; some realists also claim that to develop a true theory of international relations, one must give precedence to the system as opposed to focusing on individual states. Do globalists operating from the world-system perspective in fact share the realist view as to what constitutes the international system? There are some interesting parallels, particularly if one closely examines Wallerstein's work.

First, some realists acknowledge that Wallerstein is attempting to develop a systems level theory, although he emphasizes economic factors over political variables.[17]

Second, Wallerstein explicitly recognizes the importance of **anarchy,** a concept of critical importance to many realist writers. Recall that anarchy simply refers to the absence of a superordinate or central political authority. Wallerstein notes that "the absence of a single political authority makes it impossible for anyone to legislate the general will of the world-system and hence to curtail the capitalist mode of production."[18] Anarchy, therefore, is defined in political terms for both Wallerstein, who notes the absence of a single world empire, and those realists who discuss the importance of the absence of any central authority in the world.

The implications of anarchy for the realist and globalist are quite different, however, as evidenced by the latter part of the quotation: "to curtail the capitalist mode of production." For the realist, anarchy leads one to examine international political stability, war, and balance-of-power politics involving major states. For the globalist, the economic ramifications of political anarchy are paramount. The political anarchy of the interstate system facilitates the development and expansion of world capitalism because no single state can control the *entire* world economy. The result is an economic division of labor involving a core, a periphery, and a semi-periphery that is the focal point of globalist analysis. Political anarchy becomes a backdrop for an extensive analysis of capitalist dynamics.

Finally, Wallerstein addresses the issue of the international distribution of capabilities or power. Once again, it would appear that Wallerstein has much in common with the realists. The following quotation is illustrative:

> Of course, we shall find on closer inspection that there are periods where one state is relatively quite powerful and other periods where power is more diffuse and contested, permitting weaker states broader ranges of action. We can talk then of the relative tightness or looseness of the world-system as an important variable and seek to analyze why this dimension tends to be cyclical in nature, as it seems to have been for several hundred years.[19]

There is, however, a major difference in how realists and Wallerstein use this notion of a distribution of capabilities.

For Wallerstein, *the very existence* of a particular distribution of power or capabilities cannot be explained without reference to the underlying *economic* order. In other words, he would argue that realists spend a great deal of time talking about the balance of power but that they fail to appreciate that there are important economic processes at work that are critical in accounting for the particular distribution of capabilities or balance of power in the first place!

In sum, despite sharing a similar systems vocabulary, the use and relative importance of these concepts is quite different. For a globalist such as Wallerstein, merely focusing on the distribution of capabilities among states is insufficient if one wishes to comprehend fully the nature of the world-system. The international system has always been comprised of weak and strong political units. Differential power alone is not the defining characteristic of the system. Once again, what is critical for the Wallersteinian globalist is the fact that the key aspect of the system is its capitalist nature, the existence of global class relations, and the various functions states and societies perform in the world economy. Capitalism has been the defining attribute of the international system since the sixteenth century. It is capitalism that helps to account for a core, a periphery, and a semi-periphery. It is capitalism that provides the critical environment in which states and classes operate by constraining, shaping, and channeling behavior. Some states and classes are rewarded. Others are doomed to play subordinate roles in a worldwide division of labor determined by the dictates of capitalism. So, although states and politics are certainly important to the globalist, they must be analyzed in the context of the world capitalist system.

Political, Economic, and Social Factors

As noted in Chapter One, realists understand the importance of economic factors, but they focus on power, the balance of power, and political explanations of international relations. Pluralists interested in transnationalism emphasize political, economic, and social factors, depending on the issue. And globalists tend to stress economic factors as underlying or driving politics.

These are generalizations, and as with all generalizations, they are subject to qualification. All globalists emphasize economic factors in their conceptions of the world-system, but the degree of their emphasis varies. There even has been recent debate as to whether the capitalist mode of production has been overemphasized. At one extreme, there is Wallerstein, who is claimed by critics to have reduced the derivation and operation of the state system to economics. Other globalists, although accepting the logic of the world capitalist system approach, stress the interdependence of political and economic **variables.** Christopher Chase-Dunn, for example, argues that "the capitalist mode of production exhibits a single logic in which both political-military power" and exploitative economic processes "play an integrated role."[20] Patrick McGowan states that "distinctions between economic and political processes represent false dichotomies. . . . Accumulation, imperialism, and conflict can be considered part of a single dynamic whereby a hegemonic core state in an increasingly competitive world-system attempts to ensure its own stability, prosperity, and primacy."[21] Political processes, however, are still basically derivative of the world capitalist mode of production, or they are placed in the context of economic structures and processes. Chase-Dunn, for example, develops the argument that "both the attempts and the failures of imperium can be understood as responses to the pressures of uneven development in the world-economy. . . . The interstate system is dependent on the institutions and opportunities presented by the world market for its survival."[22]

Johan Galtung goes one step further in his perspective on imperialism, which has had a major impact on globalists.[23] In examining the mechanisms of imperialism that cause and perpetuate the tremendous inequality within and among nations, Galtung parts company with Marx and Lenin in that for him imperialism is not simply an economic relation arising out of capitalism. Imperialism is a structural relation of dominance defined in political, economic, military, cultural, and communication terms. These types of imperialism have to be seen in their totality. It is not enough for international relations scholars to be preoccupied with only political and military factors, or economists to restrict their focus to economic factors. The entire structure of dominance has to be comprehended.

Equally important, Galtung argues that one must look *inside* societies to understand the effects of interactions *among* them. Imperialism means, for example, that elites in **center** nations dominate and collaborate with elites in **periphery** nations to the disadvantage of the majority of people in the latter. This would be a political effect of imperialism. Economic effects would include the production of only a few commodities by a periphery state, and trade being concentrated with a particular center state. Equal emphasis, however, is given to other forms of imperialism.

CHANGE

Many international relations scholars are interested in understanding system change. A common distinction is between changes *of* the system and lesser changes *within* an existing system that retains its basic characteristic. For globalists, changes within the world-system appear to fall into three categories. First, there are changes in the actors' positions within the world capitalist economy. As Wallerstein states: "There is constant and patterned movement between groups of economic actors as to who shall occupy various positions in the hierarchy of production, profit, and consumption."[24] The Dutch empire of the seventeenth century, for example, gave way to British domination, and eventually the United States rose to prominence in the twentieth century. Despite different core powers, however, the hierarchical nature of the system remains the same.

Second, some scholars identify phases or cycles of capitalist growth and contraction that affect all societies. A period of relative social stability and increasing economic stagnation precedes twenty or thirty years of rapid economic growth. This is then followed by another two or three decades of economic decline, followed again by expansion. Overproduction, a key factor discussed by Hobson, is central to the interplay of economic, social, and political forces.[25]

Third, there is what has been termed a *structural transformation* of the system. This term refers to the historical and geographical expansion of the world capitalist system, incorporating new areas of the globe and nonintegrated sectors of the world economy.[26] Although the term *transformation* is used, these changes could still be viewed as changes within the system because the capitalist mode of production, although perhaps changing its character, is still capitalist. In sum, the globalist view of the world capitalist system is hardly static. The world-system is dynamic, reflecting a myriad of activities and changes.[27]

But what about changes *of* the capitalist system? World-system theorists point to one major historical occurrence: the transformation of feudalism into capitalism in sixteenth-century Europe. What are the chances of going beyond capitalism? Globalists are ambivalent on this point. Wallerstein may entitle one article "The Rise and Future Demise of the World Capitalist System," but he also refers to "The Limited Possibilities of Transformation within the Capitalist World Order."[28] Wallerstein's work in general stresses slow but inexorable changes of the world capitalist system.

Other globalists point to possible transformational processes that might make significant system change possible. Such non-Marxist scholars as Hayward Alker and Johan Galtung, for example, downplay the notion of constraints that supposedly limit the evolution of alternative world orders. Alker sees change occurring through the dialectical clash of world forces and different visions of world futures. These contradictory world-order contenders (capitalist power balancing, Soviet socialism, collective self-reliance, and corporatist authoritarianism) make system transformation possible. For his part, Galtung sees the international system as open and subject to change. He even speculates on the decline not only of the nation-state but also of multinational corporations and even any world government that may be constructed in the distant future.[29]

What role does human volition play in system change? At one extreme there are scholars who apparently see large-scale historical processes as relatively immune from the actions of human beings. A strong dose of determinism seems to be reflected in their work. They are challenged by critics who downplay constraints. Some of these critics call for revolutions to end capitalist exploitation. They argue that despite the "particularity" of Latin America or other Third World regions that is emphasized by dependency theorists, these areas remain consistent with the patterns of capitalist development discussed by Marx. The "subordinated classes," they claim, have been neglected by some globalists in favor of a focus on exchange relations among societies. Such critics state that class contradictions and the intensification of class conflict still make possible the type of worker revolution discussed by Marx. Hence, these authors have taken the more voluntarist position in a long-standing Marxist debate on the potential for revolution in the Third World—that revolutionaries can help produce world-system change.[30]

Some world-system theorists take an intermediate position. Powerful "structures of domination" are acknowledged, but so also is the permanent struggle among classes. As Henrique Cardoso states of dependency theory: "Instead of accepting the existence of a determined course in history, there is a return to conceiving of it as an open-ended process. Thus, if structures delimit the range of oscillation, the actions of humans, as well as their imagination, revive and transfigure these structures and may even replace them with others that are not predetermined."[31] Similarly, Terence Hopkins and Immanuel Wallerstein argue that the study of the capitalist world economy is the "theoretical side of the practical work of transforming the modern world-system into the socialist world-order that modern social change has made at once politically necessary and historically possible."[32] In this formulation, there is room for human political will to effect transformation. Thus, if one accepts globalists at their word (and some critics do not), globalist theory is not determinist. It allows for (and even requires) political action.

GLOBALISTS AND THEIR CRITICS: AN OVERVIEW

The globalist literature has been subject to a great deal of criticism by specialists in international relations and comparative politics. Much of the criticism is harsh, particularly of dependency theorists and Immanuel Wallerstein's ambitious work. Much of this criticism also perhaps reflects ideological biases. We first discuss some of the more telling critiques and then present rebuttals from globalists.

The Question of Causality

Some critics question whether dependency creates economic and social backwardness (as globalists claim), or whether it is economic and social backwardness that leads to a situation of dependency. In short, there is no agreement on causality—whether dependency is the *cause* of backwardness or whether it is the *effect* of this condition.

Reliance on Economics

Critics have argued that some globalists have reduced the operation of the international system down to the process of capital accumulation and related dynamics. What of other, noneconomic explanations of imperialism and relations among states? Are not political and strategic motives equally or even more important? For example, how can one account for nineteenth-century European states scrambling for economically low-value pieces of terrain such as present-day Chad or lifeless Pacific atolls? What was the economic motive? If the competitive interstate system is derived from the capitalist mode of production, how does one explain similar competitive behavior among political units in precapitalist eras before the fifteenth century? For example, recall Thucydides' discussion of the Peloponnesian War that lends support to the validity of such notions as anarchy and the security dilemma. This suggests the autonomy of the political realm and a distinctly political dynamic involving competition among sovereign units well before the emergence of a world capitalist system.

The economic variable, critics claim, cannot carry the very great explanatory weight assigned to it. Insights generated from the contemplation of international relations over the centuries should not be ignored. Realists, for example, would argue that if anything it is the international political-security system that largely determines the international economic system, not the other way around.

System Dominance

Despite globalist references to internal factors, critics claim that there is an excessive globalist reliance on international factors in explaining poverty and dependence in the periphery and that domestic variables are downplayed. The cruder dependency work, it is argued, is too sweeping in its claims, blaming virtually every Third World political, economic, and social problem on the northern industrialized states. Lack of economic growth, social unrest, and repressive governments are all laid at the doorstep of the richer capitalist countries.

Theoretical Rigidity

The criticism of economics and system dominance as bases for causality logically leads to the following: It is claimed that individual cases are examined solely in terms of general theoretical constructs such as "dependency" or "world capitalist system." A society's experiences are reduced to or explained in terms of one or two concepts. Major political, economic, and social changes all supposedly fall under the general explanatory logic of a term such as *dependency*. Furthermore, rather than modifying the theories or concepts in light of empirical evidence (often supposedly lacking) or questions raised by case studies, it is claimed that case studies are used by globalists only when they appear to provide evidence to support the line of argument. There is no tension between theory and findings, little questioning of the framework, and an unwillingness to consider alternative hypotheses. Such criticisms, however, could just as easily be leveled at work associated with both the realist and pluralist images.

Accounting for Anomalies

It is also argued that the globalists are unable to account for Third World countries that have been relatively economically successful: Venezuela, Brazil, Singapore, South Korea. In addition there is the greatest success story of any non-European, non-North American country: Japan. What is it about these countries that has allowed them to escape abject poverty? Nor are they examples of autonomous development. In fact, they seem to have benefited greatly from international ties.

In response, it should be noted that no theory can be expected to explain everything. The virtue of good theorizing is that it points out and accounts for commonalities, what particular cases have in common. Anomalies are expected and do not detract from the utility of the theory if it can adequately be explained why a unique case does not fit the general pattern.

Critics comment, however, that globalists such as Wallerstein and the dependency theorists simply group all anomalies under the concept of the semi-periphery, a theoretically and empirically poorly defined concept. Furthermore, what of the insights of authors who argue that there are certain advantages to backwardness when a state is trying to catch up economically with more advanced states? What of the work by scholars who emphasize the importance of different types of state structures, political and social coalitions, and shifting alliances in accounting for the differential modernization success of various countries?[33] Such literature is ignored, it is argued, because the globalist perspective refuses to give due consideration to domestic factors that are not the result of capitalist dynamics.

Defining Alternatives and Science as Ideology

It is argued that some globalists have done a poor job in defining reasonable alternative world futures, let alone strategies, for LDCs to pursue. What is meant, for example, by the call for autonomous development? Is such a goal feasible? How is it to be achieved? What would a world socialist system entail? Would redistributive policies of a world government be combined with political repression and the abuse of power?

Critics also charge that value preferences infuse the globalist work. Globalists, however, are not apologetic for their normative commitment to fundamental changes in the relations between the North and the South. As one noted writer has stated, in analyses of dependency relations "there is no presumption of scientific neutrality." Such works are considered to be "more true because they assume that, by discerning which are the historical agents capable of propelling a process of transformation . . . , these analyses thus grasp the meaning of historical movement and help to negate a given order of domination."[34]

Critics of the dependency literature in particular believe that much of the work seeks less to explain underdevelopment than to unite Third World nationalists and socialists against the West by providing a politically attractive doctrine packaged in social science terms that blames all LDC problems on outside powers. By diverting attention from domestic sources of underdevelopment that have little to do with external factors, the dependency theorists, it is claimed, actually help to perpetuate the very problem they seek to resolve.

Responses

Why has the globalist literature—when it has not been totally ignored—received such a great deal of criticism? Is it simply because it is deserving of such critical scrutiny? Three comments are in order.

First, it is not surprising that most of the criticism comes from scholars working within mainstream North American social science. The vocabulary of the globalist literature is alien to many of these scholars. Analyses based on Marxian insights and categories are still generally viewed with distrust in North American universities and often dismissed out of hand. And although some of the globalist work is characterized as being ideological, globalists have similarly surmised that the attacks on them are based less on dispassionate critiques and more on the value preferences of the reviewer. Ideological biases are wrapped in the cloak of supposedly objective criticisms.

Second, it was pointed out that a number of critics charge that the dependency literature in particular has been insufficiently empirical, failing to marshal evidence based on the dictates of scientific behavioralism. Where's the data, they ask? In fact, it is claimed that the empirical testing of selective hypotheses from the dependency literature indicates that these hypotheses do not hold up.

Dependency theorists respond that such a charge is based on the assumption that the behavioralist methods are the *only* means to comprehend reality. In point of fact, critics argue, there are alternative **epistemological** premises or assumptions from which one can start that question the value of formal hypothesis testing with its often exclusive focus on what can be measured, counted, and added. As one dependency theorist notes:

> The divergence is not merely methodological-formal. It is, rather, at the very heart of studies of dependency. If these studies do in fact have any power of attraction at all, it is not merely because they propose a methodology to substitute for a previously existing paradigm or because they open up a new set of themes. It is principally because they do this from a *radically critical* viewpoint.[35]

Furthermore, many of these supposed empirical tests of dependency hypotheses completely ignore location and timing—the spatial and temporal context in which development occurs. They are, in other words, nonhistorical empirical tests of globalist hypotheses. Empirical tests cognizant of the historical context, by contrast, are said to support dependency propositions.[36] In addition, much of the world-system literature has actually been conspicuously empirical in a number of crossnational studies.[37]

Finally, some of the more insightful criticisms of the globalist literature are not based on antipathy toward the work but are meant to strengthen it by pointing out its weaknesses.[38]

To conclude, judging by the international relations textbooks currently on the market, it is apparent that the globalist perspective is not considered mainstream. Realist and pluralist writers dominate the literature, but this certainly does not mean that the globalist image of international relations is unimportant or undeserving of the student's attention. Its contribution to increased understanding of the world around us should not be seen only as a function of its degree of popularity with professors and textbook publishers. By providing a very different, challenging, and provocative perspective on world politics, it is worthy of attention. After all, as Thomas Kuhn has noted, dominant scientific paradigms of one particular period have a tendency to decay. What is at one time considered to be heretical or at the fringes of "normal science" may one day itself become the prevailing orthodoxy.[39] At a minimum, the globalist perspective should encourage the student of international relations to analyze critically the realist and pluralist images and the assumptions on which they are based. At the maximum, globalist writers have provided challenging hypotheses concerning the dynamics and development of the international system.

NOTES

1. As Robert L. Heilbroner states, "The entire contribution of Marxism to social thought rests ultimately on its effort to penetrate the veil of appearances to discover the hidden essence of things, the web of relations that is the real ground of reality and not the surface manifestations that are its facade." *Marxism: For and Against* (New York: W. W. Norton, 1980), p. 49.
2. Terence K. Hopkins, Immanuel Wallerstein and associates, "Patterns of Development of the Modern World-System," in *World-System Analysis: Theory and Methodology*, ed. Hopkins, Wallerstein, and associates (Beverly Hills, CA: Sage Publications, 1982), p. 72.
3. John A. Hobson, *Imperialism: A Study* (Ann Arbor: University of Michigan Press, 1965), pp. 85–86.
4. For example, see Lenin's "What Is to Be Done?" in *The Lenin Anthology*, ed. Robert C. Tucker (New York: W. W. Norton, 1975), pp. 12–114.
5. Others who would later write in this tradition would argue that revolutionaries play more of a role than mere catalysts. They can actually create the conditions for revolution; the "subjective" can create the "objective." This is most explicit in the writings, for example, of Che Guevara, although one also finds shades of it in Mao Zedong's writings on guerrilla warfare. As Karl Marx argued, "Men make their own history, but they do not make it just as they please; they do not make it under circumstances chosen by themselves, but under circumstances directly found, given, and transmitted from the past. The tradition of all dead generations weighs heavily like a nightmare on the brain of the living." "The Eighteenth Brumaire of Louis Bonaparte" in *The Marx-Engels Reader*, ed. Robert C. Tucker (New York: W. W. Norton, 1972), p. 436.
6. Rosa Luxemburg, *Reform or Revolution* (New York: Pathfinder Press, 1970, 1973), p. 72. The original publication was in German in 1898 and 1899.
7. *Ibid.*, p. 29.
8. Rosa Luxemburg, *The Accumulation of Capital* (New Haven, CT: Yale University Press, 1951).
9. For important early discussions, see Leon Trotsky, *The Russian Revolution* (New York: Doubleday, 1959); N. I. Bukharin, *Imperialism and World Econ-*

omy (New York: International Publishers, 1929); and Eduard Bernstein, *Evolutionary Socialism* (New York: B. W. Huebsch, 1911).

10. W. W. Rostow, *The Process of Economic Growth*, 2d ed. (New York: W. W. Norton, 1962).

11. The classic statement is found in Max Weber, *The Protestant Ethic and the Spirit of Capitalism* (New York: Scribner's, 1958).

12. Raul Prebisch, *Towards a Dynamic Development Policy for Latin America* (New York: United Nations, 1963).

13. Theotonio dos Santos, "La crisis del desarrollo y las relaciones de dependencia en America Latina," in *La Dependencia politico-economica de America Latina*, ed. H. Jaguaribe et al. (Mexico, 1970), p. 180, as cited in J. Samuel Valenzuela and Arturo Valenzuela, "Modernization and Dependency: Alternative Perspectives in the Study of Latin American Underdevelopment," *Comparative Politics* 10, 4 (July 1978): 544.

14. Osvaldo Sunkel, "Big Business and Dependencia: A Latin American View," *Foreign Affairs* 50, 3 (1972): 519-20.

15. Fernando Henrique Cardoso and Enzo Faletto, *Dependency and Development in Latin America* (Berkeley: University of California Press, 1979), p. xvi. See also three works by Samir Amin, *Imperialism and Unequal Development* (New York: Monthly Review Press, 1977); *Neo-Colonialism in West Africa* (New York: Monthly Review Press, 1974); and *Accumulation on a World Scale: A Critique of the Theory of Underdevelopment* (New York: Monthly Review Press, 1974). See also Walter Rodney, *How Europe Underdeveloped Africa* (London: Bogle l'Ouverture, 1973); Arghiri Emmanuel, *Unequal Exchange* (New York: Monthly Review Press, 1972); A. G. Frank, *World Accumulation, 1492-1789* (New York: Monthly Review Press, 1978).

16. Immanuel Wallerstein, *The Modern World-System I: Capitalist Agriculture and the Origins of the European World-Economy in the Sixteenth Century* (New York: Academic Press, 1974); and *The Modern World-System II: Mercantilism and the Consolidation of the European World-Economy, 1600-1750* (New York: Academic Press, 1980). For a discussion of the non-Marxist elements upon which Wallerstein's work is based, see Robert Brenner, "The Origins of Capitalist Development: A Critique of Neo-Smithian Marxism," *New Left Review* 104 (July-August 1977): 25-92.

17. Kenneth N. Waltz, *Theory of International Politics* (Reading, MA: Addison-Wesley, 1979), p. 38.

18. Immanuel Wallerstein, *The Capitalist World-Economy* (Cambridge: Cambridge University Press, 1979), p. 69.

19. *Ibid.*, p. 25.

20. Christopher Chase-Dunn, "Interstate System and Capitalist World-Economy: One Logic or Two?" in *World System Structure: Continuity and Change*, ed. W. Ladd Hollist and James N. Rosenau (Beverly Hills, CA: Sage Publications, 1981), p. 31

21. Patrick J. McGowan with Bohdan Kordan, "Imperialism in World-System Perspective: Britain 1870-1914," in *World System Structure*, ed. Hollist and Rosenau, p. 78.

22. Chase-Dunn, "Interstate System and Capitalist World-Economy," pp. 50-51.

23. Johan Galtung, "A Structural Theory of Imperialism," *Journal of Peace Research* 2 (1971): 81-98.

24. Wallerstein, *Capitalist World-Economy*, p. 67.
25. Hopkins and Wallerstein, "Structural Transformations of the World-Economy," in *World-System Analysis*, pp. 121–122. For a discussion of cycles, see also Wallerstein, *Modern World-System II*, Chapter 1.
26. *Ibid.*, p. 123.
27. For the argument that a new version of capitalism is emerging, see Robert J. S. Ross and Kent Trachte, "The Theory of Global Capitalism and Change in the World System: The New Leviathan." Paper presented at the annual meeting of the International Studies Association, March 1985, Washington, DC.
28. Immanuel Wallerstein, "The Rise and Future Demise of the World Capitalist System" *Comparative Studies in Society and History* 16, no. 4 (September 1974): 387–415, and his "Dependence in an Interdependent World: The Limited Possibilities of Transformation Within the Capitalist World Economy," *African Studies Review* 18, no. 1 (April 1974): 1–26.
29. Hayward R. Alker, Jr., "Dialectical Foundations of Global Disparities," in *World System Structure*, ed. Hollist and Rosenau, pp. 80–109; Johan Galtung, "Global Processes and the World in the 1980s," in *World System Structure*, ed. Hollist and Rosenau, pp. 110–138. Chase-Dunn (also in Hollist and Rosenau, p. 43) states that transformation might involve the dissolution of states, the elimination of economic exchanges between national territories, or the creation of a world stage.
30. Augustin Cueva, "A Summary of Problems and Perspectives of Dependency Theory," *Latin American Perspectives* 3, 4 (Fall 1976): 12–16. On the need to build a revolutionary party, see Raul A. Fernandez and Jose F. Ocampo, "The Latin American Revolution: A Theory of Imperialism, Not Dependence," *Latin American Perspectives* 1 (Spring 1974): 30–61.
31. Fernando Henrique Cardoso, "The Consumption of Dependency Theory in the United States," *Latin American Research Review* 12, 3 (1977): 10–11.
32. Hopkins and Wallerstein, *World-System Analysis*, p. 8.
33. See, for example, Alexander Gerschenkron, *Economic Backwardness in Historical Perspective* (New York: Praeger, 1965); Barrington Moore, *Social Origins of Dictatorship and Democracy* (Boston, MA: Beacon Press, 1966); Theda Skocpol, *States and Social Revolutions* (New York: Cambridge University Press, 1979).
34. Henrique Cardoso, "The Consumption of Dependency Theory," p. 16. See also the comments by James A. Caporaso, "Introduction," *International Organization* 32, 1 (Winter 1978): 2–3. A special issue on dependence and dependency.
35. *Ibid.*
36. David Sylvan and associates, "The Peripheral Economies: Penetration and Economic Distortion," in *Contending Approaches to World System Analysis*, ed. William R. Thompson (Beverly Hills, CA: Sage Publications, 1983), pp. 79–111. See also Raymond Duvall et al., "A Formal Model of Dependencia Theory: Structure and Measurement," in *From National Development to Global Community*, ed. Richard Merritt and Bruce Russett (London: George Allen & Unwin, 1981), pp. 312–50.
37. See John W. Meyer and Michael T. Hannan, eds., *National Development and the World System: Educational, Economic, and Political Change, 1950–1970* (Chicago: University of Chicago Press, 1979); Albert Bergesen,

ed., *Studies of the Modern World-System* (New York: Academic Press, 1980); Richard Rubinson, "The World Economy and the Distribution of Income Within States: A Cross-National Study," *American Sociology Review* 41 (1976): 638–59; and Christopher Chase-Dunn, "The Effects of International Economic Dependence on Development and Inequality: A Cross-National Study," *American Sociological Review* 40 (1975): 720–38.

38. See, for example, Theda Skocpol, "Wallerstein's World Capitalist System: A Theoretical and Historical Critique," *American Journal of Sociology* 82, 5 (March 1977): 1075–91.

39. Thomas S. Kuhn, *The Structure of Scientific Revolutions* (Chicago: University of Chicago Press, 1970).

SUGGESTED READINGS

Alker, Hayward R. "The Dialectical Foundations of Global Disparities." *International Studies Quarterly* 25, 1 (March 1981): 69–98.

Alker, Hayward R., and Thomas J. Biersteker. "The Dialectics of World Order: Notes for a Future Archeologist of International Savoir Faire." *International Studies Quarterly* 28 (1984): 121–42.

Amin, Samir. *Accumulation on a World Scale.* New York: Monthly Review Press, 1978.

————, ed. *Dynamics of Global Crisis.* New York: Monthly Review Press, 1982.

————. *Imperialism and Unequal Development.* New York: Monthly Review Press, 1977.

————. *Neo-Colonialism in West Africa.* New York: Monthly Review Press, 1976.

————. *Unequal Development: An Essay on the Social Formations of Peripheral Capitalism.* New York: Monthly Review Press, 1977.

Andrews, Bruce. "The Political Economy of World Capitalism: Theory and Practice." *International Organization* 36, 1 (Winter 1982): 135–63. A review essay.

Bergesen, Albert, ed. *Crises in the World-System.* Beverly Hills, CA: Sage Publications, 1983.

————, ed. *Studies of the Modern World-System.* New York: Academic Press, 1980.

H. Bernstein, ed. *Underdevelopment and Development: The Third World Today.* London: Penguin, 1976.

Bodenheimer, Susanne. "Dependency and Imperialism: The Roots of Latin American Underdevelopment." *Politics and Society* 1, 3 (May 1971): 327–57.

Bornschier, Volker. "Multinational Corporations and Economic Growth." *Journal of Development Economics* 7 (June 1980): 191–210.

Brenner, Robert. "The Origins of Capitalist Development: A Critique of Neo-Smithian Marxism." *New Left Review* 104 (July–August 1977): 25–92.

Caporaso, James A. "Dependence, Dependency, and Power in the Global System: A Structural and Behavioral Analysis." *International Organization* 32, 1 (Winter 1978): 13–44.

————. "Dependency Theory: Continuities and Discontinuities in Development Studies." *International Organization* 34, 4 (Autumn 1980): 605–28. A review essay.

Cardoso, Fernando Henrique. "Associated-Dependent Development: Theoretical and Practical Implications." In *Authoritarian Brazil*, edited by Alfred Stepan. New Haven, CT: Yale University Press, 1973.

———. "Dependency and Development in Latin America." *New Left Review* 74 (July-August 1972): 83–95.

———. "Imperialism and Dependency in Latin America." In *Structures of Dependency*, edited by Frank Bonilla and Robert Girling. Stanford, CA: Stanford Institute of Political Studies, 1973.

Casanova, Pablo Gonzalez. "The Economic Development of Mexico." *Scientific American* 243, 3 (September 1980): 192–204.

Chase-Dunn, Christopher. "Comparative Research on World-System Characteristics." *International Studies Quarterly* 23, 4 (December 1979): 601–23.

———. "The Effects of International Economic Dependence on Development and Inequality: A Cross-National Study." *American Sociological Review* 40 (1975): 720–38.

Chase-Dunn, Christopher, and Richard Rubinson. "Toward a Structural Perspective on the World-System." *Politics and Society* 7, 4 (1977): 453–76.

Chilcote, Ronald H., ed. *Dependency and Marxism: Toward a Resolution of the Debate*. Boulder, CO: Westview Press, 1982.

———. "Dependency: A Critical Synthesis of the Literature." *Latin American Perspectives* 1 (Spring 1974): 4–29.

Chilcote, Robert H., and Dale L. Johnson, eds. *Theories of Development: Mode of Production or Dependency?* Beverly Hills, CA: Sage Publications, 1983.

Cockcroft, James D., Andre Gunder Frank, and Dale L. Johnson, eds. *Dependence and Underdevelopment in Latin America*. New York: Anchor, 1972.

Cocks, Peter. "Towards a Marxist Theory of European Integration." *International Organization* 34, 1 (Winter 1980): 1–40.

Cohen, Benjamin J. *The Question of Imperialism*. New York: Basic Books, 1973.

dos Santos, Theotonio. *Imperialismo y dependencia*. Mexico City: Ediciones Era, 1978.

———. "The Structure of Dependence." *American Economic Review* 60, 2 (May 1970): 231–36.

Duvall, Raymond and associates, "A Formal Model of Dependencia Theory: Structure and Measurement." In *From National Development to Global Community*, edited by Richard Merritt and Bruce Russett. London and Boston: Allen & Unwin, 1981.

Emmanuel, Arghiri. *Unequal Exchange*. New York: Monthly Review Press, 1972.

Evans, Peter. *Dependent Development: The Alliance of Multinational, State, and Local Capital in Brazil*. Princeton, NJ: Princeton University Press, 1979.

Foster-Carter, Aidan. "Neo-Marxist Approaches to Development and Underdevelopment." In *Sociology and Development*, edited by Emmanuel de Kadt and Gavin Williams. London: Tavistock Press, 1974.

Frank, Andre Gunder. *Capitalism and Underdevelopment in Latin America*. London: Penguin, 1971.

———. *Crisis: In the Third World*. New York: Holmes and Meier, 1981.

———. *Crisis: In the World Economy*. New York: Holmes and Meier, 1980.

———. *Critique and Anti-Critique: Essays on Dependence and Reformism*. New York: Praeger, 1983.

————. *Latin America: Underdevelopment or Revolution*. New York: Monthly Review Press, 1969.

————. *World Accumulation, 1492-1789*. New York: Monthly Review Press, 1978.

Friedman, Edward, ed. *Ascent and Decline in the World-System*. Beverly Hills, CA: Sage Publications, 1982.

Galtung, Johan. "A Structural Theory of Imperialism." *Journal of Peace Research* 2 (1971): 81-98.

————. *Peace and World Structure*. Atlantic Highlands, NJ: Humanities Press, 1980.

————. *Peace Problems: Some Case Studies*. Atlantic Highlands, N.J.: Humanities Press, 1980.

Goldfrank, Walter L., ed. *The World-System of Capitalism: Past and Present*. Beverly Hills, CA: Sage Publications, 1979.

Hollist, W. Ladd, and James N. Rosenau, eds. *World System Structure: Continuity and Change*. Beverly Hills, CA: Sage Publications, 1981.

Hopkins, Terence K., and Immanuel Wallerstein, eds. *Processes of the World-System*. Beverly Hills, CA: Sage Publications, 1980.

Hopkins, Terence K., Immanuel Wallerstein, and associates. *World-System Analysis: Theory and Methodology*. Beverly Hills, CA: Sage Publications, 1982.

Hymer, Stephen. "The Multinational Corporation and the Law of Uneven Development." In *Economics and World Order*, edited by Jagdish Bhagwati. New York: Macmillan, 1972.

Janowitz, Morris. "A Sociological Perspective on Wallerstein." *American Journal of Sociology* 82, 5 (March 1977): 1090-1102.

Kaplan, Barbara Hockey, ed. *Social Change in the Capitalist World Economy*. Beverly Hills, CA: Sage Publications, 1978.

Kolko, Gabriel. *The Politics of War*. New York: Vintage Books, 1968.

Kolko, Joyce, and Gabriel Kolko. *The Limits of Power*. New York: Harper & Row, 1972.

Laclau, Ernesto. *Politics and Ideology in Marxist Theory*. London and New York: New Left Books and Schocken Books, 1977.

Leys, Colin. *Underdevelopment in Kenya: The Political Economy of Neo-Colonialism, 1964-71*. Berkeley: University of California Press, 1975.

McGowan, Patrick, and Stephen G. Walker. "Radical and Conventional Models of U.S. Foreign Economic Policymaking." *World Politics* 33, 3 (April 1981): 347-82.

Meyer, John W., and Michael T. Hannan, eds. *National Development and the World System: Educational, Economic, and Political Change, 1950-1970*. Chicago: University of Chicago Press, 1979.

Muñoz, Heraldo, ed. *From Dependency to Development*. Boulder, CO: Westview Press, 1981.

O'Brien, Philip. "A Critique of Latin American Theories of Dependency." In *Beyond the Sociology of Development*, edited by Ivar Oxaal, Tony Barnett, and David Booth. London: Routledge and Kegan Paul, 1975.

Political Economy of the World-System, annual. Beverly Hills, CA: Sage Publications, 1978, 1979, 1980.

Prebisch, Raul. *Towards a Dynamic Development Policy for Latin America*. New York: United Nations, 1963.

Rodney, Walter. *How Europe Underdeveloped Africa*. London: Bogle-l'Ouverture, 1973.

Rubinson, Richard. *Dynamics of World Development*. Beverly Hills, CA: Sage Publications, 1981.

————. "The World Economy and the Distribution of Income Within States: A Cross-National Study." *American Sociology Review* 41 (1976): 638–59.

Skocpol, Theda. "Wallerstein's World Capitalist System: A Theoretical and Historical Critique." *American Journal of Sociology* 82, 5 (March 1977): 1075–90.

Seers, Dudley, ed. *Dependency Theory: A Critical Assessment*. London: Frances Pinter, 1981.

Seers, Dudley, et al. *Underdeveloped Europe: Studies in Core-Periphery Relations*. Atlantic Highlands, NJ: Humanities Press, 1979.

Semmel, Bernard, ed. *Marxism and the Science of War*. New York: Oxford University Press, 1981.

Smith, Tony. "The Underdevelopment of Development Literature: The Case of Dependency Theory." *World Politics* 31, 2 (January 1979): 247–88.

Sunkel, Osvaldo. "National Development Policy and External Dependence in Latin America." *Journal of Development Studies* 61 (1969): 23–48.

Sylvan, David J. "The Newest Mercantilism." *International Organization* 35, 2 (Spring 1981): 375–93. A review essay.

Taylor, John G. *From Modernisation to Modes of Production: A Critique of the Sociologies of Development and Underdevelopment*. London: Macmillan, 1979.

Thompson, William R. *Contending Approaches in World System Analysis*. London and Beverly Hills, CA: Sage Publications, 1983.

Wallerstein, Immanuel. *Historical Capitalism*. London: Verso, 1983.

————. *The Capitalist World-Economy*. Cambridge: Cambridge University Press, 1979.

————. *The Modern World System* I. New York: Academic Press, 1974.

————. *The Modern World-System* II. New York: Academic Press, 1980.

————. *The Politics of the World-Economy*. New York: Cambridge University Press, 1984.

Wallerstein, Immanuel, and Peter C. W. Gutkind, eds. *Political Economy of Contemporary Africa*. 2d ed. Beverly Hills, CA: Sage Publications, 1985.

————. "The Rise and Future Demise of the World Capitalist System." *Comparative Studies in Society and History* 16, 4 (September 1974): 387–415.

Zolberg, Aristide R. "Origins of the Modern World System: A Missing Link." *World Politics* 33, 2 (January 1981): 253–81. A review of Wallerstein, *The Modern World-System*.

The Economic Taproot of Imperialism

J. A. Hobson

John Hobson discusses the economic taproot, or driving force, of imperialism. A high rate of savings and the power of production outstrip consumption. Industrialists and manufacturers therefore seek foreign sources of investment and markets in Third World countries to solve these problems.

No mere array of facts and figures adduced to illustrate the economic nature of the new Imperialism will suffice to dispel the popular delusion that the use of national force to secure new markets by annexing fresh tracts of territory is a sound and a necessary policy for an advanced industrial country like Great Britain. It has indeed been proved that recent annexations of tropical countries, procured at great expense, have furnished poor and precarious markets, that our aggregate trade with our colonial possessions is virtually stationary, and that our most profitable and progressive trade is with rival industrial nations, whose territories we have no desire to annex, whose markets we cannot force, and whose active antagonism we are provoking by our expansive policy.

But these arguments are not conclusive. It is open to Imperialists to argue thus: "We must have markets for our growing manufactures, we must have new outlets for the investment of our surplus capital and for the energies of the adventurous surplus of our population: such expansion is a necessity of life to a nation with our great and growing powers of production. An ever larger share of our population is devoted to the manufactures and commerce of towns, and is thus dependent for life and work upon food and raw materials from foreign lands. In order to buy and pay for these things we must sell our goods abroad. During the first three-quarters of the nineteenth century we could do so without difficulty by a natural expansion of commerce with continental nations and our colonies, all of which were far behind us in the main arts of manufacture and the carrying trades. So long as England held a virtual monopoly of the world markets for certain important classes of manufactured

From John A. Hobson, *Imperialism.* Reprinted by permission of George Allen & Unwin.

goods, Imperialism was unnecessary. After 1870 this manufacturing and trading supremacy was greatly impaired: other nations, especially Germany, the United States, and Belgium, advanced with great rapidity, and while they have not crushed or even stayed the increase of our external trade, their competition made it more and more difficult to dispose of the full surplus of our manufactures at a profit. The encroachments made by these nations upon our old markets, even in our own possessions, made it most urgent that we should take energetic means to secure new markets. These new markets had to lie in hitherto undeveloped countries, chiefly in the tropics, where vast populations lived capable of growing economic needs which our manufacturers and merchants could supply. Our rivals were seizing and annexing territories for similar purposes, and when they had annexed them closed them to our trade. The diplomacy and the arms of Great Britain had to be used in order to compel the owners of the new markets to deal with us: and experience showed that the safest means of securing and developing such markets is by establishing 'protectorates' or by annexation. The value in 1905 of these markets must not be taken as a final test of the economy of such a policy; the process of educating civilized needs which we can supply is of necessity a gradual one, and the cost of such Imperialism must be regarded as a capital outlay, the fruits of which posterity would reap. The new markets might not be large, but they formed serviceable outlets for the overflow of our great textile and metal industries, and, when the vast Asiatic and African populations of the interior were reached, a rapid expansion of trade was expected to result.

"Far larger and more important is the pressure of capital for external fields of investment. Moreover, while the manufacturer and trader are well content to trade with foreign nations, the tendency for investors to work towards the political annexation of countries which contain their more speculative investments is very powerful. Of the fact of this pressure of capital there can be no question. Large savings are made which cannot find any profitable investment in this country; they must find employment elsewhere, and it is to the advantage of the nation that they should be employed as largely as possible in lands where they can be utilized in opening up markets for British trade and employment for British enterprise.

"However costly, however perilous, this process of imperial expansion may be, it is necessary to the continued existence and progress of our nation[1]; if we abandoned it we must be content to leave the development of the world to other nations, who will everywhere cut into our trade, and even impair our means of securing the food and raw materials we require to support our population. Imperialism is thus seen to be, not a choice, but a necessity."

The practical force of this economic argument in politics is strikingly illustrated by the later history of the United States. Here is a country which suddenly broke through a conservative policy, strongly held by both political parties, bound up with every popular instinct and tradition, and flung itself into a rapid imperial career for which it possessed neither the material nor the moral equipment, risking the principles and practices of liberty and equality by the establishment of militarism and the forcible subjugation of peoples which it could not safely admit to the condition of American citizenship.

Was this a mere wild freak of spread-eaglism, a burst of political ambition on the part of a nation coming to a sudden realization of its destiny? Not at all. The spirit of adventure, the American "mission of civilization," were as forces making for Imperialism, clearly subordinate to the driving force of the economic factor. The dramatic character of the change is due to the unprecedented rapidity of the industrial revolution in the United States from the eighties onwards. During that period the United States, with her unrivalled natural resources, her immense resources of skilled and unskilled labour, and her genius for invention and organization, developed the best equipped and most productive manufacturing economy the world has yet seen. Fostered by rigid protective tariffs, her metal, textile, tool, clothing, furniture, and other manufactures shot up in a single generation from infancy to full maturity, and, having passed through a period of intense competition, attained, under the able control of great trust-makers, a power of production greater than has been attained in the most advanced industrial countries of Europe.

An era of cut-throat competition, followed by a rapid process of amalgamation, threw an enormous quantity of wealth into the hands of a small number of captains of industry. No luxury of living to which this class could attain kept pace with its rise of income, and a process of automatic saving set in upon an unprecedented scale. The investment of these savings in other industries helped to bring these under the same concentrative forces. Thus a great increase of savings seeking profitable investment is synchronous with a stricter economy of the use of existing capital. No doubt the rapid growth of a population, accustomed to a high and an always ascending standard of comfort, absorbs in the satisfaction of its wants a large quantity of new capital. But the actual rate of saving, conjoined with a more economical application of forms of existing capital, exceeded considerably the rise of the national consumption of manufactures. The power of production far outstripped the actual rate of consumption, and, contrary to the older economic theory, was unable to force a corresponding increase of consumption by lowering prices.

This is no mere theory. The history of any of the numerous trusts or combinations in the United States sets out the facts with complete distinctness. In the free competition of manufactures preceding combination the chronic condition is one of "over-production," in the sense that all the mills or factories can only be kept at work by cutting prices down towards a point where the weaker competitors are forced to close down, because they cannot sell their goods at a price which covers the true cost of production. The first result of the successful formation of a trust or combine is to close down the worse equipped or worse placed mills, and supply the entire market from the better equipped and better placed ones. This course may or may not be attended by a rise of price and some restriction of consumption: in some cases trusts take most of their profits by raising prices, in other cases by reducing the costs of production through employing only the best mills and stopping the waste of competition.

For the present argument it matters not which course is taken; the point is that this concentration of industry in "trusts," "combines," etc., at once limits the quantity of capital which can be effectively employed and increases the share of profits out of which fresh savings and fresh capital will spring. It is quite evident that a trust which is motived by cut-throat competition, due to an excess of capital, cannot normally find inside the "trusted" industry employment for that portion of the profits which the trust-makers desire to save and to invest. New inventions and other economies of production or distribution within the trade may absorb some of the new capital, but there are rigid limits to this absorption. The trust-maker in oil or sugar must find other investments for his savings: if he is early in the application of the combination principles to his trade, he will naturally apply his surplus capital to establish similar combinations in other industries, economising capital still further, and rendering it ever harder for ordinary saving men to find investments for their savings.

Indeed, the conditions alike of cut-throat competition and of combination attest the congestion of capital in the manufacturing industries which have entered the machine economy. We are not here concerned with any theoretic question as to the possibility of producing by modern machine methods more goods than can find a market. It is sufficient to point out that the manufacturing power of a country like the United States would grow so fast as to exceed the demands of the home market. No one acquainted with trade will deny a fact which all American economists assert, that this is the condition which the United States reached at the end of the century, so far, as the more developed industries are concerned. Her manufactures were saturated with capital and could absorb no more. One after another they sought refuge from the waste of competition in "combines" which secure a measure of profitable peace by restricting the quantity of operative capital. Industrial and financial princes in oil, steel, sugar, railroads, banking, etc., were faced with the dilemma of either spending more than they knew how to spend, or forcing markets outside the home area. Two economic courses were open to them, both leading towards an abandonment of the political isolation of the past and the adoption of imperialist methods in the future. Instead of shutting down inferior mills and rigidly restricting output to correspond with profitable sales in the home markets, they might employ their full productive power, applying their savings to increase their business capital, and, while still regulating output and prices for the home market, may "hustle" for foreign markets, dumping down their surplus goods at prices which would not be possible save for the profitable nature of their home market. So likewise they might employ their savings in seeking investments outside their country, first repaying the capital borrowed from Great Britain and other countries for the early development of their railroads, mines and manufactures, and afterwards becoming themselves a creditor class to foreign countries.

It was this sudden demand for foreign markets for manufactures and for investments which was avowedly responsible for the adoption of Imperialism as a political policy and practice by the Republican party to which the great industrial and financial chiefs belonged, and which belonged to them. The adventurous enthusiasm of President Theodore Roosevelt and his "manifest destiny" and "mission of civilization" party must not deceive us. It was Messrs. Rockefeller, Pierpont Morgan, and their associates who needed Imperialism and who fastened it upon the shoulders of the great Republic of the West. They needed Imperialism because they desired to use the public resources of their country to find profitable employment for their capital which otherwise would be superfluous.

It is not indeed necessary to own a country in order to do trade with it or to invest capital in it, and doubtless the United States could find some vent for their surplus goods, and capital in European countries. But these countries were for the most part able to make provision for themselves: most of them erected tariffs against manufacturing imports, and even Great Britain was urged to defend herself by reverting to Protection. The big American manufacturers and financiers were compelled to look to China and the Pacific and to South America for their most profitable chances; Protectionists by principle and practice, they would insist upon getting as close a monopoly of these markets as they can secure, and the competition of Germany, England, and other trading nations would drive them to the establishment of special political relations with the markets they most prize. Cuba, the Philippines, and Hawaii were but the *hors d'œuvre* to whet an appetite for an ampler banquet. Moreover, the powerful hold upon politics which these industrial and financial magnates possessed formed a separate stimulus, which, as we have shown, was operative in Great Britain and elsewhere; the public expenditure in pursuit of an imperial career would be a separate immense source of profit to these men, as financiers negotiating loans, shipbuilders and owners handling subsidies, contractors and manufacturers of armaments and other imperialist appliances.

The suddenness of this political revolution is due to the rapid manifestation of the need. In the last years of the nineteenth century the United States nearly trebled the value of its manufacturing export trade, and it was to be expected that, if the rate of progress of those years continued, within a decade it would overtake our more slowly advancing export trade, and stand first in the list of manufacture-exporting nations.[2]

This was the avowed ambition, and no idle one, of the keenest business men of America; and with the natural resources, the labour and the administrative talents at their disposal, it was quite likely they would achieve their object.[3] The stronger and more direct control over politics exercised in America by business men enabled them to drive more quickly and more straightly along the line of their economic interests than in Great Britain. American Imperialism was the natural product of the economic pressure of a sudden advance of capitalism which could not find occupation at home and needed foreign markets for goods and for investments.

The same needs existed in European countries, and, as is admitted, drove Governments along the same path. Over-production in the sense of an excessive manufacturing plant, and surplus capital which could not find sound investments within the country, forced Great Britain, Germany, Holland, France to place larger and larger portions of their economic resources outside the area of their present political domain, and then stimulate a policy of political expansion so as to take in the new areas. The economic sources of this movement are laid bare by periodic trade-depressions due to an inability of producers to find adequate and profitable markets for what they can produce. The Majority Report of the Commission upon the Depression of Trade in 1885 put the matter in a nutshell. "That, owing to the nature of the times, the demand for our commodities does not increase at the same rate as formerly; that our capacity for production is consequently in excess of our requirements, and could be considerably increased at short notice; that this is due partly to the competition of the capital which is being steadily accumulated in the country." The Minority Report straightly imputed the condition of affairs to "over-production." Germany was in the early 1900's suffering severely from what is called a glut of capital and of manufacturing power: she had to have new markets; her Consuls all over the

TABLE 1   Export Trade of United States, 1890–1900

Year	Agriculture	Manufactures	Miscellaneous
	£	£	£
1890	125,756,000	31,435,000	13,019,000
1891	146,617,000	33,720,000	11,731,000
1892	142,508,000	30,479,000	11,660,000
1893	123,810,000	35,484,000	11,653,000
1894	114,737,000	35,557,000	11,168,000
1895	104,143,000	40,230,000	12,174,000
1896	132,992,000	50,738,000	13,639,000
1897	146,059,000	55,923,000	13,984,000
1898	170,383,000	61,585,000	14,743,000
1899	156,427,000	76,157,000	18,002,000
1900	180,931,000	88,281,000	21,389,000

world were "hustling" for trade; trading settlements were forced upon Asia Minor; in East and West Africa, in China and elsewhere the German Empire was impelled to a policy of colonization and protectorates as outlets for German commercial energy.

Every improvement of methods of production, every concentration of ownership and control, seems to accentuate the tendency. As one nation after another enters the machine economy and adopts advanced industrial methods, it becomes more difficult for its manufacturers, merchants, and financiers to dispose profitably of their economic resources, and they are tempted more and more to use their Governments in order to secure for their particular use some distant undeveloped country by annexation and protection.

The process, we may be told, is inevitable, and so it seems upon a superficial inspection. Everywhere appear excessive powers of production, excessive capital in search of investment. It is admitted by all business men that the growth of the powers of production in their country exceeds the growth in consumption, that more goods can be produced than can be sold at a profit, and that more capital exists than can find remunerative investment.

It is this economic condition of affairs that forms the taproot of Imperialism. If the consuming public in this country raised its standard of consumption to keep pace with every rise of productive powers, there could be no excess of goods or capital clamorous to use Imperialism in order to find markets: foreign trade would indeed exist, but there would be no difficulty in exchanging a small surplus of our manufactures for the food and raw material we annually absorbed, and all the savings that we made could find employment, if we chose, in home industries.

There is nothing inherently irrational in such a supposition. Whatever is, or can be, produced, can be consumed, for a claim upon it, as rent, profit, or wages, forms part of the real income of some member of the community, and he can consume it, or else exchange it for some other consumable with some one else who will consume it. With everything that is produced a consuming power is born. If then there are goods which cannot get consumed, or which cannot even get produced because it is evident they cannot get consumed, and if there is a quantity of capital and labour which cannot get full employment because its products cannot get consumed, or which cannot even get produced because it is evident they cannot get consumed, the only possible explanation of this paradox is the refusal of owners of consuming power to apply that power in effective demand for commodities.

It is, of course, possible that an excess of producing power might exist in particular industries by misdirection, being engaged in certain manufactures, whereas it ought to have been engaged in agriculture or some other use. But no one can seriously contend that such misdirection explains the recurrent gluts and consequent depressions of modern industry, or that, when over-production is manifest in the leading manufactures, ample avenues are open for the surplus capital and labour in other industries. The general character of the excess of producing power is proved by the existence at such times of large bank stocks of idle money seeking any sort of profitable investment and finding none.

The root questions underlying the phenomena are clearly these: "Why is it that consumption fails to keep pace automatically in a community with power of production?" "Why does under-consumption or over-saving occur?" For it is evident that the consuming power, which, if exercised, would keep tense the reins of production, is in part withheld, or in other words is "saved" and stored up for investment. All saving for investment does not imply slackness of production; quite the contrary. Saving is economically justified, from the social standpoint, when the capital in which it takes material shape finds full employment in helping to produce commodities which, when produced, will be consumed. It is saving in excess of this amount that causes mischief, taking shape in surplus capital which is not needed to assist current consumption, and which either lies idle, or tries to oust existing capital from its employment, or else seeks speculative use abroad under the protection of the Government.

But it may be asked, "Why should there be any tendency to over-saving? Why should the owners of consuming power withhold a larger quantity for savings than can be serviceably employed?" Another way of putting the same question is this, "Why should not the pressure of present wants keep pace with every possibility of satisfying them?" The answer to these pertinent questions carries us to the broadest issue of the distribution of wealth. If a tendency to distribute income or consuming power according to needs were operative, it is evident that consumption would rise with every rise of producing power, for human needs are illimitable, and there could be no excess of saving. But it is quite otherwise in a state of economic society where distribution has no fixed relation to needs, but is determined by other conditions which assign to some people a consuming power vastly in excess of needs or possible uses, while others are destitute of consuming power enough to satisfy even the full demands of physical efficiency. The following illustration may serve to make the issue clear. "The volume of production has been constantly rising owing to the development of modern machinery. There are two main channels to carry off these products— one channel carrying off the product destined to be consumed by the workers, and the other channel carrying off the remainder to the rich. The workers' channel is in rock-bound banks that cannot enlarge, owing to the competitive wage system preventing wages rising *pro rata* with increased efficiency. Wages are based upon cost of living, and not upon efficiency of labour. The miner in the poor mine gets the same wages per day as the miner in the adjoining rich mine. The owner of the rich mine gets the advantage—not his labourer. The channel which conveys the goods destined to supply the rich is itself divided into two streams. One stream carries off what the rich 'spend' on themselves for the necessities and luxuries of life. The other is simply an 'overflow' stream carrying off their 'savings.' The channel for spending, i.e. the amount wasted by the rich in luxuries, may broaden somewhat, but owing to the small number of those rich enough to indulge in whims it can never be greatly enlarged, and at any rate it bears such a small proportion to the other channel that in no event can much hope of avoiding a flood of capital be hoped for from this division. The rich will never be so ingenious as to spend enough to prevent over-production. The great safety overflow channel which has been continuously more and more widened and deepened to carry off the ever-increasing flood of new capital is that division of the stream which carried the savings of the rich, and this is not only suddenly found to be incapable of further enlargement, but actually seems to be in the process of being dammed up."[4]

Though this presentation over-accentuates the cleavage between rich and poor and over-states the weakness of the workers, it gives forcible and sound expression to a most important and ill-recognised economic truth. The "over-flow" stream of savings is of course fed not exclusively from the surplus income of "the rich"; the professional and industrial middle classes, and to some slight extent the workers, contribute. But the "flooding" is distinctly due to the automatic saving of the surplus income of rich men. This is of course particularly true of America, where multi-millionaires rise quickly and find themselves in possession of incomes far exceeding the demands of any craving that is known to them. To make the metaphor complete, the overflow stream must be represented as re-entering the stream of production and seeking to empty there all the "savings" that it carries. Where competition remains free, the result is a chronic congestion of productive power and of production, forcing down home prices, wasting large sums in advertising and in pushing for orders, and periodically causing a crisis followed by a collapse, during which quantities of capital and labour lie unemployed and unremunerated. The prime object of the trust or other combine is to remedy this waste and loss by substituting regulation of output for reckless over-production. In achieving this it actually narrows or even dams up the old channels of investment, limiting the overflow stream to the exact amount required to maintain the normal current of output. But this rigid limitation of trade, though required for the separate economy of each trust, does not suit the trust-maker, who is driven to compensate for strictly regulated industry at home by cutting new foreign channels as outlets for his productive power and his excessive savings. Thus we reach the conclusion that Imperialism is the endeavour of the great controllers of industry to broaden the channel for the flow of their surplus wealth by seeking foreign markets and foreign investments to take off the goods and capital they cannot sell or use at home.

The fallacy of the supposed inevitably of imperial expansion as a necessary outlet for progressive industry is now manifest. It is not industrial progress that demands the opening up of new markets and areas of investment, but mal-distribution of consuming power which prevents the absorption of commodities and capital within the country. The over-saving which is the economic root of Imperialism is found by analysis to consist of rents, monopoly profits, and other unearned or excessive elements of income, which, not being earned by labour of head or hand, have no legitimate *raison d'être*. Having no natural relation to effort of production, they impel their recipients to no corresponding satisfaction of consumption: they form a surplus wealth, which, having no proper place in the normal economy of production and consumption, tends to accumulate as excessive savings. Let any turn in the tide of politico-economic forces divert from these owners their excess of income and make it flow, either to the workers in higher wages, or to the community in taxes, so that it will be spent instead of being saved, serving in either of these ways to swell the tide of consumption—there will be no need to fight for foreign markets or foreign areas of investment.

Many have carried their analysis so far as to realise the absurdity of spending half our financial resources in fighting to secure foreign markets at times when hungry mouths, ill-clad backs, ill-furnished houses indicate countless unsatisfied material wants among our own population. If we may take the careful statistics of Mr. Rowntree[5] for our guide, we shall be aware that more than one-fourth of the population of our towns is living at a standard which is below bare physical efficiency. If, by some economic readjustment, the products which flow from the surplus saving of the rich to swell the overflow streams could be diverted so as to raise the incomes and the standard of consumption of this inefficient fourth, there would be no need for pushful Imperialism, and the cause of social reform would have won its greatest victory.

It is not inherent in the nature of things that we should spend our natural resources on militarism, war, and risky, unscrupulous diplomacy, in order to find markets for our goods and surplus capital. An intelligent progressive community, based upon substantial equality of economic and educational opportunities, will raise its standard of consumption to correspond with every increased power of production, and can find full employment for an unlimited quantity of capital and labour within the limits of the country which it occupies. Where the distribution of incomes is such as to enable all classes of the nation to convert their felt wants into an effective demand for commodities, there can be no over-production, no under-employment of capital and labour, and no necessity to fight for foreign markets.

The most convincing condemnation of the current economy is conveyed in the difficulty which producers everywhere experience in finding consumers for their products: a fact attested by the prodigious growth of classes of agents and middlemen, the multiplication of every sort of advertising, and the general increase of the distributive classes. Under a sound economy the pressure would be reversed: the growing wants of progressive societies would be a constant stimulus to the inventive and operative energies of producers, and would form a constant strain upon the powers of production. The simultaneous excess of all the factors of production, attested by frequently recurring periods of trade depression, is a most dramatic exhibition of the false economy of distribution. It does not imply a mere miscalculation in the application of productive power, or a brief temporary excess of that power; it manifests in an acute form an economic waste which is chronic and general throughout the advanced industrial nations, a waste contained in the divorcement of the desire to consume and the power to consume.

If the apportionment of income were such as to evoke no excessive saving, full constant employment for capital and labour would be furnished at home. This, of course, does not imply that there would be no foreign trade. Goods that could not be produced at home, or produced as well or as cheaply, would still be purchased by ordinary process of international exchange, but here again the pressure would be the wholesome pressure of the consumer anxious to buy abroad what he could not buy at home, not the blind eagerness of the producer to use every force or trick of trade or politics to find markets for his "surplus" goods.

The struggle for markets, the greater eagerness of producers to sell than of consumers to buy, is the crowning proof of a false economy of distribution. Imperialism is the fruit of this false economy; "social reform" is its remedy. The primary purpose of "social reform," using the term in its economic signification, is to raise the wholesome standard of private and public consumption for a nation, so as to enable the nation to live up to its highest standard of production. Even those social reformers who aim directly at abolishing or reducing some bad form of consumption, as in the Temperance movement, generally recognise the necessity of substituting some better form of current consumption which is more educative and stimulative of other tastes, and will assist to raise the general standard of consumption.

There is no necessity to open up new foreign markets; the home markets are capable of indefinite expansion. Whatever is produced in England can be consumed in England, provided that the "income" or power to demand commodities, is properly distributed. This only appears untrue because of the unnatural and unwholesome specialisation to which this country has been subjected, based upon a bad distribution of economic resources, which has induced an overgrowth of certain manufacturing trades for the express purpose of effecting foreign sales. If the industrial revolution had taken place in an England founded upon equal access by all classes to land, education and legislation, specialisation in manufactures would not have gone so far (though more intelligent progress would have been made, by reason of a widening of the area of selection of inventive and organising talents); foreign trade would have been less important, though more steady; the standard of life for all portions of the population would have been high, and the present rate of national consumption would probably have given full, constant, remunerative employment to a far larger quantity of private and public capital than is now employed.[6] For the over-saving or wider consumption that is traced to excessive incomes of the rich is a suicidal economy, even from the exclusive standpoint of capital; for consumption alone vitalises capital and makes it capable of yielding profits. An economy that assigns to the "possessing" classes an excess of consuming power which they cannot use, and cannot convert into really serviceable capital, is a dog-in-the-manger policy. The social reforms which deprive the possessing classes of their surplus will not, therefore, inflict upon them the real injury they dread; they can only use this surplus by forcing on their country a wrecking policy of Imperialism. The only safety of nations lies in removing the unearned increments of income from the possessing classes, and adding them to the wage-income of the working classes or to the public income, in order that they may be spent in raising the standard of consumption.

Social reform bifurcates, according as reformers seek to achieve this end by raising wages or by increasing public taxation and expenditure. These courses are not essentially contradictory, but are rather complementary. Working-class movements aim, either by private cooperation or by political pressure on legislative and administrative government, at increasing the proportion of the national income which accrues to labour in the form of wages, pensions, compensation for injuries, etc. State Socialism aims at getting for the direct use of the whole society an increased share of the "social values" which arise from the closely and essentially cooperative work of an industrial society, taxing property and incomes so as to draw into the public exchequer for public expenditure the "unearned elements" of income, leaving to individual producers those incomes which are necessary to induce them to apply in the best way their economic energies, and to private enterprises those businesses which do not breed monopoly, and which the public need not or cannot undertake. These are not, indeed, the sole or perhaps the best avowed objects of social reform movements. But for the purposes of this analysis they form the kernel.

Trade Unionism and Socialism are thus the natural enemies of Imperialism, for they take away from the "imperialist" classes the surplus incomes which form the economic stimulus of Imperialism.

This does not pretend to be a final statement of the full relations of these forces. When we come to political analysis we shall perceive that the tendency of Imperialism is to crush Trade Unionism and to "nibble" at or parasitically exploit State Socialism. But, confining ourselves for the present to the narrowly economic setting, Trade Unionism and State Socialism may be regarded as complementary forces arrayed against Imperialism, in as far as, by diverting to working-class or public expenditure elements of income which would otherwise be surplus savings, they raise the general standard of home consumption and abate the pressure for foreign markets. Of course, if the increase of working-class income were wholly or chiefly "saved," not spent, or if the taxation of unearned incomes were utilised for the relief of other taxes borne by the possessing classes, no such result as we have described would follow. There is, however, no reason to anticipate this result from trade-union or socialistic measures. Though no sufficient natural stimulus exists to force the well-to-do classes to spend in further luxuries the surplus incomes which they save, every working-class family is subject to powerful stimuli of economic needs, and a reasonably governed State would regard as its prime duty the relief of the present poverty of public life by new forms of socially useful expenditure.

But we are not here concerned with what belongs to the practical issues of political and economic policy. It is the economic theory for which we claim acceptance—a theory which, if accurate, dispels the delusion that expansion of foreign trade, and therefore of empire, is a necessity of national life.

Regarded from the standpoint of economy of energy, the same "choice of life" confronts the nation as the individual. An individual may expend all his energy in acquiring external possessions, adding field to field, barn to barn, factory to factory—may "spread himself" over the widest area of property, amassing material wealth which is in some sense "himself" as containing the impress of his power and interest. He does this by specialising upon the lower acquisitive plane of interest at the cost of neglecting the cultivation of the higher qualities and interests of his nature. The antagonism is not indeed absolute. Aristotle has said, "We must first secure a livelihood and then practise virtue." Hence the pursuit of material property as a reasonable basis of physical comfort would be held true economy by the wisest men; but the absorption of time, energy, and interest upon such quantitative expansion at the necessary cost of starving the higher tastes and faculties is condemned as false economy. The same issue comes up in the business life of the individual: it is the question of intensive *versus* extensive cultivation. A rude or ignorant farmer, where land is plentiful, is apt to spread his capital and labour over a large area, taking in new tracts and cultivating them poorly. A skilled, scientific farmer will study a smaller patch of land, cultivate it thoroughly, and utilise its diverse properties, adapting it to the special needs of his most remunerative markets. The same is true of other businesses; even where the economy of large-scale production is greatest there exists some limit beyond which the wise business man will not go, aware that in doing so he will risk by enfeebled management what he seems to gain by mechanical economies of production and market.

Everywhere the issue of quantitative *versus* qualitative growth comes up. This is the entire issue of empire. A people limited in number and energy and in the land they occupy have the choice of improving to the utmost the political and economic management of their own land, confining themselves to such accessions of territory as are justified by the most economical disposition of a growing population; or they may proceed, like the slovenly farmer, to spread their power and energy over the whole earth, tempted by the speculative value or the quick profits of some new market, or else by mere greed of territorial acquisition, and ignoring the political and economic wastes and risks involved by this imperial career. It must be clearly understood that this is essentially a choice of alternatives; a full simultaneous application of intensive and extensive cultivation is impossible. A nation may either, following the example of Denmark or Switzerland, put brains into agriculture, develop a finely varied system of public education, general and technical, apply the ripest science to its special manufacturing industries, and so support in progressive comfort and character a considerable population upon a strictly limited area; or it may, like Great Britain, neglect its agriculture, allowing its lands to go out of cultivation and its population to grow up in towns, fall behind other nations in its methods of education and in the capacity of adapting to its uses the latest scientific knowledge, in order that it may squander its pecuniary and military resources in forcing bad markets and finding speculative fields of investment in distant corners of the earth, adding millions of square miles and of unassimilable population to the area of the Empire.

The driving forces of class interest which stimulate and support this false economy we have explained. No remedy will serve which permits the future operation of these forces. It is idle to attack Imperialism or Militarism as political expedients or policies unless the axe is laid at the economic root of the tree, and the classes for whose interest Imperialism works are shorn of the surplus revenues which seek this outlet.

NOTES

1. And why, indeed, are wars undertaken, if not to conquer colonies which permit the employment of fresh capital, to acquire commercial monopolies, or to obtain the exclusive use of certain highways of commerce?" (Loria, *Economic Foundations of Society*, p. 267).
2. Post-war conditions, with the immense opportunities afforded for export of American goods and capital brought a pause and a temporary withdrawal from imperialist policy.
3. "We hold now three of the winning cards in the game for commercial greatness, to wit—iron, steel and coal. We have long been the granary of the world, we now aspire to be its workshop, then we want to be its clearinghouse." (The President of the American Bankers' Association at Denver, 1898.)
4. *The Significance of the Trust,* by H. G. Wilshire.
5. *Poverty: A Study of Town Life.*
6. The classical economists of England, forbidden by their theories of parsimony and of the growth of capital to entertain the notion of an indefinite expansion of home markets by reason of a constantly rising standard of national comfort,

were early driven to countenance a doctrine of the necessity of finding external markets for the investment of capital. So J. S. Mill: "The expansion of capital would soon reach its ultimate boundary if the boundary itself did not continually open and leave more space" *(Political Economy).* And before him
Ricardo (in a letter to Malthus): "If with every accumulation of capital we
could take a piece of fresh fertile land to our island, profits would never fall."

Imperialism: The Highest Stage of Capitalism

V. I. Lenin

*Lenin explains the scramble for colonies by capitalist states. His intel-
lectual debt to Hobson is obvious.*

IMPERIALISM AS A SPECIAL STAGE OF CAPITALISM

Imperialism emerged as the development and direct continuation of the
fundamental attributes of capitalism in general. But capitalism only
became capitalist imperialism at a definite and very high stage of its
development, when certain of its fundamental attributes began to be
transformed into their opposites, when the features of a period of transition from cpaitalism to a higher social and economic system began to
take shape and reveal themselves all along the line. Economically, the
main thing in this process is the substitution of capitalist monopolies for
capitalist free competition. Free competition is the fundamental attribute
of capitalism, and of commodity production generally. Monopoly is
exactly the opposite of free competition; but we have seen the latter
being transformed into monopoly before our very eyes, creating large-
scale industry and eliminating small industry, replacing large-scale industry by still larger-scale industry, finally leading to such a concentration of
production and capital that monopoly has been and is the result: cartels,
syndicates and trusts, and merging with them, the capital of a dozen or
so banks manipulating thousands of millions. At the same time monopoly, which has grown out of free competition, does not abolish the latter,
but exists over it and alongside of it, and thereby gives rise to a number

of very acute, intense intagonisms, friction and conflicts. Monopoly is the transition from capitalism to a higher system.

If it were necessary to give the briefest possible definition of imperialism we should have to say that imperialism is the monopoly stage of capitalism. Such a definition would include what is most important, for, on the one hand, finance capital is the bank capital of a few big monopolist banks, merged with the capital of the monopolist combines of manufacturers; and, on the other hand, the division of the world is the transition from a colonial policy which has extended without hindrance to territories unoccupied by any capitalist power, to a colonial policy of monopolistic possession of the territory of the world which has been completely divided up.

But very brief definitions, although convenient, for they sum up the main points, are nevertheless inadequate, because very important features of the phenomenon that has to be defined have to be especially reduced. And so, without forgetting the conditional and relative value of all definitions, which can never include all the concatenations of a phenomenon in its complete development, we must give a definition of imperialism that will embrace the following five essential features:

1) The concentration of production and capital developed to such a high stage that it created monopolies which play a decisive role in economic life.
2) The merging of bank capital with industrial capital, and the creation, on the basis of this "finance capital," of a "financial oligarchy."
3) The export of capital, which has become extremely important, as distinguished from the export of commodities.
4) The formation of international capitalist monopolies which share the world among themselves.
5) The territorial division of the whole world among the greatest capitalist powers is completed.

Imperialism is capitalism in that stage of development in which the dominance of monopolies and finance capital has established itself; in which the export of capital has acquired pronounced importance; in which the division of the world among the international trusts has begun; in which the division of all territories of the globe among the great capitalist powers has been completed. . . .

In this matter of defining imperialism, however, we have to enter into controversy, primarily, with K. Kautsky, the principal Marxian theoretician of the epoch of the so-called Second International—that is, of the twenty-five years between 1889 and 1914.

Kautsky, in 1915 and even in November 1914, very emphatically attacked the fundamental ideas expressed in our definition of imperialism. Kautsky said that imperialism must not be regarded as a "phase" or stage of economy, but as a policy; a definite policy "preferred" by finance capital; that imperialism cannot be "identified" with "contemporary capitalism"; that if imperialism is to be understood to mean "all the phenomena of contemporary capitalism"—cartels, protection, the domination of the financiers and colonial policy—then the question as to whether imperialism is necessary to capitalism becomes reduced to the "flattest tautology"; because, in that case, "imperialism is naturally a vital necessity for capitalism" and so on. The best way to present Kautsky's ideas is to quote his own definition of imperialism, which is diametrically opposed to the substance of the ideas which we have set forth. . . .

Kautsky's definition is as follows:

> Imperialism is a product of highly developed industrial capitalism. It consists in the striving of every industrialist capitalist nation to bring under its control and to annex increasingly big *agrarian* (Kautsky's italics) regions irrespective of what nations inhabit those regions. . . .

Imperialism is a striving for annexations—this is what the *political* part of Kautsky's definition amounts to. It is correct, but very incomplete, for politically, imperialism is, in general, a striving towards violence and reaction. For the moment, however, we are interested in the *economic* aspect of the question, which Kautsky *himself* introduced into *his* definition. The inaccuracy of Kautsky's definition is strikingly obvious. The characteristic feature of imperialism is *not* industrial capital, *but* finance capital. It is not an accident that in France it was precisely the extraordinarily rapid development of *finance* capital, and the weakening of industrial capital, that, from 1880 onwards, gave rise to the extreme extension of annexationist (colonial) policy. The characteristic feature of imperialism is precisely that it strives to annex *not only* agricultural regions, but even highly industrialized regions (German appetite for Belgium; French appetite for Lorraine), because 1) the fact that the world is already divided up obliges those contemplating a *new* division to reach out for *any kind* of territory, and 2) because an essential feature of imperialism is the rivalry between a number of great powers in the striving for hegemony, *i.e.*, for the conquest of territory, not so much directly for themselves as to weaken the adversary and undermine *his* hegemony. (Belgium is chiefly necessary to Germany as a base for operations against England; England needs Bagdad as a base for operations against Germany, etc.). . . .

Kautsky's definition is not only wrong and un-Marxian. It serves as a basis for a whole system of views which run counter to Marxian theory and Marxian practice all along the line. . . . The fact of the matter is that Kautsky detaches the politics of imperialism from its economics, speaks of annexations as being a policy "preferred" by finance capital, and opposes to it another bourgeois policy which, he alleges, is possible on this very basis of finance capital. According to his argument, monopolies in economics are compatible with non-monopolistic, non-violent, non-annexationist methods in politics. According to his argument, the territorial division of the world, which was completed precisely during the period of finance capital, and which constitutes the basis of the present peculiar forms of rivalry between the biggest capitalist states, is compatible with a non-imperialist policy. The result is a slurring-over and a blunting of the most profound contradictions of the latest stage of capitalism, instead of an exposure of their depth; the result is bourgeois reformism instead of Marxism. . . .

Kautsky writes: "from the purely economic point of view it is not impossible that capitalism will yet go through a new phase, that of the extension of the policy of cartels to foreign policy, the phase of ultra-imperialism," *i.e.,* of a super-imperialism, a union of world imperialisms and not struggles among imperialisms; a phase when wars shall cease under capitalism, a phase of "the joint exploitation of the world by internationally combined finance capital."

Is "ultra-imperialism" possible "from the purely economic point of view" or is it ultra-nonsense? . . .

Compare . . . the vast diversity of economic and political conditions, the extreme disparity in the rate of development of the various countries, etc., and the violent struggles of the imperialist states, with Kautsky's silly little fable about "peaceful" ultra-imperialism. Is this not the reactionary attempt of a frightened philistine to hide from stern reality? Are not the international cartels which Kautsky imagines are the embryos of "ultra-imperialism" . . . an example of the division and the *re-division* of the world, the transition from peaceful division to non-peaceful division and vice versa? Is not American and other finance capital, which divided the whole world peacefully, with Germany's participation for example, in the international rail syndicate, or in the international mercantile shipping trust, now engaged in *re-dividing* the world on the basis of a new relation of forces, which has been changed by methods *by no means* peaceful?

Finance capital and the trusts are increasing instead of diminishing the difference in the rate of development of the various parts of world economy. When the relation of forces is changed, how else, *under capitalism,* can the solution of contradictions be found, except by resorting to violence . . . ?

Capitalism is growing with the greatest rapidity in the colonies and in overseas countries. Among the latter, *new* imperialist powers are emerging (e.g., Japan). The struggle of world imperialism is becoming more acute.

It is well known that the development of productive forces in Germany, and especially the development of the coal and iron industries, has been much more rapid during this period than in England—not to mention France and Russia. In 1892, Germany produced 4,900,000 tons of pig iron and Great Britain produced 6,800,000 tons; in 1912, Germany produced 17,600,000 tons and Great Britain 9,000,000 tons. Germany, therefore, had an overwhelming superiority over England in this respect.

We ask, is there *under capitalism* any means of removing the disparity between the development of productive forces and the accumulation of capital on the one side, and the division of colonies and "spheres of influence" for finance capital on the other side—other than by resorting to war . . .

The imperialism of the beginning of the twentieth century completed the division of the world among a handful of states, each of which today exploits (*i.e.*, draws super-profits from) a part of the world only a little smaller than that which England exploited in 1858. Each of them, by means of trusts, cartels, finance capital, and debtor and creditor relations, occupies a monopoly position in the world market. Each of them enjoys to some degree a colonial monopoly. (We have seen that out of the total of 75,000,000 sq. km. which comprise the *whole* colonial world, 65,000,000 sq. km., or 86 per cent, belong to six great powers; 61,000,000 sq. km., or 81 per cent, belong to three powers.) . . .

Embryonic imperialism has grown into a dominant system; capitalist monopolies occupy first place in economics and politics; the division of the world has been completed. On the other hand, instead of an undisputed monopoly by Great Britain, we see a few imperialist powers contending for the right to share in this monopoly, and this struggle is characteristic of the whole period of the beginning of the twentieth century. . . .

THE CRITIQUE OF IMPERIALISM

By the critique of imperialism, in the broad sense of the term, we mean the attitude toward imperialist policy of the different classes of society as part of their general ideology.

The enormous dimensions of finance capital concentrated in a few hands and creating an extremely extensive and close network of ties and relationships which subordinate not only the small and medium, but also even the very small capitalists and small masters, on the one hand, and the intense struggle waged against other national state groups of financiers for the division of the world and domination over other countries, on the other hand, cause the wholesale transition of the possessing classes to the side of imperialism. The signs of the times are a "general" enthusiasm regarding its prospects, a passionate defence of imperialism, and every possible embellishment of its real nature. . . .

Bourgeois scholars and publicists usually come out in defence of imperialism in a somewhat veiled form, and obscure its complete domination and its profound roots; they strive to concentrate attention on partial and secondary details and do their very best to distract attention from the main issue by means of ridiculous schemes for "reform," such as police supervision of the trusts and banks, etc. Less frequently, cynical and frank imperialists speak out and are bold enough to admit the absurdity of the idea of reforming the fundamental features of imperialism. . . .

The question as to whether it is possible to reform the basis of imperialism, whether to go forward to the accentuation and deepening of the antagonisms which it engenders, or backwards, towards allaying these antagonisms, is a fundamental question in the critique of imperialism. As a consequence of the fact that the political features of imperialism are reaction all along the line, and increased national oppression, resulting from the oppression of the financial oligarchy and the elimination of free competition, a petty-bourgeois-democratic opposition has been rising against imperialism in almost all imperialist countries since the beginning of the twentieth century. . . .

In the United States, the imperialist war waged against Spain in 1898 stirred up the opposition of the "anti-imperialists," the last of the Mohicans of bourgeois democracy. They declared this war to be "criminal"; they denounced the annexation of foreign territories as being a violation of the Constitution, and denounced the "Jingo treachery" by means of which Aguinaldo, leader of the native Filipinos, was deceived (the Americans promised him the independence of his country, but later they landed troops and annexed it). They quoted the words of Lincoln:

> When the white man governs himself, that is self-government; but when he governs himself and also governs another man, that is more than self-government—that is despotism.

But while all this criticism shrank from recognizing the indissoluble bond between imperialism and the trusts, and, therefore, between imperialism and the very foundations of capitalism; while it shrank from joining up with the forces engendered by large-scale capitalism and its development—it remained a "pious wish."

. . . Here is an example of Kautsky's economic criticism of imperialism. He takes the statistics of the British export and import trade with Egypt for 1872 and 1912. These statistics show that this export and import trade has developed more slowly than British foreign trade as a whole. From this Kautsky concludes that:

> We have no reason to suppose that British trade with Egypt would have been less developed simply as a result of the mere operation of economic factors, without military occupation. . . . The urge of the present-day states to expand . . . can be best promoted, not by the violent methods of imperialism, but by peaceful democracy.

. . . Kautsky departed from Marxism by advocating what is, in the period of finance capital, a "reactionary ideal," "peaceful democracy," "the mere operation of economic factors," for *objectively* this ideal drags us back from monopoly capitalism to the non-monopolist stage, and is a reformist swindle.

Trade with Egypt (or with any other colony or semi-colony) "would have grown more" *without* military occupation, without imperialism, and without finance capital. What does this mean? That capitalism would develop more rapidly if free competition were not restricted by monopolies in general, by the "connections" or the yoke (*i.e.*, also the monopoly) of finance capital, or by the monopolist possession of colonies by certain countries?

Kautsky's argument can have no other meaning; and *this* "meaning" is meaningless. But suppose, for the sake of argument, free competition, without any sort of monopoly, *would* develop capitalism and trade more rapidly. Is it not a fact that the more rapidly trade and capitalism develop, the greater is the concentration of production and capital which *give rise* to monopoly? And monopolies have *already* come into being—precisely *out of* free competition! Even if monopolies have now begun to retard progress, it is not an argument in favor of free competition, which has become impossible since it gave rise to monopoly.

Whichever way one turns Kautsky's argument, one will find nothing in it except reaction and bourgeois reformism.

Even if we modify this argument and say . . . that the trade of the British colonies with the mother country is now developing more slowly than their trade with other countries, it does not save Kautsky; for it is *also* monopoly and imperialism that is beating Great Britain, only it is the monopoly and imperialism of another country (America, Germany). It is known that the cartels have given rise to a new and peculiar form of protective tariffs, *i.e.*, goods suitable for export are protected (Engels noted this in Vol. III of *Capital*). It is known, too, that the cartels and finance capital have a system peculiar to themselves, that of "exporting goods at cut-rate prices," or "dumping," as the English call it; within a given country the cartel sells its goods at a high price fixed by monopoly; abroad it sells them at a much lower price to undercut the competitor, to enlarge its own production to the utmost, etc. If Germany's trade with the British colonies is developing more rapidly than that of Great Britain with the same colonies, it only proves that German imperialism is younger, stronger and better organized than British imperialism, is superior to it. But this by no means proves the "superiority" of free trade, for it is not free trade fighting against protection and colonial dependence, but two rival imperialisms, two monopolies, two groups of finance capital that are fighting. The superiority of German imperialism over British imperialism is stronger than the wall of colonial frontiers or of protective tariffs. To use this as an argument in favor of free trade and "peaceful democracy" is banal, is to forget the essential features and qualities of imperialism, to substitute petty-bourgeois reformism for Marxism. . . .

Kautsky's theoretical critique of imperialism has nothing in common with Marxism and serves no other purpose than as a preamble to propaganda for peace and unity with the opportunists and the social-chauvinists, precisely for the reason that it evades and obscures the very profound and radical contradictions between monopoly and free competition that exist side by side with it, between the gigantic "operations" (and gigantic profits) of finance capital and "honest" trade in the free market, the contradictions between cartels and trusts, on the one hand and non-cartelised industry, on the other, etc.

The notorious theory of "ultra-imperialism," invented by Kautsky, is equally reactionary. . . .

> Cannot the present imperialist policy be supplanted by a new, ultra-imperialist policy, which will introduce the common exploitation of the world by internationally united finance capital in place of the mutual rivalries of national finance capital? Such a new phase of capitalism is at any rate conceivable. Can it be achieved? Sufficient premises are still lacking to enable us to answer this question.

. . . The only objective, *i.e.*, real, social significance Kautsky's "theory" can have, is that of a most reactionary method of consoling the masses with hopes of permanent peace being possible under capitalism, distracting their attention from the sharp antagonisms and acute problems of the present era, and directing it towards illusory prospects of an imaginary "ultra-imperialism" of the future. Deception of the masses—there is nothing but this in Kautsky's "Marxian" theory.

Indeed, it is enough to compare well-known and indisputable facts to become convinced of the utter falsity of the prospects which Kautsky tries to conjure up before the German workers (and the workers of all lands). Let us consider India, Indo-China and China. It is known that these three Colonial and semi-colonial countries, inhabited by six to seven hundred million human beings, are subjected to the exploitation of the finance capital of several imperialist states: Great Britain, France, Japan, the U.S.A., etc. We will assume that these imperialist countries form alliances against one another in order to protect and extend their possessions, their interests and their "spheres of influence" in these Asiatic states; these alliances will be "inter-imperialist" or "ultra-imperialist" alliances. We will assume that *all* the imperialist countries conclude an alliance for the "peaceful" division of these parts of Asia; this alliance would be an alliance of "internationally united finance capital." As a matter of fact, alliances of this kind have been made in the twentieth century, notably with regard to China. We ask, is it "conceivable," assuming that the capitalist system remains intact—and this is precisely the assumption that Kautsky does make—that such alliances would be more than temporary, that they would eliminate friction, conflicts and struggle in all and every possible form?

This question need only be stated clearly enough to make it impossible for any other reply to be given than that in the negative; for there can be *no* other conceivable basis under capitalism for the division of spheres of influence, of interests, of colonies, etc., than a calculation of the *strength* of the participants in the division, their general economic, financial, military strength, etc. And the strength of these participants in the division does not change to an equal degree, for under capitalism the development of different undertakings, trusts, branches of industry, or countries cannot be *even.* Half a century ago, Germany was a miserable, insignificant country, as far as its capitalist strength was concerned, compared with the strength of England at that time. Japan was similarly insignificant compared with Russia. Is it "conceivable" that in ten or twenty years' time the relative strength of the imperialist powers will have remained *un*changed? Absolutely inconceivable.

Therefore, in the realities of the capitalist system . . . no matter what form they may assume, whether of one imperialist coalition against another, or of a general alliance embracing *all* the imperialist powers, are *inevitably* nothing more than a "truce" in periods between wars. Peaceful alliances prepare the ground for wars, and in their turn grow out of wars; the one is the condition for the other, giving rise to alternating forms of peaceful and nonpeaceful struggle out of *one and the same* basis of imperialist connections and the relations between world economics and world politics. . . .

Kautsky's toning down of the deepest contradictions of imperialism, which inevitably becomes the embellishment of imperialism, leaves its traces in this writer's criticism of the political features of imperialism. Imperialism is the epoch of finance capital and of monopolies, which introduce everywhere the striving for domination, not for freedom. The result of these tendencies is reaction all along the line, whatever the political system, and an extreme intensification of existing antagonisms in this domain also. Particularly acute becomes the yoke of national oppression and the striving for annexations, *i.e.*, the violation of national independence (for annexation is nothing but the violation of the right of nations to self-determination). Hilferding justly draws attention to the connection between imperialism and the growth of national oppression.

> In the newly opened up countries themselves, [he writes] the capitalism imported into them intensifies contradictions and excites the constantly growing resistance against the intruders of the peoples who are awakening to national consciousness. This resistance can easily become transformed into dangerous measures directed against foreign capital. The old social relations become completely revolutionized. The age-long agrarian incrustation of "nations without a history" is blasted away, and they are drawn into the capitalist whirlpool. Capitalism itself gradually procures for the vanquished the means and resources for the emancipation and they set out to achieve the same goal which once seemed highest to the European nations: the creation of a united national state as a means to economic and cultural freedom. This movement for national independence threatens European capital just in its most valuable and most promising fields of exploitation, and European capital

can maintain its domination only by continually increasing its means of exerting violence.

To this must be added that it is not only in newly opened up countries, but also in the old, that imperialism is leading to annexation, to increased national oppression, and, consequently, also to increasing resistance. . . . Let us suppose that a Japanese is condemning the annexation of the Philippine Islands by the Americans. Will many believe that he is doing so because he has a horror of annexations as such, and not because he himself has a desire to annex the Philippines? And shall we not be constrained to admit that the "fight" the Japanese are waging against annexations can be regarded as being sincere and politically honest only if he fights against the annexation of Korea by Japan, and urges freedom for Korea to secede from Japan?*

Kautsky's theoretical analysis of imperialism, as well as his economic and political criticism of imperialism, are permeated *through and through* with a spirit, absolutely irreconcilable with Marxism, of obscuring and glossing over the most profound contradictions of imperialism. . . .

THE PLACE OF IMPERIALISM IN HISTORY

We have seen that the economic quintessence of imperialism is monopoly capitalism. This very fact determines its place in history, for monopoly that grew up on the basis of free competition, and precisely out of free competition, is the transition from the capitalist system to a higher social-economic order. We must take special note of the four principal manifestations of monopoly capitalism, which are characteristic of the epoch under review.

Firstly, monopoly arose out of the concentration of production at a very advanced stage of development. This refers to the monopolist capitalist combines, cartels, syndicates and trusts. We have seen the important part that these play in modern economic life. At the beginning of the twentieth century, monopolies acquired complete supremacy in the advanced countries. And although the first steps towards the formation of the cartels were first taken by countries enjoying the protection of high tariffs (Germany, America), Great Britain, with her system of free trade, was not far behind in revealing the same basic phenomenon, namely, the birth of monopoly out of the concentration of production.

Secondly, monopolies have accelerated the capture of the most important sources of raw materials, especially for the coal and iron industries, which are the basic and mostly highly cartelised industries in capitalist society. The monopoly of the most important sources of raw materials has enormously increased the power of big capital, and has sharpened the antagonism between cartelised and non-cartelised industry.

Thirdly, monopoly has sprung from the banks. The banks have developed from modest intermediary enterprises into the monopolists of finance capital. Some three or five of the biggest banks in each of the foremost capitalist countries have achieved the "personal union" of industrial and bank capital, and have concentrated in their hands the disposal of thousands upon thousands of millions which form the greater part of the capital and income of entire countries. A financial oligarchy, which throws a close net of relations of dependence over all the economic and political institutions of contemporary bourgeois society without exception—such is the most striking manifestation of this monopoly.

Fourthly, monopoly has grown out of colonial policy. To the numerous "old" motives of colonial policy, finance capital has added the struggle for the sources of raw materials, for the export of capital, for "spheres of influence," i.e., for spheres for profitable deals, concessions, monopolist profits and so on; in fine, for economic territory in general. When the colonies of the European powers in Africa, for instance, comprised only one-tenth of that territory (as was the case in 1876), colonial policy was able to develop by methods other than those of monopoly—by the "free grabbing" of territories, so to speak. But when nine-tenths of Africa had been seized (approximately by 1900), when the whole world had been divided up, there was inevitably ushered in a period of colonial monopoly and, consequently, a period of particularly intense struggle for the division and the redivision of the world.

The extent to which monopolist capital has intensified all the contradictions of capitalism is generally known. It is sufficient to mention the high cost of living and the oppression of the cartels. This intensification of contradictions constitutes the most powerful driving force of the transitional period of history, which began from the time of the definite victory of world finance capital.

Monopolies, oligarchy, the striving for domination instead of striving for liberty, the exploitation of an increasing number of small or weak nations by an extremely small group of the richest or most powerful nations—all these have given birth to those distinctive characteristics of imperialism which compel us to define it as parasitic or decaying capitalism. More and more prominently there emerges, as one of the tendencies of imperialism, the creation of the "bond-holding" (rentier) state, the usurer state, in which the bourgeoisie lives on the proceeds of capital exports and by "clipping coupons." It would be a mistake to believe that this tendency to decay precludes the possibility of the rapid growth of capitalism. It does not. In the epoch of imperialism, certain branches of industry, certain strata of the bourgeoisie and certain countries betray, to a more or less degree, one or other of these tendencies. On the whole, capitalism is growing far more rapidly than before. But this growth is not only becoming more and more uneven in general; its unevenness also manifests itself, in particular, in the decay of the countries which are richest in capital (such as England). . . .

NOTE

* [This] pamphlet . . . was written in Zurich in the spring of 1916 . . . with an eye to the tsarist censorship. . . .
"In order to show, in a guise acceptable to the censors, how shamefully the capitalists and the social-chauvinist deserters (whom Kautsky opposes with so much inconsistency) lie on the question of annexations, in order to show with what cynicism they *screen* the annexations of *their* capitalists, I was forced to quote as an example—Japan! The careful reader will easily substitute Russia for Japan, and Finland, Poland, Courland, the Ukraine, Khiva, Bokhara, Estonia or other regions peopled by non-Great Russians, for Korea."—quoted from Lenin's "Preface to the Russian Edition," written in Petrograd, April 26, 1917.

Modernization and Dependency

J. Samuel Valenzuela and Arturo Valenzuela

The authors discuss alternative approaches to explaining Third World underdevelopment.

The end of World War II marked the beginning of fundamental transformations in world affairs. The defeat of the Axis powers and the devastating toll which the war had exacted on Britain and the European allies propelled the United States into a position of economic and military preeminence. However, the United States' power did not go unchallenged. The Soviet Union was able to influence the accession of power of socialist regimes throughout Eastern Europe and Chinese Communists defeated their Western-backed adversaries to gain control of the most populous nation on earth. These events called for an urgent strategy to revitalize the economies of the Western nations. With massive U.S. public and private economic investment, Western Europe and Japan soon recovered from the ravages of war.

But World War II ushered in another important change whose global implications would not be felt for some years to come. The weakening of the European powers and the logic of a war effort aimed at preserving

From "Modernization and Dependency: Alternative Perspectives in the Study of Latin American Underdevelopment," *Comparative Politics,* 10 (July 1978), 535–57, ©The City University of New York.

self-determination, marked the final collapse of the vast colonial empires of the nineteenth century and the establishment of a multiplicity of states each claiming sovereign and independent status. The "new nations" soon drew the attention of U.S. policymakers concerned with the claim that Marxism presented the best and most logical road to full incorporation into the modern world. They also captured the attention and imagination of U.S. scholars who in the pursuit of knowledge, as well as the desire to influence government policy, began to produce a vast literature on the "developing" nations. For many economists the solution was another Marshall plan designed for the Third World. But other social scientists argued that fundamental differences between the developmental experience of Europe and the less developed countries mitigated against success of such a strategy. It was not simply a matter of reconstruction but one of development and, as such, a fundamental question needed answering before policy recommendations could be advanced: Why was there such a stark contrast in the developmental experience of a few Western countries and most of the rest of the world?

The answer to this question led to the development of the "modernization perspective." Elaborated by a few economists and by anthropologists, sociologists, and political scientists, this perspective argued that it was essential to consider the cultural characteristics of "new" nations in determining their potential for development. These "noneconomic" factors became the cornerstone of a conceptual framework which would influence the U.S. response to the Third World.[1] Though "Latin Americanists" did not write the major theoretical or conceptual works of the modernization literature, that perspective soon became the dominant approach influencing the methodology and conclusions of the most important and trend-setting studies.

U.S. scholars, however, were not the only ones preoccupied with the difficulties of applying neoclassical economic assumptions to the developmental problems of Latin America. In international agencies, notably the United Nations Economic Commission for Latin America, and university research centers, Latin American social scientists tried to come to grips with the widespread economic stagnation which affected the region in the postwar period. Working separately, often with little communication, scholars in various disciplines soon turned to the broader and more basic question of the roots of Latin American underdevelopment. Many intellectual strands came together in the 1960s with the elaboration of a more general and comprehensive conceptual framework. The "dependency perspective" became the dominant approach in most Latin American intellectual circles by the mid to late 1960s.

It is revealing that the most important writings of the "dependency perspective" still have not been translated into English, over a decade after the first mimeographed drafts began to circulate in Santiago. Dependency analysis became known in the United States and Europe not through the writings of Latin Americans but through interpreters such as André Gunder Frank whose work differs substantially from that of important authors in the field such as F. H. Cardoso, O. Sunkel, and T. dos Santos.[2]

Modernization and dependency are two sharply different perspectives seeking to explain the same reality. They originated in different areas, with different evaluative judgments, different assumptions, different methodologies, and different explanations.[3] The purpose of this review essay is not to describe the origins of the two perspectives, their "extra scientific" elements, but to compare their conceptual approaches to the study of Latin America. As such, it will be necessary to consider the two perspectives as "ideal types," accentuating important characteristics of each framework in a manner not found in any particular author. There is a good deal of variety and several polemics (particularly in the dependency literature) stemming from disagreements over the emphasis given to key elements of the conceptual framework, the operationalization of concepts, and the way in which certain processes occur empirically. Though the essay will mention some of the controversies within each perspective, its purpose is to draw broad comparisons and to provide some judgment as to the relative utility of these competing frameworks in explaining Latin American underdevelopment.

THE MODERNIZATION PERSPECTIVE

This review will examine the modernization perspective's conceptual framework by drawing on the work of some of its most important authors, and then illustrate the use of that framework in the study of Latin America. This format is dictated by the fact, noted earlier, that specialists on Latin America failed to contribute important theoretical efforts to the field.[4] Though there are several explanations for this failure, one of the most compelling is that Latin America's close (particularly cultural) ties to the West made it more difficult by contrast with Asia and Africa, to point to obvious differences with the European experience. Indeed, the early theorizing made a distinction between Western and non-Western experiences, and, as J. Martz noted, "the Latin Americanist inevitably wondered if his own region was included."[5] That fact, however, did not prevent students of Latin America from drawing extensively on the modernization literature to interpret Latin American development.

Assumptions

The basic building blocks of the modernization perspective are parallel tradition–modernity ideal types of social organization and value systems, distinctions borrowed from nineteenth-century sociology.[6] Since societies are understood to move from tradition to modernity, the ideal typical dichotomy constitutes the polar ends of an evolutionary continuum, though at some point incremental changes give way to the qualitative jump into modernity. The location of this point is unclear; and yet, Third World countries, including those of Latin America, are perceived to be below the threshold of modernity, with a preponderance of traditional features.

The specific elements included in the two polarities vary substantially in the literature. The traditional society is variously understood as having a predominance of ascriptive, particularistic, diffuse, and affective patterns of action, an extended kinship structure with a multiplicity of functions, little spatial and social mobility, a deferential stratification system, mostly primary economic activities, a tendency toward autarchy of social units, an undifferentiated political structure, with traditional elitist and hierarchical sources of authority, etc. By contrast, the modern society is characterized by a predominance of achievement; universalistic, specific, and neutral orientations and patterns of action; a nuclear family structure serving limited functions; a complex and highly differentiated occupational system; high rates of spatial and social mobility; a predominance of secondary economic activities and production for exchange; the institutionalization of change and self-sustained growth; highly differentiated political structures with rational legal sources of authority; and so on.[7]

The literature assumes that the values, institutions, and patterns of action of traditional society are both an expression and a cause of underdevelopment and constitute the main obstacles in the way of modernization. To enter the modern world, underdeveloped societies have to overcome traditional norms and structures opening the way for social, economic, and political transformations. For some authors modernization derives from a greater differentiation of societal functions, institutions, and roles and the development of new sources of integration. For others, modernization is based more on the actual transformation of individuals through their assimilation of modern values.[8] But in general, the primary source of change is discussed in terms of innovations, that is, the rejection of procedures related to traditional institutions, together with the adoption of new ideas, techniques, values, and organizations. Innovations are pursued by innovators and the group that assumes this role inevitably clashes with defenders of the old order. The struggle is over two different ways of life.[9]

In describing the assumptions of the modernization literature, it is important to note that the modern pole of the parallel ideal types is the pivotal conceptual and analytical point because it best approximates the characteristics that societies must attain in order to develop. The traditional end of the dichotomy is largely a residual category, established by logical opposition to the modern end. In turn, the basic features of the modern pole are derived from characteristics attributed to those countries already considered modern. Moreover, since in the process of modernization all societies will undergo by and large similar changes, the history of the presently modern nations is taken as the source of universally useful conceptualization. Thus, as historian C. Black notes, "Although the problems raised by generalizations from a rather narrow base (the now modern countries) must be acknowledged, the definition of modernity takes the form of a set of characteristics believed to be applicable to all societies. This conception of modernity, when thought of as a model or ideal type, may be used as a yardstick with which to measure any society."[10] G. Almond adds that to study modernization in the non-Western areas the political scientist needs to "master the model of the modern, which in turn can only be derived from the most careful empirical and formal analysis of the functions of the modern Western polities."[11]

These assumptions are logically consistent with the view that the impetus to modernize in the now developed countries was the result of endogenous cultural and institutional transformations, while change in the late developers results primarily from exogenous stimuli, that is, the diffusion of modern values and institutions from the early modernizers. Modernizing Third World elites are understood to be guided by the Western model adopting and adapting its technology; assimilating its values and patterns of action; importing its financial, industrial, and educational institutions; and so on. Western colonialism, foreign aid, foreign educational opportunities, overseas business investments, the mass media, etc., are all important channels for the transmission of modernity. For some writers this means that the world is converging toward a uniform and standardized culture resembling that of the United States and Western Europe.[12]

Though, as will be noted below, there is disagreement on the extent to which traditional features will disappear, there is broad agreement on the notion that individual developing countries must in some way replicate the path followed by the early modernizers. The principal difference between already developed countries and developing ones is not in the nature of the process, but in the speed and intensity making it possible for the late modernizers to "skip stages" or "telescope time."[13] Despite the fact that the modernization perspective stresses the importance of the worldwide context in its analysis of social change, the basic historical setting for modernization is the nation state. As Black notes, "Societies in the process of modernization must . . . be considered both as *independent* entities, the traditional institutions of which are being adapted to modern functions, and also as societies under the influence of many *outside* forces."[14] The world is fragmented, and yet bound by intersocietal communication. It is, in the words of Dankwart Rustow, a "world of nations."[15]

Finally, it is clear that the stress on the differences in values from one context to another has some important implications for the modernization perspective's concept of human nature. The characteristic of developed societies which has received the most attention in the literature is the presumed "rationality" of both leaders and followers. Indeed, W.

Moore has recently argued that modernization is best understood as "the process of rationalization of social behavior and social organization." Rationalization, or the "institutionalization of rationality," is defined as the "normative expectation that objective information and rational calculus of procedures will be applied in pursuit or achievement of any utilitarian goal. . . . It is exemplified but not exhausted in the use of sophisticated technology in construction and production."[16] As such, modernization theorists agree with the assumption of economic rationality implicit in the economic growth models of traditional economic theory. But as Moore noted in a 1950s article, where they differ with traditional economics is in the assumption that rational behavior is a universal human characteristic. By contrast with the developed countries, attitudes and values in developing nations are such that individuals "behave in ways that are 'irrational' or 'non-rational' as judged on economic grounds."[17] This explains why Bolivian businessmen will not take risks with their capital, preferring to put money in Swiss banks. Or why Ecuadorians will study law rather than enter a more lucrative career in business or technology.

In concluding this section, it is necessary to note that from the very outset certain elements of the modernization perspective came into criticism from scholars who shared its basic assumptions. It is revealing that much of the criticism came from researchers who were experts in many of the features of individual "traditional" societies. They were uncomfortable with the arbitrary designation of a wide variety of phenomena as "traditional," with little concern for the rich, complex, and often strikingly different characteristics subsumed under that vague concept. They argued that many belief systems and institutional arrangements with no common referent in the United States or Western Europe could indeed have modernizing functions. J. Gusfield has summarized many of the relevant arguments adding that even in modern societies certain traditional characteristics may survive or gain renewed importance.[18] These arguments do not, however, constitute a rejection of the assumptions of the modernization perspective but an illustration of their use. Despite the title of his article, Gusfield does not argue that tradition and modernity are "misplaced polarities." Gusfield simply points to a confusion in the use of terms and their misapplication in concrete situations. He continues to accept the assumptions that tradition and modernity are valid theoretical polarities and that tradition in its many ramifications is the basic obstacle to modernization. If a particular society or region experiences significant economic growth, what was thought to be an other-worldly religion undermining rational economic behavior may in fact be a creed capable of promoting instrumental values conducive to modernization. There can be a "modernity of tradition."[19]

Recent amendments to the modernization perspective are extensions of the same internal critique. Reflecting the sobering reality of the 1970s with many studies pointing to an ever increasing gap between rich and poor nations,[20] several modernization writers have questioned the earlier belief in an inevitable and uniform process leading to the convergence of societies on economic as well as social and political grounds.[21] Others, while not questioning the inevitability of the process, point more forcefully than before to its disruptive and negative effects which affect the "latecomers" much more seriously than the "surviviors."[22] It still remains the case that to modernize, however good or inevitable that process may be, it is by definition necessary to overcome traditional values and institutions and substitute them for more modern ones.

Latin America and the Modernization Perspective

Mainstream U.S. scholarship on Latin America has implicitly or explicitly drawn on the modernization perspective to explain Latin American underdevelopment. Often contrasting the Latin American experience to that of the United States or Western Europe, it has argued that traditional attitudes and institutions stemming from the colonial past have proven to be serious, if not fatal, stumbling blocks to any indigenous effort to develop economically, socially, or politically. The values of Catholicism, of large Indian populations, or of aristocratic rural elites have contributed to "irrational" patterns of behavior highly detrimental to modernization.

One of the most influential statements is S. M. Lipset's "Values, Education and Entrepreneurship," the introductory essay to the best-selling text *Elites in Latin America*. Lipset draws directly from T. Parsons and D. McClelland in arguing that:

> The relative failure of Latin American countries to develop on a scale comparable to those of North America or Australasia has been seen as, in some part, a consequence of variations in value systems dominating these two areas. The overseas offspring of Great Britain seemingly had the advantage of values derivative in part from the Protestant Ethic and from the formation of "New Societies" in which feudal ascriptive elements were missing. Since Latin America, on the other hand is Catholic, it has been dominated for centuries by ruling elites who created a social structure congruent with feudal social values.[23]

In his article Lipset concentrates primarily on explaining economic underdevelopment as a function of the lack of adequate entrepreneurial activity. The lack of instrumental behavior, weak achievement orientations, and the disdain for the pragmatic and material have prevented the rise of a risk-taking business sector oriented toward rational competitive and bureaucratic enterprise. The educational system has only served to perpetuate the problem by continuing to socialize the population with inappropriate attitudes. "Even [in Argentina] the second most developed Latin American country . . . the traditional landed, aristocratic disdain for manual work, industry, and trading, continues to affect the educational orientations of many students."[24] Lipset cites a whole host of studies, many of which were based on survey research in Latin America, to conclude that "the comparative evidence from the various nations of the Americas sustains the generalization that cultural values are among the major factors which affect the potentiality for economic development."[25] Recent textbooks on Latin America have clearly been influenced by such observations. Thus, R. Adie and G. E. Poitras note that "there is in Latin America a social climate in which the very rewards which have spurred on the entrepreneurs in, for example, North America, are consistently deemphasised . . . socioeconomic change dependent on business activities . . . cannot necessarily be expected to follow the same path as it has elsewhere."[26]

The late K. H. Silvert, one of the leading authorities on Latin America, wrote extensively on the impact of traditional values not only on Latin America's economic but also its political performance. He made it very clear that Latin America's experience had to be judged by the more advanced countries. In a recently reprinted article he asked, "What else is one to do other than define development by the selection of certain characteristics of the already developed states?" On the basis of implicit comparisons with his own society, Silvert goes on to say that "there is something in the quality of the Latin American man and his culture which has made it difficult for him to be truly modern . . . which has made this part of the Western world so prone to excesses of scoundrels, so politically irrational in seeking economic growth, and so ready to reach for gimmicks."[27] Judgments such as those led him to argue, during the heyday of the Alliance for Progress, that the United States should "tip the domestic political scales" in the direction of "modernizing groups." "Moneys spent on the kind of education, for instance, which will attract persons of a modern mentality can be confidently expected to assist the general move toward development. Moneys spent in bettering or certifying the positions of students of a traditional cast will only make more robust the anti-development sectors. . . . If help can be extended to the attitudinally developed in such countries, then it should be done. Otherwise assistance merely certifies non-development or invites unpredictable revolution."[28]

Similar sentiments are expressed by R. Scott, another prominent Latin Americanist. Scott notes that the "inability of Latin America's political structures to act as efficient integrating mechanisms . . . suggests that the only real solution in the long run is to alter the value system of the people."[29] A recent text echoes that theme: "A traditional psychocultural world does indeed predominate in Latin America. . . . To depict collective attitudes and value traits as basically traditional does help to explain much of political life south of the Rio Grande. . . ."[30]

The assumption that the key to Latin American society can be found in its cultural values is not only characteristic of the literature of the 1960s and of a rash of new textbooks aimed at the college market,[31] it has also found renewed currency in the writings of a number of U.S. historians and political scientists. In what has become known as the "new corporatism," an effort is being made to explain economic, social, and especially political features of Latin American countries by stressing the durability of Catholic and "Thomistic" values. Authoritarian political patterns, corporativist economic organizations, and the disdain for democratic and liberal values are the results of a "distinct tradition." H. Wiarda, a prominent representative of this "new" trend in the literature, has argued "largely untouched by the great revolutionary movements—social, economic, religious, political, intellectual—that we associate with the emergence of the modern order, the Iberic and Latin American nations remained locked in this traditional pattern of values and institutions that postponed and retarded development."[32]

Wiarda maintains that the focus on Latin American corporatism represents a significant departure from the modernization school. He bases his claim on the fact that he stresses the importance of studying Latin America on its "own terms," without advocating the desirability or inevitability of change along United States or Western European lines. He thus questions the convergence thesis noting that "many traditional societies, and particularly those of the Iberic Latin nations, have proved remarkably permeable and flexible, assimilating at various points more 'modern' and 'rational' elements, but without losing their characteristics."[33] But this position differs little from the well-established "modernity of tradition" argument referred to earlier. Wiarda merely provides an example of the concrete application of the tradition–modernity dichotomy to the Latin American case; he does not question the basic assumptions of the perspective. The impressive examples of economic development, which have occurred from time to time in Latin America are simply due to the adaptability of some traditional values and institutions to outside influences. And yet, however remarkable the "permeability" of tradition in Latin America, it is implicit in Wiarda's argument that it has been the exception rather than the rule. Otherwise, Latin America would not have fallen behind in the road of development.

THE DEPENDENCY PERSPECTIVE

Like the modernization perspective, the dependency perspective resulted from the work of many different scholars in different branches of the social sciences. Much of the work proceeded in an inductive fashion. This was the case with economists working in ECLA who first sought to explain the underdevelopment of Latin America by focusing on the unequal terms of trade between exporters of raw materials and exporters of manufactured goods. ECLA "doctrine" called for a concerted effort to diversify the export base of Latin American countries and accelerate industrialization efforts through import substitution. However, the continued difficulties with that model of development soon led to a focus on the internal constraints to industrialization, with an emphasis on factors such as the distorting effects of unequal land tenure patterns and the corrosive results of an inflation best explained by structural rather than monetary variables. Soon these two trends came together when scholars, such as Osvaldo Sunkel, combined the early emphasis on external variables with the internal constraints to development.[34]

But this dependency perspective was anticipated by Latin American historians who had been working for years on various aspects of economic history. Studies such as those of Sergio Bagú stressed the close interrelation of domestic developments in Latin America and developments in metropolitan countries. And in Brazil, sociologists such as Florestan Fernandes, Octávio Ianni, Fernando Henrique Cardoso, and Theotônio dos Santos also turned to broad structural analyses of the factors of underdevelopment. The fact that many of these scholars found themselves in Santiago in the 1960s only contributed to further development of the perspective.

In its emphasis on the expansive nature of capitalism and in its structural analysis of society, the dependency literature draws on Marxist insights and is related to the Marxist theory of imperialism. However, its examination of processes in Latin America imply important revisions in classical Leninist formulations, both historically and in light of recent trends. The focus is on explaining Latin American underdevelopment, and not on the functioning of capitalism, though some authors argue that their efforts will contribute to an understanding of capitalism and its contradictions.

Assumptions

The dependency perspective rejects the assumption made by modernization writers that the unit of analysis in studying underdevelopment is the national society. The domestic cultural and institutional features of Latin America are in themselves simply not the key variables accounting for the relative backwardness of the area, though, as will be seen below, domestic structures are certainly critical intervening factors. The relative presence of traditional and modern features may, or may not, help to differentiate societies; but it does not in itself explain the origins of modernity in some contexts and the lack of modernity in others. As such, the tradition–modernity polarity is of little value as a fundamental working concept. The dependency perspective assumes that the development of a national or regional unit can only be understood in connection with its historical insertion into the worldwide political-economic system which emerged with the wave of European colonizations of the world.

This global system is thought to be characterized by the unequal but combined development of its different components. As Sunkel and Paz put it:

> Both underdevelopment and development are aspects of the same phenomenon, both are historically simultaneous, both are linked functionally and, therefore, interact and condition each other mutually. This results . . . in the division of the world between industrial, advanced or "central" countries, and underdeveloped, backward or "peripheral" countries. . . .[35]

The center is viewed as capable of dynamic development responsive to internal needs, and as the main beneficiary of the global links. On the other hand, the periphery is seen as having a reflex type of development; one which is both constrained by its incorporation into the global system and which results from its adaptation to the requirements of the expansion of the center. As Theotônio dos Santos indicates:

> Dependency is a situation in which a certain number of countries have their economy conditioned by the development and expansion of another . . . placing the dependent countries in a backward position exploited by the dominant countries.[36]

It is important to stress that the process can be understood only by reference to its historical dimension and by focusing on the total network of social relations as they evolve in different contexts over time. For this reason dependence is characterized as "structural, historical and totalizing" or an "integral analysis of development."[37] It is meaningless to develop, as some social scientists have, a series of synchronic statistical indicators to establish relative levels of dependence or independence among different national units to test the "validity" of the model.[38] The unequal development of the world goes back to the sixteenth century with the formation of a capitalist world economy in which some countries in the center were able to specialize in industrial production of manufactured goods because the peripheral areas of the world which they colonized provided the necessary primary goods, agricultural and mineral, for consumption in the center. Contrary to some assumptions in economic theory the international division of labor did not lead to parallel development through comparative advantage. The center states gained at the expense of the periphery. But, just as significantly, the different functions of center and peripheral societies had a profound effect on the evolution of internal social and political structures. Those which evolved in the periphery reinforced economies with a narrow range of primary exports. The interdependent nature of the world capitalist system and the qualitative transformations in that system over time make it inconceivable to think that individual nations on the periphery could somehow replicate the evolutionary experience of the now developed nations.[39]

It follows from an emphasis on global structural processes and variations in internal structural arrangements that contextual variables, at least in the long run, shape and guide the behavior of groups and individuals. It is not inappropriate attitudes which contribute to the absence of entrepreneurial behavior or to institutional arrangements reinforcing underdevelopment. Dependent, peripheral development produces an opportunity structure such that personal gain for dominant groups and entrepreneurial elements is not conducive to the collective gain of balanced development. This is a fundamental difference with much of the modernization literature. It implies that dependence analysts, though they do not articulate the point explicitly, share the classical economic theorists' view of human nature. They assume that individuals in widely different societies are capable of pursuing rational patterns of behavior; able to assess information objectively in the pursuit of utilitarian goals. What varies is not the degree of rationality, but the structural foundations of the incentive systems which, in turn, produce different forms of behavior given the same process of rational calculus. It was not attitudinal transformations which generated the rapid industrialization which developed after the Great Depression, but the need to replace imports with domestic products. Or, as Cardoso points out in his studies of entrepreneurs, it is not values which condition their behavior as much as technological dependence, state intervention in the economy, and their political weakness vis-à-vis domestic and foreign actors.[40] What appear as anomalies in the modernization literature can be accounted for by a focus on contextual processes in the dependence literature.

It is necessary to underscore the fact that dependency writers stress the importance of the "way internal and external structural components are connected" in elaborating the structural context of underdevelopment. As such, underdevelopment is not simply the result of "external constraints" on peripheral societies, nor can dependency be operationalized solely with reference to clusters of external variables.[41] Dependency in any given society is a complex set of associations in which the external dimensions are determinative in varying degrees and, indeed, internal variables may very well reinforce the pattern of external linkages. Historically it has been rare for local interests to develop on the periphery which are capable of charting a successful policy of self-sustained development. Dominant local interests, given the nature of class arrangements emerging from the characteristics of peripheral economies, have tended to favor the preservation of rearticulation of patterns of dependency in their interests.

It is also important to note that while relations of dependency viewed historically help to explain underdevelopment, it does not follow that dependent relations today necessarily perpetuate across the board underdevelopment. With the evolution of the world system, the impact of dependence relations can change in particular contexts. This is why

Cardoso, in studying contemporary Brazil, stresses the possibility of "associated-dependent development," and Sunkel and Fuenzalida are able to envision sharp economic growth among countries most tied into the contemporary transnational system.[42] Because external-internal relations are complex, and because changes in the world system over time introduce new realities, it is indispensable to study comparatively concrete national and historical situations. As Anibal Quijano says, "The relationships of dependency . . . take on many forms. The national societies in Latin America are dependent, as is the case with the majority of the Asian, African and some European countries. However, each case does not present identical dependency relations."[43] The dependency perspective has thus concentrated on a careful historical evaluation of the similarities and differences in the "situations of dependency" of the various Latin American countries over time implying careful attention to "preexisting conditions" in different contexts.[44]

The description of various phases in the world system and differing configurations of external-internal linkages, follow from this insistence on diachronic analysis and its application to concrete cases. The dependency perspective is primarily a historical model with no claim to "universal validity." This is why it has paid less attention to the formulation of precise theoretical constructs, such as those found in the modernization literature, and more attention to the specification of historical phases which are an integral part of the framework.

The dependency literature distinguishes between the "mercantilistic" colonial period (1500–1750), the period of "outward growth" dependent on primary exports (1750–1914), the period of the crisis of the "liberal model" (1914–1950), and the current period of "transnational capitalism."

As already noted, because of the need for raw materials and foodstuffs for the growing industrialization of England, Germany, the United States, and France, Latin American productive structures were aimed from the outset at the export market. During the colonial period, the economic specialization was imposed by the Iberian monarchies. As Bagú notes in his classic study, "Colonial production was not directed by the needs of national consumers, and not even by the interests of local producers. The lines of production were structured and transformed to conform to an order determined by the imperial metropolis. The colonial economy was consequently shaped by its complementary character. The products that did not compete with those of Spain or Portugal in the metropolitan, international or colonial markets, found tolerance or stimulus. . . ."[45] During the nineteenth century, exports were actively pursued by the politically dominant groups. The independence movement did not attempt to transform internal productive structures; it was aimed at eliminating Iberian interference in the commercialization of products to and from England and northern Europe. The logic of the productive system in this period of "outwardly directed development," in ECLA's terms, was not conducive to the creation of a large industrial sector. Economic rationality, not only of individual entrepreneurs but also of the system, dictated payments in kind and/or extremely low wages and/or the use of slavery, thus markedly limiting the internal market. At the same time, the accumulation of foreign exchange made relatively easy the acquisition of imported industrial products. Any expansion of exports was due more to political than economic factors and depended on a saleable export commodity, and plenty of land and labor, for its success.

There were, however, important differences between region and countries. During the colonial period these are attributable to differences in colonial administrations, natural resources, and types of production. During the nineteenth century a key difference was the degree of local elite control over productive activities for export. Though in all countries elites controlled export production initially (external commercialization was mainly under foreign control), towards the end of the century in some countries control was largely relinquished to foreign exploitation. Where this occurred, the economic role of local elites was reduced considerably, though the importance of this reduction varied depending both on the degree to which the foreign enclave displaced the local elite from the export sector and the extent to which its economic activities were diversified. Concurrently, the state bureaucracy expanded and acquired increasing importance through regulations and taxation of the enclave sector. The state thus became the principal intermediary between the local economy and the enclave, which generally had little *direct* internal secondary impact. Other differences, especially at the turn of the century, are the varying importance of incipient industrialization, the size and importance of middle- and working-class groups, variations in export products, natural resources, and so on.[46]

The world wars and the depression produced a crisis in the export-oriented economies through the collapse of external demand, and therefore of the capacity to import. The adoption of fiscal and monetary policies aimed at supporting the internal market and avoiding the negative effects of the external disequilibrium produced a favorable climate for the growth of an industrial sector under national auspices. The available foreign exchange was employed to acquire capital goods to substitute imports of consumer articles.[47] The early successes of the transition to what ECLA calls "inwardly directed development" depended to a large extent on the different political alliances which emerged in the various national settings, and on the characteristics of the social and political structures inherited from the precrisis period.

Thus, in the enclave situations the earliest developments were attained in Mexico and Chile, where middle- and lower-class groups allied in supporting state development policies, ultimately strengthening the urban bourgeoisie. The alliance was successful in Chile because of the importance of middle-class parties which emerged during the final period of export-oriented development, and the early consolidation of a trade union movement. The antecedents of the Mexican situation are to be found in the destruction of agricultural elites during the revolution. Such structural conditions were absent in other enclave situations (Bolivia, Peru, Venezuela, and Central America) where the internal development phase began later under new conditions of dependence, though in some cases with similar political alliances (Bolivia, Venezuela, Guatemala, Costa Rica). Throughout the crisis period agrarian-based and largely nonexporting groups were able to remain in power, appealing in some cases to military governments, and preserving the political scheme that characterized the export-oriented period.

In the nonenclave situations, considerable industrial growth was attained in Argentina and Brazil. In the former, export-oriented agrarian entrepreneurs had invested considerably in production for the internal market and the contraction of the export sector only accentuated this trend. In Brazil the export-oriented agrarian groups collapsed with the crisis and the state, as in Chile and Mexico, assumed a major developmental role with the support of a complex alliance of urban entrepreneurs, nonexport agrarian elites, popular sectors, and middle-class groups. In Colombia the export-oriented agrarian elites remained in power and did not foster significant internal industrialization until the fifties.[48]

The import substituting industrialization attained greatest growth in Argentina, Brazil, and Mexico. It soon, however, reached its limits, given the parameters under which it was realized. Since capital goods for the establishment of industrial parks were acquired in the central nations, the success of the policy ultimately depended on adequate foreign exchange supplies. After reaching maximum growth through the accumulation of foreign exchange during the Second World War, the industrialization programs could only continue—given the available political options— on the basis of an increased external debt and further reliance on foreign investments. This accumulation of foreign reserves permitted the success of the national-populist alliances in Argentina and Brazil which gave the workers greater welfare while maintaining investments. The downfall of Perón and the suicide of Vargas symbolized the end of this easy period of import substitution.

But the final blow to "import substitution" industrialization came not from difficulties in the periphery but further transformations in the center which have led, in Sunkel's term, to the creation of a new "transnational" system. With rapid economic recovery the growing multinational corporations sought new markets and cheaper production sites for their increasingly technological manufacturing process. Dependency consequently acquired a "new character" as Dos Santos noted, which would have a profound effect on Latin America. Several processes were involved resulting in (1) the investment of centrally based corporations in manufactures within the periphery for sales in its internal market or, as Cardoso and Faletto note, the "internationalisation of the internal market"; (2) a new international division of labor in which the periphery acquires capital goods, technology, and raw materials from the central nations, and export profits, along with its traditional raw materials and a few manufactured items produced by multinational subsidiaries; and (3) a denationalization of the older import substituting industries established originally.[49] Although the "new dependence" is in evidence throughout the continent, the process has asserted itself more clearly in the largest internal markets such as Brazil, where the weakness of the trade-union movement (the comparison with Argentina in this respect is instructive) coupled with authoritarian political structures has created a singularly favorable investment climate.

In subsequent and more recent works writers in the dependency framework have pursued different strategies of research. Generally speaking, the early phases of the historical process have received less attention, though the contribution of I. Wallerstein to an understanding of the origins of the world system is a major addition to the literature.[50] Most writers have preferred to focus on the current "new situation" of dependence. Some have devoted more attention to an effort at elaborating the place of dependent capitalism as a contribution to the Marxist analysis of capitalist society. Scholars in this vein tend to argue more forcefully than others that dependent capitalism is impossible and that socialism provides the only historically viable alternative.[51] Others have focused more on the analysis of concrete cases of dependence, elaborating in some detail the various interconnections between domestic and foreign forces, and noting the possibility of different kinds of dependent development.[52] Still others have turned their attention to characterizing the nature of the new capitalist system, with particular emphasis on the emergence of a "transnational system" which is rendering more complex and problematic the old distinctions of center and periphery.[53] Particularly for the last two tendencies, the emphasis is on the design of new empirical studies while attempting to systematize further some of the propositions implicit in the conceptual framework.

SUMMARY AND CONCLUSIONS

Modernization and dependency are two different perspectives each claiming to provide conceptual and analytical tools capable of explaining the relative underdevelopment of Latin America. The object of inquiry is practically the only thing that these two competing "visions" have in common, as they differ substantially not only on fundamental assumptions, but also on methodological implications and strategies for research.

Though there are variations in the literature, the *level of analysis* of a substantial tradition in the modernization perspective, and the one which informs most reflections on Latin America, is behavioral or microsociological. The primary focus is on individuals or aggregates of individuals, their values, attitudes, and beliefs. The dependency perspective, by contrast, is structural or macrosociological. Its focus is on the mode of production, patterns of international trade, political and economic linkages between elites in peripheral and central countries, group and class alliances and conflicts, and so on. Both perspectives are concerned with the process of development in national societies. However, for the modernization writer the national society is the basic *unit of analysis,* while the writer in a dependence framework considers the global system and its various forms of interaction with national societies as the primary object of inquiry.

For the dependency perspective, the *time dimension* is a crucial aspect of what is fundamentally a historical model. Individual societies cannot be presumed to be able to replicate the evolution of other societies because the very transformation of an interrelated world system may preclude such an option. The modernization potential of individual societies must be seen in light of changes over time in the interactions between external and internal variables. The modernization perspective is obviously concerned about the origins of traditional and modern values; but, the time dimension is not fundamental to the explanatory pretensions of a model which claims "universal validity." Without knowing the source of modernity inhibiting characteristics, it is still possible to identify them by reference to their counterparts in developing contexts.

At the root of the differences between the two perspectives is a fundamentally different *perception of human nature.* Dependency assumes that human behavior in economic matters is a "constant." Individuals will behave differently in different contexts not because they are different but because the contexts are different. The insistence on structures and, in the final analysis, on the broadest structural category of all, the world system, follows logically from the view that opportunity structures condition human behavior. Modernizationists, on the other hand, attribute the lack of certain behavioral patterns to the "relativity" of human behavior; to the fact that cultural values and beliefs, regardless of opportunity structures, underlie the patterns of economic action. Thus, the *conception of change* in the modernization perspective is a product of innovations which result from the adoption of modern attitudes among elites, and eventually followers. Though some modernization theorists are now more pessimistic about the development potential for such changes, modernizing beliefs are a prerequisite for development. For dependency analysts the conception of change is different. Change results from the realignment of dependency relations over time. Whether or not development occurs and how it occurs is subject to controversy. Given the rapid evolution of the world system, dependent development is possible in certain contexts, not in others. Autonomy, through a break in relations of dependency, may not lead to development of the kind already arrived at in the developed countries because of the inability to recreate the same historical conditions, but it might lead to a different kind of development stressing different values. Thus, the *prescription for change* varies substantially in the dependency perspective depending on the ideological outlook of particular authors. It is not a logical consequence of the historical model. In the modernization perspective the prescription for change follows more automatically from the assumptions of the model, implying greater consensus.

From a methodological point of view the modernization perspective is much more parsimonious than its counterpart. And the focus of much of the literature on the microsociological level makes it amenable to the elaboration of precise explanatory propositions such as those of D. McClelland or E. Hagen. Dependency, by contrast, is more descriptive and its macrosociological formulations are much less subject to translation into a simple set of explanatory propositions. Many aspects of dependency, and particularly the linkages between external phenomena and internal class and power relations are unclear and need to be studied with more precision and care. For this reason the dependency perspective is an "approach" to the study of underdevelopment rather than a "theory." And yet, precisely because modernization theory relies on a simple conceptual framework and a reductionist approach, it is far less useful for the study of a complex phenomenon such as development or underdevelopment.

But the strengths of the dependency perspective lie not only in its consideration of a richer body of evidence and a broader range of phenomena, it is also more promising from a methodological point of view. The modernization perspective has fundamental flaws which make it difficult to provide for a fair test of its own assumptions. It will be recalled that the modernization perspective draws on a model with a "universal validity" which assumes that traditional values are not conducive to modern behavioral patterns of action. Given that underdevelopment, on the basis of various economic and social indicators, is an objective datum, the research task becomes one of identifying modernizing values and searching for their opposites in underdeveloped contexts.

In actual research efforts, the modernity inhibiting characteristics are often "deduced" from impressionistic observation. This is the case with much of the political science literature on Latin America. However, more "rigorous" methods, such as survey research, have also been employed, particularly in studies of entrepreneurial activity. Invariably, whether through deduction or survey research, less appropriate values for modernizations such as "arielismo" (a concern for transcendental as opposed to material values) or "low-achievement" (lack of risk-taking attitudes) have been identified thus "confirming" the hypothesis that traditional values contribute to underdevelopment. If by chance the use of control groups should establish little or no difference in attitudes in a developed and underdeveloped context, the research instrument can be considered to be either faulty or the characteristics tapped not the appropriate ones for identifying traditional attitudes. The latter alternative might lead to the "discovery" of a new "modernity of tradition" literature or of greater flexibility than anticipated in traditional norms or of traditional residuals in the developed country.

The problem with the model and its behavioral level of analysis is that the explanation for underdevelopment is part of the preestablished conceptual framework. It is already "known" that in backward areas the modernity inhibiting characteristics play the dominant role, otherwise the areas would not be backward. As such, the test of the hypothesis involves a priori acceptance of the very hypothesis up for verification, with empirical evidence gathered solely in an illustrative manner. The focus on individuals simply does not permit consideration of a broader range of contextual variables which might lead to invalidating the assumptions. Indeed, the modernity of tradition literature, which has pointed to anomalies in the use of the tradition-modernity "polarities," is evidence of how such a perspective can fall victim to the "and so" fallacy. Discrepancies are accounted for not by a reformulation, but by adding a new definition or a new corollary to the preexisting conceptual framework.

Much work needs to be done within a dependency perspective to clarify its concepts and causal interrelationships, as well as to assess its capacity to explain social processes in various parts of peripheral societies. And yet the dependency approach appears to have a fundamental advantage over the modernization perspective: It is open to historically grounded conceptualization in underdeveloped contexts, while modernization is locked into an illustrative methodological style by virtue of its very assumptions.

ACKNOWLEDGMENTS

Arturo Valenzuela wishes to acknowledge the support of the Ford Foundation and of the Institute of Development Studies at the University of Sussex, which made the completion of this paper possible during his tenure as a Visiting Fellow at IDS.

NOTES

1. See Manning Nash's foreword to the anniversary issue of *Economic Development and Cultural Change*, XXV (1977, supplement), in honor of Bert Hoselitz, one of the first economists to stress "noneconomic" factors in development. See his *Sociological Aspects of Economic Growth* (New York, 1960) which was translated into twenty-five languages by the U.S. Department of State. Myron Weiner's *Modernization: The Dynamics of Growth* (New York, 1966) is a good collection of essays by prominent modernization writers which were first prepared for the "Voice of America."

2. The principal works in the dependency perspective are Fernando Henrique Cardoso and Enzo Faletto, *Dependencia y desarrollo en América Latina* (Mexico, 1969) and Osvaldo Sunkel and Pedro Paz, *El subdesarrollo latinoamericano y la teoría del desarrollo* (Mexico, 1970). The former soon will be published in English, while the latter is not scheduled for translation despite the fact that the Spanish version is in its ninth printing. Because of the language "barrier" André Gunder Frank is often thought to be the founder of the dependency school. See for example Adrian Foster-Carter, "From Rostow to Gunder Frank: Conflicting Paradigms in the Analysis of Underdevelopment," *World Development,* IV (March 1976), 1975, where Frank is referred to as "Copernicus" of a new paradigm. In fact, Frank draws extensively on Latin American scholars in studies such as *Capitalism and Underdevelopment in Latin America* (New York, 1967). He and other "interpreters" such as Susanne Bodenheimer ("Dependency and Imperialism" *Politics and Society,* I, May, 1970), present oversimplified and often distorted views of much of the Latin American contribution. On this point see Cardoso, "The Consumption of Dependency Theory in the United States," *Latin American Research Review,* XII, No. 3. Frank's work was, however, extensively read and discussed in Latin American universities.
3. Though modernization and dependence can be thought of as alternative paradigms, we prefer the term "perspective" because in Thomas Kuhn's terms the social sciences are preparadigmatic, only approximating a "normal science." See Kuhn, *The Structure of Scientific Revolutions* (Chicago, 1970).
4. This is less true for developmental economics and anthropology than for sociology and political science. Economists like Hoselitz and Everett Hagen (*On the Theory of Social Change* [Homewood, Ill., 1962]) drew in part on Latin American field research. Robert Redfield's *The Folk Cultures of Yucatan* (Chicago, 1941) is considered one of the classics. The most important sociological work was done by Gino Germani, although his most important studies were never translated. See his *Política y sociedad en una época de transición* (Buenos Aires, 1968). For an intelligent overview of his work, as well as that of Cardoso, see Joseph A. Kahl, *Modernization, Exploitation and Dependency in Latin America* (New Brunswick, N.J., 1976).
5. John Martz, "Political Science and Latin American Studies: A Discipline in Search of a Region," *Latin American Research Review,* VI (Spring 1971), 78.
6. For antecedents of the modernization literature, see the work of scholars such as Maine, Tonnies, Durkheim, Weber and Redfield.
7. For surveys of the literature, see Frank Sutton, "Social Theory and Comparative Politics," in Harry Eckstein and David Apter, eds., *Comparative Politics* (New York, 1963), and Daniel Lerner, "Modernization: Social Aspects," *International Encyclopedia of the Social Sciences* (1968).
8. See the excellent distinction made by Alejandro Portes between "development as social differentiation" and "development as the enactment of values" in Portes, "On the Sociology of National Development: Theories and Issues," *American Journal of Sociology,* LXXXII (July 1976). Examples of the former are Neil J. Smelser, "The Modernization of Social Relations," in Weiner, *Modernization* and "Mechanisms of Change and Adjustment to Change," in Jason Finkle and Robert Gable, eds., *Political Development and Social Change* (New York, 1971); and Talcott Parsons' companion volumes, *Societies: Evolutionary and Comparative Perspectives* and *The System of Mod-*

ern Societies (Englewood Cliffs, N.J., 1966 and 1971, respectively). Examples of the latter are Hagen, On the Theory of Social Change; and David McClelland, The Achieving Society (Princeton, 1961) and "The Psychological Causes and Consequences of Modernization: An Ethiopian Case Study," Economic Development and Cultural Change, XXV (1977, supplement). See also Alex Inkeles and David Smith, Becoming Modern (Cambridge, Mass., 1974). Inkeles and Smith take particular care to point out that their study does not demonstrate a causal relationship between the emergence of modern attitudes and modernizing transformations, for which McClelland takes them to task in the above cited article. But if all they establish is that people who work in modern settings have modern values, then their laborious research effort is circular and pointless.

9. See Cyril Black, The Dynamics of Modernization (New York, 1966), pp. 68–75.

10. Ibid., pp. 53–54.

11. Gabriel Almond, "Introduction: A Functional Approach to Comparative Politics," in Almond and James S. Coleman, The Politics of the Developing Areas (Princeton, 1960), p. 64. Statements such as these have led to the criticism that modernization is an ethnocentric approach. But rather than pointing out their ethnocentricity, it is more important to indicate that they reflect an assumption which becomes a key methodological option, ethnocentric or otherwise.

12. For the view that modernization is an exogenous process leading to convergence see Lerner, The Passing of Traditional Society (New York, 1958) and Clark Kerr, et al., Industrialism and Industrial Man (Cambridge, Mass., 1960).

13. See Kalman H. Silvert, The Conflict Society: Reaction and Revolution in Latin America (New York, 1966), p. 261.

14. Black, p. 50 (emphasis added).

15. Dankwart A. Rustow, A World of Nations (Washington, D.C., 1967).

16. Wilbert Moore, "Modernization and Rationalization: Processes and Restraints," Economic Development and Cultural Change, XXV (1977, supplement), pp. 34–35.

17. Wilbert Moore, "Motivational Aspects of Development," in Amitai and Eva Etzioni, eds., Social Change (New York, 1964), p. 292. See also his "Social Change" in the International Encyclopedia of the Social Sciences (1968).

18. J. Gusfield, "Tradition and Modernity: Misplaced Polarities in the Study of Social Change," American Journal of Sociology, LXXII (January 1967).

19. Lloyd I. and Susanne H. Rudolph, The Modernity of Traditional Development in India (Chicago, 1967). Another work in this vein is Robert Ward and Dankwart A. Rustow, eds., Political Modernization in Japan and Turkey (Princeton, 1964).

20. For example see Irma Adelman and Cynthia Morris, Economic Growth and Social Equity in Developing Countries (Stanford, 1973).

21. S. N. Eisenstadt, Tradition, Change and Modernity (New York, 1973) and Moore, "Modernization and Rationalization."

22. Marion Levy, Jr., Modernization: Latecomers and Survivors (New York, 1972).

23. Seymour Martin Lipset, "Values, Education and Entrepreneurship," in Lipset and Aldo Solari, eds., Elites in Latin America (New York, 1963). For another study in which Lipset expresses similar views about Latin America, while

extolling the opposite values in the United States, see his *The First New Nation* (New York, 1963).

24. Lipset, "Values, Education and Entrepreneurship," p. 19.
25. Ibid., p. 30. Some of the studies cited include T. C. Cohran, "Cultural Factors in Economic Growth," *Journal of Economic History,* XX (1974); T. R. Fillol, *Social Factors in Economic Development: The Argentine Case* (Cambridge, Mass., 1961); B. J. Siegel, "Social Structure and Economic Change in Brazil," in Simon Kuznets, et al., *Economic Growth: Brazil, India, Japan* (Durham, N.C., 1955); and W. P. Strassman, "The Industrialist," in John J. Johnson, ed., *Continuity and Change in Latin America* (Stanford, 1964).
26. R. Adia and G. E. Poitras, *Latin America: The Politics of Immobility* (Englewood Cliffs, N.J., 1974), pp. 73–75. For similar views see pp. 252–53 and W. R. Duncan, *Latin American Politics: A Developmental Approach* (New York, 1976), p. 240.
27. Silvert, "The Politics of Social and Economic Change in Latin America," in Howard J. Wiarda, ed., *Politics and Social Change in Latin America: The Distinct Tradition* (Amherst, Mass., 1974), pp. 160–62.
28. Silvert, *The Conflict Society,* p. 271. For a definition of "modern man" see p. 265. In the preface Arthur Whitacker, a well known historian, noted that the book should be made "required reading for anyone who wishes to express an opinion" on the alliance.
29. R. Scott, "Political Elites," in Lipset and Solari, pp. 133–34.
30. Duncan, p. 240. Scott emphasizes cultural determinants in later writings. See his edited volume, *Latin American Modernization Problems* (Urbana, Ill., 1973). The role of traditional features in explaining economic and political patterns in Latin America was stressed by the best known studies of the 1960s. For a sampling see the articles in the collections edited by Johnson, *Continuity and Change,* and by D. B. Heath and R. N. Adams, *Contemporary Cultures and Societies in Latin America* (New York, 1965). See also Stanislav Andreski, *Parasitism and Subversion: The Case in Latin America* (New York, 1966); George Blanksten, "The Politics of Latin America," in Almond and Coleman, *The Politics of the Developing Areas;* J. Mander, *The Unrevolutionary Society* (New York, 1969); Luis Mercier Vega, *Roads to Power in Latin America* (New York, 1969); and Martin Needler, *Latin American Politics in Perspective* (Princeton, 1967). Crude applications of modernization concepts to particular cases include Frank Jay Moreno, *Legitimacy and Stability in Latin America: A Study of Chilean Political Culture* (New York, 1969) and James Payne, *Patterns of Conflict in Colombia* (New Haven, 1968). Some important authors, however, took different approaches, much closer to those of the dependency perspective. See Merle Kling, "Toward a Theory of Power and Political Instability in Latin America," *Western Political Quarterly,* IX (1956); Charles Anderson, *Politics and Economic Change in Latin America* (Princeton, 1967); Richard Adams, *The Second Sowing; Power and Secondary Development in Latin America* (San Francisco, 1967); and Douglas Chalmers, "Developing on the Periphery: External Factors in Latin America Politics," in James Rosenau, ed., *Linkage Politics* (New York, 1969). The reader by James Petras and Maurice Zeitlin, eds., *Latin America: Reform or Revolution?* (New York, 1968), also provided a differing perspective incorporating many writings of Latin American scholars.

31. Besides the Adie and Poitras and the Duncan works cited above, see also C. F. Denton and L. L. Preston, *Latin American Politics: A Developmental Approach* (New York, 1975); and Needler, *An Introduction to Latin American Politics: the Structure of Conflict* (Englewood Cliffs, N.J., 1977). For one of the few alternative texts see Petras, *Politics and Social Structure in Latin America* (New York, 1970).

32. Wiarda, Howard J., *Politics and Social Change in Latin America*, p. 269. Another important contribution to this literature is Frederick Pike and T. Stritch, eds., *The New Corporatism; Social-Political Structures in the Iberian World* (South Bend, Ind., 1974). Not all writers interested in corporatism draw primarily on cultural variables. Philippe C. Schmitter explicitly rejects what he considers to be the circularity of that approach. See his essay, "The Century of Corporatism?" in Pike and Stritch.

33. Wiarda, Howard J., "Toward a Framework for the Study of Political Change in the Iberic-Latin Tradition: the Corporative Model," *World Politics*, XXV (January 1973).

34. See Osvaldo Sunkel, "Politica nacional de desarrollo y dependencia externa," *Estudios Internacionales*, I (April 1967). For reviews of the dependency literature see Norman Girvan, "The Development of Dependency Economics in the Caribbean and Latin America: Review and Comparison," *Social and Economic Studies*, XXII (March 1973); Ronald H. Chilcote, "A Critical Synthesis of the Dependency Literature," *Latin American Perspectives*, I (Spring 1974); and Philip O'Brien, "A Critique of Latin American Theories of Dependence," in I. Oxaal, et al., eds., *Beyond the Sociology of Development* (London, 1975).

35. Sunkel and Paz, *El Subdesarrollo Latinoamericano*, p. 6.

36. Theotonio dos Santos, "La crisis del desarrollo y las relaciones de dependencia en América Latina," (Mexico, 1970), p. 180. See also his *Dependencia y cambio social* (Santiago, 1970) and *Socialismo o Fascismo: El nuevo carácter de la dependencia y el dilema latinoamericano* (Buenos Aires, 1972).

37. Sunkel and Paz, p. 39; Cardoso and Faletto, *Dependencia y desarrollo, chap. 2.*

38. This is the problem with the studies by Robert Kaufman, et al., "A Preliminary Test of the Theory of Dependency," *Comparative Politics*, VII (April 1975), pp. 303-30, and C. Chase–Dunn, "The Effects of International Economic Dependence on Development and Inequality: A Cross National Study," *American Sociological Review*, XL (December 1975). It is interesting to note that Marxist scholars make the same mistake. They point to features in the dependency literature such as unemployment, marginalization, etc., noting that they are not peculiar to peripheral countries but characterize capitalist countries in general. Thus "dependency" is said to have no explanatory value beyond a Marxist theory of capitalist society. See Sanjaya Lall, "Is Dependence a Useful Concept in Analyzing Underdevelopment?" *World Development*, III (November 1975) and Theodore Weisskopf, "Dependence as an Explanation of Underdevelopment: A Critique," (paper presented at the Sixth Annual Latin American Studies Association Meeting, Atlanta, Georgia, 1976). The point of dependency analysis is not the relative mix at one point in time of certain identifiable factors but the evolution over time of structural relations which help to explain the differential development of capitalism in different parts of the world. As a historical model it cannot be

tested with cross national data. For an attempt to differentiate conceptually contemporary capitalism of the core and peripheral countries, and thus more amenable to such criticism, see Samir Amin, *Accumulation on a World Scale* (New York, 1974).

39. Some authors have criticized the focus of the literature on the evolution of the world capitalist system. David Ray, for example, has argued that "Soviet satellites" are also in a dependent and unequal relationship vis-à-vis the Soviet Union and that the key variable should not be capitalism but "political power." Robert Packenham has also argued that the most important critique of the dependency literature is that it does not consider the implications of "power." See Ray, "The Dependency Model of Latin American Underdevelopment: Three Basic Fallacies," *Journal of Interamerican Studies and World Affairs,* XV (February 1973) and Packenham, "Latin American Dependency Theories: Strengths and Weaknesses," (paper presented to the Harvard-MIT Joint Seminar on Political Development, February, 1974), especially pp. 16–17, 54. This criticism misses the point completely. It is not power relations today which cause underdevelopment, but the historical evolution of a world economic system which led to economic specialization more favorable to some than others. It is precisely this concern with the evolution of world capitalism which has led to the preoccupation in the dependency literature with rejecting interpretations stressing the "feudal" rather than "capitalist"nature of colonial and post colonial Latin American agriculture. On this point see Sergio Bagú, *Economía de la sociedad colonial* (Buenos Aires, 1949); Louis Vitale, "América Latina: Feudal o Capitalista?" *Revista Estrategia,* III (1966) and *Interpretación Marxista de la historia de Chile* (Santiago, 1967); and E. Laclau, "Feudalism and Capitalism in Latin America," *New Left Review,* LXVII (May-July 1971). A brilliant recent exposition of the importance of studying the evolution of the capitalist world system in order to understand underdevelopment which focuses more on the center states than on the periphery is Immanuel Wallerstein, *The Modern World System: Capitalist Agriculture and the Origins of the European World Economy in the Sixteenth Century* (New York, 1974).

40. Fernando Henrique Cardoso, *Empresario industrial e desenvolvimento economico no Brazil* (São Paulo, 1964) and *Ideologías de la burguesía industrial en sociedades dependientes* (Mexico, 1971).

41. Cardoso and Faletto, *Dependencia y desarrollo,* p. 20. Indeed Cardoso argues that the distinction between external and internal is "metaphysical." See his "Teoría de la dependencia o análisis de situaciones concretas de dependencia?" *Revista Latinoamericana de Ciencia Política,* I (December 1970), p. 404. The ontology implicit in such an analysis is the one of "internal relations." See Bertell Ollman, *Alienation: Marx's Conception of Man in Capitalist Society* (London, 1971). This point is important because both Frank and the early ECLA literature were criticized for their almost mechanistic relationship between external and internal variables. Frank acknowledges this problem and tries to answer his critics in *Lumpenbourgeoisie and Lumpendevelopment* (New York, 1967). "Tests" of dependency theory also attribute an excessively mechanical dimension to the relationship. See Kaufman, et al., "A Preliminary Test of the Theory of Dependency."

42. Fernando Henrique Cardoso, "Associated Dependent Development: Theoretical Implications," in Alfred Stepan, ed., *Authoritarian Brazil* (New Haven,

1973), and Sunkel and Edmundo Fuenzalida, "Transnational Capitalism and National Development" (London). It is thus incorrect to argue that dependency analysts ignore the evidence of certain kinds of economic growth. For fallacies in the dependency literature see Fernando Henrique Cardoso, "Las contradicciones del desarrollo asociado," *Desarrollo Económico,* IV (April-June 1974).

43. Aníbal Quijano, "Dependencia, cambio social y urbanización en América Latina," in Cardoso and F. Weffort, eds., *América Latina: Ensayos de interpretación sociológico político* (Santiago, 1970).
44. Cardoso and Faletto, *Dependencia y desarrollo,* pp. 19–20; Sunkel and Paz, *El subdesarrollo latinoamericano,* pp. 5, 9.
45. Bagú, *Economía de la sociedad colonial,* pp. 122–23.
46. On industrialization see A. Dorfman, *La industrialización en América Latina y las políticas de fomento* (Mexico, 1967).
47. See M. de C. Tavares, "El proceso de substitución de importaciones como modelo de desarrollo reciente en América Latina," in Andres Bianchi, ed., *América Latina: Ensayos de interpretación económica* (Santiago, 1969).
48. For detailed discussions of nonenclave versus enclave situations see Cardoso and Faletto and Sunkel and Paz.
49. Osvaldo Sunkel, "Capitalismo transnacional y desintegración nacional en América Latina," *Estudios Internacionales,* IV (January-March 1971) and "Big Business and Dependencia: A Latin American View," *Foreign Affairs,* L (April 1972); Cardoso and Faletto; dos Santos, *El nuevo carácter de la dependencia* (Santiago, 1966).
50. Wallerstein, *The Modern World System.*
51. V. Bambirra, *Capitalismo dependiente latinoamericano* (Santiago, 1973); R. M. Marini, *Subdesarrollo y revolución* (Mexico, 1969); F. Hinkelammert, *El subdesarrollo latinoamericano: un caso de desarrollo capitalista* (Santiago, 1970).
52. Cardoso, "Teoría de la dependencia." A recent trend in dependency writings attempts to explain the current wave of authoritarianism in Latin America as a result of economic difficulties created by the exhaustion of the easy import substituting industrialization. The new situation leads to a process of development led by the state and the multinational corporation, which concentrates income toward the top, increases the levels of capital accumulation and expands heavy industry; the old populist alliances can therefore no longer be maintained. See Theotonio dos Santos, *Socialismo o fascismo: el nuevo carácter de la dependencia y el dilema latinoamericano* (Buenos Aires, 1972); Guillermo O'Donnell, *Modernization and Bureaucratic Authoritarianism: Studies in Latin American Politics* (Berkeley, 1973); Atilio Borón, "El fascismo como categoria histórica: en torno al problema de las dictaduras en América Latina," *Revista Mexicana de Sociología,* XXXIV (April-June 1977); the effects of this situation on labor are explored in Kenneth P. Erickson and Patrick Peppe, "Dependent Capitalist Development, U.S. Foreign Policy, and Repression of the Working Class in Chile and Brazil," *Latin American Perspectives,* III (Winter 1976). However, in the postscript to their 1968 book, Cardoso and Faletto caution against adopting an excessively mechanistic view on this point, against letting "economism kill history"; Cardoso and Faletto, "Estado y proceso politico en América Latina," *Revista Mexicana de Sociología,* XXXIV (April-June 1977), p. 383. Articles with dependency per-

spective appear frequently in the *Revista Mexicana de Sociología* as well as in *Latin American Perspectives.*
53. Sunkel, "Capitalismo transnacional y desintegración nacional en América Latina," and Sunkel and Fuenzalida, "Transnational Capitalism and National Development."

Big Business and Dependencia: A Latin American View

Osvaldo Sunkel

The author argues that foreign corporations have denationalized Latin American countries. The importance of local businesses is reduced as a result of foreign control over markets. As with other dependency theorists, it is not a question of lack of economic growth as much as it is uneven development that has increased the gap between the rich and the poor, the cities and impoverished countryside. To the author, such effects are the result of the expansion of the world capitalist system to include Latin America.

I

The winds of economic nationalism are blowing strong in Latin America. . . . The recent burst of nationalism is in fact a reaction to long-term and increasingly intolerable dependence on foreigners. The development strategy of industrialization as a substitute for imports was supposed to free the economy from its heavy reliance on primary exports, foreign capital and technology. It has not only failed to achieve these aims, but has in fact aggravated the situation and nature of "dependencia."

In its initial period, from 1930 to around 1955, the strategy stimulated the growth of a significant manufacturing industry and of the corresponding national entrepreneurial class. But subsequently industry was taken over to a large extent by foreign subsidiaries, with the result that much of the benefit expected from industrialization has gone abroad in payment for capital equipment and in a transfer of profits, royalties and other financial payments. This has effectively denationalized and eroded the local entrepreneurial class. Although the massive penetration of foreign firms has accelerated growth rates, especially industrial, it has also accentuated the uneven nature of development: on the one hand, a partial process of modernization and expansion of capital-intensive activities; on the other, a process of disruption, contraction and disorganization of traditional labor-intensive activities.

Disguised and open unemployment—that process of internal polarization and segregation which has been termed "marginalization"—has therefore been rising; together they account for levels estimated at over 25 percent, and they are still increasing. Owing to this and to the fact that the development strategies pursued aimed at the formation and strengthening of a reliable middle class, income seems at least as heavily concentrated in the hands of the wealthy as it was 20 years ago, allowing them consumption levels and patterns similar to those of the middle classes of developed countries, while the gap between high and low incomes in towns and in the countryside appears in most cases to have widened.

Things obviously went wrong with the development policies and strategy pursued after the Second World War. In a nutshell, the essence of its logic was that rapid economic growth could be achieved by protecting and stimulating industry, which eventually, and with the aid of appropriate government action, would induce the modernization of other sectors of the economy. This, in turn, would improve the social conditions of the people, more or less following the pattern of the industrial revolution in Western Europe and North America.

Apparently something important had been overlooked which hindered both the implementation and even an adequate understanding of the process. In the conventional approach to underdevelopment, the unit of analysis has always been the national economy in isolation, treated as if it existed in an international vacuum. Myrdal, Singer, Nurkse, as well as Prebisch and numerous economists from underdeveloped countries and U.N. agencies such as the Economic Commission for Latin America and the United Nations Conference on Trade and Development (UNCTAD) have emphasized the significance of the foreign trade structure of these countries—raw material exports and manufactured imports—as causing instability, stagnation, deteriorating terms of trade and balance-of-payments difficulties. They have also pointed to foreign financing and technical aid as having a significant influence on the rate of growth and the equilibrium of the underdeveloped economy.

New studies of "dependencia" in industry and related sectors have led to a greater recognition of its nature and effects. To begin with, local development and modernization are seen not in isolation but as part of the development of an international capitalist system, whose dynamic has a determining influence on the local processes. Therefore, foreign factors are seen not as external but as intrinsic to the system, with manifold and sometimes hidden or subtle political, financial, economic, technical and cultural effects inside the underdeveloped country. These contribute significantly to shaping the nature and operation of the economy, society and polity, a kind of "fifth column" as it were. Thus, the concept of "dependencia" links the postwar evolution of capitalism internationally to the discriminatory nature of the local process of development, as we know it. Access to the means and benefits of development is selective; rather than spreading them the process tends to ensure a self-reinforcing accumulation of privilege for special groups as well as the continued existence of a marginal class.

In other words, this approach considers the capitalist system as a whole, as a global international system, within which national economies—nation–states—constitute sub-systems. These are not completely separated from each other but partially overlapping, owing to the fact that national economies interpenetrate each other to some extent in terms of productive facilities, technologies, consumption patterns, ideologies, political parties, cultural activities, private and government institutions. According to this approach, it is no longer possible to assume that underdevelopment is a moment in the evolution of a society which has been economically, politically and culturally autonomous and isolated.

The present international panorama of countries at different levels of development is not simply an aggregate of individual historical performances; the development process is not simply a race which started somewhere before the industrial revolution and in which some countries reached advanced stages while others stagnated or moved slower. The "dependencia" analysis maintains that one of the essential elements of the development of capitalism has been, from the outset, the creation of an international system which brought the world economy under the influence of a few European countries, plus the United States from the late nineteenth century onwards. Development and underdevelopment, in this view, are simultaneous processes: the two faces of the historical evolution of the capitalist system.

II

During the colonial period, in order to extract the precious metals and obtain the tropical products needed by the metropolis, Europeans interfered with existing social relationships and reorganized local economies on the basis of slavery and other forms of forced labor. This created the basis for agrarian structures and institutions which have survived in some form until today. During the nineteenth and first half of the twentieth century, the industrial revolution in Europe and later in the United States created a world economic system where Europe and the United States invested heavily in the production of food and raw materials in the rest of the world, while specializing at home in the production of manufactures. In Latin America, to the agrarian colonial heritage was added specialization in the export of staples and raw materials and with another set of socio-economic and political structures and institutions, including the new dominant élites.

The breakdown of the nineteenth-century model of international economic relations during the two World Wars and the Great Depression opened for Latin American economies the period of import-substituting industrialization. This meant, in the larger countries of the region, the formation by the middle of the 1950s of a significant manufacturing sector, complete with its entrepreneurial class, professional and technical groups and industrial proletariat, as well as the necessary and ancillary government and private financial, marketing and educational agencies.

But during this period, while Europe was being ravaged by war and economic crisis, the U.S. economy developed into the most powerful center in the capitalist world and expanded into the economies of both developed and underdeveloped countries, bringing about very substantial changes, particularly in the latter. At the same time the U.S. economy experienced important changes in its internal structure. Government intervention expanded considerably within the United States, accelerating growth, reducing cyclical fluctuations and contributing to a fantastic development of science and technology; all this helped produce large business conglomerates. Vast economic, technological and therefore political power has enabled the multinational corporation, through the control of the marketing and communication processes, to induce consumers and governments to buy the products which it is technologically able to produce in ever-growing quantities. Within certain limits it is thus able to plan the development of consumption.

These institutional developments in the United States are reflected abroad as the new multinational corporations spread throughout the international economy. Their activities follow a fairly definite pattern: first, they export their finished products; then they establish sales organizations abroad; they then proceed to allow foreign producers to use their licenses and patents to manufacture the product locally; finally, they buy off the local producer and establish a partially or wholly owned subsidiary. In the process a new structure of international economic relations is emerging, where trade between national firm Z of country A and national firm Y of country B is replaced by the internal transfers of Firm Z to countries A and B, while firm Y vanishes from the picture.

As a consequence, free-market forces and/or national policies are gradually superseded by the multinational firm's plan. It is estimated that for the decade 1960–70 around a fourth of all manufacturing exports from the United States were intra-firm transfers, and this proportion is rising quickly. Moreover, while previously only the international primary product market was an oligopoly, this is now also becoming true of the international market in manufactures. For the underdeveloped countries this means that outside control, formerly applied only to their exports, is also increasingly exercised over their imports. Lastly, the intervention by government agencies in the developed countries, which paved the way for business expansion in their national markets, now is being repeated internationally, as these agencies intervene increasingly in "world markets"—which is really a euphemism for other countries' markets—to support and protect the expansion of their firms.

The greatly extended economic role of the state takes essentially two forms: direct, bilateral, government-to-government relationships on the one hand, and international, multilateral economic organizations on the other. The bilateral relationship between a dominant and a dependent country corresponds closely to mercantilistic formulas. The dominant country tries to establish, enlarge and preserve exclusive privileges for its business interests, granting in exchange support of various kinds to the local social groups with which it is associated. The instruments of domination in bilateral relationships are well known: tied loans, technical aid, preferential arrangements with regard to transportation, communications, foreign investment, tariffs and so on. The multilateral relationship consists of a maze of international economic organizations. Some would like to see these set up in a hierarchical system, with organizations like the World Bank and the International Monetary Fund (IMF), where developed countries have a decisive influence, at the top. Regional organizations like the Organization of American States (OAS), which exist within one hegemonic system, and organizations among the developed countries such as the European Community would be kept independent from outside influence. World organizations where each country has one vote would be relegated to a rather weak position, much as are the organizations among underdeveloped countries of one region, the Latin American Free Trade Association (LAFTA) and the Organization of African Unity (OAU). Meanwhile, it has not been possible to create a formal global organization of underdeveloped countries—only the informal UNCTAD group, orginally 77, now over 100.

Efforts to reorganize international relations to correspond to the transformation in the structure of the world economy have been clearly discernible in recent reports dealing with international cooperation. This is not surprising, since it should be the function of the superstructure to provide the ideological rationale for the system, as well as to lay down the rules of the game and provide the institutional means for policing its implementation. The following quotation constitutes a good statement of an apologist for these trends:

> The international corporation is acting and planning in terms that are far in advance of the political concepts of the nation–state. As the Renaissance of the fifteenth century brought an end to feudalism, aristocracy and the dom-

inant role of the Church, the twentieth-century Renaissance is bringing an end to middle-class society and the dominance of the nation–state. The heart of the new power structure is the international organization and technocrats who guide it. Power is shifting away from the nation–state to international institutions, public and private. Within a generation about 400 to 500 international corporations will own about two-thirds of the fixed assets of the world.[1]

III

Following the transformations that have occurred in the new centers of the capitalist world—the U.S., European and Japanese economies—the system of international economic relations has experienced fundamental institutional and structural changes. As a consequence, the internal economic, social and political structures of the dependent underdeveloped countries have also experienced fundamental transformations. These transformations are the main factors behind the rising nationalism in Latin America.

As mentioned earlier, the large expansion of the U.S. multinational corporation in Latin America really gained momentum around the mid-1950s; but only in the late 1960s did it reach the stage of the wholesale process of buying up local firms and integrating affiliates closely with headquarters and with each other. A study of the operations of 187 transnational corporations in Latin America shows that while in 1945 there were only 74 of these firms with manufacturing subsidiaries in the region, in 1967 the number of their subsidiaries in the region had increased from 182 to 950, and the total number of subsidiaries from 452 to 1,914.[2]

This process has profoundly affected the Latin American economy and society. While in the earlier period foreign investment in these countries manifested itself mainly in primary production and public utilities, in the postwar period extractive subsidiaries grew from only 38 to 56. The fundamental impact has therefore been in the manufacturing and related sectors, which have expanded considerably since the 1930s. In their growth they were faced with the need of starting almost from scratch to obtain a specialized labor force, highly qualified technicians, entrepreneurs, equipment, raw materials, financial resources, organizations for marketing, distribution, publicity, sales and credit, as well as technical ability to carry out all these tasks. In the process of industrial growth and diversification, these countries have been increasingly incorporating these elements from foreign sources.

From the nineteen-thirties through the early nineteen-fifties, particularly in the larger countries, immigrants and local entrepreneurs provided most of the skilled personnel; capital and financing came mainly from public sources, both national and foreign; know-how and technology were acquired through the purchase of licenses and technical assistance. All these producers contributed to the formation and strengthening of private entrepreneurship and industry. But in recent years there has been a reversal of these trends. Subsidiaries of foreign firms have provided a complete package of entrepreneurship, management, design technology, financing and marketing. This has been the local counterpart of the institutional transformation indicated earlier in the mature capitalist countries and in the international economy.

On a more general level, import-substituting industrialization constitutes another way of setting the underdeveloped economies within the framework of a reorganized world economic system. The new system is formed, as before, on the basis of dominant (developed) economies and dependent (underdeveloped) economies, increasingly linked to each other through growing transnational interlocking of production structures and consumption patterns.

In the plants, laboratories, design and publicity departments, as well as in the planning, decision-making, personnel and finance organizations that constitute its headquarters—always located in an industrialized country—the transnational corporation develops: (1) new products; (2) new ways of producing those products; (3) the new machinery, equipment and innovative methods necessary to produce them; and (4) the publicity needed to create their markets. In the underdeveloped country, the corporation establishes the subsidiaries necessary for the marketing, assembling or routine production of those goods. The import-substitution process of industrialization has therefore become the corporation's strategy for penetration of foreign protected markets, supported by external public and private credit, international technical assistance and ideological advice in respect to development policies and strategies.

Let us look at some of the economic effects of this process through the words of Professor Harry Johnson:

> The corporation . . . has no commerical interest in diffusing its knowledge to potential native competitors, nor has it any interest in investing more than it has to in acquiring knowledge of local conditions and investigating ways of adapting its own productive knowledge to local factor/price ratios and market conditions. Its purpose is not to transform the economy by exploiting its potentialities (especially its human potentialities) for development. . . . The main contribution of direct foreign investment will be highly specific and very uneven in its incidence.[3]

A. O. Hirschman, on his part, has pointed out that direct private foreign investment, by taking over local firms and displacing local entrepreneurship, may be harming the quality of local factors of production. Moreover, given the "complete package" character of subsidiaries, the foreign contribution may not be complementary but may instead be competitive with local factors of production, retarding or preventing their growth, and therefore decreasing the quantity of local inputs. His conclusion: "Private foreign investment is a mixed blessing, and the mixture is likely to become more noxious at the intermediate stage of development which characterizes much of present-day Latin America."[4]

The massive expansion and branch-plant nature of direct foreign investment has in fact some highly negative effects. In the first place, there is the process of vertical integration between the subsidiary and the headquarters. This means that flows of goods, finance, technology, etc. generally take place within firms, which have a natural tendency to prefer their own branches or affiliates as partners in any transaction, even if the country's interests are different. Their tendency is not to integrate with local suppliers or to share or adapt their technology, as Johnson points out. Furthermore, there is usually a market-sharing agreement among headquarters and the various subsidiaries and affiliates, which often means that branch plants are not allowed to export. Even the integration process in LAFTA or the Central American Common Market gives the subsidiaries located in the member countries a further opportunity to diminish the position of national firms.

Secondly, subsidiaries within one country tend to integrate horizontally, to conglomerate among themselves. Gaining control of finance, credit, markets and publicity means a considerable capacity to influence consumption patterns, not only of the higher income groups which can afford their goods, but also of lower income groups by way of the "trickling down" effect, thereby completely distorting their consumption patterns.

The control of the commanding heights of the economy also means, of course, the capacity to influence the allocation of resources in the public sector, frequently in the direction of providing infrastructure needed for subsidizing the expansion of the foreign subsidiary. It also implies the capacity to acquire significant financial resources, private and public, with which to finance local expansion and foreign remittances, almost without the need of net additional foreign capital. In fact, between 1963 and 1968 only nine percent of the total funds used by the Latin American subsidiaries of the U.S. corporations came from abroad. This, together with their negligible contribution to exports, inevitably leads to a serious balance-of-payments problem.

In the third place, foreign subsidiaries are usually able to extract oligopolistic profits from the exploitation of consumer and supplier markets. Moreover, as they keep most of their international transactions within the boundaries of the firm, there is a strong tendency to remit excess profits by manipulating the prices, kinds and quantities of these transactions.

Finally, the activities of subsidiaries in underdeveloped countries follow a definite life cycle. At the beginning the foreign firm may make a substantial contribution in capital, skilled personnel, technology, management, etc. But over time the cash outflow becomes larger than the inflow. Moreover, among the various alternative ways of obtaining external cooperation, direct foreign investment in the form of wholly owned subsidiaries is the one that has the smallest educational effect because of its policy of retaining its monopoly of skills and technology. It is only as a consequence of the process of the country's development that local personnel learn modern management and technological skills. Eventually, the corporation's net contribution to the development capabilities of the country becomes negligible or even negative. When the technology of the activities in which the firm operates becomes standardized and well known, the subsidiary becomes an "obsolete" form of foreign ownership from the point of view of its contribution to the resources, abilities and technology of the country.

IV

While these and other negative economic effects illustrate clearly the "mixed blessing" that private foreign investment represents, it is the socio-political consequences that are of far greater importance and of a much more explosive character.

The massive penetration of subsidiaries of foreign firms into the industrial, financial, marketing and distribution activities has fundamentally changed the ownership pattern in most Latin American countries. Foreign firms have acquired a dominant position among medium and large firms in many if not all the main sectors of private economic activity. This implies a basic change in the social structure and the political system. As the economist Celso Furtado has pointed out:

> The process of forming a local entrepreneurial class has been interrupted. The best talents that emerge from local industries are being absorbed into the new managerial class. ... National independent entrepreneurship is ... restricted to secondary activities or to pioneering ventures which, in the long run, simply open up new fields for the future expansion of the multinational corporation. ... The elimination of the national entrepreneurial class necessarily excludes the possibility of self-sustained national development, along the lines of the classical capitalist development.[5]

In other words, a significant part of the national bourgeoisie is being transformed into a private transnational technocracy, losing legitimacy as part of a national ruling class.

But Furtado's observation may be extended to all groups and social classes to gain a clearer perception of the crisis which is affecting the nation–state in Latin America. At the level of production, this crisis makes itself felt through the massive and extraordinarily dynamic penetration of the transnational firm with its subsidiaries and affiliates; at the technological level, by the large–scale introduction of highly capital-intensive techniques; at the cultural and ideological level, by the over-whelming and systematic promotion and publicity of conspicuous consumption capitalism; and at the concrete level of development policies and strategies, by the pressure of national and international interests in favor of an industrialization process aimed basically at providing consumer goods for the high-income groups.

This process of so-called modernization implies the gradual replacement of the traditional production structure, which is labor-intensive, by another of much higher capital intensity. Under these conditions, the process incorporates into the new institutions and structures the individuals and groups that are apt to fit into the kind of rationale which prevails there. It also expels those individuals and groups that have no place in the new productive structure or lack the ability to adapt to it. Therefore, this process not only prevents the formation of a national entrepreneurial class, but also limits and erodes the middle classes generally (including intellectuals, scientists and technocrats) and even creates privileged and underprivileged sectors within the working class, adding another serious difficulty to the creation of a strong labor movement.

In this process, some national entrepreneurs are coopted as executives into the new subsidiaries; some professionals, forming part of the technical staff, and some specially trained employees are incorporated. The rest are left out. Part of the qualified labor supply will be brought in and the remainder excluded, adding to the growing problem of unemployment and underemployment. The effects of the disintegration of each social class have important consequences for social mobility. The marginal entrepreneur will probably be added to the ranks of small businessmen, or will abandon independent activity and become a middle-class employee. The segregated sectors of the middle class will probably form a group of frustrated lower-middle-class people trying to maintain appearances without much possibility of upward mobility and terrified by the prospect of proletarianization. The unemployed or underemployed workers will increase the numbers of those marginal to the economy and society, as in the lower middle class. Growing pools of resentment and frustration will certainly accumulate in both middle and lower classes.

Corresponding to this downward mobility there is also an upward mobility of a selective and discriminatory character. Some unemployed or underemployed are incorporated into the working class, some workers rise to the lower ranks of the middle classes and some sectors of the middle classes become small or medium-sized entrepreneurs. This upward movement probably tends to depress the wage levels, at least of unskilled workers and employees, and increases the anguish of the lower-middle and working classes.

Corresponding to this internal mobility is an international mobility between the internationalized sectors of developed and underdeveloped countries; these constitute in fact an international market for skilled labor. One side of this mobility is the outward "brain drain"; the obverse is the flow of experts and administrators sent into the underdeveloped countries to oversee the process of modernization and development described earlier. There may also be a flow of underemployed from Latin America in response to demands for low-salaried employees in developed countries.

V

The crisis of the nation–state which has been outlined above also affects the main institutions of society: the state, the armed forces, political parties, the universities, the Church. In Latin America, different countries have reacted in various ways to this crisis. In Brazil, leading groups and classes seem to have accepted "dependencia" and marginalization as inevitable and necessary ingredients of the process of development and modernization. An increasing share of the ownership and control of national resources and activities is being turned over to foreign firms and the government apparatus is being put at their disposal. This means not only the provision of infrastructural investments necessary for their expansion, but also the political and police repression needed to suppress the growing reaction and resentment to advancing denationalization, widening inequality and increasing marginalization. This development model could perhaps best be described as Dependent State Capitalism.

In other countries, owing to the different nature of preexisting local conditions and other elements which cannot be analyzed here, certain social classes have reacted to the crisis by trying to oppose the above-mentioned trends. To do this they are trying to regain control over the economy. But this implies, in the first place, taking away the control of the state from the social groups which are more closely associated with the development strategy of Dependent State Capitalism. In the case of Peru this has been done by the nationalist elements among the military, and in Chile by a government elected with the support of large sectors of the working class and important sections of the middle class.

Having taken over the control of the state, these groups face three essential development tasks in correcting the main malformation inherited from the historical process of interaction with the international system: in the first place, this means transforming the agrarian structure, which is the fundamental root of inequality, marginalization and stagnation; second, using the primary export sector, which represents an underdeveloped country's most important source of capital accumulation, to support the expansion of heavy and consumer industries; and, finally, the reorganization of the industrial sector, essentially in order to orient it away from satisfying the conspicuous consumption of the minority into satisfying the basic needs of the majority.

In this process of structural reform, many well-established local and foreign interests will be affected. If there are foreign investments in the agricultural sector, they will be affected by agrarian reform. If there are foreign investments in the primary export sector, whether agricultural or mining, they will be affected by the need to control these fundamental sources of foreign financing. If there are foreign investments in the industrial and related sectors, as there increasingly are, the reorientation of industrial policy will affect subsidiaries of foreign firms. As the present level of industrial development has rested to a large extent on the power structures built around the main local and foreign industrial and commercial monopolies and the banking system, they are also bound to be taken over by the state. This will mean nationalizations and renegotiations with foreign interests.

It is interesting to note that international public opinion has more or less become accustomed to the idea that structural reforms are necessary in agriculture, so much so that underdeveloped countries are urged to go ahead with agrarian reform. If foreign interests are involved, there may be protests but they would be considerably attenuated by the recognized need for an agrarian reform.

Even in the field of primary export activities it is being accepted that our nations have the right to control their most essential resources, and that the policies of subsidiaries of foreign firms do not necessarily coincide with the best long-term interests of the country. It seems, as Hirschman points out, that at a certain level of industrial and general development, our countries are also beginning to reassert their own interests in the fields of manufacturing, commerce and banking, where the foreign penetration is now greatest. The conflict of interest with foreign private investment in these sectors will be more or less intense according to whether the country will choose a socialistic development path, as in Chile; some rather progressive variety of state capitalism, as seems to be the case in Peru; or some less well-defined and more moderate variety, as in most other countries.

Whatever the case, the era of "creating favorable business conditions for direct foreign investment" as a general policy seems to be coming to an end. But even then, as is seen more and more with the socialist countries, possible cooperation with foreign firms is not totally excluded, even though there will certainly be little place for wholly owned subsidiaries of foreign firms or private foreign investment of the traditional kind. What is opening up is a new era of hard bargaining and negotiations, of pragmatic and detailed considerations of specific cases, of weighing the conditions offered by Japan, Europe, the socialist countries and the United States, of building up alliances with countries with similar interests (the Andean Pact, the Special Co-ordination Commission of Latin America, the Organization of the Petroleum Exporting Countries), etc. In short, what we are seeing is the assertion of the national interest of our countries in their international economic relations. The aim is greater autonomy, in order to achieve development without "dependencia" and without marginalization. To achieve this goal, the asymmetrical nature of the present system of international economic relations must first undergo a thorough reform.

NOTES

1. A. Barber, "Emerging New Power: The World Corporation," *War/Peace Report,* October, 1968, p. 7.
2. J. W. Vaupel and Joan P. Curham, "The Making of Multinational Enterprise." Boston: Harvard University Division of Research, 1969.
3. Harry G. Johnson, "The Multi-National Corporation as an Agency of Economic Development: Some Exploratory Observations," in Barbara Ward, Lenore d'Anjou and J. D. Runnalls, "The Widening Gap; Development in the 1970's." New York: Columbia University Press, 1971, pp. 244 and 246.
4. Albert O. Hirschman, "How to Divest in Latin America, and Why," *Essays in International Finance,* No. 76, Princeton University, November 1969.
5. Celso Furtado, "La concentración del poder económico en los EE. UU. y sus proyecciones en América Latina," *Estudios Internacionales,* Año I, no. 3–4, Santiago, 1968.

The Consumption of Dependency Theory in the United States

Fernando Henrique Cardoso

The author discusses how dependency theory has been misinterpreted in the United States, identifying what he sees as distortions, simplifications, and questionable criticisms.

If an observer from outer space had landed his UFO at any meeting of Latin Americanists during the last few years, he would have had to agree with the structural anthropologists. He would have said that at these meetings, versions of the same myth are constantly repeated: dependency and development, exploitation and wealth, backwardness and sophisticated technology, unemployment and extreme concentration of income. Somewhat wearily, our creature from space would have com-

From *Latin American Research Review,* 12 (1977), no. 3: 7–24. Reprinted by permission.

mented: "The brains of these beings appear to limit their images and thoughts to binary opposites." Returning to the debate on the meaning of analyses of dependency gives one the sensation of entering a discussion in which imagination is bound by preestablished models. Nevertheless, as though I were one of the "founding fathers" of dependency, I endorse the ceremonial consumption of the theme. How to escape from this uncomfortable position?

A little while ago, in Princeton, I was present at a talk by an English anthropologist, recently knighted by the Queen. With his characteristic irony, Sir Edmund Leach told how he tried to stifle his own amusement at the ceremonial rite to which he had to submit, by comparing his consecration at the Court of St. James to sacrificial ceremonies on the high plains of Burma. His talk was entitled, "Once a Knight is Enough." Nevertheless, the irony, mingled with erudition and with pious respect for the ritualized reenactment of a moment of passage from the condition of "commoner" to that of member of a noble order (which, even if it is not sacred, has something of the distinction that is reserved for the upper ranks of the hierarchy), could not conceal the fact that the ritual and the symbolic renaming to which he was submitted did hold some kind of meaning for him. The scientific consumption of the rite of passage did not eliminate its force. The game of comparative-formal analysis did not expose the political and social interests that underlay these ritual ceremonies but simply reaffirmed the universal value of them.

By using the title "Consumption of Dependency," and at the same time participating in this critico-commemorative celebration (which is, naturally, a more plebeian ceremony than the English knighting ritual), do I not run the same risk? There is no way to deny it. I hope, nevertheless, to maintain a sufficiently critical (and self-critical) position to avoid merely consenting to the ritual consumption of the theme.

The risk of ceremonial celebration becomes greater as studies of dependency arouse a certain movement of conversion among social scientists. Susanne Bodenheimer, grasping the critical power that these studies contained, gave wider currency to some of these formulations (since she wrote in English, which is the Latin of our times) and presented them as a *new* paradigm.[1] From that point on (although it was not her fault), what had been an endeavor to be *critical* and to maintain the *continuity* of previous historical, economic, sociological, and political studies in Latin America was transformed into an article for consumption in various versions that include references to the original myth but in large measure constitute the expression of a quite distinct intellectual universe from that which gave it birth.

Every myth requires a simple structure and a moment of revelation. The first, drastic simplification carried out by some popularizers of these studies was to treat them as a sort of mental thunderclap that occurred at a given time and place. Now the discussion revolves around the question of in whose head the thunderclap was produced; with that kind of beginning, the celebratory aspect is inevitable. Each interpreter seeks to locate his prophet. However, anyone who is aware of the social nature of thought knows that every new paradigm results from a complex discussion among persons, institutions, and groups, which in the modern world are located in different countries. With time, the discussion is enriched and provokes internal controversies.[2]

However, after establishing the immediate origins of the "dependency paradigm," popularizers who are not aware of the process of intellectual production attempt to describe its prehistory. Here, two principal currents are generally cited: ECLA, and the Marxian and neo-Marxian North American current (Baran, Sweezy, and Gunder Frank). At times, some spice is added to the debate by saying that the *dependentistas* (a term that makes me shudder) are of distinct ideological hues; there are those who are closer to ECLA (and to the "petty-bourgeois nationalism" that is supposed to have been derived from ECLA's research work), and there are those who adopt a position of more authentic opposition to capitalism and are thus more influenced by the above-mentioned Marxian economists prior to the dependentistas. These assertions are plausible—indeed, perhaps they are typologically correct—but they do not correspond to the intellectual history of these ideas as it really happened.

The analyses of dependency situations in Latin America done in the second half of the sixties did not represent new methodological propositions. What happened was that a current which was already old in Latin American thought managed to make itself heard in the discussions that were taking place in institutions normally closed to it: ECLA, the universities, some government planning agencies, and—last but not least—the North American academic community.

As for the renovating influence of the North American neo-Marxian current, if it was real (principally the contribution of Baran), it was certainly not greater than that of Marx himself, and it did not "reveal" anything not already present in the perspective of critical Latin American thought before 1960. In practically all the principal Latin American intellectual centers, a critique of the critics was also developed which paralleled the development of a current of analysis and interpretation based on Prebisch and Furtado (and, along with or before them, Nurkse, Hans Singer, Myrdal, and Hirschman—to cite just a few of the authors who opposed "orthodox" theories justifying the nonindustrialization of the region in view of the comparative advantages that might be obtained with agricultural production for export). It arose within ECLA itself, at times explicitly, as in the studies by Ahumada and Aníbal Pinto dealing with Chile and the concentration of benefits from technological progress, or in the essays of Medina Echevarria on the social conditions of development and on the "instrumental rationality" of the developmentalist approach. At other times the critique of the critics was implicit in the work of intellectuals who, in the universities or in political movements, emphasized not only the "obstacles" and the "distortions" of capitalist development (often inspired by structural-functionalist analysis), but also the inequality of opportunities and wealth that was inherent in forms of development derived from the expansion of capitalism and the strengthening of imperialism.

Historians Sergio Bagu and Caio Prado, Jr.; sociologists Florestan Fernandes, Pablo González Casanova, and Jorge Graciarena; and economists Armando Córdoba, Antonio García, and Alonso Aguilar are examples of efforts to present alternatives both to orthodox analyses and to what we might call the ECLA-Keynesian analyses. A rereading of the *Revista Brasiliense,* published in Brazil in the 1950s—and there were journals of the same sort published in almost all the cultural centers of the area—shows that criticism of structural-functionalism and Keynesianism occurred in Latin America at the same time as the criticism of "orthodoxy" was being elaborated. In an effort to develop a double-edged critique, a few groups of intellectuals in Santiago in the mid-1960s took up the ECLA problematic and tried to redefine it radically, while seeking to avoid "vulgar Marxism." To compare what ECLA predicted as the outcome of industrialization with what was in fact happening was easy. It was more difficult to propose an alternative that could not be limited to methodological-formal critique; one that, starting from the analysis of historical-social processes, would be able to define an alternative problematic and break with both the prevailing "economicism" of analyses of development and the "apoliticism" of sociological analyses. How was that to be accomplished?

A study of the history of ideas in the twentieth century would show that each generation of critical intellectuals seeks to revive Marxism with a new breath of life. The crust of so-called "vulgar Marxism"—"economic determinism," "mechanistic" analysis, the difficulty of capturing social movement due to conceptions that give a deterministic weight to the structures, etc.—is so recurring that it must have something to do with Marxism itself. From time to time things are shaken up by rereading the classics, by some new interpretation, or by the support that some author outside the tradition of dialectical thought lends to Marxian analysis. In the 1950s and the beginning of the 1960s, this bridge was made by Sartre and by the publication in French of *History and Class Consciousness* by Lukacs. It took years to emerge from the impasse between dialectics and the notions of "project" and "possible consciousness."[3] For those like myself who had undergone prior training in Dilthey, Weber, and Mannheim, the preoccupation with ideology and its incorporation in analysis came to be constant and was frequently equivocal. In the following generation, Althusser reread Marx in another way and structuralism nearly killed the movement of dialectics. Later (and in a few countries, like Argentina, even as early as the sixties), Gramsci appeared as a liferaft for those who wanted to understand the political processes, ideology, the will in history, etc., and avoid drowning in the abovementioned "deviations" of mechanistic Marxism.

Studies of dependency, then, constitute part of this constantly renewed effort to reestablish a tradition of analysis of economic structures and structures of domination; one that would not suffocate the historical process by removing from it the movement which results from the permanent struggle among groups and classes. Instead of accepting the existence of a determined course in history, there is a return to conceiving of it as an open-ended process. Thus, if structures delimit the range of oscillation, the actions of humans, as well as their imagination, revive and transfigure these structures and may even replace them with others that are not predetermined. These studies also had a peculiarity within this tradition of criticism: instead of limiting themselves to the theoretical-abstract plane, they sought to utilize the historical-structural, "non-vulgar" method to analyse concrete situations. And instead of limiting their studies to the analysis of circumscribed problems, they sought (returning to the theme of development) to define questions relevant to national politics and to the relations between the central capitalist economies and the dependent and nonindustrialized periphery, following in this respect the tradition of the ECLA perspective. It did not interest them merely to describe abstractly the consequences of the accumulation of capital and of its expansion at the global level; they also posed questions arising from the historically determined point of view of dependent societies: What are the forces that operate in them, and what are their objectives? How and under what conditions is it possible to overcome a given situation of dependency?

Thus, an initial reevaluation of the manner in which the consumption of dependency theories occurs in the U.S. must reconsider the point of view from which the "new paradigm" was established, through the work of a group of intellectuals at ILPES (Latin American Institute for Economic and Social Planning, at ECLA) and CESO (Center for Socioeconomic Studies, University of Chile). Some intellectuals in these organizations played a certain role in the proposal of a set of themes and in the critique of Keynesianism and of structural-functionalism—a role to be discussed further on—but they did *not* propose any *new* methodology.[4]

Once the methodological contribution of the dependentistas has been limited and the possible influence of North American Marxism on proposing studies of dependency has been redefined, it is necessary to look at the contribution of André Gunder Frank to the themes of dependency. Some of his studies in *Capitalism and Development in Latin America* had great critical impact and were contemporary with the elaboration of what is called here the "theory of dependency." Earlier works, such as his paper criticizing the thesis about Brazilian agrarian dualism, may have been stimulating, but frequently missed the point as far as proposing new themes is concerned.

The central question in Brazilian discussions concerning the past nature of social relations in rural areas and their specific weight in determining a certain type of sociohistorical formation was not a debate between the partisans of the existence of a feudal structure and those who believed that "since colonial times" the concept of capitalism best described the existing social relations and forms of production. Nor was it a debate between precapitalism and capitalism *tout court* (although this discussion was more common). These propositions lost their force when confronted with the concern of those who tried to characterize the mode of production that prevailed in the past by taking colonial slave-holding into account. Except for the crudest of the evolutionist Marxists (who really did see "feudalism" as an important characteristic of Brazilian society), the discussion had for a long while centered on slaveholding colonial production and on the specific nature of a social formation which, although created by the expansion of mercantile capitalism, was based on slave-labor relations and reserved the most dynamic part of its output for the internal market.[5] (This outlook is already noticeable in the works of Gilberto Freyre, dating from the 1930s, despite their commemorative quality.) Gunder Frank simplified the debate, disdained the specificity of the situation (a procedure contrary to that of the dependentistas), and failed to attempt any sort of theoretical scheme of a dialectical type that might draw together the general and the particular in a specific whole. With the masterful polemics that are his special skill, he mortally wounded the dualists and blamed the confusion, sometimes correctly and sometimes not, on Marxists and ECLA theorists.

Nevertheless, the paradigm of dependency is consumed in the U.S. as though its contribution to the historical debate had been centered on a critique of Latin American feudalism. That is, some of Gunder Frank's works are taken to mark the beginning of a "new" perspective in Latin America. Bagu, Caio Prado, Simonsen, Celso Furtado, Florestan Fernandes, Alonso Aguilar, and many others, had already written on the colonial period or on the structure of agricultural production for export, basing their analyses on considerably more complex themes than the simple duality between feudalism and capitalism.

The second distortion produced in the consumption of dependency theories concerns the relationship between the social, economic, and political structures of the dependent countries and the international capitalist system. Dependency analyses in the years 1965–68 were preoccupied much less with the external conditioning of the Latin American economies, which was taken for granted, than with the development of a type of analysis that could grasp the political alliances, the ideologies, and the movement of structures within the dependent countries. How was this to be done? The "vulgar" current was predominant in analyses that regarded imperialism and external economic conditioning as the substantive and omnipresent explanation of every social or ideological process that occurred. Certain political forces endorsed that formulation for tactical reasons. Clearly the target of the struggle was evident—North American imperialism, and the allied camp was also clearly defined—everyone, except the agro-exporting latifundists linked to imperialism.

The dependentistas put the question the other way around: social movement cannot be theoretically represented by means of a "mechanical" opposition between the internal and the external, in which the latter cancels out the existence of the former. The approach ought to be historical, and it therefore starts from the emergence of social formations. Underdevelopment then comes to be seen not merely as a process which is concomitant of the expansion of mercantile capitalism and recurs under industrial capitalism, but as one which is actually generated by them. The approach ought also to emphasize the *specificity* of dependency situations, as against societies in countries of the economic center. In other words, although the social formation underlying situations of dependency is the product of the expansion of capitalism, it is distinguishable from the classical pattern to the extent that "slaveholding colonialism," or some other form of colonial exploitation, is present as the basis of the articulation between dependent and dominant societies. On the other hand, after the passage from the colonial situation to situations of dependency of national states, it is observed that: (a) the passage implies the creation of states in answer to the interests of local property-owning classes; (b) these, however, have their structural situation defined within the larger framework of the international capitalist system and are thus connected and subordinated to the conquering bourgeoisies of the western world and to those classes which succeed them; in this way alliances are established *within the country,* even though in contradictory form, to unify external interests with those of the local dominant groups; and (c) as a consequence, the local dominated classes suffer a kind of double exploitation.

The "movement" that had to be understood, then, was that deriving from the contradictions between the external and the internal, viewed in this complex fashion and summed up in the expression "structural dependency." If imperialism was embodied in the penetration of foreign capital (invasions by Americans in the Caribbean, by the English in South America, etc.), it also implied a structural pattern of relations that "internalized" the external and created a state which was formally sovereign and ready to be an answer to the interests of the "nation," but which was simultaneously and contradictorily the instrument of international economic domination. Certainly, the phases and forms of capitalist expansion (colonial-mercantile, mercantile-financial and industrial-financial capitalism, oligopolist forms of "multinationalized" capitalism, etc.) are constituent parts of dependency situations, but the latter are explicable only when those forms cease to be taken as an entelechy or as an abstract and general conditioning factor, and reappear concretely in the analysis of their articulation in each local economy at different moments of time. This process was to be explained not as the "abstract" unreeling of forms of accumulation, but as a historicosocial process through which certain classes impose their domination over others, certain factions of classes ally or oppose themselves to others in political struggles. In this struggle, what appears at first as inevitable because of the "logic of capitalism" is revealed without disguise: one side wins or loses, one form or another of dependency is maintained or makes way for another, the general conditions for capitalist development are sustained or reach their limits, and other forms of social organization are foreseen as a historical possibility.

Thus, right from the initial propositions,[6] dialectical analysis was the point of departure. What was significant was the "movement," the class struggles, the redefinitions of interest, the political alliances that maintained the structures while at the same time opening the possibility of their transformation. The structures were regarded as relations of contradiction, and therefore dynamic.[7]

This aspect of the relations between the internal and the external was quickly accepted and was put forward, with slight variations, in various works.[8] The most competent North American commentators took note of these propositions and saw in them something new.[9] New it certainly was, but within the spirit of efforts that, every ten or fifteen years, in different countries, attempt to recall that dialectical analysis should above all be analysis of contradictions, of the reproduction of forms of domination, and, at the same time, of the transformation and expansion of a given economic form or type of society.

In the process of disseminating these studies in the U.S., however, the characterization of dependency acquired local color. There was a preoccupation with the denunciation of forms of "foreign aid"—the intervention of the CIA in foreign policy, the invisible and Machiavellian hand of the multinationals, etc.—a politically legitimate preoccupation that emphasized real aspects of the contemporary historical process. Little by little, however, this ended by reestablishing the priority of the external over the internal (which may be well-founded), and it led in the end to the elimination of the dynamic proper to dependent societies as a relevant explanatory factor (which is not acceptable). Once again, in metaphysical fashion, the two terms of the opposition—external and internal—were separated, and the opposition passed from dialectical to structural-mechanical, when it was not conceived of in terms of antecedent causes and inert consequences.

The most general and formal of Gunder Frank's works are taken as though they were his best, the formal definition of dependency furnished by Theotonio dos Santos is appended, the problematic of "sub-imperialism" and "marginality" is sometimes inserted, one or another of my works or Sunkel's is footnoted, and the result is a "theory of dependency"—a straw man easy to destroy.

Therefore, instead of demanding an empirico-analytical effort of reconstructing a "concrete whole" with the abovementioned characteristics, dependency came to be consumed as a "theory," implying a corpus of formal and testable propositions. I was always reluctant to use the expression "theory of dependency" because I was afraid of formalizing the approach. Nevertheless, Latin Americans and North Americans began to make the effort to create a "theory." The Latin American authors who moved in that direction were nearly all of Marxist inspiration; although they yielded to the glorious temptation to construct a theory (a temptation that led them to formulate abstract formal definitions and elaborate typologies),[10] they nevertheless held on to the concern for establishing "laws of movement" of "dependent capitalism."[11] In my opinion, they did not always succeed in their difficult undertaking, since there was even a difficulty in logic to be overcome: how to establish a legitimacy that, by definition, is contained in a separate and distinct situation? On the other hand, some North American specialists began clamoring for "internal consistency" in the theory of dependency and established a body of hypotheses deduced from the principle of dependency in order to test them empirically. In this type of reformulation of dependency, the concepts must be one-dimensional and precise and must refer to clearly established variables. With their help it ought to be possible to measure the continuum that goes from "dependency" to "independence" and to characterize variable degrees of dependency.[12]

However, this kind of definition of the notion of dependency also modifies the "theoretical field" of its study: instead of making a dialectical analysis of historical processes, conceiving of them as the result of struggles between classes and groups that define their interests and values in the process of the expansion of a mode of production, history is formalized; the specific contribution that these analyses of dependency might make from a methodological point of view (that is, the idea of contradiction) is withdrawn. The ambiguity, the contradictions, and the more or less abrupt "breaks" in reality are reduced to "operational dimensions" which, by definition, are univocal but static. The result is somewhat like a dialogue between two deaf people, in which one group says: give me precise concepts, with clear dimensions, and I will tell you, after testing them, if the relationships among the variables defined within their theoretical framework conform to the hypotheses which you propose. The other group says: I am not interested in defining univocal concepts; what interests me is pointing out contradictions and formulating relationships in which the *same* thing is transformed into *the other* by means of a process which takes place in time and which brings certain classes or fragments of classes into relation with others through struggle and opposes them to rival blocs—for example, how one and *the same* "national" bourgeoisie is internationalized into *something else,* or how "public servants" are transformed into the "state bourgeoisie" by redefining the allied and enemy camps. In this analytical perspective, processes involve changes in quality and not merely in degree.

The divergence is not merely methodological-formal. It is, rather, at the very heart of studies of dependency. If these studies do in fact have any power of attraction at all, it is not merely because they propose a methodology to substitute for a previously existing paradigm or because they open up a new set of themes. It is principally because they do this from a *radically critical* viewpoint.

Indeed, by admitting that structures have movement and that changes cannot be explained through factors conceived of only as external (which act as conditioning of and interfering in the social process), the dependentistas affirm the existence of domination and struggle. The question, "How does the *transition* from one situation of dependency to another occur?" or "How can situations of dependency be eliminated?" ought to be asked in terms of "Who are the classes and groups which, in the struggle for control or for the reformulation of the existing order (through parties, movements, ideologies, the state, etc.), are making a given structure of domination historically viable or are transforming it?" In these analyses, therefore, there is no presumption of scientific "neutrality." They are to be considered more "true" because they assume that, by discerning which are the historical agents capable of propelling a process of transformation and by providing those agents with theoretical and methodological tools for their struggles, these analyses thus grasp the meaning of historical movement and help to negate a given order of domination.

They are therefore *explanatory because they are critical.* In any case, there is no intention to put "arbitrary" in place of "objective" knowledge. What is intended is an approach that accepts and starts from the idea that history is movement and that structures are the result of impositions; even though these impositions may become crystallized, they contain tensions among classes and groups which always make them, at least potentially, dynamic.

In the struggle that takes place among the components of a structure there are no "dimensions" or "variables" at stake, but tensions between interests, values, appropriations of nature and society, all of which are unequal and in opposition. Therefore, when speaking of "dependent capitalist development," one speaks necessarily and simultaneously of socioeconomic exploitation, unequal distribution of income, the private appropriation of the means of production, and the *subordination* of some economies to others. On the other hand, one also necessarily inquires into the conditions under which this order of affairs is negated.

To sum up, then, studies of dependency continue a live tradition in Latin American thought, reinvigorated in the 1960s by the proposition of themes and problems defined in a theoretical-methodological field not only distinct from what inspired Keynesian and structural-functionalist analyses (the theory of modernization, and of the stages of development that would repeat the history of the industrialized countries), but radically distinct with respect to its inherent critical component. If this kind of study acquired force and penetrated the contemporary intellectual world, it was because it explained more accurately certain changes occurring in Latin America, while certain changes in the countries of the center itself (above all the U.S.), beginning in the 1960s, brought out clearly the inadequacy of the assumptions of structural-functionalism. The protest of American blacks, the war in Vietnam and the movement in opposition to it, the counterculture, the student movement, the feminist movement, etc., all demanded paradigms that were more sensitive to the historical process, to social struggles, and to the transformation of systems of domination. In such a perspective, analyses of dependency correspond better to this search for new models of explanation, not only in order to comprehend what is happening in Latin America, but also what is happening in the U.S.

Up to this point, I have somewhat inelegantly been putting the blame for all the misunderstandings on the consumers of dependency theory, as though the reestablishment of the original myth would resolve all the problems. An ill-disposed critic might quickly respond that I not only content myself with the ritualization of the theme, with more indulgence than Sir Edmund Leach, but I even aspire if not to "true prophethood" at least to being one of the most zealous of apostles.

However, if there have been so many distortions in the consumption, it is because the original production was not clear regarding several of these points, and may even have included, in latent form, much that later appeared as simplification and inconsistency. I shall not repeat here what I have already said in previous works. I want merely to emphasize that, if it is to be judged on the basis of its own assumptions, the point of view of dependency ought to be confronted with at least three types of question:

1. Have dependency studies been able to whet the imagination so that discussion is opened on themes and forms of comprehending reality which are compatible with the contemporary historical process?

2. Does the theoretical representation of the dynamic of this process proposed by dependency studies permit us to comprehend the forms of capitalist expansion on the periphery and realistically to make out the alternatives to it?

3. Do the studies enable us to define the classes and groups that give life to dependent structures through their political struggles? Do they make it possible to go beyond the structural frame of reference in order to clarify the relations between ideologies and social and political movements in specific political conjunctures, so as to assist action to transform reality?

As for the first question, if the initial studies of dependency possessed any novelty, it certainly was not the affirmation that dependency exists, but it was rather the characterization and the search for an explanation of *emerging forms of dependency*. The studies sought to show the meaning of the industrialization of the periphery (and thus the formation of an internal market, since in Latin America this process did not involve the construction of mere export-manufacturing enclaves), under the control of what later came to be called "multinational corporations." The recognition of the effects of this process—the "new dependency"[13]—was the point of departure for reflection on this theme. Today, this appears to constitute another banality. Nevertheless, in Latin America up to the end of the decade of the 1950s there was a deeply rooted conception that the international economic trusts were not interested in the industrialization of the periphery, since they exported finished goods there; their fundamental interest was the control and exploitation of primary agricultural and mineral products. The theory of imperialism reinforced this point of view, which was moreover consistent, at least in part with what happened up to that point. The anti-imperialist struggles were at the same time struggles for industrialization. The local states and national bourgeoisie seemed to be the potential historical agents for capitalist economic development, which in turn was looked upon as a "necessary stage" by a considerable part of critical opinion.

The dependentistas showed that a kind of industrialization was occurring under the control of the multinationals, and they drew certain conclusions from it. There was even an attempt to propose a more general model of the process, to characterize a "transnational capitalism" and to estimate its effects, not only on the periphery, but also on the very center of the capitalist economies.[14]

The revision proposed on the basis of these perspectives—that of the industrialization of the periphery and the internationalization of internal markets—made it possible to generalize the criticisms of the theory that the national bourgeoisies could repeat the function they served in the center as the leaders of the capitalist process in underdeveloped countries. It also displayed the insufficiencies of the theory of modernization and the expectation that there would be stages of development identical to and in the same sequence as those in Europe. From that point on, the question of the state came to be reformulated, and the role of the bureaucracy (and what later on I called the "state bourgeoisies") came to be discussed in greater depth.[15] On the other hand, thanks to the characterization of the specific form of capitalist industrial development on the periphery—where what dominated was oligopolistic-corporative production oriented toward consumption by the high-income classes—numerous hypotheses were advanced and some studies were made on the theme of marginality and of the formation and behavior of the working class.[16]

On balance, the effect of dependency theories on the sociological imagination seems to me to have been positive. Thanks to these theories (but not exclusively so, since the ECLA group had already pointed in that direction), attention was called to a thematic frame that ceased to see capitalist development on the periphery as a mere "consequence" of accumulation of capital in the center, and began dealing with the historical form that this process acquired in dependent societies.

I have more reservations concerning the explanations proposed in many of these studies to account for the historical process. I shall limit myself to one question that has served to divide the dependentistas; that is, the question of the form of analysis of the movement provoked by the expansion of capitalism on the periphery. Here there are two polar modalities (although I simplify somewhat) to conceive of the process of capitalist development:

1. There are those who believe that "dependent capitalism" is based on the hyper-exploitation of labor, that it is incapable of broadening the internal market, that it generates constant unemployment and marginality, and that it presents a tendency to stagnation and a kind of constant reproduction of underdevelopment (thus Gunder Frank, Marini, and to a certain extent, dos Santos).

2. There are those who think that, at least in some countries of the periphery, the penetration of industrial-financial capital accelerates the production of relative surplus-value; intensifies the productive forces; and, if it generates unemployment in the phases of economic contraction, absorbs labor-power in the expansive cycles, producing, in this aspect, an effect similar to capitalism in the advanced countries, where unemployment and absorption, wealth and misery coexist.

Personally I believe the second is more consistent, although the "dependent-associated development" model is not generalizeable to all the periphery. At times the "theory of dependency" is thought to be impugned, or contradictions are seen in it, when it is pointed out that there can be *development* and *dependence* and that there exist more dynamic forms of dependence than those characterizing enclave or quasi-colonial situations (even allowing greater degrees of maneuver to the national states and to the bourgeoisies locally associated to the state and to the multinationals). The argument most commonly used is that in this case a relationship of "interdependence" comes into being. Nevertheless, when one examines the relationship between the economies of "dependent-associated development" and the central economies, it is not hard to perceive that the international division of labor persists, based on very unequal degrees of wealth, on unequal forms of appropriation of the international surplus, and on the monopolization of the dynamic capitalist sectors by the central countries. All of which leaves no doubt about the distinction between central and dependent economies. The sectors of production of capital goods and the generation of new technologies, which are the most revolutionary sectors at the level of productive forces and are decisive in the scheme of extended reproduction of capital, remain in the central nuclei of the multinational firms. And the external debt is oscillating but continuous in the dependent countries.

Finally, in this very summary balance, I also find very debatable the analyses produced up to now to categorize the "historical agents" of social transformations. Both the "stagnationist" or "underconsumptionist" authors—who believe that the internal market is insufficient to make way for the capitalist-dependent expansion—as well as those favorable to the possibility of capitalist development in certain countries of the periphery, have generated up to now a relatively impoverished political analysis. Either they emphasize the "structural possibility" of revolution and go on to discuss the overcoming of dependency in terms of a historical horizon in which socialism appears as the result of growing crises peculiar to a stagnating capitalism, or they foresee a "new barbarism" and display an inclination for repeating clichés that explain little. Those who do not share either idyllic or catastrophic vision (and I am one of them) are reticent concerning the political alternatives. At any rate, the "catastrophists" make a "mechanico-formal" analysis, and the latter either reveal a good will toward an "autonomous capitalism" (although it is not clear how it can be brought about), or they sketch out their hopes of a socialism whose historical *persona* is not described in their analysis, nor perhaps in reality.

Both the mechanico-formal style of those who believe in the ultimate aims of history, guaranteed by the *necessary* structural incapacity of dependent capitalism to expand and reproduce itself, and the elliptical style of those who wish to escape this Frankenstein politics, lead the critics of dependency to the conviction that a catastrophic vision of history or permanent indefinition must be inherent outcomes of this kind of analysis. To avoid this, they ask that better dimensions be defined, so that degrees of dependency may be measured. With these, they think it is possible to demonstrate that as long as the local states increase their capacity to regulate the economy and counterbalance the multinationals, the area of independence will enlarge.

I do not agree with the idea that to improve the quality of analysis, the theory of dependency should be formalized so that, after testing hypotheses derived from this formalization, one could venture out into the world waving the banner of the percentage of variance explained by each factor within the situation of dependence. Instead of asking for analyses within the mold of empiricist structural-functionalism, it would be better to ask for an improvement in the quality of historical-structural analyses.

In saying this, however, I do not want to endorse the ingenuous expectation that theories about dependency explain *everything* or that, if they do not yet explain everything, it is because the method has been badly applied. It is necessary to have a sense—I will not say of proportion—but of the ridiculous, and to avoid the simplistic reductionism so common among the present-day butterfly collectors who abound in the social sciences and who stroll through history classifying types of dependency, modes of production, and laws of development, with the blissful illusion that their findings can remove from history all its ambiguities, conjectures, and surprises. It is necessary, on the contrary, to have the patience for research disciplined by a dialectic that is neither listless nor complacently constructing abstract and general formulations that seek to be taken for syntheses. Luckily, as much as social scientists strive to enclose the structural possibilities of history in their own constructs, history continually makes us *dupes de nous-mêmes,* and astonishes us with unexpected revelations.

NOTES

1. Susanne J. Bodenheimer, *The Ideology of Developmentalism: The American Paradigm Surrogate for Latin American Studies* (Beverly Hills, California: Sage Publications, 1971), esp. "Toward a New Conceptual Framework: The Dependency Model," pp.34–40.
2. Some original formulations of dependency studies try to avoid the simplistic presentation of the subject. The same is true for some commentators. Several books and papers are available in English about "dependency theory." See, for a historical view on Latin American sociology, Joseph A. Kahl, *Modernization, Exploitation, and Dependency in Latin America* (New Brunswick, New Jersey: Transaction Books, 1976). For an extensive review of Latin American literature on dependency, Ronald Chilcote and Joel Edelstein, *Latin America: The Struggle with Dependency and Beyond* (New York: John Wiley and Sons, 1974), "Introduction," pp. 1–87. For some criticism and an alternative but not incompatible perspective, see Albert Hirschman, "A generalized Linkage Approach to Development with Special Reference to Staples," mimeographed, 1975. For a critique and a summary assuming another paradigm, Robert Packenham, "Latin American Dependency Theories: Strengths and Weaknesses," mimeographed. For brief, but consistent summaries, Philip O'Brien, "A Critique of Latin American Theories of Dependency," mimeographed, Glasgow Institute of Latin American Studies; and Juan E. Corradi, "Cultural Dependency and the Sociology of Knowledge: The Latin American Case," in *Ideology and Social Change in Latin America,* ed. June Nash and Juan Corradi. For an overview and bibliography, see Frank Bonilla and Robert Girling, *Structures of Dependency* (Stanford, California: Stanford University Press, 1973).
3. The debate between the "humanistic" and the "ontological" approaches in the interpretation of Marxist dialectics has influenced most of the attempts to use this methodology by Brazilian social scientists. The methodological introduction to my Ph.D. dissertation, "Capitalismo e escravidão no Brasil meridional" (São Paulo, DIFEL, 1962), for instance, expresses this mood. On the other hand, the concept of "project," with all its metaphysical implications, was also behind most of the publications of the influential Brazilian Institute for High Studies (ISEB) since the fifties.
4. The methodology of the book *Dependência e Desenvolvimento* (whose first version was an ILPES document) is quite close to the methodology that I used in previous studies on slavery and capitalism, as well as in research on problems of development and entrepreneurship in Brazil (see, for instance, *Desenvolvimento Econômico e Empresário Industrial no Brasil;* [São Paulo: DIFEL, 1964]). Several other Latin American authors have published since the early fifties attempting to revitalize the dialectical approach.
5. Brazilian literature on this topic is considerable. The classic studies are the well-known books by Roberto Simonsen, Caio Prado, and Celso Furtado on the colonial economy. From the sociological viewpoint, Florestan Fernandes's analysis of slave society and the "ancien régime" provides insight-

ful interpretations. All those books (as well as Octavio Ianni, *As metamorfoses do escravo* [São Paulo: DIFEL, 1963] and my own book on slave society in Southern Brazil) were already published when Gunder Frank discussed his thesis on "feudalism" and "capitalism."

6. This is the perspective of interpretations proposed in F. H. Cardoso and Enzo Faletto, *Dependência e Desenvolvimento* (Santiago: ILPES, 1967). The draft version was distributed in Santiago in 1965.

7. In spite of that, the usual conception of a static analysis of structures leads to misinterpretations of some of my writings. In criticism I have been considered a structuralist in the Levi-Strauss tradition, or even a defender of a non-class-struggle style of analysis. See, for this kind of naive understanding of the methodology that I propose, John Myer, "A Crown of Thorns: Cardoso and the Counter-Revolution," *Latin American Perspectives* 2, no. 1 (Spring 1975).

8. Theotonio dos Santos, for instance, presents a similar view in the study he wrote after the discussion in Santiago of the essay written by Faletto and myself *(Dependencia e Desenvolvimento)*. See dos Santos, *El nuevo carácter de la dependencia* (Santiago: Cuadernos de Estudios Socio-Económicos 10, Centro de Estudios Socio-Económicos [CESO], Universidad de Chile, 1968). In other essays that dos Santos published after his first comprehensive writing about "la nueva dependencia," the same pattern of dialectical and non-mechanical connection between external and internal interests is described in a simple and clear way. See especially, "La crisis de la teoría del desarollo y las relaciones de dependencia en América Latina," in Helio Jaguaribe et al., *La dependencia político-económica de América Latina* (México: Siglo Veintiuno Editores, 1970), pp. 147–87.

9. See, apart from Kahl's book which is more comprehensive in historical terms and is not limited to the discussion on dependency, Bodenheimer, *The Ideology of Developmentalism* and Chilcote and Edelstein, *Latin America*. See also, Packenham, "Latin American Dependency Theories," pp. 4–5.

10. Even dos Santos proposes a formal (and thus static and nonhistorical) definition of dependency in his well known article "The Structure of Dependency" (*American Economic Review* 60, no. 2 [1970]: 231–36). Vania Bambirra also succumbed to the temptation of helping dos Santos to develop a "theory of dependency" or of dependent capitalism, as the latter suggested in his essay "La crisis de la teoría." The result of that attempt was a new typology of forms of dependency and some formal possibilities of structural changes. See Vania Bambirra, *El capitalismo dependente latinoamericano* (México: Siglo Veintiuno Editores, 1974). Bambirra misinterprets the analysis of situations of dependency suggested by Faletto and me when she refers to them as if we were proposing "types" of dependency.

11. The preoccupation with "laws of transformation"—in the Marxist tradition—is quite clear in dos Santos, as well as in Bambirra's book. Rui Mauro Marini, in "Brazilian Sub-imperialism" (*Monthly Review* 9 [February 1972]: 14–24), and *Sub-desarrollo y revolución* (México: Siglo Veintiuno Editores, 1969), refers also to some kind of historical laws. But Marini's views are more analogical-formal than historical-structural and his presentation of dependent capitalism's characteristics (in terms of overexploitation of the labor force and permanent crisis of capital realization) does not fit with the real historical process.

12. Examples of this are Packenham's criticism of dependency studies and, correspondingly, his contributions towards evaluating the performance of states and economies in terms of degrees of independence. See, especially, his article "Trends in Brazilian Dependency since 1964," unpublished. Others, in spite of more adequate understanding about the theoretical meaning of dependency studies, have committed methodological fallacies. One example is the quite provocative paper by Chris Chase-Dunn, "The Effects of International Economic Dependency on Development and Inequalities: A Cross-national Study," unpublished. The author makes comparisons between *different* situations of dependency as if they form part of the same continuum of dependency-independence. The analysis becomes, thus, formal and ahistorical. Even in Durkheim's approach to comparative analyses, some compatibility among structures being analyzed is required to validate the results. Furthermore, in a *historical*-structural approach, the specificity of concrete situations is a precondition for any analytical formulation. Nevertheless, Chase-Dunn does not take into account the basic distinctions between class and political structures in an enclave type of economy, a nationally controlled export economy, and an associated-dependent industrialized one. Mixing data drawn from distinct situations of dependency, he intends to validate or to criticize statements that have been presented as characteristic of specific forms of dependency. I am not arguing against the use of statistics or empirical (historical) data as a means of validation or rejection of theories. I am criticizing the inadequate use of them, in methodological and theoretical terms.

Some other papers present mistakes similar to the above, with an additional characteristic: they replace the theoretical views of dependentistas by the "common-sense meaning of the term" (dependency and imperialism). The pretext for this is the lack of precision in the literature. By precision these authors mean a positivistic approach. After redefining the "theory of dependency" according to their own conceptions they intend to submit it to "empirical test," confronting hypotheses with data. Which hypotheses, how to categorize data, and who are the authors submitted to proof depends, of course, on the arbitrary choice of these empirical and objective cultivators of science. See, for instance, Raymond Duval and Bruce Russett, "Some Proposals to Guide Research on Contemporary Imperialism," unpublished.

13. See *Dependencia y Desenvolvimento,* last chapter, "The New Dependency." Dos Santos took these ideas and developed the characterization in *El nuevo carácter de la dependencia.* Nevertheless, several critics and commentators have not realized the implications of what is *new* in the dependency situations of industrialized Third World countries. Bodenheimer, for instance, kept the perspective of the expansion model of one phase of imperialism as the main feature of "la nueva industrialización": "The international system *today* is characterized by: advanced industrial capitalism . . . the dominant nations need raw materials and, more important, commodities and capital markets" ("Dependency and Imperialism: The Roots of Latin American Underdevelopment," in *Readings in U.S. Imperialism,* ed. K. T. Fann and Donald C. Hodges [Boston: Porter Sargent, 1971]). p. 161. Moreover, Bodenheimer's concept of the "infra-structure of dependency" relates basically to the multinational corporations. Thus, again, the *external* forces are supposed to reshape internal structures without internal mediation: "The infra-

structure of dependency may be seen as the functional equivalent of a formal colonial apparatus," sustained by client-classes which play, in "modern" Latin America, the historical role of a "comprador bourgeoisie" (see pp. 161–63). In this approach the functional-formalistic method is alive again, not because of the use of the expression "functional equivalent" by itself, but because Bodenheimer is comparing situations (the "colonial" and the "modern capitalist") constructed without historical content, as Gunder Frank sometimes does when he refers to feudalism and capitalism.

14. In this respect, the most influential essay was Osvaldo Sunkel, "Transnational Capitalism and National Disintegration in Latin America," *Social and Economic Studies* (University of the West Indies) 22, no. 1 (March 1973). Celso Furtado wrote some recent articles on contemporary capitalism, stressing the reorganization of the international market under the control of multinationals and its consequences for international political domination.

15. The importance of state bureaucracy and state enterprises in Latin America was stressed by several dependentistas. See, dos Santos, "La crisis de la teoría del desarollo," and "Dependencia económica y alternativas de cambio en América Latina" (*Revista Mexicana de Sociología* 32, no. 2 [March-April 1970]: 416–63). My own views on the subject can be found in *Autoritarismo e Democratizacão* (Rio de Janeiro: Paz e Terra, 1975). See, for more recent developments in the discussion of the role of the state, the insightful essay by Guillermo O'Donnell, "Reflexiones sobre las tendencias generales de cambio en el Estado burocrático-autoritario" (Buenos Aires: CEDES, 1975; to appear in LARR 13, no. 1. Marcos Kaplan published pioneering essays on the nature of the state in dependent societies. See, esp., his "Estado, dependencia externa y desarrollo en América Latina" (*Estudios Internacionales* 2, no. 2 [July-September 1968]: 179–213). Francisco Weffort published a well known, illuminating essay on "State and Masses" (*Revista Latinoamericana de Sociología* [*Buenos Aires, 1977*]).

16. This is not the occasion to recall the discussion on "marginality," to which Anibal Quijano and José Nun have contributed. Recent research and criticism seem to reorient the discussion by assuming other hypotheses with respect to employment, marginality, and industrialization. See Paul Singer as well as Elizabeth Balan and Lucio Kowarick in various issues of CEBRAP's *Cuadernos* and *Estudios*. Vilmar Faria in his Ph.D. dissertation "Urban Marginality as a Structural Phenomenon: An Overview of the Literature" (Harvard University, 1976), not only summarizes previous discussions, but proposes new approaches to the subject, taking into consideration empirical evidence and theoretical elaborations on the question of employment and capitalist development, without the "stagnationist" bias.

Patterns and Perspectives of the Capitalist World-Economy

Professor Wallerstein outlines key concepts and propositions associated with the world-capitalist system.

1. THE NATURE OF THE WORLD-ECONOMY

1.1. The concept world-economy (*économie-monde* in French) should be distinguished from that of world economy (*économie mondiale*) or international economy. The latter concept presumes there are a series of separate "economies" which are "national" in scope, and that under certain circumstances these "national economies" trade with each other, the sum of these (limited) contacts being called the international economy. Those who use this latter concept argue that the limited contacts have been expanding in the 20th century. It is thus asserted that the world has become "one world" in a sense it wasn't prior to the 20th century.

By contrast, the concept "world-economy" assumes that there exists an "economy" wherever (and if but only if) there is an ongoing extensive and relatively complete social division of labor with an integrated set of production processes which relate to each other through a "market" which has been "instituted" or "created" in some complex way. Using such a concept, the world-economy is not new in the 20th century, nor is it a coming together of "national economies," none of the latter constituting complete divisions of labor. Rather, a world-economy, capitalist in form, has been in existence in at least part of the globe since the 16th century. Today, the entire globe is operating within the framework of this singular social division of labor we are calling the capitalist world-economy.

1.2. The capitalist world-economy has, and has had since its coming into existence, boundaries far larger than that of any political unit. Indeed, it seems to be one of the basic defining features of a capitalist

Reprinted with permission of Immanuel Wallerstein and *Contemporary Marxism,* No. 9 1984 (Synthesis Publications, San Francisco © 1984. Originally prepared for Seminar on Culture and Thought in the Transformation of the World (third international seminar of the United Nations University Project on Socio-Cultural Development Alternatives in a Changing World), held in Algiers, 13–17 December 1981.

world-economy that there exists no political entity with ultimate authority in all its zones.

Rather, the political superstructure of the capitalist world-economy is an interstate system within which and through which political structures called "sovereign states" are legitimized and constrained. Far from meaning the total autonomy of decision-making, the term "sovereignty" in reality implies a formal autonomy combined with real limitations on this autonomy, which are implemented both via the explicit and implicit rules of the interstate system and via the power of other states in the interstate system. No state in the interstate system, even the single most powerful one at any given time, is totally autonomous—but obviously some enjoy far greater autonomy than others.

1.3. The world-economy is a complex of cultures—in the sense of languages, religions, ideologies—but this complex is not haphazard. There exists a *Weltanschauung* of imperium, albeit one with several variants, and there exist cultures of resistance to this imperium.

1.4. The major social institutions of the capitalist world-economy—the states, the classes, the "peoples," and the households—are all shaped (even created) by the ongoing workings of the world-economy. None of them are primordial, in the sense of permanent, pre-existing, relatively fixed structures to which the working of the capitalist world-economy are exogenous.

1.5. The capitalist world-economy is a *historical* social system. It came into existence, and its genesis must be explained. Its existence is defined by certain patterns—both cyclical rhythms and secular trends—which must be explicated. It is highly probable that it will one day go out of existence (become transformed into another type of historical social system), and we can therefore assess the historical alternatives that are before us.

2. THE PATTERNS OF THE WORLD-ECONOMY

All historical structures constantly evolve. However, the use of any concept is a capturing in fixed form of some continuing pattern. We could not discern the world, interpret it, or consciously change it unless we used concepts, with all the limitations that any reification, however slight, implies.

2.1. The world-economy has a capitalist mode of production. This is an empirical statement. Although there have been other world-economies (as defined above) known in history, the modern one of which we are speaking is the only one which has survived over a long period of time without either disintegrating or being transformed into a world-empire (with a singular political structure). This modern one has had a capitalist mode of production—that is, its economy has been dominated by those who operate on the primacy of endless accumulation, such entrepreneurs (or controllers of production units) driving from the arena those who seek to operate on other premises. Since only one world-economy has survived over a long period of time, and since this one has been capitalist in form, we may suspect that the two phenomena are theoretically linked: that a world-economy to survive must have a capitalist mode of production, and inversely that capitalism cannot be the mode of production except in a system that has the form of a world-economy (a division of labor more extensive than any one political entity).

2.2. The capitalist world-economy has operated via a social relationship called capital/labor, in which the surplus created by direct producers has been appropriated by others either at the point of production or at the most immediate market place, in either case by virtue of the fact that the appropriators control the "capital" and that their "rights" to the surplus are legally guaranteed. The extractors of surplus-value may in many cases be individuals, but they have tended increasingly to be collective entities (private or state corporations).

2.3. Once surplus-value has been extracted, it has yet to be "distributed" among a network of beneficiaries. The exchange processes of the "market" are one mode through which this redistribution occurs. In particular, the structure of the world-economy permits an unequal exchange of goods and services (primarily trans-state), such that much of the surplus-value extracted in the peripheral zones of the world-economy is transferred to the core zones.

2.4. The exchange of products containing unequal amounts of social labor we may call the core/periphery relationship. This is pervasive, continuing, and constant. There tend to be geographical localizations of productive activities such that core-like production activities and periphery-like production activities tend each to be spatially grouped together. We can thus, for shorthand purposes, refer to some states as core states and others as peripheral states.

2.5. Insofar as some states function as loci of mixed kinds of production activities (some core-like, some periphery-like), we can speak of such states as semi-peripheral. There always exist semi-peripheral zones.

2.6. While the pattern of a spatial hierarchy of production processes within the capitalist world-economy is a constant, the position of any given state is not, since there have been regular partial relocations of core-like and periphery-like economic activities.

2.7. Since what makes a production process core-like or periphery-like is the degree to which it incorporates labor-value, is mechanized, and is highly profitable, and all these characteristics shift over time for any given product because of "product cycles," it follows that no product is inherently core-like or periphery-like, but has that characteristic for a given time. Nonetheless, there are always some products which are core-like and others which are periphery-like at any given time.

2.8. Because the imperatives of accumulation operate via the individual decisions of entrepreneurs, each seeking to maximize his profit—the so-called anarchy of production—there is an inherent tendency to the expansion of absolute volume of production in the world-economy. Profit can, however, only be realized if there is effective demand for the global product. World effective demand, however, is a function of the sum of political arrangements in the various states (the result of prior class struggles), which determine the real distribution of the global surplus. These arrangements are stable for intermediate periods of time. Consequently, world supply expands at a steady rate while world demand remains relatively fixed for intermediate periods. Such a system must result, and historically has resulted, in recurring bottlenecks for accumulation, which are translated into periods of economic stagnation. The A-phases of expansion and the B-phases of stagnation seem to have occurred historically in cycles of 40–55 years (sometimes called "Kondratieff cycles").

2.9. Each period of stagnation has created pressures to restructure the network of production processes and the social relations that underlie them in ways that would overcome bottlenecks to accumulation. Among the mechanisms that have operated to renew expansion are:

a. reduction of production costs of former core-like products by further mechanization and/or relocation of these activities in lower-wage zones;
b. creation of new core-like activities ("innovation"), which promise high initial rates of profit, thus encouraging new loci of investment;
c. an intensified class struggle both within the core states and between groups located in different states such that there may occur at the end of the process some political redistribution of world surplus to workers in core zones (often by means of fully proletarianizing hitherto semi-proletarian households) and to bourgeois in semi-peripheral and peripheral zones, thereby augmenting world effective demand;
d. expansion of the outer boundaries of the world-economy, thereby creating new pools of direct producers who can be involved in world production as semi-proletarianized workers receiving wages below the cost of reproduction.

2.10. States in which core-like activities occur develop relatively strong state apparatuses which can advance the interests of their bourgeoisies, less by protection (a mechanism of the medium-strong seeking to be stronger) than by preventing other states from erecting political barriers to the profitability of these activities. In general, states seek to shape the world market in ways that will advance the interests of some enterpreneurs against that of others.

2.11. There seem to be cycles as well, within the interstate system. On three separate occasions, one state has been able to achieve what may be called a hegemonic position in the world-economy: the United Provinces, 1620–1650; the United Kingdom, 1815–1873; the United

States, 1945–1967. When producers located within a given state can undersell producers located in other core states in the latter's "home market," they can over time transform this production advantage into one in the commercial arena and then into one in the financial arena. The combined advantages may be said to constitute hegemony and are reflected as well in a political-military advantage in the interstate system. Such hegemonies are relatively short-lived, since the production advantages cannot be sustained indefinitely and mechanisms of the balance of power intrude to reduce the political advantage of the single most powerful state.

2.12. The core states in general, and the hegemonic state when one exists in particular, seek to reinforce the advantages of their producers and to legitimize their role in the interstate system by imposing their cultural dominance on the world. To some extent, this occurs in the easily visible form of language, religion, and mores, but more importantly this occurs in the form of seeking to impose modes of thought and analysis, including in particular the paradigms that inform philosophy and the sciences/social sciences.

3. THE SECULAR TRENDS OF THE WORLD-ECONOMY

The patterns of the world-economy may be at first glance cyclical in form, but they are not perfectly cyclical. The world-economy has a historical development which is structural and can be analyzed in terms of its secular trends.

3.1. The drive to accumulate leads to the constant deepening of the capitalist development. The search to reduce long-term costs of production leads to a steady increase in the degree to which production is mechanized. The search for the least expensive source of factors of production (including as an expense delays in time in acquiring access) leads to a steady increase in the degree to which these factors (land, labor, and goods) are commodified. The desire to reduce barriers to the process of accumulation leads to a steady increase in the degree to which economic transactions are contractualized. It is important to recognize two things about these processes of mechanization, commodification, and contractualization.

3.1.1. While there are regular increases in the world-economy taken as a whole of the degree of mechanization, commodification, and contractualization, the pattern is not linear but stepwise, each significant advance leading to overall expansion, and each overall stagnation leading to a restructuring of the world-economy such that there is further advance.

3.1.2. The capitalist development of the world-economy at the world level is far from complete in the 20th century. These processes are still in full operation.

3.2. The recurring stagnations of the world-economy, which have led to the regular restructuring of this world-economy, have involved as part of restructuring the expansion of the "outer" boundaries of the world-economy, a process which, however, has been nearly completed as of now. This expansion, which was central to world history of the past several hundred years, gradually eliminated from the globe other kinds of historical social systems, creating the historically unique situation of there being, for all effects and purposes, a single social division of labor on the earth.

3.3. The steady but still incomplete commodification of labor, side by side with the now largely completed expansion of the outer boundaries of the world-economy, accounts for the shape of two of the major institutional structures of the capitalist world-economy: the classes and the households.

3.3.1. The commodification of labor ultimately means a structure in which direct producers have no access to the means of production except by selling their labor-power on a market; that is, they become proletarians. Although the percentage of direct producers who are full-lifetime proletarians has been growing worldwide over time, nonetheless, even today such proletarians are still probably no more than half of the world's work force.

3.3.2. The commodification of land and capital ultimately means a structure in which controllers of land or capital (including "human capital") have no access to the maintenance and reproduction of land and capital except by pursuing an active policy of maximizing the accumulation of capital; that is, they become bourgeois. In the 20th century, there are very few who control land or capital—directly (individually) or indirectly (collectively)—who are not bourgeois, that is, persons whose economic raison d'être is the accumulation of capital.

3.3.3. Hence, we have a situation in which a part but not all of the direct producers are (full-lifetime) proletarians (the other part we may designate as "semi-proletarians"), but most of the controllers of land and capital are bourgeois.

3.3.4. The creation of two large worldwide classes has led to the molding of appropriate household structures as the member-units of these classes. We mean by household the unit which, over a longish (30–50 year) period, pools the income of all its members, from whatever source and in whatever form is this income.

3.3.5. The "semi-proletarian" household, so extensive in peripheral zones of the world-economy, permits the wage-employment of some of its members for parts of their lives at wages below the proportionate cost of reproduction by pooling this wage-income with that received from subsistence, petty commodity, rental, and transfer income. This is what is meant by "super-exploitation" (since in this case the employer of the wage-laborer is receiving not merely the surplus-value created by the wage-laborer, but that which other members of the household are creating).

3.3.6. The proletarian household, tending to receive wage-income approximating the real costs of reproduction (no less but also not much more) tends to move in the direction of more "nucleated" households, sloughing off *affines* and others not defined as pulling their full weight.

3.3.7. The bourgeois household, seeking to maximize the use of capital, the direct control of which tends to increase by age, and utilizing the family structure as the primary mechanism of avoiding social redistribution, tends to take the form of extended, multilocal households.

3.4 The steady (now largely completed) expansion of the outer boundaries of the world-economy, combined with the continuing competition among bourgeois for advantage in the capitalist world-economy, accounts for the shape of the other two major institutional structures of the capitalist world-economy: the states and the peoples.

3.4.1. The drive of bourgeois for competitive advantage has led to increasing definition ("power") of the states as political structures and increasing emphasis on their constraint by the interstate system. This push for a "strong" state (strong vis-à-vis both other internal loci of power and vis-à-vis other states and external nonstate forces) has been greatest and therefore most efficacious in those states with core-like production activities. The strong state has been the principal mechanism by which the bourgeois controlling these core-like production activities have been able a) to limit and moderate the economic demands of their national work forces, b) to shape the world market so as to compete effectively with bourgeoisies located in other states, and c) to incorporate new zones into the world-economy, thus constantly re-creating new centers of peripheral production activities.

3.4.2. The increasing definition of state structures has led to the shaping, reshaping, creation, destruction, revival of "peoples." To the extent that these "peoples" are defined by themselves (and by others) as controlling or having the "moral" right to control state structures, these "peoples" become "nations." To the extent that they are not defined as having the right to control a state structure, these people become "minorities" or "ethnic groups." Defining given states as nation–states is an aid in strengthening the state. Such a definition requires emphasizing one "people" and de-emphasizing, even destroying (conceptually or literally), others. This is particularly important for semi-peripheral states seeking to transform their structural role in the world-economy. Various groups have interests supporting and opposing any particular nation–state definition. "Nationalism" is a mechanism both of imperium/integration and of resistance/liberation. The peoples are not haphazardly defined but neither are they simple and unfixed derivations from a historical past. They are solidarity groupings whose boundaries are a matter of constant social transmittal/redefinition.

3.5. As the classes come to be defined vis-à-vis the developing division of labor in the world-economy and the peoples come to be defined vis-à-vis the increasing rationalized interstate system, the locational concentration of various oppressed groups gives rise over time to anti-systemic movements. These movements have organized in two main forms around two main themes: the social movement around "class" and the national movement around "nation" or people.

3.5.1. The seriously anti-systemic (or revolutionary) forms of such movements first emerged in *organized* form in the 19th century. Their general objective, human equality, was by definition incompatible with the functioning of the capitalist world-economy, a hierarchical system based on uneven development, unequal exchange, and the appropriation of surplus-value. However, the political structure of the capitalist world-economy—the fact that it was not a single unit but a series of sovereign states—pressed the movements to seek the transformation of the world-system via the achievement of political power within separate states. The organization of these anti-systemic movements at the state level had contradictory effects.

3.5.2. Organization at the state level for the social movement was ideologically confusing from the beginning, as it counterposed the logical and ideological necessity of worldwide struggle (proletarian internationalism) against the immediate political need of achieving power within one state. Either the social movement resisted "nationalism" and was rendered inefficacious or it utilized nationalism and then faced ambiguously the so-called "national question"—that is, the "nationalisms" of the "minorities" within the boundaries of the state. Whatever the tactic of a given social movement, the achievement of partial or total state power involved power in a structure constrained by the interstate system, hence unable by itself to transform the system entirely (that is, to withdraw totally from the capitalist world-economy).

3.5.3. Organization at the state level created dilemmas for the national movements as well. The smaller the zone within which the national movement defined itself, the easier the access to state power but the less consequential. Hence, all national movements have oscillated in terms of the unit of definition, and the various "pan-" movements have had limited success. But defeats of "pan-" movements have tended to dilute the anti-systemic thrust of particular national movements.

3.5.4. In general, both social and national movements have had a difficult time reconciling long-run anti-systemic objectives and short-run "developmentalist" or "catching-up" objectives, which tend to reinforce rather than undermine the world-system. Nonetheless, the collective momentum of the social and national movements over time has been anti-systemic in effect, despite the "reformism" or "revisionism" of the various movements taken separately. Furthermore, the collective momentum of these movements has been such as to confound increasingly the social and national movements, which has in fact been a source of additional strength.

3.6. The unfolding of the institutional structures of the world-system—the classes, the states, the peoples, the households—has been reflected in the cultural mosaic of the world-system, whose pattern has been increasingly that of the tension between imperium and resistance.

3.6.1. As the axial division of labor became more pronounced and more unequal, the need to facilitate its operation through the allocation of work forces and the justification of inequality led to an ideology of racism that became the central organizing cultural theme of the world bourgeoisie. The existence of superior groups (whether in particular instances these groups were defined as Caucasians or Anglosaxons or other variants on this theme) became a method of simple *triage* in job and income allocation.

3.6.2. Whereas racism has served as a mechanism of worldwide control of direct producers, the bourgeoisie of strong core states (and particularly of the hegemonic power) sought also to direct the activities of the bourgeois of other states and various middle strata worldwide into channels that would maximize the close integration of production processes and the smooth operation of the interstate system such that the accumulation of capital was facilitated. This required the creation of a world bourgeois cultural framework that could be grafted onto "national" variations. This was particularly important in terms of science and technology, but quite important too in the realm of political ideas and of the social sciences.

3.6.3. The concept of a neutral "universal" culture to which the cadres of the world division of labor would be "assimilated" (the passive tense being important here) hence came to serve as one of the pillars of the world-system as it historically evolved. The exaltation of progress, and later of "modernization," summarized this set of ideas, which served less as true norms of social action than as status-symbols of obeisance and of participation in the world's upper strata.

3.6.4. Resistance to this cultural assimilationism was to be found among competitive bourgeois in semi-peripheral and nonhegemonic core states and took the form of asserting the autonomy of "national" traditions and/or antipathy to structural generalizations in the domain of ideas. It also took the form of reinforcing alternative world linguistic groupings to the hegemonic one (in practice, of English).

3.6.5. More fundamental cultural resistance on the part of anti-systemic movements has come slowly to take the form of positing civilizational alternatives to dominant cultural forms. In particular, it has counterdistinguished civilizations (plural) to civilization (singular and imperial).

4. THE SYSTEM IN CRISIS

4.1. A system that has cyclical patterns has recurring downturns, whatever we wish to call them. We have argued the regularity of world economic stagnations as one of the patterns of the capitalist world-economy.

But insofar as there are also mechanisms that regularly bring these stagnations to an end and relaunch world economic expansion, we cannot count these cyclical downturns as crises, however much they are perceived as such by the individuals living through them.

4.2. Rather, a "crisis" is a situation in which the restitutive mechanisms of the system are no longer functioning well, and therefore the system will either be transformed fundamentally or disintegrate. It is in this sense that we could talk for example of the "crisis of feudalism" in Europe in the period 1300–1450, a crisis whose resolution was the historic emergence of a capitalist world-economy located in that particular geographic arena. We may say that this capitalist world-economy in turn entered into a long "crisis" of a comparable nature in the 20th century, a crisis in the midst of which we are living.

4.3. The causes of the crisis are internal to the system, the result of the contradictions built into the process.

4.3.1. One of the mechanisms whereby the world-economy has overcome its downturn phases has been the expansion of the outer boundaries of the world-economy, but this is a process which has inbuilt limits which are nearly reached.

4.3.2. Another of the mechanisms whereby the world-economy has overcome its downturn phases has been the expansion of world effective demand, in part through proletarianization of the direct producers, in part by redistribution of the surplus among the world bourgeoisie.

4.3.2.1. Proletarianization is also a process that has inbuilt limits. While they have hardly yet been reached, the process has been speeding up, and one can foresee it reaching its asymptote within the coming century.

4.3.2.2. Redistribution of the surplus among the bourgeoisie is itself the result of bourgeoisification, which has entailed an increase of the total percentage of the world population who are bourgeois. If one distinguishes between the small group of bourgeois who control most of the fixed capital and the much larger group of bourgeois who control principally human capital, the growth and social concentration of the latter group have resulted in their acquisition of considerable political power in core states. They have been able, as the price of their political support for the world-system as a system, to ensure that an increasing proportion of the appropriated surplus will be redistributed to them, reducing over the long run the rate of profit to the holders of fixed capital.

4.4. Increasing proletarianization and the increasing constraint on individual mobility because of the degree to which definitions of peoples have been linked to position in the world-economy have led to the rise of the anti-systemic movements. These movements have a cumulative effect which may be said to draw a logarithmic curve. We have entered into the phase of acute escalation.

4.5. The fact that we are in a systemic crisis and have been in one at least since the Russian Revolution—which was its symbolic detonator and has always been seen as such—does not mean that the capitalist development of the world-economy has come to an end. Quite the contrary. It is as vigorous as ever, perhaps more so. This is indeed the prime cause of the crisis. The very vigor of capitalist development has been and will continue to be the main factor that exacerbates the contradictions of the system.

4.6. It is therefore not the case that the crisis will be imminently resolved. A crisis of a system is a long, slow, difficult process, and for it to play itself out over a 150-year period is scarcely surprising. We have little perspective on it as we are amidst it, and we therefore tend to exaggerate each minor fork in the road. There is some constructive value in being overly optimistic in a short run, but the negative side of such exaggeration is the disillusionments it breeds. A crisis is best navigated by a cool, long-run strategy. It cannot however be totally planned, as the crisis itself gives rise to new possibilities of human action.

5. PROSPECTIVES

There are three different logics which are playing themselves out in the present world crisis. The outcome will be the result of their interaction.

5.1. There is the logic of socialism.

5.1.1. The capitalist development of the world-economy itself moves toward the socialization of the productive process. There is an *organizational* (as opposed to a political) imperative in which the full achievement of capitalist relations of production—through its emphasis on the increase of relative surplus-value and the maximum efficiency (free flow) of the factors of production—pushes toward a fully planned single productive organizational network in the world-economy.

5.1.2. Furthermore, the political logic of the appropriation of surplus by the few leads to the growth of the anti-systemic movements and therefore toward the spread of socialist values among the world's direct producers.

5.1.3. Finally, the structure of the world-economy (multiple states within the division of labor) has created the possibility of socialist political movements coming to power in individual states, seeking to "construct socialism." Despite the fact that their continued location in the capitalist world-economy and the interstate system seriously constrains the kinds of transformations they can effectuate within boundaries of a given state, their attempts to approximate in various ways a socialist order create additional institutional pressures on the world-system to move in the direction of socialism.

5.2. There is also the logic of domination.

5.2.1. Insofar as the powerful have, by definition, more power than the mass of the world population, and insofar as the process of transformation is slow and contradictory, it creates much opportunity for the ruling strata (the world bourgeoisie) to invent modes of continuity of power and privilege. The adoption of new social roles and new ideological clothing may be a route for existing dominant strata to perpetuate themselves in a new system. It is certainly the logic of domination that dominant groups seek to survive even a "crisis." As the landowning hero of de Lampedusa's *Il Gattopardo* says: "We must change everything in order that everything remain the same."

5.2.2. In the process of the world bourgeoisie seeking to retain their power, they may engage in policies which lead to a nuclear world war. This could bring about a demise of the present system in a manner that would destroy much of the forces of production and thereby make a socialist world order far less structurally feasible.

5.3. There is a logic of the civilizational project.

5.3.1. While the capitalist world-economy has been the first and only social system that has managed to eliminate from the earth all contemporaneous social systems, this has been historically true only for a very recent period of time. We could regard it as simply the conquest by Western Europeans of the globe. In this case, in the long run of history, the political and technological supremacy of the West constitutes a short interval and, from the perspective of alternative "civilizational" centers, might be thought of as a transitory and aberrant interlude. There is thus a drive for a restituted civilizational balance, which the very process of capitalist development of the world-economy makes more urgent and more realizable.

5.3.2. How a restituted civilizational balance fits in, however, with world socialism on the one hand and the drive of world ruling strata to survive on the other is not at all clear.

5.4. We live facing real historical alternatives. It is clear that the capitalist world-economy cannot survive, and that as a historical social system it is in the process of being superseded. The forces at play are also clear, as are the secular trends. We can struggle for our preferences. We can analyze probabilities. But we cannot foretell, because we cannot yet know for certain how the conjuncture of forces at play will constrain the directions of change and even less can we know what new possibilities of human liberation they will afford. The only thing of which we may be certain is that our present activity will be a major factor in the outcome of the crisis.

CHAPTER FIVE

Normative Considerations and International Relations Theory

In recent years, textbooks on international relations have been conspicuous for the absence of much discussion of **normative** or value considerations.[1] This is a rather strange turn of events in that the intellectual traditions underlying realism, pluralism, and globalism are a blend of normative (what *should* be the case?) and **empirical** questions (what *is* the case?). For writers as divergent as Machiavelli, Kant, Carr, Madison, or Marx it was inconceivable to discuss politics without at least some attention to the relation between facts and values. The two were thought by them to be inseparable.

In this chapter, we raise some of the issues and value considerations central to an understanding of normative international relations theory. When, if ever, is war just, and what is just conduct in war? Is the global distribution of wealth equitable, and if not, what authoritative steps should be taken to alter the status quo? On what moral bases should statesmen make foreign policy choices? It is not our intention here to delve deeply into such complex questions, an enterprise well beyond the scope of this effort. Over the centuries, many international relations theorists have grappled with value questions, and we want to alert the reader to some of the most critical of these.

Second, we also want to recognize normative international relations theory building as a legitimate enterprise worthy of more scholarly efforts than has been the case in recent years. As discussed in Chapter One, normative theory differs fundamentally from empirical theory. Propositions in normative theory that deal with what *ought* to be are not subject to the formal empirical tests of hypotheses about what *is*, which is the realm of empirical theory. This fact does not make normative theory any less important, however. Choices among competing alternatives made by policymakers are informed not just by knowledge of what *is* or could be but also by a rationale for what *ought* to be. Developing the basis for such value choices is the domain of normative theory.

Finally, value orientations are present even among empirical theorists in all three international relations images we identify. *What* is studied and *how* it is studied are preferences that vary from theorist to theorist across all three images. True, empirical theorists try to minimize the effect of individual value bias through objective testing of hypotheses, but personal values cannot be filtered out completely. We have recognized these value preferences in previous chapters, but we find it useful to identify them explicitly in this chapter as well.

MORAL CHOICE: ALTERNATIVE CRITERIA

Various criteria exist for providing guidance as to what constitutes **moral** choice in international relations. The **relativist** position—that values are not universal in character but are specific to a particular culture, situation, or set of circumstances—holds that such universal criteria cannot be devised or discerned. This relativist view is rejected by those who hold to **Kantian, utilitarian,** and **social contract** bases for moral choice. If what is *right* is so variable as potentially to mean so many different things to the relativist, then does it really mean anything?

Relativist thinking is, therefore, a rejection of the universalist tradition in Western thought that has its roots in ancient Stoic and Roman writings. For example, the Roman orator Cicero (106–43 B.C.) states that "true law is right reason in agreement with nature; it is of universal application, unchanging and everlasting." He asserts: "Justice is one; it binds all society, and is based on one law." Indeed, he observes: "Justice does not exist at all if it does not exist in Nature."[2]

This universalism was the basis for the idea of a law common to the nations of the Roman empire. That values transcend a single community or state, thus having truly global reach *and* that they are revealed in scripture or can be discovered as part of natural law by use of right reason would be central to the thought of Augustine, Aquinas, and other religious writers of the Middle Ages. As discussed in Chapter Two, Grotius and others would provide a secular basis for international law—whether based on general principles, customary international practice, the writings of jurists, or treaties or conventions voluntarily undertaken by states. The important point, however, is that values exist that are applicable to all leaders and their states.

Immanuel Kant (1724–1804), whose work has already been mentioned in Chapter Three, is best known for his writings on ethics and reason, but he also addressed war and peace in international society. According to Kant, the individual has free will to choose the correct moral course, clearly a **voluntarist** position. Individual behavior is not predetermined, but the individual is obligated, nevertheless, to follow the moral law that is discoverable through the proper exercise of reason. What this means is that the individual is to treat other human beings as ends worthy in themselves, not just as means. Moreover, the correct prescription for moral conduct is knowable by the individual and amounts to those precepts that have universally binding character.[3]

It is this universal dimension in Kantian ethics that is also the basis for his thinking on international relations. The Kantian ideal was a cosmopolitan international society of individuals, states, or other actors following ethical principles and aiming toward perfection. In other words, "right reason" is to be used to discern obligations stemming from a universal law that transcends the laws made by individual states. This was to be the path toward "perpetual peace"—a world free of war. A federation of peaceful states could (but would not necessarily) come to be established as a response to the very real security needs of states.

By contrast to Kantian ethics, the writings of Jeremy Bentham (1748–1832), John Stuart Mill (1806–1873), and others focus on attaining the greatest good for the greatest number as the principal criterion of utilitarian thought. A "society is rightly ordered," according to utilitarians, if "its major institutions are arranged so as to achieve the greatest net balance of satisfaction."[4] In principle, utilitarian and Kantian criteria may provide a philosophical basis for international law because the application of these criteria transcends the boundaries of any given state or society. In practice, however, given the present division of the world into separate, sovereign states with very different perspectives on global issues, it is not clear that either Kantian or utilitarian ethics *can*, as a practical matter, be the basis for constructing some radically new and just world order.

Yet another approach to finding a guide to right behavior is that of the social contract: that individuals may voluntarily agree to bind or obligate themselves to some set of principles. In Rousseau's stag hunt discussed in Chapter Two, the hunters in a state of nature can be understood as maximizing individual, short-term self-interest by going for the hare. In a Hobbesian world of no sovereign authority to compel collaboration or to force the honoring of contracts, no other outcome can be expected. On the other hand, by making assumptions different from Hobbes about human beings in a hypothetical state of nature, there is at least the possibility that the hunters may agree to upgrade their common interest by collaborating to hunt the stag. Such agreement is a social contract in its most primitive form. Binding obligations are made as a voluntary, positive act.

Building on this approach as a means to finding justice, for example, John Rawls asks what would be considered fair if individuals were in a state of nature and none knew in advance what one's place in society, class position, or social status would be. Behind this common "veil of ignorance" about outcomes, what principles of **distributive justice** would these hypothetically free agents choose?

One principle taken from Rawls' analysis is that "all social values—liberty and opportunity, income and wealth, and the bases of self-respect—are to be distributed equally unless an unequal distribution of any, or all, of these values is to everyone's advantage."[5] Beyond that, socioeconomic inequality is admissible only if it benefits everyone in society and if there is an equal opportunity for everyone to acquire those positions associated with unequal rewards. Whether one extends such propositions as the basis for global justice for individuals or for states as if they were individuals is not altogether clear. Rawls himself makes no such claim. Indeed, he formulates a "conception of justice for the basic structure of society" and observes that "the conditions of the law of nations may require different principles arrived at in a somewhat different way."[6] Nevertheless, Rawls' notion of justice could conceivably provide the philosophical basis for the demands of poor Third World countries for a new international economic order designed to reduce the gap between **North** and **South.**

If social contract theory cannot be applied to states as if they were persons, it cannot be a source of moral or legal obligations among states. If one allows it, however, to be applied to states (as if they were individual persons) social contract becomes the basis for a **positivist** interpretation of international law. Among positivists, international law and the obligation to follow other international rules or norms stem not from natural law or religious notions but from affirmative actions taken by states. Kantian, utilitarian, or other principles may be part of the calculus of deciding which rules are to be made binding, but it is the voluntary contract, or choice, made by states in the form of a treaty, convention, or customary practice (so routine in performance as to amount to an implicit contract) that creates the obligation. That there is no higher authority to enforce obligations undertaken by states makes them no less binding in principle.

Values, therefore, are not new to the study of international relations. They may be addressed in terms of "right reason" to discern obligations stemming from some natural law. Alternatively, they may conform more closely to a positivist approach to constructing international law—that treaties, for example, are binding *(pacta sunt servanda)* and that such obligations *ought* to be kept. The Kantian perspective in particular contrasts sharply with the views of Machiavelli and Hobbes described in Chapter Two. Although values and value choices certainly are present in classic realism, power and the balance of power have clearly been the more important considerations in this tradition. It is, however, incorrect to view power and values as if they were mutually exclusive approaches to international politics. As E. H. Carr noted:

The utopian who dreams that it is possible to eliminate self-assertion from politics and to base a political system on morality alone is just as wide of the mark as the realist who believes that altruism is an illusion and that all political action is self-seeking.[7]

In short, international politics involves a blend of values and power, utopianism and realism. Such a perspective can be found in virtually all the intellectual precursors and influences discussed in this book. There is disagreement, however, as to the relative importance of values and power, and which values should be pursued.[8]

THE PROBLEM OF JUSTICE AND WAR

One fairly well developed area that stands as an exception to our general observation of the paucity of normative international relations theory is that which deals with the morality of war itself *(jus ad bellum)* and the ethical constraints within any given war *(jus in bello)*. Scholars have pondered the subject, building on a tradition in Western thought extending to the writings of St. Augustine (354–430 A.D.) and before. Contrary to the absolute pacifism of early Christians, Augustine addressed war as something that was to be avoided but that was sometimes necessary: "It is the wrong-doing of the opposing party which compels the wise man to wage wars."[9] The corpus of just war theory grew with additions made by Aquinas, Suarez, Vittoria, and other political philosophers of the medieval period. That we can develop a theory of just war through the exercise of right reason and right conduct are philosophical assumptions underlying normative theory on armed conflict.

Perhaps not surprisingly, given their preoccupation with national security issues, much contemporary thinking on just war has occurred primarily among realists. Not all realists would accept the Machiavellian characterization of war as something useful for acquiring or maintaining rule and that, if postponed, might work only to the advantage of the enemy. A Machiavellian principle underscored by Clausewitz is that war is decidedly not a legitimate end in itself but is merely a means used to achieve essentially political purposes. That war should not be waged without "legitimate" purpose—that it should at least be subordinate to the political objective or serve some national interest—can be understood as a limited but nevertheless moral statement in itself.

Defense against unprovoked aggression is generally conceded (except by absolute pacifists) to be a legitimate political objective justifying war. Nevertheless, in just-war thinking, war is a last resort to be undertaken only if there appears to be some chance of success. The death and destruction wrought by war are to be minimized consistent with achieving legitimate military purposes. Indeed, there can be no positive moral content in war unless legitimate political objectives and military purposes are served. Following conventional military logic, the purpose in any war is to destroy or substantially weaken an enemy's war-making capability. Military necessity, so defined, however, does not justify the use of means disproportionate to the ends sought or the use of weapons that are indiscriminate or that cause needless human suffering. Moreover, the lives of noncombatants are to be spared.[10]

Realists of Grotian persuasion look for rules or law that constrain states, statesmen, and soldiers in the exercise of their war powers. Beginning with the Hague Conventions in the late nineteenth and early twentieth centuries, a large body of treaties and conventions based largely on earlier just-war thinking has come into force, providing the basis for the contemporary law of war. There are difficulties, however, beyond the usual problem of no international enforcement authority and the problems of defining aggression and dealing with insurgencies, in which the legitimacy of the parties is in question. Quite apart from such concerns, however, the focus on limits in just-war theory and international law are seen by some theorists to be impractical in an age dominated by weapons of mass destruction. Moreover, some theorists question whether just war theory can be used to legitimate deterrence doctrines that argue that in order to maintain peace one must threaten devastation on a global scale.[11]

ALTERNATIVE IMAGES AND FOREIGN POLICY CHOICE

The relative emphasis placed on *order, justice, freedom,* and *change*—values that are part of foreign policymaking and that have a direct bearing on international politics—varies widely among realists, pluralists, and globalists. Realist concern with power and the balance of power is closely related to value commitments of statesmen who see order as essential to national security. If they are committed further to the avoidance of war, they may see their task as one of managing conflict and seeking to maximize accomplishment of state objectives, however constrained by states comprising the balance. Following Machiavelli, the realist sees national security or the national interest—at a minimum, survival in an anarchic world—as the *raison d'état* justifying state policy.

Justice and freedom may also be valued by realists, particularly those of Grotian persuasion, but even they must first confront the realities of power among states. Some states rise in power relative to others, and other states decline. Power and the balance of power persist, nevertheless. Changes in international politics occur within the international system or among states, but the anarchic nature of the international system (or of international politics) remains as a constant condition. Fundamental change of the international system that would alter the anarchy of sovereign states remains a possibility, but to most realists this seems unlikely to occur any time soon. Moreover, consistent with liberal thought that, as discussed in Chapter Three, has also had major impact on the pluralist school, there is a preference among many realists for a world order in which states are "free"—that is, not constrained by any superior authority. There is, then, a conservative value bias among realists that leads most of them to view schemes for new world orders as so much wishful thinking, products of utopian thought and divorced from reality.

To some extent, the value bias among pluralists is also conservative, if not to the same degree. To pluralists, change tends to be evolutionary and incremental. If change is to be willed, then *reformist*, not *revolutionary*, measures are the appropriate ones. Pluralist theories, given the fragmentation of states and proliferation of actors that are their starting point, focus on the formation of coalitions and countercoalitions, whether within a state or across national borders. This is hardly the environment for radical changes that would require greater societal unity or at least a strong and unitary leadership. Faction against faction, governmental department against governmental department—the Madisonian formula underlying the American Constitution—is not the means to sweeping change. There are simply too many obstacles (or potential obstacles in the form of opposing groups or factions) to make change easy to come by.

Although for different theoretical reasons and to a different degree, pluralists therefore share with realists a conservative bias and a predisposition toward order as a desired value. Many pluralists, however, place greater emphasis on democratic notions of *freedom* and *justice* for individuals, groups, and societies than they do on order within and among states, although all three are desired values. Richard Falk, for example, identifies four values to be maximized as part of his World Order Models Project: "minimization of collective violence; maximization of economic well-being; maximization of social and political justice; and maximization of ecological quality."[12] To minimize collective violence, order remains important to Falk, but his focus quickly shifts to social and welfare issues that need to be addressed as part of the world order. The pluralism in Falk's approach is evident in his characterization of it as "a transnational social movement dedicated to global reform."[13]

Justice, especially *distributive* justice, is a central concern not only to a number of pluralists but also to many globalists. Rawls presents a non-Marxist formulation that supports the normative preferences of both pluralists like Falk and those globalists who focus on inequalities in the distribution of wealth between North (industrial) and South (less-developed) countries. Globalists of Marxist persuasion do not need Rawls, of course, given their own long-standing moral concern with exploitative class relations and associated prescriptions for overturning what they see as the existing, unjust world order.

To many globalists, reformism and incremental change are merely prescriptions for maintaining the status quo. If justice is to be served, what may be needed is revolutionary change that sweeps out an unjust world order and replaces it with one that allows for an equitable distribution of wealth and resources. Whether understood as exploitation of peasants and workers by an international **bourgeoisie** or domination by highly industrial core states and societies over poor, industrially underdeveloped peripheral states, the answer is always the same: justice requires change. Order, peace, and individual freedom will only be established after fundamental (or revolutionary) change of the existing order has been effected.

RATIONALITY AND FOREIGN POLICY CHOICE

Foreign policy choice is the domain in which values apply directly. On the basis of some set of criteria, decisionmakers choose authoritatively among competing alternatives. The rational model, often a critical element in realist thinking, amounts to policymakers' ordering of alternatives, making decisions, and taking actions to achieve the most *efficient* outcome in terms of ends sought. This process is not value-free. First, determining the objective or ends to be sought obviously involves value choices.[14] Second, the idea that the means chosen to achieve these goals should be the most efficient, the best, or even just "good enough" is itself a value underlying the decision-making calculus. Finally, even if statesmen can reach a consensus on what general values should be pursued internationally, there may be honest disagreement as to how these values are to be defined and implemented. A good example of this problem involves human rights.

Notwithstanding a Universal Declaration of Human Rights in 1948 and a number of human rights conventions since then, there remains no real consensus among governments on which criteria should apply in approaching questions of human rights: which rights are to be protected, the relative importance or weight of different values when they conflict, and whose rights—individuals, groups, classes, states—take precedence. As Ernst Haas comments: "Rights come in various hues and stripes."[15] Indeed, the Jeffersonian tradition in American politics predisposes U.S. decisionmakers to emphasize political and civil rights of individuals. As a consequence, economic, social and cultural rights of groups and classes that receive greater emphasis in many other countries tend to be downgraded or ignored by makers of American foreign policy. Rights claimed by other states to be due them as *sovereign* entities also receive less American emphasis when prerogatives exercised by them are seen as infringing on individual rights.[16]

In sum, contrary to what one might first presume, the rational model of foreign policy decisionmaking is by no means a value-free approach, particularly given the wide range of values pursued by statesmen and different views as to how a particular value should be defined and implemented. As has been discussed in Chapters One and Three, many pluralists challenge whether foreign policy decision making can ever conform to a rational model when the actors involved are various organizations and small groups of individuals and when decisions are typically the outcome of bargaining, compromise, "end-running," or related tactics. Each separate actor may act rationally to achieve its own goals and values, but this is not the same thing as assuming that statesmen act rationally to achieve the goals or interests of the entire state and society. Similarly, some globalists may question the rationality of a decision-making or foreign policy process that, from their point of view, is dominated by narrow class interests. Whatever may be the rationality of individuals, institutions, or classes in maximizing or serving their own values or interests, the outcome for the whole may be suboptimal or less than the best.

VALUES, CHOICES, AND THEORY

Normative theory is relevant to each of the images and associated empirical theories we discuss in this book to the extent that one finds allowance for the exercise of human will within them. How much can statesmen affect the course of events? If those statesmen are driven internally, consistent with some psychological theories, or if they are severely constrained by their external environment, then normative theory plays a reduced, if any, role in their decision making. On the other hand, if human beings do have some degree of control over their affairs, including international relations, and if empirical theories take this effect of the will into account and exclude determinist "inevitabilities," then normative international relations theory ought not to be as neglected as it has been in recent years.

A central argument made in this book is that the image and set of assumptions one holds concerning international relations do affect interpretations—the sense one makes of facts and the causal explanations or predictions one offers. Realists evaluate what they see in a manner that is different from those persons holding what we have labeled pluralist and globalist images of international relations. Nor are these three images necessarily the last word. Other competing images may emerge and in time supersede the three discussed in this volume.

Although it is important to come to an understanding of biases or perspectives associated with any particular image of international relations, we are by no means making the argument that knowledge of international relations is a function only of prior assumptions, preferences, or values. Reality will not so easily be subordinated to myth, however deeply held or sacred these myths may seem. When what we see as facts contradict the image we hold, then it is the image that should be altered or even overturned to accommodate new information.[17] Our knowledge of international relations is imperfect and various biases color our vision, but facts have a way of breaking down our preconceptions when these preconceptions are fallacious. Scientific skepticism about claims to truth forces testing of various propositions or hypotheses with historical or other empirical data. Whether in the natural or social realms, scientific progress that enhances our knowledge of the world is painfully slow, but it is persistent.

NOTES

1. One can draw a distinction between normative and value considerations, perhaps seeing values as just one part of normative theory. Indeed, one can see that some normative considerations are nonmoral ones, as when an artist uses the terms *ought* and *right* in an esthetic context that does not have the moral content usually associated with these words. For our purposes, however, we use the terms *normative, moral,* and *value* interchangeably.
2. See, for example, Cicero, "'The Republic' and 'The Laws'" in William Ebenstein, *Great Political Thinkers,* 4th ed. (New York: Holt, Rinehart and Winston, 1969), pp. 136–38.
3. According to Kant, one should exercise free will and act according to the "categorical imperative" whereby one acts "according to the maxim which you can at the same time will to be a universal law." Moreover, one should "treat humanity, in your own person, and in the person of everyone else as an end as well as a means, never merely as a means." The literature on Kant is vast, and no attempt is made to summarize it here. We are particularly drawn, however, to the late Hannah Arendt's *Lectures on Kant's Political Philosophy* (Chicago: University of Chicago Press, 1982). There are numerous translations of what is perhaps Kant's most important contribution to the international relations literature, his *Perpetual Peace.*
4. See John Rawls, *A Theory of Justice* (Cambridge, MA: Harvard University Press, 1971), p.22.
5. *Ibid.,* p. 62.
6. *Ibid.,* p. 8.
7. E. H. Carr, *The Twenty Years' Crisis, 1919–1939* (New York: Harper & Row, 1964), p. 97.
8. Part of an effort to revive and develop normative international relations theory is a relatively recent study by Charles R. Beitz. See his *Political Theory and International Relations* (Princeton, NJ: Princeton University Press, 1979).
9. See, for example, St. Augustine, "The City of God" in Ebenstein, *Great Political Thinkers,* pp. 181–84.
10. Noncombatancy, particularly if "innocents" are involved, may be construed as conveying an absolute immunity. As a practical matter, however, attacks in war on what are understood to be legitimate military targets are usually accompanied by some collateral death and destruction. Following the logic of just war, however, such effects should always be minimized.

11. See, for example, Louis René Beres, *Mimicking Sisyphus: America's Countervailing Nuclear Strategy* (Lexington, MA: Lexington Books, 1983).
12. See Richard A. Falk, *A Study of Future Worlds* (New York: Free Press, 1975), pp. 11–30.
13. Richard A. Falk, *The End of World Order: Essays on Normative International Relations* (New York: Holmes and Meier, 1983), p. 53.
14. For an excellent summary of theories of rational choice, see Anthony Heath, *Rational Choice and Social Exchange: A Critique of Exchange Theory* (London: Cambridge University Press, 1976). See also Mancur Olson, *The Logic of Collective Action: Public Goods and the Theory of Groups* (Cambridge, MA: Harvard University Press, 1971), and William Riker, *The Theory of Political Coalitions* (New Haven, CT: Yale University Press, 1962).
15. See Ernst B. Haas, *Global Evangelism Rides Again: How to Protect Human Rights Without Really Trying* (Berkeley, CA: Institute of International Studies, 1978), pp. 1–23.
16. Thus, sovereign state jurisdiction exercised by the USSR over its citizens clashed with what was claimed by the U.S. government to be a fundamental human right of those Jews wishing to emigrate to the West.
17. Thomas Kuhn, for example, did not argue that one paradigm was as good as another. To the contrary, it was when anomalies accumulated to the point at which the empirical validity of a perspective was undermined that an alternative paradigm, one better able to account for such anomalies, would emerge. See Kuhn's *The Structure of Scientific Revolutions*, 2nd ed. (Chicago: University of Chicago Press, 1970).

SUGGESTED READINGS

Ajami, Fouad. "The Global Logic of the Neoconservatives." *World Politics* 30, 3 (April 1978): 450–468. A review of Tucker, *The Inequality of Nations.*

Arendt, Hannah. *On Violence.* New York: Harcourt, Brace and World, 1970.

———. *Lectures on Kant's Political Philosophy.* Edited by Ronald Beiner. Chicago: University of Chicago Press, 1982.

Aron, Raymond. *Peace and War: A Theory of International Relations.* Translated by Richard Howard and Annette Baker Fox. New York: Doubleday, 1966 and Praeger Publishers, 1968. See especially Chapters 20 and 21.

Aron, Raymond, and associates. *Scientists in Search of Their Conscience.* Edited by Anthony R. Michaelis and Hugh Harvey. Berlin and New York: Springer-Verlag, 1973.

Ashley, Richard K. "Political Realism and Human Interests." *International Studies Quarterly.* 25, 2 (June 1981): 204–36.

Beitz, Charles R. "Bounded Morality: Justice and the State in World Politics." *International Organization.* 33, 3 (Summer 1979): 405–24. A review essay on Walzer, *Just and Unjust Wars* and Brown and Shue, *Food Policy.*

———. "Economic Rights and Distributive Justice in Developing Societies." *World Politics* 33, 3 (1981): 321–46.

———. "Justice and International Relations." *Philosophy and Public Affairs* 4, 4 (Summer 1975).

———. *Political Theory and International Relations.* Princeton, NJ: Princeton University Press, 1979.

Bindschedler-Robert, Denise. *A Reconsideration of the Law of Armed Conflicts.* New York: Carnegie Endowment for International Peace, 1971.

Bondurant, Joan V. *Conquest of Violence: The Gandhian Philosophy of Conduct.* Berkeley, CA: University of California Press, 1971.

Brierly, J. L. *The Law of Nations: An Introduction to the International Law of Peace.* 6th ed. Edited by Sir Humphrey Waldock. New York and Oxford: Oxford University Press, 1963.

Brown, Peter G. and Henry Shue, eds. *Food Policy: The Responsibility of the United States in the Life and Death Choices.* New York: Free Press, 1977.

Bull, Hedley. "Recapturing the Just War for Political Theory." *World Politics* 31, 4 (July 1979): 588–99. A review of Walzer, *Just and Unjust Wars.*

Burton, John W. *Dear Survivors.* London: Frances Pinter; Boulder, CO: Westview Press, 1982.

———. *Deviance, Terrorism and War.* New York: St. Martin's Press, 1979.

Carr, E. H. *The Twenty Years' Crisis, 1919–1939.* New York: Harper & Row, 1964.

Cohen, Raymond. *International Politics: The Rules of the Game.* New York: Longman, 1981.

Deutsch, Karl W., and Stanley Hoffmann, eds. *The Relevance of International Law.* Cambridge, MA: Schankman, 1968.

Donnelly, Jack. "Human Rights and Foreign Policy." *World Politics* 34, 4 (July 1982): 574–95.

Falk, Richard A. *A Study of Future Worlds.* New York: Free Press, 1975.

———. *The End of World Order: Essays on Normative International Relations.* New York: Holmes and Meier, 1983.

———. *This Endangered Planet: Prospects and Proposals for Human Survival.* New York: Random House, 1971.

———. "The World Order Models Project and Its Critics." *International Organization.* 32, 2 (Spring 1978): 531–45.

Farer, Tom J. "The Greening of the Globe: A Preliminary Appraisal of the World Order Models Project (WOMP)." *International Organization.* 31, 1 (Winter 1977): 129–47.

Friedrich, Carl Joachim. *Inevitable Peace.* Cambridge, MA: Harvard University Press, 1948.

Gallie, W. B. *Philosophers of Peace and War: Kant, Clausewitz, Marx, Engels, and Tolstoy.* Cambridge: Cambridge University Press, 1978.

Haas, Ernst B. *Global Evangelism Rides Again: How to Protect Human Rights Without Really Trying.* Berkeley: University of California Institute of International Studies, 1978.

———. *Human Rights and International Action: The Case of Freedom of Association.* Stanford, CA: Stanford University Press, 1970.

Herz, John H. *The Nation–State and the Crisis of World Politics.* New York: David McKay, 1976.

———. "Political Realism Revisited." *International Studies Quarterly.* 25, 2 (June 1981): 182–97.

Hoffmann, Stanley, *Duties Beyond Borders: On the Limits and Possibilities of Ethical International Politics.* Syracuse, NY: Syracuse University Press, 1981.

Jacobson, Harold K. "The Global System and the Realization of Human Dignity and Justice." *International Studies Quarterly.* 26, 3 (September 1982): 315–32.

Johansen, Robert C. "Human Rights in the 1980s: Revolutionary Growth or Unanticipated Erosion." *World Politics.* 35, 2 (January 1983): 286–314. A review essay.

Johnson, James Turner. *Just War Tradition and the Restraint of War: A Moral and Historical Inquiry.* Princeton, NJ: Princeton University Press, 1981.

———. *Can Modern War Be Just?* New Haven, CT: Yale University Press, 1984.

Jones, Christopher D. "Just Wars and Limited Wars: Restraints on the Use of the Soviet Armed Forces," *World Politics* 28, 1 (October 1975): 44–68.

Kaplan, Morton A., ed. *Strategic Thinking and Its Moral Implications.* Chicago: University of Chicago Press, 1973.

Kennan, George F. "Morality and Foreign Policy." *Foreign Affairs.* 64, 2 (Winter 1985–1986): 205–18.

Lefever, Ernest S. *Ethics and World Politics.* Baltimore, MD: Johns Hopkins University Press, 1972.

Mendlovitz, Saul, ed. *On the Creation of a Just World Order.* New York: Free Press, 1975.

Mill, John Stuart. *Utilitarianism.* New York: E. P. Dutton, 1951. Originally published in 1861.

Niebuhr, Reinhold. *Christian Realism and Political Problems.* New York: Scribners, 1953.

O'Brien, William V. *The Conduct of Just and Limited War.* New York: Praeger, 1981.

Orwin, Clifford. "The Just and the Advantageous in Thucydides." *The American Political Science Review.* 78, 2 (June 1984): 485–94.

Osgood, Robert E. *Ideals and Self-interest in American Foreign Relations.* Chicago: University of Chicago Press, 1953.

Osgood, Robert E., and Robert W. Tucker. *Force, Order, and Justice.* Baltimore, MD: Johns Hopkins University Press, 1967.

Pettmann, Ralph. *Moral Claims in World Affairs.* New York: St. Martin's Press, 1979.

Ramsey, Paul. *The Just War: Force and Political Responsibility.* New York: University Press of America, 1968, 1983.

Rapoport, Anatol. *Strategy and Conscience.* New York: Schocken Books, 1964, 1969.

Rawls, John. *A Theory of Justice.* Cambridge, MA: Harvard University Press, 1971.

Reilly, Robert R., James V. Schall and associates. *Justice and War in the Nuclear Age.* New York: University Press of America, 1983.

Rummel, R. J. *Understanding Conflict and War:* Vol. V, *The Just Peace.* Beverly Hills, CA: Sage Publications, 1981.

Sandel, Michael J. *Liberalism and the Limits of Justice.* Cambridge: Cambridge University Press, 1982.

Singer, J. David. "The Responsibilities of Competence in the Global Village." *International Studies Quarterly.* 29, 3 (September 1985): 245–62.

Steiner, Miriam. "Human Nature and Truth as World Order Issues." *Interna-*

tional Organization 34, 3 (Summer 1980): 335-53.

Stone, Julius. "Approaches to the Notion of International Justice." In *The Future of the International Legal Order*, eds. Richard A. Falk and Cyril E. Black. Vol. I. Princeton, NJ: Princeton University Press, 1969.Tucker, Robert W. *The Inequality of Nations.* New York: Basic Books, 1976.

Tucker, Robert W. *The Inequality of Nations.* New York: Basic Books, 1976.

Wakin, Malham M., ed. *War, Morality, and the Military Profession.* Boulder, CO: Westview Press, 1979.

Walzer, Michael. *Just and Unjust Wars: A Moral Argument with Historical Illustrations.* New York: Basic Books, 1977.

Wasserstrom, Richard A. *War and Morality.* Belmont, CA: Wadsworth, 1970.

Wolfers, Arnold. "Statesmanship and Moral Choice." *World Politics* (1949): 175-95.

Young, Oran R. "Anarchy and Social Choice: Reflections on the International Polity." *World Politics* 30, 2 (January 1978), 241-63.

The Nature of Politics

E. H. Carr

The late E. H. Carr argues that the practice and study of politics require an appreciation of realism as well as utopianism, power as well as morality.

Man has always lived in groups. The smallest kind of human group, the family, has clearly been necessary for the maintenance of the species. But so far as is known, men have always from the most primitive times formed semi-permanent groups larger than the single family; and one of the functions of such a group has been to regulate relations between its members. Politics deals with the behavior of men in such organised permanent or semi-permanent groups. All attempts to deduce the nature of society from the supposed behavior of man in isolation are purely theoretical, since there is no reason to assume that such a man ever existed. Aristotle laid the foundation of all sound thinking about politics when he declared that man was by nature a political animal.

Man in society reacts to his fellow men in two opposite ways. Sometimes he displays egoism, or the will to assert himself at the expense of others. At other times he displays sociability, or the desire to cooperate with others, to enter into reciprocal relations of good-will and friendship with them, and even to subordinate himself to them. In every society, these two qualities can be seen at work. No society can exist unless a substantial proportion of its members exhibits in some degree the desire for cooperation and mutual good-will. But in every society some sanction is required to produce the measure of solidarity requisite for its maintenance; and this sanction is applied by a controlling group or individual acting in the name of the society. Membership of most societies is voluntary, and the only ultimate sanction which can be applied is expulsion. But the peculiarity of political society, which in the modern world takes the form of the state, is that membership is compulsory. The state, like other societies, must be based on some sense of common interests and

From E. H. Carr, *The Twenty Years' Crisis*. By permission of Macmillan, London and Basingstoke.

obligations among its members. But coercion is regularly exercised by a governing group to enforce loyalty and obedience; and this coercion inevitably means that the governors control the governed and "exploit" them for their own purposes.[1]

The dual character of political society is therefore strongly marked. Professor Laski tells us that "every state is built upon the consciences of men."[2] On the other hand, anthropology, as well as much recent history, teaches that "war seems to be the main agency in producing the state"; and Professor Laski himself, in another passage, declares that "our civilisation is held together by fear rather than by good-will."[3] There is no contradiction between these apparently opposite views. When Tom Paine, in the *Rights of Man,* tries to confront Burke with the dilemma that "governments arise either *out* of the people or *over* the people," the answer is that they do both. Coercion and conscience, enmity and goodwill, self-assertion and self-subordination, are present in every political society. The state is built up out of these two conflicting aspects of human nature. Utopia and reality, the ideal and the institution, morality and power, are from the outset inextricably blended in it. In the making of the United States, as a modern American writer has said, "Hamilton stood for strength, wealth, and power, Jefferson, for the American dream"; and both the power and the dream were necessary ingredients.[4]

If this be correct, we can draw one important conclusion. The utopian who dreams that it is possible to eliminate self-assertion from politics and to base a political system on morality alone is just as wide of the mark as the realist who believes that altruism is an illusion and that all political action is based on self-seeking. These errors have both left their mark on popular terminology. The phrase "power politics" is often used in an invidious sense, as if the element of power or self-assertion in politics were something abnormal and susceptible of elimination from a healthy political life. Conversely, there is a disposition, even among some writers who are not strictly speaking realists, to treat politics as the science of power and self-assertion and exclude from it by definition actions inspired by the moral consciousness. Professor Catlin describes the *homo politicus* as one who "seeks to bring into conformity with his own will the wills of others, so that he may the better attain his own ends."[5] Such terminological implications are misleading. Politics cannot be divorced from power. But the *homo politicus* who pursues nothing but power is as unreal a myth as the *homo economicus* who pursues nothing but gain. Political action must be based on a coordination of morality and power.

This truth is of practical as well as theoretical importance. It is as fatal in politics to ignore power as it is to ignore morality. The fate of China in the nineteenth century is an illustration of what happens to a country which is content to believe in the moral superiority of its own civilisation and to despise the ways of power. The Liberal Government of Great Britain nearly came to grief in the spring of 1914 because it sought to pursue an Irish policy based on moral authority unsupported (or rather, directly opposed) by effective military power. In Germany, the Frankfort Assembly of 1848 is the classic example of the impotence of ideas divorced from power; and the Weimar Republic broke down because many of the policies it pursued—in fact, nearly all of them except its opposition to the communists—were unsupported, or actively opposed, by effective military power.[6] The utopian, who believes that democracy is not based on force, refuses to look these unwelcome facts in the face.

On the other hand, the realist, who believes that, if you look after the power, the moral authority will look after itself, is equally in error. The most recent form of this doctrine is embodied in the much-quoted phrase: "The function of force is to give moral ideas time to take root." Internationally, this argument was used in 1919 by those who, unable to defend the Versailles Treaty on moral grounds, maintained that this initial act of power would pave the way for subsequent moral appeasement. Experience has done little to confirm this comfortable belief. The same fallacy is implicit in the once popular view that the aim of British policy should be "to rebuild the League of Nations, to make it capable of holding a political aggressor in restraint by armed power, and thereafter to labour faithfully for the mitigation of just and real grievances."[7] Once the enemy has been crushed or the "aggressor" restrained by force, the "thereafter" fails to arrive. The illusion that priority can be given to power and that morality will follow, is just as dangerous as the illusion that priority can be given to moral authority and that power will follow.

Before proceeding, however, to consider the respective roles of power and morality in politics, we must take some note of the views of those who, though far from being realists, identify politics with power and believe that moral concepts must be altogether excluded from its scope. There is, according to this view, an essential antinomy between politics and morality; and the moral man as such will therefore have nothing to do with politics. This thesis has many attractions, and reappears at different periods of history and in different contexts. It takes at least three forms.

(i) Its simplest form is the doctrine of non-resistance. The moral man recognises the existence of political power as an evil, but regards the use of power to resist power as a still greater evil. This is the basis of such doctrines of non-resistance as those of Jesus or of Gandhi, or of modern pacifism. It amounts, in brief, to a boycott of politics.

(ii) The second form of the antithesis between politics and morality is anarchism. The state, as the principal organ of political power, is "the most flagrant, most cynical and most complete negation of humanity."[8] The anarchist will use power to overthrow the state. This revolutionary power is, however, not thought of as political power, but as the spontaneous revolt of the outraged individual conscience. It does not seek to create a new political society to take the place of the old one, but a moral society from which power, and consequently politics, are completely eliminated. "The principles of the Sermon on the Mount," an English divine recently remarked, would mean "sudden death to civilised society."[9] The anarchist sets out to destroy "civilised society" in the name of the Sermon on the Mount.

(iii) A third school of thought starts from the same premise of the essential antithesis between morality and politics, but arrives at a totally different conclusion. The injunction of Jesus to "render unto Caesar the things that are Caesar's, and unto God the things that are God's," implies the coexistence of two separate spheres: the political and the moral. But the moral man is under an obligation to assist—or at any rate not to obstruct—the politician in the discharge of his non-moral functions. "Let every soul be subject to the higher powers. The powers that be are ordained of God." We thus recognise politics as necessary but non-moral. This tradition, which remained dormant throughout the Middle Ages, when the ecclesiastical and the secular authority was theoretically one, was revived by Luther in order to effect his compromise between reformed church and state. Luther "turned on the peasants of his day in holy horror when they attempted to transmute the 'spiritual' kingdom into an 'earthly' one by suggesting that the principles of the gospel had social significance."[10] The division of functions between Caesar and God is implicit in the very conception of an "established" church. But the tradition has been more persistent and more effective in Lutheran Germany than anywhere else. "We do not consult Jesus," wrote a German liberal nineteenth-century pastor, "when we are concerned with things which belong to the domain of the construction of the state and political economy"[11] and Bernhardi declared that "Christian morality is personal and social, and in its nature cannot be political."[12] The same attitude is inherent in the modern theology of Karl Barth, which insists that political and social evils are the necessary product of man's sinful nature and that human effort to eradicate them is therefore futile; and the doctrine that Christian morality has nothing to do with politics is vigorously upheld by the Nazi régime. This view is basically different from that of the realist who makes morality a function of politics. But in the field of politics it tends to become indistinguishable from realism.

The theory of the divorce between the spheres of politics and morality is superficially attractive, if only because it evades the insoluble problem of finding a moral justification for the use of force.[13] But it is not ultimately satisfying. Both non-resistance and anarchism are counsels of despair, which appear to find widespread acceptance only where men feel hopeless of achieving anything by political action; and the attempt to keep God and Caesar in watertight compartments runs too much athwart the deep-seated desire of the human mind to reduce its view of the world to some kind of moral order. We are not in the long run satisfied to believe that what is politically good is morally bad; and since we can neither moralise power nor expel power from politics, we are faced with a dilemma which cannot be completely resolved.[14] The planes of utopia and of reality never coincide. The ideal cannot be institutionalised, nor the institution idealised. "Politics," writes Dr. Niebuhr, "will, to the end of history, be an area where conscience and power meet, where the ethical and coercive factors of human life will interpenetrate and work out their tentative and uneasy compromises."[15] The compromises, like solutions of other human problems, will remain uneasy and tentative. But it is an essential part of any compromise that both factors shall be taken into account.

We have now therefore to analyse the part played in international politics by these two cardinal factors: power and morality.

NOTES

1. "Everywhere do I perceive a certain conspiracy of the rich men seeking their own advantage under the name and pretext of the commonwealth" (More, *Utopia*). "The exploitation of one part of society by another is common to all past centuries" (*Communist Manifesto*).
2. *A Defence of Liberty against Tyrants (Vindiciae contra Tyrannos)*, ed. Laski, Introd. p. 55.
3. Linton, *The Study of Man*, p. 240; Laski, *A Grammar of Politics*, p. 20.
4. J. Truslow Adams, *The Epic of America*, p. 112. The idea that the state has a moral foundation in the consent of its citizens as well as a power foundation was propounded by Locke and Rousseau and popularised by the American and French revolutions. Two recent expressions of the idea may be quoted. The Czecho-Slovak declaration of independence of October 18, 1918, described Austria–Hungary as "a state which has no justification for its existence, and which, since it refuses to accept the fundamental basis of modern world-organisation [i.e. self-determination], is only an artificial and unmoral construction." In February 1938, Hitler told Schuschnigg, the then Austrian Chancellor, that "a régime lacking every kind of legality and which in reality ruled only by force, must in the long run come into continually increasing conflict with public opinion" (speech in the Reichstag of March 17, 1938). Hitler maintained that the two pillars of the state are "force" and "popularity" (*Mein Kampf,* p. 579).
5. Catlin, *The Science and Method of Politics*, p. 309.
6. It is significant that the word *Realpolitik* was coined in the once famous treatise of von Rochau, *Grundsätze der Realpolitik* published in 1853, which was largely inspired by the lessons of Frankfort. The inspiration which Hitler's *Realpolitik* has derived from the lessons of the Weimar Republic is obvious.
7. Winston Churchill, *Arms and the Covenant*, p. 368. The argument that power is a necessary motive force for the remedy of "just" grievances is further developed on pp. 209–216.
8. Bakunin, *Œuvres*, i. p. 150; cf. vi. p. 17: "If there is a devil in all human history, it is this principle of command and authority."
9. The Dean of St. Paul's, quoted in a leading article in *The Times*, August 2, 1937.
10. R. Niebuhr, *Moral Man and Immoral Society*, p. 77.
11. Quoted in W. F. Bruck, *Social and Economic History of Germany*, p. 65.
12. Bernhardi, *Germany and the Next War* (Engl. transl.), p. 29.

13. "Force in the right place," as Mr. Maxton once said in the House of Commons, is a meaningless conception, "because the right place for me is exactly where I want to use it, and for him also, and for everyone else." (House of Commons, November 7, 1933: *Official Record,* col. 130). Force in politics is always the instrument of some kind of group interest.

14. Acton was fond of saying that "great men are almost always bad men," and quotes Walpole's dictum that "no great country was ever saved by good men" (*History of Freedom,* p. 219). Rosebery showed more acuteness when he remarked that "there is one question which English people ask about great men: Was he 'a good man'?" (*Napoleon: The Last Phase,* p. 364).

15. R. Niebuhr, *Moral Man and Immoral Society,* p. 4.

Against Realism

Michael Walzer

Professor Walzer makes a case for the importance of considering questions of morality and justice in the study and conduct of international affairs. He criticizes what he argues is insufficient attention to these matters on the part of realists.

For as long as men and women have talked about war, they have talked about it in terms of right and wrong. And for almost as long, some among them have derided such talk, called it a charade, insisted that war lies beyond (or beneath) moral judgment. War is a world apart, where life itself is at stake, where human nature is reduced to its elemental forms, where self-interest and necessity prevail. Here men and women do what they must to save themselves and their communities, and morality and law have no place. *Inter arma silent leges:* in time of war the law is silent.

Sometimes this silence is extended to other forms of competitive activity, as in the popular proverb, "All's fair in love and war." That means that anything goes—any kind of deceit in love, any kind of violence in war. We can neither praise nor blame; there is nothing to say. And yet we are rarely silent. The language we use to talk about love and war is so rich with moral meaning that it could hardly have been developed except through centuries of argument. Faithfulness, devotion, chastity, shame, adultery, seduction, betrayal; aggression, self-defense, appeasement, cruelty, ruthlessness, atrocity, massacre—all these words are judgments, and judging is as common a human activity as loving or fighting.

It is true, however, that we often lack the courage of our judgments, and especially so in the case of military conflict. The moral posture of mankind is not well represented by that popular proverb about love and war. We would do better to mark a contrast rather than a similarity: before Venus, censorious; before Mars, timid. Not that we don't justify or condemn particular attacks, but we do so hesitantly and uncertainly (or loudly and recklessly), as if we were not sure that our judgments reach to the reality of war.

THE REALIST ARGUMENT

Realism is the issue. The defenders of *silent leges* claim to have discovered an awful truth: what we conventionally call inhumanity is simply humanity under pressure. War strips away our civilized adornments and reveals our nakedness. They describe that nakedness for us, not without a certain relish: fearful, self-concerned, driven, murderous. They aren't wrong in any simple sense. The words are sometimes descriptive. Paradoxically, the description is often a kind of apology: yes, our soldiers committed atrocities in the course of the battle, but that's what war does to people, that's what war is like. The proverb, all's fair, is invoked in defense of conduct that appears to be unfair. And one urges silence on the law when one is engaged in activities that would otherwise be called unlawful. So there are arguments here that will enter into my own argument: justifications and excuses, references to necessity and duress, that we can recognize as forms of moral discourse and that have or don't have force in particular cases. But there is also a general account of war as a realm of necessity and duress, the purpose of which is to make discourse about particular cases appear to be idle chatter, a mask of noise with which we conceal, even from ourselves, the awful truth. It is that general account that I have to challenge before I can begin my own work, and I want to challenge it at its source and in its most compelling form, as it is put forward by the historian Thucydides and the philosopher Thomas Hobbes. These two men, separated by 2,000 years, are collaborators of a kind, for Hobbes translated Thucydides' *History of the Peloponnesian War* and then generalized its argument in his own *Leviathan*. It is not my purpose here to write a full philosophical response to Thucydides and Hobbes. I wish only to suggest, first by argument and then by example, that the judgment of war and of wartime conduct is a serious enterprise.

The Melian Dialogue

The dialogue between the Athenian generals Cleomedes and Tisias and the magistrates of the island state of Melos is one of the high points of Thucydides' *History* and the climax of his realism. Melos was a Spartan colony, and its people had "therefore refused to be subject, as the rest of the islands were, unto the Athenians; but rested at first neutral; and afterwards, when the Athenians put them to it by wasting their lands, they entered into open war."[1] This is a classic account of aggression, for to commit aggression is simply to "put people to it" as Thucydides describes. But such a description, he seems to say, is merely external; he wants to show us the inner meaning of war. His spokesmen are the two Athenian generals, who demand a parley and then speak as generals have rarely done in military history. Let us have no fine words about justice, they say. We for our part will not pretend that, having defeated the Persians, our empire is deserved; you must not claim that having done no injury to the Athenian people, you have a right to be let alone. We will talk instead of what is feasible and what is necessary. For this is what war is really like: "they that have odds of power exact as much as they can, and the weak yield to such conditions as they can get."

It is not only the Melians here who bear the burdens of necessity. The Athenians are driven, too; they must expand their empire, Cleomedes and Tisias believe, or lose what they already have. The neutrality of Melos "will be an argument of our weakness, and your hatred of our power, among those we have rule over." It will inspire rebellion throughout the islands, wherever men and women are "offended with the necessity of subjection"—and what subject is not offended, eager for freedom, resentful of his conquerors? When the Athenian generals say that men "will everywhere reign over such as they be too strong for," they are not only describing the desire for glory and command, but also the more narrow necessity of inter-state politics: reign or be subject. If they do not conquer when they can, they only reveal weakness and invite attack; and so, "by a necessity of nature" (a phrase Hobbes later made his own), they conquer when they can.

The Melians, on the other hand, are too weak to conquer. They face a harsher necessity: yield or be destroyed. "For you have not in hand a match of valor upon equal terms . . . but rather a consultation upon your safety. . . . " The rulers of Melos, however, value freedom above safety: "If you then to retain your command, and your vassals to get loose from you, will undergo the utmost danger: would it not in us, that be already free, be great baseness and cowardice, if we should not encounter anything whatsoever rather than suffer ourselves to be brought into bondage?" Though they know that it will be a "hard matter" to stand against the power and fortune of Athens, "nevertheless we believe that, for fortune, we shall be nothing inferior, as having the gods on our side, because we stand innocent against men unjust." And as for power, they hope for assistance from the Spartans, "who are of necessity obliged, if for no other cause, yet for consanguinity's sake and for their own honor to defend us." But the gods, too, reign where they can, reply the Athenian generals, and consanguinity and honor have nothing to do with necessity. The Spartans will (necessarily) think only of themselves: "most apparently of all men, they hold for honorable that which pleaseth and for just that which profiteth."

So the argument ended. The magistrates refused to surrender; the Athenians laid siege to their city; the Spartans sent no help. Finally, after some months of fighting, in the winter of 416 B.C., Melos was betrayed by several of its citizens. When further resistance seemed impossible, the Melians "yielded themselves to the discretion of the Athenians: who slew all the men of military age, made slaves of the women and children; and inhabited the place with a colony sent thither afterwards of 500 men of their own."

The dialogue between the generals and the magistrates is a literary and philosophical construction of Thucydides. The magistrates speak as they well might have done, but their conventional piety and heroism is only a foil to what the classical critic Dionysius calls the "depraved shrewdness" of the Athenian generals.[2] It is the generals who have often seemed unbelievable. Their words, writes Dionysius, "were appropriate to oriental monarchs . . . but unfit to be spoken by Athenians. . . . " Perhaps Thucydides means us to notice the unfitness, not so much of the words but of the policies they were used to defend, and thinks we might have missed it had he permitted the generals to speak as they probably in fact spoke, weaving "fair pretenses" over their vile actions. We are to understand that Athens is no longer itself. Cleomedes and Tisias do not represent that noble people who fought the Persians in the name of freedom and whose politics and culture, as Dionysius says, "exercised such a humanizing influence on everyday life." They represent instead the imperial decadence of the city state. It is not that they are war criminals in the modern sense; that idea is alien to Thucydides. But they embody a certain loss of ethical balance, of restraint and moderation. Their statesmanship is flawed, and their "realistic" speeches provide an ironic contrast to the blindness and arrogance with which the Athenians only a few months later launched the disastrous expedition to Sicily. The *History*, on this view, is a tragedy and Athens itself the tragic hero.[3] Thucydides has given us a morality play in the Greek style. We can glimpse his meaning in Euripides' *The Trojan Women*, written in the immediate aftermath of the conquest of Melos and undoubtedly intended to suggest the human significance of slaughter and slavery—and to predict a divine retribution:

> How ye are blind
> Ye treaders down of cities, ye that cast
> Temples to desolation, and lay waste
> Tombs, the untrodden sanctuaries where lie
> The ancient dead; yourselves so soon to die![4]

But Thucydides seems in fact to be making a rather different, and a more secular, statement than this quotation suggests, and not about Athens so much as about war itself. He probably did not mean the harshness of the Athenian generals to be taken as a sign of depravity, but rather as a sign of impatience, toughmindedness, honesty—qualities of mind not inappropriate in military commanders. He is arguing, as Werner Jaeger has said, that "the principle of force forms a realm of its own, with laws of its own," distinct and separate from the laws of moral life.[5] This is certainly the way Hobbes read Thucydides, and it is the reading with which we must come to grips. For if the realm of force is indeed distinct and if this is an accurate account of its laws, then one could no more criticize the Athenians for their wartime policies than one could criticize a stone for falling downwards. The slaughter of the Melians is explained by reference to the circumstances of war and the necessities of nature; and again, there is nothing to say. Or rather, one can *say* anything, call necessity cruel and war hellish; but while these statements may be true in their own terms, they do not touch the political realities of the case or help us understand the Athenian decision.

It is important to stress, however, that Thucydides has told us nothing at all about the Athenian decision. And if we place ourselves, not in the council room at Melos where a cruel policy was being expounded, but in the assembly at Athens where that policy was first adopted, the argument of the generals has a very different ring. In the Greek as in the English language, the word *necessity* "doubles the parts of indispensable and inevitable."[6] At Melos, Cleomedes and Tisias mixed the two of these, stressing the last. In the assembly they could have argued only about the first, claiming, I suppose, that the destruction of Melos was necessary (indispensable) for the preservation of the empire. But this claim is rhetorical in two senses. First, it evades the moral question of whether the preservation of the empire was itself necessary. There were some Athenians, at least, who had doubts about that, and more who doubted that the empire had to be a uniform system of domination and subjection (as the policy adopted for Melos suggested). Secondly, it exaggerates the knowledge and foresight of the generals. They are not saying with certainty that Athens will fall unless Melos is destroyed; their argument has to do with probabilities and risks. And such arguments are always arguable. Would the destruction of Melos really reduce Athenian risks? Are there alternative policies? What are the likely costs of this one? Would it be right? What would other people think of Athens if it were carried out?

Once the debate begins, all sorts of moral and strategic questions are likely to come up. And for the participants in the debate, the outcome is not going to be determined "by a necessity of nature," but by the opinions they hold or come to hold as a result of the arguments they hear and then by the decisions they freely make, individually and collectively. Afterwards, the generals claim that a certain decision was inevitable; and that, presumably, is what Thucydides wants us to believe. But the claim can only be made afterwards, for inevitability here is mediated by a process of political deliberation, and Thucydides could not know what was inevitable until that process had been completed. Judgments of necessity in this sense are always retrospective in character—the work of historians, not historical actors.

Now, the moral point of view derives its legitimacy from the perspective of the actor. When we make moral judgments, we try to recapture that perspective. We reiterate the decision-making process, or we rehearse our own future decision, asking what we would have done (or what we would do) in similar circumstances. The Athenian generals recognize the importance of such questions, for they defend their policy certain "that you likewise, and others that should have the same power which we have, would do the same." But that is a dubious knowledge, especially so once we realize that the "Melian decree" was sharply opposed in the Athenian assembly. Our standpoint is that of citizens debating the decree. What *should* we do?

We have no account of the Athenian decision to attack Melos or of the decision (which may have been taken at the same time) to kill and enslave its people. Plutarch claims that it was Alcibiades, chief architect of the Sicilian expedition, who was "the principal cause of the slaughter . . . having spoken in favor of the decree."[7] He played the part of Cleon in the debate that Thucydides does record, that occurred some years earlier, over the fate of Mytilene. It is worth glancing back at that earlier argument. Mytilene had been an ally of Athens from the time of the Persian War; it was never a subject city in any formal way, but bound by treaty to the Athenian cause. In 428, it rebelled and formed an alliance with the Spartans. After considerable fighting, the city was captured by Athenian forces, and the assembly determined "to put to death . . . all the men of Mytilene that were of age, and to make slaves of the women and children; laying to their charge the revolt itself, in that they revolted not being in subjection as others were. . . . "[8] But the following day the citizens "felt a kind of repentance . . . and began to consider what a great and cruel decree it was, that not the authors only, but that the whole city should be destroyed." It is this second debate that Thucydides has recorded, or some part of it, giving us two speeches, that of Cleon upholding the original decree and that of Diodotus urging its revocation. Cleon argues largely in terms of collective guilt and retributive justice; Diodotus offers a critique of the deterrent effects of capital punishment. The assembly accepts Diodotus' position, convinced apparently that the destruction of Mytilene would not uphold the force of treaties or ensure the stability of the empire. It is the appeal to interest that triumphs—as has often been pointed out—though it should be remembered that the occasion for the appeal was the repentance of the citizens. Moral anxiety, not political calculation, leads them to worry about the effectiveness of their decree.

In the debate over Melos, the positions must have been reversed. Now there was no retributivist argument to make, for the Melians had done Athens no injury. Alcibiades probably talked like Thucydides' generals, though with the all-important difference I have already noted. When he told his fellow citizens that the decree was necessary, he didn't mean that it was ordained by the laws that govern the realm of force; he meant merely that it was needed (in his view) to reduce the risks of rebellion among the subject cities of the Athenian empire. And his opponents probably argued, like the Melians, that the decree was dishonorable and unjust and would more likely excite resentment than fear throughout the islands, that Melos did not threaten Athens in any way, and that other policies would serve Athenian interests and Athenian self-esteem. Perhaps they also reminded the citizens of their repentance in the case of Mytilene and urged them once again to avoid the cruelty of massacre and enslavement. How Alcibiades won out, and how close the vote was, we don't know. But there is no reason to think that the decision was predetermined and debate of no avail: no more with Melos than with Mytilene. Stand in imagination in the Athenian assembly, and one can still feel a sense of freedom.

But the realism of the Athenian generals has a further thrust. It is not only a denial of the freedom that makes moral decision possible; it is a denial also of the meaningfulness of moral argument. The second claim is closely related to the first. If we must act in accordance with our interests, driven by our fears of one another, then talk about justice cannot possibly be anything more than talk. It refers to no purposes that we can make our own and to no goals that we can share with others. That is why the Athenian generals could have woven "fair pretenses" as easily as the Melian magistrates; in discourse of this sort anything can be said. The words have no clear references, no certain definitions, no logical entailments. They are, as Hobbes writes in *Leviathan*, "ever used with relation to the person that useth them," and they express that person's appetites and fears and nothing else. It is only "most apparent" in the Spartans, but true for everyone, that "they hold for honorable that which pleaseth them and for just that which profiteth." Or, as Hobbes later explained, the names of the virtues and vices are of "uncertain signification."

> For one calleth wisdom, what another calleth fear; and one cruelty what another justice; one prodigality, what another magnanimity . . . etc. And therefore such names can never be true grounds of any ratiocination.[9]

"*Never*"—until the sovereign, who is also the supreme linguistic authority, fixes the meaning of the moral vocabulary; but in the state of war, "*never*" without qualification, because in that state, by definition, no sovereign rules. In fact, even in civil society, the sovereign does not entirely succeed in bringing certainty into the world of virtue and vice. Hence moral discourse is always suspect, and war is only an extreme case of the anarchy of moral meanings. It is generally true, but especially so in time of violent conflict, that we can understand what other people are saying only if we see through their "fair pretenses" and translate moral talk into the harder currency of interest talk. When the Melians insist that their cause is just, they are saying only that they don't want to be subject; and had the generals claimed that Athens deserved its empire, they would simply have been expressing the lust for conquest or the fear of overthrow.

This is a powerful argument because it plays upon the common experience of moral disagreement—painful, sustained, exasperating, and endless. For all its realism, however, it fails to get at the realities of that experience or to explain its character. We can see this clearly, I think, if we look again at the argument over the Mytilene decree. Hobbes may well have had this debate in mind when he wrote, "and one [calleth] cruelty what another justice. . . . " The Athenians repented of their cruelty, writes Thucydides, while Cleon told them that they had not been cruel at all but justly severe. Yet this was in no sense a disagreement over the meaning of words. Had there been no common meanings, there could have been no debate at all. The cruelty of the Athenians consisted in seeking to punish not only the authors of the rebellion but others as well, and Cleon agreed that that would indeed be cruel. He then went on to argue, as he had to do given his position, that in Mytilene there were no "others." "Let not the fault be laid upon a few, and the people absolved. For they have all alike taken arms against us. . . . "

I cannot pursue the argument further, since Thucydides doesn't, but there is an obvious rejoinder to Cleon, having to do with the status of the women and children of Mytilene. This might involve the deployment of additional moral terms (innocence, for example); but it would not hang—any more than the argument about cruelty and justice hangs— on idiosyncratic definitions. In fact, definitions are not at issue here, but descriptions and interpretations. The Athenians shared a moral vocabulary, shared it with the people of Mytilene and Melos; and allowing for cultural differences, they share it with us too. They had no difficulty, and we have none, in understanding the claim of the Melian magistrates that the invasion of their island was unjust. It is in applying the agreed-upon words to actual cases that we come to disagree. These disagreements are in part generated and always compounded by antagonistic interests and mutual fears. But they have other causes, too, which help to explain the complex and disparate ways in which men and women (even when they have similar interests and no reason to fear one another) position themselves in the moral world. There are, first of all, serious difficulties of perception and information (in war and politics generally), and so controversies arise over "the facts of the case." There are sharp disparities in the weight we attach even to values we share, as there are in the actions we are ready to condone when these values are threatened. There are conflicting commitments and obligations that force us into violent antagonism even when we see the point of one another's positions. All this is real enough, and common enough: it makes morality into a world of good-faith quarrels as well as a world of ideology and verbal manipulation.

In any case, the possibilities for manipulation are limited. Whether or not people speak in good faith, they cannot say just anything they please. Moral talk is coercive; one thing leads to another. Perhaps that's why the Athenian generals did not want to begin. A war called unjust is not, to paraphrase Hobbes, a war misliked; it is a war misliked for particular reasons, and anyone making the charge is required to provide particular sorts of evidence. Similarly, if I claim that I am fighting justly, I must also claim that I was attacked ("put to it," as the Melians were), or threatened with attack, or that I am coming to the aid of a victim of someone else's attack. And each of these claims has it own entailments, leading me deeper and deeper into a world of discourse where, though I can go on talking indefinitely, I am severely constrained in what I can say. I must say this or that, and at many points in a long argument this or that will be true or false. We don't have to translate moral talk into interest talk in order to understand it; morality refers in its own way to the real world.

Let us consider a Hobbist example. In Chapter XXI of *Leviathan*, Hobbes urges that we make allowance for the "natural timorousness" of mankind. "When armies fight, there is on one side, or both a running away; yet when they do it not out of treachery, but fear, they are not esteemed to do it unjustly, but dishonorably." Now, judgments are called for here: we are to distinguish cowards from traitors. If these are words of "inconstant signification," the task is impossible and absurd. Every traitor would plead natural timorousness, and we would accept the plea or not depending on whether the soldier was a friend or an enemy, an obstacle to our advancement or an ally and supporter. I suppose we sometimes do behave that way, but it is not the case (nor does Hobbes, when it comes to cases, suppose that it is) that the judgments we make can only be understood in these terms. When we charge a man with treason, we have to tell a very special kind of story about him, and we have to provide concrete evidence that the story is true. If we call him a traitor when we cannot tell that story, we are not using words inconstantly, we are simply lying.

STRATEGY AND MORALITY

Morality and justice are talked about in much the same way as military strategy. Strategy is the other language of war, and while it is commonly said to be free from the difficulties of moral discourse, its use is equally problematic. Though generals agree on the meaning of strategic terms— entrapment, retreat, flanking maneuver, concentration of forces, and so on—they nevertheless disagree about strategically appropriate courses of action. They argue about what ought to be done. After the battle, they disagree about what happened, and if they were defeated, they argue about who was to blame. Strategy, like morality, is a language of justification. Every confused and cowardly commander describes his hesitations and panics as part of an elaborate plan; the strategic vocabulary is as available to him as it is to a competent commander. But that is not to say that its terms are meaningless. It would be a great triumph for the incompetent if they were, for we would then have no way to talk about incompetence. No doubt, "one calleth retreat what another calleth strategic redeployment. . . . " But we do know the difference between these two, and though the facts of the case may be difficult to collect and interpret, we are nevertheless able to make critical judgments.

Similarly, we can make moral judgments: moral concepts and strategic concepts reflect the real world in the same way. They are not merely normative terms, telling soldiers (who often don't listen) what to do. They are descriptive terms, and without them we would have no coherent way of talking about war. Here are soldiers moving away from the scene of a battle, marching over the same ground they marched over yesterday, but fewer now, less eager, many without weapons, many wounded: we call this a retreat. Here are soldiers lining up the inhabitants of a peasant village, men, women, and children, and shooting them down: we call this a massacre.

It is only when their substantive content is fairly clear that moral and strategic terms can be used imperatively, and the wisdom they embody expressed in the form of rules. Never refuse quarter to a soldier trying to surrender. Never advance with your flanks unprotected. One might construct out of such commands a moral or a strategic war plan, and then it would be important to notice whether or not the actual conduct of the war conformed to the plan. We can assume that it would not. War is recalcitrant to this sort of theoretical control—a quality it shares with every other human activity, but which it seems to possess to an especially intense degree. In *The Charterhouse of Parma,* Stendhal provides a description of the battle of Waterloo that is intended to mock the very idea of a strategic plan. It is an account of combat as chaos, therefore not an account at all but a denial, so to speak, that combat is accountable. It should be read alongside some strategic analysis of Waterloo like that of Major General Fuller, who views the battle as an organized series of maneuvers and counter-maneuvers.[10] The strategist is not unaware of confusion and disorder in the field; nor is he entirely unwilling to see these as aspects of war itself, the natural effects of the stress of battle. But he sees them also as matters of command responsibility, failures of discipline or control. He suggests that strategic imperatives have been ignored; he looks for lessons to be learned.

The moral theorist is in the same position. He too must come to grips with the fact that his rules are often violated or ignored—and with the deeper realization that, to men at war, the rules often don't seem relevant to the extremity of their situation. But however he does this, he does not surrender his sense of war as a human action, purposive and premeditated, for whose effects someone is responsible. Confronted with the many crimes committed in the course of a war, or with the crime of aggressive war itself, he searches for human agents. Nor is he alone in this search. It is one of the most important features of war, distinguishing it from the other scourges of mankind, that the men and women caught up in it are not only victims, they are also participants. All of us are inclined to hold them responsible for what they do (though we may recognize the plea of duress in particular cases). Reiterated over time, our arguments and judgments shape what I want to call *the moral reality of war*—that is, all those experiences of which moral language is descriptive or within which it is necessarily employed.

It is important to stress that the moral reality of war is not fixed by the actual activities of soldiers but by the opinions of mankind. That means, in part, that it is fixed by the activity of philosophers, lawyers, publicists of all sorts. But these people don't work in isolation from the experience of combat, and their views have value only insofar as they give shape and structure to that experience in ways that are plausible to the rest of us. We often say, for example, that in time of war soldiers and statesmen must make agonizing decisions. The pain is real enough, but it is not one of the natural effects of combat. Agony is not like Hobbist fear; it is entirely the product of our moral views, and it is common in war only insofar as those views are common. It was not some unusual Athenian who "repented" of the decision to kill the men of Mytilene, but the citizens generally. They repented, and they were able to understand one another's repentance, because they shared a sense of what cruelty meant. It is by the assignment of such meanings that we make war what it is—which is to say that it could be (and it probably has been) something different.

What of a soldier or statesman who does not feel the agony? We say of him that he is morally ignorant or morally insensitive, much as we might say of a general who experienced no difficulty making a (really) difficult decision that he did not understand the strategic realities of his own position or that he was reckless and insensible of danger. And we might go on to argue, in the case of the general, that such a man has no business fighting or leading others in battle, that he ought to know that his army's right flank, say, is vulnerable, and ought to worry about the danger and take steps to avoid it. Once again, the case is the same with moral decisions: soldiers and statesmen ought to know the dangers of cruelty and injustice and worry about them and take steps to avoid them.

HISTORICAL RELATIVISM

Against this view, however, Hobbist relativism is often given a social or historical form: moral and strategic knowledge, it is said, changes over time or varies among political communities, and so what appears to me as ignorance may look like understanding to someone else. Now, change and variation are certainly real enough, and they make for a tale that is complex in the telling. But the importance of that tale for ordinary moral life and, above all, for the judgment of moral conduct is easily exaggerated. Between radically separate and dissimilar cultures, one can expect to find radical dichotomies in perception and understanding. No doubt the moral reality of war is not the same for us as it was for Genghis Khan; nor is the strategic reality. But even fundamental social and political transformations within a particular culture may well leave the moral world intact or at least sufficiently whole so that we can still be said to share it with our ancestors. It is rare indeed that we do not share it with our contemporaries, and by and large we learn how to act among our contemporaries by studying the actions of those who have preceded us.

The assumption of that study is that they saw the world much as we do. That is not always true, but it is true enough of the time to give stability and coherence to our moral lives (and to our military lives). Even when world views and high ideals have been abandoned—as the glorification of aristocratic chivalry was abandoned in early modern times—notions about right conduct are remarkably persistent: the military code survives the death of warrior idealism. I shall say more about this survival later on, but I can demonstrate it now in a general way by looking at an example from feudal Europe, an age in some ways more distant from us than Greece of the city states, but with which we nevertheless share moral and strategic perceptions.

Three Accounts of Agincourt

Actually, the sharing of strategic perceptions is in this case the more dubious of the two. Those French knights so many of whom died at Agincourt had notions about combat very different from our own. Modern critics have still felt able to criticize their "fanatical adherence to the old method of fighting" (King Henry, after all, fought differently) and even to offer practical suggestions: the French attack, writes Oman, "should have been accompanied by a turning movement around the woods. . . . "[11] Had he not been "overconfident," the French commander would have seen the advantages of the move. We can talk in a similar way about the crucial moral decision that Henry made toward the end of the battle, when the English thought their victory secure. They had taken many prisoners, who were loosely assembled behind the lines. Suddenly, a French attack aimed at the supply tents far in the rear seemed to threaten a renewal of the fighting. Here is Holinshed's sixteenth century account of the incident (virtually copied from an earlier chronicle):

> . . . certain Frenchmen on horseback . . . to the number of six hundred horsemen, which were the first that fled, hearing that the English tents and pavilions were a good way distant from the army, without any sufficient guard to defend the same . . . entered upon the king's camp and there . . . robbed the tents, broke up chests, and carried away caskets and slew such servants as they found to make any resistance. . . . But when the outcry of the lackeys and boys which ran away for fear of the Frenchmen . . . came to the king's ears, he doubting lest his enemies should gather together again, and begin a new field; and mistrusting further that the prisoners would be an aid to his enemies . . . contrary to his accustomed gentleness, commanded by sound of trumpet that every man . . . should incontinently slay his prisoner.[12]

The moral character of the command is suggested by the words "accustomed gentleness" and "incontinently." It involved a shattering of personal and conventional restraints (the latter well-established by 1415), and Holinshed goes to some lengths to explain and excuse it, stressing the king's fear that the prisoners his forces held were about to rejoin the fighting. Shakespeare, whose *Henry V* closely follows Holinshed, goes further, emphasizing the slaying of the English servants by the French and omitting the chronicler's assertion that only those who resisted were killed:

> *Fluellen*. Kill the [b]oys and the baggage! 'Tis expressly against the law of arms. 'Tis as arrant a piece of knavery, mark you now, as can be offert.[13]

At the same time, however, he cannot resist an ironical comment:

> *Gower*. . . . they have burned and carried away all that was in the king's tent, wherefore the king most worthily hath caused every soldier to cut his prisoner's throat. O, 'tis a gallant king!

A century and a half later, David Hume gives a similar account, without the irony, stressing instead the king's eventual cancellation of his order:

> . . . some gentlemen of Picardy . . . had fallen upon the English baggage, and were doing execution on the unarmed followers of the camp, who fled before them. Henry, seeing the enemy on all sides of him, began to entertain apprehensions from his prisoners; and he thought it necessary to issue a general order for putting them to death; but on discovering the truth, he stopped the slaughter, and was still able to save a great number.[14]

Here the moral meaning is caught in the tension between "necessary" and "slaughter." Since slaughter is the killing of men as if they were animals—it "makes a massacre," wrote the poet Dryden, "what was a war"—it cannot often be called necessary. If the prisoners were so easy to kill, they were probably not dangerous enough to warrant the killing. When he grasped the actual situation, Henry, who was (so Hume wants us to believe) a moral man, called off the executions.

French chroniclers and historians write of the event in much the same way. It is from them that we learn that many of the English knights refused to kill their prisoners—not, chiefly, out of humanity, rather for the sake of the ransom they expected; but also "thinking of the dishonor that the horrible executions would reflect on themselves."[15] English writers have focused more, and more worriedly, on the command of the king; he was, after all, their king. In the later nineteenth century, at about the same time as the rules of war with respect to prisoners were being codified, their criticism grew increasingly sharp: "a brutal butchery," "cold-blooded wholesale murder."[16] Hume would not have said that, but the difference between that and what he did say is marginal, not a matter of moral or linguistic transformation.

To judge Henry ourselves we would need a more circumstantial account of the battle than I can provide here.[17] Even given that account, our opinions might differ, depending on the allowance we were willing to make for the stress and excitement of battle. But this is a clear example of a situation common in both strategy and morality, where our sharpest disagreements are structured and organized by our underlying agreements, by the meanings we share. For Holinshed, Shakespeare, and Hume—traditional chronicler, Renaissance playwright, and Enlightenment historian—and for us too, Henry's command belongs to a category of military acts that requires scrutiny and judgment. It is *as a matter of fact* morally problematic, because it accepts the risks of cruelty and injustice. In exactly the same way, we might regard the battle plan of the French commander as strategically problematic, because it accepted the risks of a frontal assault on a prepared position. And, again, a general who did not recognize these risks is properly said to be ignorant of morality or strategy.

In moral life, ignorance isn't all that common; dishonesty is far more so. Even those soldiers and statesmen who don't feel the agony of a problematic decision generally know that they should feel it. Harry Truman's flat statement that he never lost a night's sleep over his decision to drop the atomic bomb on Hiroshima is not the sort of thing political leaders often say. They usually find it preferable to stress the painfulness of decision-making; it is one of the burdens of office, and it is best if the burdens appear to be borne. I suspect that many officeholders even experience pain simply because they are expected to. If they don't, they lie about it. The clearest evidence for the stability of our values over time is the unchanging character of the lies soldiers and statesmen tell. They lie in order to justify themselves, and so they describe for us the lineaments of justice. Wherever we find hypocrisy, we also find moral knowledge. The hypocrite is like that Russian general in Solzhenitsyn's *August 1914*, whose elaborate battle reports barely concealed his total inability to control or direct the battle. He knew at least that there was a story to tell, a set of names to attach to things and happenings, so he tried to tell the story and attach the names. His effort was not mere mimicry; it was, so to speak, the tribute that incompetence pays to understanding. The case is the same in moral life: there really is a story to tell, a way of talking about wars and battles that the rest of us recognize as morally appropriate. I don't mean that particular decisions are necessarily right or wrong, or simply right or wrong, only that there is a way of seeing the world so that moral decision-making makes sense. The hypocrite knows that this is true, though he may actually see the world differently.

Hypocrisy is rife in wartime discourse, because it is especially important at such a time to appear to be in the right. It is not only that the moral stakes are high; the hypocrite may not understand that; more crucially, his actions will be judged by other people, who are not hypocrites, and whose judgments will affect their policies toward him. There would be no point to hypocrisy if this were not so, just as there would be no point to lying in a world where no one told the truth. The hypocrite presumes on the moral understanding of the rest of us, and we have no choice, I think, except to take his assertions seriously and put them to the test of moral realism. He pretends to think and act as the rest of us expect him to do. He tells us that he is fighting according to the moral war plan: he does not aim at civilians, he grants quarter to soldiers trying to surrender, he never tortures prisoners, and so on. These claims are true or false, and though it is not easy to judge them (nor is the war plan really so simple), it is important to make the effort. Indeed, if we call ourselves moral men and women, we must make the effort, and the evidence is that we regularly do so. If we had all become realists like the Athenian generals or like Hobbists in a state of war, there would be an end alike to both morality and hypocrisy. We would simply tell one another, brutally and directly, what we wanted to do or have done. But the truth is that one of the things most of us want, even in war, is to act or to seem to act morally. And we want that, most simply, because we know what morality means (at least, we know what it is generally thought to mean). . . .

NOTES

1. This and subsequent quotations are from Hobbes' *Thucydides*, ed. Richard Schlatter (New Brunswick, N.J., 1975), pp. 377–85 (*The History of The Peloponnesian War*, 5:84–116).
2. Dionysius of Halicarnassus, *On Thucydides*, trans. W. Kendrick Pritchett (Berkeley, 1975), pp. 31–33.
3. See F. M. Cornford, *Thucydides Mythistoricus* (London, 1907), esp. ch. XIII.
4. *The Trojan Women*, trans. Gilbert Murray (London, 1905), p. 16.
5. Werner Jaeger, *Paideia: the Ideals of Greek Culture*, trans. Gilbert Highet (New York, 1939), I, 402.
6. H. W. Fowler, *A Dictionary of Modern English Usage*, second ed., rev. Sir Ernest Gowers (New York, 1965), p. 168; cf. Jaeger, I, 397.
7. *Plutarch's Lives*, trans. John Dryden, rev. Arthur Hugh Clough (London, 1910), I, 303. Alcibiades also "selected for himself one of the captive Melian women . . . "
8. Hobbes' *Thucydides*, pp. 194–204 (*The History of the Peloponnesian War*, 3:36–49).
9. Thomas Hobbes, *Leviathan*, ch. IV.
10. *The Charterhouse of Parma*, I, chs. 3 and 4; J. F. C. Fuller, *A Military History of the Western World* (n.p., 1955), II, ch. 15.
11. C. W. C. Oman, *The Art of War in the Middle Ages* (Ithaca, N.Y., 1968), p. 137.
12. Raphael Holinshed, *Chronicles of England, Scotland, and Ireland*, excerpted in William Shakespeare, *The Life of Henry V* (Signet Classics, New York, 1965), p. 197.
13. *Henry V*, 4:7, ll. 1–11.
14. David Hume, *The History of England* (Boston, 1854), II, 358.
15. René de Belleval, *Azincourt* (Paris, 1865), pp. 105–06.
16. See the summary of opinions in J. H. Wylie, *The Reign of Henry the Fifth* (Cambridge, England, 1919), II, 171ff.
17. For an excellent and detailed account, which suggests that Henry's action cannot be defended, see John Keegan, *The Face of Battle* (New York, 1976), pp. 107–12.

Values and Paradigm Change: The Elusive Quest for International Relations Theory

Richard W. Mansbach and Yale H. Ferguson

The authors present a sobering assessment of the current state of the international relations discipline and the role of values.

It is difficult to find a major work on international relations that either does not urge that the discipline synthesize a new paradigm or does not itself offer such a paradigm.[1] Implicit in such works is the assumption that the "constellation of beliefs, values, techniques, and so on shared by the members"[2] of the international relations fraternity is undergoing change in the manner in which science, according to Thomas Kuhn, evolves, for example, that our basic understanding of the world around us is growing even as theoretical consensus breaks down.

Kuhn's analysis of the natural sciences suggests that when a discipline is confronted by significant and unanswerable anomalies, it ultimately enters a period of crisis during which an existing paradigm is replaced by another that can effectively overcome these anomalies. For Kuhn, understanding and knowledge proceed progressively; earlier paradigms become no more than historical curiosities to subsequent generations of scholars. "Why," asks Kuhn, "should the student of physics, for example, read the works of Newton, Faraday, Einstein, or Schrodinger, when everything he needs to know about these works is recapitulated in a far briefer, more precise, and more systematic form in a number of up-to-date textbooks?"[3] For a discipline in need of confidence that progress is indeed occurring, Kuhn's analysis provides a confidence-building rationale for apparent disarray. After all, "during a preparadigm period, when there is a multiplicity of competing schools, evidence of progress is very hard to find," and "during periods of revolution . . . doubts are repeatedly expressed about the very possibility of continued progress if one or another of the opposed paradigms is adopted."[4]

There is thus actually more at stake for those who claim that our discipline is a science than the outcome of methodological controversies. The claim to scientific status among scholars of international relations appears to be necessary for many of us to maintain a sense of intellectual and institutional well-being in the face of disciplinary adversity. To the extent that we can manage to keep up our faith in James Rosenau's asser-

Published from Margaret P. Karns, *Persistent Patterns and Emergent Structures in a Waning Century*, Praeger, 1986.

tion "that the same methods that unraveled the mysteries of atomic structure can reveal the dynamics of societal behavior,"[5] we may also continue to trust that progress is taking place despite the theoretical chaos around us.

Our intention is not to reopen the "science" versus "traditionalist" controversy,[6] but rather to suggest that there are sufficient differences between the evolution of theoretical change in the social sciences, including international relations, and Kuhn's version of the natural sciences that his analysis may not be applicable. If that is the case, our perception of progress may be illusory. In addition, we wish to describe briefly a most un-Kuhnian version of the way in which ideas emerge and compete in international relations.

THE SOURCE AND ROLE OF VALUES

Kuhn himself highlights the most significant difference between the natural and social sciences when he notes "the unparalleled insulation of mature scientific communities from the demands of the laity and of everyday life."[7]

> In this respect . . . the contrast between natural scientists and many social scientists proves instructive. The latter often tend, as the former almost never do, to defend their choice of a research problem . . . chiefly in terms of the social importance of achieving a solution.[8]

In other words, the work of the social scientist is generally infused by a commitment to serve the needs of the society of which he/she is a member.

The importance of Kuhn's observation was appreciated two decades before by E. H. Carr when he wrote:

> The science of international politics has . . . come into being in response to a popular demand. It has been created to serve a purpose. . . . At first sight, this pattern may appear illogical. Our first business, it will be said, is to collect, classify and analyse our facts and draw out inferences; and we shall then be ready to investigate the purpose to which our facts and our deductions can be put. The processes of the human mind do not, however, appear to develop in this logical order. . . . Purpose, which should logically follow analysis, is required to give it both its initial impulse and its direction.[9]

Thus, the facts that scholars amass and the phenomena with which they preoccupy themselves are selections derived initially from a set of specific normative concerns. In proceeding in this fashion, they inevitably decide to ignore other facts and phenomena. If they choose to take cognizance of the latter at a future date, that choice reflects a shift in normative concerns rather than a paradigm change in the Kuhnian sense.[10] Carr sees this as a condition of the physical sciences as well, but notes correctly how much more difficult it is to isolate facts from values in social science:

> The purpose is not, as in the physical sciences, irrelevant to the investigation and separable from it: it is itself one of the facts. In theory, the distinction may no doubt still be drawn between the role of the investigator who establishes the facts and the role of the practitioner who considers the right course of action. In practice, one role shades imperceptibly into the other. Purpose and analysis become part and parcel of a single process.[11]

This synthesis of purpose and analysis is clearly in evidence in R. J. Rummel's autobiographical reflection, which could probably be echoed by many in our profession. "My lifelong superordinate goal," Rummel declares, "has been to eliminate war and social violence; only by understanding this goal's genesis and enveloping cognitive structure can Dimensionality of Nations Project (DON) research and my current reorientation be grasped. For to me science or quantitative research are not the aims, but tools to be pragmatically applied to doing something about war."[12] How different from this was the normative commitment of the German historian Heinrich Von Treitschke when he thundered that the "grandeur of history lies in the perpetual conflict of nations, and it is simply foolish to desire the suppression of their rivalry.[13] How well these contrasting admissions reveal the starkly different normative climates of the societies in which they were written!

In many ways, Jacob Bronowski's arguments against the "naturalistic fallacy" in the natural sciences are, if anything, even more germane to the social sciences. Bronowski suggests that normative consequences inhere in scientific discovery for at least three reasons.[14] The first is that discovery reveals that certain forms of conduct are "obviously ridiculous" and that one ought to tailor one's own actions so as not to be ridiculous. The second is that science informs us of our capabilities as human beings and "that it is right that we should practice those gifts." Finally, and most importantly for Bronowski, scientists must behave in certain ways in order to learn what is true, which is the object of their calling: "What is the good of talking about what is, when in fact you are told how to behave in order to discover what is true. 'Ought' is dictated by 'is' in the actual inquiry for knowledge. Knowledge cannot be gained unless you behave in certain ways."[15]

In large measure, theoretical debates among political scientists reflect different normative commitments that are indirectly revealed in competing claims over which actors should be studied, which level of analysis is most appropriate, which variables are critical, and which issues are most pressing. What is striking about these debates and what distinguishes them from debates in the natural sciences is that essentially the same arguments and emphases tend to recur over and over again through time, despite superficial changes in concepts and language. As we shall suggest, such debates recur because they revolve around enduring normative themes.[16] The key assertions of realism and idealism, for example, have been present in intellectual discourse about international relations at least since Thucydides.

Thucydides's *Melian Dialogue* and Thrasymachus's argument with Socrates in Plato's *Republic* are enduring reflections of the antimony between power and justice. Centuries of European political theorists served the roles of "realists" and "idealists." Machiavelli and those later known as Machiavellians consciously propounded their versions of realism in contrast to the so-called idealists of their time.[17] The old realist-idealist debate is currently manifested in debates among structural realists, neo-Marxists, and unrepentant neofunctionalists.

Although the normative elements in these debates are, perhaps, less evident in contemporary international relations discourse than in the past, owing to conscious efforts of social scientists to be "scientific" and "value-free," the debates are no less value-laden than their precursors. Dominant schools of thought in international relations are as much a part of the *Zeitgeist* of their age as are dominant theories of art and literature; all are part of the *ductus* of a culture.[18] Indeed, the contemporary devotion to science in international relations is a phenomenon that will always be associated with the late twentieth-century United States and the numerous symbols of its "modernity"—pragmatism, technology, nonrepresentational art, functional architecture, and so forth. All reflect a similar ethos, fully as much as did *The Trojan Women* of Euripides and Thucydides's *History*.[19]

Whatever the prospects, then, for applying the scientific method to studying political phenomena, political science will continue to develop more like one of the arts than one of the sciences unless or until political scientists can isolate themselves from the milieu whose problems they seek to address. This, we believe, is an impossible task and probably not one worth undertaking.

THE REALIST "PARADIGM"

Scholars of international relations who are content to view their discipline as evolving in a Kuhnian manner are wont to cite the fate of realism, which, they claim, once assumed the role of a paradigm but has had to give way in the face of persistent anomalies. It is certainly the case that in the years following World War II, realism came to dominate the field. It even had an "exemplar" in Hans J. Morgenthau's *Politics Among Nations* (1948); and, in general, textbooks from the 1940s to the end of the 1960s tended to share realist assumptions.[20] Realist theory, especially as articulated by Morgenthau, was at once elegant and parsimonious, but the theory did not achieve ascendancy simply because it was able to account for anomalies that its competitors had failed to explain. In fact, so-called idealist and Marxist theory can explain the outbreak of World War II quite as convincingly as can realism. Although the facts of history do not change, dominant interpretations do vary as those facts are viewed through changing normative lenses. And normative disputes of this ilk are anchored in genuine political and policy quarrels among practitioners seeking to cope with life and death issues; such disputes are not the stuff of ivory towers alone. In recent years, this phenomenon has been most clearly reflected in analyses of the Cold War, but it was equally characteristic of analyses of earlier wars as well.

Realists accused Western statesmen in the interwar period of having "deprecated" power in favor of legal and moral solutions to the problems of their time. In doing so, according to realists, idealists confused theory with practice and confounded scientific with normative analysis. Yet, for the most part, the supposedly offending statesmen were quite as aware of the balance of power as their realist critics but were as unable as are contemporary analysts to assess that balance in a manner that could provide clear policy guidelines. In addition, they were conscious of the role that balance-of-power politics had played in bringing about the conflagration of 1914. Furthermore, national power, as Morgenthau himself notes, includes such unmeasurable elements as "national character," "national morale," "the quality of diplomacy," and "the quality of government."[21] Diplomats' efforts to formulate policy sought to account for these several factors, yet realist criticisms come perilously near to focusing only on military factors. Ultimately, Morgenthau admits that the calculation of national power "is an ideal task and, hence, incapable of achievement,"[22] and this admission forces us to ask why realists think that they could have done better. Ironically, the factor that was least understood by interwar politicians was one for which realists cannot account: the motives and personality of Hitler, who refused to behave according to the dictates of balance of power. History revealed to the realists (and to many of the practitioners of that time as well) that the interwar statesmen should have acted differently. Unfortunately, theory that can provide answers only retrospectively is of limited value.

The victory of realism after World War II, then, supports the notion that theory in international relations evolves somewhat differently than does the almost dialectical manner in which Kuhn views paradigm change in the natural sciences.[23] Realism was not merely a product of "the recognition that nature has somehow violated the paradigm-induced expectations,"[24] but also represented a condemnation of earlier norms brought about by the revolutionary effects of the war. For Kuhn, a paradigm shift occurs not because the natural universe itself changes but because something about that universe is revealed for which the existing paradigm cannot account. In contrast, realism achieved ascendancy because the political universe itself changed after 1945. The occurrence of World War II served less to reveal anomalies in an existing paradigm than to provide normative justification for the claims of power thinkers who had been competing with "idealist" rivals for centuries. In the same way, World War I had previously provided normative justification for Wilsonians to assert the superiority of moral universalism over "narrow nationalists" and "balance-of-power" advocates, and the early years of the interwar period seemed to represent the final victory of the Gladstone-Cobden school over the adherents of Disraeli.

For their part, twentieth-century realists were not especially innovative theoretically; nor did they claim to be, as reflected in their repeated references to eighteenth-century European political practice and the ideas of Alexander Hamilton as sources of their wisdom.[25] It was not, then, that they could account for anomalies in an existing body of thought, but that they eloquently asserted the normative superiority of the national interest over universalism. The key to their victory lay less in the power of their assumptions than in the claim that their work was "empirical and pragmatic"[26] and that they could discern a "science of international politics."[27] For a number of reasons, this claim exercised a powerful attraction in the years after World War II; the soil was indeed fertile for what Morgenthau declared to be "another great debate."[28] Realism entailed a rejection of ideologies such as those that had legitimized the excesses of the previous years, as well as of those institutional and legal efforts to eliminate world conflict that had failed in the 1920s and 1930s. Moreover, realism meshed nicely with the United States' self-image at a time that the country had so clearly emerged as *primus inter pares* in the global system.[29]

U.S. science and economic productivity had won the war, and the atom bomb would secure the peace. Of course, pragmatism, positivism, faith in scientific advancement, and free enterprise themselves constituted an ideology, but one that appeared to be objective and rational. In this context, realism was especially attractive because it, too, appeared to offer an alternative to ideological and moralistic analysis. "Intellectually," declared Morgenthau, "the political realist maintains the autonomy of the political sphere, as the economist, the lawyer, the moralist maintain theirs,"[30] a claim that served the paradigmatic purpose of providing disciplinary boundaries and predicted the reductionist preferences of later scholars. Although, like Machiavelli, realists were accused of being amoral, like Machiavelli, they, in fact, provided a rather clear set of moral and prescriptive dicta that constituted the obligations of official decision makers seeking to serve the national interest. Indeed, one of the ironies of the realist triumph is that the realists were able to make a powerful moral case against their intellectual adversaries by asserting the value-free character of their theories, while simultaneously providing moral and prescriptive guidelines for a generation of scholars and statesmen.

Surveys have shown that Morgenthau is the political theorist whose ideas have been most familiar to U.S. policymakers.[31] Bernard Brodie writes of a "strong and rigid . . . professional tradition" among them, holding that the intrusion of moral considerations is "inherently mischievous, that is . . . likely to cause the warping of what otherwise would be trimly correct thinking about foreign affairs."[32] Richard J. Barnet summarizes this position:

> Those who run nations cannot be unselfish, generous, or even honest in the jungle world of international relations because such impulses are not reciprocated. To recognize external limits on discretion is to compromise the interests of the American people and of future generations for whom the statesman is supposed to act as trustee.

To the realist, he continues, "what was expedient also became right. . . . Neither God, law, world opinion, right reason, or any other outside standard was recognized as a limit on their own discretion, for that discretion, they convinced themselves, would be exercised in pursuit of the highest moral values."[33]

In justifying expediency, realism neatly reinforced the ideological tenet of "pragmatism" that has been central to U.S. culture and for policymakers who are the product of that culture. For instance, David Halberstam reports:

> In the early days of the [Kennedy] Administration [the word pragmatism] had been used so frequently that David Brinkley, writing the introduction of an early book of portraits of the Kennedy people, would dwell on that single word, and note that at an early Washington cocktail party a woman had gone around the room asking each of the hundred people there if he was a pragmatist.[34]

Pragmatism is an example of what might be termed "the attitude of ideology toward itself," advancing as it does the proposition that "practical" responses to the "real world" should take precedence over the dictates of ideology (other than pragmatism). In fact, pragmatism has regularly allowed decision makers to conceal from themselves the ideological premises behind their policies and, less often, to congratulate themselves on the "rightness" of their policies when the dictates of ideology and the demands of the "real world" have seemed to coincide. The concealing function of pragmatism has been enhanced by its links to the realist concept of the "national interest," purporting as it does to provide an "objective" standard for national policy. Of course, as numerous critics have pointed out, this supposed standard is so vague that its interpretation cannot help but involve a highly subjective judgment. Arnold Wolfers states:

> Political formulas such as 'national interest' may not mean the same thing to different people. They may not have precise meaning at all. Thus, while appearing to offer guidance and a basis for broad consensus they may be permitting everyone to label whatever policy he favors with an attractive and possibly deceptive name.[35]

Realism thus provided the legerdemain through which the sow's ear of the pragmatist's expediency could be converted into the silk purse of the pursuit of the national interest.

The realist's association of the national interest concept with the "struggle for power," in turn, has reinforced yet another aspect of what Richard Barnet sees as part of the U.S. tradition, a phenomenon that he terms "bureaucratic machismo." He writes: "One of the first lessons a national security manager learns after a day in the bureaucratic climate of the Pentagon, State Department, White House, or CIA is that toughness is the most highly prized virtue." U.S. officials have customarily adopted a self-consciously "tough," "hard-nosed" brand of decision making and evidenced a profound distrust of policies favored by "soft-headed," "liberal" "idealists" and "intellectuals."[36]

Many intellectuals, too, were influenced by realism. Realism's apparent rejection of institutional and legal mechanisms and its assertion of the value-free nature of theory were instrumental in encouraging the behavioral and scientific revolutions in international politics. Morgenthau's assertion that realism "requires indeed a sharp distinction between the desirable and the possible"[37] was, especially in the 1960s, repeated by a generation of scholars who believed that it was possible to separate values from the study of political phenomena. For the most part, these scholars retained the assumptions of realism and, in retrospect, performed the task of "normal science" in the Kuhnian sense.[38] Their contributions were primarily methodological rather than theoretical and served to institutionalize and legitimize realism's key assumptions.

THE VICISSITUDES OF THEORY: THE DECLINE OF REALISM

The 1970s witnessed a concerted assault on the several realist assumptions—the centrality of the unitary state as actor, the autonomy of the international and domestic realms of politics, and the existence of the single issue of managing power—accompanied by an implicit "declaration of independence" from the doctrine.

Among the principal lines of attack were those that highlighted nonrational sources of decision makers' behavior,[39] the impact of situations on decision making,[40] the importance of bureaucratic politics and organizational behavior,[41] the significance of transnationalism and interdependence,[42] the role of nonstate actors,[43] and the influence of issues on behavior.[44] In a word, realism was no longer a "disciplinary matrix."[45]

None of the above phenomena identified by these scholars as detracting from realism was new, and none was in any sense "discovered" in the 1970s. For example, as regards nonrational sources of behavior, even as realism was in the ascendant the ideas of Freud were entering the discipline,[46] the evolution of the containment policy and the reorganization of the U.S. defense and foreign policy establishment were providing clear cases of the impact of situation and bureaucracies,[47] the integration of Western Europe was revealing some of the implications of interdependence and transnationalism;[48] the emergence of revolutionary and anticolonial movements and of multinational corporations reflected the potential roles of nonstate actors, while the appearance of a North–South axis, alongside an East–West axis, illustrated the role of issues.[49]

What had changed was the frame of reference of scholars and the ethos of the society in which they were working. Although many factors were involved in bringing about these changes, the decline in U.S. hegemony symbolized by Vietnam, the growing salience of nonmilitary problems with an economic or environmental basis, and growing fears of nuclear war encouraged scholarly criticisms that were grounded in an unarticulated criticism of realist norms.

The Vietnam debacle suggested that the elements of power were even more obscure than had been realized, that national power was contextual, and that military capabilities had limited utility. Successive energy crises highlighted the existence of fragile economic interdependence and the finite nature of key resources. Endemic stagflation in the West pointed to the central role of economics in national power, reinforced the growing sense of interdependence, and focused attention upon issues without any evident military dimension. In many ways, successive environmental traumas had the same effects. Finally, the demise of détente and the achievement of technomilitary breakthroughs unleashed dormant fears in the United States and Europe regarding the adequacy of nuclear deterrence as a formula for managing conflict.

These events promoted a shift in the nature of political vocabulary and dialogue. That altered vocabulary emphasized the linked fate of humanity as a whole, processes and interactions only partly controlled by national decision makers, and potential outcomes in which the differences between "winning" and "losing" were unclear. For the most part, these were precisely the concerns that had motivated political thinkers after 1919 and had shaped their vocabulary and dialogue.

Although a feedback loop of sorts is obviously involved, political dialogue is most accurately seen as a reflection, rather than a cause, of the normative temper of an era. It is the shift in that temper, rather than the appearance of anomalies, that seems to stimulate paradigm shifts in international relations. Such a shift occurs under conditions of rapid change and stressful events that generate an atmosphere of unpredictability and instability, a sense that somehow new and baleful forces are at work that will alter existing conditions in ways not as yet fully apprehended. In these circumstances, prior patterns of behavior and standard procedures no longer seem able to perform the tasks for which they were established or appear unsuited for new tasks that are identified.

Although the causal sequence remains unclear, such periods seem to be associated with the genesis of sharply different religious, scientific, social, and ideological concepts; qualitative technological changes; and major unanticipated events, especially wars and environmental disasters. Often these occur together, though not necessarily so. Fifth-century Greece was one such period. This era witnessed the development of tragedy by the Athenian poets, the philosophic relativism of the Sophists, the introduction of empirical diagnosis by Hippocrates of Cos, the development of mining at Mount Laurion (which provided precious metals for a monied economy), the earthquake and helot revolt in Sparta (464 B.C.), the plague in Athens (430 B.C.), and the Peloponnesian War. These developments provided the bases for Thucydides's view of the world. The late fifteenth through the early seventeenth century in Europe was another tumultuous period. A renewal of the plague; the rise of Protestantism; the ideas of Brahe, Galileo, and Kepler regarding the physical universe; the spread of movable type; the rifling of guns and the boring of cannons; and, finally, the Thirty Years' War—all combined to constitute a sharp break with the past and to usher in fundamental revisions of the normative order. Changes of such magnitude pointed to new issues in need of resolution and/or new opportunities to be exploited.

Intervening between changing conditions and revision of the normative order are perceptions of linkages among stakes at issue in the global arena and the hierarchy of issues on the global agenda.[50] Fears of value deprivation and/or identification of new opportunities for value satisfaction occur as old stakes disappear and new ones emerge. Although these processes are continuous, they are especially intense during periods of potential or actual shifts in the global status hierarchy when the enfeeblement of high-status actors encourages challenges to an existing distribution of stakes and the energizing of low-status actors spurs their ambition.[51] Thus, the dramatic increase in German industrial and military strength and significant medical advances in the second half of the nineteenth century, coupled with the relative decline of Great Britain and France, made available as stakes territories in Africa that previously had been seen as preempted or qualitatively inaccessible. Similarly, the decline of traditional trade unions in the West and the growing obsolescence of traditional industries at a time of recession and high unemployment in the 1980s have transformed into stakes many social and economic benefits that until recently were regarded as sacrosanct.

As new stakes become available for, and old ones removed from, contention, new issues emerge, old ones are redefined, and the salience of issues on the global agenda may shift dramatically. Changes in issue salience redirect attention toward the values that underlie the newly important issues and away from values that are associated with declining issues.[52] Accordingly, the value of prosperity, which had dominated the value hierarchy during the Great Depression, became a secondary concern with the outbreak of World War II and its aftermath, during which time physical security and freedom became principal preoccupations. As memories of the war receded in the 1960s and 1970s and the relative salience of key issues continued to change, values like peace, health, and human dignity assumed greater importance.

Changes in the global agenda of issues and in the value hierarchy invariably produce new normative emphases, which are reflected in what we have called the normative temper of an era. Normative shifts occur along several dimensions, often at the same time. Among the most important of these are mutability–immutability, optimism–pessimism, competitiveness–community, and elitism–nonelitism.

Mutability–immutability is the degree to which it is believed that human affairs and the conditions that shape them can or will be purposefully modified. In traditional cultures, the status quo in human affairs is accepted as inevitable and unchanging and the conditions in which humans find themselves are viewed as not subject to manipulation. Arguments that attribute behavior to the supernatural or to human nature commonly assume immutability. By contrast, modern Western science assumes almost unlimited mutability. The normative implication of a belief in immutability is that efforts to change the human condition are, at best, a waste of time and, at worst, dangerous and illusory. In any event, such efforts ought not to be made. Realism in its several versions tends to view political conditions as relatively immutable, whether owing to "human nature" (Morgenthau), "original sin" (Niebuhr), or system anarchy (Waltz). Although realists accept that alterations in the distribution of power continuously occur, they see a struggle for power as a permanent feature of international politics. Nowhere is this emphasis on immutability more succinctly expressed than in Morgenthau's observation that, "human nature, in which the laws of politics have their roots, has not changed since the classical philosophies of China, India, and Greece endeavored to discover these laws. Hence novelty is not necessarily a virtue in political theory, nor is old age a defect."[53]

This emphasis leads realists to criticize those who seek to reform prevailing conditions; such individuals are "divorced from the facts . . . and informed by prejudice and wishful thinking," and the laws of politics, rooted as they are in human nature, are "impervious to our preferences."[54] In the United States and Europe, at least, such an emphasis found ready acceptance after World War II with the apparent failure of bold experiments like the League of Nations. Those who sought to make fundamental changes were dismissed as "idealists." Even Marxism–Leninism, with its putative belief in the march of history and the uplifting of humankind, seemed to have lost its vigor in Stalin's conservative empire. Since experimentation entailed an element of peril, "prudence" became the prescriptive hallmark of realism. The prudent leader understands the immutability of historical laws, and eschews bold efforts to transform humankind or the global system.

Optimism–pessimism constitutes a second key normative dimension. Unlike mutability–immutability, which describes the degree to which it is believed that change can be engineered by human intervention, optimism–pessimism refers to the direction in which change is taking place, whether such change is the consequence of purposeful modification or not. More simply, it describes the answer given to the question, Are conditions likely to improve or not? Nevertheless, as the previous discussion of realism suggests, those who see conditions as relatively immutable are also likely to view change in a distinctly pessimistic light. After all, if the forces of change cannot be governed and directed, change itself is likely to be fickle, unpredictable, and ultimately dangerous. There are, of course, significant exceptions to this intellectual propensity. Classical Marxists, for example, view history itself as an engine of progress governed by laws of economic development that will in time improve the human condition. As Kenneth Waltz points out, even those who start from an assumption that human nature is relatively immutable can be divided into "optimists" and "pessimists."[55] There are obviously degrees of immutability that allow for varying assessments of the potential for change.

Overall, however, optimism is at least partly a function of belief in mutability. Natural and behavioral scientists and social reformers share a common acceptance of the possibility that conditions and behavior can be improved by the accumulation of knowledge and the application of that knowledge. (How clearly this emerges from the passages cited earlier from Bronowski!) The normative implication of such optimism is that it is the obligation of those with knowledge and insight to apply these for the benefit of humanity.[56] In the context of political life, liberalism tends to be associated with optimism and conservatism with pessimism.[57]

It is no coincidence that intellectual optimism and scientific advance are associated with eras and places in which the norms of a culture were also characterized by a wave of optimism—Renaissance Italy, late eighteenth-century France, Edwardian England, and pre-Depression United States. While pessimism encourages political conservatism and inertia, waves of optimism inspire great efforts to give history a push. Political revolutions, for example, generally occur in the context of growing optimism, or at least a belief that the improvement of conditions is probable once the weight of existing institutions is swept away. As the historian George Soule observed:

> When the people are in their most desperate and miserable condition, they are often least inclined to revolt, for then they are hopeless. . . . Only after their position is somewhat improved and they have sensed the possibility of change, do they revolt effectively against oppression and injustice. What touches off insurrection is hope, not lack of it, rising confidence, not bleak suffering.[58]

Wordsworth's description in book 12 of *Prelude* of his feelings at the time of the French Revolution captures perfectly the optimism of that era:[59] "Bliss was it in that dawn to be alive,/But to be young was very heaven!"

In the context of international relations theory, the ascendance of realism reflected in part a rejection of the prevailing optimism of the 1920s and early 1930s. Yet realism is not a doctrine of unrelieved gloom. Realists do see it as possible to ameliorate the effects of international conflict by the judicious management of power. Indeed, some neorealists, like Kenneth Waltz, can be regarded as cautiously optimistic.[60] As a whole, advocates of a scientific approach to the discipline in the 1960s, while retaining many of realism's critical assumptions, reflected an increasing optimism about the prospects for overcoming the most dangerous problems of international relations insofar as the methods of the natural sciences were to be applied to an understanding of them. However, growing fears about environmental, political, and economic trends in the early 1970s produced a renewal of pessimism that was perhaps most vividly reflected in Robert Heilbroner's *Inquiry into the Human Prospect:*

> At this stage of our inquiry, with the full spectacle of the human prospect before us, the spirit quails and the will falters. We find ourselves pressed to the very limit of our personal capacities, not alone in summoning up the courage to look squarely at the dimensions of the impending predicament, but in finding words that can offer some plausible relief in a situation so bleak. There is now nowhere to turn other than to those private beliefs and disbeliefs that guide each of us through life.[61]

And this pessimism was a significant aspect of the revolt against realism and the reemergence of doubts regarding the ultimate prospects for a science of international relations.

A third normative variable that is central to international relations theory is that of *competitiveness–community,* that is, the degree to which welfare and/or deprivation is perceived in relative or absolute terms. Are evaluations of status and value satisfaction made in comparison with others, or are they made in terms of an absolute level that changes over time? The former emphasizes competition for scarce resources, and the latter linked fates and interdependence. When evaluation is made in relative terms, it implies that greater value satisfaction can be achieved only at the expense of others; changes in the absolute level of well-being matter less than the distribution of costs and benefits. Outcomes are viewed in zero-sum, rather than positive- or negative-sum, terms.

It is commonly argued that the emphasis on competition intensifies as perceptions of scarcity grow. This is not, however, necessarily the case. Highly competitive doctrines such as Adam Smith's version of capitalism or late nineteenth-century Social Darwinism became popular in exuberantly expansionist eras. In contrast, recent doctrines of interdependence and "limits to growth," which are at least in part based on perceptions of scarcity, emphasize the shared condition of humankind and the absolute nature of value enhancement and deprivation. Nor does there seem to be any necessary connection between competitiveness–community and optimism–pessimism, despite the common assertion that pessimism encourages competitive evaluations.

Realism, with its emphasis on national interest, clearly falls on the competitive end of the spectrum. Morgenthau's definition of international politics "as a continuing effort to maintain and to increase the power of one's own nation and to keep in check or reduce the power of other nations"[62] highlights the realist emphasis on the relative nature of status and security in the global system. Although there is an implication that a scarcity of political goods conditions the intensity of competition, it is the absence of central power and trust that is fundamental in the analysis. Efforts to equate the national interest with a global interest through international law and organization are dismissed as "legalistic-moralistic,"[63] "too wildly improbable,"[64] or, more generally, idealistic. Efforts to achieve justice must, in the realist vision, give way to the more basic search for security that can limit the prospect of relative loss with scant possibility for universal gain.[65]

In practice, emphasizing competitive elements in global politics necessitates undervaluing prospects for international, supranational, or transnational organization, whether formal or informal. Actors that are more powerful, wealthier, or more skillful should, it is implied, see to their own well-being and security before concerning themselves with some "abstract" global good unless it can somehow be shown that the two are identical.[66]

The devaluation of the norm of equality by those who emphasize competition tends as well to make them relatively elitist in their perceptions of global politics. This normative dimension entails perceptions of who ought to be involved in the making of decisions and the management of issues. Elitists emphasize that the possession of some attribute— wealth, power, skill, and so forth—renders some individuals or groups legitimate leaders (and others, followers).

Among international relations theorists, elitism takes the form of an assertion that certain actors in the global system are and ought to be responsible for significant outcomes that affect the system as a whole. An elitist emphasis can be manifested at different levels of analysis. At the system level, for instance, it may assume the form of claims that the discipline should limit its focus to "sovereign" entities and exclude nongovernmental and transnational interactions. In more extreme form, it may implicitly or explicitly entail the assertion that only the governments of "great powers" or "superpowers" matter and that the interests and aspirations of minor states can (and, by implication, ought to) be ignored except in unusual circumstances.

Realist admiration for the virtues of the eighteenth-century balance of power is elitist in this sense. Among contemporary scholars, Kenneth Waltz's unabashed preference for bipolarity is perhaps the clearest expression of the elitist norm.[67] Waltz believes that the world has remained fundamentally bipolar since 1945 and, more importantly, thinks this is a virtue. He argues persuasively that bipolarity ensures greater stability than any alternative structure and appears to restrict himself to empirical and prescriptive analysis. However, there is a clear, if unstated, normative position underlying the analysis. For both Waltz and realists in general, the avoidance of catastrophic war is the most important of values. In order to secure this, they are prepared to assume as irrational the value hierarchies of those for whom the risks of war might be preferable to the perpetuation of unbearable political, economic, and social conditions. They assume that the great powers are somehow more responsible than lesser powers, presumably because the former have so much more to lose than the latter. The poor or the weak might be tempted to behave rashly and promote instability in order to improve their status. Whether this argument takes the form of opposition to nuclear proliferation or praise for the ability of the balance of power to preserve the independence of major states, it is profoundly conservative and elitist. In effect, it is an international version of the argument that there should be a property or educational qualification for voting in democracies.[68]

The Wilsonian critique of balance-of-power politics was dismissed by realists as utopian because it did not sufficiently take account of the role of power in international relations. Yet, however "unscientific" Woodrow Wilson's analysis of international politics was, what probably incensed realists most was his denunciation of the prevailing elitist ethic. It is not simply that Wilson denounced aristocratic rule within states, but also that he rejected a condominium of the great powers. His assertion of the rights of nationalities and ethnic minorities, along with his praise of democracy and the rights of small states, constituted a brief in favor of greater participation in global decision making. There is an irony in the fact that although Wilson was accused of being naive for advocating such participation, he effectively predicted what has become an elemental process in the global politics of the late twentieth century.

At a different level of analysis, elitism may also take the form of assertions that foreign policy should be left in the hands of small coteries of professional diplomats. The arguments are often made in the context of expressions of concern about the possibility of formulating consistent and farsighted foreign policy. Thus, Walter Lippmann saw the "devitalization of the governing power" as "the malady of democratic states,"[69] and Alexis de Tocqueville concluded that "a democracy can only with great difficulty regulate the details of an important undertaking, persevere in a fixed design, and work out its execution in spite of serious obstacles."[70] For their part, realists consistently lament the passing of the age of the professional diplomat and the onset of the era of mass politics. George Kennan believes that "a good deal of our trouble seems to have stemmed from the extent to which the executive has felt itself beholden to short-term trends of public opinion in the country and from . . . the erratic and subjective nature of public reaction to foreign-policy questions",[71] and Morgenthau cites as one of his "four fundamental rules": "The government is the leader of public opinion, not its slave."[72] In sum, the elitist bias of realists is characteristic of their perception of all levels of analysis, just as Wilson's antielitist bent was present in his views of both internal and external political life.

Historically, most societies have been characterized by the presence of several normative strands simultaneously competing with one another. For this reason, theories of international relations that reflected one or another extreme have rarely monopolized scholarly discourse. For every self-professed Machiavellian, there has been an anti-Machiavellian; and Jeremy Bentham and Richard Cobden flourished alongside the nineteenth-century advocates of balance of power and imperialism. However, for reasons noted earlier, the normative temper of any era is likely to have distinctive emphases. Typically, if these are extreme in one period, a compensating shift will take place during the following period. These shifts are reflected in changing fashions in the social sciences, including international relations.

Such a shift has been underway since the early 1970s. In its postwar heyday, realism emphasized immutability, pessimism, competitiveness, and elitism. These emphases were at least partly the product of a global preoccupation with the value of security in the wake of World War II, and this preoccupation was manifested in the overriding salience of a single critical issue, the Cold War.[73] Having emerged from a catastrophic conflict that had been inflicted by the aggressive behavior of a small group of dissatisfied and expansionist actors, publics and governments were ready to embrace policies and theories that focused upon the prevention of war through strength.

By the 1970s, the salience of the Cold War issue had begun to recede, permitting renewed attention to be paid to a host of other global issues that had been "hidden" in the previous years. These issues involved disputes and concerns revolving around global resource allocation, the maintenance of postwar prosperity, and environmental decay.[74] Many were, of course, not new issues but issues that had been quietly managed after the war by international institutions and regimes that had been constructed largely by U.S. efforts. The growing prominence of these issues in the 1970s, however, was especially the product of a decline in the preoccupation with security in a military sense that accompanied the flowering of détente, along with an intensified sense of potential deprivation of other base values. In a more general sense, their prominence grew as the United States found itself increasingly less able to dominate unilaterally key international regimes like oil and money.

In this climate, realism and the norms it reflected seemed less relevant.[75] The decline in cold war anxieties was largely responsible for reducing, at least in the West, the belief in human immutability and competitiveness, and the emergence of power centers other than Washington and Moscow necessarily diluted the atmosphere of postwar elitism.

There was, however, little change along the dimension of optimism–pessimism because even as acute anxieties concerning some survival issues eased, new anxieties about other survival issues increased.

Such change in the global agenda and shift in normative emphases were reflected in the breakdown of consensus about international relations theory and the proliferation of new approaches, frameworks, and theories that rejected some or all of the realist assumptions. There was a retreat from grand theory and an impulse to the investigation of specific issues and cases in inductive fashion. The nonmilitary nature of many issues encouraged the introduction of concepts and ideas from allied disciplines, especially economics, psychology, biology, and sociology; and this increased doubts about the disciplinary autonomy of political science. Although the heterogeneity and ecumenical nature of postrealist international relations scholarship makes it difficult to generalize, some of the key concepts have been "linkage," "interdependence," "regimes," "political economy," and "transnationalism."[76]

The shift in normative emphases that is reflected in postrealism is perhaps best seen in the work of Robert Keohane, who seeks explicitly to graft such concepts onto realist insights about power.[77] Among other reasons, Koehane is especially interesting because he has been a prolific writer during the 1970s and early 1980s, has been unusually self-conscious regarding the evolution of his ideas, and has openly discussed the normative content of those ideas. Keohane regards international relations as more mutable than do realists, viewing a significant degree of cooperation among actors through international regimes as both possible and desirable. He is relatively sanguine about postwar developments, while taking pains to preclude accusations of "idealism," and he views global society through less elitist and competitive lenses than did his realist precursors.

Will these new concepts and ideas provide the bases for a new paradigm for international relations in the Kuhnian sense? If our analysis of the sources of intellectual change is correct, the answer is probably no. Even as major syntheses of postrealist theory are emerging, such as Keohane's *After Hegemony,* it appears that the agenda of global issues is once more in transition, with military security concerns and East–West relations beginning to assume greater salience since the late 1970s. Concomitantly, an upturn in economic conditions in the West and the prolonged oil glut have reduced anxieties about these matters even though the international economic system continues to face serious threats (for example, debt repayment). Barring major war or some other systemwide catastrophe, we would anticipate a partial return to realist norms, though realism is unlikely to achieve the dominance it once enjoyed. Its resurgence was in part forecast by the impact that Waltz's *Theory of International Politics* and its reassertion of the primacy of structural realism had on the discipline when it appeared in 1979.[78]

Keohane's own work is another harbinger of this trend. While retaining some of the language and insights of scholars who had predicted a decline in the autonomy of nation-states, the growing irrelevance of military security issues, and the inevitable growth of regional and global cooperation on functional or neofunctional lines, he carefully asserts his debt to realism. "My analysis has assumed that governments calculate their interests minutely on every issue facing them. It has not relied at all on assumptions about the 'public interest' or the General Will; no idealism whatever is posited."[79]

CONCLUSION

This brief analysis of the sources and nature of evolving theory in international relations is self-consciously gloomy about the prospects for developing a cumulative science in the discipline. Notwithstanding significant advances in data collection and method, it views the discipline as mired in an unceasing set of theoretical debates in which competing empirical assertions grow out of competing normative emphases that have their roots in a broader sociocultural milieu. Dominant norms tend to vary through time, along with shifts in perceptions of the sources of value deprivation and satisfaction; such norms therefore reflect the hierarchy of issues on the global political agenda.

This analysis suggests, therefore, that what we believe to be the dominant theories of an age are more the products of ideology and fashion than of science in the Kuhnian sense. If the natural sciences somehow evolve in linear fashion regardless of their social and cultural context, "knowledge" generation in the social sciences—including international relations—may more closely resemble that in the humanities, which is inevitably infused by the ethos of its era. International relations will therefore continue to be characterized by a welter of competing theories that reflect significant political, subjective, and normative differences until the global system enters a new period of rapid and stressful change.[80] At that point, a dominant theory, resembling a Kuhnian paradigm, may emerge for some period of time, after which the cycle will resume.

NOTES

1. Some of the same issues that we address here echo concerns expressed by Stanley Hoffmann almost 25 years ago. Hoffmann, "International Relations: The Long Road to Theory," *World Politics* 13 (April 1961):346–77.
2. Thomas Kuhn, *The Structure of Scientific Revolutions*, expanded ed. (Chicago: University of Chicago Press, 1970), p. 175.
3. Ibid., p. 165.
4. Ibid., p. 163.
5. James N. Rosenau, *The Scientific Study of Foreign Policy* (New York: Free Press, 1971), p. vii.

6. See Klaus Knorr and James N. Rosenau (eds.), *Contending Approaches to International Politics* (Princeton, NJ: Princeton University Press, 1969).

7. Kuhn, *Structure of Scientific Revolutions*, p. 164.

8. Ibid., p. 164.

9. E. H. Carr, *The Twenty Years' Crisis 1919–1939* (New York: St. Martin's Press, 1962), p. 2.

10. By norms, we refer to considerations that are viewed as morally compelling.

11. Carr, *Twenty Years' Crisis*, p. 4.

12. R. J. Rummel, "The Roots of Faith," in James N. Rosenau (ed.), *In Search of Global Patterns* (New York: Free Press, 1976), p. 11.

13. "The State Idea," in M. G. Forsyth, H. M. A. Keens-Soper, and P. Savigear (eds.), *The Theory of International Relations: Selected Texts from Gentili to Treitschke* (New York: Atherton Press, 1970), p. 327.

14. Jacob Bronowski, *The Origins of Knowledge and Imagination* (New Haven, CT: Yale University Press, 1978), pp. 127–29.

15. Ibid., p. 129.

16. For a similar approach, see F. Parkinson, *The Philosophy of International Relations: A Study in the History of Thought* (Beverly Hills, CA: Sage, 1977). The varied normative cleavages in classical Greece are discussed in E. R. Dodd's *The Greeks and the Irrational* (Berkeley: University of California Press, 1964).

17. See Friedrich Meinecke, *Machiavellism: The Doctrine of Raison d'Etat and Its Place in Modern History*, trans. Douglas Scott (New Haven, CT: Yale University Press, 1957). Significant idealists in the European tradition might include Dante, Emeric Cruce, the Duc de Sully, William Penn, the Abbe de Saint Pierre, Rousseau, and Kant.

18. See Jose Ortega Y Gasset, *The Dehumanization of Art and Other Essays on Art, Culture and Literature* (Princeton, NJ: Princeton University Press, 1948), p. 4.

19. See Lionel Trilling, *Beyond Culture* (New York: Harcourt Brace Jovanovich, 1965), p. 81.

20. See James E. Dougherty and Robert L. Pfaltzgraff, Jr., *Contending Theories of International Relations: A Comprehensive Survey*, 2nd ed. (New York: Harper & Row, 1981), pp. 10 and 45, fn. 38.

21. Hans J. Morgenthau, *Politics Among Nations*, 5th ed. (New York: Alfred A. Knopf, 1973), pp. 128–49.

22. Ibid., p. 152.

23. Relatively little has been written regarding the utility of Kuhn's framework to international relations. For contrasting views concerning its utility, see Richard Smith Beal, "A Contra-Kuhnian View of the Discipline's Growth," in *In Search of Global Patterns*, pp. 158–61, Arend Lijphart, "The Structure of the Theoretical Revolution in International Relations," *International Studies Quarterly* 18 (1974):41–74. However, the "paradigm" concept is increasingly accepted, though often in a purely metaphorical sense. Of special interest in this regard is the recent work of Hayward R. Alker, Jr. See Alker and Thomas J. Biersteker, "The Dialectics of World Order: Notes for a Future Archeologist of International Savoir Faire," *International Studies Quarterly* 28 (1984):121–42.

24. Kuhn, *Structure of Scientific Revolutions*, pp. 52–53.

25. See Morgenthau, *Politics Among Nations*, p. 169. Realists were especially enamored of European balance-of-power practice, frequently alleging that

Americans had been able to ignore this practice—at their peril—because of the fortunate circumstances of geography. See Robert E. Osgood, *Ideals and Self-Interest in America's Foreign Relations* (Chicago: University of Chicago Press, 1953).

26. Morgenthau, *Politics Among Nations,* p. 3.
27. Ibid., p. 16.
28. Hans J. Morgenthau, "Another Great Debate: The National Interest of the United States," *American Political Science Review* 46 (December 1952):961–88.
29. Realists have correctly pointed out that a people's self-image is not always compatible with the "realities" of power. This insight has provided the basis of theories based on status equilibrium and disequilibrium.
30. Morgenthau, *Politics Among Nations,* p. 11.
31. See Robert A. Packenham, *Liberal America and the Third World: Political Development Ideas in Foreign Aid and Social Science* (Princeton, NJ: Princeton University Press, 1973), p. 245.
32. Bernard Brodie, *War and Politics* (New York: Macmillan, 1973), pp. 368, 365.
33. Richard J. Barnet, *The Roots of War* (New York: Atheneum, 1972), p. 65.
34. David Halberstam, *The Best and the Brightest* (New York: Random House, 1972), p. 69.
35. Arnold Wolfers, *Discord and Collaboration* (Baltimore: Johns Hopkins University Press, 1962), p. 147.
36. Barnet, *Roots of War,* pp. 109–120.
37. Morgenthau, *Politics Among Nations,* p. 7.
38. Kuhn, *Structure of Scientific Revolutions,* p. 34. Perhaps the best analysis of the work of behavioral and quantitative scholars in this context is by John Vasquez, *The Power of Power Politics: A Critique* (New Brunswick, NJ: Rutgers University Press, 1983).
39. See Robert Jervis, *Perception and Misperception in International Politics* (Princeton, NJ: Princeton University Press, 1976).
40. See Charles F. Hermann, *Crises in Foreign Policy* (Indianapolis: Bobbs-Merrill, 1969).
41. See Graham Allison, *Essence of Decision: Explaining the Cuban Missile Crisis* (Boston: Little, Brown, 1971); Morton H. Halperin, *Bureaucratic Politics and Foreign Policy* (Washington, D.C.: Brookings Institution, 1974).
42. See Robert O. Keohane and Joseph Nye, Jr., *Transnational Relations and World Politics* (Cambridge, MA: Harvard University Press, 1972), and *Power and Interdependence: World Politics in Transition* (Boston: Little, Brown, 1977).
43. See Richard W. Mansbach, Yale H. Ferguson, and Donald E. Lampert, *The Web of World Politics: Nonstate Actors in the Global System* (Englewood Cliffs, NJ: Prentice-Hall, 1975).
44. See Edward L. Morse, *Modernization and the Transformation of International Relations* (New York: Free Press, 1976); Richard W. Mansbach and John A. Vasquez, *In Search of Theory: A New Paradigm for Global Politics* (New York: Columbia University Press, 1981).
45. Kuhn, *Structure of Scientific Revolutions,* p. 182. See also his "Second Thoughts on Paradigms," in F. Suppe (ed.), *The Structure of Scientific Theories* (Urbana: University of Illinois Press, 1971), pp. 462–63, and *The Essential Tension* (Chicago: University of Chicago Press, 1977), pp. xvi–xxiii.

46. See Harold D. Lasswell, *World Politics and Personal Insecurity* (New York: McGraw-Hill, 1935).

47. See Samuel P. Huntington, *The Common Defense* (New York: Columbia University Press, 1961); Warner R. Schilling, Paul Hammond, and Glenn Snyder (eds.), *Strategy, Politics, and Defense Budgets* (New York: Columbia University Press, 1962).

48. See Ernst B. Haas, *The Uniting of Europe: Political, Social and Economic Forces* (Stanford, CA: Stanford University Press, 1958).

49. See Bruce M. Russett, *Trends in World Politics* (New York: Macmillan, 1965); Raymond Vernon, *Sovereignty at Bay: The Multinational Spread of U.S. Enterprises* (New York: Basic Books, 1971).

50. For a discussion of these variables and the manner in which they function, see Mansbach and Vasquez, *In Search of Theory,* pp. 59–63, 87–124.

51. "Actor" in this context should not be equated with "state" or "government." Rather the concept refers to any purposive group that behaves in a collective and autonomous fashion.

52. "Values" are subjective constructs that express human aspirations for self-improvement. Cf. Harold J. Lasswell and Abraham Kaplan, *Power and Society* (New Haven, CT: Yale University Press, 1950), pp. 55–56 and Ted Robert Gurr, *Why Men Rebel* (Princeton, NJ: Princeton University Press, 1970), pp. 24–26.

53. Morgenthau, *Politics Among Nations,* p. 4.

54. *Ibid.*

55. Kenneth N. Waltz, *Man, the State, and War* (New York: Columbia University Press, 1959), p. 18ff.

56. Among natural scientists, Freudian psychologists may be viewed as relative pessimists owing to the dark forces that they see as inherent in the human psyche and the putative intractability of these forces. Nevertheless, even this relative pessimism has been recently and eloquently challenged by Bruno Bettelheim. See Bettelheim, *Freud and Man's Soul* (New York: Knopf, 1983), esp. p. 103ff. See also Erich Fromm, *Beyond the Chains of Illusion* (New York: Simon & Schuster, 1962), p. 174ff.

57. See Waltz, *Man, the State, and War.* Richard K. Ashley characterizes "neo-realist" theory as lending "itself wonderfully well to becoming an apologia for the status quo, an excuse for domination." "The Poverty of Neorealism," *International Organization,* 38 (Spring 1984):257.

58. George Soule, *The Coming American Revolution* (New York: Macmillan, 1935), p. 20. See also Crane Brinton, *The Anatomy of Revolution* (New York: Norton, 1938).

59. By contrast, Edmund Burke in his *Reflections on the Revolution in France* represented the views of a pessimist whose conservatism would not allow him to accept uncontrolled change.

60. See Kenneth N. Waltz, "The Stability of a Bipolar World," *Daedalus* 93 (Summer 1964):881–909, and his *Theory of International Politics* (Reading, MA: Addison-Wesley, 1979).

61. Robert Heilbroner, *An Inquiry into the Human Prospect* (New York: W. W. Norton, 1975), pp. 136–37.

62. Morgenthau, *Politics Among Nations,* p. 231.

63. George F. Kennan, *American Diplomacy 1900–1950* (Chicago: University of Chicago Press, 1951), p. 82.

64. James Burnham, *The Machiavellians* (Chicago: Henry Regnery, 1943), p. 34.

65. For an effort to find a middle path, see Hedley Bull, *The Anarchical Society: A Study of Order in World Politics* (New York: Columbia University Press, 1977). For his part, Robert O. Keohane seeks to provide a less stringent and abstract definition of self-interest based on "a less egotistical formulation of the concept" in his *After Hegemony: Cooperation and Discord in the World Political Economy* (Princeton, NJ: Princeton University Press, 1984), pp. 110, 110–32.

66. The distinction between these two emphases reflects the problem of private versus collective benefits. See Mancur Olson, Jr., *The Logic of Collective Action* (Cambridge, MA: Harvard University Press, 1965).

67. Kenneth N. Waltz, "International Structure, National Force, and the Balance of World Power," *Journal of International Affairs* 21 (1967):215–31, and his "Stability of a Bipolar World."

68. For an excellent critique of Morgenthau's version of balance of power that shows how its empirical and prescriptive elements become entangled, see Inis L. Claude, Jr., *Power and International Relations* (New York: Random House, 1962), pp. 25–37.

69. Walter Lippmann, *The Public Philosophy* (New York: Mentor, 1955), p. 29.

70. Alexis de Tocqueville, *Democracy in America, Vol. 1* (New York: Alfred A. Knopf, 1945), p. 234.

71. Kennan, *American Diplomacy,* p. 81.

72. Morgenthau, *Politics Among Nations,* p. 547.

73. See Mansbach and Vasquez, *In Search of Theory* pp. 110–13. The concept of "critical issue" has been analyzed largely in the context of U.S. politics and has to date received little attention in international relations. At present, the process in which a single all-encompassing issue arrives at the apex of the global agenda is only poorly understood.

74. See Dennis Pirages, *A New Context for International Relations: Global Eco-politics* (North Scituate, MA: Duxbury Press, 1978).

75. See Richard K. Ashley, "The Poverty of Neorealism," *International Organization,* 38 (Spring 1984):232.

76. See Keohane and Nye, *Transnational Relations*; Ole R. Holsti, Randolph M. Siverson, and Alexander George (eds.), *Change in the International System* (Boulder, CO: Westview/Praeger, 1980); Stephen D. Krasner (ed.), *International Regimes* (Ithaca, NY: Cornell University Press, 1983); John Gerard Ruggie (ed.), *The Antinomies of Interdependence: National Welfare and the Division of Labor* (New York: Columbia University Press, 1983).

77. Keohane, *After Hegemony,* esp. pp. 5–17.

78. Kenneth N. Waltz, *Theory of International Politics* (Reading, MA: Addison-Wesley, 1979). In "The Poverty of Neorealism," Ashley argues that a new synthesis—"neorealism"—has already emerged to replace classical realism, and he declares: "In the United States of the 1980s, neorealism and its structural theory of hegemony frames the measured discourse and ritual of a generation of graduate students in international politics" (p. 227). In addition, Ashley provides something of a *Weltgeist* interpretation for this development by viewing it as paralleling "structuralist triumphs in such fields as linguistics, sociology, anthropology, and philosophy" (p. 234). While some of his criticisms of neorealism are telling (for example, reliance on economic logic and revival of state centricity), his argument is diluted by a self-conscious pole-

micism and opacity of style. See Robert G. Gilpin's response, "The Richness of the Tradition of Political Realism," *International Organization,* 38 (Spring 1984): esp. p. 289. Nevertheless, Ashley correctly sees a renewed emphasis upon immutability (structural dominance), pessimism, competitiveness, and elitism (hegemony).

79. Keohane, *After Hegemony,* p. 105.
80. Training in the discipline will therefore continue to be characterized by diversity, and this in turn will tend to perpetuate competition among theories.

.

CHAPTER SIX

Conclusion

We conclude with several observations concerning the current state of the international relations discipline. A constant lament among scholars and students is that the field consists of a confusing array of competing perspectives and conceptual approaches. Professors have trouble deciding which theories to emphasize from this intellectual smorgasbord in a ten- to fifteen-week class, and students have to wrestle with the problem of coming to terms with vast amounts of material for upcoming exams. The basic question we pose is whether the field is becoming less fragmented—whether there are indications of movement toward a greater degree of consensus on how to approach the study of international phenomena. One could argue that this is not a burning issue, and in fact a multiplicity of interests, methods, paradigms, concepts, and value preferences is actually beneficial and should be applauded. Greater unity, it is feared, could result in uniformity and the intellectual tyranny of a dominant paradigm or school of thought. Hence, eclecticism is to be encouraged, and any signs of uniformity regarded with suspicion.

No one would argue against diversity per se—it is the lifeblood of scientific enquiry. Seemingly unrelated research may some day come together to help explain a significant aspect of international relations. The concern, however, is whether diversity might more appropriately be described as parochialism. Scholars at times engage in narrowly focused research programs that ignore alternative conceptual approaches, develop specialized jargon that unintentionally serves to confuse and mystify the uninitiated, and unduly restrict their course syllabus to literature that reinforces their own value and theoretical preferences. It is to overcome parochialism, encourage communication among scholars, and stimulate the growth of cumulative knowledge on such important issues as war and peace that has led scholars to search for common threads that may serve to bring a greater degree of unity to the field, not some desire to stifle alternative perspectives or create some sort of paradigmatic Leviathan. Are there any indications of increasing unity or coherence in the discipline of international relations? We believe there is some evidence in three areas: underlying images, theory building, and normative concerns.

UNDERLYING IMAGES

By simply positing the existence of three basic images that influence theory building, we have in effect argued that a certain degree of coherence already exists in the international relations discipline. A logical follow-up question is whether it is possible to combine elements of the three perspectives to provide a more comprehensive and integrated approach to the study of international politics that draws on the strengths of all three images. Simply combining all the actors and assumptions would result in a conceptual grab bag with contradictory elements. But what about a more careful selection of certain insights and assumptions? This could possibly result in creative and fruitful theory building.

To date, calls for such a synthesis have involved combining elements of realism and pluralism. Two scholars whose earlier work is associated with pluralism, Robert Keohane and John Ruggie, have indicated why such a synthesis is desirable and how it might be achieved.[1] Both argue that in attempting to construct a theory of international relations, one must begin with the realist emphasis on power and the state. Recent structural analyses of international politics that stress the importance of the system provide the critical context, they argue, in which pluralist insights and actors are to be analyzed. By itself, realism is inadequate in explaining recent patterns of interaction and changes in the world political economy. The same is true of pluralism. Realist systemic theory, however, provides a necessary "first cut," or context, within which international regimes, transnational actors, the political structure of states, bureaucratic politics, and the perceptions of decisionmakers are examined. Some of the best work in the pluralist image, it is noted, takes explicit account of the international system within which such actors and domestic institutions operate.

What of the globalists? Can their work perhaps also be combined with elements of the other two perspectives? There appears to be some common ground. First, as noted in Chapter Four, pluralists and globalists have a common interest in political economy, transnational actors and processes, and welfare issues. It was argued, however, that they deal with these topics in fundamentally different ways.

Second, and more important, globalists very often focus on hegemonic states or groups of states that reflect the distribution of power during a particular historical epoch. This is also characteristic of many realist analyses. Some globalists, however, might contend that this use of state-centered analysis is an exception and that a focus on broader patterns of social, economic, and political domination tends to be the norm. Nevertheless, a number of observers have noted an affinity between realist and globalist discussions of hegemony when it comes to explaining particular international events and outcomes.[2]

Third, it should be recalled that both the realist and globalist images of world politics have proponents of structural, systemic analysis such as Immanuel Wallerstein and Kenneth Waltz. The former, however, emphasizes economic structures and processes, whereas the latter emphasizes political, military, and economic components of power and capabilities.

Finally, John Ruggie has made the interesting observation that modern political relations as exemplified by the nation–state (the realist preoccupation) as well as modern modes of capitalist production (a concern for many globalists) are both derived from the same historical factors: the redefinition of property rights toward the end of the medieval era, which occurred simultaneously with the emergence of the principle of sovereignty as a legitimation for the interstate order.[3] If realism (emphasizing political factors) and globalism (emphasizing economic factors) are both derived from similar roots, is it possible that they may be at least partially reconciled?

Our expectations should remain suitably modest. A problem that is difficult to overcome concerns the basic incommensurability of the three images.[4] First, the topics addressed are often incommensurable. Realists may examine balances of power, pluralists decision-making processes, and globalists patterns of domination. Different topics may require not only the use of different levels of analysis but also conflicting assumptions. Second, meanings are often incommensurable, the same term being defined in different ways by different theorists. The concept of imperialism is a good example. Morgenthau defined it as "a reversal of the power relations between two or more nations," and Lenin defined it as "the highest stage of capitalism."[5] Finally, there is the problem of competing normative prescriptions often embedded in alternative images and theories. At the extreme, this might mean the adoption of a particular research program designed to produce results consistent with the expectations of a private or public funding agency. More commonly, the relative attractiveness of a realist or globalist explanation of imperialism, for example, may be based on a student's personal value preferences than on critical scholarly scrutiny.

THEORY BUILDING

In Chapter One we noted that we did not find the traditionalist–behavioralist debate of the late 1960s on the issue of appropriate methodology to be of overwhelming importance. In the 1980s, scholars still have not reached a consensus on the relative merits of quantitative versus non-quantitative research, in-depth single-case studies versus an examination of multiple cases, or inductive as opposed to deductive approaches to theory building. Each still has its advocates and practitioners. There appears to be, however, a growing consensus on a number of other issues concerning theory building. These may appear to be modest points of convergence, but they do represent changes over the past twenty years.

First, pure empiricism in the form of mere correlation of variables is in general disrepute. Studies involving bivariate and multivariate relations flourished in the 1960s, and it was assumed that various patterns in and of themselves told us something significant about international relations. Such studies have been criticized for simply seeking out that which is easily quantifiable, ignoring the larger context within which states interact and failing to relate the empirical efforts to more general theoretical constructs or research programs. This supposedly hampered the goal of cumulative research.

Second, there is a heightened awareness of the need to take into account the structure of the international system when engaged in theorizing. According to Kenneth Waltz's influential formulation, the existence of anarchy and various distributions of capabilities constrain and influence states and other actors to behave in certain ways. Simply examining state interactions is insufficient.[6]

Finally, there has been greater emphasis on theoretical rigor, which requires explicitly stating one's theoretical assumptions, delineating causal links, and noting the types of evidence to be used in testing propositions and hypotheses. This may all seem commonsensical and basic to any theoretical effort. In fact, very often work fails to meet such standards of theoretical rigor.[7]

NORMATIVE CONCERNS

Some scholars of international relations are quite explicit about their normative concerns. J. David Singer, for example, states, "Specialists in world affairs have a special responsibility to not only teach and conduct high-quality research, but to address the major problems confronting the global village. . . . The human condition is, on balance, morally unacceptable. Too many of our fellows continue to die prematurely from war, terrorism, assassination, poverty, starvation, disease, and even more of them suffer untold misery, pain, and degradation en route to the grave."[8] Few scholars would disagree that the ultimate goal of research should be to contribute to the storehouse of knowledge in an effort to ameliorate if not eliminate the scourge of war and poverty. The road may be difficult, the degree of commitment may vary, but few persons would probably care to admit even to themselves that they had no interest in furthering our understanding of the problems faced by the global community. The choice of a particular research topic may reflect a normative concern, but we believe that there is also a general consensus in the discipline that the final product should be the result of a good-faith effort to avoid allowing personal values to affect directly the construction of models, gathering of data, empirical testing of hypotheses and propositions, and interpretation of results. A normative commitment to improving our understanding of global problems does not sanction conducting biased research.

Finally, as we noted in Chapter Five, some scholars are concerned with developing normative theories. Although both empirical and normative theorists may be motivated by such similar concerns as the devastation wrought by war, they operate in different domains. Normative theorists hope to provide the logical or philosophical bases for value choices facing decisionmakers and others. We consider work in both domains to be important. In this regard, we applaud a recent upsurge in interest in normative international relations theory while, at the same time, we call for continued efforts to develop better empirical theory.

NOTES

1. See Keohane's "Theory of World Politics" in this volume and John Gerard Ruggie, "Continuity and Transformation in the World Polity: Toward a Neorealist Synthesis," *World Politics,* 35, 2 (January 1983):261–85. See also Robert O. Keohane, *After Hegemony: Cooperation and Discord in the World Political Economy* (Princeton, NJ: Princeton University Press, 1984).
2. See, for example, Robert Brenner, "The Origins of Capitalist Development: A Critique of Neo-Smithian Marxism," *New Left Review* 104 (July-August 1977):25–92; David J. Sylvan, "The Newest Mercantilism," *International Organization* 35, 2 (Spring 1981):375–93. As Keohane notes, the globalist Fred Block and the realist Robert Gilpin "both emphasize the role of U.S. hegemony in creating order after the Second World War and the disturbing effects of the erosion of American power." Keohane, *After Hegemony,* p. 42.
3. Ruggie, "Continuity and Transformation," p. 281. As he argues: "Despite its defects, Waltz's model is powerful and elegant. And, as I have suggested, its defects can be compensated for in a suitably amended and augmented neorealist formulation. Such a formulation would also go some way toward subsuming the major competing systemic theories." P. 285.
4. The following discussion is based on Stephen D. Krasner, "Toward Understanding in International Relations," *International Studies Quarterly,* 29, 2 (June 1985):138–140.
5. Krasner uses the imperialism example to illustrate the problem of competing normative prescriptions, but it is just as relevant to the problem of incommensurability in meaning.
6. Kenneth N. Waltz, *Theory of International Politics* (Reading, MA: Addison-Wesley, 1979).

7. For a discussion covering these and other points, see the articles by Bruce Bueno de Mesquita, Robert Jervis, and Stephen Krasner in *International Studies Quarterly*, 29, 2 (June 1985).

8. J. David Singer, "The Responsibilities of Competence in the Global Village," *International Studies Quarterly*, 29, 3 (September 1985):245, 259.

Glossary

abstraction A general idea, principle, or concept without physical or tangible quality. International relations theorists sometimes write of systems, the balance of power, and equilibrium—examples of abstractions that may be useful to the theorist who wishes to explain or account for political or other phenomena.

action A movement or physical act, as when the state or its decisionmakers take some concrete step in a given situation. An action is the practical expression of policy. See also **policy, interaction.**

actor A participant or player. The state is considered by realists to be the principal actor in international relations; other nonstate actors include transnational actors such as multinational corporations and banks. See also **rational, unitary, transnational,** and **transgovernmental** actors.

aggregation The bringing together of parts into a single whole, as when the state is understood to be a *unitary* actor. Pluralists tend to see the state not as a single, unitary whole but as many parts, thus disaggregating or breaking the state apart into its component institutions, groups, and individual persons.

amoral Morally neutral; without moral content. See also **moral.**

anarchic See **anarchy.**

anarchy The absence of political authority. International politics or the international system are said to be anarchic in that there is no central or superordinate authority over states.

anthropology The scientific study of humankind, including its physical, social, and cultural origins and development.

appeasement The policy of allowing another state to have what it wants—an attempt to avoid aggression by that state; for an example, see **learning.**

assumption A premise or statement taken to be true without empirical or factual proof. The theorist typically makes assumptions as the starting point in developing a given theory. For example, some balance-of-power theorists make assumptions about the state as principal, unitary, and rational actor.

asymmetry, asymmetric Not symmetrical; lacking precise correspondence or relation between or among components. An interdependence relation is said to be asymmetric if Party A is more dependent on Party B than Party B is on Party A.

autarky An independent posture of self-sufficiency without dependence on other actors. Autarky occurs when a state attempts as a matter of policy to exist in economic isolation from other states.

authority A legitimate right to direct or command and to make, decide, and enforce rules. The term *authority* has a moral or legal quality and, as such, can be distinguished from control by brute force or by coercion. See also **power.**

autonomous development See **development.**

balance of payments Accounting concept by which the international economic transactions (inflows and outflows) of states and their corporate and private elements are tracked. Balance of payments includes export and import of goods and services (balance of trade), capital investment and other "invisible" or financial flows, and gold or other financial reserve transactions. "Balance" is achieved when gold or other financial reserves flow in or out to cover differences in the other accounts as when a country exporting more than it imports receives foreign currency that it can hold as a financial reserve.

balance of power   A key concept among realists that refers to a condition of equilibrium among states. Realists differ on whether the equilibrium or balance among states is (a) created by statesmen or (b) occurs quite apart from the will of statesmen as an inherent characteristic of international politics. Balance-of-power considerations may be used by decisionmakers as justification for a given foreign policy. Some critics have noted that the multiple definitions or meanings of balance of power diminish its utility as a concept in international relations theory.

behavior   The actions and interactions among units; the behavior of policymakers or of states. *Behavioralism* refers to a way to study politics or other social phenomena that focuses on the actions and interactions among units by using scientific methods of observation to include quantification of variables whenever possible. A practitioner of *behavioralism* is often referred to as a *behavioralist. Behaviorism* refers to the ideas held by those behavioral scientists who consider only observed behavior as relevant to the scientific enterprise and who reject what they consider to be metaphysical notions of "mind" or "consciousness."

behavioralism   See **behavior.**

bipolar, bipolarity   The condition of having two poles as when the distribution of power or capabilities in international politics is said to be *bipolar.* Some theorists consider the contemporary international political system to have a bipolar *structure*—the United States and the Soviet Union. Others consider it to be multipolar or to conform to some other characterization. See also **structure.**

bourgeoisie   The capitalist (and, at the time of its emergence, the "middle") class. The class defined in Marxian terms by its relation to the means of production—its ownership of capital, including factories and other machinery of production in a capitalist economic mode. A member of this class is sometimes referred to as a *bourgeois.*

bureaucracy   The administrative arm of government staffed primarily by appointed, nonelected officials. A given governmental agency may be referred to as a bureaucracy, whereas the generic category of such agencies may be referred to as the bureaucracy. An individual member of a bureaucracy or administrator is sometimes referred to as a *bureaucrat.* Bureaucracy, bureaucrat, and bureaucratic are words sometimes used to convey negative connotations about government, but most academic usage is merely descriptive of the governmental administrative function.

bureaucratic politics   The formulation of policy is a function of the competition among opposing individuals who represent diverse governmental institutions. Coalitions and counter-coalitions typically form as a part of the process of bureaucratic politics. See also **organizational process.**

capitalism   An economic system or mode of production that emphasizes private ownership of the means of production and a free market. One who owns the means of production is a capitalist, or *bourgeois.* See also **bourgeoisie.**

causality B occurs on account of A, which precedes it in time. A produces or is responsible for the subsequent occurrence of B. In this sequence, A is the *cause* and B is the *effect*. Some causes have multiple effects, as when A causes B, C, and D. Some effects have multiple causes, as when effect T is caused by Q, R, and S. Some causes may be *necessary*, but not *sufficient* to produce a given effect, as when A is necessary to cause D but will not do so unless B or C is also present (thus, A and B or A and C are *necessary and sufficient* causes of D). Some causes are sufficient in themselves to produce a given effect, as when the presence of A always produces B. An *efficient* cause is the factor immediately responsible for a given effect, whereas a *permissive* cause may refer to an underlying condition that allows a certain effect to be produced (Kenneth Waltz, for example, argues that international anarchy is the permissive cause of—the absence of any obstacle to—war whereas other factors proximate to a particular situation, such as misperception in a crisis, are among the efficient causes of a given war). Some theorists reject causality as an abstract or metaphysical notion: One can observe B as coming after or following A in terms of time, but that does not prove that A is a "cause" of B.

causal modeling The depiction, such as by a computer simulation or diagram, of sequential relations among two or more variables and how they result in a particular event, action, or outcome, including the relative importance or "weight" of each variable in producing a particular outcome. Causal models depict cause-effect relations, as in a model of an arms race that hypothesizes a causal connection between the decision of the Soviet Union to increase the level of its military expenditure and an increase in the later military expenditure of the United States in an action-reaction sequence. The Soviet Union's actions, it may be hypothesized, caused the United States to react in a similar fashion, resulting in an overall increase in the amount of money devoted to military expenditures and producing, in turn, similar reaction by the Soviet Union—in effect, an arms race spiral.

center The term used especially by many dependency theorists to refer to First World or the industrialized countries in the global political economy— Japan and the countries in Europe and North America. Also sometimes used to refer to the elites or dominant classes. See also **core** and **periphery.**

city-state A political entity composed of a city and its surrounding territory as in the city-states of ancient Greece (Sparta, Athens, Corinth, etc.) or Renaissance Italy (Florence, Venice, Padua, etc.)

class A stratum of society with an identifiable characteristic or set of characteristics that differentiate it from another stratum. In Marxian usage, the term is defined by relations to the means of production. Under capitalism the *bourgeoisie* is defined by its ownership of capital (not only money but, significantly, the factories and machinery that are the means of production), and the *proletariat*, or working class, is defined by its labor. Under feudalism, the *aristocracy* is defined by its ownership of land, and the *serfs*, or peasants, by their labor.

class conflict A concept associated with Marxism that emphasizes the inevitable clash of interests between strata, or classes, defined in terms of their relations to the means of production (i.e., how goods are produced). Marx, for example, analyzed the conflict between the *bourgeoisie* (owners of capital, especially factories and machinery of production) and the *proletariat*, or workers, who were being exploited by the bourgeoisie. Marx argued that eventually exploitation would reach the point at which a proletarian revolution would occur and the power of the bourgeoisie would be broken. See **proletarian revolution, Marxism.**

coalition   A combination or alliance of individuals, factions, or states, including both temporary and more enduring groupings of actors around a common interest or purpose.

cognition   The process by which human beings come to know or acquire knowledge through perception, reasoning, and (some would say) intuition. The term *cognitive* refers to this process.

cognitive dissonance   A concept developed by Leon Festinger wherein human beings tend not to perceive what is contrary to their preconceived or previously held perspectives. To avoid cognitive dissonance, individuals either (a) unconsciously screen out information or evidence that contradicts what they already believe to be true, or (b) interpret such discordant information in such a way as to support their preconceptions.

collective goods theory   Relates to the allocation of, and payment for, goods that, once provided, cannot easily be denied to others and that whose use does not deny their use to others. Providing national security or international security through alliances has been described by some theorists as collective goods. Collective goods are referred to by some as public goods. See also **public choice theory.**

colonialism   See **imperialism.**

communism   A mode of production in Marxist thought that is to be achieved after the passing of capitalism and a socialist transition period. Communism is a classless society in which each person produces according to his or her ability and receives or consumes according to need. In Marxist thought, given the absence of classes, the state as an instrument of class domination ceases to exist.

communist   An individual committed to the eventual attainment of communism, particularly through revolutionary means that would lead to the overthrow of capitalism.

comparative advantage   The concept that holds that countries specialize in the production of those goods and services which they produce most efficiently. In a free trade environment there would be, according to theory, a global specialization or division of labor with aggregate productivity maximized. As critics point out, however, free trade theory does not address such matters as equity in the distribution of wealth. Some dependency theorists see free trade theory as the vehicle by which Third World countries are kept in a status of dependency and precluded from development.

complex interdependence   A term developed by Robert Keohane and Joseph Nye that refers to the multiple transnational channels that connect societies, including interstate, transgovernmental, and transnational relations. The resulting relations are extremely complex with economic interests assuming far greater importance than in classic realism. See also **interdependence.**

comprador class   A term referring originally to the stratum of native businessmen in various Asian countries (including China) who served as local agents for foreign, colonial business interests. In contemporary usage, it refers to the aggregate of business elites in a Third World country or countries who maintain close links with their counterparts in the industrial countries of the First World. Particularly in Marxist usage, the term is used to explain relations of exploitation by the bourgoisie of Third World workers and peasants.

compromise Reaching accommodation or settlement between or among parties. A process typically involving give and take and concessions by one or more of the parties.

concept An idea of a general or abstract nature; sometimes referred to as a *construct*. Such concepts as *power, interdependence, order, justice,* and *peace* are used in the construction of international relations theories.

conceptual See **conceptualization.**

conceptualization The process of creating general ideas or concepts.

condition A set of circumstances or state of being. An underlying condition of international politics, for example, is the absence of a single or central source of authority. When a given population has established a sense of community, this can be described as a condition.

conflict Disagreement; the opposition or clash of units. Conflicts may be nonviolent or at varying degrees or levels of violence. Some theorists see the management of conflicts that cannot be resolved as being central to maintaining peace. Conflict of interest among states or other actors is a widely used concept.

constant A factor that does not vary. See **variable.**

constitutionalism The liberal idea that individual freedom is served by constraining the power or authority of government and setting formal limits, whether written or unwritten.

construct Used synonymously with *concept*. A construct can be understood as an abstraction created or put together often out of simpler elements. See **concept.**

core A term used synonymously with *center;* a reference to the industrialized countries in the global political economy. The term is also sometimes used to refer to the elites or dominant classes. See also **center** and **periphery.**

correlation An association between two, or among more than two, variables, of such a nature that a change in one seems to be tied or related to a change in another. A correlation among variables does not necessarily mean that they are causally linked. See also **causality, variable.**

cost A loss as opposed to a benefit; something paid as opposed to something received. The concept is central to game theory, including coalition and alliance formation. Costs may be distributed asymmetrically or unevenly among the actors in interdependence relations.

counterintuitive Against, or contrary to, what is thought to be true. See **intuition, intuitive.**

decision Making a choice among often competing alternatives or options; making a judgment or drawing a conclusion. A *rational* decision-making process is one in which alternative means to achieve certain objectives are evaluated and the option or options best (or at least satisfactorily) leading to the attainment of these objectives are selected. See also **policy,** which can be understood as being composed of both *decisions* and *actions.*

decision making See **decision.**

dependency A situation in which the economies of Third World countries are conditioned by and subordinate to the economic development, expansion, and contraction of the economies of advanced capitalist states. It is a situation of exploitation and is examined in a historical context. Domestic constraints and structures (such as land tenure patterns) are also critical in inhibiting balanced economic development.

dependent variable The thing that is to be explained or accounted for. Some theorists have tried to explain, or find the causes of, war, which is their dependent variable. See also **variable, independent variable.**

description A verbal statement that provides an understanding or meaning. Description is often differentiated from *explanation* or *prediction*, which are understood to be *theoretical* tasks. Thus, *theory* is considered to be different from mere *description*. From this perspective, description is a necessary but pretheoretical task.

détente An easing or relaxation of tensions as when the relations between the superpowers are said to be less tense. The Cold War was said to have given way in the late 1960s and 1970s to a period of détente.

determinism, deterministic A philosophical view that what we observe inevitably occurs as the consequence of factors over which human beings have no volition or control. Most social theorists who accept the characterization or who can be labeled as *determinists* do not reject totally the role of human will, as the strict definition of determinism would imply, but they do allow much less freedom of action for individuals to affect outcomes than those theorists labeled as *voluntarists*. The determinism–voluntarism issue among social science theorists has its analog in theological disputes over determinism or predestination on the one hand and free will on the other. See also **voluntarism.**

deterrence Psychological effect on an opponent that results in a decision not to take some act such as attacking or starting a war. Deterrence is thought to be achieved either through fear of retaliatory punishment or through rational calculation that taking this action will not succeed in achieving intended objectives or that the costs of doing so will be too high.

development The process associated with the industrialization of societies. *Modernization* is a term sometimes used synonymously with *development*, but some theorists differentiate between the two. For some, *modernization* refers to societal values and processes that undergo major changes from preindustrial traditional society, including the effects of industrialization, whereas *development* refers to the building of societal or governmental administrative infrastructure more capable of coping with increasing demands brought on by the modernization process. *Autonomous* development occurs in isolation, or independent of what is going on outside of a given country, a circumstance more difficult to achieve in the contemporary period than may have been true in the nineteenth-century. *Reflexive* development, when and if it occurs, is responsive to external economic conditions and may well be dependent on them.

diachronic Refers to a study over a period of time; sometimes referred to as a *longitudinal* study, as in a study of the causes of war between 1815 and 1945. See also **synchronic.**

dialectic, dialectical A form of reasoning or argument that juxtaposes contradictory ideas with the goal of resolving the contradiction and thus moving closer to the truth. The term is associated with the ancient Greek philosophers, the German philosopher Hegel, and Karl Marx. Marx substituted materially based class conflict and the contradictions between means and modes of production for the clash of ideas. Whereas Hegel argued that the dialectical clash of ideas moved history forward, Marx focused on the importance of material forces. See also **class conflict, proletarian revolution, Marxism, means of production, modes of production.**

diffuse Dispersed widely; not concentrated or narrowly focused. When a state is said to be a functionally diffuse actor, it performs a multitude of functions. The opposite of functionally diffuse is to be functionally specific or more narrowly focused.

diplomacy The process or art of communication among states and their statesmen in international relations; negotiation, including positive inducements or persuasive tactics, compromise, threats, or other measures understood to be part (or tools) of diplomacy. Diplomacy is the state's political or policy element in the conduct of its foreign relations. The terms *diplomat* and *diplomatic* have a positive connotation, referring in common parlance to peaceful, nonwarlike approaches. As a technical term, *diplomacy* includes the threat or imposition of punishment or sanctions as tactics that may be employed by the diplomat in addition to (or in place of) more positive inducements.

disaggregation See **aggregation.**

distributive justice The question of the rightness of (or moral criteria associated with) the allocation of scarce resources, particularly material or economic resources. The rightness of a particular distribution of wealth or profit could be subject to normative standards of distributive justice. See also **justice, normative.**

dyad, dyadic As between two units. See **interdependence.**

East In a contemporary East–West context, East usually refers to the Soviet Union and other Marxist-Leninist countries, mainly those in Eastern Europe. A more traditional meaning is the Orient or countries of Asia. Variants are the Far East (the countries of East Asia, including China, Japan, and the Koreas), the Middle East (originally referring to such south Asian countries as India and Pakistan, but now more commonly used to refer to Egypt, Israel, Jordan, Syria, Saudia Arabia, and neighboring countries), and the Near East (originally referring to countries in North Africa and Arabia; now more commonly referred to as the Middle East). See also **East–West.**

East–West In contemporary usage, East–West usually refers to conflict between capitalist, industrial democracies of the First World or West (including West Europe, North America, and paradoxically even Japan) and the Marxist-Leninist countries of the Second World, or East (including the USSR and other Marxist-Leninist countries, mainly those in Eastern Europe, but sometimes including China, particularly in the Maoist years). The more traditional meaning of East–West refers to Europe and the Americas as "West" and Asia as "East"—the meaning in Kipling's observation that East is East and West is West and never the twain shall meet. See also **East** and **West.**

EC See **European Communities.**

econometrics Quantitative techniques used in economic analysis.

efficient cause See **causality.**

elite The upper stratum or strata of a society.

empirical, empirically Factual or known through observation. Propositions or hypotheses may be subject to empirical or factual test to determine whether observed "facts" are consistent with what is predicted.

endogenous factor   See **system.**

epistemology   Refers to the study of how one knows or how one acquires knowledge.

equilibrium   When various elements of a system are in balance. When disturbed, some systems are said to have an inherent tendency to restore this balance or equilibrium. For example, when a state or group of states upset the balance of power, other states respond in opposition, restoring the balance.

Ethnocentrism   An inward-looking tendency or favorable disposition toward the people or nation with which one identifies, particularly when it is seen as superior to others.

European Communities (EC)   Refers to European collaborative activity or international organization in several issue areas—the European Coal and Steel Community (ECSC), the European Economic Community (EEC), and the European Atomic Energy Community (EURATOM).

exogenous factor   See **system.**

explanation   See **theory.**

factor analysis   A quantitative technique by which the analyst tries to identify underlying and related elements or factors (usually as part of a causal explanation of some observed phenomenon or phenomena).

federalism   See **world federalism.**

feedback   A concept in systems theory and communication theory (or cybernetics) by which responses to decisions or actions taken are returned by affected elements to the sender or taker of these decisions or actions, thus allowing for corrective actions.

feudal, feudalism   A system of political, social, and economic organization that existed in Europe from approximately the ninth to approximately the fifteenth centuries. Reciprocal rights and duties were expected between the lord and his vassals—for example, protection of the vassal by the lord in return for the vassal's giving up a percentage of his crops. Feudalism is viewed in Marxist usage as a mode of production dominant in the Middle Ages and that preceded capitalism. See also **modes of production.**

First World   See **Third World.**

force   Usually refers to efforts undertaken by states in an attempt to compel others to take a certain course of action or to cease an action. The term usually means the use of armed or military force.

foreign policy   Refers to external affairs, particularly to decisions and actions taken by states in their dealings with other states or such "external" actors as international organizations, multinational corporations, and other transnational actors.

functionalism, functionalist   A focus on purposes or tasks, particularly those performed by organizations. Some theorists have explained the growth of organizations, particularly international organizations, as a response to an increase in the number of purposes or tasks demanding attention. *Neofunctionalism* as a theory of regional integration emphasizes the political calculation and pay-off to elites who agree to collaborate in the performance of certain tasks. See also **integration, spillover.**

functionally diffuse   See **diffuse.**

fungibility   The condition that exists when one element or unit has no unique identity and can easily be exchanged or replaced by another of like nature.

Money is said to be fungible (for example, funds in a national budget can easily be shifted from one account to another when cuts are made in one area of the budget to fund increases in another). Whether the power of states, like money, is fungible and can readily be transferred from one issue area to another is a point of some dispute among international relations theorists.

game theory A decision—making approach based on the assumption of actor rationality in a situation of competition. Each actor tries to maximize gains or minimize losses under conditions of uncertainty and incomplete information, which requires each actor to rank order preferences, estimate probabilities, and try to discern what the other actor is going to do. In a two-person *zero-sum* game, what one actor wins the other loses; if *A* wins 5, *B* loses 5, and the sum is zero. In a two-person, *non-zero-sum* or *variable sum* game, gains and losses are not necessarily equal; it is possible that both sides may gain. This is sometimes referred to as a *positive-sum* game. In some games, both parties can lose, and by different amounts or to a different degree. So-called *n-person* games include more than two actors or sides. Game theory has contributed to the development of models of deterrence and arms race spirals, but it is also the basis for work concerning the question of how collaboration among competitive states in an anarchic world can be achieved: The central problem is that the rational decision for an individual actor such as a state may be to "defect" and go it alone as opposed to taking a chance on collaboration with another state actor. Dealing with this problem is a central concern of much of the literature on international regimes, regional integration, and conflict resolution. See also **anarchy, rational, theory.**

general theory See **theory.**

globalism, globalist As used in this volume, *globalism* refers to an image of politics different from *realism* and *pluralism*. Globalism focuses on the importance of economy, especially capitalist relations of dominance or exploitation, to understanding world politics. The globalist image is influenced by Marxist analyses of exploitative relations, although not all globalists are Marxists. Dependency theory, whether understood in Marxist or non-Marxist terms, is categorized here as part of the globalist image. Also included is the view that international relations are best understood if one sees them as occurring within a world-capitalist system. See also **image.**

government The law-making, judicial, administrative, and enforcement apparatus of a state.

Grotian Refers to the influence of Hugo Grotius, seventeenth-century Dutch scholar usually identified as the father of international law. The Grotian view is that international relations, although lacking central authority, can be subject to rules or norms, some of which have the binding character of law, that are expressly or tacitly agreed to by states.

groupthink According to Irving Janis: a "mode of thinking that people engage in when they are deeply involved in a cohesive in-group, when the members' strivings for unanimity override their motivation to realistically appraise alternative courses of action." Indicators of groupthink include social pressure to enforce conformity, limiting discussion to a few alternatives, failing to reexamine initial decisions, and making little attempt to seek information from outside experts who may challenge a preferred policy.

hegemony, hegemon Relations of dominance as when a major power exercises hegemony over countries within its sphere of influence. A state exercising hegemony is sometimes referred to as a *hegemon*. An alternative characterization reflecting preeminent position for a state, but not necessarily implying dominance, is to refer to it as a leader exercising leadership of other states within its sphere. The difference between hegemony and leadership is often a subtle distinction and perhaps more a matter of nuance or connotation intended by the user of the terms. See also **hegemonic stability.**

hegemonic stability   The view that stability in international relations stems from the presence of hegemony or dominance. The absence of hegemony or hegemons would imply a lack of order in the relations among states whether in commercial activities (trade, the exchange of money, and investment), social issues, or security concerns. See also **hegemony.**

heuristic   Refers to the illustrative value of some device or schematic presentation. Such a presentation is not intended as an actual or precise, empirically verified representation of relations among variables in a model, but it is useful for gaining a better understanding of some concept or set of concepts under investigation.

high politics   Refers to matters of security, particularly the strategic interests of states. Realists have tended traditionally to draw a distinction between such high political concerns and those dealing with socioeconomic or welfare issues of lesser interest to statesmen—the so-called *low politics.*

Hobbesean   Deriving from the influence of Thomas Hobbes, seventeenth-century English philosopher, who characterized anarchic politics—the absence of a sovereign or central authority—as producing grave threat to individual security. The absence of central authority in international relations in this Hobbesean view poses a security threat to all states to which they may respond internally by strengthening their power positions, or externally by forming alliances. International security in the Hobbesean view rests, therefore, more on power and the balance of power than on law and other rules or norms.

hypothesis, hypotheses   (plural) A proposition usually relating two or more variables (such as "Arms races cause wars") but subject to empirical or factual test. In one view, hypotheses may be verified or confirmed to the extent that tests do not show the hypothesis to be false. Repeated tests, including *replication* of earlier work, increase confidence in the correctness of the original hypothesis, although it is always subject to being shown to be false in subsequent tests and thus can never be confirmed with 100% certainty. A *null* hypothesis, the starting point, is a proposition in which no relation between or among variables is specified (as in "There is no relation between arms races and the onset of war") in contrast to a *working* hypothesis in which such a relation is specified. If one's empirical tests show no relation, then the null hypothesis is retained and the working hypothesis is rejected.

idealist   One who sees such values or human preferences as justice or a desire for world peace as potentially decisive and capable of overcoming obstacles to their realization. Referred to by critics as utopian, in that the idealist does not understand the realities that constrain human choice. An idealist considers ideas as having important causal effects as opposed to others who see power or material factors as being the determinants of political outcomes.

ideal (pure) type   A concept developed by the German sociologist Max Weber to describe an extreme, or pure, case that is not found in this form anywhere but that serves as an analytical benchmark useful in comparing real-world cases. Strictly defined, ideal types for democracy or modern and traditional societies are constructed by theorists even though the actual cases they examine are, at best, only approximations of the conditions they specify.

ideology A belief system or set of ideas or values usually held as a matter of conviction. Ideological views are usually not subjected to the same standards of empirical test as are theories and associated hypotheses. Marxism-Leninism as ideology offers not only explanation and prediction of world politics but also a means for interpreting social relations.

idiographic A detailed study of a particular case or event. See also **nomothetic.**

IGO An abbreviation used to designate international, governmental organizations in which membership is composed of states—for example, the United Nations and its affiliated agencies. See also **INGO.**

image As used in this book, an image refers to a general perspective of international relations and world politics that consists of certain assumptions about actors and processes. See also **realism, pluralism, globalism.**

imperialism In its classic meaning, a position or policy of preeminence or dominance with respect to foreign elements, as in the Roman, Ottoman, or British empires. Imperialism in earlier centuries involved the establishment of colonies, which led to so-called *colonialism.* Although most of these colonies have become formally independent states, the relations of economic, social, cultural, and even political dominance by the former colonial power remain— so-called *neocolonialism.* Some theorists also contend that contemporary imperialism involves economic and other forms of exploitation or dominance by multinational corporations in less developed countries. Marxist theories of imperialism tend to emphasize the economic dynamics of capitalism and associated class relations.

incrementalism A step-by-step rather than a comprehensive, all-encompassing, sweeping approach. In an incremental decision-making process, decisions are often deferred until information on which to base a choice has been maximized (or until not making a decision would foreclose certain options and thus, in effect, be a decision in itself).

independent variable A factor used to explain some outcome. See also **variable, dependent variable.**

INGO An abbreviation used to designate international, nongovernmental organizations, those in which membership is composed of private individuals and groups, but usually *not* states or their governments. Examples are the International Red Cross and the World Council of Churches. See also **IGO.**

indeterminacy The degree to which an outcome cannot be predicted with a reasonable degree of confidence or is subject to seemingly random influences. There may be a great deal of indeterminacy in voluntarist theories that maximize the effect of human choice or volition. See also **determinism, voluntarism.**

indeterminate solution Refers to problems in which the outcome cannot be predicted with much, if any, confidence, as when the influence of variables appears to have random effect. See also **indeterminacy.**

integration The coming together of separate states or other political units under a common authority. Integration may occur as an international or regional phenomenon with varying degrees of authority given to institutions established to deal with common issues or problems facing member states.

Integration can be viewed either as *process* or as *outcome* that reflects and encourages cooperation among states operating under conditions of international anarchy (i.e., lack of common government). Research on integration has tended to focus on the assignment of economic and social tasks to regional or international authorities. Earlier theories of regional integration saw political union as a possible outcome of collaboration in economic or social issues. See also **functionalism, ramification, spillover.**

interaction An exchange between two, or among more than two, units as in the *interactions* of states, groups, classes, or individuals. By contrast, *actions* do not refer to the back-and-forth of an exchange but to steps or measures taken by a state, group, class, individual or other unit. See also **action.**

interdependence, interdependent A relation or relations between two (a *dyadic* relation) or among more than two units in which one is *sensitive* or *vulnerable* to the decisions or actions of the other or others. The flow of capital or money to or from one country may respond to (or be *sensitive* to) changes in the interest rates in other countries—so-called *sensitivity interdependence.* To the extent that one unit may be adversely affected by decisions or actions of another, it is said to be *vulnerable* to the other unit or units, as when State *A* depends on State *B* as the principal source of its oil supply and thus is vulnerable or would be adversely affected by its cutoff. To many theorists, such *vulnerability interdependence* is to be minimized or avoided altogether. Interdependence may be *symmetric* (affecting both or all sides equally), but it is more likely to be *asymmetric* (with effects varying from actor to actor). State *A* may be more dependent on a supply of oil from State *B* than State *B* is on the security of its investments in State *A.* See also **complex interdependence, balance of power.**

interest That which is of importance to a unit (state, class, group, or individual), usually including, as a minimum, its survival. *National* interest refers to matters of importance to a state. Some theorists have found the concept of national interest to be too vague; they prefer to substitute the notion that states do formulate certain objectives that can be identified more easily. Others view the national interest as little more than what leaders say it is.

interest group liberalism An approach to politics that emphasizes competing groups or institutions. Not only is interest group liberalism thought to be an accurate description of democratic politics, particularly in the United States, but is is also thought by many to be the way politics *should* be conducted. See also **liberalism.**

international Specifically, relations between or among states. More loosely, it is a reference to matters outside a state, which has led to the synonymous usage by many persons of the terms *international politics* and *world politics.*

International Court of Justice Located in the Hague; a principal organ of the United Nations. See **international law.**

international law A body of rules considered to be binding on states and other actors even though there is no central enforcement authority to assure compliance. Sources of international law include treaties or covenants made by states, customary practice, generally accepted principles, and the writings of jurists. International courts such as the International Court of Justice interpret international law and apply it to individual cases brought by states. National courts and enforcement systems (those of individual states) are the primary mechanisms for dealing with international law. International law (particularly that based on treaty commitments) may have precedence over domestic laws that conflict with such international obligations.

international organization An institution composed of states as members (for example, the United Nations [UN], European Communities [EC], and the Warsaw Treaty Organization [WTO or Warsaw Pact]). More broadly, the term refers to patterns of behavior or structures and actors that cross or go beyond national frontiers.

international politics The *political* focus is on choices made by actors with authority to do so on issues external to states or that cross the frontiers or boundaries of state jurisdiction. *International politics* is often used synonymously with *world politics* or *international relations*, although these terms do have separate, more precise meanings. See also **international relations.**

international regimes See **regime.**

international relations The total of political, social, economic, cultural, and other interactions among states (and even nonstate) actors. *International politics* can be understood to be a part (or subset) of international relations, although the terms *international relations, world politics,* and *international politics* are often used synonymously. See also **international politics.**

intuition, intuitive That which is held, assumed, or seems to be true *a priori* (beforehand). The term refers to a view that usually has not been subject to formal or empirical test but merely seems to make sense. See also **counterintuitive.**

jus ad bellum See **just war.**

jus in bello See **just war.**

justice In common usage, that which is right, fair, or equitable for (or pertaining to relations among) individuals, groups, classes, states, or other units. See also **distributive justice, just war.**

just war Normative theory referring to conditions under which (1) states rightfully go to war *(jus ad bellum)* with just cause, as in self-defense in response to aggression, when the decision to go to war is made by legitimate authority in the state, as a last resort after exhausting peaceful remedies, *and* with some reasonable hope of achieving legitimate objectives; (2) states exercise right conduct in war *(jus in bello)* when the means employed are proportional to the ends sought, when noncombatants are spared, when weapons or other means that are immoral in themselves are not used (typically those that are indiscriminate or cause needless suffering), *and* when actions are taken with a *right intention* to accomplish legitimate military objectives and to minimize collateral death and destruction. Many of these principles of just war are part of the body of international law and thus are legally binding on states and their agents.

Kantian Deriving from the influence of Immanuel Kant, eighteenth-century East Prussian philosopher whose ethical writings emphasized certain *categorical imperatives* as being universal, morally binding norms such as the obligation to treat other human beings as ends important in themselves and not merely as means. In normative international relations theory, the Kantian preference was for a cosmopolitan world society, perhaps a world federation based on universal values in which perpetual peace would be maintained.

law In domestic and international politics, the term refers to authoritative rules that are binding on those subordinate to them. In the natural sciences, the term refers to a general statement that specifies some regularity, as in Newton's second law of motion that force is equal to the time derivative of momentum: $F = d(mv)/dt = m(dv/dt) = ma$. Such specificity of relations among variables and constants has been elusive in the social sciences, and theorists have had to be content with identifying tendencies and generating what are at best "law-like" statements.

LDC Abbreviation for *less*-developed country. In some usages, LDC refers to *lesser*-developed country. See also **Third World, South.**

learning Inferences or lessons drawn from the experiences of states (and statesmen) that guide future policy choices. For example, correctly or incorrectly (the inference is disputed by some), statesmen "learned" that appeasement of aggressors does not make such states less aggressive but may actually whet their appetites for more aggressive behavior (the case usually cited is appeasement of Hitler's Germany in 1938 when diplomats, meeting in Munich and wishing to avoid war, allowed the Germans to annex that portion of western Czechoslovakia inhabited primarily by Germanic peoples). Statesmen may "learn" the benefits of international collaboration as opposed to going it alone, an inference that might lead them to create new and expand existing international organizations.

legitimacy The implication of the existence of *right*, as when a government is said to have, or have been granted, a right to govern based on such criteria as its popular acceptance, the legal or constitutional processes that brought it to, or maintains it in, a position of authority, traditional grounds as in the divine right of kings, or the charismatic quality of its leadership that commands a following and thus contributes to its popular acceptance. See also **authority.**

less-developed country, lesser-developed country (LDC) A country in Latin America, Africa, Asia or the Pacific that is in the early stages of industrialization or that has not yet industrialized to the extent that Japan and countries in Europe and North America have. See also **North-South.**

levels of analysis Individuals, groups, state and society, or international system as separate points of focus. Such levels help scholars to be systematic in their approach to understanding international relations. In explaining a phenomenon such as war, for example, the theorist may identify possible causes as being some characteristic or characteristics of the international system, states and their societies, groups or individuals. In accounting for or explaining such a phenomenon, one may look both within a unit such as a state as well as how the unit relates to its external environment, which are different levels of analysis.

Leviathan The biblical beast of gargantuan proportions used as a metaphor by Thomas Hobbes to refer to the state—the supreme authority that provides order and security to individuals living under its sway; also the title of Hobbes' classic work. See also **Hobbesean.**

liberalism Political philosophy with origins in the seventeenth and eighteenth centuries that emphasizes individual liberty to be achieved through a minimal state. A *laissez-faire* government, one that provides for law and order (sometimes referred to as a "night watchman" state) but otherwise constrained or not granted authority to infringe on the rights of individuals, is said to be a liberal government. In both domestic and international economy, this classic liberalism implies commitment to free market principles without government intervention, including free trade policies and unconstrained commercial activities both at home and abroad. In contemporary American political usage, influenced by President Franklin Roosevelt and those who have followed him, *liberalism* usually means enhancing individual rights and well-being through government action or government programs—a substantial departure from the *laissez-faire* of classic liberalism. See also **interest group liberalism.**

linkage Coupling among units or issues as in ties that cross state boundaries and thus link internationally or transnationally the domestic elements (corporations, groups, individuals, etc.) of various states. In another sense, various policies may be tied to one another in such a way that international trade policy is affected by changes in international monetary policy (linkages sometimes referred to as "policy interdependence"). The term *linkage* has also been used to describe foreign policy connections, as when a government ties negotiations with another government in one field (such as progress in arms control) to behavior by that government in another field (such as demonstration that it will not intervene in the affairs of some third state).

longitudinal See **diachronic.**

low politics See **high politics.**

Machiavellian, Machiavellianism, Machiavellism Deriving from the influence of Niccolo Machiavelli, the sixteenth-century Florentine political philosopher. In its perjorative meaning, the term refers to unprincipled behavior by statesmen or other state agents who aim to achieve certain objectives deemed to be in the state's interest. In this view, the ends of the state (its survival and its continuing security) may justify means or actions taken for these purposes, even though the same means might otherwise be considered immoral or illegal.

macrotheory See **theory.**

Madisonian Deriving from the influence of James Madison, often referred to as the "father of the U.S. Constitution." Madison's ideas (along with those of such other Federalists as Alexander Hamilton and John Jay) on the separation of powers among various branches of government and the division of powers between central and state governments were central to framing the U.S. Constitution.

Marxism A body of thought inspired by the German Karl Marx. It emphasizes the *dialectical* unfolding of historical stages. It stresses the importance of economic and material forces and *class analysis*. It predicts that contradictions inherent in each historical epoch eventually lead to the rise of a new dominant class. The era of capitalism, according to Marx, is dominated by the *bourgeoisie* and will give way to a *proletarian*, or working class, revolution and an era of *socialism* in which the workers own the *means of production* and move toward a classless, *communist* society in which the state, historically a tool of the dominant class, will wither away. A number of contemporary theorists have drawn on Marxian insights and categories of analysis—an influence most evident in work on *dependency* and the *world capitalist system*. See also **dialectic, means of production, proletarian revolution, class, world capitalist system, bourgeoisie, socialism.**

means of production A concept particularly associated with Marxist analyses that refers to factors essential to the production of goods—combinations of land, labor, and capital. Classes are defined in Marxian terms as relations to the means of production: The feudal aristocracy owned land, the bourgeoisie own capital (including factories and machines), and the proletariat is defined by its labor. See also **class, modes of production.**

methodology The approach one takes to an academic study; modes of research and analysis, as in the use of historical case and comparative case studies, or the use of statistics as in formal hypothesis testing or causal modeling of variables. See also **causal modeling.**

microtheory See **theory.**

minimum winning coalition The smallest number of actors needed to agree to a policy or course of action in order to put it into effect. See also **game theory.**

MNC See **multinational corporation.**

modernization See **development.**

modes of production The organization of the economy for the production of goods, as in such historical epochs identified by Marx as slavery, feudalism, and capitalism. According to Marx, as technology has advanced, the mode of production has also changed—feudalism being a more productive mode than slavery and capitalism being more productive than feudalism.

monopoly Occurs when a firm has solitary or complete control of a market. Marx noted an increasing concentration of capital or a tendency toward monopoly in advanced capitalism.

moral Principles of right and wrong in one's behavior.

multinational corporation (MNC) A firm usually with headquarters in one country but with production facilities in more than one country. Because they operate across national borders, MNCs are among those units referred to as transnational actors. See also **transnational.**

multipolar, multipolarity A distribution of power in the international system with more than two centers or "poles" such as a world in which there are five principal or major powers.

nation A group of people with a common identity. A nation coterminous with state boundaries is referred to as a *nation-state,* although in common language the terms *nation, state,* and *nation-state* are used synonymously. It is possible for there to be a nation without a single state—for example, a *non-state nation* such as the Palestinian and Kurdish peoples in the Middle East. Some states such as the USSR contain more than one nation and are usually referred to as multinational states.

nation-state See **nation.**

national interest See **interest.**

national security Issues dealing with the survival, welfare, and protection of a state.

national self-determination The view that a people with a common identity have the right to be independent from outside control, as in establishing a state for such a national group. National self-determination has been an important rallying cry for Third World countries that have demanded an end to colonial rule.

NATO The North Atlantic Treaty Organization; a mutual defense organization founded in 1949 by the United States, Canada, and Western European countries. There are currently sixteen members.

natural law, universal law A philosophical view dating back to at least the times of the ancient Greeks that posits there are laws inherent in nature that transcend any laws made by mere mortals. All leaders and all forms of government, it is argued, are bound by these laws, and they should not be violated. Some scholars have dealt with natural law as a means to develop a body of international law to govern the relations among states.

neocolonialism See **imperialism.**

neofunctionalism See **functionalism, spillover.**

neorealism A label applied to those realists who are interested in explaining state behavior under conditions of anarchy and who emphasize the importance of the structure of the international system and how this influences and constrains state behavior. The term may also have negative connotations in the eyes of some critics who claim that the neorealists have neglected the importance of values and norms as stressed by earlier realists such as Hans Morgenthau and E. H. Carr. Neorealists deny the validity of such charges, and some even reject the neorealist label. See also **structure, structural determinist.**

nomothetic Related to finding general or universal laws as in the study of numerous, different cases over time. See also **idiographic.**

non-state actors International actors other than governments, such as multinational corporations, international banks, terrorist groups, the Red Cross. Pluralists with a transnationalist perspective on international relations emphasize the importance of such non-state actors. See also **transnational.**

non-zero-sum See **game theory.**

normative, norm A principle of right action; a standard to guide behavior, as in norms or obligations governing the conduct of war, transit on the high seas, diplomacy, trade and commerce. Normative judgments are often equated to value judgments and the idea of what *ought* to be; some norms may have the binding character of international law.

North See **North-South.**

North-South Terms meant to distinguish between the advanced industrialized states of the northern hemisphere and the poorer states of the southern hemisphere. The South is also referred to as the Third World. Some authors include the Soviet Union and Eastern Europe as part of the North, but most others restrict the definition to Western Europe, Japan, and North America. Debate and discussion revolve around the question of how can the North-South economic gap be bridged and what, if any, obligation the North has toward the South.

n-person game See **game theory.**

oligopoly An economic market in which a few firms control the production (or distribution) of certain goods or services. Marx and Lenin argued that capitalism tended to move toward greater concentration of capital, resulting in oligopolies.

operationalize, operationalization see **variable.**

operational code The world view or belief system of foreign policy elites. The pathbreaking work was by Nathan Leites on the Bolsheviks and was later developed by Alexander George and others.

optimal In the context of decision-making, the best possible outcome.

organizational process A model developed by Graham Allison to distinguish *bureaucratic politics* from organizational process—the institutional perspectives, routines, standard procedures, and processes of particular bureaucracies.

pacta sunt servanda Latin for "treaties are binding"; the idea that treaties or formal covenants are legally binding even in the absence of a central authority to enforce adherence to them.

paradigm A pattern, model, or perspective that helps one organize and guide research. A paradigm may include key assumptions about the world and the best way to go about understanding it. The concept was central in Thomas Kuhn's influential *The Structure of Scientific Revolutions* (1962) and has since been applied to the social sciences. According to Kuhn, a scientific era is characterized by a dominant paradigm that represents "normal science"; the majority of scholars work within this paradigm, often accepting the assumptions of the paradigm in an unquestioning manner. These assumptions have an impact on how research is conducted and the resultant scholarly work.

parsimonious theory A theory that contains only a few elements yet can explain or predict a wide variety of phenomena. See also **theory, hypothesis.**

partial theory See **theory.**

peace A wide variety of definitions exist, including the absence of war; a situation of security, order, or stability; harmonious relations among states. For some theorists, it means worldwide collaboration to solve common global problems.

perception, perceptual Awareness of the world through the medium of the senses. In international relations, the literature on deterrence and crisis situations, for example, often deals with the importance of perception and misperception.

periphery The less-developed countries or areas of Asia, Latin America, and Africa. In the dependency literature, the periphery is dominated by the *center*, which consists of the economically and politically dominant countries of the world (usually viewed as North America, Western Europe, and Japan). The literature on the world capitalist system has applied the concept of periphery back to the origins of capitalism in Europe. The periphery plays a subordinate but important role in a worldwide capitalist division of labor by providing raw materials and cheap labor. As capitalism expanded, countries that at one time were part of the center slipped into peripheral or semiperipheral status. See also **semiperiphery, core, and center.**

permissive cause See **causality.**

phenomenology A philosophical term with various complex meanings one of which is the classification and description of phenomena, including identification of the formal structures of phenomena as part of an attempt to establish their scientific foundations.

phenomenon, phenomena (plural) An observed or observable occurrence.

pluralism, pluralist As used in this book, pluralism refers to an image of international relations that assumes that non-state actors are important entities in international relations. The state is not necessarily a rational and unitary actor but is composed of a multitude of competing bureaucracies, individuals, and groups. The agenda of world politics is extensive and goes well beyond security concerns. Much of the work on decision-making and transnationalism falls within the pluralist image as the result of a focus on a multiplicity of factors and actors. See also **image.**

policy A decision or a course of action chosen from alternatives.

politburo The supreme policy and decision-making body of the Soviet Union and other Marxist-Leninist states; an organ of the Communist Party.

political economy There are at least two major ways in which this term is used in international relations research: (1) the view that politics and economics are inextricably linked, leading one to study the interrelations of political and economic variables, and (2) the use of economic models of rationality to explain political actions. For example, some theorists use economic models of rationality in order to determine under what conditions international collaboration can be achieved among states.

politics, political Numerous definitions have been offered including the processes that determine who gets what, when, and how (Harold Lasswell), the authoritative allocation of values (Easton), or simply authoritative choice.

polity In common usage, a political system such as the American polity or the Canadian polity. In the original Aristotelian usage, the term referred to an ideal form of government.

positive-sum game See **game theory.**

positivist The view that laws stem only from the actions of those having the political authority to make them rather than being the derivation of divine or natural law. In science, the view that knowledge comes from empirical testing of propositions or hypotheses against evidence or facts.

power Capabilities, or the relative capabilities, of actors such as states. The ability to control or influence outcomes or the actions of others. Central to realist works on international relations. For more detailed discussion, see the text.

prediction See **theory.**

proletarian See **proletarian revolution, proletariat.**

proletarian revolution A Marxist concept referring to the rising up of the working class, or proletariat, and the overthrow of the capitalist system dominated by the bourgeoisie who own capital—the factors, industries, and banks. The revolution, is, theoretically, the result of contradictions internal to the nature of capitalism.

proletariat A Marxist concept referring to a particular class or stratum of people, in this case the working class. The proletariat is usually viewed as being in opposition to the bourgeois class, which owns the means of production. See also **Marxism, means of production.**

prophecy See **self-fulfilling prophecy.**

psychohistory The study of historically significant individuals through the analysis of what is known about their personality and psychological development.

psychology The study of the mind and its impact on behavior. See also **social psychology.**

public choice theory The use of economic methods to analyze what are essentially political problems (issues involving choices or decisions by political authorities). See also **collective goods theory.**

pure type See **ideal type.**

ramification A concept developed by David Mitrany in his work on functionalist integration: Successful collaboration by states in one particular technical area would encourage the expansion of collaboration into other areas. Mitrany hypothesized that if states became increasingly integrated in a number of technical or functional areas, the cost of breaking these ties (such as by going to war) would be high enough to prevent such actions from occurring in the first place. See also **functionalism, spillover.**

rational To act rationally requires a rank ordering of preferred goals, consideration of all feasible alternatives to attain those goals in the light of existing capabilities, and consideration of the costs and benefits associated with using particular methods to attain particular goals. The assumption is often made in international relations research that actors do, indeed, act rationally. The assumption is made in order to develop hypotheses and to produce insights on world politics. See **decision, action, policy.**

rationality See **rational.**

realism, realist A perspective on international relations that focuses on the state as unitary and rational actor and on the actions and interactions of states. Realists attempt to understand patterns of conflict and collaboration under conditions of anarchy or lack of common government. Security issues are usually the most important for realists. *National interest* or objectives, *power* and *balance of power* are key concepts for most realists. See also **image.**

Realpolitik A German term referring to power politics. It emphasizes policies based more on practical power considerations and less on moral or ethical considerations. The attainment and maintenance of state security in a hostile world through power or balance-of-power politics is viewed as the primary goal of leaders.

reductionism An analytic approach leading to oversimplification and incompleteness of explanation. In some usages, the term refers to explanations that look only within a unit, such as state or individual, ignoring the environment within which the unit is immersed and the interaction of that unit with elements in its environment. Reducing the explanation of some phenomenon such as war among states to something deep within the human psyche (as being, for example, at the level of synapses between nerve endings) is an extreme example of *reductio ad absurdum*—explanation reduced to an absurd degree of oversimplification and incompleteness—as if one could explain the recurrence of war among states purely in neurological terms. Similarly, theorists who have tried to explain revolution solely in social or social-psychological terms, ignoring economic, political, and other factors, have been criticized for reductionism.

reformism The idea that revolution or the violent overthrow of an existing capitalist political-economic order is not necessary, but that change can occur incrementally and nonviolently. The possibility of evolving toward socialism by peaceful means such as parliamentary methods or the creation of trade unions is a tenet of reformism. The issue of reformism is one reason the socialist movement split in the late nineteenth and early twentieth centuries. V. I. Lenin and Rosa Luxemburg argued that the reformist policies of Karl Kautsky, Eduard Bernstein, and others were wrong. Lenin believed that capitalism could not be reformed to benefit the working class, that a revolution was required. See **proletarian revolution.**

regime, international regime In its domestic context, an existing governmental or constitutional order defined in terms of sets of rules and institutions established to govern relations among individuals, groups, or classes within a state. In its international context, the term is defined as voluntarily agreed upon sets of principles, norms, rules, and procedures around which actor expectations converge in a given area of international relations. The literature on international regimes blossomed in the 1970s. Scholars argued that international collaboration was obviously not restricted to formal international organizations such as the United Nations—cooperation was necessary in monetary and trade areas, telecommunications, air traffic control, and a whole host of areas of greater and lesser importance.

reified, reification Giving a concrete reality to what is in fact an abstract concept of analysis. For example, some critics claim that realists have reified the state, attributing to it human characteristics such as rationality, or treating the state as if it operated in the international arena like an actual human being. The concept of system, used by some realist, pluralist, and globalist theorists, has also been criticized on similar grounds.

relativist, relativism A view that what is true varies from individual to individual, group to group, and context to context. See **natural law.**

satisficing A less-than-optimal choice that does not completely maximize the values or goals one is pursuing but is good enough; work on decision-making shows that people often choose the first viable option that is minimally acceptable.

Second World See **Third World.**

security dilemma A term coined by John Herz: In an anarchic international system, State *A* may sincerely increase its level of defense spending only for defensive purposes and self-preservation, but it is rational for other states to assume the worst and impute aggressive intentions to State *A*. They therefore also increase their level of arms, leading State *A* to feel insecure and contemplate a further increase in military spending. Hence, by initially trying to enhance its own security, State *A* sets in motion a process that results ironically in its feeling less secure. In another usage, the term merely refers to the security problem faced by all states in a world without central authority or lack of common government among states. See also **anarchy, self-help.**

self-fulfilling prophecy To predict a particular outcome and then choose policies or actions that help to bring about the predicted outcome even though this is not the intended effect. For example, predicting that State *B* will increase support for a war of national liberation against an ally of State *A*, State *A* provides its ally with more military assistance to combat rebels, resulting in State *B*'s feeling it is necessary to increase its support for the guerrillas. State *A*'s prophecy that State *B* will increase support for the guerrillas hence becomes self-fulfilling.

self-help In the international arena, there is no superordinate authority, world government, or "Leviathan" to ensure order or to see that all parties to an agreement keep their end of a bargain. Each state must look after its own security and not assume the help of other states. See also **anarchy.**

semi-periphery As used by world capitalist system theorists (see Chapter 4), term refers to those countries or regions that occupy an intermediate position between core and peripheral areas. The semi-periphery is engaged in a mix of activities, some associated with the core and some with the periphery. It serves as an outlet for investment when wages, and thus the cost of production, in core areas become too high. The semi-periphery may at one time have been a core or peripheral area, or it may be moving into either status. See also **bourgeoisie, class conflict.**

sensitivity interdependence See **interdependence.**

social contract A philosophical idea used by theorists such as Thomas Hobbes,

John Locke, and Jean Jacques Rousseau to justify their preference for a particular type of political order. Living in an imaginary "state of nature"—a condition without any social or political structure—individuals contract with one another to create a political community or society governed by certain rules. For Hobbes, the social contract resulted in the establishment of a sovereign or central authority who is given the task of maintaining order. In international relations, however, no such sovereign exists. See also **self-help, security dilemma.**

socialism Ownership of the means of production and distribution of goods by the society or the people as a whole (the public) rather than by private individuals. In a more limited form of socialism, only major industries and utilities are publicly owned. In some usages, socialism refers not only to public ownership of the means of production; it also includes public welfare programs and government acts in the name of the people in carrying out these programs. In Marxist thought, socialism is a stage or mode of production between capitalism and communism.

social psychology The study of the mental processes of individuals and how they relate to their environment, especially to other individuals and groups. Behavior is explained by the interaction of individual and environment, not solely by elements within an individual's psyche.

sociology The study of society, particularly social groups and classes and relations among them.

South See **North–South.**

sovereign, sovereignty The supreme, independent, and final authority. The attribute of a state that refers to its right to exercise complete jurisdiction over its own territory. In international relations, states as sovereign units have a right to be independent or autonomous with respect to other states. States may differ in their power, but as sovereign entities all are legal equals.

spillover In the regional integration literature, a concept referring to a process whereby successful collaboration by states in one technical area leads to the realization by state authorities that it is in their rational self-interest to expand collaboration into related fields. Thus, progress in reducing barriers to trade may depend on, and lead to, further progress in rules facilitating the exchange of money among states. As used by Ernst Haas, the term refers to a process whereby states upgrade or collaborate in issue areas of common interest, similar to the concept of ramification. See also **ramification.**

state A legal entity composed of territory, a population, and an administration or government. It possesses sovereignty and recognition by other states. See also **government, sovereignty.**

structural See **structure**

structural determinist One who believes that the structure of the international system largely determines the behavior of individual states and that there is very little effective choice for leaders of states. The term is usually used in a negative or critical sense against realists, neorealists, and some Marxists. Few, if any, theorists would admit to complete structural determinism in their theories, but some do assign greater weight to structure as a determinant of the behavior of states and other actors. See also **system, structure, neorealism, realism, Marxism.**

structure The arrangement of parts of a whole, as in the structure of the international system being defined in terms of the distribution of capabilities or power among states. The international system structure, following this usage, may be bipolar, multipolar, or unipolar. Some theorists look for underlying structure associated with the anarchy of the system—the lack of central authority. For others, structure refers to observed patterns of behavior as among states, although still others contend that such a definition confuses underlying *structure* with *behavior*, or the interactions of states—concepts that are, and should be, kept analytically separate. Some theorists of dependency and the world capitalist system use the term *structure* to describe relations or mechanisms of dominance, dependence, and exploitation. See also **system, behavior, bipolar, multipolar, structural determinist.**

suboptimal See **optimal.**

supranational Beyond or above the state. For example, a world government would be a supranational authority that governs the relations among states.

synchronic Refers to a study of phenomena at a given point in time as opposed to over a period of time. See also **diachronic.**

synthesis Putting together parts to make a whole.

system A set of interrelated parts or an arrangement of units connected in such a way as to form a unity or whole; an abstract concept used by many theorists to bring order to their work. The use of the term varies. For example, some theorists see the *international* system as being composed of states and other actors, whereas some authors see world capitalism as a system composed of classes with conflicting interests. Some systems are said to be *open* to external influences, whereas others are *closed* systems. Factors external to a system that may effect it are *exogenous*, whereas those internal to the system are often referred to as *endogenous* factors. Some systems are said to have certain inherent qualities or attributes such as a tendency toward balance or equilibrium, although not all systems theorists assign such automaticity to systems. Some theorists use systems merely as taxonomies, or frameworks, for organizing research and analysis.

systemic See **system.**

taxonomy, taxonomies A classification as in a categorization of states as democratic, socialist, or fascist.

teleology, teleological That phenomena are to be explained by the purposes they serve. In systems theory, for example, it is teleological to argue that the need for a system to return to some natural state of equilibrium causes units within the system to behave the way they do. It may be that unit interactions within a system have a tendency to produce equilibrium, but it is teleological in effect to reverse the causal flow and argue that this systemic purpose (equilibrium) somehow causes the behavior of actors within the system to occur so as to achieve this result. Similarly, some functionalist theories have been criticized to the extent that they are also teleological.

terms of trade The ratio of a country's average export prices to its average import prices, especially regarding merchandise trade. When import prices rise faster than export prices, the terms of trade worsen. This is said to be the case for most less-developed countries since the 1950s; the prices of raw materials have generally lagged behind the prices of imported manufactured goods from developed countries.

theory A set of interrelated propositions that aims to *explain* or *predict* phenomena, thereby attempting to make the world more intelligible. *Explanation* involves accounting for, or understanding causes of, such phenomena as war, arms races, and regional integration. In a loose sense, *prediction* amounts merely to forecasting, but in a strict sense it implies explanation sufficient to anticipate outcomes, given the presence of certain variables or conditions (for example, theories that would predict war as the outcome of arms races). *General* theories attempt a comprehensive or complete explanation of some phenomenon, whereas *partial* theories are often understood as initial steps or attempts to explain narrower aspects of the phenomenon under investigation. There are considerable differences about the use of the terms *microtheory* and *macrotheory*. Most theorists use the term *microtheory* to refer to partial theories and *macrotheory* to refer to grand theory that would, for example, explain all of international relations. For a more extensive discussion, see the text. See also **parsimonious theory, hypothesis.**

Third World The economically less-developed (or underdeveloped) states of Asia, Africa, and Latin America. The *First World* includes the more industrially developed states in North America, Western Europe, Japan, Australia, and New Zealand; the *Second World* consists of Marxist-Leninist countries, mainly the Soviet Union and its Eastern European allies. Some theorists have identified the poorest of the less-developed countries as constituting a *Fourth World*. See also **North–South, East, West,** and **East–West.**

traditionalism A mode of thinking about international relations that emphasizes the studying of such disciplines as diplomatic history, international law, and philosophy in an attempt to develop better insights. Traditionalists tend to be skeptical of behavioralist approaches that are confined to strict scientific standards that include formal hypothesis testing and, usually, the use of statistical analysis. See also **behavior, methodology.**

transformation, system transformation A *fundamental* change in the system, as in a shift from a multipolar to a bipolar world or vice versa. The creation of a world government to replace an anarchic system of sovereign states would be such a system transformation. In a domestic context, the overthrow of the bourgeoisie by the proletariat would be considered a transformation of the political, social, and economic order.

transgovernmental Relations involving links, ties, or even coalitions among bureaucratic or other official actors of different states. To the extent that these are effective, they may be a means for bypassing central government authorities in each state, although some theorists consider such circumvention of authority more an exception to the usual pattern in which the state remains unitary and speaks with one voice. See also **transnational.**

transnational, transnationalism Interactions and coalitions across state boundaries that involve such diverse nongovernmental actors as multinational corporations and banks, church groups, and terrorist networks. In some usages, transnationalism includes both nongovernmental as well as *transgovernmental* links. The term *transnational* is used both to label the actor (for example, a transnational actor) or a pattern of behavior (for example, an international organization that acts *transnationally*—operates across state borders). Theorists focusing on transnationalism often deemphasize the state as primary and unitary actor. See also **transgovernmental.**

uneven development A concept used by Marxists and other theorists that emphasizes capitalism's unequal spread of global economic benefits. In Lenin's *Imperialism,* for example, he argued that the increasing concentration of capital in advanced capitalist states led to monopolies and cartels that sought foreign investments once national markets were exhausted. This spread of capitalism inevitably resulted in the exploitation of colonies. In the present period, uneven development continues to characterize not only individual national economies but the capitalist world as a whole. Both domestically and internationally, benefits accrue to the few.

unitary Undivided, whole. In many realist analyses, states are viewed as unitary actors.

units of analysis That which is being studied, such as a state.

utilitarians, utilitarianism A doctrine developed in the nineteenth century that postulated that the greatest happiness of the greatest number should be the aim of all action. The term can also mean a belief that the value of anything is determined solely by its utility. Utilitarian thinking as applied to theory building tends to emphasize a rational decision-making process in which actors seek to maximize benefit or minimize cost.

utopian See **idealist.**

values Refers to the way things *ought* to be quite apart from the way things *are*. Political values would include preferences with respect to liberty, equality, order and so on. A value is an estimate made of the worth or goodness of a goal or action. Also refers to measures as in numerical values. See also **normative.**

variable A characteristic of an object or class of objects that may take on different values. The variable may be quantitative (such as height) or qualitative (such as marital status). In international relations research, for example, the class of objects may be states and the variable military power. Researchers wish to *operationalize* a variable, which means finding a way to measure the variable. Military power may be operationalized, for example, by using such indicators as number of nuclear weapons, amount of the gross national product devoted to military expenditures, or number of persons under arms. A *dependent variable* is simply what one is trying to explain, such as the frequency and intensity of war since 1800. *Independent variables* are factors that may help to explain or predict the dependent variable.

variable sum game See **game theory.**

voluntarism, voluntarist A philosophical position that reality is created by human will; that humans can affect, if not control, their destinies. In international relations, it generally means that decisionmakers have effective choice and are able to influence outcomes. As used in this volume, voluntarism is in opposition to the philosophical idea of determinism. See also **determinism.**

vulnerability interdependence See **interdependence.**

war To engage in hostilities and military operations, usually for some political purpose. War among states is *interstate* war; war between opposing parties within a state is *civil* war; war involving irregulars and unconventional tactics is *guerrilla* war. The explanation of war is traditionally the primary concern of scholars of international relations.

welfare issues Socioeconomic and other issues associated with improving the living conditions and standards of people.

West Generally, the countries of North America, Western Europe, and, paradoxically, Japan because of its level of industrial development and its links to other advanced capitalist states. See **East–West.**

world capitalist system An approach to international relations that emphasizes the impact of the worldwide spread of capitalism; a focus on class and economic relations and the division of the world into a core, periphery, and semi-periphery. See also **core, periphery, semi-periphery, class.**

world federalism   The goal of individuals favoring a world government that would have authority in certain areas over constituent states.

world politics   See **international relations.**

zero-sum game   See **game theory.**

INDEX

A

Alker, Hayward, 415
alliance, 35-36, 45, 49, 52, 55, 57, 97, 177-80, 182-83, 363, 381, 418
Allison, Graham, 203-205, 282
anarchy, 4, 12, 38, 42, 48-51, 98, 101, 132, 137, 147, 158, 195-96, 200, 206, 209, 213, 215, 361-62, 399, 411-12, 416, 524, 580
Aquinas, St. Thomas, 520, 523
arms race, 43, 49
Ashley, Richard, 66, 134-35, 160
assumption, vii, 5-14, 32-34, 192-93, 383-84, 399-401, 419, 521, 523, 527, 578-80
Augustine, *see* St. Augustine
Axelrod, Robert, 157

B

balance of power, 1, 34-36, 40, 43, 50-56, 58, 64, 66, 78, 96-103, 105-15, 126, 129, 137-40, 209, 211-13, 229, 383, 411-13, 524, 567-68, 579
  bipolarity-multipolarity, 54-55, 177-78, 213, 567-68
Baldwin, David, 148, 150
Barnet, Richard, 560
behavioralists, 2, 13, 579
Belassa, Bela, 367-68
Bentham, Jeremy, 521, 569
Bentley, Arthur, 197

Bernstein, Eduard, 405-406
Bodenheimer, Susanne, 490
Brecher, Michael, 272
Brodie, Bernard, 559
Brzezinski, Zbigniew, 61
Bueno de Mesquita, Bruce, 4, 45, 55, 147, 149
Bull, Hedley, 92
bureaucratic politics, 154, 193, 203, 211-12, 214, 234-38, 309-21, 344, 561, 578
Burns, Arthur Lee, 108-109
Burton, John W., 118-19, 352

C

capabilities, 33, 40, 44-46, 50, 56, 137, 180, 412, 580
capitalism, 9-10, 399ff.
Cardoso, Henrique Fernando, 415, 461, 463-64, 466, 489
Carr, E. H., vii, 40-44, 66, 119, 123, 144, 193, 519, 522-23, 533, 555-56
center, 366, 401, 414, 462
change, 55, 58-60, 64-66, 115-26, 127-28, 130, 141-44, 158-60, 196, 212-13, 215, 380, 399, 401, 414-16
Chase-Dunn, Christopher, 413, 505
Cicero, 520
class conflict, 401, 415
Claude, Inis, 362
Clausewitz, Carl von, 40, 101, 523
CMEA, 45

cobweb image, 206, 211, 352, 357-61
cognition, 154, 200-202, 250-54
collective goods theory, 13
comparative advantage, 403
comprador class, 409
Cooper, Richard, 366
core, 410, 412, 414, 510ff.
crisis, *see* decision making
Cuban missile crisis, 266-71, 282-332
cycles of war, 59-60

D

Dahl, Robert, 197
decison making, 6, 13, 42-43, 53, 152, 192-
    94, 197-205, 212, 216, 225ff, 526-27,
    543ff, 579
  crises, 4, 140-41, 193-202, 244-81, 561
dependency, 10, 12, 14, 209, 366, 399-401,
    406-409, 415-19, 452ff., 477ff., 489ff.
determinism, 5, 53-54, 62-63, 65, 146, 202,
    210, 403, 405-406, 415, 527
deterrence, 35, 50, 108-109, 244-45, 289-90,
    302-304, 315, 379, 388, 524
Deutsch, Karl, 54-55, 362-64
dialectic, 402
Diesing, Paul, 136, 140-41, 143, 145-46,
    152-54, 272
distributive justice, 522
dos Santos, Theotonio, 461-62, 466, 496

E

ECLA 406-407, 460, 464-65, 491-95, 500
econometrics, 13
EEC, 362
empirical, viii, 2, 4, 22, 46, 55, 134, 175, 186,
    199, 225-27, 380, 405, 419, 519-20, 527-
    28, 559, 580-81
ethics, 37

F

factor analysis, 47
Falk, Richard, 525
feedback, 213
Ferguson, Yale H., 554
First World, 401
foreign policy, vii, 2, 6, 8-9, 11, 43, 50, 52,
    97, 192, 195, 198-205, 211, 225ff, 244ff,
    282ff, 332ff, 524-27
Frank, Andre Gunder, 491-94, 496

functionalism, *see* integration
Furtado, Celso, 485, 494

G

Galtung, Johan, 364, 413-15
game theory, 13, 50, 98-101, 107, 140,
    368
  nonzero sum, 94, 108, 383
  positive-sum, 401
  zero-sum, 94, 207, 340, 382, 401, 566
George, Alexander, 149, 154, 200
Gilpin, Robert, 12, 65, 115, 136, 141-46,
    158-60
globalism, vii, 2, 9-10, 56, 399-426, 525-27,
    578-79
Gourevitch, Peter, 153
Grotius, Hugo, 39-40, 92-93, 95, 193, 210,
    520, 524
groupthink, 201-202, 247, 271

H

Haas, Ernst B., 53, 105, 117, 207-209, 362-
    65, 526
Halberstam, David, 560
Harsanyi, John, 149
hegemonic stability, 57-58
Hermann, Charles, 246, 249
Herz, John, 109, 134, 159-60
high politics, 7, 10, 33, 57, 193, 384, 400
Hilferding, Rudolph, 404
Hobbes, Thomas, 38-41, 48, 88, 93-95, 207,
    361-62, 521-22, 540ff
Hobson, John, 402-403, 414, 427
Hoffmann, Stanley, 11, 111-13, 127, 228,
    286-87
Holsti, K. J., 117
Holsti, Ole, 154, 157, 200, 231, 244
Hopkins, Terence, 415
human rights, 526
Hume, David, 194, 551
hypothesis, 3-4, 46, 55, 116-17, 127, 129,
    160, 167, 417, 419, 519, 528, 580

I

idealists, 2, 34, 41, 61-62, 559, 567, 570
image, vii-viii, 2-3, 5-16, 60-61, 66, 213-
    16, 380, 527, 578-79
imperialism, 117, 185, 402-405, 413-14,
    416, 427ff, 441ff, 461, 579

systems, 117, 132, 134, 140, 143–44, 150, 153–54, 158, 212, 411, 578–79, 581
Third World, 65, 193, 399ff, 427, 522
Thucydides, 34–36, 39–40, 49, 51, 58, 78, 119, 130–34, 142–43, 145–46, 205, 416, 540ff, 557
Tocqueville, Alexis de, 198
traditionalists, -ism, 2, 13, 379, 579
transformation, 64, 66, 208, 213, 215, 332ff, 414–16, 418
transgovernmental, 155, 204–10, 393–94
transnational, vii, 6, 8, 10, 12, 32, 127, 155, 192–94, 197, 204–10, 212, 216, 334–35, 346, 348, 363, 379, 384, 393–94, 401, 413, 525, 561–62, 570, 578
Truman, David, 197
Tucker, Robert, 362

U

UNCTAD, 406, 478, 481
uneven/unequal development, 400, 410, 413, 462
unit of analysis, 6, 14, 196, 209, 402
utilitarians, 194, 520–22
utopian, 41, 213, 523, 525, 533ff

V

Valenzuela, Arturo, 452
Valenzuela, J. Samuel, 452
values, viii, 5, 22–23, 34, 39, 519–38, 554ff, 557, 581
Vasquez, John A., 127

voluntarism, 5, 52–54, 202, 210, 213, 215, 405–406, 415, 521
von Neumann, John, 98–99

W

Wallerstein, Immanuel, 12, 145, 410–16, 418, 507, 579
Waltz, Kenneth N., 3, 11, 42, 52–55, 106–108, 116, 130, 132–33, 135–40, 143, 145–47, 152, 154, 157, 226, 361, 374, 564–68, 579–80
Walzer, Michael, 539
war, 1, 39–43, 45, 47–48, 50–52, 54–55, 58–62, 64–65, 106–107, 115ff, 158–60, 167–91, 195, 202, 207, 213–15, 362, 380, 383, 403–405, 411, 519, 523–24, 539ff, 577, 580–81
Weber, Max, 2
Wight, Martin, 118
Wolfers, Arnold, 226, 228, 230, 362, 560
world capitalist system, 9–10, 399, 409–14, 417, 479, 507ff
world society, 352ff
Wright, Quincy, 3, 168, 248

Y

Young, Oran, 365

Z

zero-sum game, *see* game theory